8-75

NORMAN
INSTITUTIONS

NORMAN INSTITUTIONS

CHARLES HOMER
HASKINS

FREDERICK UNGAR PUBLISHING CO.
NEW YORK

First published 1918

Republished 1960 by arrangement with the author's estate

Second Printing, 1967

Printed in the United States of America

Library of Congress Catalog Card No. 60-8569

TO THE SPIRIT OF FRANCE
HUMANE UNFLINCHING
CLEAR AND FREE
THESE STUDIES IN FRENCH HISTORY
ARE DEDICATED

PREFACE

THE institutions of the duchy of Normandy occupy a unique place in the history of Europe. They have their local interest, giving character and distinctness to an important region of France; they furnished models of orderly and centralized administration to the French kings after the conquest of the duchy by Philip Augustus; and they exerted an influence of the first importance upon the constitutional and legal development of England and the countries of English law. Normandy was thus the channel through which the stream of Frankish and feudal custom flowed to England; it was the training ground where the first Anglo-Norman king gained his experience as a ruler, and the source whence his followers drew their ideas of law and government; and during nearly a century and a half of personal union with England it afforded a constant example of parallel development. In the larger view the effects of Norman institutions upon English lands are the most significant, and these naturally possess the principal interest for English and American students of history. The following studies were undertaken in the first instance for the purpose of seeking light on the constitutional development of England, and while they necessarily include many matters which bear on this but indirectly, their original purpose has determined their scope and character. They begin with the earliest trustworthy information respecting the government of Normandy; they end with the loss of the duchy's originality and independence.

A constitutional history of Normandy in this period is, in any full or adequate sense, an impossibility for lack of sufficient information. Normandy can offer no parallel to the abundance and continuity of the English public records; however great their original volume and importance, the documentary sources of Norman history have suffered sadly from war and revolution and neglect, until only fragments remain from which to spell out some chapters of the story, It will be necessary more than once to revert to this fundamental fact; [1] it is emphasized here as conditioning the nature of this volume. We cannot trace a full development, but must confine ourselves to such periods and topics as have left materials for their treatment, and some of these must await the results of more minute and special study.

The continuity of Norman constitutional development has, nevertheless, been kept steadily in view, and however fragmentary and inadequate the result, it is believed that light has been thrown upon some of the dark corners of Norman history. There is here given for the first time a comprehensive description of the government of Normandy under William the Conqueror, with special reference to conditions on the eve of the Conquest of England, and certain new conclusions are suggested respecting the military, fiscal, and judicial organization of the duchy. The weakness of the rule of Robert Curthose is made more evident by a systematic study of his charters. What is said of the government of Henry I rests for the most part upon new evidence and points to new conclusions. The persistence of Norman institutions under Angevin rule is shown, and the parallel development of England and Normandy under Henry II is examined. New facts are brought out respecting the establishment of the jury under Geoffrey Plantagenet and Henry II, and other points will be apparent to the special investigator. No attempt has been made to restate matters already well established, notably by the masterly researches of Stapleton, Brunner, and Delisle, but careful attention has been paid to their writings as well as to more recent works, such as those of Valin and Powicke. That the results of the parallel labors of students of English history, notably Maitland and Round, have been freely used will be seen from the frequent recurrence of their names in the notes and the index. Certain chapters, as indicated in each case, have already appeared in the *American Historical Review* and the *English Historical Review*,[2] by whose permission they are here utilized; but these have

[1] See especially Appendix A.

[2] A summary of these articles has been prepared by M. Jean Lesquier for early publication in the *Bulletin de la Société des Antiquaires de Normandie*. See also my

been carefully revised from the sources and considerably expanded by the use of new matter. Unpublished documents and special discussions will be found in the appendices, which are supplemented by facsimiles of certain charters of special interest. The documentary publications of the past ten years have relieved the volume of many texts which had been gathered for its purposes, while the appendices have been further reduced by reason of the difficulties of collation under present circumstances.

So far as this book contains new results, it rests primarily upon a systematic exploration of the documentary sources of Norman history, which in its early stages was made possible by a grant from the Carnegie Institution of Washington and in its later months was aided by the Woodbury Lowery Fellowship of Harvard University. Begun in 1902, these researches have been prosecuted under certain inevitable disadvantages of distance and interruption, and it has been possible to conduct them only because of the generous and unfailing helpfulness of French archivists and librarians and the patience and good will of their assistants. Space forbids a full list of those who have given such aid, but I must express my special indebtedness to MM. Georges Besnier, archivist of the Calvados, R.-N. Sauvage, librarian of Caen, L. Dolbet, late archivist of the Manche, and J.-J. Vernier, archivist of the Seine-Inférieure. For access to material in private hands my thanks are due to the Marquis de Mathan, at Saint-Pierre-de-Semilly, to the proprietors of the Bénédictine de Fécamp, and, in the days before the Separation Law, to the abbé L. Deslandes, of Bayeux cathedral, and the episcopal authorities of Séez and Coutances. At Paris I must acknowledge my constant obligation to the learning and friendship of a distinguished Norman scholar, M. Henri Omont, of the Bibliothèque Nationale, and to those who administer under his direction its great collections of manuscripts. I owe much to the advice and encouragement of the late Léopold Delisle, and in continuing his work M. Élie Berger has generously placed at my disposal the

paper, *Quelques problèmes de l'histoire des institutions anglo-normandes*, read before the Congrès du Millénaire normand (Rouen, 1911); and my *Normans in European History* (Boston, 1915).

proofs of the second volume of the *Recueil des actes de Henri II*.
My thanks are also due to MM. Maurice Prou and Ferdinand
Lot of Paris, to Mr. H. W. C. Davis, of Balliol College, Oxford,
to my colleagues Professors Edwin F. Gay and Charles H. Mc-
Ilwain, and particularly to Professor George B. Adams of Yale
University.   The Harvard Library has been generous in providing books of a sort not ordinarily accessible in the United States;
and Mr. George W. Robinson, Secretary of the Graduate School
of Arts and Sciences of Harvard University, has rendered valuable assistance in the correction of the proof sheets.

If the book has been over-long in the making, this has not been
without compensations for the author. He has had time to linger
over the great Norman chroniclers with his students and to try
his conclusions in the give and take of seminary discussion. He
has made the personal acquaintance of a number of workers in
the field of Norman history, and has enjoyed several summers of
study and research in some of the pleasant places of the earth.
And as the work comes to a close, the memories which it recalls
are not so much of dusty *fonds d'archives* or weary journeys on
the Ouest-État, as of quiet days of study in provincial collections,
long evenings of reflection by the Orne or the Vire or in the
garden of some cathedral city, and rare afternoons at Chantilly
with Léopold Delisle, now gone the way of the Norman historians
and chancellors on whom he lavished so much labor and learning.
Requiescant a laboribus suis, opera enim illorum sequuntur illos!
To these historians of an elder day must now be added friends and
students whose end has come recently and all too soon, French
and English scholars of promise and already of fulfillment, American scholars in the making, martyrs to a common cause which is
higher than scholarship and dearer than life itself. May their
works likewise follow them!

CAMBRIDGE, December, 1917.

CONTENTS

CHAPTER I

CHAPTER II

CHAPTER V

CHAPTER VI

APPENDICES

FACSIMILES

LIST OF ABBREVIATIONS

A. H. R. . . . . *American Historical Review.* New York, 1895– .

B. É. C. . . . . *Bibliothèque de l'École des Chartes.* Paris, 1839– .

Davis . . . . H. W. C. Davis, *Regesta Regum Anglo-Normannorum,* i. Oxford, 1913.

Delisle . . . . Léopold Delisle, *Recueil des actes de Henri II, roi d'Angleterre et duc de Normandie, concernant les provinces françaises et les affaires de France,* introduction. Paris, 1909.

Delisle-Berger . . . . Ditto, tomes i, ii, *oeuvre posthume revue et publiée par Élie Berger.* Paris, 1916– .

Delisle, *Cartulaire normand* . . . . Léopold Delisle, *Cartulaire normand de Philippe-Auguste, Louis VIII, Saint Louis, et Philippe-le-Hardi,* in *Mémoires des Antiquaires de Normandie,* xvi (1852).

Delisle, *S.-Sauveur* . . . . Léopold Delisle, *Histoire du château et des sires de Saint-Sauveur-le-Vicomte.* Valognes, 1867.

Deville, *Analyse* . . . . . . Étienne Deville, *Analyse d'un ancien cartulaire de Saint-Étienne de Caen.* Évreux, 1905, reprinted from *Revue catholique de Normandie,* xv.

E. H. R. . . . . *English Historical Review.* London, 1886– .

H. F. . . . . *Recueil des historiens des Gaules et de la France.* Paris, 1738– .

La Roque . . . . Gilles-André de La Roque, *Histoire généalogique de la maison de Harcourt.* Paris, 1662.

Le Prévost, *Eure* . . . . Auguste Le Prévost, *Mémoires et notes pour servir à l'histoire du département de l'Eure.* Évreux, 1862–1869.

Livre noir . . . . *Antiquus Cartularius Ecclesiae Baiocensis (Livre noir),* ed. V. Bourrienne. Paris, 1902–1903.

Lot, *S.-Wandrille* . . . . . Ferdinand Lot, *Études critiques sur l'abbaye de Saint-Wandrille.* Paris, 1913.

M. A. N. . . . . *Mémoires de la Société des Antiquaires de Normandie.* Caen, 1824– .

M. G. H. . . . . *Monumenta Germaniae Historica.* Hanover, etc., 1826– .

Neustria Pia. . . . . Arthur Du Monstier, *Neustria Pia seu De omnibus et singulis Abbatibus et Prioratibus totius Normaniae.* Rouen, 1663.

Pollock and Maitland Sir Frederick Pollock and Frederic W. Maitland, *The History of English Law before the Time of Edward I.* Second edition, Cambridge, 1898.

Powicke . . . . F. M. Powicke, *The Loss of Normandy.* Manchester, 1913.

Round . . . . J. Horace Round, *Calendar of Documents preserved in France illustrative of the History of Great Britain and Ireland,* i, 918–1206. London, 1899.

Sauvage, *Troarn* . . . . . R. N. Sauvage, *L'abbaye de Saint-Martin de Troarn.* Caen, 1911; and *Mémoires des Antiquaires de Normandie,* xxxiv.

Stapleton . . . . Thomas Stapleton, *Magni Rotuli Scaccarii Normanniae sub Regibus Angliae.* London, 1840–1844.

Valin . . . . Lucien Valin, *Le duc de Normandie et sa cour (912–1204).* Paris, 1910.

Vernier . . . . J.-J. Vernier, *Chartes de l'abbaye de Jumièges.* Rouen, 1916.

Manuscripts cited without further indication of place are in the Bibliothèque Nationale.

NORMAN
INSTITUTIONS

NORMAN INSTITUTIONS

CHAPTER I

NORMANDY UNDER WILLIAM THE CONQUEROR[1]

THE Anglo-Norman state of the twelfth century is one of the most interesting phenomena in the history of European institutions. Whether in the extent and cohesion of its territory, in the centralized authority of its rulers, or in the precocity and vigor of its administrative system, whose many-sided activity can still be traced in writ and roll and exchequer record, the Anglo-Norman kingdom finds no parallel in the western Europe of its time. Moreover, on its institutional side at least, it was no local or temporary affair. Themselves the product of a variety of elements — Anglo-Saxon, Danish, Frankish, not to mention the more immediate Norman and Angevin — the contemporary influence of Anglo-Norman institutions extended from Scotland to Sicily, while their later outgrowths are to be seen in the imitation of Norman practices by the kings of France, as well as in the whole fabric of English government.

Of the two sets of institutions which were suddenly brought into contact in 1066 and continued side by side under the same rulers for a century and a half, those of Normandy are much the more obscure. It is not, of course, implied that investigation of the Anglo-Saxon period has reached its limits: within twenty years the labors of Maitland and Liebermann, of Round and Vinogradoff — to mention no others — have shown what can be done, and what remains to be done, by a more scientific study of the Domesday survey and the legal sources and by a wider view of the relations of England to the Continent, and we are likely to see further additions to our knowledge in these directions. Still the

[1] Revised and expanded from *A. H. R.*, xiv. 453–476 (1909), incorporating also the special study of knight service in *E. H. R.*, xxii. 636–649 (1907). A summary was read before the International Congress of the Historical Sciences at Berlin in August 1908, and before the American Historical Association at Richmond in December 1908.

mere mention of these scholars and the sources which are at their disposal shows the great advantage of England over Normandy, both before and after the Conquest. It is only natural that the history of Normandy should generally have been approached, as in the classic researches of Léopold Delisle, from the point of view of France rather than of England, and although it is forty years since Brunner first showed the way to a broader study of Anglo-Norman legal history, little has been done to apply his method to new materials and other problems. The paucity of sources is, of course, the great obstacle. Normandy has no Domesday and no dooms. Its earliest law book, the older part of the *Très Ancien Coutumier*, dates from the very end of the twelfth century, and while there are indications of the existence of a distinctly Norman body of custom before 1066,[2] the only formulation of the law of the Conqueror's day is a brief statement of certain of the ducal rights drawn up four years after his death by order of his sons.[3] There is almost no contemporary evidence for the tenth century, when even grants of land were made orally without any written record,[4] and although Dudo of Saint-Quentin is useful so far as he reflects the conditions of his own age, about the year 1000, for the greater part of the eleventh century we have only narratives put together two or three generations later. Our main reliance must be upon the charters, and even here, such has been the destruction of Norman records, the body of materials is less than for contemporary England or for such adjacent regions as Anjou and Flanders, and is notably small for the earlier part of the Conqueror's

[2] 'Donavi apud Argentias leuvam iuxta morem patriae nostrae': charter of Robert I for Fécamp, Appendix B, no. 10. 'Consuetudines quoque et servicia omnia que de terra exeunt secundum morem Normannie': Delisle, *S.-Sauveur-le-Vicomte*, pièces, no. 24. In 1074 Roger, earl of Hereford, is tried 'secundum leges Normannorum': Ordericus Vitalis, ed. Le Prévost, ii. 264.

[3] The so-called *Consuetudines et iusticie*, Appendix D. On the sources of early Norman law see now E.-J. Tardif, *Étude sur les sources de l'ancien droit normand*, i (Rouen, 1911), who emphasizes the canons of councils as a source of secular law.

[4] L. Valin, *Le duc de Normandie*, p. 145; Lot, *S.-Wandrille*, p. lxi. The criticism of Dudo has at last been made by H. Prentout, *Étude critique sur Dudon de S.-Quentin et son histoire des premiers ducs normands* (Paris, 1916); cf. *A. H. R.*, xxii. 432 f. The two principal historians of the later eleventh century, William of Poitiers and William of Jumièges, are of slight use for the study of institutions. On the evidence for the reign of Robert I see Appendix C.

reign.[5] A large part of this documentary material is still un-printed and unsifted, and we cannot use it in full security until it has been collected and tested monastery by monastery, after the admirable example set by Lot in the case of Saint-Wandrille.

For the present any treatment of early Norman history must be provisional, and we can never hope to understand the interaction of Frankish and Scandinavian elements in the tenth century or the government of the first dukes.[6] For lack of sufficient earlier evidence, the study of Norman institutions must begin about half a century before the Conquest of England, with the chronicle of Dudo and the charters of the later years of Richard II. Even for this period we shall find the material too fragmentary to yield conclusions on many points, and we shall need to supplement it from the more abundant, but still meager, records of the latter part of William the Conqueror's reign. Ideally what we should most wish is a picture of Normandy at the moment of the invasion of England; but as a practical problem we shall find it hard enough to piece out some account of the government of Normandy if we use all the sources of the Conqueror's reign, defining wherever possible the points that can be established as prior to 1066, and those also which are anterior to his accession as duke.

First of all, it is plain that Norman society in 1066 was a feudal society, and one of the most fully developed feudal societies in Europe.[7] Feudalism, however, may mean many different

---

[5] See in general Appendix A. H. W. C. Davis, *Regesta Regum Anglo-Normannorum*, begins with 1066 and includes only a portion of the Norman charters of the Conqueror; cf. *A. H. R.*, xix. 594–596. The Bibliothèque Nationale possesses (MS. Lat. n. a. 1243) a collection of copies of William I's charters made by Achille Deville, which, though far from complete, is of considerable convenience.

[6] See, however, for this period Tardif, *Étude sur les sources*, pp. 7 f., 19–21; Prentout, *Étude sur Dudon*, pp. 415–424. Prentout's *Étude* treats in detail the narrative history of the early dukes, which is also sketched in his *Essai sur les origines et la fondation du duché de Normandie* (Paris, 1911).

[7] See J. Flach, *Les origines de l'ancienne France*, iii. 88, who singles out Normandy, Flanders, and the county of Barcelona as the earliest feudal states in France, and assigns the preëminence to Normandy as ' berceau à l'état féodal en France.' The question of the feudal relation of the Norman dukes to the French crown lies outside the limits of the present volume. Consult F. Lot, *Fidèles ou vassaux?*, ch. 6; Flach, in *Comptes-rendus de l'Académie des Sciences Morales et Politiques*, clxxxi. 138–165 (1914); Prentout, *Étude sur Dudon*, p. 207 ff.

things,[8] and we must seek to determine what specifically feudal institutions then existed, keeping in mind always those which are significant with reference to subsequent English developments. Vassalage and dependent tenure meet us on every hand, and while there are holdings for life [9] and the word allod occurs, though not always with a very exact technical meaning,[10] the greater part of the land seems to be held by hereditary tenure of some lord. There are degrees of such tenure, and in some instances subinfeudation is well advanced,[11] but it is impossible to say whether all land was supposed to be held ultimately of the duke. Some measure of the extent to which feudal ideas had gone in early Normandy may be got from the indications of their disintegrating influence upon the Church. Before 1046 a provincial council prohibits bishops from granting the lands and revenues of the clergy as benefices to laymen,[12] and the need of such legislation appears from the case of Bishop Robert of Coutances, who gave cathedral prebends as fiefs to his relatives.[13] The feudal relation might be created out of other ecclesiastical rights besides land, as when the bishop of Bayeux and the bishop of Séez granted in fee the episcopal *consuetudines* of several parishes,[14]

[8] Cf. Pollock and Maitland, *History of English Law*, i. 67; G. B. Adams, *Anglo-Saxon Feudalism*, in *A. H. R.*, vii. 11–35. Pollock and Maitland's chapter on Norman law, though brief, contains the best account of conditions before the Conquest, and it is not necessary to repeat what is there said of feudal tenure. M. Rabasse, *Du régime des fiefs en Normandie au moyen âge* (Paris, 1905), is of no value for the early period and is confused for the later.

[9] E. g., Collection Moreau, xxi. 8, 9, 25, 30.

[10] See William's grant to Saint-Julien de Tours (1063) of the allod of Roncheville as his vassal Adam had held it: Delisle-Berger, *Henri II*, no. 137; L.-J. Denis, *Les chartes de S.-Julien de Tours*, no. 29. Various instances of *alodium* in this period will be found in Lot, *S.-Wandrille*.

[11] *Infra*, pp. 16, 21.

[12] Council of Rouen (1037–1046), c. 10: Mansi, *Concilia*, xix. 753; Bessin, *Concilia Rotomagensis Provinciae*, i. 42.

[13] Before 1048, *Gallia Christiana*, xi. instr. 218. Cf. also in the cartulary of the chapter of Rouen (MS. Rouen 1193, ff. 31, 54v) the account 'quomodo villa de Duverent de dominicatu archiepiscopatus exiit': *Archaeological Journal*, iii. 6; Valin, pièces, no. 1.

[14] *Gallia Christiana*, xi. instr. 63, 335; Denis, *Chartes de S.-Julien de Tours*, no. 24 (1053). Cf. also Ordericus, ii. 26, iii. 473, v. 183; Imbart de la Tour, in *Revue historique*, lxviii. 49.

or the archbishop of Rouen turned an archdeaconry into an hereditary fief.[15]

That the Norman barons before the Conquest held their lands from the duke by military service has been clearly shown by Brunner [16] and the authors of the *History of English Law*,[17] but it

[15] Ordericus, ii. 132; *infra*, note 17.

[16] *Die Entstehung der Schwurgerichte*, p. 131, note 3. Waitz had declared (Göttingen *Nachrichten*, 1866, p. 95 f.) that we knew nothing of Norman feudal law before 1066.

[17] Pollock and Maitland, i. 69–72. Cf. H. Lagouëlle, *La conception juridique de la propriété foncière dans le très-ancien droit normand* (Paris, 1902), p. 114 ff. The following instances may be added to those cited by these authors: A vassal of Richard the Good makes the following grant to Saint-Père de Chartres: ' tres milites concedo cum beneficiis suis qui sic vocantur, Rollo et Angoht et Unbeina, ut inde persolvant liberum servitium ' (*Cartulaire*, i. 108; cf. pp. 109, 40, 146, 152). Robert I confirms to Saint-Wandrille land purchased ' ab Hugone archidiacono qui eam ex me tenebat in beneficio,' and ' terram Durandi militis quam prefato abbati cum servicio filiorum ipsius dedi ': Lot, *S.-Wandrille*, pièces, no. 14. He grants to Fécamp, giving their names, ' quidam homines mei scilicet milites cum omnibus sibi pertinentibus . . . etiam alios milites ': Appendix B, no. 10. Robert also gave La Croix ' in beneficium cuidam militum suorum nomine Adelelmo ' (Round, *Calendar*, no. 709), and granted to Mont-Saint-Michel half of Guernsey ' quam quidam fidelis noster nomine Nigellus in beneficio tenet ' (*ibid.*, no. 705; Delisle, *S.-Sauveur*, pièces, no. 9). Richard de Beaufou grants to Saint-Amand ' unum feudum laici c. acrarum quod Anschitillus presbyter tenet ' (*Monasticon*, vii. 1101; La Roque, iii. suppl., 2). For the Conqueror's reign before 1066 see his grant, *ca.* 1048, of ' terram Atzelini equitis mei,' Lot, *S.-Wandrille*, no. 26; his charter of 1063 for Tours (' equites huius terre qui servierunt Adam serviant Sancto Iuliano '), Denis, *Chartes de S.-Julien*, no. 29 (= Delisle-Berger, *Henri II*, no. 137); *Cartulaire de S.-Ymer*, no. 1; *Livre noir de Bayeux*, nos. 1, 5; Round, *Calendar*, no. 1109; Pommeraye, *Histoire de S.-Ouen*, pp. 424, 460; the grants to Fécamp copied in the Collection Moreau, xxii. 108v, xxv. 249; the cartulary of Préaux (Archives of the Eure, H. 711), nos. 301, 320, 429, 439; and the grant to Jumièges by Gislebertus of ' benefitium Alsvillam scilicet quam a predicto meo domino militans obtineo ' (original in the Archives of the Seine-Inférieure; Vernier, no. 25).

The statements of the chroniclers are in themselves of doubtful value, but taken in connection with the passages in the charters they offer supplementary evidence of some interest. Thus Ordericus (ii. 397) says that Fulk, dean of Évreux, 'ex paterna hereditate feudum militis possedit,' and mentions the grant to Saint-Évroul by another Fulk of ' archidiaconatum quoque quem in feudo ab antecessoribus suis de archiepiscopo Rotomagensi tenebat ' (ii. 132). In 1056 or 1057 a judgment was rendered ' in curia S. Ebrulfi ' depriving one of the abbey's knights of 'omnem feudum quem ipse de S. Ebrulfo tenebat ' (ii. 60). The dealings of Saint-Évroul with Baudri de Bocquencé (ii. 74 f.) are also interesting in relation to feudal justice and service, fealty, and castle guard. Feudal relations are also mentioned in the *Vita altera Herluini* (Mabillon, *Acta SS. Ordinis S. Benedicti*, vi. 2, p. 356).

has not been established that their military service had been
definitely fixed in amount or assessed against specific pieces of
land, and the problem requires at this point somewhat detailed
examination.

The question whether a system of knights' fees existed in Normandy before 1066 can best be approached from the side of the
ecclesiastical holdings. In England, Round has called attention
to " the appearance from the earliest period to which our information extends of certain quotas of knight service, clearly arbitrary in amount, as due from those bishops and abbots who held
by military service "; [18] and he has shown that these quotas were
fixed shortly after the Conquest by the arbitrary act of the king.
In this the Conqueror may have been instituting something new
or may have simply followed previous Norman practice, and it is
from many points of view interesting to compare with the English
inquest of 1166 the earliest statement of the service due from the
Norman tenants-in-chief, the returns collected by Henry II in
1172.[19] In these the service of the ecclesiastical tenants is given
as follows: —

Episcopus Abrincensis debet servicium v militum de Abrincensi, et de
honore Sancti Philiberti v milites.

Episcopus de Costanciis, servicium v militum, et ad suum servicium xiii
milites, [id est debet capere servicium xiii militum pro exercitu, et similiter
de aliis].

Episcopus Baiocensis, servicium xx militum, et ad suum servicium cxx
milites.

Episcopus Sagiensis, servicium sex militum.

Episcopus Lexoviensis, servicium xx militum, et ad suum servicium xxx
milites et terciam partem unius militis, et preter hec habet x milites in
banleuca Lexoviensi, qui remanent ad custodiendam civitatem donec retrobannus summoneatur, et tunc ibunt cum propriis expensis episcopi. Idem
habet ii milites de dono regis Henrici filii Matildis, scilicet in Mesnilio Odonis
et in Corbespina.

Abbas Fiscannensis, servicium x militum, et ad suum servicium xiii milites
et tres partes unius militis.

Abbas Bernaii, ad suum servicium ii milites.

Abbas Gemeticensis, servicium iii militum, et preter hoc ad suum servicium i militem in Esmalevilla, quem comes Hugo le Bigot ei difforciat.

[18] *Feudal England*, p. 298.
[19] *H. F.*, xxiii. 693–699; *Red Book of the Exchequer*, pp. 624–645. Those who
made no returns are mentioned at the end; the list includes the archbishop of Rouen
and the bishop of Évreux, but no abbot.

Abbas Montis Rothomagi, servicium vi militum et tres partes unius militis.

Abbas de Monte Sancti Michaelis, servicium vi militum in Abrincensi et Costanciensi et i militem in Baiocassino, quem faciunt vavassores nisi fuerint in exercitum.

Abbas Cadomensis, servicium i militis, de feodo de Taillebois.

Abbas Sancti Ebrulfi, servicium ii militum, et preter hoc feodum Rogeri Gulafre, quod Guillelmus Paganelli habet de rege in vadio, unde difforciat servicium abbatis.

Abbas Sancti Wandregisili, servicium iiiior militum.

Abbas Sancti Audoeni de Rothomago, servicium vi militum, et ad suum servicium quatuordecim milites.

Abbas de Bernaio habet de feodo suo ii milites.

Abbas Sancti Dyonisii, servicium i militis, de feodo Bernevallis.

Abbatissa de Mosterviller, servicium iii militum, et ad suum servicium v milites et terciam partem unius militis.

The *servitia debita* of this list are smaller than those of the English bishops and abbots, and, perhaps for this reason, the group of five knights is not quite so much in evidence, but the most striking thing is the small number of monastic foundations which owe military service to the duke. If we deduct Saint-Denis, which is not Norman, and Saint-Étienne of Caen, which is evidently assessed not as a barony but for a fief which has come into its possession,[20] there remain only nine monastic baronies in a land where religious houses were numerous and closely subjected to the duke's control.[21] Upon what principle had these nine been selected ? Not, as we might expect, because they were the monasteries which had been founded by the dukes, for La Trinité-du-Mont and Saint-Évroul were established by the duke's vassals, and such important ducal foundations as Cerisy, Caen, and Montebourg are not included. The explanation must be sought in some other direction, and the most natural one is that of age. None of the nine was established after 1050; except Saint-Évroul, all are older than the Conqueror's accession. Jumièges, Fécamp, Mont-Saint-Michel, Saint-Ouen, and Saint-Wandrille were restored under the early dukes; Bernai goes back to the reign of Richard II, La Trinité and Monti-

[20] Cf. the fief held by Saint-Évroul in addition to its normal assessment. The fief of Taillebois does not appear in the early charters enumerating the possessions of Saint-Étienne. Seven knights at Grainville were granted to Saint-Ouen between 1055 and 1066: Le Prévost, *Eure*, ii. 38.

[21] Cf. H. Böhmer, *Kirche und Staat in England und in der Normandie*, p. 31 f.

villiers to that of Robert, while Saint-Denis had held Berneval since 968.[22] It is true that these are not the only monasteries which claimed to be earlier than Duke William, but it is not clear that any of the other abbeys which were independent in 1172 was sufficiently organized and endowed at the time of William's accession to be assigned definite military obligations. Saint-Taurin of Évreux, which is undoubtedly older, was subjected to Fécamp by Robert I in exchange for the independence of Montivilliers; Cerisy, though begun in 1032, owed its completion to William; if Saint-Amand goes back to 1030, which is disputed, its church was not dedicated till 1078; Préaux is barely earlier than Robert's departure for Jerusalem; Herluin may have founded his monastic community in 1034, but he did not establish it at Bec until some years later.[23] The list of 1172 is essentially a list of the oldest monasteries of the duchy. If this be the case, it is altogether likely that the erection of these into baronies owing definite quotas of military service took place in this same early period — if not while they were the only monastic establishments, at least while they were still the most important ones. Moreover, since the early years of William's reign were hardly a favorable time for so marked a manifestation of ducal authority, this step may well have been taken before the death of Robert the Magnificent, whether entirely in his reign or partly in that of his predecessors we have no means of knowing. Then, for some reason which likewise escapes us,[24] Saint-Évroul was added after its foundation in 1050, thus completing the list as we have it in 1172.[25]

[22] It claimed to have received it from Rollo: *H. F.*, ix. 731; cf. Dudo of Saint-Quentin, ed. Lair, p. 171.

[23] In the absence of a critical study of the early monastic history of Normandy the dates of these foundations are often uncertain. The chief authorities are the documents in the *Gallia Christiana* and *Neustria Pia*; Ordericus, ii. 9 ff., with Le Prévost's notes; Robert of Torigni, ed. Delisle, ii. 184 ff.; and his continuation of William of Jumièges, bk. vii, c. 22 (ed. Marx, p. 252). Cf. E. Sackur, *Die Cluniacenser*, ii. 41–54; and the monastic histories enumerated in Sauvage, *Troarn*, pp. xlv–xlix.

[24] Probably because the lands granted to the abbey already rendered knight service to the duke. Cf. note 30 below.

[25] The returns of 1172 do not cover arrière vassals. The Norman monasteries which appear as arrière tenants in the registers of the French kings in the early thirteenth century are likewise early foundations. Thus Lire dates from 1046, Troarn from *ca.* 1050, and Cormeilles from *ca.* 1060. See *H. F.*, xxiii. 617, 705, 714 f.

This conclusion with respect to the early existence of the monastic baronies in Normandy may be reached by a different route by examining the account of the creation of the barony of Saint-Évroul which has fortunately been preserved in the long confirmation of that abbey's privileges and possessions granted by Henry I in 1128:—[26]

Concedo etiam eis et confirmo totam villam de Cueleio cum ecclesia et omnibus pertinentiis eius de donis sepe dictorum Roberti et Hugonis de Grentemaisnil, que est feodum unius lorice, et aliud feodum lorice de dono Willelmi Geroiani quod est inter Tolchetam et villam que Villaris dicitur et appellatur Bauchencaium, de feodo de Mosterol, de quibus predictus Willelmus pater meus, cum assensu et voluntate Theoderici abbatis eiusdem loci primi post tempora Sancti Ebrulfi et predictorum Roberti et Hugonis de Grentemaisnil et dicti Willelmi Geroiani avunculi eorum predicte abbatie fundatorum, baroniam unam constituit ad servitium suum et heredum suorum faciendum in exercitibus et aliis negotiis suis per totam Normanniam, ita tamen quod Ric. de Cueleio et Baldricus filius Nicholai milites, quibus memoratus abbas Theodericus illa duo feoda loricarum in hereditatem de se tenenda donavit cum assensu dicti W. patris mei, servitium illud facere tenebuntur quisque pro feodo suo cum equis et armis et cum expensis suis, et heredes eorum, quando abbas S. Ebrulfi a me submonitus fuerit et ipsi ab abbate, et habebunt rationabiles tallias pro exercitibus et aliis negotiis meis in Normannia concessas. Si vero de servitio illo defecerint et abbas submonitionem suam adversus eos probare poterit, in eorum corpora et catalla a me et successoribus meis capietur emenda et abbas relevamenta et placita habebit et alia iura que habent barones Normannie in feodis loricarum suarum. . . . Item de donis Ernaudi Geroiani totam terram que est inter Tolchetam et Carentonam, que est de feodo Escalfoii, quam dedit Theodericus abbas Baldrico filio Nicholai tenendam de se per servitium unum vavassoris, quotiens habere voluerit, cum nemore Baldrici. . . .

As Theodoric was abbot from 1050 to 1057 and William Géré departed for Italy before 1056,[27] it thus appears that Saint-Évroul was erected into a barony by the duke shortly after its revival and reëndowment in 1050, and in any case not later than 1056. The abbot's military service was fixed at two knights and assessed against two of its holdings, Cullei and Bocquencé, which were with the duke's consent granted as knights' fees to Richard de Cullei and Baudri son of Nicholas respectively, Baudri also receiving a piece of land between Touquette and the Charentonne in return for a vavassor's service. These statements are in general

[26] *Gallia Christiana*, xi. instr. 204–210.
[27] Ordericus, ii. 56–63; William of Jumièges, ed. Marx. p. 178.

accord with what we know from other sources. Two knights are the quota of Saint-Évroul in the inquest of 1172 and the later Norman returns,[28] and they are charged against the fiefs of Cullei and Bocquencé in the registers of Philip Augustus.[29] Now Cullei and 'Bocquencé as the duke's archer Baudri had held it,'[30] as well as the land between Touquette and the Charentonne, appear as possessions of the abbey in Duke William's charters of 1050,[31] where, however, Bocquencé is said to have been bought from Ernaud Géré. The successor of Theodoric, elected in 1059, soon had trouble with Baudri de Bocquencé, but after this had been settled Ordericus declares 'tam ipse quam Rodbertus filius eius usque in hodiernum diem pro terra de Balgenzaio solummodo monachis militavit.'[32] Toward the end of the eleventh century the son Robert appears as lord of the honor,[33] and a suspicious charter of the early years of Henry II records the settlement, in favor of the monks, of a dispute between them and their knight Roger de Bocquencé concerning the services due for a knight's fee at Bocquencé and 'quadam vavassoria terre que est inter Tolquetam et Carentonam.'[34] Cullei appears as a knight's fee in a charter of Henry I, where it is granted to Nigel d'Aubigny.[35]

There are, it is true, some difficulties with regard to Henry I's charter of 1128. Although it was printed by the editors of the *Gallia Christiana* 'ex authentico,' the original has disappeared in the wreck of the abbey's archives; it was not copied into any of

---

[28] *H. F.*, xxiii. 694, 710; *supra*, p. 9.   [29] *H. F.*, xxiii. 637.

[30] If Baudri the archer had held Bocquencé as a knight's fee of the duke, we can easily see why the duke should insist upon the continuance of the military service when the fief passed into the abbot's control — a possible explanation of the singling out of Saint-Évroul as the only monastery among the later foundations which was held to render military service to the duke. There is a discrepancy with respect to the various Baudris. The Baudri de Bocquencé of whom Ordericus speaks was the son of Baudri the German, not of Nicholas, and Le Prévost identifies the grantee of the abbey's fief with Baudri de Guitry, whose father's name was Nicholas. Ordericus, ii. 75-76, iii. 38, 199, 248, note; Le Prévost, *Eure*, ii. 224 f.; Lot, *S.-Wandrille*, nos. 16, 27.

[31] Printed in Ordericus, v. 173-180. Cf. ii. 33, 35.

[32] *Ibid.*, ii. 75.   [33] *Ibid.*, v. 184.

[34] Archives of the Orne, H. 564; cartulary of Saint-Évroul (MS. Lat. 11055), no. 21; Round, *Calendar*, nos. 638, 639; Delisle-Berger, no. 513.

[35] Ordericus, v. 200; Round, *Calendar*, no. 627.

the extant cartularies, nor is it mentioned by Ordericus. The form of dating is exceptional, and the other final clauses are an obvious imitation of a papal bull. Moreover, it awakens suspicion to find that all of the witnesses appear in earlier charters for Saint-Évroul,[36] and that one of them, William Bigot, went down in the White Ship in 1120.[37] On the whole, however, there does not seem to be sufficient reason for considering the charter a forgery, though it is quite probable that it has undergone something of the retouching of which there are indications in certain charters of Henry II for Saint-Évroul.[38] If we assume that the list of witnesses has been correctly printed, still the name of William de Sai which precedes might easily have caused the scribe to substitute William Bigot for his brother Hugh, who is well known in the charters of the later years of Henry I — a kind of blunder which may be seen in an original charter of Henry I for Saint-Étienne, issued two or three years later.[39] Imitations of papal forms are not unparalleled in Norman documents of this period,[40] and the issue of the charter in a provincial council is a sufficient explanation of the unusual style of dating. We know from Ordericus that the abbot of Saint-Évroul was present at the council in which the charter was granted, and as his monastery was one of the largest holders of the parish churches and tithes which this council prohibited monasteries from receiving at the hands of laymen,[41] it would be natural for the abbot to secure at once from the king a detailed enumeration and confirmation of the abbey's possessions, clothed with all the formalities which the council could give. Even if the initial and final clauses be rejected as spurious, the body of the charter, compared with earlier charters for the same

---

[36] Ordericus, v. 199, 204.   [37] *Ibid.*, iv. 418.

[38] See Round, *Calendar*, p. 224, note; Delisle, *Henri II*, p. 316 f.

[39] Archives of the Calvados, H. 1834, no. 13-5 *bis; infra*, p. 96. Here John, bishop of Séez, appears as Robert between Robert de Sigillo and Robert, earl of Gloucester.

[40] For illustrations from 1131 see Henry's charter for Séez, Appendix F, no. 11; the letter of Geoffrey, dean of Rouen, in Martène and Durand, *Thesaurus Anecdotorum*, i. 380; and a charter of John, bishop of Séez, in *Gallia Christiana*, xi. instr. 160. The presence of the papal legate at the council of 1128 might have had some influence on the form of Henry's charter.

[41] Ordericus, iv. 496 f.

house,[42] gives no occasion for suspicion. Such comparison shows moreover that even if the charter be declared a fabrication, it contains elements of unquestionable genuineness, while for the passage printed above concerning the knights' fees there is internal evidence that it was reproduced from an older document. The preservation of the names of the original tenants of Cullei and Bocquencé with their obligations expressed in the future tense, as if Duke William were still speaking, constitutes an anachronism which could hardly arise if Henry were making his own statement of the abbey's service, or if a forger were making the statement for him, but would be natural enough if he, or a later compiler, were incorporating into his charter the Conqueror's own formulation of the terms on which these knights' fees were to be held.

If the confirmation of Henry I has thus preserved for us the original terms of the grant of Cullei and Bocquencé, certain of its phrases acquire special significance. The exact regulation of such matters as summons and individual liability (*quisque pro feodo suo*), the proviso that the service is to be at the vassal's cost, and the reference to the rights of his other barons in their knights' fees, all imply that Duke William is dealing with no new or exceptional arrangements but with an institution which has been adjusted and defined as the result of considerable experience of the points which needed guarding. Even if it be held that these provisions represent only the language of Henry I's day, there is no reason to suppose that the erection of Saint-Évroul into a barony was anything unique or in advance of the duke's policy elsewhere. Indeed, the fact that the abbey had just been restored and reëndowed makes it probable that William was here extending to Saint-Évroul a system which was already in force in other ecclesiastical baronies.

That the military obligations of the Norman bishops, all of whom are expected to make return in 1172, had been fixed quite as early as those of the abbots is of course altogether likely,[43] but

[42] Ordericus, v. 173–207; *Monasticon*, vii. 1079.
[43] Two knights of the bishop of Lisieux attest a charter as early as the reign of Richard II: *M. A. N.*, xiii. 11.

the evidence is somewhat different from that in the case of the monasteries. The earliest detailed account which has been preserved of the tenants and obligations of a great Norman fief, the Bayeux inquest of 1133,[44] relates to the lands of a bishop, and the conditions of tenure therein set forth are those which prevailed in the latter part of the eleventh century. The returns, it is true, simply state that the inquest was held immediately after the death of Richard Fitz-Samson, who died in Easter week, 1133,[45] to determine what services were owing to the duke and the bishop from the bishop's knights and vavassors; but it is clear that this was part of a comprehensive inquest which covered the whole extent of the bishop's rights and possessions, and sought to determine how they had been held in Bishop Odo's time (1050-1097).[46] The matter is thus stated in an early charter of Henry II:

Quoniam ecclesia Baiocensis post mortem Odonis episcopi [tum] per subsequentium episcoporum impotentiam cum per eorumdem negligentiam et per venditiones et donationes et commutationes ab ipsis factas fere ad nichilum redacta erat, ne funditus ecclesia predicta destrueretur provide Henricus rex, avus meus, instituit ut iuramento antiquorum hominum qui rem norant recognoscerentur tenedure iam dicte ecclesie sicut fuerant in tempore predicti Odonis, tam in dominicis quam in feodis militum, vavassorum, et rusticorum. Ipsius equidem tempore hec omnia iurata sunt et recognita et sepedicte ecclesie precepto eius resignata et munimine carthe sue, quocunque modo a possessione ecclesie alienata essent, reddita sunt et confirmata.[47]

According to these returns, the bishop owes the duke ten knights for service to the king of France and twenty for the duke's own service in Normandy, the proportion being in the first case one knight for every ten who owe service to the bishop, and in the second case one knight for every five. Groups of five or multiples of five make up the greater part of the bishop's own military force, which according to the proportions just given should be 100

---

[44] Printed in *M. A. N.*, viii. 425-431; Béziers, *Mémoires . . . du diocèse de Bayeux*, i. 142; and *H. F.*, xxiii. 699-702, which furnishes the best text. Le Prévost's copy 'sur une copie collationnée faite en 1637,' is in MS. Lat. n. a. 1837, p. 282. A summary of these returns is appended to the Norman returns of 1172: *H. F.*, xxiii. 699; *Red Book of the Exchequer*, pp. 645-647.

[45] Ordericus, v. 31.

[46] *Infra*, Chapter VI.

[47] *Livre noir*, i. 20, no. 14. See also the writ and charter of Geoffrey, nos. 16, 39, and the bull of Lucius II, no. 157.

knights, but in fact amounts to a long hundred of 120.[48] These had plainly been the obligations in the days of Bishop Odo, but there is no direct intimation that they had been so fixed in the period of his episcopate which fell before the Conquest. The history of one of the bishop's honors, however, indicates that its military obligations had been fixed even before Odo's day, and it is safe to assume that the amount of the bishop's service to the duke had been determined at least as early as the amount due to the bishop from his vassals. The honor in question had formerly belonged to Grimald, one of the conspirators defeated at Val des Dunes in 1047, who died a traitor in the duke's prison at Rouen.[49] In 1074 William the Conqueror granted to the bishop of Bayeux in demesne Grimald's forfeited honor, which included Plessis and certain other lands,

> Que omnia olim tenuit supradictus Grimoldus et de quibus eidem sancte ecclesie quam supra diximus servivit.[50]

What disposal was made of these lands we learn from the inquest of the bishop's military tenures in 1133:

> Episcopus vero de eodem feodo fecit septem prebendas et retinuit in dominium suum manerium de Plesseyo cum foresta de Montpinchon. De reliquo vero honoris Grimoudi habet episcopus servitium octo militum cum terra de Bougeyo et de Dampvou, que fuit de predicto feodo dimidium militis, quam terram Guillelmus de Albigneyo tenebat de Grimoudo in maritagio cum sorore Grimoudi. De hiis autem militibus servit episcopus regi sicut de feodis que comes Glocestrie tenet de episcopo.[51]

William d'Aubigny, accordingly, must have held Danvou and Bougy of Grimald, who held them of the bishop, before the treason of 1047, a clear example of early subinfeudation. It is entirely possible that the assessment of half a knight's service by which his descendants held these lands [52] was not made until later, but the language of the inquest indicates that they had been held as half a knight's fee in Grimald's time, and the fractional amount of the

---

[48] It so appears in the returns of 1172, quoted above (p. 8); but the actual returns of 1133 give only 117¾, and the abstract of them in the *Red Book* 119½.

[49] See Wace, ed. Andresen, ii, lines 4219–4242; and the Bayeux inquest.

[50] *Livre noir*, no. 3; *M. A. N.*, xxx. 700, from the *Livre blanc* of Saint-Florent; incomplete in *Gallia Christiana*, xi. instr. 65. Cf. *Livre noir*, no. 155.

[51] *H. F.*, xxiii. 700.   [52] *Ibid.*, xxiii. 702.

service would seem to imply the existence of a knight's fee which had been divided before or at the time of the grant to William.

There is also reason for thinking that as early as Grimald's time the honor owed the service of ten knights. In the inquest of 1133, as just quoted, the bishop owes service to the duke for the enfeoffed portion of this honor in the same proportion as the earl of Gloucester for his holdings, namely, for every ten knights that the earl holds of the bishop two knights for the duke's own service and one knight for the service to the king of France. Such an arrangement evidently presupposes a group of five knights or some multiple of five, such as we find in the case of the earl of Gloucester and the other greater tenants of the bishop, and we should expect the honor of Plessis, like the earl's honor of Évrecy and several honors in the later Norman inquests,[53] to contain ten knights' fees. In 1133, it is true, it furnishes but eight knights, but these are charged against the portion remaining after the bishop has created seven prebends and retained the manor of Plessis and the forest of Montpinçon in demesne, so that Grimald's honor must have supported more than eight knights when it came into the bishop's hands in 1074. The number may not have been ten, but it was pretty certainly a multiple of five. Remembering that this service was the amount due to the bishop and not that due to the duke, who received only one-fifth of it, we must conclude that it was assessed when the holder of the honor 'served the church' of Bayeux, not when the honor was in the duke's hands, so that we are carried back to Grimald's time or before. If the assessment of Plessis antedates 1047, so in all probability does that of such other fiefs of the bishop as can be traced back to the beginning of William's reign, as, for instance, the honor of Évrecy and the Suhard fief.[54] And if the bishop's groups of five and ten knights

[53] *H. F.*, xxiii. 694, 695, 700.

[54] See Bishop Hugh's charter of 1035–1037 in the *Livre noir*, no. 21; Delisle, *S.-Sauveur*, no. 13. Haimon's fief of Évrecy is also mentioned by Wace, ed. Andresen, ii, line 4044. See also the witnesses to Bishop Hugh's charter of 1042 for Préaux, Mabillon, *Annales*, iv. 444. That the bishop had tenants by military service before 1050 is also apparent from a charter of Bishop Hugh preserved in the Archives of the Seine-Inférieure (*fonds* Jumièges, charters of Rouvray) and printed by Le Prévost, *Eure*, iii. 45; Vernier, no. 8.

go back to so early a time, so, it is altogether likely, does his own service of twenty knights to the duke.

If the preceding line of inference is valid, the Bayeux inquest is important, not only in lending support to the conclusions already reached with regard to the existence of ecclesiastical baronies and knights' fees before 1066, but also in confirming Round's view that " the Normans were familiar with *servitium debitum* in terms of the ten-knight unit when they landed in England." [55] Round seems indeed to consider this point well established, but his only authority is Wace's account of the deliberations of 1066; and, after the destructive criticism to which Wace, in another connection, has been subjected by him,[56] it is hardly necessary to point out how little value 'a mere late compiler' has for the events and conditions of that year. The Bayeux returns are a better sort of evidence, and they not only show clearly the prevalence of the five- and ten-knight unit in Bishop Odo's time, but render it probable that part, if not the whole, of this scheme of tenures is of still earlier origin. If statements of later chroniclers were to be accepted as conclusive, we should not overlook a passage in a writer earlier than Wace, the report in Ordericus of the deathbed speech of William the Conqueror in which he mentions the assessment of an arbitrary service of one hundred knights upon Count Guy of Ponthieu, when vassalage was imposed upon him in 1056.[57]

Fortunately the bishopric of Avranches offers evidence which is still clearer and more direct. In the inquest of 1172 the bishop owes five knights for his lands in the Avranchin and five for the barony of Saint-Philbert-sur-Risle, in the diocese of Lisieux. Now the barony of Saint-Philbert came to the church of Avranches as a gift of Bishop John in 1066, being half of his paternal inheritance from Raoul d'Ivry, and in the Conqueror's charter of that year

[55] *Feudal England*, p. 259 f.

[56] *Ibid.*, pp. 399–418. Round admits that in the passage in question the figures " are far too large, and savor of poetic license " (p. 260, note).

[57] ' Widonem vero comitem Baiocis quandiu placuit in carcere habui et post duos annos hominium ab eo tali tenore recepi ut exinde mihi semper fidelis existeret et militare servitium ubi iussissem cum centum militibus mihi singulis annis exhiberet ' (Ordericus, iii. 237). Cf. a charter of 1071–1082 confirming the acquisition by Marmoutier ' de feudo unius militis nomine Serlonis ' (Round, *Calendar*, no. 1211).

confirming the gift it appears that this was a fief of five knights and was thereafter to be held as such of the bishops of Avranches.[58] Evidently the whole had hitherto been an honor of ten knights. Moreover, by thus fixing the date of the acquisition of this supplementary obligation, we establish as anterior to 1066 the assignment of the service of five knights for the original holdings of the bishopric in the Avranchin.

Besides defining the amount and distribution of the ordinary feudal service, the Bayeux returns of 1133 include castle guard,[59] the equipment and service of vavassors, and the aids and reliefs due to the bishop,[60] on all which points, as Guilhiermoz has shown,[61] they yield remarkably early and significant information. Their importance, especially for the student of contemporary

[58] The Conqueror's charter is found in full in a *vidimus* in the Archives Nationales, JJ. 71, no. 90; and is printed by Le Prévost, *Eure*, iii. 183, where the date, which rests also upon internal evidence (comet, dedication of the Abbaye aux Hommes, signature of Archbishop Maurilius), is incorrectly printed as 1076. E. A. Pigeon, *Le diocèse d'Avranches*, ii. 660, gives only an extract.

[59] On castle guard see Round, *Calendar*, no. 319; Ordericus, ii. 74; and the decisions of Robert of Bellême's court in the *Chartrier rouge* of Troarn (MS. Lat. 10086), f. 180, 182v, 186v. On its appearance in England after the Conquest, see Round, in *Archaeological Journal*, lix. 144.

[60] On reliefs cf. Round, no. 320. Other early examples of vavassors will be found in Round, nos. 319, 639; Le Prévost, *Eure*, iii. 467; *Revue catholique de Normandie*, x. 49; *Neustria Pia*, p. 587; *Monasticon*, vii. 1074; Lot, *S.-Wandrille*, no. 38; *Bulletin de la Société historique de l'Orne*, v. 62, 68. The following notice in the *Livre blanc* of Saint-Martin of Séez (f. 47 of the original) illustrates also other matters of tenure: ' Cum Willelmus de Daraio anno ab incarnatione domini m ᵐᵒ. lxxx ᵐᵒ. octavo ex divino iuditio nimia corporis infirmitate aggravatus emori timeret, . . . donavit quicquid de sua terra dominica Stephanus metearius tenebat et colebat, et insuper tantum de suo alio dominio sine calumpna quieto quod plenarie sufficeret ad unam carrucam preter prata de ponte de Roca que ipse etiam donavit, necnon etiam terra Fulcoun quam predicti monachi a prefato Willelmo in feodo, nec in feudo ut prius sed in elemosina sicut cetera donavit. Namque affirmando rectum esse dicebat ut qui suis filiis centum vavassores dimittebat sibi atque monachis cum quibus victurus atque moriturus erat unum saltim ex illis proprie et solute retineret.' . . .

[61] *Essai sur l'origine de la noblesse* (Paris, 1902), pp. 185, note 34; 187, note 36; 267, note 37; 268, note 40; 275, notes 56, 57; 286, note 90; 292, note 102; 312, note 164. The earliest mention of reliefs which I have found is in a charter of Roger de Clera, anterior to 1066, for Saint-Ouen (Collection Moreau, xxii. 118, from the original; Le Prévost, *Eure*, iii. 467): 'nec retinui ex ipsa terra preter les reilies de vavassoribus.'

English institutions, is naturally increased when it is seen that the conditions they describe are those of the latter part of the eleventh century. As an illustration of this, let us take one of the points in the history of feudal institutions which most needs clearing up, the matter of the forty days' service. This was certainly the normal amount in Normandy in the twelfth century, and seems to have passed thence to the other continental domains of the Plantagenets;[62] but while its prevalence in England has generally been assumed, it has recently been asserted that even "its theoretic existence can hardly be proved for England out of any authoritative document."[63] Now the earliest mention of the forty days' limit so far noted is found in the Bayeux inquest, where it appears as the regular period for the service due to the king of France as well as for that owed to the duke within the confines of Normandy.[64] The same period is found in upper Normandy in a Saint-Amand charter of the Conqueror's reign, which is also interesting as bringing out the distinction between complete equipment and 'plain arms' which appears for the first time elsewhere [65] in the Bayeux inquest:

Ego Baldricus annuente domino Willelmo Anglorum rege et Normannorum duce clamo quetum sanctimonialibus de Sancto Amando Rothomagi servicium duorum militum quod quadraginta diebus debent per annum de feudo Bascheville donec ego vel meus heres reddamus .xxx. libras Rodmesinorum quas Sancto Amando et sanctimonialibus debeo pro sorore mea Elisabeth que ibi effecta est monacha. Testes sunt Gilbertus, Alannus, Radulfus fil[ius] Heluini, Robertus de Bothes, Ricardus de Boievilla, Willelmi regis, (*sic*) Baldrici. Ante hoc vademonium predicti milites sic erant in servicio parati: unus horum totis armis, alter vero ad plainas armas.[66]

From still another part of Normandy, between 1070 and 1081, we have another example of the forty days' limit, this time as applied to watch and ward. Here, if we may trust the natural interpretation of the possessive pronouns, we also find the principle, later well known, that the forty days' service is at the vas-

---

[62] Guilhiermoz, p. 275 f.   [63] Pollock and Maitland, i. 254.

[64] *H. F.*, xxiii. 699–700.

[65] Guilhiermoz, pp. 185–188.

[66] From a *vidimus* of Philip the Fair of 1313; Archives of the Seine-Inférieure, *fonds* Saint-Amand. The word *plainas* is badly rubbed, but only the penultimate letter is uncertain.

sal's expense, but any other service is at the cost of the lord.[67] The document, which comes from the cartulary of Mont-Saint-Michel,[68] contains so many points of interest that it is worth reprinting in full:

Conventio inter abbatem et Guillelmum Paginellum.

Haec carta narrat conventionem Baiocis factam coram regina inter abbatem de Monte Sancti Michaelis et Guillelmum Paginellum. Si Willelmus Paginellus habet guerram de illa terra quam rex Anglorum dedit sibi cum femina sua, conventio est quoniam Hugo de Bricavilla quadraginta diebus illi faciet de guarda vel custodia sese septimum de caballaribus ad suum cibum. Et nepos illius Hugonis similiter faciet si in parage terram suam tenuerit secundum hoc quod tenebit. Rursus si Guillelmus Paginellus illum Hugonem submonuerit, cum duobus equitibus eum in sua familia ad suum cibum habuerit vel filium suum, si liber erit de submonitione abbatis. Nec si[c] eum donnus abbas semper habebit quin Guillelmus Paginellus hoc habeat. Et ita equidem habebit in sua familia nepotem Hugonis et Robertum de Cantelupo et Guillelmum Becheth et illum qui honorem Scollant habebit. Et si vindictam vel placitum habuerit ad faciendum, homines quos tenet de Sancto Michaele ita habebit quod in sero erunt ad suas domos. Et si homines sibi deficient de his serviciis que hic sunt divisa, rectum sibi facient ad unam mansionum quas tenet de Sancto Michaele. Auxilium accipiet de terra quam tenet de Sancto Michaele pro sui corporis captione aut pro sua terra, si forisfecerit eam erga regem vel abbatem, vel pro filio huius femine de qua est hereditas si captus fuerit in servitio regis vel abbatis de quo est fedus, aut pro una sola filia maritanda quam habet de hac femina. Conventio est quoniam Guillelmus Paginellus in terra quam tenet de abbate statuet unum hominem apud quem abbas mittet pro submonitionibus quas habet facere ipse abbas in terra quam Guillelmus Paginellus tenet de illo. Qui si bene submonitiones fecerit et ille remaneat quem monuerit, abbas suam forisfacturam inde accipiet. Quod si in illo submonitore remanet submonitio, abbati decem et octo solidos emendabit et abbas postea per suum legatum submonitionem suam fecerit. Conventio est quoniam Willelmus Paginellus unoquoque anno duodecim quercus ad suum cois accipiet in silva de Longa Villa usque ad aquam que dicitur Ars, nec plus habet accipere nisi per abbatem fecerit. Conventio est quoniam abbas de Monte unoquoque anno dat illi unum provendarium de cera vel viginti solidos, et est in cois abbatis dare quale horum maluerit, et hoc pro relevationibus de Cantelupo et pro pastura de Lalande, si homines de Cantelupo possunt illam de raisneer in curia Guillelmi Paginelli. De Lavidande, quam Willelmus Paginellus inter-

[67] Guilhiermoz, p. 275.

[68] MS. 210 of the library of Avranches, f. 95; there are also two copies of the fifteenth century in the remnant of a cartulary of Saint-Pair preserved in the Archives of the Manche, *fonds* Mont-Saint-Michel, ff. 1v, 5v. Printed by Stapleton, in *Archaeologia*, xxvii. 27 (1838); Round, *Calendar*, no. 714. Cf. P. Chesnel, *Le Cotentin et l'Avranchin sous les ducs de Normandie* (Caen, 1912), pp. 211–219.

rogat in fedo, dum venit in Monte Sancti Michaelis est in respectu donec coram rege. Conventio est de septem paribus de honore quem Willelmus Paginellus tenet de abbate de Monte Sancti Michaelis quoniam submonuerit illos in sua curia, qui si sponte sua ambulare voluerint ibunt si liberi erunt de servicio abbatis. Si vero ire noluerint, hoc debet Guillelmus Paginellus de raisneer in curia abbatis per homines qui sunt de honore quem accepit cum sua uxore qui illos viderunt in suo servicio per consuetudinem antecessorum suorum. Huius cause testes existunt presul Abrincensis Michael, episcopus Sagiensis Robertus, Rogerius de Montegomerii, Richardus proconsul, Rogerius de Bellomonte, Hubertus de Ria, Unfredus de Bohon, Hubertus de Portu, Turgisus de Tracei, Alveredus Malbedenc, Gaufredus de Sai.

The document is not always so explicit as we could wish, but certain points are fairly clear. We see the Conqueror disposing of the hand of an heiress who holds an honor of the abbey of Mont-Saint-Michel, and her husband receiving aids, reliefs, and suit of court from the men of the honor. The aids are carefully defined: the lord may have an aid for his ransom from captivity or for redeeming his forfeited land from the duke or abbot, for marrying one daughter, or for ransoming his son if captured in the service of the duke or abbot. The last is noteworthy, suggesting that the aid for knighting the eldest son may have developed comparatively late with the growing importance of the institution of knighthood. The mention of tenure *in parage* would be important, if it were more specific, with reference to the parage of Domesday and the early history of the tenure in Normandy, where it seems to be otherwise unknown before Henry II.[69]

In all these feudal arrangements, the ultimate supremacy of the duke is clearly recognized. Even under the weak rule of Robert Curthose a declaration of liege fealty to the bishop of Bayeux contains an express reservation of the ducal rights; [70] while the whole system of assessing knight service is a convincing manifestation of the duke's power and authority. Moreover, the duke's right of calling out the general levy of the country in case of invasion

[69] Cf. Pollock and Maitland, ii. 264; Maitland, *Domesday Book and Beyond*, pp. 145–146; Guilhiermoz, *Origine de la noblesse*, p. 214 ff.; Round, in *Victoria History of Hampshire*, i. 441; Génestal, *Le parage normand* (Caen, 1911); Powicke, *The Loss of Normandy*, pp. 98–102.

[70] See the elaborate agreement between the bishop and Ranulf, *vicomte* of the Bessin, drawn up doubtless shortly after Bishop Odo's return in 1087, in *Livre noir*, no. 76; Round, no. 1435. The early mention of ' fidelitas ligia ' is noteworthy.

appears clearly in the Bayeux returns, where it is found under the name of *retrobannus*, or *arrière-ban*, by which it is later known; and it is specifically reserved in one of William's charters for Saint-Étienne.[71] From the care with which his vassals reserve this obligation as regards their dependents and even their townsmen,[72] it would seem that the duke held the lords responsible for producing their men when occasion arose.[73] Materials are lacking for any comparison of this system with the Anglo-Saxon *fyrd*, but it is highly probable that the familiarity of the Norman kings with the *arrière-ban* in the duchy made natural that preservation of the *fyrd* which is usually set down to deliberate desire to maintain Anglo-Saxon popular institutions. It should also be noted that the ordinance which, a century later, is generally said to have 'recreated and rearmed this ancient force' of the *fyrd*,[74] the Assize of Arms of Henry II, is drawn on the same lines as an earlier assize for Henry's continental dominions.[75]

Certain distinctive characteristics of feudal tenure in Normandy would doubtless stand out more clearly if we could compare them in detail with the feudal arrangements established by the Norman conquerors of southern Italy and Sicily. Unfortunately, evidence on this point is lacking for the South in the eleventh century, and while we now know that the substance of the South-Italian *Catalogus baronum*[76] belongs to the reign of King Roger and thus antedates the English *cartae* of 1166 as well

[71] Delisle, *Cartulaire normand*, no. 826. Cf. Guilhiermoz, pp. 289–292, where the text of the Bayeux returns is emended. Wace (ed. Andresen, ii, lines 5205 ff.) mentions the calling out of the peasants against the king of France in 1058.

[72] Ordericus, iii. 36, 39.

[73] Cf. the Worcestershire custom, Maitland, *Domesday Book and Beyond*, p. 159. On the *fyrd* in general see P. Vinogradoff, *English Society in the Eleventh Century*, p. 22 ff.

[74] Stubbs, *Select Charters*, eighth edition, p. 154; *Constitutional History*, i. 632.

[75] Benedict of Peterborough, i. 269; Guilhiermoz, *l. c.*, pp. 225–227.

[76] See the text in Del Re, *Cronisti e scrittori sincroni* (Naples, 1845), i. 571–616; and my discussion of its date and contents, *E. H. R.*, xxvi. 655–664 (1911). A similar conclusion regarding the date was reached independently by Giulio de Petra: *Rendiconti della R. Accademia di Archeologia di Napoli*, 1911, p. 35; *Supplemento all' opera* 'Le Monete delle Due Sicilie,' ed. Cangiati, March–June, 1912. Cf. Miss Evelyn Jamison, *The Norman Administration of Apulia and Capua* (*Papers of the British School at Rome*, vi, 1913), pp. 258, 338–341.

as the Norman inquest of 1172, we are in no position to apply it
to the conditions of an earlier time. The *Catalogus baronum*, however, is based upon the fundamental Norman institutions of the
knight's fee, the groups of five and ten knights, and the *arrière-
ban*, while other evidence shows the existence of the feudal aids
and the forty days' period of service; and these parallelisms are so
close that they can be satisfactorily explained only by treating the
feudalism of the South as an offshoot from the parent stem in
Normandy in the early period of Norman expansion.

Intimately connected with feudal tenure is the matter of feudal
jurisdiction. First of all, there is the jurisdiction which is strictly
feudal, the justice of the feudal lord over his tenants. Robert of
Bellême has an important court of his barons.[77] The monks of
Saint-Évroul have their court, in which they may declare the forfeiture of a fief.[78] The honor of Ralph Taisson has its barons, who
can be summoned to record against encroachment the title of the
abbey of their lord's foundation.[79] The honor which William
Painel holds of the abbot of Mont-Saint-Michel has a court of
seven peers, who owe service according to the custom of their
ancestors, and there are also separate courts for his manors.[80]
Besides this feudal justice, there is the jurisdiction which is fran-
chisal, arising from the grant of public rights by the sovereign, the
justice which men will one day say has nothing in common with
the fief. We cannot in the eleventh century draw the line separating these two sorts of jurisdiction with the sharpness which later
feudal law permits;[81] the justice of the feudal lord may owe some-

[77] Archives of the Orne, H. 2150; Bry, *Histoire du pays et comté du Perche* (Paris,
1620), pp. 82, 103; Round, *Calendar*, no. 654; Vernier, no. 34.

[78] *Ca.* 1056, Ordericus, ii. 60, 75. Cf. Round, no. 713 (Mont-Saint-Michel);
the stipulation of suit of court, *supra*, p. 22; Chevreux and Vernier, *Les archives
de Normandie et de la Seine-Inférieure* (Rouen, 1911), no. 7 (= Round, no. 116);
Le Prévost, *Eure*, iii. 209; Vernier, no. 24.

[79] *Gallia Christiana*, xi. instr. 65 (*ca.* 1070).

[80] *Supra*, p. 22. The number seven suggests the usual number of the Frankish
scabini from whom the peers of feudal courts seem to have been derived; probably
it is these same seven who owe the military service due from the honor.

[81] Cf. Esmein, *Cours d'histoire du droit français*, eleventh edition, p. 293 ff.;
Maitland, *Domesday Book and Beyond*, p. 80.

thing to royal grant, and the holder of the franchise may not always be able to point to the act which created it, yet the distinction seems thus early justified by the facts.

We must at the outset give up any attempt to follow the Norman franchises back into Frankish days. Doubtless Norman churches enjoyed the immunity which all such bodies were supposed to possess under Louis the Pious,[82] and some had more specific privileges;[83] but the nature and development of the immunity is obscure enough in those regions which have preserved an unbroken series of such grants,[84] and in Normandy the coming of the invaders not only made a wide gap in our records, but produced important changes in the holders of land and probably in the rights exercised over it. The clearest case of continuity is furnished by Berneval-sur-Mer, which had been a dependency of Saint-Denis under the Frankish kings and was confirmed to the abbey by the first Norman dukes.[85] This confirmation was repeated by Richard I in 968 in a charter which grants full immunity and all rights exercised in Berneval by count or viscount, *vicarius* or *centenarius*.[86] When we come to the charters of the eleventh century, the clause of immunity, though reminiscent of Frankish models, is shorter and more general. Richard II grants to Fécamp[87] and Jumièges[88] the possession of their lands "without any disturbance of any secular or judicial authority whatever, as property belonging to the demesne fisc," and the same phrases appear, omitting the reference to the fisc, in his charters

[82] H. Brunner, *Deutsche Rechtsgeschichte*, ii. 291.

[83] Lot, *S.-Wandrille*, no. 4; *H. F.*, viii. 650 (Saint-Ouen).

[84] For the literature of the controversy, see Brunner, *l. c.*, ii. 287 ff.; A. Meister, *Deutsche Verfassungsgeschichte*[2] (in his *Grundriss*, 1913), pp. 77–80; G. von Below, *Der deutsche Staat des Mittelalters* (Leipzig, 1914), i. 252–261.

[85] Böhmer-Mühlbacher, *Regesten der Karolinger*, nos. 60 (58), 190 (186); Dudo of Saint-Quentin, ed. Lair, p. 171.

[86] *H. F.*, ix. 731; cf. Lot, *Les derniers Carolingiens*, p. 57.

[87] 'Haec omnia . . . concedo . . . ut habeant, teneant, et possideant absque ulla inquietudine cuiuslibet secularis vel iudiciarię potestatis sicuti res ad fiscum dominicum pertinentes.' Original in Musée de la Bénédictine at Fécamp, no. 2 *ter; Neustria Pia*, p. 217. See Appendix B, where the documents relative to the Fécamp immunity are discussed.

[88] Cartulary no. 22, f. 7, and *vidimus* of 1499 and 1529 in Archives of the Seine-Inférieure; Vernier, no. 12 (i. 40).

for Bernai[89] and Saint-Ouen.[90] The clause is not found in Richard's grant to Mont-Saint-Michel, but appears in the charter of Robert I,[91] who likewise made the sites of Saint-Amand and La Trinité-du-Mont 'immune from the judicial exaction of his authority.'[92] I have found no such clauses in any new grant after Robert's time, though phrases are common which grant such protection as is enjoyed by the duke's demesne.[93]

How much, if any, actual authority these vague grants of immunity conveyed, it is impossible to say. Except in the very early instance of Berneval, they make no direct grant of fees or jurisdiction, and if they are more than a pious formula, it would seem that their primary purpose was to assure the duke's protection. It is altogether likely that, in Normandy as elsewhere, such phrases persist in documents after they have lost all real meaning.[94] In any event it must be borne in mind, as one of the few points upon which there is general agreement, that the Frankish immunity itself, whatever its ultimate effects in establishing private jurisdictions, did not create exemption from the authority of the count,[95] so that, apart from the question of any devolution of royal rights to the Norman dukes, they would still as counts [96] retain some control of the great religious establishments. That the clauses of immunity in the charters of the Norman dukes were not intended as a general grant of the duke's judicial powers is

[89] Le Prévost, *Eure*, i. 285; *Neustria Pia*, p. 399.

[90] Pommeraye, *Histoire de S.-Ouen* (Rouen, 1662), p. 405; Valin, p. 222.

[91] *M. A. N.*, xii. 111 (Round, no. 705).

[92] *Cartulaire de la Trinité-du-Mont de Rouen*, no. 1; *Monasticon*, vii. 1101; Valin, p. 223.

[93] Brunner, *Schwurgerichte*, p. 238 ff. The charter of Richard I for Saint-Taurin of Évreux is said to have granted 'tantam libertatem in curia Sancti Taurini quantam suis hominibus in sua curia ': Bonnin, *Cartulaire de Louviers*, i. 2, where we have only a later notice, not the act itself (Prentout, *Étude critique sur Dudon de S.-Quentin*, p. xxiv, note).

[94] E. Stengel, *Die Immunitäts-Urkunden der deutschen Könige* (Innsbruck, 1902); M. Kroell, *L'immunité franque* (Paris, 1910), p. 303 ff.

[95] Brunner, *Deutsche Rechtsgeschichte*, ii. 166, 300, 302; G. Seeliger, *Die Bedeutung der Grundherrschaft* (Leipzig, 1903), p. 80 ff.; Kroell, *l. c.*, pp. 217, 249 ff.; Dopsch, *Die Wirthschaftsentwickelung der Karolingerzeit* (Weimar, 1912–1913), ii. 95 ff.

[96] On the use of count as a title of the Norman dukes, see Lappenberg, *Geschichte Englands*, ii. 18; Vernier, i. 75; and the charters of Robert I cited in Appendix C, note 39.

shown by the practice,[97] which appears as early as Richard II, of granting, sometimes in the very documents which contain the immunity clause, the ducal *consuetudines* in specified places. Thus Richard II's charter to Bernai conveys the duke's *consuetudines* in all the *villae* possessed by the monastery,[98] and his charter for Jumièges grants his customs, here styled *consuetudines comitatus*, in three places.[99] The term is, of course, a general one, [100] comprising tolls, market rights, and a great variety of rights of exploitation other than the profits of justice, but it specifically includes 'laws and forfeitures' in Richard's grant of the customs of the Mount to Mont-Saint-Michel,[101] and its jurisdictional content is more exactly defined in documents to which we shall come in a moment. We may say provisionally that when the duke wished to convey jurisdiction, he made a grant of the ducal *consuetudines*, but we can understand what this means only when we have examined what judicial rights the duke had to grant.

It is commonly asserted by modern writers [102] that the duke of Normandy was the only feudatory of the French crown who suc-

[97] This point is overlooked by Valin, p. 223, in his argument from the later interpretation of monastic immunities.

[98] Le Prévost, *Eure*, i. 285.

[99] 'Ex quibus nostro tempore donavit per nostrum consensum Rotbertus archiepiscopus frater noster omnes consuetudines que ad comitatum pertinent quas ipse ex nostro iure possidebat. . . . In Vado Fulmerii unum alodarium et omnes consuetudines quas ex iure comitatus in omnibus terris ipsius loci tenebam. . . . Pro quo et nos donavimus omnes consuetudines que ex ipsa terra pertinebant ad nos.' Cartulary 22 in Archives of the Seine-Inférieure, ff. 7–11; *vidimus* of 1499 and 1529 in same archives; Vernier, no. 12. Cf. *Neustria Pia*, p. 323; Delisle-Berger, no. 527; *Monasticon*, vii. 1087; Le Prévost, *Eure*, ii. 296; and the long and interesting list of *consuetudines* of the count of Maine at Château-du-Loir in *Archives historiques du Maine*, vi. 34.

[100] Cf. Flach, *Origines de l'ancienne France*, i. 203; and notes 109, 163, below.

[101] *Neustria Pia*, p. 378; *M.A.N.*, xii. 110; Round, no. 702. Cf. the Conqueror's charter in *Cartulaire de S.-Père de Chartres*, i. 168. On the other hand his charter for Saint-Désir mentions 'consuetudinibus et forisfactis' (*Gallia Christiana*, xi. instr. 203). Undefined ducal grants of *consuetudines* will be found in *Livre noir*, no. 1; *Revue catholique de Normandie*, x. 49; La Roque, iii. 26; *Cartulaire de Notre-Dame de Chartres*, i. 86; Sauvage, *Troarn*, p. 349 f.; Collection Moreau, xxi. 110 (Saint-Ouen).

[102] Brussel, *Usage des fiefs* (Paris, 1750), i. 253; A. Luchaire, *Manuel des institutions françaises*, pp. 245, 256. Valin, pp. 60, 182–193, also criticizes the current view, but in too juristic a fashion, overlooking the early evidence cited below, which was

ceeded in retaining for himself the monopoly of *haute justice* throughout his dominions. Now if we mean by *haute justice* what the lawyers of the thirteenth century meant, jurisdiction by virtue of which the duel could be held and penalty of death or mutilation inflicted, this statement is far from correct, for so-called pleas of the sword are often held by the duke's vassals [103] and the duel is waged in their courts.[104] If, on the other hand, we mean that a baron could possess such pleas only by virtue of a ducal grant, and that certain of them were never granted, the statement will probably hold. For the pleas of the sword in the twelfth century we have a list drawn up under Henry II, which can be supplemented by certain chapters of the *Très Ancien Coutumier* [105] and confirmed by the Exchequer Rolls. This list, however, expressly says that murder belongs " to the duke alone or to those to whom he or his ancestors have granted it," and it is plain that the same limitation is intended to qualify others of the pleas enumerated. The matter is clearer in the inquest of 1091, which gives a statement, including fewer pleas but professedly incomplete, of the 'customs and justice' exercised by William the Conqueror in the duchy. Assault in the duke's court or on the way to and from it, offenses committed in the host or within a week of its setting forth or its return, offenses against pilgrims, and violations of the coinage — these place the offender in the duke's mercy and belong exclusively to his jurisdiction.[106] On the other hand, it appears from the same inquest that there are other offenses, such as attacks on houses (*hainfara*), arson, rape, and unwarranted seizure of sureties, jurisdiction over which belongs in some places to the duke

printed in 1908 and 1909. His theory of the late development of ducal sovereignty has been answered by Powicke, *Loss of Normandy*, pp. 80–84.

[103] See *B. É. C.*, xiii. 108–109; Stapleton, *Magni Rotuli*, i, p. xxxiii; and the texts cited below.

[104] See, for example, the duels held in the court of the abbot of Jumièges in 1056, Mabillon, *Annales Ordinis S. Benedicti*, iv. 519; and in the court of Roger of Beaumont, *Gallia Christiana*, xi. instr. 202.

[105] Ed. Tardif, cc. 70 (inquest), 15, 16, 35, 53, 58, 59; cf. 67, 69. Cf. Pollock and Maitland, ii. 455; and *infra*, p. 187.

[106] Appendix D, cc. 1–3, 12, 13. The protection of the plow by the duke, as we find it in the *Très Ancien Coutumier*, likewise goes far back into Norman, if not into Scandinavian, history. Dudo, ed. Lair, pp. 171–172; Wilda, *Strafrecht*, p. 245; council of Rouen, 1096, c. 2.

and in others to his barons; [107] and we find arson, rape, and *hain-fara* among the *consuetudines* which Duke William, in the year of his marriage, granted to the abbot of Préaux.[108] Similar pleas were doubtless included in the *consuetudines de sanguine* granted by the Conqueror to Bec, which possessed jurisdiction over murder and mayhem among the ' royal liberties ' it enjoyed under Henry I; [109] and while there were probably local differences, as in Anglo-Saxon England, where Domesday shows curious parallels to the Norman forfeitures,[110] it is evidently jurisdiction over crimes of this sort which is conferred by the ducal grants of *consuetudines* to monasteries. The great lay lords might also have such customs; indeed the forfeiture of life and limb in baronial courts is presupposed in the inquest of 1091.[111] The counts of Évreux and Mortain have blood-justice; [112] the count of Eu has justice in the hundred of Saint-Pierre-sur-Dive over all forfeitures except the duke's army and coinage; [113] Robert, count of Meulan,

[107] Cc. 9, 10.

[108] Appendix D, p. 279; Valin, pièces, no. 2. Kings Robert I and Philip I enumerate ' sanguinem, raptum, incendium, homicidium ' among the *consuetudines* of Micy: Pfister, *Robert le Pieux*, no. 68; Prou, *Actes de Philippe I*, no. 77.

[109] ' Predicto monasterio tradidit idem comes Normannie omnes consuetudines de sanguine et theloneo quas habebat circa ipsum monasterium ': before 1066, MS. Lat. 12884, f. 177; cf. E. Porée, *Histoire du Bec*, i. 327, 367, 646. The relevant portion of the charter of Henry I for Bec (Round, *Calendar*, no. 375) is printed below in Chapter III, note 21; see also the charter on the next page establishing the jurisdiction of Fécamp over homicide and arson by grant of Henry's predecessors. Cf. also Robert I's grant of Harfleur ' cum sanguine ' to Montivilliers (*Gallia Christiana*, xi. instr. 326); the Conqueror's grant of ' leugam cum sanguine ' to the monks of Saint-Benoit (Prou and Vidier, *Recueil des chartes de S.-Benoit-sur-Loire*, no. 78); and Henry I's charter for Saint-Pierre-sur-Dive, where, however, pleas relating to the army and the coinage are expressly reserved (*Gallia Christiana*, xi. instr. 157). John, abbot of Fécamp (1028–1079), grants a piece of land ' retenta publica iustitia in consilio nostro ': Collection Moreau, xxi. 25.

[110] Cf. Pollock and Maitland, ii. 454; Maitland, *Domesday Book and Beyond*, pp. 87–88; Vinogradoff, *English Society in the Eleventh Century*, p. 111 ff.

[111] C. 8.

[112] Count Richard of Évreux (d. 1067) gives ' Deo et Sancto Taurino tres consuetudines quas habebat in terra Sancti Taurini, videlicet sanguinem, septeragium (sesteragium ?), et thelonagium.' ' Little Cartulary ' of Saint-Taurin, Archives of the Eure, H. 793, no. 26. For Mortain see *B. É. C.*, xiii. 108, note.

[113] *Gallia Christiana*, xi. instr. 156–158; cf. col. 203. See also Countess Adeliza's grant of ' omnem vicecomitatum . . . et omnes consuetudines ' to Auchy-Aumale: *Archaeologia*, xxvi. 359.

gives the abbot of Préaux, in Salerne, his " forfeitures which according to human law are collected by ancient custom from homicides, thieves, and such others as are capitally convicted," and in another district *hainfara*, arson, and *ullac*.[114] The privileged area of the *banleuca* also existed.[115]

Whatever view one may hold as to the relative development of seigniorial jurisdiction on the two sides of the Channel before the Conquest, there was one field in which England had much to learn from Normandy, that of ecclesiastical justice. We have the Conqueror's word for it that in England " the episcopal laws had not been observed properly nor according to the precepts of the sacred canons," [116] and it is generally recognized that we must seek in Normandy the principles underlying the ordinance separating the spiritual and temporal courts which he issued within ten years of his accession to the English throne. Of course the Norman precedents must not be scanned too narrowly without due regard to the jurisprudence of the Roman Church as a whole, but it is significant that in this period this jurisprudence came to England through Norman prelates and Norman manuscripts, as has been clearly shown in the case of the Pseudo-Isidorian decretals.[117] What the Norman practice then was we can in some measure discern from the canons of the council of Lillebonne, issued by an assembly of prelates and barons held by William's command in 1080.[118] Freeman, it is true, with his splendid indifference

[114] Cartulary of Préaux (Archives of the Eure, H. 711), nos. 68, 347; MS. Lat. n. a. 1929, no. 250; Le Prévost, *Eure*, iii. 97 (cf. on p. 96 the grant of Roger of Beaumont); Valin, pièces, no. 4. For *ullac* see Appendix D, note 16. Tithes of the baron's forfeitures are frequently granted to monasteries, e. g., Le Prévost, *Eure*, i. 408 (= Lot, *S.-Wandrille*, no. 41); *Gallia Christiana*, xi. instr. 129.

[115] See *infra*, p. 49.

[116] Liebermann, *Gesetze*, i. 485, ii. 440, 531; Stubbs-Davis, *Select Charters* (1913), p. 99.

[117] See the account of MS. 405 of Trinity College, Cambridge, brought from Bec to Canterbury by Lanfranc, and its derivatives, in H. Böhmer, *Die Fälschungen Erzbischof Lanfranks von Canterbury* (Leipzig, 1902), pp. 61–65. Norman copies of Pseudo-Isidore will be found in MS. Lat. 3856 and MSS. 701–703 at Rouen. For decretals of Alexander II addressed to the bishop of Coutances, see Jaffé-Löwenfeld, nos. 4479, 4480.

[118] Teulet, *Layettes du Trésor des Chartes*, i. 25, no. 22, from an early copy in the

to such ecclesiastical matters as were not architectural, says that, apart from the renewal of the Truce of God, this council merely pronounced " a great number of enactments of the usual kind ";[119] but when we recall that Henry II began his great struggle with the church by decreeing that the provisions of the council of Lillebonne should be observed,[120] we shall hardly dismiss so lightly an authoritative statement of the law of the Conqueror's day on matters of church and state. Unfortunately, these decrees, while affording abundant evidence respecting the existence of a system of ecclesiastical courts, leave us in the dark on some of the matters we most need to understand. Besides the enforcement of the Truce of God, the bishop has cognizance of offenses committed in churches and churchyards, including the disturbance of worship and assaults on those going to and from church. He has his fines from criminous and delinquent clerks and from offending members of a clerk's household, and dwellers within the church enclosure are likewise subject to the ' episcopal laws.' Of the offenses of laymen from which the bishop has his fine, specific mention is made of adultery, incest, desertion, divination, assaults upon priests or monks, and the burning of their houses. A fine is also due from those who fail at the ordeal or are excommunicated for resistance to justice. The question throughout is one of fines to be paid the bishop, and while in secular justice it is a fairly safe rule that he who has the fines will also have the jurisdiction, it is entirely possible that for certain offenses the bishop should have had fines from laymen who were convicted in secular tribunals, just as he had from those who denied their guilt and failed at the ordeal, and, later, from violators of the Truce of God convicted in the duke's court.[121] It is hardly likely, for example, that the fine to the bishop was the only penalty for slaying a clerk.

Archives Nationales attested by the seal of Henry I; Ordericus, ii. 316–323; Bessin, *Concilia Rotomagensis Provinciae*, i. 67; Mansi, xx. 555. Cf. Tardif, *Étude sur les sources de l'ancien droit normand*, i. 39–43.

[119] *Norman Conquest*, 2d edition, iv. 657.

[120] Robert of Torigni, i. 336; see *infra*, Chapter V, note 83. The importance of the council is realized by H. W. C. Davis, *England under the Normans and Angevins*, pp. 527, 533, but his interpretations of its canons are not always sound.

[121] Bessin, *Concilia*, i. 81; *Très Ancien Coutumier*, c. 71; Round, no. 290.

Little is said of the relation of the clerk to lay courts, either in civil or in criminal matters. With respect to his secular holding the priest is subject to the court of his lord, although if the question concerns the church he can have it brought before his bishop. Violations of the forest laws by clerks are beyond the sphere of the bishop's authority, and it would seem from the decree of an earlier council that a clerk who exposed himself to the blood-feud could be attacked after due notice to his bishop.[122] A well known passage of William of Poitiers indicates that the Conqueror was in the habit of interfering when the sentence of the court Christian seemed to him too light, and inflicting discipline on the bishop or archdeacon as well as on the culprit; [123] but specific instances of this sort are lacking. When the archdeacons of the diocese of Bayeux consult Lanfranc respecting the case of a priest who had committed homicide in self-defense, the question is not one of punishment at their hands, but simply how soon, if at all, the offender can be restored to his priestly functions.[124] In another case, before William, archbishop of Rouen, a priest convicted of a variety of offenses suffers degradation and the loss of his benefice.[125]

Throughout the canons of Lillebonne runs the assertion of the ultimate authority of the duke. The council attempts no innovation: duke, barons, and bishops are to have the customs and justice which they have enjoyed under William and his father, but

[122] ' Ut etiam clerici arma non ferant nec assaliant vel assaliantur nisi ipsi promeruerint, neque etiam tunc nisi facta proclamatione apud episcopum rationabiliter ': Council of Lisieux (1064), c. 5, in *Journal des savants*, 1901, p. 517.

[123] Ed. Duchesne, p. 194; Migne, cxlix. 1241. The participation of the duke in ecclesiastical discipline is also implied in Richard II's charter for Mont-Saint-Michel: *Neustria Pia*, p. 378.

[124] Lanfranc, *Ep.* 62, Migne, cl. 550. Cf. Migne, cxlvii. 266 (1061).

[125] ' Notum sit omnibus quod Gausfredus presbyter de Verliaco . . . ad iudicium utrinque venerunt coram Guillelmo Rotomagensi archiepiscopo presbyter scilicet et monachi. . . . Ibi presbyter accusatus atque convictus de multis criminibus tam per se ipsum perpetratis quam sua consensione per quendam filium suum, videlicet de furtis, de sacrilegiis, de fornicationibus, et de contaminatione ecclesie sue, cum se de his nulla posset ratione purgare, ab ordine suo depositus est ab archiepiscopo. . . . Veniens in curiam regis Anglorum apud castrum Nielfam guerpivit coram omnibus totum omnino beneficium vel quicquid reclamare poterat ullo modo in ecclesia nostra de Verliaco. Insuper coram tota ipsa curia iuravit non se quicquam eorum ultra reclamaturum.' MS. Baluze 77, f. 61, from cartulary of Marmoutier.

the judicial privileges are held by virtue of the duke's concession, and in case of dispute as to their extent the court of the duke is to decide.[126] The bishop's rights over laymen were a matter of custom, and varied from place to place. In many parishes the charters show that he had, in whole or in part, lost his jurisdiction, for the episcopal fines and forfeitures were valuable rights, like his synodal dues and visitation fees,[127] and were often granted in fief to laymen [128] or handed over to monasteries in the form of exemption from episcopal *consuetudines*,[129] just as ducal *consuetudines* were granted by the duke. Thus Fécamp claimed certain churches free from the jurisdiction of the archbishop of Rouen,[130] and by privilege of Archbishop Robert the monks of Saint-Père of Chartres held the church of Fontenay in the Vexin free from bishop and archdeacon.[131]   Robert I was said to have given Mont-Saint-Michel the 'episcopal laws' in half of Guernsey.[132] The abbess of La Trinité had the fines from episcopal forfeitures in two parishes of Caen,[133] and the abbot of Saint-Étienne had similar

[126] So the author of the *Acta archiepiscoporum* says of William, after the difficulties between the archbishop and the monks of Rouen in 1073: ' In his omnibus semper apud ipsum cautum extitit ne quid sibi archiepiscopus quasi sub ecclesiastico vigore in causis huius ecclesie insolenter arrogaverit.' Mabillon, *Vetera Analecta*, p. 226; *Gallia Christiana*, xi. 35. On the author see Vacandard, in *Revue catholique de Normandie*, iii. 121 ff.

[127] On which cf. the protest of the canons of Chartres in *H. F.*, x. 498; and Fulbert of Chartres, *Epistolae*, nos. 48, 115 (Migne, cxli. 225, 265).

[128] *Supra*, notes 12–15. Cf. council of Rouen, 1096, c. 6: ' Nullus laicus habeat consuetudines episcopales vel iustitiam que pertinet ad curam animarum ' (Ordericus, iii. 473). For England cf. the grant of ' placita hominum de christianitate ' in Davis, no. 71.

[129] *Gallia Christiana*, xi. instr. 73, 126, 231; *Neustria Pia*, pp. 339, 431; Sauvage, *Troarn*, p. 356; Delisle, *S.-Sauveur*, pièces, nos. 46, 48; *Musée des archives départementales*, no. 25 (Lessay); Bry, *Histoire du Perche*, p. 70. The following grant of 1053 is more specific: ' aecclesiam Sancte Marie de Berlo et altare et omnes reditus eorum, decimas scilicet, primitias, sepulturam, sinodalia, circada, et omnes forfacturas ad ipsam aecclesiam pertinentes, hoc est: sacrilegium, latrocinium, infracturam cimiterii, et cum omnibus commissis episcopo pertinentibus ' (charter of William of La Ferté-Macé, Denis, *Chartes de S.-Julien de Tours*, no. 24; *Revue catholique*, i. 168).

[130] See Appendix B.

[131] *Cartulaire*, ed. Guérard, i. 115; *Gallia Christiana*, viii. instr. 297.

[132] Cartulary (MS. Avranches 210), f. 106v.

[133] *Gallia Christiana*, xi. instr. 71.

privileges.[134] In such cases the bishop sought to retain the ultimate authority, whose symbol, the administration of the ordeal at his cathedral church, was specifically reserved to him by the council of Lillebonne; [135] yet two years later the abbot of Saint-Wandrille established in the duke's court his ancient right to administer the ordeal in the four parishes subject to his jurisdiction.[136] That the bishop's jurisdiction was comprehensive and attendance at his court no light matter, appears from the case of Mont-Saint-Michel: the residents of the Mount complained of their frequent summons to Avranches as parties or witnesses in the bishop's court in all matters *contra christianitatem*, and of the bishop's refusal to accept excuses in time of invasion or storm, so that they were constantly being fined or punished on this account; until in 1061 the bishop consented to make the abbot his archdeacon for the Mount, reserving to himself, however, the administration of the ordeal, the hearing of matrimonial causes, and the

[134] *Gallia Christiania*, xi. instr. 73; charter of Odo, bishop of Bayeux (copies in Archives of the Calvados, H. 1825; MS. Fr. n. a. 20218, f. 6): 'Trado ista que hic determino, videlicet de omnibus in prefatis ecclesiis domibus terris habitatoribus omnium forisfacturarum de criminalibus peccatis vel de non criminalibus prodeuntium pecuniam et de ipsis omnibus habitatoribus de non criminalibus peccatis penitentie iniunctionem. Addo etiam ut ex ipsis criminalibus peccatis quandocumque in prefatis ecclesiis domibus terris audiri contigerint ab archidiacono Baiocensi, abbas vel prior predicti cenobii, non ipse super quo crimen auditum fuerit, moneatur et ibidem ab utroque disposito termino congruo ac prefixo die conveniant monachus et archidiaconus et in ipsa parrochia in qua crimen auditum fuerit predictis presentibus inquiratur, inquisito discutiatur, et discusso, si inde iudicium portandum prodierit vel cognitio peccati potuerit, Baiocensis ecclesia ut decet requiratur vel causa examinationis vel gratia consequende reconciliationis.' Cf. the similar charter of Geoffrey, bishop of Coutances (in charter of Archbishop William, copied in Archives of the Calvados, H. 1825): ' De his autem omnibus supradictis si placitum contingat, in curia abbatis Cadomi agatur et forisfacturam si contingat abbas habebit. Si iudicium inde portandum prodierit, ad Hulmum ut constitutum est requiratur, vidente archidiacono, et penitentia detur.' Early in the twelfth century Abbot Eudo 'separavit Robertum Blundum ab uxore sua coram Osberto archidiacono, qui fuit ibi in loco episcopi Ricardi filii comitis,' bishop of Bayeux (Deville, *Analyse*, p. 32).

[135] See the charters quoted in the preceding note, and the arrangement between the archbishop of Rouen and Bec, *Gallia Christiana*, xi. instr. 17. There is a curious account of the holding of an ordeal at Bayeux before archdeacons, by order of the duke's court, in *Archaeologia*, xxvii. 26. William's ordinance separating the temporal and spiritual courts in England likewise reserves the ordeal for the cathedral.

[136] Bessin, *Concilia*, i. 76; Lot, *S.-Wandrille*, no. 39 (cf. no. 40).

imposition of sentence in other cases.[137] It appears from other documents that matrimonial matters were an important part of the work of the courts Christian.[138]

The duke's assertion of authority over church courts and his interference, at the council of Lillebonne, in the enforcement of sacerdotal celibacy [139] are only one phase of an ecclesiastical

[137] ' Cogebantur enim venire Abrincas ad respondendum de quacunque accusatione contra christianitatem, nec excusare poterat eos mare insurgens nec Britonum insidie quia preveniri ac provideri poterant, et ita sepe in forifacta et emendationes episcopales incidebant et sepe iuramentis fatigabantur. . . . Episcopus vero prefatus, ut erat animo et genere nobilis, petitioni abbatis annuit et archidiaconum suum in Monte eum fecit, ita tamen ut quod bene non faceret vel non posset episcopus corrigeret Abrincis et ecclesiastico iuditio terminaret. De coniugiis autem illicitis si qui legales testes procederent, apud episcopum audirentur et per sacramentum ipsorum lege dissolveretur quod contra legem presumptum erat. De criminalibus culpis venirent ad iuditium et sententiam episcopi confessi vel convicti coram suo archidiacono, excommunicati ab episcopo ad eius satisfactionem et absolutionem venirent. Iuditium ferri igniti et aque ferventis Abrincis portaretur.' MS. Lat. 14832, f. 183v; Migne, cxlvii. 265; Pigeon, *Le diocèse d'Avranches*, ii. 658. It should be noted that Richard II's charter had granted to the abbot all ducal and episcopal *consuetudines* in the Mount, including ' omnes leges omnesque forisfacturas clericorum ac laicorum virorum ac mulierum eiusdem burgi ' in terms which suggest a later interpolation (Cartulary, f. 21v; *Neustria Pia*, p. 378; Mabillon, *Annales*, iv. 651. Cf. the description of these liberties in the *Roman du Mont-Saint-Michel*, lines 2406 ff.). On the other hand, the statement of the rights of the bishop of Avranches over the abbeys of his diocese, preserved in a MS. of the twelfth century in the Vatican (MS. Regina 946, f. 73v) states the matter from the bishop's point of view: ' Salva est autem episcopo Abrincensi in predicta abbatia in omnibus canonica iusticia.' See Appendix K.

The agreement of 1061 is of possible interest in relation to the use of synodal witnesses in Normandy; see Chapter VI, note 119.

[138] See the case from Caen cited in note 134, *supra;* Barret, *Cartulaire de Marmoutier pour le Perche*, no. 18 (1092–1100); and the notice of the grant by the *vicomtes* to Saint-Sauveur of freedom ' ab omnibus placitis et querelis, videlicet de trevia, de adulteriis, et de omnibus aliis rebus que pertinent ad christianitatem, ita ut monachi habeant placita in curia sua omnemque emendacionem' (Delisle, *S.-Sauveur*, pièces, no. 46). The penance imposed by the bishop of Séez upon the slayer of three pilgrims to Mont-Saint-Michel illustrates another phase of the bishop's jurisdiction: Lanfranc, *Epistolae*, no. 9 (Migne, cl. 517). Cf. an agreement of 1084 between the count of Anjou and the bishop of Angers: L. Halphen, *L'Anjou au XIe siècle*, p. 314, no. 242.

[139] H. Böhmer, *Kirche und Staat in England und in der Normandie* (Leipzig, 1899), p. 127 f. On p. 36, note 2, he questions the authenticity, in its present form, of the canon of Lillebonne (c. 3) which deals with this subject. The last sentence is somewhat perplexing, but it appears in the text as confirmed by Henry I (Teulet, *Layettes*, i, no. 22) and may perhaps mean that the judgment of parishioners and the

supremacy to which the eleventh century affords no parallel.[140] A familiar passage of Eadmer [141] assigns a Norman origin to the customs which the Conqueror established with respect to church matters in England — control over councils and appointments, necessity of the king's approval for the excommunication of his barons and for the reception of letters or legates from Rome — and there is little to add to what is already known concerning his policy in these respects in Normandy.[142] William was regularly present at the meetings of church councils, and their decrees were issued with his sanction. He not only appointed the bishops and abbots, like the stronger princes of his time, but was able on occasion to secure their deposition. The monasteries were under the special protection of the duke, and this was so effective as to leave little room in Normandy for the *avoués* who play so large a part in monastic and feudal history elsewhere.[143] No bishop succeeded in getting permanent possession of a county or even in acquiring the full rights of a count in his episcopal city, where the presence of the *vicomte* was a constant reminder of the duke's authority and might, as at Rouen in 1073, even serve to protect the prelate in time of disturbance.[144] If we may judge by the case of the see of

penalty prescribed in the preceding clause had been forced by the king upon the unwilling bishops.

[140] "Das landesherrliche Kirchenregiment war hier mithin viel stärker entwickelt, als in den anderen Staaten des Kontinents: " Böhmer, p. 33. The absence of such control over the bishops was a constant source of weakness to Normandy's powerful neighbor, the count of Flanders: Lot, *Études sur le règne de Hugues Capet*, p. 219.

[141] *Historia Novorum*, p. 9; Liebermann, *Gesetze*, i. 520.

[142] Böhmer's discussion is the best. The council of Lisieux of 1064, discovered and published by Delisle (*Journal des savants*, 1901, p. 516), should be added to his list of councils. On the appointment of bishops see also Imbart de la Tour, *Les élections épiscopales dans l'église de France* (Paris, 1891), pp. 247, 273, 291–294, 455.

[143] Brussel, *Usage des fiefs*, ii. 810; F. Senn, *L'institution des avoueries ecclésiastiques en France* (Paris, 1903), p. 95 ff.; both of whom insist too absolutely upon the exclusion of the *avoué* from early Normandy. See Valin, pp. 85–88; and Sauvage, *Troarn*, p. 61. The absence of the *vidame* is also noteworthy: Senn, *L'institution des vidamies* p. 98 f. See, however, below, p. 167.

[144] *Gallia Christiana*, xi. 34; on the date see Vacandard, *Revue catholique*, iii. 118 (1893). Geoffrey de Montbray had no land in Coutances when he became bishop, and was obliged to purchase what he needed from the duke: *Gallia Christiana*, xi. instr. 219. The bishop of Lisieux had greater freedom: Stapleton, i, p. clxix; H. de Formeville, *Histoire de l'ancien évêché-comté de Lisieux* (Lisieux, 1873), pp. dxlvii, 315.

Bayeux, [145] the bishops lost rather than gained by the anarchy of the Conqueror's successor, and when bishops appear taking an important part in secular affairs in the twelfth century, it is as the agents and justices of the duke and not as his rivals.

One function of the Norman ecclesiastical courts found no occasion for its exercise in England,[146] namely their enforcement of the Truce of God. Introduced into Normandy in its Flemish form early in the Conqueror's reign,[147] the Truce was reaffirmed by councils of 1064 and 1080 and elaborated at the council of Rouen in 1096. The original penalties were ecclesiastical and their imposition was the duty of the bishop and his deputies: before 1067 the bishop of Évreux is trying to punish monks for its infraction;[148] under Henry I the bishop's claim to his fine is clearly recognized;[149] and as late as 1233 the bishop of Avranches and his rural deans assert their immemorial right to hold *placita treuge*.[150] The duke, however, has likewise an interest in maintaining so important an adjunct to public order: the council of Lillebonne provides that the lord of the land shall aid the bishop in coercing recalcitrant offenders, and, failing his aid, the *vicomte* of the duke shall take the matter into his hands; while by 1135 the punishment of serious violations has become the function of the ducal

[145] *Livre noir*, pp. xli, xlii.

[146] On the absence of the Truce of God in England, see F. Liebermann, *Ueber die Leges Edwardi Confessoris*, p. 59 ff.; Pollock and Maitland, i. 75 f. Their conclusions do not seem to me invalidated by what Powicke says on the subject (*Loss of Normandy*, p. 94), although his general views on the Norman phase of the question appear sound. Cf. Liebermann, *Gesetze*, ii. 687 f.

[147] Bessin, *Concilia*, i. 39; Mansi, xix. 597; cf. *Gallia Christiana*, xi. instr. 202; *Acta Sanctorum*, August, iv. 834; *Analecta Bollandiana*, xxii. 438; *M. G. H.*, *Scriptores*, viii. 403. On the date of the council, which is not later than 1047 and is probably of 1042 or 1043, see Tardif, *Étude*, p. 29 f., where the parallelism with the Flemish form of the text is overlooked. The latest edition of the Norman ordinance, that of the *M. G. H.*, *Constitutiones et Acta Publica*, i. 600, does not pay sufficient attention to Norman MSS., such as MS. Rouen 1383, f. 9, a MS. of the eleventh century from Jumièges, or MS. Lat. 1928, f. 173v (used by Bessin). The provisions of the various councils are analyzed by Tardif, p. 30 ff.

[148] Migne, cxliii. 1387.

[149] *Tres Ancièn Coutumier*, c. 71; Round, no. 290. Cf. Delisle, in *B. É. C.*, xiii. 102.

[150] L. Auvray, *Registres de Grégoire IX*, no. 1308; Collection Moreau, mclxxxviii. 68.

court, and the bishop's interest is merely pecuniary.[151] "As it appears in the first part of the *Très Ancien Coutumier*, the Truce of God has almost become the peace of the duke." [152]

While, however, the ducal authority welcomed such aid in the difficult task of maintaining order, it did not owe its supremacy to an ecclesiastical principle imported from without; Normandy was not one of the countries where the *Landfrieden* sprang from the *Gottesfrieden*. In the reign of Robert I we see the duke's messenger separating combatants and putting them under oath to abide by the decision of his court,[153] while their repression of disorder and their rigorous administration of justice are the constant refrain of Dudo's eulogies of the first three dukes.[154] From the Conqueror's reign we have his law limiting the blood feud in 1075,[155] and the numerous restrictions upon private war formulated in the *Consuetudines et iusticie*.[156] According to these no one was allowed to go out to seek his enemy with hauberk and standard and sounding horn. Assaults and ambushes were not permitted in the duke's forests, nor could a joust be made an occasion for an ambuscade. Captives were not to be taken in a feud, nor could arms, horses, or property be carried off from a combat. Burning, plunder, and waste were forbidden in pursuing claims to land, and, except for open crimes, no one could be condemned to loss of limb save by judgment of the proper ducal or baronial court. Moreover castles and strongholds could be built only by the duke's license and were required to be handed over to him on demand, and he could also exact hostages as a guarantee of a baron's loyalty.[157] Coinage was his,[158] and everything relating

---

[151] *Supra*, note 149.   [152] Tardif, p. 49.

[153] *Vita Herluini*, in Mabillon, *Acta Sanctorum Ordinis S. Benedicti*, vi. 2, p. 348.

[154] Ed. Lair, pp. 171, 183, 196, 200 f., 205, 245, 248, 255, 259, 261–264, 266, 268 f., 272, 280, 290–293. On the nature of their legislation against disorder see Tardif, *Étude*, pp. 14–21.

[155] Duchesne, p. 1018; see below, Appendix D, note 9. Cf. the restrictions upon private war in the case of clerks, council of Lisieux, 1064, cc. 5, 7 (*Journal des savants*, 1901, p. 517). On the Conqueror's early legislation see Tardif, *Étude*, p. 31 f.   [156] Appendix D.

[157] Respecting the Conqueror's control over castles compare William of Jumièges (bk. vii, c. 1, ed. Marx, p. 115 f.) on the beginning of his reign with Ordericus (iii. 262) on conditions after his death.   [158] Appendix D, p. 280.

thereto. There was, we have already seen, a well developed ducal jurisdiction, and the maintenance of the duke's judicial supremacy was only one form of the persistent assertion of his ultimate authority over his barons. The extermination of disorder and violence was doubtless less complete than the Conqueror's panegyrists would have us believe,[159] but the peace of the duke was already a fact as well as a theory.

An authority such as the Conqueror wielded in church and state required a considerable income for its maintenance, and while there are no fiscal records for Normandy earlier than 1180, it is possible to trace back to William's time most of the sources of revenue which appear in detail in the Exchequer Rolls a century later.[160] The duke had his domains and forests, scattered throughout the duchy and sometimes of considerable extent, which might yield a money rent as well as a great variety of payments in kind. He had his mills, such as the eight ' fiscal mills ' on the Eau de Robec at Rouen, his salt-pans, his fishing-rights at certain points on the rivers and on the coast, and his monopoly of the taking of whales and other ' great fish.' Wreck and treasure-trove were his, as well as the profits of coinage.[161] He had large possessions in certain towns — he could sell half of Coutances to its bishop [162] — in addition to tolls, rights over markets and fairs, and other urban *consuetudines*.[163] *Bernagium* for his hunting dogs was a burden on

[159] William of Poitiers, ed. Duchesne, p. 193 (Migne, cxlix. 1240); Ordericus, ii. 177; Wace, ed. Andresen, lines 5348–5352.

[160] See the classical study of Delisle, *Des revenus publics en Normandie au douzième siècle*, in *B. É. C.*, x. 173–210, 257–289, xi. 400–451, xiii. 97–135. On the domain of the early dukes, see Prentout, *Étude sur Dudon*, p. 265.

[161] On the ducal rights over coinage, see Appendix D.

[162] *Gallia Christiana*, xi. instr. 219.

[163] E. g., in a charter of 1068 for Troarn, ' in Falesia totam terram Wesman et consuetudines eius ad regem pertinentes ': Sauvage, *Troarn*, p. 350. The following, relating to Bayeux, is more specific: ' Et ille bene scit domos infra civitatem et terram extra civitatem positam semper fuisse quietas ab omni consuetudine Normannorum principis, scilicet theloneo, gildo, molta molendinorum, et custodia vigiliarum, et dominus predicte terre si faceret adducere vinum suum de Argencis esset quietus suum carragium apud Cadomum et apud Baiocas ' (*Archaeologia*, xxvii. 27). For Caen see H. Legras, *Le bourgage de Caen* (Paris, 1911), pp. 39–42, 52, 74 ff.

the land,[164] as was also an exaction called *gravaria*.[165] The fines and forfeitures of justice and the receipts from feudal dues were naturally important.

How the revenues of the Norman dukes were collected and administered is a question of great interest, particularly to the student of English institutions. Since the days of the *Dialogue on the Exchequer* [166] there have not been wanting those who have maintained that the English Exchequer was organized on the model of an earlier Norman institution; and while recent investigations have traced portions of the Exchequer system back to Anglo-Saxon times [167] and have suggested that an elaborate fiscal system is more likely to have grown out of the collection of a heavy tax like Danegeld than out of the more ordinary and miscellaneous set of revenues which we have just enumerated,[168] the possibility of Norman influence upon the English Exchequer has by no means been eliminated from the discussion. The Norman evidence, it is true, is of the most meager sort,[169] the absence of anything like the Domesday survey being the greatest gap; but the argument from silence is especially dangerous where the destruction of records has been so great as in Normandy, and it is well to bear in mind that, save for the accident which has preserved a single Pipe Roll of Henry I, the existence of the English Exchequer is barely known before Henry II. A ducal treasury appears in Normandy as early as Richard II, who gives a hundred pounds from his *camera* to redeem lands of Saint-Bénigne of Dijon,[170] and

[164] *Infra*, Appendix D, p. 279; Round, *Calendar*, no. 2; *Monasticon*, vii. 1074; *Liber Albus* of Le Mans, no. 1; charter of William I for Saint-Étienne, Archives of the Calvados, H. 1830, 2–2 (' quietum ab omni gravaria et bernagio '); charter of William Rufus for Bec, Davis, *Regesta*, no. 425 (*infra*, p. 82).

[165] DuCange, *Glossarium*, under ' gravaria '; Stapleton, i, pp. lxxxvii, xcvii, cxxviii, clxxxi; P. de Farcy, *Abbayes de l'évêché de Bayeux*, Cerisy, p. 81 f. (before 1066); Round, *Calendar*, nos. 117, 1175; *B. É. C.*, xiii. 120–122.

[166] Bk. i, c. 4, ed. Hughes, Crump, and Johnson, p. 66.

[167] See especially Round, *Commune of London*, p. 62 ff.; and R. L. Poole, *The Exchequer in the Twelfth Century* (Oxford, 1912), chs. 2, 3.

[168] Vinogradoff, *English Society in the Eleventh Century*, p. 140.

[169] The name exchequer appears in Normandy in a document of *ca.* 1130: Round, *E. H. R.*, xiv. 426; *infra*, Chapter III, note 18. An exchequer roll of 1136 was cited in the eighteenth century, *M. A. N.*, xvi, p. xxx. See below, p. 175.

[170] ' Tactus pater meus divina inspiratione dedit de camera sua predicto Attoni

grants to Fécamp permanently the tithe of his *camera*.[171] The latter grant, which has come down in the original, is particularly interesting, for the duke goes on to define the *camera* as comprising everything given to him " by reason of the service of anything, whether lands purchased or fines or gifts or any sort of transaction " — in other words, any extraordinary or occasional addition to his treasure.[172] The profits of coinage are separately reckoned, and the *fiscalis census* and " what are anciently called customs " are expressly excluded. It would be rash to attempt to define too closely the content of the *census* and the customs, but the *census* must at least have covered the returns from the demesne and forests, and the customs would naturally include the profits of tolls and markets and justice — altogether much the sort of thing which was later comprised within the farm of the *vicomté* or *prévôté*. The duke plainly knows the difference between his ordinary and his extraordinary sources of income. So a century and a half later we find that returns from the mint and receipts of the *camera* are separately accounted for; the Exchequer Rolls record only the revenues gathered by the local officers.

Can we discover in the eleventh century any indication of system in the collection of these fixed sources of revenue ? We may dismiss at the outset, as the report of a later age, Wace's picture of Richard II shut up in a tower with his *vicomtes* and *prévôts* and

centum libras nummorum.' Charter of Robert I, MS. 1656 of the Bibliothèque Sainte-Geneviève at Paris, p. 46; printed, inaccurately, in Deville, *Analyse*, p. 34. Cf. Appendix C, no. 4.

[171] ' Concedo etiam decimas monetę nostrae ex integro et decimas nostrę camerę, videlicet de omnibus quęcumque michi alicuius rei servitio dabuntur, videlicet aut emptarum terrarum aut emendarum aut cuiuslibetcumque negotii sive dono muneris gratis dati excepto fiscali censu et exceptis his quae costumas antiquitus dicunt. Do et decimas telonei de burgo qui dicitur Cadumus.' Charter of 1027 for Fécamp, Musée de la Bénédictine, no. 2 *ter; Neustria Pia*, p. 217; *infra*, Appendix B, no. 5. The grant of the toll of Caen shows that tolls are not included in the receipts of the *camera*. Cf. the grant by Robert I of ' decimam denariorum suorum ' to the canons of Rouen: Le Prévost, *Eure*, ii. 520.

[172] So when Nigel grants Ceaux to Mont-Saint-Michel a payment is made to William I's *camera:* ' Pro cuius rei concessu dedit prefato Guillelmo centum et 1ta libras quas accepit Radulfus camerarius ' (MS. Avranches 210, f. 107); cf. the *cubicularii* who are ordered to make a payment from Robert's treasury (William of Jumièges, ed. Marx, p. 107); and the *ministri camere sue* who draw up the description of William's treasure in 1087 (*De obitu Willelmi, ibid.*, p. 146).

going over their accounts; [173] but it is nevertheless possible, by working back from documents of the twelfth century, to reach certain conclusions with respect to the fiscal system of the Conqueror's reign. In the first place it is clear that the farm of the *vicomté* existed under William I, for we know from a charter of Henry I that certain fixed items in the later rolls, to wit twelve pounds in the farm and twenty shillings in the toll of Argentan and sixty shillings and tenpence in the toll of Exmes, had been settled as alms to the canons of Séez by grant of his father and mother.[174] Permanent charges of this sort, either in the form of tithes or of definite amounts, are frequently recorded against the farms in the Norman rolls of the twelfth century, as in the English Pipe Rolls of the same period, but whereas in the English rolls such fixed alms are of recent creation, in Normandy they can often be traced back into the eleventh century. Thus Saint-Wandrille produced charters of Richard II to secure its title to the tithes of the toll of Falaise, Exmes, Argentan,[175] and the Hiesmois, of the *vicomtés* and tolls of Dieppe and Arques, and of the fair of Caen.[176] By grant of the same prince Fécamp received the tithe of the toll of Caen,[177] and Jumièges the tithes of the *prévôtés* of Bayeux and

---

[173] Ed. Andresen, lines 2009–2012. The early form of the passage (William of Jumièges, ed. Marx, p. 89) speaks merely of ' quarumdam rerum publicarum totius Neustrie . . . generale placitum.' Cf. *E. H. R.*, xxxi. 151.

[174] ' Preterea duodecim libras in firma nostra de Argentomo et viginti et unum solidos in teloneo eiusdem ville et sexaginta solidos et decem denarios de teloneo meo de Oximis, que dederunt pater meus et mater mea ecclesie Sagiensi ad victum canonicorum duorum, quod antiquitus in elemosinam statutum fuerat:' MS. Alençon 177, f. 98; MS. Lat. 11058, f. 8. See the charter in full in Appendix F, no. 11; and cf. *infra*, Chapter III. These items are duly charged in the rolls of 1180 and 1184: Stapleton, i, pp. lxxxviii, xcvi, cxxxii, 39, 50, 103; Delisle, *Henri II*, p. 334.

[175] In the later rolls this has become a fixed rent of 15 pounds: *M. A. N.*, xvi, p. xii; Delisle, *Henri II*, p. 334.

[176] See the charges in Stapleton, i, pp. xcvi, ci, cviii, cxxiii, cxxxii, 39, 50, 57, 68, 90, 103; and the charters in Lot, *S.-Wandrille*, no. 11 ABCD, who shows their late origin (pp. lxxxii f., xcvi f.). Note, however, the grant of the tithe of the markets of the Hiesmois by Robert I in no. 14.

[177] See above, note 171; Stapleton, i, pp. xxiv, c, 56. Saint-Taurin, later a dependency of Fécamp, received from Richard I the tithe of the *vicomté* of Évreux, but this passed out of the duke's hands and does not appear in the rolls: ' Little Cartulary," ff. 57, 115v; Bonnin, *Cartulaire de Louviers*, i. 1; *Gallia Christiana*, xi. instr. 138; Martène and Durand, *Thesaurus Anecdotorum*, i. 154. The tithe of

the Bessin.[178] The abbey of Cerisy received its tithes, as granted by Robert I and confirmed by the Conqueror in 1042, from the *vicomtés* of the Cotentin, Coutances, and Gavray, and from a number of the ducal forests.[179] By authority of William I the nuns of Saint-Amand had the tithe of Barfleur, of Saint-James, and of the *modiatio* of Rouen; [180] those of La Trinité had two-thirds of the tithe of the *prévôté* of Caen; the bishop of Coutances had the tithe of the toll of Cherbourg, and the canons of Cherbourg the tithe of the ducal mills in Guernsey.[181] Specific grants make their appearance in the same reign: besides the above mentioned grant to Séez William gives, before 1066, to the nuns of Montivilliers a hundred shillings in the *prévôté* of Caen.[182] In none of these cases does the original grant use the word farm, although the duke's revenues at Barfleur and in the *vicomtés* of the Cotentin, Coutances, and Gavray are expressly stated to be in money, but it is altogether likely in view of the charter to Séez that the *vicomtés* and *prévôtés* were farmed in the Conqueror's time. This was almost certainly true in the case of Avranches, from whose farm of £80 twenty were regularly credited at the Exchequer on account of the ducal manor of Vains and its appurtenances, which had been granted by the Conqueror to Saint-Étienne. If the farm had been established after the date of this grant, it would have been stated net, instead of recording to no purpose the deduction for what was no longer a source of ducal income, so

Avranches, granted to the cathedral by Robert I (Pigeon, *Le diocèse d'Avranches*, ii. 667), does not appear in the rolls, for similar reasons.

[178] *Neustria Pia*, p. 323; *Monasticon*, vii. 1087; Delisle-Berger, no.527; Stapleton, i. 7, 40; Vernier, i. 40, ii. 23.

[179] *Neustria Pia*, p. 432; *Monasticon*, vii. 1073; Farcy, *Abbayes de l'évêché de Bayeux*, p. 78; Appendix C, no. 3.

[180] *Monasticon*, vii. 1101; Stapleton, i. 37, 40.

[181] Stapleton, i, pp. c, 56, lxxxiii, 30, lxxvii, 27. The tithe of Moulins (*ibid.*, pp. cxxxiv, 105) also went back to a grant approved by William before 1066: *Cartulaire de S.-Père de Chartres*, i. 146.

[182] *Gallia Christiana*, xi. instr. 328; Stapleton, i. pp. c, 56. The Conqueror also assigned against this *prévôté* twelve prebends for his hospital at Caen, and similar charges were made against the *prévôté* of Bayeux: Stapleton, i, pp. lxi, ci; cf. Henry II's charter for the lepers of Bayeux, Delisle-Berger, no. 689.

The duke's officers also pay tithes and fixed charges granted by his barons on tolls which have subsequently come into his hands. *B. É. C.*, x. 178, 196; Stapleton, i, pp. lxiv, cxviii, 8, 14, 17, 82. Cf. *Dialogus de Scaccario*, bk. ii, c. 10.

that we must infer the existence of this farm under the Conqueror.[183] In any event, in order to make grants of tithes of fixed amounts, the duke must have been in the habit of dealing with these local areas as fiscal wholes and not as mere aggregates of scattered sources of income; the unit was the *vicomté* or *prévôté*, and not the individual domain. He can tithe the revenue from such a district as he can tithe the receipts of his *camera*. One other point of interest deserves to be mentioned in connection with these entries of fixed alms, the fact, namely, that wherever the matter can be tested, the various fixed charges are entered under each account in chronological order.[184] This cannot be mere chance, nor is it likely that a later exchequer official would have sufficient historical interest to rearrange them chronologically; it is much more probable that when each grant was made it was entered, probably on a central record similar to the later exactory roll. If this is the correct explanation, it follows that where the list begins with the grants of Richard II and continues with those of William, [185] the entries were made as early as the Conqueror's time. There would be nothing surprising in the existence of a record of amounts due and allowances to be made; such a roll is the natural part of the system of farms and fixed alms which we have found under the Conqueror, if not of the state of affairs existing under Richard II.[186]

Whatever weight may be attached to these inferences, it would seem clear that in the matter of fiscal organization Normandy was well in advance of neighboring lands such as the county of Anjou or the royal domain.[187] The Capetian charters of the

---

[183] See the inquest of 1171 in Delisle, *Henri II*, p. 345; and my observations in *E. H. R.*, xxvi. 327. For the grant of Vains as confirmed by Robert II, see *infra*, Appendix E, no. 1.

[184] Stapleton, i. 7, 30, 38, 39, 50, 56, 68, 70, 90, 97, 103, 111; *M. A. N.*, xvi. 109.

[185] E. g., Stapleton, i. 39, 56.

[186] Compare the early development of a fiscal system in Flanders: H. Pirenne, *Histoire de Belgique*, i. 109.

[187] A comparative study of fiscal arrangements in the eleventh century is much needed. The charters of the Angevin counts are listed by L. Halphen, *Le comté d'Anjou au XI*e* siècle* (Paris, 1906); those of Robert I and Henry I by C. Pfister, *Études sur le règne de Robert le Pieux* (Paris, 1885), and F. Soehnée, *Catalogue des actes d'Henri I*er* (Paris, 1907). The charters of Philip I are now accessible in the admirable edition of Maurice Prou, *Recueil des actes de Philippe I*er* (Paris, 1908).

eleventh century, for example, indicate fairly primitive economic conditions. The kings are liberal in granting lands and exemptions and rights of exploitation, but fixed grants of money are rare and small in amount, and are nearly always charged against an individual domain or a specific source of revenue rather than, as in Normandy, against the receipts from a considerable district.[188] Whereas the Conqueror's grants give evidence of a considerable money income, the ruder economy, or *Naturalwirthschaft*, of the Capetian kings is shown by the prevalence, well into the twelfth century, of fixed charges which are paid in kind — the tithe of the royal cellars and granaries at Auvers and Poissy,[189] two *sétiers* of salt in the granaries of Perche, fourteen *muids* of grain in the mills of Bourges, or twenty *muids* of wine from the vineyards of Vorges and Joui.[190] It is thoroughly characteristic of the condition of eleventh-century Normandy that the dukes should be sparing in conferring extensive franchises and rights of exploitation, while they were generous in permanent grants of money from the income which their own officers collected.

In local government the distinctive feature of the Norman system is the presence of a set of officers who are public officials, rather than mere domanial agents, and are in charge of administrative districts of considerable extent. As has been anticipated in the account of Norman finance, the chief local officer of the

[188] The nearest parallels to the Norman grants among the grants of the Capetian kings are the gift by Robert I to the church of Étampes of ten *sous* of ' census de fisco regali Stampensi ' (*H. F.*, xi. 579; Soehnée, no. 73), and the grant by Henry I to Saint-Magloire of the tithe of the port of Montreuil, where however the tithe of the money had already been granted to another monastery and the tithe of beer to a third: Tardif, *Monuments historiques*, no. 262; Soehnée, no. 33.

[189] Prou, *Philippe I*, no. 63; A. Luchaire, *Louis VI* (Paris, 1890), no. 350.

[190] *Cartulaire de Nogent-le-Rotrou*, no. 117; Luchaire, *Louis VI*, nos. 224, 621; cf. nos. 557, 628, 630. The Norman grants of wine from the *modiatio* of Rouen are different, being from the proceeds of a toll (levied on every hundred *modii*) instead of from an ordinary storehouse or vineyard. See particularly the Conqueror's charter (before 1055) giving Saint-Amand ' decimam mee modiationis de Rothomago' (*vidimus* in Archives of the Seine-Inférieure); and cf. *B. É. C.*, xi. 424; Beaurepaire, *La Vicomté de l'Eau de Rouen* (Rouen, 1856), p. 19. For an early Norman grant in produce, later paid in money, see the gift of Richard II in Le Prévost, *Eure*, ii. 413; or Stapleton, i, p. cxxxvii.

eleventh century was the *vicomte*, and the principal local division the *vicomté*.[191] The older Frankish areas, *pagus*,[192] *centena*,[193] and *vicaria*,[194] have not wholly disappeared, and in some cases the *vicaria* may have become the *vicecomitatus*,[195] but the *vicomte* is a far more important personage than the *voyer* of neighboring lands,[196] and the territory which he rules is considerably larger. Whether the Norman *vicecomes* contributed anything more than his name to the Anglo-Norman sheriff, is a question to which no satisfactory answer can be given until we know more of the functions of both officials.[197] The *vicomte* is a military leader, commanding the duke's troops and guarding his castles;[198] he is charged with the maintenance of order, and may proclaim the duke's ban;[199] he collects the ducal revenues for his district, including the customary dues from the demesne;[200] and he administers local justice in the duke's name,[201] assisting the bishop in the enforcement of the Truce of God[202] and doubtless exercising the

[191] The prevalence of the *vicomté* as the local division appears from the council of Lillebonne, c. 1, as well as from the frequent mention of *vicomtes* in charters from all parts of Normandy.

[192] See particularly Le Prévost, *Anciennes divisions territoriales de la Normandie*, in *M. A. N.*, xi. 1–59, reprinted in his *Eure*, iii. 485–544. Cf. Powicke, *Loss of Normandy*, p. 61 ff.

[193] *M. A. N.*, xxx. 668; *Gallia Christiana*, xi. instr. 158; cf. Valin, p. 97.

[194] Stapleton, i, p. lxxxi; ' extra vieriam Belismi,' charter of Robert of Bellême, Archives of the Orne, H. 2150; Denis, *Chartes de S.-Julien de Tours*, no. 29.

[195] E. Mayer, *Deutsche und französische Verfassungsgeschichte* (Leipzig, 1899), i. 357. Their equivalence is implied in Ordericus, ii. 470; and in a charter of the *vicomte* of Mantes in 1117 (Lot, *S.-Wandrille*, no. 57).

[196] For Anjou see Halphen, *Moyen Age*, xv. 297–325.

[197] Cf. Stubbs, *Constitutional History*, i. 292, note. On the Anglo-Saxon sheriff see now W. A. Morris, *E. H. R.*, xxxi. 20–40 (1916).

[198] Delisle, *S.-Sauveur*, pp. 2–3, and pièce 34, where Néel the elder holds the castle of Le Homme ' quia vicecomes erat eiusdem patrie.'

[199] *Gallia Christiana*, xi. 34; Bessin, *Concilia*, i. 63 (1073).

[200] Delisle, *S.-Sauveur*, no. 35; Round, *Calendar*, nos. 1169, 1170.

[201] See the account in Ordericus of the *vicomte* of Orbec (iii. 371) and particularly the cases at Neaufle ' in curia Roberti Normannorum comitis . . . coram Guillelmo Crispino illius terre vicecomite ' (Le Prévost, *Eure*, ii. 506) and ' in curia regis Anglorum apud castrum Nielfam ' (Bibliothèque Nationale, MS. Baluze, 77, f. 61). William Crispin is also mentioned as *vicomte* of the Vexin in Migne, *Patrologia*, cl. 737; and in MS. Tours 1381, f. 25v. See Porée, *Histoire du Bec*, i. 178 ff.; J. Armitage Robinson, *Gilbert Crispin* (Cambridge, 1911), p. 13 ff.

[202] Council of Lillebonne, c. 1.

jurisdiction comprised in the *consuetudines vicecomitatus*.[203] He is a frequent attendant at the duke's *curia*, witnessing charters and taking part in the decision of cases,[204] and he may be specially commissioned to hold a sworn inquest [205] or execute the decision of the court.[206] The office might become hereditary, as in the Bessin and the Cotentin,[207] but the annual farm was still due and the duke's control seems to have been maintained.[208] The evidence is not sufficient to enable us to define the relations between the *vicecomitatus* and the *prepositura* in the eleventh century, but it seems probable that they were " from the first convertible names for the same description of jurisdiction, however qualified in extent," [209] in somewhat the same way as the offices of *prévôt* and *voyer* in contemporary Anjou.[210] The scattered *prepositi* who appear in the charters [211] are plainly not men of importance, and, as in the case of the *thelonearii* [212] and *gravarii*,[213] the texts do not always make it possible to distinguish ducal from baronial agents.

Beyond certain names of foresters,[214] we get no light on the forest administration, but it is evident that the ducal forests are

[203] See above, notes 99, 108, 113.

[204] See below, note 280.

[205] *Gallia Christiana*, xi. instr. 65.

[206] *Archaeological Journal*, iii. 6; Le Prévost, *Eure*, iii. 184.

[207] Stapleton, i, p. lvii; Lambert, *Les anciens vicomtes de Bayeux*, in *Mémoires de la Société d'Agriculture de Bayeux*, viii, 233 ff.; Delisle, *S.-Sauveur*, ch. 1; Valin, p. 97; Chesnel, *Le Cotentin et l'Avranchin*, pp. 114–134.

[208] Ordericus implies the removability of the local officials when he says of the Conqueror, in 1067: ' Optimosque iudices et rectores per provincias Neustrie constituit ' (ii. 177).

[209] Stapleton, i, p. lxi; cf. *B. É. C.*, xi. 402.

[210] Where the *prévôt* is the more important of the two but exercises the same functions as the *voyer*: *Moyen Age*, xv. 297 ff. For the Capetian *prévôt* see Luchaire, *Institutions monarchiques*, i. 209–212, 219–235; Fliche, *Le règne de Philippe Ier*, pp. 158–162.

[211] Le Prévost, *Eure*, i. 141, 460, ii. 393; Round, *Calendar*, no. 713; *Cartulaire de la Trinité de Rouen*, nos. 24, 27, 42, 44, 51; Denis, *Chartes de S.-Julien*, no. 29.

[212] *Gallia Christiana*, xi. instr. 66; Pommeraye, *Histoire de S.-Amand*, p. 79; *Cartulaire de la Trinité*, no. 16.

[213] *Cartulaire de la Trinité*, nos. 16, 73, 80; Round, no. 1175; *Revue catholique de Normandie*, vii. 432; Stapleton, i, p. clxxxi.

[214] Round, nos. 1169, 1175; *Cartulaire de la Trinité*, nos. 7, 28, 47, 49, 51, 64, 79; Le Prévost, *Eure*, i. 286, 562; Lot, *S.-Wandrille*, no. 37; *M. G. H.*, *Scriptores*, viii. 401; *Revue catholique de Normandie*, x. 47.

already extensive and important, and are subject to the special jurisdiction which goes back to the Frankish forest ban [215] and will develop into the forest code of the Anglo-Norman kings. We hear of pleas of the forest,[216] though we do not know by whom they were held; such assaults as are lawful elsewhere are forbidden in the forests,[217] and for offenses against the forest law even priests cannot claim their exemption.[218]

Of municipal institutions before 1066 the surviving evidence is exceedingly scanty and unsatisfactory. ' The conspiracy which is called a commune ' came no nearer Normandy than Le Mans,[219] and the small beginnings of less independent forms of urban life have left few traces indeed. The men of Rouen traded with London as early as the reign of Ethelred II,[220] and had their own wharf at Dowgate under Edward the Confessor; [221] but we know nothing of their form of government before the days of Henry II. Caen is an important ducal town under Richard II, and in the following half-century *burgi* spring up in various parts of the duchy,[222] foreshadowing " the grand scheme of burghal colonization initiated by the Conqueror's tenants-in-chief " in England.[223]

[215] Waitz, *Deutsche Verfassungsgeschichte*, ii. 2, p. 316, iv. 128 ff.; Liebermann, *Ueber Pseudo-Cnuts Constitutiones de Foresta*, pp. 17, 19; Thimme, *Forestis*, in *Archiv für Urkundenforschung*, ii. 114 ff. (1908); and the searching criticism of C. Petit-Dutaillis, in *B. É. C.*, lxxvi. 97–152 (1915). The view suggested in the text in 1909 has been established and more fully developed by Petit-Dutaillis, *Les origines franco-normandes de la* ' forêt ' *anglaise*, in *Mélanges Bémont* (Paris, 1913), pp. 59–76; cf. his translation of Stubbs, ii. 757–849; and Prou in *Journal des savants*, 1915, pp. 241–253, 310–320, 345–354.

[216] Charters of Robert and William for Cerisy, *Neustria Pia*, p. 431 f. The count of Mortain also had forest courts: *B. É. C.*, xi. 444.

[217] *Consuetudines et iusticie*, c. 7.

[218] Council of Lillebonne, c. 8.

[219] Luchaire, *Les communes françaises* (1911), pp. 225, 228 f., 252; R. Latouche, *Histoire du comté du Maine pendant le Xe et le XIe siècle* (Paris, 1910), pp. 88–95.

[220] Liebermann, *Gesetze*, i. 232.

[221] E. de Fréville, *Mémoire sur le commerce maritime de Rouen* (Rouen, 1857), i. 90, ii. 12; Round, *Calendar*, no. 109.

[222] See in general Génestal, *La tenure en bourgage* (Paris, 1900), especially p. 233 ff.; and for Caen, the excellent study of H. Legras, *Le bourgage de Caen* (Paris, 1911), p. 39. Robert I is said to have granted at Caen 'unum burgarium ad pontum': Appendix B, no. 10 (B). Cf. the ' burgarii Rotomagenses,' *ca.* 1040, in Lot, *S.-Wandrille*, no. 18*bis*.

[223] Bateson, *E. H. R.*, xv. 74.

Already Cormeilles has its *leges* with such definiteness that they can be granted to the new *bourg* of Auffai,[224] and the laws of Breteuil, whatever they may have been at this period, were stiffening into form for their triumphal progress through England to the Welsh border and to Ireland.[225] The privileged area of a league about a town or castle, the *leugata* or *banleuca*, of which we find traces in Norman England,[226] is also found in early Normandy. Robert I grants this privilege at Argences: *leuvam iuxta morem patriae nostrae propter mercatum ipsius villae.*[227] Other early examples are at Cambremer,[228] Condé,[229] Conches,[230] and Lisieux.[231] The league of Brionne is even said to have been measured out at Tunbridge with the same rope.[232]

The organization of the ducal household can be sketched only in provisional fashion until the whole body of contemporary charters has been collected and their witnesses critically sifted. In general the history of the Norman *curia* is parallel to that of the contemporary Capetian establishment, in which the great officers emerge during the reign of Henry I and become firmly placed under Philip I.[233] Barely known under Richard II and

---

[224] Ordericus, iii. 42.

[225] Mary Bateson, *The Laws of Breteuil*, in *E. H. R.*, xv–xvi. Her reconstruction of the laws has been criticized by Hemmeon, *Burgage Tenure in Mediaeval England* (*Harvard Historical Studies*, xx), pp. 166–172.

[226] Domesday, i. 5b–9 (Kent), 303b (York); charter for Battle Abbey, new Rymer, i. 1, p. 4; cf. Maitland, *Domesday Book and Beyond*, p. 281; Pollock and Maitland, i. 583; C. Gross, *Gild Merchant*, ii. 30; *Ramsey Chronicle*, pp. 214, 224.

[227] Appendix B, no. 10.

[228] *Livre noir*, no. 21 (1036); cf. nos. 39, 43, 44.

[229] *Neustria Pia*, p. 425.   [230] *Gallia Christiana*, xi. instr. 128.

[231] *Ibid.*, p. 203; *Neustria Pia*, p. 585. For later examples see Delisle, *Étude sur l'agriculture*, p. 40 f.; Round, no. 124; Legras, *Caen*, p. 38.

[232] Robert of Torigni in William of Jumièges, ed. Marx, p. 289. The *leuca Brionie* is mentioned in the Conqueror's charter for Jumièges (*Neustria Pia*, p. 324; Vernier, i. 99) and in a grant to Bec (Porée, *Histoire du Bec*, i. 647).

[233] See Luchaire, *Institutions monarchiques*, i. 160 ff.; and particularly the careful lists in Prou, *Actes de Philippe I*, pp. cxxxvi–cli; and the discussion in A. Fliche, *Philippe Ier*, pp. 112–120. The preëminence of the four chief officers is not so clear in Normandy, but L. W. Vernon Harcourt, *His Grace the Steward* (London, 1907), p. 6, tends to exaggerate the difference between the two courts. Valin, pp. 141–151, does not treat this subject in any detail. Round, The *King's Serjeants* (London, 1911), is concerned almost wholly with the later period.

Robert I,[234] the principal officers of the Norman household are already established in the early part of the Conqueror's reign, but they are not yet clearly distinguished from lesser dignitaries of the same title,[235] and further study is needed to determine their succession, functions, and relative importance. Ralph of Tancarville the chamberlain,[236] Gerald the seneschal,[237] and Hugh of Ivry the butler [238] are familiar figures at William's court; the constable,

[234] ' Rotselinus camberarius,' in original of Richard II for Saint-Ouen, before 1024 (*Musée des archives départementales*, no. 21); ' Roztelinus cubicularius,' Lot, *S.-Wandrille*, no. 12; ' Odo constabularius' of Richard II, in charter for Jumièges in Archives of the Seine-Inférieure (Vernier, i. 40); ' Turoldus comitisse Gunnoris camerarius,' *Cartulaire de la Trinité*, no. 4. For the rare indications of household officers under Robert I, see *infra*, Appendix C. The *vicomtes* are more prominent than the household officers in the charters of these dukes, e. g., Le Prévost, *Eure*, i. 285.

[235] Cf. Stubbs, *Constitutional History*, i. 373, note 1; and Schubert's study of the imperial household, *Mitteilungen des Instituts*, xxxiv. 427-501 (1913).

[236] Round, nos. 73, 196, 711, 1165-1167; Le Prévost, *Eure*, iii. 468; Denis, *Chartes de S.-Julien*, no. 24; *Livre noir de Bayeux*, nos. 1, 5; *Cartulaire de la Trinité*, nos. 7, 38, 39; *Gallia Christiana*, xi. instr. 60f., 68 f., 72, 201, 328; A. Deville, *Essai historique sur S.-Georges-de-Bocherville* (Rouen, 1827), p. 62 (' Radulfus autem meus magister auleque et camere mee princeps '); cf. Lot, *S.-Wandrille*, no. 14. He appears as late as 1079 according to the Cartulary of Jumièges, no. 22, f. 22(cf. Vernier, i. 108), and the office passed to his descendants.

For other chamberlains see Davis, *Regesta*, pp. xxiv-xxvi; and the mention of Corbuzzo (*Cartulaire de la Trinité*, no. 75); Robert (Round, no. 87; *Gallia Christiana*, xi. instr. 71); and William (*ibid.*, 67, 71).

[237] For the various seneschals of this period see Vernon Harcourt, pp. 7-21; Davis, p. xxiii f.; neither of whom mentions Robert the seneschal, witness to the foundation charter of Sigy before 1047 (original in Archives of the Seine-Inférieure, *fonds* Saint-Ouen; d'Achery, *Spicilegium*, iii. 400; Pommeraye, *Histoire de S.-Ouen*, p. 460). Examples of two holders of the title in the same document are Osbern and Ansfred in Lot, *S.-Wandrille*, no. 13; William Fitz Osbern and Gerald in cartulary of Saint-Ouen (28*bis*), no. 338.

[238] Before 1066: Round, nos. 73, 81, 1167; charter for Jumièges, Vernier, no. 25; Pommeraye, *S.-Amand*, pp. 77, 79; Le Prévost, *Eure*, i. 149, 562; La Roque, iii. 26; *Cartulaire de la Trinité*, nos. 38, 39. For later instances, see Davis, p. xxvii; Round, nos. 91, 93, 421; *Gallia Christiana*, xi. instr. 71 f., 329; Sauvage, *Troarn*, p. 456; Collection Moreau, xxx. 190v (1071); *Cartulaire de la Trinité*, no. 47; Archives of the Seine-Inférieure, G. 8739 (1075, issued by the Queen during William's absence in England). Roger of Ivry also was butler: Davis, *l. c.* Before 1066 we likewise find ' Giraldus pincerna ' in a charter of Fécamp (Collection Moreau, xxii. 109v); ' Girardus comitis botellarius ' (Préaux cartulary, no. 438); ' Gerardus pincernarum magister comitis Willelmi ' (*Gallia Christiana*, xi. instr. 12; *Cartulaire de S.-Père de Chartres*, i. 176).

though mentioned under Robert I, is apparently of less importance,[239] and the marshal is just traceable.[240] Of lesser men of the
palace the *hostiarius* is noteworthy.[241] The mention of the chamberlain in fiscal matters [242] indicates at least one of his functions;
whether the seneschalship of Osbern and his son William had any
connection with their titles of *procurator principalis domus, comes
palatii,* and *magister militum,* is an open question.[243] Whatever
the duties of the household officers, they do not seem to have had
any fixed place or order in the ducal charters, where they appear,
if at all, scattered among the other witnesses who sign these none
too regular documents.[244]

The clerical element in the household naturally centered in the
duke's chapel, which was the point of departure for the development of the secretarial and fiscal sides of the central administration; but while we have the names of several of William's early
chaplains,[245] some of whom became bishops in Normandy or in

[239] Under Robert I the office was held by Turold, under William by Hugh de
Montfort: *infra,* p. 275; Davis, p. xxvi.

[240] Davis, p. xxvi f.; Round, in *Victoria History of Hampshire,* i. 430. Ilbert
the Marshal (*Cartulaire de la Trinité,* no. 2) may also have been a ducal officer.

[241] 'Rotgerius hostiarius' before 1024 (*Musée des archives départementales,* no. 21);
' Turoldus hostiarius ' in 1053 (*Cartulaire de la Trinité,* no. 37); 'Theodericus hos-
tiarius' before 1060 (Pigeon, *Le diocèse d'Avranches,* ii. 668); ' Rogerius hostiarius '
(Delisle, *S.-Sauveur,* no. 41).

[242] *Supra,* note 172.

[243] Vernon Harcourt, pp. 11–15, who, however, argues vainly against William's
having been seneschal. See below, note 289. To say, as this author says (p. 9),
that Osbern " was a mere household officer, procurator and dapifer, not an officer
of state," is to misunderstand the nature of the development.

[244] See however a charter of 1066 in *Cartulaire de la Trinité,* no. 39, attested by
William Fitz Osbern, Gerald the seneschal, Ralph the chamberlain, and Hugh the
butler. Cf. no. 38; Pommeraye, *S.-Amand,* p. 82; and Mabillon, *Annales,* v. 593
(1070). See also Round, no. 1167, printed in Bertrand de Broussillon, *La maison
de Laval* (Paris, 1895), i. 35, a charter of 1055 which is somewhat suspicious.

[245] Theobald, Baldwin (bishop of Évreux in 1066), and Herfast (chancellor after
1068) witness as chaplains an early charter in Round, *Calendar,* no. 1165; Delisle,
S.-Sauveur, no. 19. Other chaplains before 1066 are Robert (*Gallia Christiana,* xi.
instr. 327); Stephen (at Mont-Saint-Michel, in 1054, cartulary of Mont-Saint-
Michel, f. 65; cf. *Gallia Christiana,* xi. instr. 159); Gilbert Maminot, later bishop
of Lisieux (Ordericus, ii. 122); and the Bayeux group mentioned in the following
note. Isembert had been chaplain of Robert I before he became abbot of La
Trinité: William of Jumièges, ed. Marx, p. 108. For William's later years see
Davis, *Regesta,* pp. xviii–xxi; and the long list in no. 22 of his calendar (1068).

England, very little is known of their secular duties. Certain churches seem to have been constituted chapelries for the chaplains' support,[246] so that the office had some degree of continuity, and the ducal clerks of these days show something of the skill in acquiring desirable houses and lands which is characteristic of their successors in the twelfth century.[247] If the Norman dukes had a chancery, it was doubtless closely connected with the chapel, so that the absence, save for two charters of Richard II,[248] of any mention of a chancellor before 1066 does not preclude the existence of some sort of a chancery. Chancery and chapel were not completely differentiated in Frankish days,[249] and at the court of Philip I the chancellor sometimes attested simply as chaplain;[250] while it should be remembered that the Conqueror's first chancellor in England, Herfast, had long been his chaplain in

[246] ' Temporibus Ricardi comitis Normannie et Rotberti eius filii et Willelmi filii predicti Rotberti fuit quidam eorum capellanus Baiocis Ernaldus nomine, potens in prediis et domibus infra civitatem et extra civitatem que emerat suo auro atque suo argento. Quo mortuo tempore Willelmi Normannorum ducis Stephanus nepos predicti Ernaldi iure hereditario successit in hereditatem sui avunculi dono Willelmi Normannorum ducis.' After Stephen's death and a suit in the king's court the king ' accepit in suum dominium possessionem Stephani et dedit eam regine, et regina dedit michi concessu regis domos et duodecim acras terre que iam predixi et ortos et omnia que habuerat Stephanus de suo alodio, nam alias res eiusdem Stephani que pertinebant ad ecclesiam Sancti Iohannis que erat capella regis dederat iam rex Thome suo clerico nondum archiepiscopo.' Notice of Rainald the chaplain, MS. Lat. n. a. 1243, f. 80; MS. Fr. 4899, p. 292; printed in *Archaeologia*, xxvii. 26. This *capellaria* was later held by Samson (*Livre noir*, no. 4), doubtless the royal chaplain of that name who became bishop of Worcester in 1096. Both Samson and his brother Thomas were canons and treasurers of Bayeux. For other possessions of Rainald see *Gallia Christiana*, xi. instr. 69, 328 f.; for his later history, Davis, p. xx, and attestations in Collection Moreau, xxix. 89.

[247] Cf. Round, *Bernard the King's Scribe, E. H. R.*, xiv. 417–430.

[248] ' Hugo cancellarius scripsit et subscripsit ': charter for Fécamp, Musée de la Bénédictine, no. 2 *ter; Neustria Pia*, p. 215; Appendix B, no. 5. ' Odo cancellarius scripsit et subscripsit ': charter for Dudo of Saint-Quentin, *Gallia Christiana*, xi. instr. 284; *Nouveau traité de diplomatique*, iv. 225, v. 760. The charter of 1011 for Saint-Ouen (Pommeraye, *Histoire de S.-Ouen*, p. 422) which contains the words ' Dudo capellanus composui et scripsi ' is an evident forgery; but an authentic charter of 1006 for Fécamp (Musée, no. 1; Appendix B, no. 2) has ' ego Wido notarius iussu domni Richardi illustrissimi ducis . . . hoc testamentum scripsi.'

[249] On the whole subject of the Frankish chapel see Lüders, *Capella*, in *Archiv für Urkundenforschung*, ii. 1–100; Bresslau, *Urkundenlehre²*, i. 406 ff.

[250] Prou, *Actes de Philippe I*, p. lv.

Normandy,[251] where he is called chaplain as late as 1069, apparently after his entrance upon the English chancellorship.[252] On the whole, however, under William as under his father, a chancery seems to have been lacking in fact as well as in name before 1066. Few of his charters bear a chaplain's attestation, and only one mentions its author, a certain ' Frater Robertus ' who seems to have been a monk of Saint-Wandrille.[253] Something remains to be done in the palaeographical study of the few extant originals, but in general there is no regularity of type, and local authorship is indicated by the style of the duke's documents and by the frequency with which he is content to affix his signature to the charters of others.[254] There is no trace or mention of a ducal seal.[255] After the Conquest, the existence of a chancery is well established, and it seems plain that the English tradition, such as it was,[256]

[251] Davis, p. xvi.

[252] Round, no. 77, dated 1069, whereas, if we accept the authenticity of no. 22 in Davis, he is chancellor in 1068. So Osmund, chaplain in 1074 (Davis, no. 76), may have borne the title of chancellor in the preceding year (*ibid.*, no. 70). Davis, p. xvii, seems to me too rigid in denying the impossibility of such an alternation of title, which meets us two generations later under Geoffrey Plantagenet (*infra*, Chapter IV, p. 137).

[253] 'Ego frater Rodbertus scripsi et subscripsi': original in MS. Lat. 16738, no. 4; Lot, *S.-Wandrille*, no. 20 (1037 1055). Cf. ' Robertus scriptor ' in a charter for Saint-Amand (Pommeraye, *Histoire de S.-Amand*, p. 78); ' Rodbertus clericus ' in an early charter for Jumièges (Vernier, no. 20); 'Godbertus clericus' in Le Prévost, *Eure*, i. 562 (1063).

[254] For a convincing illustration, see Lot, *S.-Wandrille*, nos. 30 and 31 (1051), and the editor's notes. Another example, also an original, is in *M. A. N.*, xxx. 670 (Round, no. 1109). On the absence of clear evidence for a Norman chancery before the Conquest, see Stevenson, in *E. H. R.*, xi. 733, note 5; and compare the interesting observations of Pirenne on the documents of the counts of Flanders, *Mélanges Julien Havet*, pp. 733–748.

[255] The mention of William's seal in the notice of the foundation of Cherbourg (*Gallia Christiana*, xi. instr. 229; *Revue catholique*, x. 47) must be taken with caution. In any case the date is long after 1035, the year indicated by Stevenson, *E. H. R.*, xxvii. 4, note, who remarks the absence of any Norman seals anterior to 1066 save the one of Richard II described by the authors of the *Nouveau traité*, iv. 226.

[256] For the external history of the Anglo-Saxon chancery, see Davis, pp. xi–xv; for the conditions under which documents were drawn up, Hubert Hall, *Studies in English Official Historical Documents*, p. 163 ff. See also Stevenson, in *E. H. R.*, xi. 731–744. The subject is far from being exhausted; one of the necessary topics of investigation is the private charters of the period, studied region by region and monastery by monastery.

strongly asserted itself. There is no reason for assuming more than one such bureau for William's dominions, indeed the hypothesis of a 'Norman chancery' [257] runs counter to all that we know of the essentially personal relation of king and chancellor at this time and for long thereafter; and writs fly in either direction across the Channel. [258] A regular succession of chancellors can now be traced, [259] but their documents have yet to be subjected to the close diplomatic examination which alone can determine the influence of Anglo-Saxon precedents, the survival of local authorship, and the actual processes of the chancery. Until the more abundant English evidence has been more adequately utilized, Norman investigation must perforce wait.

Of the *curia* in the wider sense before 1066 it is likewise impossible to speak with the definiteness which it deserves as an antecedent of the English *curia regis*. A comparison of the names of the witnesses to William's charters does not show any great degree of fixity in his entourage. The bishops, when present, sign after the members of the ducal family. Then comes a small group of counts and men of high rank — the counts of Évreux and Mortain, Roger of Beaumont, Roger of Montgomery, William Fitz Osbern — followed by household officers, *vicomtes*, and others. [260] These are the elements which constitute the *curia*, but their function is attestation rather than assent, and, except for the few cases where the charter is expressly declared to be issued in such a gathering, [261] it is impossible to say when the *primates* or *proceres*

[257] Davis uses this ill-advised phrase, p. xviii f. Note the presence of the king's chancellor Osmund at Bonneville in Davis, no. 70, and, still on the Continent, in nos. 76 and 114.

[258] 'Rex Willelmus . . . mandavit de Normannia in Angliam episcopo Constantiarum et R. de Oilli per breves suos': Round, *Feudal England*, p. 157; cf. *Textus Roffensis*, ed. Hearne, p. 145. For an example of such a writ see Davis, no. 98. A letter from William in England to Matilda in Normandy is assumed in Delisle, *S.-Sauveur*, no. 35 (Round, no. 1170), and one is printed in *Revue catholique*, x. 348 (Round, no. 1175; Davis, no. 161). The writ of summons is mentioned in Normandy, *ca.* 1077: 'per me vel per brevem meum abbatem summoneam' (*Gallia Christiana*, xi. instr. 66; Davis, no. 105).

[259] Davis, pp. xvi–xviii.

[260] On the *curia* under Robert I see the analysis of the charters in Appendix C. On resemblances to the Frankish *conventus*, Tardif, *Étude sur les sources*, i. 6.

[261] Hariulf, ed. Lot, p. 185; Martène and Durand, *Thesaurus*, i. 252; Ordericus,

have met as an assembly. Beyond the old custom of holding an assembly at Fécamp at Eastertide,[262] our knowledge of the duke's itinerary is too fragmentary to show any such regularity in the court's meetings as we find in England after the Conquest.[263] The *curia* was brought together for purposes of counsel on matters which ranged from a transfer of relics [264] to the invasion of England,[265] and for judicial business. As a judicial body the charters reveal its activity chiefly in cases concerning a monastery's title to land [266] — for the duke's protection naturally carried with it access to his court — but it plainly has wider functions growing out of the judicial supremacy of the duke. It may try barons for high crimes.[267] Disputes respecting the limits of ecclesiastical and baronial jurisdiction must be brought before it,[268] and it is the

ii. 40. Cf. what Maitland has to say of the ' consent ' of the witan, *Domesday Book and Beyond*, pp. 247–252.

[262] William of Jumièges, ed. Marx, p. 340; Lot, *Fidèles ou vassaux?*, p. 262. We find an Easter court at Fécamp in 1032 (Ordericus, iii. 223); 1028 or 1034 (Appendix B, no. 7); *ca.* 1056 (Round, no. 1109); 1066 (Le Prévost, *Eure*, i. 149); 1067 (Duchesne, *Scriptores*, p. 211); 1075 (Ordericus, ii. 303); 1083 (MS. Rouen 1193, f. 30v). No place is mentioned in *Cartulaire de la Trinité de Rouen*, no. 82, issued at the Easter court of 1080. The great privileges of Richard II for the Norman monasteries were granted at a *curia* held at Fécamp in August (*Neustria Pia*, pp. 215, 398; Le Prevost, *Eure*, i. 285; Appendix B, no. 5), and Robert I held a *curia* there in January, 1035 (*Gallia Christiana*, xi. instr. 327).

[263] The scanty list in Coville, *Les États de Normandie* (Paris, 1894), p. 250 f., is based solely on the chroniclers. William's itinerary after 1066 (Davis, p. xxi f.) shows how little Norman evidence there is for Valin's assertion (p. 103) that the three assemblies were held regularly each year. Now and then there is evidence of the duke's presence at Rouen at or near Christmas: 1032 (Migne, *Patrologia*, clxii. 1165 f.); 1054 (Round, no. 710); 1070 (? Davis, no. 56); 1074 (*ibid.*, no. 75). Liebermann, *The National Assembly* (Halle, 1913), p. 82, considers the three assemblies in England as ' a French novelty ' of the Conqueror. See, however, L. M. Larson, *The King's Household* (Madison, 1904), p. 200 f.

[264] *Acta Sanctorum*, February, i. 193 (Richard I).

[265] Freeman, *Norman Conquest*, iii. (1875) 290 ff.

[266] ' Si per illam calumniam damnum aliquod ipsi monachi habuerint, duas reclamationes in mea corte vel curia faciant:' Robert I for Fécamp, Appendix B, no. 7. See Delisle, *S.-Sauveur*, nos. 35, 36, 42; Hariulf, ed. Lot, p. 224; *Cartulaire de la Trinité*, no. 82; Ordericus, ii. 310; Deville, *Analyse*, p. 20; Round, *Calendar*, nos. 78, 116, 165, 711, 712, 1114, 1170–1172, 1190, 1212. On certain of these cases cf. Davis, p. xxix.

[267] Ordericus, ii. 433. Cf. the case of the abbot of Saint-Évroul, *ibid.*, ii. 81; and Round, no. 713.

[268] Council of Lillebonne, end.

obvious place for the settlement of other difficulties between the greater tenants, so that it may even be agreed that a case shall be respited until it can come before the duke.[269] The *curia* is a place of record for agreements,[270] and may itself order a sworn record to be made and attested.[271] It may send officers to partition land.[272] Evidence is secured by oath,[273] ordeal,[274] and the wager of battle,[275] and it is altogether probable that the sworn inquest was employed.[276] Where the account is at all explicit, we usually find certain members rendering the decision of the court, sometimes merely as *Urteilfinder* after the case has been heard before the whole *curia*,[277] sometimes as a separate body before which the proceedings are conducted.[278] This does not necessarily involve any stability of organization or specialization of function, but there are indications that more of a beginning had been made in this direction in Normandy than, for example, in the neighboring county of Anjou.[279] Among the men who act as judges we regularly find one or more bishops and a *vicomte*,[280] members of the

[269] ' Est in respectu donec coram rege,' 1070–1081, *supra*, p. 22. The passage is somewhat obscure (cf. Round, *Calendar*, no. 714), but the meaning of *coram rege* is plain.

[270] Round, nos. 713, 1171 (of 1063, printed in Bertrand de Broussillon, *La maison de Laval*, i. 38), and the charter cited in the preceding note. Cf. the following, from a charter of William as duke: ' Me petierunt canonici precepique ut coram Geraldo dapifero meo firmaretur eorum conventio, quod factum est.' A. Deville, *Essai historique sur S.-Georges-de-Bocherville*, p. 71.

[271] *Gallia Christiana*, xi. instr. 65 (Davis, no. 117).

[272] Valin, pièces, no. 1 (= *Archaeological Journal*, iii. 6), under Richard II; Le Prévost, *Eure*, iii. 184 (1066).

[273] *Livre noir*, no. 21; *M. A. N.*, xv. 196, xxx. 681.

[274] Bertrand de Broussillon, *La maison de Laval*, i. 39 (Round, no. 1172); Ordericus, ii. 433; *Mémoires de la Société d'Agriculture de Bayeux* (1845), iii. 125; *Archaeologia*, xxvii. 26; Lot. *S.-Wandrille*, no. 39.

[275] Lot, *S.-Wandrille*, no. 37 (Round, no. 165).

[276] Brunner, *Schwurgerichte*, p. 270; Pollock and Maitland, i. 143; Valin, p. 200. The existence of the sworn inquest has mainly to be inferred from its appearance in England shortly after the Conquest and in Normandy in the twelfth century. See *infra*, Chapter VI.

[277] Round, no. 1190. On this practice see G. B. Adams, in *Columbia Law Review*, April, 1913, note 30.

[278] Delisle, *S.-Sauveur*, nos. 36, 42; Round, no. 1114; Pigeon, *Le diocèse d'Avranches*, ii. 673.

[279] For Anjou see Halphen, in *Revue historique*, lxxvii. 282.

[280] Delisle, *S.-Sauveur*, nos. 13, 35, 36, 42; Round, no. 1190. The bishops are

two classes which had most occasion to become acquainted with the law, and while we do not yet hear of a body of justices and a chief justiciar, it is not impossible that something of the sort may have existed. At the very beginning of William's reign the bishop of Bayeux makes complaint before the archbishop of Rouen, Count Odo of Brittany, Neal the *vicomte, aliique seniores iusticiam regni obtinentes;*[281] in a case between 1055 and 1066 the judges are Robert, count of Mortain, the archbishop, the bishops of Évreux and Lisieux, and the abbot of Fécamp;[282] in three other cases the archbishop of Rouen and Roger of Beaumont appear among the judges.[283] In 1077 Lanfranc, who had attended the dedication of Saint-Étienne a fortnight earlier, heard a plea between Osbern Giffard and Abbot William,[284] doubtless by special order of the duke. Bishop Geoffrey of Coutances, described by his biographer as immersed in the business of the king and the *curia*,[285] is found in three of the small number of charters where the names of the judges are given,[286] and it would not be surprising if he served a Norman apprenticeship for his work as judge and Domesday commissioner in England.[287] It is clear that, contrary to Freeman's view of the exclusion of ecclesiastics from the Norman

prominent in Round, no. 78; in no. 1114 the bishops and abbots are the judges; in no. 116, two abbots and five laymen. The *curiae* in which the *vicomte* appears may in some cases have been local. Cf. note 201.

[281] *Livre noir*, no. 21; Delisle, *S.-Sauveur*, no. 13. Delisle, p. 3, considers these men to have been regents; Stapleton, i, p. xxiv, note o, calls them justiciars. Cf. G. B. Adams, in *Yale Law Journal*, April, 1914, note 39.

[282] Pigeon, *Le diocèse d'Avranches*, ii. 673.

[283] Round, nos. 78, 1190; *Archaeologia*, xxvii. 26. Cf. Mabillon, *Annales*, v. 593.

[284] Deville, *Analyse*, p. 20. We have no record of the writ under which he acted, but we have (Davis, no. 98) one of the same year addressed to him in England.

[285] *Gallia Christiana*, xi. instr. 219.

[286] Delisle, *S.-Sauveur*, nos. 36, 42: Round, no. 78 (Davis, nos. 92, 123, 132); all subsequent to 1066. In the first two instances he is at the head of the body. The writ in Round, no. 464 (Davis, no. 97), evidently relates to England and not to Normandy, for an examination of the original in the Archives of the Calvados shows that the archbishop's initial is not J but L (i. e., Lanfranc).

[287] On his work in England see Round, *Feudal England*, pp. 133–134, 138, 157, 460; Stubbs, *Constitutional History*, i. 375; Adams, *The Local King's Court in the Reign of William I*, in *Yale Law Journal*, April, 1914.

curia,[288] the bishops took an active part in its proceedings, and it is probably among them, rather than in the office of seneschal, that we should seek the origin of the English justiciarship.[289] So, while there is not much evidence for the sending of special justices to hold a local court, the Norman origin of this practice " is not likely to be questioned." [290]

In this sketch of Norman institutions under the Conqueror it has been necessary here and there, especially in studying the *curia* and the judicial supremacy of the duke, to use evidence later than 1066, and just to that extent the possibility exists that the result is vitiated by influences from England or by the changed conditions of the Conqueror's later years. William reigned fifty-two years in Normandy, and this long period must have seen notable changes in the institutions of the duchy, changes which we are no longer in a position to trace as a whole, even to the extent of contrasting the earlier and the later years of the reign. All that is now possible is to seek to indicate at each point the dates of the individual bits of evidence used. But while there was development under William, we do not know to what extent there was innovation; and, scanty as are the earlier sources, they indicate that much of the account would hold true of the reign of

---

[288] *Norman Conquest*, i (1877). 174, iii (1875). 290.

[289] Stubbs's view of the derivation of the justiciarship from the seneschalship (*l. c.*, i. 375) has also been criticized by Vernon Harcourt, *His Grace the Steward*, pp. 11–18, but on the untenable ground that William Fitz Osbern " was never dapifer to William." In addition to the statements of the chroniclers, which Harcourt seeks to explain away, Fitz Osbern witnesses as dapifer, along with the dapifer Gerald, in a charter for Saint-Ouen (Collection Moreau, xxii. 110v, from the original; Cartulary of Saint-Ouen, in Archives of the Seine-Inférieure, 28*bis*, no. 338), and issues a charter for Saint-Denis in which he styles himself ' ego Willelmus Osberni filius consul et dapifer Willelmi Anglorum regis ' (Archives Nationales, LL. 1158, p. 590). For the genealogy of the family see *Revue catholique de Normandie*, xix. 261. A William Fitz Osbern, apparently a canon of Rouen, attests in 1075 (Archives of the Seine-Inférieure, G. 8739). On the English justiciars in this reign see Davis, p. xxviii.

[290] Adams, in *Yale Law Journal*, April, 1914, p. 18. The clearest cases are the inquest held at Caen 'iuxta preceptum regis' by Richard, *vicomte* of Avranches, 1070–1079 (*Gallia Christiana*, xi. instr. 65; Davis, no. 117), and the ordeal held at Bayeux ' precepto regis ' and reported to the king 1067–1079 (*Archaeologia*, xxvii. 26).

Robert I and even of that of Richard II.[291] Under Robert there was feudal tenure; probably also military service had been assessed, at least upon the monasteries. Under his father, besides the survivals of the older phrases of immunity, there are specific grants of ducal jurisdiction. Already the duke has a *camera* and distinguishes between his regular and irregular sources of income, already he makes permanent grants from the revenue of his tolls and *vicomtés*. He has certain household officers, even in two instances a so-called chancellor who disappeared with him,

[291] For the sources concerning Robert I, see Appendix C. The principal charters of Richard II, few of which throw light on the institutions of the period, are as follows:

Dotalicium Iudithe: Martène and Durand, *Thesaurus*, i. 122. Cf. *Dotalicium Adele:* d'Achery, *Spicilegium* (Paris, 1723), iii. 390.

Bernai, foundation, August, 1025 (1027). *Neustria Pia*, p. 398; Le Prévost, *Eure*, i. 284. On the date see Appendix B, no. 5.

Chartres cathedral. D'Achery, iii. 386; *Cartulaire de Notre-Dame de Chartres*, ed. Lépinois and Merlet, i. 85.

Saint-Père de Chartres. Three charters: *Cartulaire*, ed. Guérard, i. 92, 93, 106; the original of the third is in MS. Lat. 9221, no. 4.

Fécamp. Three charters, all original. See Appendix B, nos. 2, 3, 5.

Jumièges. (1) General confirmation: cartulary 22 in Archives of the Seine-Inférieure, f. 7; *vidimus* of 1499 and 1529 in the same archives; copy in MS. Lat. n. a. 1245, f. 165; substance in confirmation of Henry II, *Neustria Pia*, p. 323; *Monasticon*, vii. 1087; Delisle-Berger, no. 527; on the date see Appendix B, no. 5. (2) Attests exchange with Saint-Vaast: Pfister, *Robert le Pieux*, no. 72. (3) Attests grant of Albert, abbot of Micy: original in Archives of the Seine-Inférieure; Mabillon, *Vetera Analecta*, p. 431; Bry, *Histoire du Perche*, p. 51. (4) Confirms priory of Longueville, 1012: *Gallia Christiana*, xi. instr. 283. These four charters are now published by Vernier, nos. 12 (cf. 111), 10, 9, 7.

Lisieux cathedral. *M. A. N.*, xiii. 9; H. de Formeville, *Histoire de l'évêché-comté de Lisieux*, i, p. ccccxlii; V. Hunger, *Histoire de Verson*, pièces, no. 2.

Marmoutier. Delisle, *S.-Sauveur*, no. 3; *Revue catholique*, vii. 423; the original is noted in *B. É. C.*, xvii. 405.

Mont-Saint-Michel. (1) Appointment of Hildebert as abbot, 1009: original in Archives of the Manche, H. 14982; Martène and Durand, *Thesaurus*, i. 124. (2) Grant of Verson, etc.: cartulary, f. 22v; Archives Nationales, JJ. 66, no. 1494; *M. A. N.*, xii. 108; Round, no. 701. (3) Grant of Saint-Pair, etc.: cartulary, f. 20; JJ. 66, no. 1493; Mabillon, *Annales* (1739), iv. 651; Round, no. 702; *Neustria Pia*, p. 378; *M. A. N.*, xii. 109. (4) Attests charter of his mother Gonnor: *M. A. N.*, xii. 108; Delisle, *S.-Sauveur*, no. 2; Round, no. 703. 2–4 in Hunger, *Verson*, nos. 1, 3, 4.

Saint-Ouen. Various originals in Archives of the Seine-Inférieure and copies in Collection Moreau, xviii, and MS. Lat. 5423 (many of the early documents are false). See, in part, *Musée des archives départementales*, no. 21; Chevreux and

and he holds his court at Fécamp at Easter and other great occasions.[292]

If, in conclusion, we try to summarize the constitution of Normandy on the eve of the invasion of England, certain features stand out with reasonable clearness. The organization of Norman society is feudal, with the accompaniments of feudal tenure of land, feudal military organization, and private justice, but it is a feudalism which is held in check by a strong ducal power. The military service owing to the duke has been systematically assessed and is regularly enforced. Castles can be built only by the duke's license and must be handed over to him on demand. Private war and the blood feud are carefully restricted, and private jurisdictions are restrained by the reserved jurisdiction of the duke and by the maintenance of a public local administration. The duke keeps a firm hand on the Norman church, in the matter both of appointments and of jurisdiction. He holds the monopoly of coinage, and is able to collect a considerable part of his income in money. The administrative machinery, though in many respects still primitive, has kept pace with the duke's authority. His local representative, the *vicomte*, is a public officer and not a domanial agent; his revenues are regularly collected; and something has been done toward creating organs of fiscal control and of judicial administration. The system shows strength, and it shows organizing power. In some directions, as in the fixing of military obligations, this organizing force may have been at work before the Conqueror's time, but much must have been due to his efforts.

Vernier, *Les archives de Normandie*, no. 1; Martène and Durand, i. 121; Le Prévost, *Eure*, ii. 164, 413; Pommeraye, *Histoire de S.-Ouen*, p. 403 ff.

Saint-Quentin, 1015. Hémeré, *Augusta Viromandorum*, p. 107; *Gallia Christiana*, xi. instr. 284; *Nouveau traité de diplomatique*, iv. 226 f.

Saint-Riquier. D'Achery, *Spicilegium* (1723), ii. 332; Hariulf, ed. Lot, p. 185. Saint-Wandrille. Lot, *S.-Wandrille*, nos. 9–12.

Séez cathedral. Attests charter of William of Bellême: library of Alençon, MS. 177, f. 28; MS. Lat. 11058, f. 2.

Grants are cited for Montivilliers (*Gallia Christiana*, xi. instr. 326) and Saint-Bénigne of Dijon (Le Prévost, *Eure*, ii. 323; *Analecta Divionensia*, ix. 175; Deville, *Analyse*, p. 34).

[292] Note particularly the large number of witnesses to the charter for Bernai, among others all the bishops of the province and thirteen *vicomtes*: Le Prévost, *Eure*, i. 284.

Stark and stern and wrathful, whether we read of him in the classic phrases of William of Poitiers or in the simple speech of the Old English Chronicle, the personality of William the Conqueror stands out preëminent in the midst of a conquering race, but it does not stand alone. The Norman barons shared the high-handed and masterful character of their leader, and the history of Norman rule in southern Italy and Sicily shows that the Norman genius for political organization was not confined to the dukes of Rouen.[293] It was in England, however, that this constructive talent found its chief opportunity, and there, as in Normandy, the directing hand was that of the sovereign, who, like his followers, found a wider field for qualities of state-building which he had already shown at home.

The organization of England by the Normans and the problem of the extent of Norman influence upon its government form no part of our subject, but must be left, after this attempt to fill in the Norman background, to the historian of English institutions. Of him we may, however, ask that he proceed with due regard to the interaction of Normandy and England during the union which continued, with scarcely an interruption, for nearly a century and a half after 1066, and to the parallel constitutional development of the duchy which it is the purpose of the following chapters to examine.

[293] The Norman kingdom of Sicily lies beyond the limits of the present volume. I have tried to sketch its European position in my *Normans in European History*, chapters 7 and 8; and I have discussed certain of its institutions in *E. H. R.*, xxvi. 433–447, 641–665. See also my paper at the Millenary Congress, *Quelques problèmes de l'histoire des institutions anglo-normandes* (Rouen, 1911), pp. 7-10; and *infra*, Chapter III, p. 111 f., Chapter VI, pp. 232–234.

CHAPTER II

NORMANDY UNDER ROBERT CURTHOSE AND WILLIAM RUFUS

THE strength of the Conqueror's system of government in Normandy was to be severely tested during the reign of his son Robert Curthose.[1] Whatever amiable and knightly qualities contemporaries were willing to ascribe to Robert, no one appears to have considered him a strong or even a prudent ruler, and his indolence, instability, and easy-going irresponsibility soon earned for him such epithets as the soft duke, the lazy duke, and the sleepy duke. Lack of governance was writ large over his reign, and its results are set forth in the gloomy picture of the state of Normandy drawn by the fullest of contemporary narratives, that of Ordericus Vitalis.[2] It is a dreary tale of private war, murder, and pillage, of perjury, disloyalty, and revolt, for which the good monk finds a parallel only in the worst days of Israel. Destruction fell especially upon the peasants and upon the possessions of the church: " that which the locust hath left hath the cankerworm eaten, and that which the cankerworm hath left hath the caterpillar eaten." [3] And when the nuns of Holy Trinity at Caen came to reckon up their losses year after year in land and cattle and produce and rents and men, their matter-of-fact summary is more

[1] There is no modern account of this period of Norman history. The sketch of Robert Curthose by G. LeHardy, in the *Bulletin de la Société des Antiquaires de Normandie*, x. 1–184 (1882), is partisan and quite inadequate; at my suggestion a critical biography is being prepared by Charles W. David, of the University of Washington. Freeman's *William Rufus* is useful for the narrative history of the period.

[2] Ed. Le Prévost, iii. 261, 289–291, 351, 357, 412, 463, 473, 475 f., iv. 98 f., 101, 106, 163, 172, 178–182, 192, 199 f., 206, 219–221, 227 f.; and his verses in *Annuaire-Bulletin de la Société de l'histoire de France*, 1863, ii. 1–7. See also William of Malmesbury, *Gesta Regum*, pp. 460, 462, 473 f.; and cf. Freeman, *William Rufus*, i. 190, 195, ii. 367 f., 394; and Sauvage, *Troarn*, pp. 21 f., 71.

[3] Ordericus, iii. 357.

eloquent of the Norman anarchy than are many pages of the
chronicler: [4]

Willelmus comes Ebroicensis ex quo rex Willelmus finivit aufer[t] Sanctę
Trinitati et abbatissę et dominabus .vii. agripennos vineę et duos equos et
.xx. solidos Rotomagensium nummorum et salinas de Escrenevilla et unoquoque anno .xx. libras de Gauceio et de Bavent. Ricardus filius Herluini
duas villas, Tassilei et Montboen. Willelmus camerarius filius Rogeri de
Candos decimam de Hainovilla. Willelmus Baivel .xx. boves quos sumpsit
apud Osbernivillam. Robertus de Bonesboz eandem villam depredavit.
Robertus de Uz terram de .iiii. puteis et de Cierneio. Willelmus Bertrannus
duos vavasores et eorum decimam et .v. solidos quoque anno apud Colum-
bellas. Ricardus de Corceio .iiii^{or}. libras et .xx. oves. Nigellus de Oillei .ii.
boves. Rogerus de Avesnes in equis et in denariis et in aliis rebus .viiii.
libras. Robertus Pantolf in denariis et in aliis rebus .vi. libras. Willelmus
Iudas .xx. solidos. Rogerus dispensator et Rogerus de Scutella .xi. boves et
.ii^{os} equos et predam de Folebec, et homines vulneraverunt et verberaverunt
in pace. Robertus de Molbrai .lxviii. libras quoque anno post mortem regis.
Eudo vicecomes .xx. boves. Adelofdus camerarius episcopi Baiocensis terram de Anglicivilla. Ranulfus vicecomes Ricardus de Corceio .xv. libras
de terra de Grandicampo, et Ranulfus idem et iii. boves et .ii. equos de
Duxeio et de Aneriis et .v. acros annone in Aneriis et decimam de Boivilla.
Ingelrannus prata de Grai. Comes Henricus pedagium accepit de Chetel-
hulmo et de omni Constantino et super hoc facit operari homines Sanctę
Trinitatis de eadem villa et patria ad castella suorum hominum. Alveredus
de Ludreio aufert Sanctę Trinitati tres boves apud Teuvillam et terram de
eadem villa devastat. Et Willelmus de Veteri ponto prata de predicta villa.
Et Hulmum aufertur Sanctę Trinitati iniuste. Adeloldus predictus camerarius episcopi aufert annonam de Grandicampo et quamplures alias. Hugo
de Redeveris aufert .v. modios vini et vineam quoque anno ad Vernun.
Fulco de Aneriis .i. equum et viii. solidos et iii. minas de favis et omnem
terram devastat ita quod nullus ibi lucrari potest. Willelmus Bertrannus
accepit de Osbertivilla duos boves et postea viros misit in carcerem. Willelmus de Rupieres accepit boves et porcos domne abbatissę et homines super
terram eius interfecit. Idem Willelmus pecuniam metatoris abbatissę de
Ruvvres accepit et annonam fecit inde ferri et apud Ranvillam duos viro[s]
interfecit et complures vulneravit; et item Robertus de Guz aufert ei unum
equum apud Monboen. Hugo Paganus aufert abbatissę silvam de Salan et
sacerdotem verberavit in pace, et Willelmus Gernun silwam incidit et evellit
quantum potest. Ranulfus frater Igeri saisiavit terram abbatissę super hoc
quod ipsa sibi terminum respondendi dederat et inquirendi si deberet ei inde
rectum facere. Brenagium autem interrogant et Rainaldus Landun et alii
ministri abbatisse et monent eam placitare. Inde Robertus de Genz aufert ei

---

[4] Cartulary, MS. Lat. 5650, f. 39v–40v. The list of excommunicates in the
Benedictional of Archbishop Robert, ed. H. A. Wilson (London, 1903), p. 166, which
seems to belong to this period, may be connected with depredations on ecclesiastical
lands.

terram de Donmaisnil et annonam inde tulit et oves et boves et alia multa, et vi adhuc detinet. Et Radulfus de Cortlandun ponit terram abbatisse in gravatoria [5] et vi vult ibi eam tenere, quod nunquam fuit amplius.

Such a record shows the weakness of the duke as well as the sufferings of the duchy. Many of the barons were in more or less constant revolt, others were easily bought away from him. Many of his own castles were denied him, and adulterine strongholds sprang up.[6] Even on these conditions Robert held but a part of Normandy. Prince Henry ruled Domfront and the Cotentin during a good part of this reign; King William won over the lands east of the Seine and proved a serious menace elsewhere.[7] Even the nominal unity of the duchy was lost.

Amidst these narratives of confusion and revolt there is small place for the machinery of government, and we are not surprised that the chroniclers are almost silent on the subject. Robert's reliance on mercenaries [8] shows the breakdown of the feudal service, which may also be illustrated by an apparent example of popular levies;[9] his constant financial necessities [10] point to the demoralization of the revenue. The rare mention of his *curia*[11] implies that it met but rarely. Still, these inferences are negative and to that extent inconclusive, and even the detailed account of Ordericus is largely local and episodic, being chiefly devoted to events in the notoriously troubled region of the south, and is also colored by the sufferings and losses of the church. Only from documentary evidence shall we get a wholly impersonal view of the ducal government.

First of all, there is something to be learned from the statement of ducal rights under the Conqueror, the so-called *Consuetudines et iusticie*, drawn up under the joint auspices of Robert and William Rufus in the summer of 1091.[12] Just as the coronation char-

[5] Du Cange, *s. v.*, cites only this passage.
[6] Cf. the Fécamp charter, Appendix E, no. 4c.
[7] Note also the cession of Gisors to Philip I as the price of his aid against William: *Gallia Christiana*, xi. instr. 18; Fliche, *Le règne de Philippe I*er, p. 293.
[8] Ordericus, iii. 266 f.; cf. William of Malmesbury, *Gesta Regum*, p. 468.
[9] Ordericus, iii. 415.
[10] *Ibid.*, iii. 267, iv. 105; cf. Wace, lines 10927 ff.
[11] Ordericus, iii. 297, 303, 381.
[12] Appendix D.

ter of Henry I offers the best picture of the abuses of the Red King's reign in England, so this inquest reflects the history of the preceding four years in Normandy. But whereas the English record shows the strength of government, the Norman shows its weakness: Henry I promises to refrain from abuses of royal authority, the Norman prince seeks by appeal to ancient precedent to recover power that has slipped from his hands. Of the ducal rights which the Conqueror upheld *maxime et viriliter*, only a portion is here recorded, but these are evidently chosen with reference to the existing situation — *quia magis necessaria sunt*. They point to the usual evils of a weak rule in this period, private war, private castles, and private coinage; emphasizing the body of restrictions upon private war which had been so carefully built up under Robert's predecessors with respect to the duke's court, army, and forests, and the actual conduct of hostilities between his barons, and asserting the right of the duke to take over his vassals' castles and prevent the building of new ones. The whole reads like a legal commentary on the narrative of Ordericus.

Another commentary, this time ecclesiastical, can be read in the canons of the council held at Rouen in February 1096, as a preliminary to the First Crusade.[13] These are concerned chiefly with the enforcement of the Truce of God, already established in Normandy and recently reënacted by the council of Clermont, but requiring amplification because of the weakness of the lay power.[14] All men from the age of twelve upward were required to take an oath to observe its provisions and to give military aid for their enforcement; and anathema was pronounced against counterfeiters and brigands and all who might give them aid or comfort. The protection of the farmer at his plow, a bit of old Scandinavian custom, received ecclesiastical sanction.[15] All churches were to hold their property as they had held it under the Conqueror. Excellent decrees, says Ordericus,[16] but of little profit to the peace of the church because of the failure of the duke's justice. At best, however, the council of Rouen was but a pale

[13] Ordericus, iii. 470–473.
[14] Cf. *supra*, Chapter I, note 147.
[15] Cf. Chapter I, note 106.
[16] iii. 473.

reflection of that of Clermont: it left untouched the problem of celibacy and the lay investiture of bishops and abbots, and placed no obstacle in the way of the shameless simony and corruption of Robert's dealings with ecclesiastical offices. The case of the bishopric of Lisieux, taken over by Ranulf Flambard for his own minor son, and later sold to William of Paci, is a particularly flagrant instance.[17]

Best of all, however, if we can but read it aright, is Robert's own commentary as written in the ducal charters of his reign. As the only surviving acts of sovereign power, these show us the ducal government in action and tell their own tale of localism and weakness. Those of which we have knowledge are the following, which are here arranged by the ecclesiastical establishments for whose benefit they were issued: [18]

1. BAYEUX cathedral. 24 April 1089, at Vernon. Various specific grants. *Livre noir*, no. 4; extract in Delisle, *Saint-Sauveur*, pièces, no. 44; Round, no. 1433; Davis, no. 308. Trigan, *Histoire ecclésiastique*, iii. 402, cites the original.

2. BAYEUX, Saint-Vigor. 1089, at Eu. Confirms the restoration of the monastery, its possessions, and the rights of the bishop over it. *Livre noir*, no. 6; *Livre rouge*, nos. 104, 105, where ' Guillelmus camerarius ' is added to the witnesses; J.-F. Faucon, *Essai historique sur le prieuré de Saint-Vigor-le-Grand* (Bayeux, 1861), p. 213; Round, no. 1434; Davis, no. 310.

3. BAYEUX, Saint-Vigor. 24 May 1096, at Bayeux. Attests charter of Bishop Odo granting Saint-Vigor to Saint-Bénigne of Dijon. Apparent original (A) and early copy containing additional material (B) in Archives of

---

[17] See Böhmer's account of the Norman church under Robert, *Kirche und Staat*, pp. 142–146; and his study of Serlo of Bayeux, in *Neues Archiv*, xxii. 701–738. The case of Turold, bishop of Bayeux, deposed for irregularities by Paschal II in 1107, should be added. See Dom G. Morin in *Revue d'histoire ecclésiastique*, v. 284–289; and W. Tavernier's biographical investigations in *Zeitschrift für französische Sprache und Litteratur*, xxxvi-xlii. For Odo of Bayeux, see further Bourrienne, in *Revue catholique de Normandie*, vii–x. On the investiture question, see further the bull of Paschal II published by Levison, in *Neues Archiv*, xxxv. 427–431; *B. É. C.*, lxxi. 465.

[18] For Robert's attestation to a charter of William Rufus for Durham during his visit to England in 1091, see Davis, *Regesta*, no. 318. For a charter of 1100–1106 confirming his brothers' grants to Bath Priory, see *Two Chartularies of the Priory of St. Peter at Bath*, ed. Hunt (Somerset Record Society, 1893), i. 47, no. 44. It must be remembered that the mention of 'Robertus comes' in a notice may refer also to the period before his father's death; e. g., Lot, *S.-Wandrille*, pp. 98–100, where I am inclined to see Robert Curthose rather than, with Lot, Robert count of Eu.

the Côte-d'Or, where a cartulary copy (no. 43) of B has inserted a confirmation by Bishop Philip d'Harcourt at the end. Printed in E. Pérard, *Recueil de pièces servant à l'histoire de Bourgogne*, p. 206 (B); U. Plancher, *Histoire de Bourgogne*, i, preuves, xxxii (B); Migne, *Patrologia*, clv. 475 (B); *Gallia Christiana*, xi. instr. 76 (B); Faucon, *Saint-Vigor-le-Grand*, p. 216 (A); *Revue catholique de Normandie*, x. 280 (translation from A, with some variants from B). Cf. *Analecta Divionensia*, ix. 200–202.

4. BAYEUX, Saint-Vigor. 24 May 1096, at Bayeux. Confirms Odo's grant of the same date.[19] Original in Bibliothèque municipale at Bayeux, titres scellés, no. 9, with fragments of applied seal; copy of the twelfth century in cartulary in Archives of the Côte-d'Or, no. 44. *Revue catholique*, x. 283 f. (= V. Bourrienne, *Odon de Conteville*, p. 132), from original; date only in Ordericus, ed. Le Prévost, iii. 265, thence in Davis, no. 376.

5. BEAUVAIS, Saint-Lucien. 14 July 1096, at Rouen 'in capitulo.' Assents to charter of Stephen, count of Aumale, granting Saint-Martin d' Auchy. *Gallia Christiana*, xi. instr. 19, apparently from lost original. According to the *Inventaire sommaire*, the Archives of the Oise possess only a late mention of this document in H. 1302.

[19] As the inaccurate reproduction of the dates of these charters has given rise to unnecessary confusion, it may be worth while to print them exactly:

Odo A: 'Anno ab incarnatione domini .m̄.xc̄.vi.° indictione .iiii.ª concurrente .vii° epacta .xxviii.ª xviiii.° anno principatus domni Roberti Vuillemi regis Anglorum filii ducis Normannię hęc cartha confirmata est et sigillo suo signata. Actum publice Baiocas mense maio die xx iiii. viiii kal. iunii luna .xxvii.'

Odo B: 'Anno ab incarnatione domini .mxcvi. indictione .iiii.ª concurrente .ii.° xviiii. anno principatus domni Roberti Willelmi regis Anglorum filii ducis Normannię hęc carta confirmata est et sigillo suo signata. Actum publice Baiocas mense maio die .xxiiii.ª eiusdem mensis .viiii kal. iunii luna .xxvii.ª feria septima bissextili anno.'

Robert: 'Anno ab incarnatione domini .m̄°xc°vi° indictione .iiii.ª concurrente .vii.° epacta .xxᵐªiii.ª .x°viiii.° anno principatus Rotberti Guillelmi regis Anglorum filii ducis Normannię hęc carta firmata est et sigillo suo signata. Actum publice Baiocas mense maio die .xx iiii. viiii. kal. iunii luna .xxªvii.ª ciclo decennovennali .x°iiii.° EGO HUGO DIVIONENSIS ĘCCLESIĘ MONACHUS IUSSU EIUS- DEM ROBERTI DUCIS NORMANNIĘ SCRIPSI ET SUBSCRIPSI VICE CANCELLARII RODULFI.'

The different elements in the date are in agreement throughout save in the case of the concurrent, which is wrongly given as seven in Robert's charter and the first version of Odo's, but is corrected to two in the second form of Odo's charter. It is noteworthy that all agree in dating Robert's reign from 1077–1078. In Robert's charter the *x* of the year of the incarnation has been almost entirely rubbed out, either by time or by some one who attempted to bring it into agreement with the generally known date of Robert's accession, and this has misled some writers into assigning the document to 1106 (*B. É. C.*, xlviii. 175 f.; *Revue catholique de Normandie*, x. 282–285). The original at Bayeux, however, still shows traces of the *x*, which is required not only by the remaining elements of the date but also by the witnesses. The epact in Odo A may have been corrected at the time, as the *v* is faint.

6. BEC. [1087-1089.] Attests charter of Roger of Beaumont for the priory of Beaumont-le-Roger. Cartulary in Bibliothèque Mazarine, MS. 1212, no. 1; MS. Lat. 13905, f. 6v; Collection du Vexin, iv. 165, xi. 256 (with a fuller list of witnesses than the cartulary). E. Deville, *Le cartulaire de Beaumont-le-Roger* (Paris, 1912), no. 1; Le Prévost, *Eure*, i. 205; Round, no. 368.

7. BEC. February 1092. Confirms the grants of his father and mother on behalf of the church of Émendreville (Saint-Sever, seat of the priory of Notre-Dame-du-Pré) and adds the tithe of the hay of his park at Rouen. Original, in poor condition, with crosses and evidently never sealed, in Archives of the Seine-Inférieure, *fonds* Bonne-Nouvelle; copy in MS. Lat. n. a. 1245, f. 34; extracts in MS. Lat. 12884, ff. 79v, 85. *Neustria Pia*, p. 613, from a copy; La Roque, iv. 1328; translated in Farin, *Histoire de la ville de Rouen* (1731), ii*. 151*. The witnesses, incompletely given in the editions, are: 'Willelmi Rotomagensis archiepiscopi, Rodberti comitis Normannorum, Eustachii comitis Boloniensis, Willelmi episcopi Dunelmensis, Willelmi de Wativilla, Roberti de Monteforti, Roberti comitis Mellentensis, Willelmi Bertranni, Ba[lduini?] filii Ans[chetilli] de Bellomonte, Simonis dapiferi, Eu[do]nis filii Turstini de Constantino, Gisleberti filii Bernardi, Roberti filii Alwardi.'

8. BEC. [1091-1092.][20] Attests grant of privileges and jurisdiction by Archbishop William. *Lanfranci Opera* (Paris, 1648), p. 332; Migne, *Patrologia*, cl. 552; *Gallia Christiana*, xi. instr. 17. Dom Jouvelin-Thibaut, in MS. Lat. 13905, f. 52, corrects the printed text and adds the important list of witnesses: 'Rotberti comitis Normannie, Willelmi archiepiscopi Rothomagensis, Gisleberti Ebroicensis episcopi, Gaufridi episcopi Constantiensis, Willelmi episcopi Dunelmensis, Odonis episcopi Baiocensis, Serlonis episcopi Sagiensis, Benedicti archidiaconi, Fulberti archidiaconi, Girardi archidiaconi, Gisleberti scolastici, Rogeri secretarii, Ricardi filii Willelmi, Rogeri fratris abbatis Cadumensis, Giraldi abbatis S. Wandregisili, Hugonis abbatis Cerasiensis, Nicholai abbatis S. Audoeni, Willelmi abbatis Cormeliensis, Gisleberti abbatis Cadumensis, Fulconis abbatis de supra Diva, Willelmi Ebroicensis comitis, Gisleberti Crispini, Rotberti de Monteforti, Rotberti comitis de Mellent, Guillelmi Crispini, Radulfi de Conchis.'

9. BEC. [1087-1096.] Attests various gifts of Gerard de Gournay. Porée, *Bec*, i. 338 f.

10. BEC. [1087-1096.] Present at grant of freedom of toll and customs by William of Breteuil, attested by Robert, count of Meulan, and Eustace, count of Boulogne. Fragment of cartulary, Archives of the Eure, H. 91, f. 75.

11. BEC. Confirms foundation of priory of Envermeu. " La première charte d' Henry Ier n' est qu' une confirmation de celle de Robert, sous qui la fondation du prieuré a dû être faite ": Dom Jouvelin-Thibault in MS. Lat. 13905, f. 80v; cf. Porée, *Bec*, i. 427, note 3.

12. BEC. Grants to Bec one-half of Saint-Philbert-sur-Risle and the church of Saint-Étienne-l'Allier. Mention in charter of Henry II: Delisle-Berger, no. 624.

[20] The fatal illness of Geoffrey of Coutances dates from August 1092, in which year also Fulk of Saint-Pierre-sur-Dive seems to have been deposed.

13. CAEN, Saint-Étienne. [Shortly after 1087.] Grant of Vains (Manche). Appendix E, no. 1.

14. CAEN, Saint-Étienne. [1091, probably.] Confirms exchange between Abbot Gilbert and William de Tornebu. Mention in Deville, *Analyse*, p. 31; cf. p. 27.

15. CAEN, Saint-Étienne. [1091, probably.] Joins with William Rufus in confirming this exchange. Modern copy, evidently incomplete, in MS. Lat. 17135, p. 12; MS. Lat. n. a. 1428, f. 3v. Mention in Deville, p. 31.

16. CAEN, Saint-Étienne. [1089–1091.] Witnesses, with William of Saint-Calais, bishop of Durham, and others, a charter of Hugh Painel granting to Saint-Étienne two-thirds of the tithe of Fontenay-le-Pesnel. MS. Lat. 17135, p. 23, from the original, now lost; MS. Caen 108, f. 10v, from lost cartulary; modern copy in Archives du Calvados. Deville, *Analyse*, p. 32; cf. C. Hippeau, *L'abbaye de Saint-Étienne de Caen* (*M. A. N.*, xxi, and Caen, 1855), p. 41.

17. CAEN, Saint-Étienne. [1096.] Attests exchange with Dijon. Appendix E, no. 2, from original.

18. CAEN, Saint-Étienne. [1101–1104.] Grant of market at Cheux (Calvados). Appendix E, no. 3, from original.

19. CAEN, La Trinité. [1087–1091.] Grant, with the consent of his brother Henry, of lands and rights near Caen and a market at Ouistreham (Calvados). MS. Lat. 5650, f. 34v. Printed by Stapleton in *Archaeological Journal*, iii. 26; Round, no. 423, omitting some of the witnesses; Davis, no. 324.

20. FÉCAMP. 7 July 1088. Restores various lands, with approval of his brother Henry. Appendix E, no. 4a, from original.

21. FÉCAMP. [After 7 July 1088.] Grant of fair at Fécamp. Appendix E, no. 4b, from original.

22. FÉCAMP. [1089–1091] at Fécamp. Renewal of preceding grants and seisin by ' hoc lignum.' Appendix E, no. 4c, from original.

23. FÉCAMP. [Before 1091.] Grant of land of Hugh Mursard. Appendix E, no. 5.

24. JUMIÈGES. 30 March 1088. Attests with his brother Henry charter of Ralph Fitz Anseré granting Beaunay and its appurtenances and the tithe of Anneville-sur-Seine (? Seine-Inférieure). Appendix E, no. 6, from original.

25. JUMIÈGES. [1091–1095] at Lisieux. Attests grant of Étables (Seine-Inférieure) by Ralph Fitz Anseré and invests therewith 'per lignum.' Appendix E, no. 7, from original.

26. LE MANS, Saint-Vincent. Grants tithe of his revenues in the castle of Fresnay-sur-Sarthe. Martène and Durand, *Veterum Scriptorum Amplissima Collectio*, i. 568; *Cartulaire de Saint-Vincent-du-Mans*, ed. Charles and Menjot d'Elbenne, no. 532.

27. MARMOUTIER. 1091. Grant of Ertald in Guernsey, ' procurante Rotberto comite Normannie.' MS. Lat. 5441, part 1, p. 199. Round, no. 1179; extract in Dupont, *Histoire du Cotentin*, i. 466, no. 6.

28. MONT-SAINT-MICHEL. 1088. Grant of a fair at Ardevon (Manche) and a house lot at Rouen. Original in MS. Lat. n. a. 1674, no. 2; cartulary at Avranches, MS. 210, f. 80v; MS. Lat. 5430A, p. 256. Published, with facsimile, by Delisle, *La commémoration du Domesday-Book à Londres* (Paris,

1886); text in *Annuaire-Bulletin de la Société de l' histoire de France*, 1886, pp. 177–184; Round, no. 717; Davis, no. 299.

29. PRÉAUX. [1087–1095.] Attests grant in Saint-Cyr-de-Salerne (Eure) by Roger de Beaumont. Cartulary in Archives of the Eure, H. 711, no. 388. Le Prévost, *Eure*, iii. 97.

30. PRÉAUX. [1087–1096.] Consents to grant of church and tithe of Le Bosgouet (Eure) by Robert of Meulan. Cartulary, f. 130v. Le Prévost, *Eure*, i. 378; cf. Delisle-Berger, no. 675.

31. ROUEN cathedral. 15 August 1095 at Rouen. Grants his right of *bernagium* in Pierreval (Seine-Inférieure). Cartulary, in Bibliothèque de Rouen, MS. 1193, ff. 47, 115v; copy therefrom in MS. Lat. n. a. 1246, f. 66; *vidimus* of 1422 in Archives of the Seine-Inférieure, G. 3680. La Roque, iii. 34, from the original now lost; [Pommeraye], *Histoire de l'église cathédrale de Rouen* (Rouen, 1686), p. 570 (mention); Round, no. 2; Davis, no. 384. Round, followed by Davis, omits the year from the date.

32. ROUEN cathedral. 1096. Grants to the church and its canon William Fitz Ogier the possessions of Osbert the priest and his sons in Neaufles-Saint-Martin (Eure). Pretended original in Archives of the Seine-Inférieure, G. 4069; *vidimus* of 1422, *ibid.*, G. 3680; copy in cartulary, f. 47. Printed, with a slight omission, in *Inventaire sommaire*, under G. 4069.

33. ROUEN, La Trinité. 1091. Attests agreement between Abbot Walter and Ralph of Bec concerning the tithe of Amfreville-la-Mi-Voie (Seine-Inférieure). A. Deville, *Chartularium Monasterii Sanctae Trinitatis*, no. 83; Davis, no. 317.

34. ROUEN, Saint-Ouen. [Before 1092.] Present at exchange *temp.* Abbot Nicholas. Cartulary 28*bis* in Archives of the Seine-Inférieure, p. 487, no. 597. Robert was also present at the translation of relics 29 April 1090: *Normanniae Nova Chronica* (*M. A. N.*, xviii), p. 8.

35. SAINT-ÉVROUL. [1087–1102.] Confirms grant of Walter, son of Goubert of Auffai, and grants a fair at Notre-Dame-du-Parc (Seine-Inférieure). Mentioned by Ordericus, iii. 40.

36. SAUMUR, Saint-Florent. [1093] at Bonneville. Notice of suit in Robert's *curia* between Lonlai and Saint-Florent, followed by sealed charter of protection addressed to Serlo, bishop of Séez. *Livre blanc* of Saint-Florent, in Archives of the Maine-et-Loire, f. 116. Ed. Marchegay, in *M. A. N.*, xxx. 682; Round, no. 1115; Davis, no. 342.

37. SÉEZ, Saint-Martin. Confirms and attests grant of tithe of rents in Argentan by Arnulf, son of Roger of Montgomery. *Livre blanc*, copy in MS. Alençon 190, f. 73v; MS. Fr. 18953, p. 27.

38. VENDÔME. 1094. Attests charter of Ivo Taillebois granting Cristot (Calvados). C. Métais, *Cartulaire de la Trinité de Vendôme*, ii. 90, no. 351; cf. iii. 42.

39. VENDÔME. 1094. Attests gifts in Audrieu (Calvados). *Ibid.*, ii. 90, no. 352.

Before subjecting this material to diplomatic study, we may note certain general facts of significance. First of all, the total is small, only thirty-nine charters, notices, and attestations for a reign of fifteen years (1087–1096, 1100–1106), only seven more than can be identified from the hand of Robert's grandfather, Robert the Magnificent,[21] who reigned less than eight years and at an epoch when the documentary habit was much less well established. It may be that later times were indifferent to preserving charters of Robert Curthose, but it is even more likely that his own age was not eager to secure them. As confirmation at his hands counted for little, none of these charters consist of general liberties or comprehensive enumerations of past grants; they are all specific and immediate. Furthermore, so far as can now be seen, the surviving documents are all authentic; privileges of the Conqueror, Henry I, or Henry II were worth fabricating, but no one seems to have thought it worth while to invent a charter of Robert. Chronologically, Robert's charters fall, with only one certain exception, in the period before his departure for the Crusade, and within this period almost wholly either in the first years of his reign, when there were late grants of his father to confirm or new matters to settle, or in the year of his departure, when certain final dispositions received his sanction; the lack of documents after his return from the East is suggestive of his political impotence. Geographically considered, the charters concern chiefly central Normandy, where Robert was strongest; at the beginning of the reign they reach as far as Mont-Saint-Michel on the one hand and Fécamp and Jumièges on the other, but for the most part they concern Bec, Préaux, and the region of Caen and Bayeux which was his last refuge. The southern border is represented by single grants for Saint-Évroul and Saint-Martin of Séez, but it is noteworthy that in the detailed list of Saint-Évroul's acquisitions in this period no mention is made of the duke's confirmation or consent.[22] Likewise significant is the absence of any evidence of the duke's supremacy in Henry's region of the Cotentin.[23] The fact that five of these

[21] See the list in Appendix C.

[22] See the roll of *ca.* 1090–1098 printed in the appendix to Ordericus, v. 182–195. His consent, however, is mentioned by William de la Ferté-Macé in a grant of 1093: Denis, *Les chartes de S.-Julien de Tours*, no. 45.

[23] See, however, for the bishop of Coutances, *Gallia Christiana*, xi. instr. 221. A charter of Ranulfus de Podiis for Héauville, Mid-Lent 1093, is granted ' tempore

charters[24] contain grants of markets or fairs is also symptomatic of Robert's careless disregard of valuable rights.

Of the thirty-nine documents only seventeen, less than one-half, are issued in Robert's name, the others being either notices of his acts or documents of his barons attested by him. Of the whole number ten at least are preserved in originals, three, that is, of the attested documents (nos. 3, 24, 25) and seven (nos. 4, 7, 18, 20, 21, 22, 28), possibly eight (no. 32), of Robert's own charters. The material is not abundant, yet it is sufficient to permit of drawing certain conclusions respecting his chancery and his government. The documents which are presented to him for attestation were naturally drawn up by the interested parties, but in the case of the duke's own charters it is natural to look for something of the regularity and system which we find in the chancery of the Conqueror's later years or of their contemporary Philip I.[25] If we fail to discover this, we shall have convincing evidence of the weakness of the administrative organization.

Externally, the originals of Robert's charters present no uniformity in size, handwriting, or mode of authentication. Each of the seven is in a different hand; only one (no. 28) has the first line in capitals. Five of the duke's charters announce the apposition of his seal (nos. 1, 2, 22, 31, 32), which is mentioned in two of the other documents (nos. 3, 36); but only two of the surviving originals preserve traces of the seal, no. 4, to which it was applied, and nos. 20–22, the three charters for Fécamp, which were tied together by a strip of white leather, secured by a large seal of grayish wax. On neither of these seals can anything be distin-

---

Roberti Normannorum comitis' (Bibliothèque de Grenoble, MS. 1402, f. 233; cf. *Revue catholique de Normandie*, vii. 438), but a bare reference of this sort is quite different from a recognition of Robert's authority such as is involved in his attestation. For such references elsewhere see the charter of William, son of William Fitz Osbern, for Lire, in Le Prévost, *Eure*, i. 356; a grant to Marmoutier ' tempore Philippi regis et Rotberti comitis Normannorum,' MS. Lat. 5441, part 2, p. 87; and a grant to Préaux, Round, no. 321.

[24] Nos. 18, 19, 21, 28, 35.

[25] No thorough study has been made of the diplomatics of William I; cf. *supra*, Chapter I, p. 53 f.; and the *Facsimiles of Royal and other Charters in the British Museum*, ed. Warner and Ellis. For Philip I, see the introduction to M. Prou, *Recueil des actes de Philippe Ier*.

guished, nor has any loose seal survived. No. 18 has a long tag projecting from the parchment of the charter, but no seal is announced nor is there now evidence that one was attached. No. 28 shows incisions such as were later made for a *double queue*, but there is no evidence that these were contemporary, no seal being announced in the document, and the crosses being evidently regarded as sufficient. Nos. 20 and 21 were evidently sealed only after no. 22 was issued and attached to them; nos. 7 and 32 were never sealed. In every case the signatures of the duke and the principal witnesses are accompanied with crosses, and it is clear that this was considered the regular and essential form of validation. Another indication of the small weight attached to Robert's seal is seen in the importance assigned to the accompanying investiture ' per lignum ' in the text of two of his charters (nos. 22, 25) and ' per unum cultellum ' in another (no. 31), forms which suggest that the ducal charter did not differ fundamentally from a private agreement.

The style of the charters shows the greatest variety. The duke entitles himself *dux Normannorum* (nos. 4, 18, 31), *dux Normannorum et comes Cenomannensium* (nos. 1, 2), *dux Normannorum et princeps Cenomannorum* (no. 13), *Normannorum atque Cenomannorum princeps* (no. 19), *Normannie princeps et Cenomannorum comes* (no. 26), *gratia Dei princeps Normannorum* (no. 7), *Dei gratia dux et princeps Normannorum* (nos. 20, 21), *Dei gratia Normannorum dux* (no. 28), *Normannorum comes* (no. 32). In no. 7 he is also *filius Willelmi gloriosi regis Anglorum*, in no. 28 *filius Willelmi gloriosissimi Anglorum regis*, in nos. 19, 31, and 32, *filius Willelmi regis Anglorum*. He witnesses as *comes* simply in nos. 20, 22, 25; as *comes Normannię*, in nos. 3, 8, 18, 24, 28; as *comes Normannorum* in nos. 7 and 17 (here also *filius Willelmi regis Anglorum*); and as *dux Normannorum* in nos. 4 and 16. Nos. 4, 13, 18, 20, 28, 32 begin with an invocation to the Trinity; nos. 7, 19, 21, 22, 31 omit it. The date is often left out and, when given, usually appears somewhere in the text. Only the charters for Bayeux (nos. 1, 2, 4) have a full dating clause at the end; only these have a well developed preamble.[26] The resemblances of

[26] But cf. also no. 26, which has a preamble and is incomplete at the end.

style in this group of charters and the similarities between nos.
13 and 18 for Saint-Étienne point directly to local authorship,
while in general the range of variation in style and form precludes
the existence of an effective chancery and indicates that the
duke's charters were ordinarily drawn up by the recipients.

This conclusion is not invalidated by the occasional mention of
a ducal chancellor or chaplain; it might even be argued that a
government which pretends to have a chancery and yet makes no
regular or effective use of it is in a weaker position than one which
frankly depends on others for its secretarial work. The charter of
1088 for Mont-Saint-Michel (no. 28), one of the most formal and
regular of Robert's charters, has at the end of the list of witnesses
' Signum R. capellani R. comitis,' in the same hand as the names
of eight other witnesses, not including the duke, but in a different
hand from that of the body of the charter. Apparently this was
drawn up by the monks, the attestations being left to the duke's
secretary. Unfortunately for purposes of comparison, we have not
the originals of the other documents in which this chaplain takes
part. In one of these, the charter for La Trinité of Caen, 1087–
1091 (no. 19), we find ' Radulfus capellanus de Airi ' in the body
of the document, and ' Signum Radulfi capellani ' among the
attestations along with other officials of the ducal household. By
15 August 1095 in a charter for Rouen he has become ' Radulfus
cancellarius ' (no. 31), a dignity which he still holds in 1096, when
he so attests in another charter for Rouen (no. 32) and when Hugh
of Flavigny signs ' vice cancellarii Rodulfi ' [27] (no. 4). Another
chaplain-chancellor is found at the same time, Arnulf of Choques,
ranking below Ralph, since he appears as chaplain in the charter
of 1095 in which Ralph is chancellor,[28] but called chancellor in
1093 and 1094 by a monk of Bec who mentions him as the duke's
messenger and intermediary.[29] It is Arnulf, formerly tutor of the

[27] See the date, above, note 19. His name suggests the clerks under Henry II,
infra, Chapter V, note 133.
[28] ' Presentibus . . . Radulpho cancellario meo Ernulfo de Cioches capellano
meo' (no. 31).
[29] *De libertate Beccensis ecclesie*, in Mabillon, *Annales* (Lucca, 1740), v.603; *Vita
Willelmi tertii abbatis*, in Migne, cl. 718; Porée, *Bec*, i. 243–245. ' Turgisus capellanus regis ', who became bishop of Avranches in 1094, attests no. 38 in that year.

duke's sister Cecily, who accompanies Robert as chaplain on the Crusade and rises to fame as patriarch of Jerusalem.[30]

Special interest attaches to the signature of Hugh of Flavigny in the charter of 24 May 1096, confirming as it does Hugh's chronicle and throwing light on the mission of Gerento, abbot of Saint-Bénigne of Dijon, to England and Normandy. Freeman,[31] it is true, relates this episode " not without a certain misgiving " because of the silence of " our own writers," especially Eadmer; but there is nothing save insular prejudice to throw doubt on the narrative of Hugh, who, having accompanied his abbot on the journey, tells of the mission to England, toward the close of 1095, for the purpose of arranging peace between William Rufus and Robert and securing reforms in the English church, and of the sojourn in Normandy until the autumn of 1096, when they journeyed with the crusaders as far as Pontarlier. There is, moreover, excellent charter evidence for Gerento's presence in Normandy in the interval, for he arranges and attests (no. 17) an exchange of possessions with Gilbert, abbot of Caen, completed in the presence of Duke Robert, and also attests the duke's charter of 1096 for Rouen cathedral (no. 32), probably issued at Rouen. His name appears here in company with that of Bishop Odo of Bayeux,[32] and it was doubtless during Gerento's visit to Normandy that preparations were made for the grant of Saint-Vigor to Saint-Bénigne, as accomplished by the charters of the bishop and duke (nos. 3 and 4) issued at Bayeux 24 May 1096. As for Hugh, his chronicle refers repeatedly to his visit to Normandy, and specifically to Rouen and Bayeux, where he spent some time,[33] while the documents show him attesting as ' Hugo capellanus ' the exchange between the abbeys of Dijon and Caen, and subscribing Robert's charter confirming the grant of Saint-

[30] *Historiens occidentaux des Croisades*, iii. 281, 302, 604, 665, iv. 232; *Gesta Francorum*, ed. Hagenmeyer, p. 481 f.; Moeller, in *Mélanges Paul Fredericq* (Brussels, 1904), pp. 194–196.

[31] *William Rufus*, ii. 588 f. See, however, F. Liebermann, *Anselm von Canterbury und Hugo von Lyon* (Hanover, 1886), p. 16. On Hugh's life and writings, see the preface to the edition of his *Chronicle* in *M. G. H., Scriptores*, viii.

[32] On Odo's visit to Dijon, see the chronicle of Saint-Bénigne, d'Achery, *Spicilegium*, ii. 395; *Analecta Divionensia*, ix. 200–202.

[33] viii. 393, 475 (general); 369, 399, 407 (Rouen); 394, 482 (Bayeux).

Vigor to Saint-Bénigne. Written in a more formal hand than the autograph of Hugh's *Chronicle*,[34] this ducal charter shows many points of difference from its Norman contemporaries. It takes over, it is true, certain phrases from Robert's earlier charter for Saint-Vigor, but the foreign authorship appears in the penal clause, the elaborate date, and the pretentious signature of Hugh, ' vice cancellarii Rodulfi,' in elongated capitals. As Ralph himself never claims a share in drafting the documents which he witnesses, this form of subscription is simply a further illustration of the preparation of Robert's documents by the parties interested in the transaction rather than by his own officers.

The disintegration of the chancery is accompanied by a corresponding decline in the ducal *curia*. The lists of witnesses do not show any great amount of continuity in the duke's entourage, still less any clearly marked official element. The archbishop of Rouen and the bishops of Évreux, Bayeux, and Lisieux appear fairly often, those of Coutances and Séez rarely, the bishop of Avranches not at all. William of Saint-Calais, bishop of Durham, who is said to have been intrusted by Robert with the administration of all Normandy,[35] attests six times (nos. 1, 2, 7, 8, 16, 38) during his Norman sojourns (1089–1094), and his successor Ranulf once in the latter part of the reign (no. 18). Of laymen, the most frequent witnesses are Robert, count of Meulan, William, count of Évreux, Robert of Montfort, William of Breteuil, William Bertran, Enguerran Fitz Ilbert, faithful to Robert to the end, when the men of Caen drove him forth in 1105,[36] and William of Arques, a monk of Molême whom Ordericus places

---

[34] See the facsimile, from the MS., now MS. Phillipps 142 in Berlin, in *Scriptores*, viii. 284; a modern reproduction would yield clearer results for purposes of comparison. It would also be interesting to compare this charter with contemporary documents for Dijon and other monasteries with which Hugh was connected. The handwriting of the exchange with Caen resembles closely that of the chronicle and the Saint-Vigor charter; if not the work of Hugh, it must have been written by one of the other monks of Dijon, two of whom sign here with Hugh and the abbot.

[35] ' A Roberto fratre regis, comite Normannorum, honorifice susceptus, totius Normannie curam suscepit ': *De iniusta vexatione Willelmi*, in Simeon of Durham, ed. Arnold, i. 194. Cf. Simeon, ii. 216, where, as C. W. David has shown (*E. H. R.*, xxxii. 384), this statement is carried over to Odo of Bayeux.

[36] Ordericus, iv. 219.

among the chief counselors of Robert's earlier years as duke.[37] Of household officials [38] we have only the merest mention of Roger of Ivry, butler of the Conqueror and still bearing this title in 1089 (no. 1); William (of Tancarville) the chamberlain (nos. 2, 18, 19); Roger Mau-Couronne 'dispensator' (no. 19) [39]; Simon 'dapifer' (no. 7); and Turold ' hostiarius ' (no. 19). The bare mention of one or two *vicomtes* [40] is the only evidence of the persistence of the local administration, while respecting the fiscal system the sources are entirely silent.[41] Once, and once only, do the charters mention a meeting of the ducal *curia*, namely in a narration of the *démêlés* of the abbot of Lonlai and the monks of Saint-Florent, Saumur, respecting the priory of Briouze.[42] A term was fixed at the duke's court at Bonneville-sur-Touques toward the close of December 1093, and on the appointed day Robert ordered his bishops and nobles to do right in the case. Upon the abbot of Lonlai and his monks making default, the duke sent a mandate of protection under seal to the bishop of Séez, in whose diocese the priory lay, and through him also ordered the abbot to respect the rights of the monks of Saint-Florent. If the original documents in this suit had been preserved, they would supply one of the noteworthy gaps in the documentary materials of the reign, the absence of any writs or *mandata*, whether executive or judicial. The mention of something of the sort in this instance saves us from the hasty inference that nothing of the kind then existed, an argument from silence which could in any event hardly be justified in view of the chances against the preservation of these smaller and more fugitive bits of parchment. Nevertheless, it cannot be without signi-

[37] Ordericus, iii. 322, 354. Cf. Delisle's note in *Annuaire-Bulletin*, 1886, p. 182; *Bulletin de la Société d'histoire de Normandie*, x. 5.

[38] Roger de Lassi, ' magister militum,' is known to us from Ordericus, iii. 411, iv. 180. Cf. Sauvage, *Troarn*, p. 88 f.

[39] Cf. Round, nos. 424, 666; *supra*, p. 63.

[40] Nos. 1, 28. Note, however, no. 13 and the survival of *bernagium*, *infra*, p. 82.

[41] Sauvage has suggested (*Troarn*, p. 226, note) that the mortgage of the duchy to William Rufus for five years for 10,000 marks may serve as a basis for estimating the annual revenue in this period. There is, however, disagreement as to the term of the pledge; see below, note 50.

[42] No. 36. Cf. the condemnation to *debilitatio membrorum* by the *curia* in Ordericus, iii. 297.

ficance that documents of this type have come down to us from the Norman administration of William Rufus and Henry I; and the least that can be said is that the administrative weakness of Robert's reign cannot produce on its behalf this most convincing evidence of the normal vigor and precision of Anglo-Norman government.

A survey of the government of Normandy under Robert Curthose must also take account of the rule of William Rufus, from 1091 to 1096 in possession of the eastern portion of the duchy and at times coöperating with Robert elsewhere, from 1096 to 1100 sole ruler during Robert's absence. Crossing early in 1091,[43] the Red King quickly established himself in the lands east of the Seine, where several of the leading barons had already espoused his cause, and he soon compelled Robert to sign a treaty relinquishing to him the counties of Eu and Aumale, the possessions of the lords of Gournay and Conches, the abbey of Fécamp, and, apparently, at the other extremity of the duchy, Cherbourg and the abbey of Mont-Saint-Michel, then in the hands of his brother Henry.[44] Until William's return to England in August of this year he and Robert seem to have exercised a kind of joint rule in Normandy. They conduct a joint expedition against Henry, whom they besiege in the Mount,[45] they appear together in a confirmation for Saint-Étienne of Caen issued probably at this time,[46] and they unite, 18 July, in holding the inquest concerning their rights and privileges which formulated the *Consuetudines et*

[43] Ordericus (iii. 365, 377) places the crossing in the week of 23 January; Florence of Worcester (ii. 27) gives February; the *Anglo-Saxon Chronicle*, Candlemas. In any case it was subsequent to 27 January, when William was at Dover (Davis, *Regesta*, no. 315).

[44] On the provisions of this agreement, see Freeman, *William Rufus*, i. 275, ii. 522–528, who calls it the ' Treaty of Caen ' on the basis of a statement by Robert of Torigni (William of Jumièges, ed. Marx, p. 270) that it was concluded there. Ordericus, however, places it at Rouen, which is geographically more probable; Robert of Torigni may have confused this with the Caen inquest of July. In any case the brothers came to terms quickly, for the siege of Henry in Mont-Saint-Michel began at Mid-Lent (Ordericus, iii. 378). In the enumeration of lands granted Cherbourg is mentioned only by the *Anglo-Saxon Chronicle*, and Florence of Worcester, who adds Mont-Saint-Michel.

[45] Freeman, i. 284–293, ii. 528–535.   [46] *Supra*, no. 15.

iusticie.[47] The harmony of all three brothers is shown later in the same year by the attestation of Robert and Henry to a charter of the Red King for Durham.[48] This state of affairs was, however, of short duration. Robert formally accused William of violating the agreement of 1091, and its sworn guarantors supported the charge. No reconciliation could be reached, and in 1094 William conducted hostile operations in Normandy from March until the end of December. Then, as before, his base lay in the region east of the Seine, but the history of the year is confused and tells us nothing of civil affairs.[49] The reconciliation of the two brothers was a special object of the mission of the Abbot Gerento of Dijon in the winter of 1095–1096; the agreement handed over the duchy to William in pledge for the ten thousand marks which he advanced to Robert for the expenses of his crusade. The terms of the transaction are known only through the chroniclers, who differ as to the period. Eadmer and Hugh of Flavigny give three years, Ordericus has five, while Robert of Torigni says William was to have Normandy until Robert's return and the repayment of the money.[50]

William Rufus entered into possession of Normandy in September 1096.[51] It is not clear whether he arrived before the crusaders had started; at least there is no evidence of a conference between the brothers on this occasion.[52] Of the four years of rule which

[47] Appendix D.

[48] Davis, *Regesta*, no. 318; W. Farrers, *Early Yorkshire Charters*, no. 928.

[49] Freeman, i. 460–470; Fliche, *Le règne de Philippe Ier*, pp. 298–301, who seeks to explain away the siege of Eu in this year on the ground of confusion with the campaign of 1091. The English chroniclers, however, are quite specific on this point. A precept of William Rufus to Bishop Robert of Lincoln dated at Eu belongs to this year or later: Davis, no. 350.

[50] See the passages collected in Freeman, i. 555.

[51] Ordericus, iv. 16. Cf. Davis, no. 377, the date of which is given as follows in the Winchester cartulary (Add. MS. 29436, f. 12): ' Hec confirmatio facta est apud Hastinges anno dominice incarnationis M°.XCVI° quando perrexi Normanniam pro concordia fratris mei Roberti euntis Ierusalem.'

[52] There is no reason for placing in this year the letter of Ives of Chartres (*Ep.* 28) upon which Freeman relies (i. 559) to prove that a conference was held under the auspices of the French king; Fliche, p. 299, places it in 1094. Apparently the Norman crusaders started after 9 September (Delisle, *Littérature latine et histoire du moyen âge*, Paris, 1890, p. 28) but before the end of the month (Ordericus, iii. 483).

remained to the Red King, the greater portion was spent in Normandy, but they were years of war, in Maine and on the perennial battle-ground of the Vexin,[53] and we hear little of the state of the duchy under him. Ordericus tells us that the new master recovered portions of the ducal domain which Robert had given away, and that he exercised to the full his ecclesiastical supremacy, but that under his iron heel Normandy at least enjoyed a brief period of order and rigorous justice to which it looked back with longing after Robert's return.[54]

It is not surprising that the documentary sources of these years should be meager; the remarkable thing is that, few as they are, the Norman charters of William Rufus tell us more of the workings of administration than do the more numerous acts of Robert Curthose. We may begin by eliminating the documents issued in England or at unknown places for the English lands of Norman religious establishments, but for convenience we may include three or four other charters which probably belong to the period before 1096. There results the following list of documents issued in or concerning Normandy,[55] which are here numbered with Roman numerals in order to avoid confusion with the preceding catalogue of acts of Robert:

I. Bec. At Rouen. Release of Surcy (Eure) from *bernagium*. Davis, *Regesta*, nos. 425, lxxiii; printed below, p. 82.

II. Caen, Saint-Étienne [probably in 1091]. Confirms exchange with William de Tornebu. *Supra* under Robert, no. 15.

---

[53] On these campaigns, see Freeman, ii. 165–256, 274–296; Fliche, pp. 301–305; R. Latouche, *Histoire du comté du Maine pendant le Xe et le XIe siècle* (Paris, 1910), pp. 45–51.

[54] iv. 16–19, 98. A returning crusader, Wigo de Marra, makes a grant to Saint-Julien of Tours in 1099, ' regnante Willelmo rege Anglorum et duce Normannorum,' and agrees 'si possum volente domino Normannie conficere et congregare feriam, quod ipsi monachi habebunt totius ferie omnium rerum decimam.' This is the latest recognition of William's dominion that I have found: Denis, *Chartes de S.-Julien de Tours*, no. 51.

[55] I have not included the following writ for Montebourg, which may be of William I or II: ' Willelmus rex Anglorum omnibus suis ministris tocius Normannie salutem. Precipio vobis ut res Sancte Marie de Monteborc quiete sint ab omni consuetudine et sine theloneo transeant quocunque venerint.' MS. Lat. 10087, no. 6. The chapter of Chartres addressed a letter of congratulation to the Red King at his accession (*B. É. C.*, xvi. 453), but he does not appear in the list of its royal benefactors (*E. H. R.*, xvi. 498).

III. CAEN, Saint-Étienne [in England, 1096–1097]. Grant of Creech in exchange for his father's crown and regalia, and general confirmation. *Vidimus* of 1424, in *Neustria Pia*, p. 638; La Roque, iv. 1334; MS. Lat. n. a. 1428, f. 4. Davis, no. 397; cf. Delisle-Berger, i. 263, note.

IV. DURHAM. At Pont de l'Arche [1096–1100]. Writ of freedom from gelds. Davis, nos. 480, xci.

V. FÉCAMP. [1094–1099.] Notice of suit between Fécamp and Saint-Florent. Davis, nos. 423, lxxiv.

VI. FÉCAMP. Writ to justiciars mentioned in the foregoing notice. Davis, nos. 424, lxxiv.

VII. FÉCAMP. At Lillebonne [1099]. Writ issued in pursuance of the same judgment to Ranulf of Durham and others. Original in Archives of the Seine-Inférieure; copy in MS. Rouen 1207, f. 16; MS. Lat. n. a. 2412, no. 46. Edited by me from the original, *E. H. R.* xxvii. 103. Round, no. 119, where it is wrongly given as of Henry I; Davis, no. 416.

VIII. LE MANS cathedral. At Saint-Sever (Émendreville) [1096–1099]. Writ confirming grants of his father. *Liber albus*, no. 2; Davis, no. 440.

IX. LINCOLN. At Pont de l'Arche [1094–1100]. Confirming grant in Binbrook. Davis, no. 473.

X. LONGUEVILLE. Grant at Bosc-Lehard (Seine-Inférieure). Mentioned in confirmations of Henry I and Henry II in Archives of the Seine-Inférieure; Round, nos. 219, 225. For the charters of Henry II see Chevreux and Vernier, *Les archives de Normandie et de la Seine-Inférieure*, plate 13; Delisle-Berger, nos. 7, 768.

XI. SAINT-ÉVROUL. At Windsor, late in 1091. General confirmation. Mentioned by Ordericus, iii. 381, cf. 41.

XII. SAUMUR, Saint-Florent. 1092. Confirms his father's grant of Ceaux. Davis, no. 158.

XIII. STOW. At Eu, perhaps in 1094. Writ to bishop of Lincoln. Davis, no. 350.

XIV. THORNEY. At Rosay[56] [1094–1099]. Writ to bishop of Lincoln and others respecting the abbey's assessment. Davis, nos. 422, lxxii.

XV. TROARN. Confirms the abbey's possessions in Normandy and England as granted by his father. Sauvage, *Troarn*, p. 363.[57]

[56] There are two places of this name in the department of the Seine-Inférieure, one in canton Bellencombre, the other in canton Ménerval. The compiler of the index to Davis unaccountably identifies Roseium with Rozoy-en-Brie, far out of William's territory; cf. Round, in *E. H. R.*, xxix. 349.

[57] There are also two spurious documents of this reign. One, dated in 1089 but written in a later style, recites that ' tres regis Willelmi pincerne nomine Gerardus Radulfus Malgerius ' have granted ' Deo et Petro et S. Audoeno infra Chatomensium fines terram quandam ' (cartulary of Saint-Ouen in Archives of the Seine-Inférieure, no. 28*bis*, p. 277, no. 340). The other (cf. *E. H. R.*, xxiv. 213, note 16), quite possibly meant for William's father, is a general charter for the abbey of Montebourg, for which the substance and most of the witnesses have been borrowed from a charter of Henry I which is printed in Delisle, *Cartulaire normand*, no. 737. The false charter (*Gallia Christiana*, xi. instr. 229; *Neustria Pia*, p. 672)

It is clear, first of all, that William Rufus brought with him to Normandy his chancellor, William Giffard,[58] who attests charters at Rouen (no. i), Pont de l'Arche (no. iv), Saint-Sever (Émendreville, no. viii), Eu (no. xiii), and Rosay (no. xiv), and who had sufficient association with Rouen cathedral to lead the canons to secure from him later a formal declaration that no chancellor or chaplain had any rights in its choir.[59] With the English chancellor naturally came the writ. There are seven writs, a goodly number under the circumstances, and one (no. vii) is preserved in the original. Five are addressed to the king's officers in England (nos. iv, vi, vii, xiii, xiv), one to officers in Maine (no. viii),[60] and one to officers in Normandy (no. i). The Norman writ runs as follows:

Willermus rex Anglorum F. veltrario et Isenbardo bernario [61] et omnibus servientibus hanc consuetudinem requirentibus salutem. Sciatis quia clamo terram Sancte Marie de Surceio omnino quietam de bernagio donec ego inquiram quomodo fuit tempore patris mei. Teste Willelmo cancellario apud Rothomagum.[62]

Here we have a document parallel in every way to its English contemporaries in its sharp, crisp form and in its assumption of regular execution as a matter of course. The question is a purely Norman one, the ancient contribution to the maintenance of the duke's hunting dogs,[63] and the officers addressed show by their titles that they are concerned with this branch of the ducal

is not found in the Montebourg cartulary (MS. Lat. 10087) but appears in the *Livre blanc*, Archives of the Manche, H. 8391, f. 1; in the cartulary of Loders, Add. MS. 15605, f. 20v, from a *vidimus* of Philip III; and in Archives of the Manche, H. 8409; MS. Lat. 12885, f. 160; MS. Fr. 5200, f. 107; and MS. Grenoble 1395, f. 3.

[58] On whom see Davis, in *E. H. R.*, xxvi. 86.

[59] MS. Rouen 1193, ff. 49, 141v; Archives of the Seine-Inférieure, G. 3623; printed in Valin, p. 258, no. 3; Round, no. 4.

[60] Robert Doisnel, one of the officers here addressed, appears later in a charter of Robert Curthose (no. 18).

[61] The text has ' brevario,' clearly a copyist's error for ' bernario.' Cf. Round, in *E. H. R.*, xxix. 354; and on the berner and the velterer, his *King's Serjeants*, p. 271 f.

[62] Fragment of Bec cartulary in Archives of the Eure, H. 91, f. 39v. Indicated in *A. H. R.*, xiv. 464, note 69; printed in Valin, p. 200, note 2. *Bernagium* is also mentioned under Robert (no. 31).

[63] *Supra*, Chapter I, note 164.

administration; but the single example suffices to show the regular mechanism of Anglo-Norman administration at work. It
should be noted that the norm taken for inquiry is the practice of
the Conqueror's time, not of Robert's; and it is probable that the
method to be employed by the king was the sworn inquest.[64]
Other Norman writs would be more than welcome as illustrating
procedure, especially in judicial matters, but so far as the general
character of the government is concerned their value would be
essentially confirmatory. In such a case a single instance establishes the whole. Moreover, in respect to the duke's justice
another set of documents bears witness to the workings of the
curia in this period and enables us to follow the course of a suit
much as in the Conqueror's time. The monks of Saint-Florent
and those of Fécamp have a dispute respecting their rights at
Steyning and Beeding, in Sussex, which they bring before the
court of William the Younger at Foucarmont. Five act as judges
on the king's part, Robert of Meulan, Eudo the seneschal, William the chancellor, William Werelwast, the king's chaplain, and
William Fitz Ogier. When the decision has been reached, the king
sends sealed letters on behalf of the abbey of Fécamp to his justiciars in England, supplemented by a later writ which has reached
us in the original (nos. v-vii). Evidently royal justice ran the
same course wherever the king was; Normandy and England
were a part of the same system.

These faint glimpses of the government of Normandy under
William Rufus are all that we have to bridge the gap between the
Conqueror and Henry I. They show us what happened when, as
again under Henry I, Normandy was subject to the ruler of England and could be treated as part of the same organization; and
if we knew nothing of the independent history of Norman institutions, we might be led to suppose that they had no vitality of their
own and were in some degree a reflection of the larger state across
the Channel. We have seen, however, the strength and vigor of
the Norman system before the Conquest of 1066, and we shall see
under Henry I the survival of the institutions of the Conqueror's
time, which was the standard to which all matters were then re-

[64] Valin, p. 200; *infra*, Chapter VI, note 103.

ferred. When we find the Exchequer of Henry I and Henry II
carefully keeping up the fiscal arrangements of the Conqueror, we
get some measure of the persistence of the ancient organization in
Normandy, and we are justified in inferring that, in local matters
at least, it was in some measure maintained even during the
disorder and weakness of Robert's reign.

CHAPTER III

THE ADMINISTRATION OF NORMANDY UNDER HENRY I[1]

THE reign of Henry I, which Round has declared perhaps the most tantalizing in English history, is equally tantalizing to the student of the history and institutions of Normandy, where the paucity of documents is even greater than in England for the same period. There is nothing in Normandy which corresponds to the Pipe Roll of 1130; the only local survey is the Bayeux inquest of 1133, examined above as a source for the feudal conditions of the eleventh century;[2] the only piece of legislation is the ordinance of 1135 which divides between the king and the bishops the fines for violating the Truce of God;[3] the destruction of the records of cathedrals and religious houses has been far greater than in England. Nevertheless the number of charters issued in Normandy or for Norman beneficiaries is still considerable and quite exceeds the possibility of such a catalogue as has been attempted for the scanty documentary remains of Robert Curthose and Geoffrey Plantagenet.[4] Until the *Regesta* of Davis shall have created a documentary and chronological basis for the study of this reign in England, it is premature to undertake a systematic treatment of its annals in Normandy.[5] For the present we must content ourselves with an exploration of the significant points in the administrative system, having regard on the one hand to the restoration of stable government after the overthrow of Robert, and on the other to such institutions of later Normandy as can be traced back to Henry's reign. Parallels and connections with England will inevitably suggest themselves.

---

[1] Revised and expanded from *E. H. R.*, xxiv. 209–231 (1909).
[2] *Supra*, Chapter I.
[3] *Très Ancien Coutumier*, ed. Tardif, c. 71; Round, *Calendar*, no. 290.
[4] See Chapters II and IV.
[5] See, however, the contributions to Henry's Norman itinerary in Appendix G.

When the victory of Tinchebrai, 28 September 1106, gave Henry complete control of the duchy, it found him already established at Bayeux, Caen, and Évreux.[6] Proceeding to Rouen, he renewed his father's privileges to the city: *paternas leges renovavit pristinasque urbis dignitates restituit*, phrases which also point to a general restoration of the Conqueror's system of government throughout the duchy.[7] Such was also the purpose of a council of barons and clergy held in mid-October at Lisieux, where, according to Ordericus,[8] Henry revoked all Robert's grants from the ducal domain and restored the possessions of the church as they had stood at the time of his father's death. General peace was reëstablished by the repression of acts of robbery and violence, and we are told that special penalties were enacted against rape and counterfeiting.[9] The destruction of adulterine castles was also systematically begun.[10] Assemblies were held at Falaise in January and at Lisieux in March of 1107, but no record of their legislation has reached us,[11] and by Easter Henry was back in

[6] Besides the narratives of the events of 1105-1106 to be found in the chroniclers — Ordericus, Henry of Huntingdon, the Peterborough chronicle, Florence of Worcester, William of Malmesbury, and Wace, who preserves certain local details — there are three contemporary pieces of importance: (1) Serlo, *De capta Baiocensi civitate*, H. F., xix, p. xci; Wright, *Anglo-Latin Poets*, ii. 241; see Böhmer, *Serlo von Bayeux*, in *Neues Archiv*, xxii. 701-738. (2) Henry's letter to Anselm after Tinchebrai, in Eadmer, *Historia Novorum*, p. 184. (3) The account of this battle by a priest of Fécamp, first printed by Delisle, Robert of Torigni, i. 129; reprinted, *E. H. R.*, xxiv. 728, and, more correctly, xxv. 295.

[7] Ordericus, iv. 233; cf. Tardif, *Étude sur les sources*, i. 45. That *paternas leges* applies to the whole duchy is clear from the repetition of the phrase in the speech which Ordericus puts in Henry's mouth in 1119 (iv. 402). Cf. the use of *laga Edwardi* in England.

[8] iv. 233.

[9] According to a statement of uncertain origin in Bessin, *Concilia*, i. 79; cf. Le Prévost's note to Ordericus, iv. 233; Tardif, *Étude*, p. 46. The penalties are similar to those proclaimed in England in 1108 and enforced severely in 1125: Florence of Worcester, ii. 57, 79; William of Malmesbury, *Gesta Regum*, p. 476; Eadmer, *Historia Novorum*, p. 193; Henry of Huntingdon, p. 246; Simeon of Durham, ii. 281; Robert of Torigni, in William of Jumièges, ed. Marx, p. 297; Suger, *Louis le Gros*, ed. Molinier, p. 47. In a charter issued at Easter 1108 Henry describes this English legislation as 'nova statuta mea de iudiciis sive de placitis latronum et falsorum monetariorum': *Calendar of Patent Rolls*, 1338-1340, p. 166; *Historians of the Church of York*, iii. 22.

[10] Ordericus, iv. 236; Suger, p. 47.   [11] Ordericus, iv. 239, 269.

England.[12] Ordericus tells us, under this same year, that the *magistratus populi* were often called to the *curia* and admonished to conform themselves to the new conditions of peace and stricter responsibility.[13] The only meeting of the *curia* of which we have formal record at this time was held at Rouen, 7 November 1106, in the archbishop's *camera*, to decide a dispute between the monasteries of Fécamp and Saint-Taurin of Évreux, which had been subjected to Fécamp by charter of Robert the Magnificent; the decision was given by the ' counsel and judgment of the bishops, abbots, and barons,' among whom appear the archbishop of Rouen, the bishops of Bayeux, Évreux, Winchester, and Durham, the abbots of Saint-Ouen, La Trinité, Jumièges, and Troarn, the archdeacons of Rouen and Évreux, Robert de Meulan, Richard de Revers, William d'Aubigny, and the king's chancellor Waldric.[14] Another suit of this same winter was decided in favor of the abbey of Bec in the presence of the archbishop and the bishops and barons of Normandy, the charter which records the result being approved by King Henry, the bishops of Bayeux and Avranches, Robert of Bellême, Robert of Meulan, Eustace of Boulogne, Henry, count of Eu, and the archdeacons of Rouen.[15]

What means were provided for maintaining the government during the king's absence is a question which we cannot answer from the chroniclers, who are quite fragmentary on events in Normandy between 1107 and 1112. The charters, however, tell us before 1108 of ducal justices in the Cotentin, and before 1109 of a chief justiciar; and, as we shall see, the *curia* meets to decide an important case in the king's absence in 1111.[16] It can hardly be an accident that before his departure in 1107 Henry gave the see of Lisieux to John, who appears at the head of the Norman *curia* in

[12] Henry of Huntingdon, p. 236.

[13] iv. 269.

[14] *Gallia Christiana*, xi. instr. 127; a fuller list of witnesses in Collection Moreau, xlii. 88. Henry's presence at Rouen is also attested for 30 November of this year by a charter witnessed by his chancellor Waldric (*Calendar of Charter Rolls*, v. 56, no. 7; *Monasticon*, iii. 384), who was about this time sought out at Rouen by the canons of Laon: Davis, in *E. H. R.*, xxvi. 88.

[15] Appendix F, no. 1.

[16] See the charters for Montebourg, Saint-Pierre-sur-Dive, and Jumièges cited below, p. 93 f.

the later years of the reign, and who had already served a long apprenticeship as judge in ecclesiastical causes in Normandy and as one of Henry's principal chaplains in England.[17] It is probable that Bishop John was, if not the head, at least an important member of the government of the duchy in these early years; but there is no definite evidence for this period, and little enough for any period, and we are compelled to study the administration of Normandy topically rather than chronologically throughout the reign. Only toward the end do the long sojourns of Henry on the Norman side of the Channel and a somewhat greater variety of evidence give us a rather more connected view.

The starting-point for any study of the government of Normandy under Henry I is the plea, published by Round in 1899, which established for the first time the existence of the Norman Exchequer *eo nomine* in this reign.[18] In this document the great

[17] Ordericus, iv. 273–275: 'A prefatis itaque magistris, quia ratione et eloquentia satis enituit, ad archidiaconatus officium promotus, ad examen rectitudinis iure proferendum inter primos resedit et ecclesiastica negotia rationabiliter diu disseruit.' Driven out of the archdeaconry of Séez by Robert of Bellême he fled to England, where 'inter precipuos regis capellanos computatus est, atque ad regalia inter familiares consilia sepe accitus est.' Note that Bishop John was not only a contemporary of Ordericus but also his diocesan.

[18] 'Isti sunt homines qui fuerunt [presentes] ubi Bernardus disrationavit versus Serlonem surdum virgultum et terram iuxta virgultum de Maton ad dominium suum, scilicet Robertus de Curci dapifer et Willelmus filius Odonis et Henricus de Pomerai et Willelmus Glastonie et Wiganus Marescallus et Robertus capellanus episcopi Luxoviensis et Robertus Ebroicensis et Martin scriba de capella. Et ibi positus fuit Serlo in misericordia regis per iudicium baronum de scaccario quia excoluerat terram illam super saisinam Bernardi, quam ante placitum istud disracionaverat per iudicium episcopi Luxoviensis et Roberti de Haia et multorum aliorum ad scaccarium. Et hoc idem testificati fuerunt per brevia sua ad hoc placitum ubi non interfuerunt quia ambo tunc infirmi fuerunt. Et cum Serlone fuerunt ibi Ricardus frater suus et [*blank*] qui hoc viderunt et audierunt et per deprecationem Bernardi Serlo admensuratus fuit de misericordia regis ad x solidos.' *E. H. R.*, xiv. 426.

Valin, pp. 125–132, labors hard to explain away this document, which upsets his whole theory of the origin and functions of the Exchequer, on the ground that it was drawn up, probably later, by a canon of Merton who introduced English terminology. Taken apart from any preconceived theory, however, it is strictly parallel to the other notices concerning the lands of Bernard the scribe which Round has printed (*l. c.*, 417–430), all of which are plainly contemporaneous records of transactions of the reign of Henry I and show no trace of tampering. The form

officers of the household — Robert de Courcy seneschal, Henry
de la Pommeraie and William Fitz Odo constables, William of
Glastonbury chamberlain,[19] and Wigan the marshal — together
with Robert the treasurer [20] and two other clerks, sit in judgment
as 'barons of the Exchequer' to determine the ownership of a
piece of land, as well as to protect possession previously established at the Exchequer before John, bishop of Lisieux, Robert de
la Haie seneschal, and others. With this clue in our hands, we
shall have little difficulty in recognizing the same body in the following charter, in which, this time under the name of the king's
curia, it sustains the appeal of the abbot of Fécamp against an
infringement of the abbey's *haute justice* [21] by the king's justices.
It is not stated that the witnesses to the charter are the members
of the court who rendered the decision, but such is doubtless the
case. The bishop of Lisieux, the two seneschals, and William of
Glastonbury are known to us as barons of the Exchequer from
the document already mentioned, while William d'Aubigny the

can also be found in St. Paul's charters of the same period: 9 *Historical MSS. Com
mission*, p. 61 f. Valin's main argument, the statement that there was no such
thing as a Norman Exchequer before 1176, will be disposed of in Chapter V. As
Powicke points out (*Loss of Normandy*, p. 85), the name is of subordinate importance; the existence of the court under Henry I is abundantly established by
the documents printed in Chapter III.

[19] The office inherited by William from his uncle Walchelin was a chamberlainship (*Monasticon*, vii. 1000). He also appears in two other documents relating to
the administration of justice in Normandy: *E. H. R.*, xiv. 424; *Livre noir*, no. 8.

[20] For proof that Robert of Évreux was treasurer, see below, p. 108 f. As the
charter there quoted shows that he was chaplain to Stephen, he cannot be the man
of this name whose son appears as a claimant for his father's land in Cornwall in
1130, so that Round's reason for dating his plea before 1130 falls.

[21] Murder and arson were pleas of the crown in Normandy, but had been conferred on certain immunists by ducal grant. See *supra*, Chapter I; and Appendix
D. For the reign of Henry I the clearest statement is found in his charter of 1134
for Bec: 'Concedimus etiam eisdem monachis ut habeant in tota parochia Becci
omnes regias libertates: murdrum, mortem hominis, plagam, mehaim, sanguinem,
aquam, et ignem, sed et latronem in Becci parochia captum undecumque fuerit, et
omnes alias regias libertates quocumque nomine vocentur, excepto solummodo
rapto, de quo honestius existimavimus seculares quam monachos iudicare:' MS.
Lat. 13905, f. 9v; MS. Lat. 1597B, f. 166v; Archives Nationales, JJ. 92, f. 17, no.
58; Round, *Calendar*, no. 375; Porée, *Bec*, i. 658 f. From a comparison of this
with the Fécamp charter printed in the text, E. Perrot, *Les cas royaux*, p. 315,
argues that the theory of pleas of the crown had not yet become permanently fixed.

butler and Geoffrey de Clinton chamberlain and treasurer [22] are well-known officers of Henry's household.

(1) H. rex Angl[orum] iustic[iis] et omnibus baronibus et vic[ecomitibus] et ministris et omnibus fidelibus suis totius terre sue salutem. Sciatis quia iuditio et consideratione curie mee per privilegium ecclesie de Fiscann[o] ex dono et concessione predecessorum meorum remanserunt Rogero abbati Fiscann[ensi] et conventui Fiscann[ensi] .xxi.[23] libre de placit[o] de quadam combustione et .xx. libre de plac[ito] de quodam homicidio factis in terra Sancte Trinitatis Fiscann[i], unde iusticia mea placitaverat et duellum tenuerat de combustione in curia mea. Ideoque precipio et volo quod amodo teneat predicta abbatia Sancte Trinitatis de Fiscann[o] omnes dignitates suas et rectitudines et consuetudines tam in placitis quam in omnibus aliis rebus, sicut umquam prefata abbatia melius et quietius et honorificentius tenuit tempore predecessorum meorum et sicut carta ecclesie testatur et sicut per breve meum precipio. T[estibus] Iohanne Lexov[iensi] episcopo et Roberto de Haia et Roberto de Curceio et Willelmo de Albeny et Galfr[edo] de Clinton[ia] et Willelmo de Glestingeberia. Apud Rothom[agum].[24]

It will be observed that the word *curia* in this charter is used of two different bodies, the household officials, probably sitting at Rouen, where the charter is issued, and the king's justices (*iusticia*), from whose jurisdiction in holding pleas of the crown the abbot claims exemption. In the following documents we see the king and his *curia* determining questions of title to land, but nothing is said of the composition of the court:

(2) H. rex Angl[orum] Ric[ardo] episcopo Baioc[ensi] et omnibus baro-nibus et fidelibus suis de Oismeis salutem. Sciatis me concessisse Deo et Sancto Martino et monachis de Troarz amodo in perpetuum totum mariscum unde placitum fuit in curia mea inter monachos predictos et Robertum de Usseio. Ipse enim Robertus predictus recognovit rectum eorum quod iniuste eam (*sic*) clamabat et illam calumpniam marisci quam habebat in eo Deo et Sancto Martino clamavit quietam coram me. Et volo et concedo et firmiter precipio ut amodo in pace et honorifice et quiete et perpetualiter teneat ecclesia supradicta totum illud mariscum absque calumpnia et teneat et habeat sicut melius et honorabilius et quietius tenet suas alias res. T[estibus] Roberto com[ite] de Mellent et Nig[ello] de Albinni. Apud Rothomagum.[25]

[22] Pipe Roll 31 Henry I, p. 37; *Monasticon*, vi. 220; *Calendar of Charter Rolls*, iii. 275.

[23] The cartulary has '.xx.'

[24] Public Record Office, Cartae Antiquae, S. 3; cartulary of Fécamp in the library at Rouen, MS. 1207, no. 7, where only the first of the witnesses is given. Valin, p. 259, prints from the cartulary.

[25] Original, formerly sealed *sur simple queue*, in Archives of the Calvados, *fonds* Troarn (Marais, liasse 2, no. 77*bis*); copy by La Rue in the Collection Mancel at

(3) Notum sit domino Normannię et omnibus hęredibus meis, baronibus, prepositis, et ministris quod ego Guillelmus comes de Pontivo cum essem apud Falesiam ante dominum meum Henricum regem Anglorum habui verbum cum Rogerio de Gratapanchia patre et filio de maresco quod calumniabantur contra Sanctum Martinum et monachos eius, et rem gestam et tanto tempore a meis antecessoribus possessam et quomodo liberam et communem regi pręfato ostendi. Diiudicavit autem rex et eius curia per verba mea et illorum Sancto Martino et monachis remanere marescum quietum et liberum et amplius non debere fieri inde contra eos calumniam. Quapropter pręcipio omnibus hęredibus meis ut hęc firmiter in perpetuum teneant. Huius finis testes mei sunt Hugo vicecomes et Robertus frater eius, Paganus filius Hugonis de Mesdavid, Guillelmus de Corcella, Ascelinus et Serlo capellani. Hęc autem facta sunt anno ab incarnatione Domini .M.C.XXIX. in Pentecosten.[26]

In the following plea [27] of the year 1111, the judges are named, but they are styled *optimates* and appear to have been taken from the great men of the duchy rather than exclusively from the royal household. Apparently the king was not present. The final agreement, dated 18 December 1138, is interesting for its reference to the justiciarship of William of Roumare, created by Stephen on his departure from Normandy toward the close of 1137,[28] and for the list of barons witnessing. The civil strife at Rouen is evidently that of 1090.[29]

(4) In nomine domini nostri Iesu Christi ad noticiam presentium et memoriam futurorum, ad evitandam in posterum rerum oblivionem et adverse partis controversiam, litteris annotamus et apicibus subsequentibus non abolendis temporibus commendamus qualiter pontificante papa Paschali anno ab incarnatione Domini .M°.C°.XI°. sub rege Henrico abbas Ursus et postea ecclesię Romane presidente papa Innocentio regnante rege Stephano abbas Willelmus anno ab incarnatione Domini .M°.C°.XXX°.VIII°. calumpniam quam heredes Clari, Balduinus videlicet et Clarus frater eius, de

Caen, MS. 159, f. 1. Now also printed in Sauvage, *Troarn*, p. 265, n. 3. Anterior to 1118, the year of the death of the count of Meulan.

[26] Original, with seal of red wax in parchment cover, attached *sur double queue*. Now also printed in Sauvage, p. 368; Valin, p. 262. This and a charter of William's son John are found, in original and copy, with the preceding.

[27] Original notice, with no sign of having been sealed, in Archives of the Seine-Inférieure, *fonds* Jumièges; copy by Bigot in MS. Lat. 10055, f. 84. Now also printed in Valin, p. 260; Vernier, no. 61. The personnel of the court is analyzed by R. de Fréville, in *Nouvelle revue historique de droit*, 1912, pp. 687–696.

[28] ' Neustrie vero iusticiarios Guillelmum de Rolmara et Rogerium vicecomitem aliosque nonnullos constituerat: ' Ordericus, v. 91. See *infra*, Chapter IV, note 15.

[29] Ordericus, iii. 351 ff. A Clarus de Rothomago appears as tenant of the bishop of Bayeux in 1133: *H. F.*, xxiii. 701.

mansione quę est apud Rothomagum turris Rainerii cognominata et a beato Audoeno Sancto Philiberto et ecclesię Gemmeticensi iure perpetuo possidenda donata, sicut principali comitis Ricardi auctoritate karta teste roboratum est, diffinierunt. Que res se ita habet: Dominante in Normannia Rotberto comite in urbe Rothomagensi gravis dissensio inter partes Pilatensium scilicet et Calloensium exorta est que multa civitatem strage vexavit et multos nobilium utriusque partis gladio prostravit. Inter quos partis Pilatensium erat quidam rebus et nomine quem supra diximus valde Clarus qui abbati et monachis Gemmeticensibus pro suo actu et merito plurimum erat carus. Hic ergo, quia domus prefata in munitiori loco consistit, rerum metuens eventum, ut ibi hospes degeret expetiit et pro sua probitate et bonitate ad tempus impetravit. Quo decedente et rege Henrico principante filius ipsius Balduinus hereditario iure mansionem ibidem violenter voluit optinere, sed abbate Ursone ęquitatem iudicii reposcente in causam vocatus et nichil rationis dicere visus, iudicio optimatum eadem domo exire et deinceps carere iussus est. Qui videlicet iudices hi fuerunt: Gaufridus Rothomagensis archiepiscopus, Iohannes Luxoviensis episcopus, Rotbertus comes Mellenti, Willelmus comes Warenne, Gislebertus de Aquila, Willelmus camerarius de Tancardivilla, Willelmus de Ferrariis.

Nonnullis postea evolutis annis cum Balduinus obisset in primordio excellentissimi regis Stephani, Clarus eiusdem frater super eodem negocio regias aures pulsare et abbatem Willelmum cepit vexare. Que causa multis locis et temporibus varie tractata est et multismodis ut penitus finiretur a nobilibus et prudentibus viris utrinque amicis elaboratum est. Tandem in hoc rei summa devenit ut idem Clarus ab abbate iiii^{or}. marchas argenti acceperit et fide data quod nec ipse nec quisquis suorum pro se vel per se de predicta domo ulterius calumpniam moveret abiuravit et filios suos qui tunc non aderant infra .xl. dies adventus eorum ab abbate conventus ad   id se inclinaturum sub eadem fide promisit. Itaque Willelmo de Roumara iusticiam regis in Normannia conservante, dominica natale Domini proxima precedente quando(?) idem natale mortalibus cunctis honorandum subsequente proxima dominica erat celebrandum, apud Rothomagum in domo que fuerat Audoeni Postelli ista pactio a Godoboldo de Sancto Victore recitata ac perorata est et pecunia Claro tradita est, sub principibus baronibus et testibus his: Ludovico abbate Sancti Georgii, Gualeranno comite Mellenti, Willelmo comite Warenne fratre eius, Hugone de Gornaco, Rotberto de Novo Burgo, Iohanne de Lunda, Rogerio de Paviliaco, Radulfo de Bosco Rohardi, Rotberto Wesnevallis, Osberno de Kailliaco, Ingelranno de Wascolio, Walterio de Cantelou, Waleranno de Mellente et Willelmo de Pinu, Iuhel consanguineo Clari, Luca pincerna, Godoboldo de Sancto Victore, Alveredo fratre eius, Stephano filio Radulfi, Radulfo filio Rotberti, Urselino de Wanteria, Radulfo de Bellomonte, Iohanne fratre eius, Radulfo filio Rainboldi. Ex parte abbatis: Gisleberto de Mara fidei susceptore, Geroldus ad barbam, Rainaldo Vulpe, Willelmo Clarello, Rotberti Filiolo, Waltero de Eudonisvilla, Radulfo Calcaterram fratre eius, Rabello filio Goscelini.

So far the evidence respecting judicial organization has been of a rather general character, but when we come to investigate the ducal justices we are on firmer ground. The existence of a regular body of Norman justices under Henry I is plain, first of all, from their enumeration with the other ducal officers in the addresses of his general charters, and is clearly seen from the writs directed *iusticiis suis Normannie* [30] and from the clause, perpetuated under Geoffrey and Henry II, *nisi feceris iusticia mea faciat.*[31] The duke's justices are mentioned as early as 1108 in a charter for Monte-bourg,[32] and about the same time — in any case not later than the following year — we find a chief justiciar, *meus proprius iusti-tiarius . . . qui super omnes alios vice mea iustitiam tenet,*[33] or,

[30] *Livre noir*, no. 8; Round, *Calendar*, nos. 107, 875. Cf. Round, no. 479; Delisle, *Cartulaire normand*, no. 737, and nos. 15, 17, and 18, printed below. The following writ, from a *vidimus* of the *vicomte* of Pontaudemer in 1338, is unprinted: ' H. rex Angl[orum] iusticiar[iis] Norm[annie] salutem. Mando vobis quod faciatis habere abbati de Fiscampo terram et prata de mariscis de Aisi ita bene et plenarie et iuste sicut comes de Mellent ea tenuit de eo tempore suo, ne super hoc inde amplius clamorem audiam. T[este] canc[ellario] apud Bonam Villam.' Archives of the Seine-Inférieure, *fonds* Fécamp, box A (Aizier).

[31] See no. 13 below, and the *Livre noir*, no. 37. A *vidimus* of Philip the Fair of 1313 offers another example: ' H. rex Angl[orum] W[illelmo] de Roumara salutem. Sicut . . abbatissa Sancti Amandi Maeelina et ecclesia sua saisite fuerunt de ecclesia sua de Roumara et de hiis que ad ecclesiam pertinent anno et die qua pater meus fuit vivus et mortuus et postea eam tenuit tempore patris et fratris mei et meo et Emma abbatissa post eam hucusque, sic precipio quod inde amodo versus nemi-nem ponatur in placito, quia hoc est statutum terre mee. Sed bene et in pace teneat sicut ecclesia sua in retro tenuit hucusque. Et nisi feceris archiepiscopus et iusticia mea facient. T[este] R[oberto] de Ver apud Rothomagum.' Archives of the Seine-Inférieure, *fonds* Saint-Amand; Archives Nationales, JJ. 49, no. 48; copy in MS. Lat. 17131, f. 100.

[32] ' Volo autem et districte precipio ne iusticie mee manum mittant pro iusticia facienda in villa Montisburgi diebus mercati sive nundinarum ': Delisle, *Cartulaire normand*, no. 737; *Calendar of Charter Rolls*, iv. 157. The charter is witnessed by Anselm, and Henry was absent from England from the summer of 1108 until after Anselm's death. The same phrase appears in a charter for Montebourg purporting to emanate from William Rufus (*Livre blanc*, in Archives of the Manche, H. 8391, f. 1; *Gallia Christiana*, xi. instr. 229; *Neustria Pia*, p. 672), but it is evident from the witnesses that this has been forged on the basis of the charter of Henry I; see *supra*, Chapter II, note 57.

[33] Charters for Saint-Pierre-sur-Dive, *Gallia Christiana*, xi. instr. 156–160. The first of these, witnessed by William, archbishop of Rouen, who died in February 1110, is anterior to Henry's departure for England in the preceding May; it may have suffered some alterations, but the original of the other charter is still pre-served in the Archives of the Calvados.

more succinctly, *iusticia mea capitalis*.[34] Ordinarily, as in the Fécamp charter printed above (no. 1) and in nos. 5 and 6 below, the word *iustitia* denotes the body of justices.[35]

What is perhaps our clearest bit of evidence respecting the justices of Henry I is contained in the 'Emptiones Eudonis,' a document of 1129–1131[36] which comprises a series of notices of the acquisitions made by Saint-Étienne of Caen under the administration of Abbot Eudo (1107–1140). Of the suits here recorded the first came before the king and the whole *curia* at Arganchy; besides the bishop of Lisieux, two of the barons who attest are household officers, namely Robert de Courcy seneschal, and William of Tancarville chamberlain (d. 1129[37]). In the second case, which is prior to 1122, we find a full court (*tocius iusticie*) of five justices sitting in the castle at Caen, where the Exchequer of

[34] This phrase occurs in a charter for Beaubec which has come down to us with the style of Henry II, but has the witnesses of a charter of Henry I and is apparently cited in a charter of Stephen which accompanies it in the cartulary: ' Prohibeo ne de aliqua possessione sua trahantur in causam nisi coram me vel coram iusticia mea capitali. Et nichil retineo in aliquo predictorum preter oraciones monachorum. T[estibus] episcopo Bern[ardo] de Sancto David, W[illelmo] de Tanc[ardivilla] cam-[erario], R[ogero ?] filio Ricardi, apud Clarendonam.' *Vidimus* of 1311 (badly faded), and *Coutumier de Dieppe* (G. 851, f. 57v), in Archives of the Seine-Inférieure; Archives Nationales, JJ. 46, f. 37v; Delisle-Berger, no. 314, as a charter of Henry II. In England the same phrase is found in a charter of Henry for Holy Trinity, London: original in Public Record Office, Ancient Deeds, AS. 317 (before 1123).

[35] Other examples are the assistance given Rabel of Tancarville by the canons of Sainte-Barbe ' erga iusticiam regis Henrici ' (Round, *Calendar*, no. 568); ' per manus iusticie mee ' (*Très Ancien Coutumier*, c. 71); a transaction under Henry II 'in castello Cadomi coram iustitia regis' (Deville, *Analyse*, p. 52); and the following notice in a cartulary of Troarn: ' Willelmus rex et Rogerius comes dederunt nobis decimam de crasso pisce Retisville, quam Robertus de Turpo nobis voluit auferre sed reddidit coactus iusticia regis Henrici' (MS. Lat. 10086, f. 5v; Sauvage, *Troarn*, p. 359).

[36] It falls between the release of Galeran de Meulan in 1129 (Simeon of Durham, ii. 283; *Anglo-Saxon Chronicle*; Ordericus, iv. 463) and the death of Richard of Coutances, 18 November 1131 (*Gallia Christiana*, xi. 874; *H. F.*, xxiii. 475). Henry was absent in England from 15 July 1129 to September 1130, and again beginning with the summer of 1131; see Appendix G.

[37] Annals of Saint-Wandrille, *Histoire littéraire de la France*, xxxii. 204. In the Pipe Roll of 1130 we find, not William, but Rabel of Tancarville. If, as seems likely, the order of notices in the ' Emptiones ' is chronological, the judgment at Arganchy was rendered before 1118, the year of the death of William, count of Évreux, who makes the grant which follows next but one.

the later twelfth century regularly held its sessions; John of Lisieux, Robert de la Haie, and Hugh de Montfort constable,[38] are among the judges, but we are hardly justified in assuming that this was a meeting of the Exchequer. The action of the justices in deputing one of their number to take surety from the disturber of the monks should be noted. The proceedings in the third case took place likewise in the castle at Caen, before the king and three justices. Here the justices are sharply distinguished from the barons,[39] and Roger Marmion, who acted as justice in the preceding case, attests simply as a baron.[40]

(5) Emit Eudo abbas a Willelmo de capella molendinum de Drocione iuxta Divam viginti duabus libris in prima emptione, de quo molendino desaisitus per Robertum Frellam dedit prefatus abbas predicto Willelmo alias .xxii[as]. libras ut ipsum molendinum contra predictum Robertum disrationaret et Sancto Stephano adquietaret. Que disratiocinatio et adquietatio facta fuit apud Argenteium ante regem Henricum ibique in presentia ipsius regis et tocius curie recognitum fuit ipsum molendinum esse de fedio regis. Cuius rei testis est rex ipse et barones ipsius, Iohannes scilicet Lexoviensis episcopus, Robertus de Curceio, Willelmus de Tancardivilla, Willelmus Pevrellus, Rainaldus de Argenteio. Testes utriusque emptionis et tocius consummationis ex parte Sancti Stephani: Robertus de Grainvilla, Warinus de Diva, Willelmus Rabodus et fratres eius. Ex parte Willelmi: Willelmus frater eius, Robertus de Hotot, Radulphus filius Ansfride, Malgerius de Bosavalle, Rainaldus filius Ase. Dedit etiam predictus abbas uxori eiusdem Willelmi pro concessione huius venditionis, quia ipsum molendinum de eius maritagio erat, xl. solidos Rotomagensium. Testes: Robertus portarius, Rogerius camerarius, Warinus Cepellus, Willelmus cocus et alii plures. . . .

Rogerius filius Petri de Fontaneto in castello Cadomi in presentia tocius iusticie reddidit Sancto Stephano terram illam et omnes decimas illas quas ipse sanctus a Godefrido avo illius et a patre suo habuerat easque eidem sancto deinceps firmiter in perpetuum tenendas concessit. Et quia idem Rogerius abbatem et monachos pro eisdem decimis sepius vexaverat, ex consideratione iusticie Gaufrido de Sublis fidem suam affidavit quod nunquam amplius damnum contrarium ac laborem inde Sancto Stephano faceret sed manuteneret et bene adquietaret. Et ut hec omnia firmissimo et indissolubili vinculo Sancto Stephano teneret, abbas et monachi societatem quam predecessores illius in monasterio habuerant illi concesserunt et insuper de caritate .xl. solidos et unum equum ei dederunt. Testes ipsa iusticia, Iohan-

[38] Round, *Geoffrey de Mandeville*, p. 326. Hugh revolted in 1122, and was kept in close confinement after his capture in 1124: Ordericus, iv. 441, 458, 463.

[39] Cf. Delisle, in *B. É. C.*, x. 273; Fréville, in *Nouvelle revue historique de droit*, 1912, p. 705 f.

[40] Roger Marmion was dead in 1130, when his son paid relief for his lands: Pipe Roll 31 Henry I, p. 111.

nes scilicet Luxoviensis episcopus, Robertus de Haia, Hugo de Monteforti, Gaufridus de Sublis, Rogerius Marmio. Ex parte Sancti Stephani: Rannulfus de Taissel et Ricardus filius eius, Radulfus de Hotot, Aigulfus de Mercato et nepotes illius. Ex parte Rogerii: Radulfus sororius eius, Anschitillus heres de Hotot, Radulfus de Iuvinneio. . . .

Huius autem ville[41] ecclesiam quam Sanctus Stephanus antiquitus in magna pace tenuerat Herbertus quidam clericus ei modis quibuscumque poterat auferre querens abbatem et monachos inde diu fortiter vexavit. Quorum vexationi Henricus rex finem imponere decernens utrisque ante se in castello Cadomi diem constituit placitandi. Die igitur constituto abbas et monachi cum omnibus que eis necessaria erant ipsi regi et iusticie placitum suum obtulerunt. Herberto autem ibi in audientia regis et tocius iusticie necnon et baronum deficiente, de prefata ecclesia ipsius regis et iusticie iudicio Sanctus Stephanus saisitus remansit, nemini deinceps amplius inde responsurus. Testes huius rei ipse rex Henricus et iusticia, Iohannes videlicet Luxoviensis episcopus, Robertus de Haia, Gaufridus de Sublis, et barones Radulfus Taisso, Rogerius Marmio, Willelmus Patricus, Robertus Carbonellus. Ex parte Sancti Stephani: Rannulfus de Taissello et filii eius Willelmus et Ricardus, Robertus de Grainvilla, Radulfus de Hotot, Warinus de Diva et filii eius.

. . . .

Has emptiones quas fecit predictus abbas et donationes quas fecerunt suprascripti barones ego Henricus rex Anglorum concedo et sigilli mei assertione confirmo. Huius rei sunt testes cum signis suis subscripti barones. Signum Henřrici regis. S. Ricardi † Baiocensis episcopi. S. Iohannis † Luxoviensis episcopi. S. Ricarřdi Constanciensis episcopi. †S. Turřgisi Abrincensis episcopi. S. Rořberti de sigillo. S. Roberřti Sagiensis episcopi. S. Roberřti comitis Gloecestrie. S. Waleranřni comitis de Mellent. S. Roberřti de Haia, S. Rogeřrii vicecomitis. S. Willelřmi de Albigneio. S. Roberřti filii Bernardi.[42]

---

[41] Siccavilla (Secqueville-en-Bessin).

[42] Original, endorsed 'Emptiones Eudonis,' in Archives of the Calvados, H. 1834, no. 13–5*bis*. The charter, which measures 57 by 66 centimeters, is ruled in dry point and divided into four columns; there is a *double queue* but no trace of a seal. (Cf. *M. A. N.*, vii. 272, no. 13; a copy by Hippeau is in MS. Lat. n. a. 1406, ff. 76–85v). The witnesses are printed by Delisle, *S.-Sauveur*, pièces, no. 47; the slip which makes John, bishop of Séez, appear as Robert between two other Roberts is not of the sort one expects in an original, and the crosses seem to have been made by the same hand, so that we may have only an early copy. There can be no doubt of the genuineness of the contents, as the substance of the notices is reproduced, without the names of justices or witnesses, in one of Henry I's great charters for Saint-Étienne in the same archives (H. 1833, no. 12–3; 63 by 52 centimeters). The witnesses of this are given by Delisle, *Cartulaire normand*, no. 828; they are identical with those of another charter for the same monastery, evidently issued at the same time (H. 1833, no. 12*bis*–3*bis*; 74 by 52 centimeters). The two are incorporated by Henry II into a single charter of extraordinary length: Delisle-Berger, no. 154. The 'Emptiones Eudones' were transcribed into the lost cartulary of Saint-

The following document of May 1133 is of greater interest for the procedure than for the composition of the king's court; unfortunately it is known only through an extract from a lost cartulary, and the omitted portions are plainly of importance. A certain Fulk, vassal of the abbot of Troarn in respect of a certain fief, also claims to hold of the abbot the entertainment of a man and a horse. The king commands the abbot to do the claimant right, and a duel is waged, doubtless in the abbot's court, and, in accordance with a practice abundantly exemplified in the later Exchequer Rolls, recorded at Caen before the king's justices, who render a decision in favor of the abbot. Fulk, or rather, as before, his guardian for him, then brings forward another claim, this time to a church and twenty acres of land, and the justices again order the abbot to do him right; but the suit is abandoned at the instance of the patron of the monastery, William, count of Ponthieu. It should be noted that while the first plea is held *per iussum regis Henrici*, Henry had been absent from Normandy for nearly two years. There was nothing to prevent the plaintiff's securing his writ from England, but it was probably granted by the justices in Normandy, as in the ensuing complaint. A notice of this kind must not be pressed too hard, but there is no indication that the procedure was exceptional, and there is interest in the suggestion which the account affords of the justices' issuing writs in the king's name and taking jurisdiction in disputes between a lord and his vassal. Such writs of right indicate that Normandy, as well as England, was already moving in the direction of the procedure found in Glanvill.[43] The case also illustrates the procedure in the wager of battle as described by Glanvill:[44] the plaintiff offers battle through a champion who still preserves the name, if not also the character, of a witness. The only justice

Étienne, a full analysis of which is in the library of Sainte-Geneviève at Paris (MS. 1656), whence it has been published by Deville, *Analyse*, pp. 44–49. The notices which mention the king's justices are quoted from Deville's text, which is incomplete and very carelessly printed, by L. W. Vernon Harcourt, *His Grace the Steward*, p. 26 f. Valin strangely overlooks the whole document.

[43] See G. B. Adams, *Origin of the English Constitution*, pp. 78–80, 94–105. Professor Adams has convinced me that in this case Fulk was the tenant, not the lord, of the abbot, as I was inclined to believe in 1909.

[44] Bk. ii, c. 3.

named besides the bishop of Lisieux is William Tanetin,[45] who appears to be acting individually when the suit is dismissed.

(6) xxiiii° folio veteris cart[arii]. Notum sit omnibus quod anno millesimo centesimo tricesimo tercio in mense maio, per clamorem Fulconis filii Fulconis et Rog[erii] Pelavillani vitrici eius qui custodiebat eum et terram illius et per iussum regis Henrici, tenuit domnus abbas Andreas placitum et rectitudinem illis de procuratu unius hominis et unius equi quem dicebant ipsum filium Fulconis debere habere ab ipso abbate in feudo cum alio feudo suo. Et in ipso placito fuit inde duellum iudicatum et captum inter Hugonem de Alimannia qui testis erat filii Fulconis et Rad[ulfum] filium Fulberti. Deinde in eodem mense apud Cad[omum] recordatum est duellum coram iusticia regis, scilicet coram Iohanne episcopo Lex[oviensi] et Willelmo Tanetin et aliis, et iudicavit curia regis quod habere non debebant quod requirebant, etc. Post finem huius duelli fecit clamorem Rog[erius] Pelavillanus coram iusticia regis quod abbas Troarnensis tollebat filio Fulconis ecclesiam de Turfredivilla [46] et .xx. acras terre, et precepit iusticia regis ut abbas rectitudinem inde teneret ill[is]. Interea venit Troarnum Willelmus comes Pontivorum dominus Troarnensis abbatie et interrogavit ipsum Rog[erium] si de hoc vellet placitare, et respondit Rog[erius] quod in pace dimittebat ex toto in finem comiti et abbati, etc., totum id est et placitum et ecclesiam et terram, coram ipso comite et Willelmo Tanetin iusticiario regis. Plures sunt testes.[47]

The activity of the justices is also seen from writs like the following, which should be compared with one in the *Livre noir* of Bayeux,[48] addressed to the bishop of Lisieux, Roger de Mandeville, and William son of Ansger, and ordering them to do full justice to the bishop of Bayeux as regards any disturbance of his rights:

(7) Henricus rex Anglorum Iohanni episcopo Lexoviensi et Rogerio de Magn[avilla] salutem. Precipio vobis ut faciatis tenere plenum rectum abbati de Cadomo de aqua de Vei[m] desicuti ipsa iacebat ad manerium in tempore patris mei, ita ne inde clamorem audiam.[49]

[45] William Tanetin appears as dapifer (of the count of Ponthieu ?) in 1127, and as tenant of the count in 1135 (Round, *Calendar*, nos. 590, 970). He is frequently mentioned in the cartulary of Troarn in documents ranging from 1117 to 1135: MS. Lat. 10086, ff. 30v, 31, 152v; Sauvage, *Troarn*, pp. xxxii, 152, 225 f.

[46] Touffréville (Calvados), canton of Troarn. Cf. Sauvage, pp. 23, 140.

[47] Troarn cartulary, MS. Lat. 10086, f. 35v; copy by the abbé La Rue in MS. Caen 64, f. 46v. Now also printed in Valin, p. 263.

[48] No. 29; also in *Livre rouge* (MS. Lat. n. a. 1828), no. 29. Anterior to 1122, when William Fitz Ansger was dead (Delisle, *Rouleaux des morts*, p. 293).

[49] Library of Sainte-Geneviève, MS. 1656, f. 20; incorrectly printed by Deville, *Analyse*, p. 18. Vains (Manche) had been granted to Saint-Étienne by the Conqueror: Appendix E, no. 1.

With respect to the personnel of the king's court the documents published above, taken with the order of precedence in the address of the king's charters,[50] fully substantiate Round's assertion that Bishop John of Lisieux was the head of the Norman Exchequer; and while the title is not given him in any document so far known, there can be no doubt that he held the office of chief justiciar. Next to the bishop, Robert de la Haie the seneschal appears as the principal member of the court, indeed the absence of these two on account of illness is the occasion of explanation.[51] Robert seems to have been the chief lay officer of the Norman administration, for his name heads the list of laymen both in the address and in the testing clause of Henry's charters except when he is preceded by some one of the rank of count.[52] When Robert de la Haie is not one of the court, the other Norman seneschal, Robert de Courcy, is the first lay member. The justiciar and the seneschal would thus seem to have been the important elements in the court.

In certain of Henry's writs we find a distinction drawn between his *iusticia Normannie* and other justices in a way which suggests at first sight the chief justiciar in contrast to his colleagues, but more probably has reference to justices who were local or were at least acting locally. Thus a writ in favor of the canons of Bayeux is addressed *iusticiis suis Normannie et Willelmo Glast[onie] et Eudoni Baiocensi et G[aufrido] de Subles.*[53] Another writ, evi-

---

[50] Round, *Calendar*, nos. 282, 569, 1436 (cf. no. 611); Ordericus, iv. 435.

[51] *E. H. R.*, xiv. 426; *supra*, note 18.

[52] *E. H. R.*, xiv. 424; *supra*, nos. 1, 5; *infra*, nos. 9, 11, 12, 14; Ordericus, iv. 435; Round, *Calendar*, nos. 107, 122, 123, 168, 197, 398, 724, 924, 998, 1191, 1388, 1436 (where Round has Richard, but the *Livre noir*, no. 34, has simply R.); *Calendar of Charter Rolls*, ii. 137; *Calendar of Patent Rolls*, 1330–1334, p. 334, 1334–1338, p. 249; *Montacute Cartulary* (Somerset Record Society, 1894), no. 164; Appendix F, nos. 10, 11. Such exceptions to the precedence of Robert in the testing clause as are found in Round, nos. 373, 375, 411, and *Monasticon*, vii. 1071, are not originals; but no. 1052 in Round (from a copy by Gaignières) and no. 828 in the *Cartulaire normand* of Delisle seem to be real exceptions. The place of Robert de la Haie in the Norman administration shows the need of serious modification in Vernon Harcourt's view of the unimportance of the seneschal's office in this reign; indeed, in view of the almost uniform precedence of the seneschals in Henry's charters, it is impossible to maintain that they show " no trace of preëminence over other household functionaries " (*His Grace the Steward*, p. 24).

[53] *Livre noir*, no. 8; U. Chevalier, *Ordinaire et coutumier de l'église de Bayeux*, p. 419; Round, *Calendar*, no. 1437.

dently issued in the vacancy of the see between 1133 and 1135, is directed *iusticiis et custodibus episcopatus Baiocensis*, who are ordered to execute a decision of the king's *curia* in a case between two of the bishop's vassals — *et nisi feceritis iusticia Norm[annie] faciat fieri*.[54] There are also writs addressed to local justices in particular districts: *iustitie et vicecomiti Archarum*,[55] *iusticiariis et ministris de Sancto Marculfo et de Varrevilla*,[56] *iusticiis Constantini, iusticiis Constantini et Valloniarum*,[57] *Algaro de Sancte Marie Ecclesia ceterisque iusticiis Constantini*.[58] In the first of these instances the justice and *vicecomes* may be one and the same, as occurs in England at this period,[59] and the same persons may be acting as justices and *custodes* in the Bayeux writ; but it is not likely that the justices and *ministri* of Saint-Marcouf were identical, and the justices of the Cotentin have no other title and are evidently royal judges for the district, whether itinerant or acting under local commissions it is impossible to say. In some instances, as when the bishop of Lisieux is associated with local magnates like Roger de Mandeville and William Tanetin, the court may have consisted of an itinerant justiciar and a local judge. In order to follow out questions connected with the local administration of justice, we should need to examine a considerable number of writs, or at least a considerable group of those relating to a particular district or religious establishment; and the Norman writs of Henry's reign are few and scattered.[60] Not all of the following documents for the abbey of Montebourg relate to the administration of justice, but they are printed here because they form an interesting group which has not as yet been published:[61]

[54] *Livre noir*, no. 37.   [56] No. 9, below.

[55] Round, *Calendar*, no. 398.   [57] No. 11, below.

[58] Henry I for Héauville, a priory of Marmoutier: *vidimus* in Archives of the Manche; copy in MS. Grenoble 1402, f. 232; printed in *Revue catholique de Normandie*, x. 350.

[59] Stubbs, *Constitutional History*, 6th ed., i. 423; Round, *Geoffrey de Mandeville*, p. 106 ff.

[60] The two most important sets of such writs are those in the *Livre noir* of Bayeux (nos. 8, 29, 34, 37, 38) and the charters and writs relating to Envermeu calendared by Round (*Calendar*, nos. 393–398). See also the writ for Saint-Père of Chartres printed below, Chapter VI, p. 223.

[61] The cartulary of Montebourg (MS. Lat. 10087) was unknown to Round, as were the valuable copies of documents relating to the Cotentin which were made by

(8) H. rex Angl[orum] vicec[omitibus] et prepositis et ministris suis tocius Costantini salutem. Precipio vobis quod non capiatis hominem aliquem vel nampnum eius aliqua occasione in mercato de Monteborc die ipso quo mercatum est, si eum alia die et alibi in terra mea eos capere poteritis. Quia nolo quod mercatum elemosine mee per occasionem destruatur. T[este] R[oberto] comite Gloec[estrie] apud Argent[onum ?] per Willelmum Glastonie.[62]

(9) H. rex Angl[orum] iusticiariis et ministris de Sancto Malculpho et de Varrevilla[63] et omnibus dominis de quibus abbatia de Monteborc tenet, salutem. Precipio quod abbatia de Monteburgo teneat omnia sua ita bene et quiete et honorifice sicut liberior abbacia tocius Normannie, et nominatim elemosinam meam terram de Foucarvilla liberam et quietam de teloneo et de verec et de omnibus consuetudinibus et de omnibus querelis. Nolo enim ut habeant occasionem mittendi manum ullo modo super elemosinam meam. Quod si quid iniurie fecerint, videat iusticia mea ne perdam rectum meum; abbacia namque est propria mea capella et ideo precipio vobis ut eam custodiatis. T[este] R[oberto] de Haia. Apud Roth[omagum].[64]

(10) H. rex Anglie R[icardo] Constantiensi episcopo et vicec[omitibus] et omnibus baronibus et fidelibus suis de Costent[ino] salutem. Sciatis me concessisse abbatie Sancte Marie Montisburgi ecclesiam de Morfarivilla[65] cum feria et terris et decimis et omnibus rebus ipsi ecclesie pertinentibus, quam Sanson de Morfarvilla predicte abbatie dedit et concessit concessione Roberti de Novo Burgo domini sui et fratrum eius. Et volo et precipio firmiter ut bene et in pace et quiete et honorifice teneat. T[estibus] Roberto de Novo Burgo et Willelmo de Albinneio. Apud Rothomagum.[66]

Pierre Mangon at the end of the seventeenth century and are now preserved in the library of Grenoble (MSS. 1390–1402). Cf. Delisle, *Les mémoires de Pierre Mangon, vicomte de Valognes*, in *Annuaire de la Manche*, 1891, pp. 11–42. Certain documents concerning the Norman possessions of Montebourg are also copied in the cartulary of Loders in the British Museum, Add. MS. 15605, excerpted in *Revue catholique de Normandie*, xvii–xix.

[62] MS. Lat. 10087, no. 8, where the writ is dated ' apud Dug.' The *vidimus* in the Archives of the Manche (H. 8426, 8527) and in the Archives Nationales (JJ. 52, f. 62, JJ. 118, f. 258); MSS. Grenoble 1395, ff. 9, 58, and 1402, f. 64v; and Add. MS. 15605 of the British Museum, ff. 13v, 14v, 26, all have ' Argent.' For the contents of the privileges of the market of Montebourg, see Delisle, *Cartulaire normand*, no. 737; *Revue catholique*, xvii. 308; *Calendar of Charter Rolls*, iv. 157.

[63] Saint-Marcouf is in the canton of Montebourg. Varreville and Foucarville are in the canton of Sainte-Mère-Église (Manche).

[64] MS. Lat. 10087, no. 9; also in *Livre blanc* (Archives of the Manche, H. 8391), f. 2; MS. Lat. 12885, f. 161; Add. MS. 15605, ff. 13v, 14v, 26. *Vidimus* in Archives of the Manche, H. 8426, 8427, 10881, and in Archives Nationales, JJ. 52, f. 62, JJ. 118, f. 258. Copies in MSS. Grenoble 1395, f. 28v, and 1402, f. 35v, and in the Baluze MSS. of the Bibliothèque Nationale, MS. 58, ff. 38, 39v. In MS. Grenoble 1395, f. 9, there is a copy of this writ (from a *vidimus* of 1315) addressed 'episcopo Const[antiensi] et iustic[iis] Norm[annie] et omnibus . . .'

[65] Montfarville (Manche), canton of Quettehou.   [66] MS. Lat. 10087, no. 10.

(11) H. rex Angl[orum] iustic[iis] Costentini et Willelmo de Bruis et forestariis suis salutem. Mando vobis atque precipio quod permittatis habere monachos de Montisburg[o] tot arbores in Bruis [67] ad focum suum quot ebdomade habentur in anno et materiem ad sua edificia et pasnagium suum quietum et omnes consuetudines suas liberas et quietas, et de tot arboribus sint quieti forestarii in placitis meis de quot garantizaverint eos monachi per suas taillias. T[este] R[oberto] comite Gloec[estrie] apud Roth[omagum] per R[obertum] de Haia. [68]

(12) H. rex Angl[orum] Ric[ardo] episcopo de Constanc[iis] et W[illelmo] de Alben[neio] salutem. Precipio ut Unfredus de Alben[neio] teneat terram suam in pace et quiete et decimam de Morsalines [69] et molendinum et quicquid habet in eadem villa, et concedo ut ecclesia de Montebo[r]c post mortem Unfredi eamdem terram habeat in quiete et pace sicut Unfridus eam eidem ecclesie dedit. T[este] R[oberto] de Haia. Apud Roth[omagum]. [70]

(13) H. rex Angl[orum] W[illelmo] de Albin[neio] salutem. Precipio quod ecclesia de Monteburgo de elemosina mea teneat terram suam de Morsalinis quam Unfridus de Adevilla ei dedit concessu patris tui ita bene et in pace et iuste et quiete sicut breve patris tui quod habet testatur. Et nisi feceris iusticia mea faciat, ne inde amplius clamorem audiam pro penuria plene iusticie vel recti. T[este] R[oberto] comite Gloec[estrie] apud Alg' per W. Filiastr[um]. [71]

(14) H. rex Angl[orum] Ric[ardo] de Ansgervilla, W. de Sancto Germano salutem. Precipio vobis quod faciatis ita iuste habere abbati de Montisburgo octavam partem ecclesie de Herrevilla [72] sicut habet octavam partem terre eiusdem ville et desicut venit in curiam meam ut illam partem disrationaret versus monachos de Haivilla et homines suos et illi defecerunt se illuc veniendi ad diem suum inde sumptum et datum; ita ne super hoc amplius clamorem inde audiam. T[este] R[oberto] de Haia per Thomam de Ponte Episcopi. Apud Rothomagum. [73]

(15) H. rex Anglie episcopo Constanc[iensi] et iustic[iis] Normannie et omnibus dominis de quibus abbatia de Montisburgo et ecclesia sua tenet, salutem. Precipio quod abbas de Montisburgo et ecclesia sua teneant terras et homines et ecclesias et decimas et molendina et consuetudines et omnia sua

---

[67] Brix (Manche), canton of Valognes.

[68] MS. Lat. 10087, no. 11; Archives of the Manche, H. 8426, 8427; Archives Nationales, JJ. 52, f. 62, JJ. 118, f. 258; MS. Grenoble 1395; f. 9; Add. MS. 15605, ff. 13v, 14. In MSS. Grenoble 1395, f. 29, and 1402, f. 35v, the writ begins: ' H. r[ex] Angl[orum] iust[iciis] Constantini et Vallon[iarum] et forestariis de Bruis.' Cf. Henry's general confirmation, Delisle, *Cartulaire normand*, no. 737.

[69] Morsalines (Manche), canton of Quettehou.

[70] MS. Lat. 10087, no. 12.

[71] *Ibid.*, no. 13.

[72] Helleville (Manche), in the canton of Les Pieux, not far from the priory of Héauville.

[73] MS. Lat. 10087, no. 14.

ita bene et in pace sicut abbatia Fiscan[ni], quod enim ad me pertinet in ea omne concessi illi in elemosina. T[este] R[oberto] de Ver. Apud Rotho-m[agum].[74]

The glimpse of the forest courts in no. 11 is interesting. Pleas of the forest are mentioned in Normandy as early as the reign of Robert I, and there is evidence of a special forest law under the Conqueror; [75] this writ shows the foresters rendering periodic account before the king's justices and offering tallies as their justification for trees that have been taken by the monks. The regarders are also mentioned in Henry's reign,[76] as are the fines and forfeitures of the forest pleas.[77]

William de Brix and Richard d'Angerville [78] are also found as royal judges in the Cotentin in a document relating to the abbey of Saint-Sauveur, where the king's justices are apparently sitting in the feudal court of Nigel the *vicomte*. That they might so sit appears from English practice, and there is also evidence that Henry's officers exercised judicial rights on the lands of the bishop of Bayeux.[79]

(16) Sciant etiam omnes quod monachi Sancti Salvatoris omnes decimas et maxime medietatem campartorum, quod est decima pro qua inceptum fuit, totius terrę Nigelli vicecomitis et suorum omnium hominum diraciocinaverunt in curia sua, quibusdam eius militibus et vavassoribus contradicentibus, quibusdam concedentibus. Et ibi nemine resistente sed omnibus adquiescentibus iudicatum est atque diffinitum tam a regis quam a Nigelli iudicibus ut abbatię extunc et deinceps recta decima et maxime medietas

[74] MS. Lat. 10087, no. 15 (where the witness appears as 'R. de Weū'); *Livre blanc* (H. 8931), f. 1v; MS. Lat. 12885, f. 161; Add. MS. 15605, ff. 13v, 14v, 26; MS. Grenoble 1395, f. 28v; *vidimus* in Archives of the Manche, H. 8426, 8427, 8692, and in Archives Nationales, JJ. 52, f. 62, JJ. 118, f. 258. In MS. Grenoble 1402, f. 35v, the witness is given as ' Ric. de Redvers.'

[75] *Supra*, Chapter I, notes 215–218.

[76] *Infra*, note 156.

[77] Appendix F, no. 17.

[78] William de Brix witnesses charters of Henry I for Saint-Étienne (Round, *Calendar*, nos. 1411, 1412; Delisle, *Cartulaire normand*, no. 828). Richard d'Angerville appears as a witness in January 1101 in the Troarn cartulary (MS. Lat. 10086, f. 149) and in 1104 in Delisle, *S.-Sauveur*, pièces, no. 46. Roger Suhart was a prominent sub-tenant of the bishop of Bayeux in 1133, *H. F.*, xxiii. 699 f. (cf. Tardif, *Coutumiers de Normandie*, i. 1, p. 112).

[79] *Livre noir*, no. 16. Cf. the presence of Henry I's judges in the court of the bishop of Exeter, *E. H. R.*, xiv. 421.

campartorum a predictis sine calumpnia redderetur. His testibus: Willelmo de Bruis, Ricardo de Ansgervilla, Rogero de Rufo Campo, Waltero de Hainou, Rogero Suhart.[80]

As regards ecclesiastical jurisdiction, Henry I seems to have adhered in general to the practice of his father, the principles of whose policy, as formulated in the canons of Lillebonne, he confirmed by the apposition of his seal.[81] Barons as well as prelates sat in the *curiae* which decided the independence of Saint-Taurin from Fécamp and the rights of Bec over Notre-Dame-du-Pré.[82] If the court which establishes the right of Geoffrey the priest to the church of Saint-Sauveur at Caen is composed of bishops and clergy, it is still the king's court and the result is transmitted to the bishop and chapter of Bayeux by royal writ.[83] For slaying in violation of the Truce of God the bishop now has a fixed fine of nine pounds; all personal property beyond this is forfeited to the king, in whose court the duel must be held and whose justices collect the fine due the bishop.[84]

The Norman evidence, like that for England in the same period, does not suffice to give a clear picture of the judicial system, yet it is plain that there is such a system and that it is creating a body of law. The justices issue writs, take sureties, try pleas of the crown, and hear possessory as well as petitory actions. If we may trust Henry I's charter for the town of Verneuil in the form in which it has reached us, the use of writs is already so common that they are granted by local officers, although the writ concerning land stands on a different footing from the others.[85] Very likely the

[80] In *pancarte* of Saint-Sauveur, British Museum, Add. Ch. 15281, formerly sealed ('sigillum Rogerii vicecomitis'). Printed by Delisle, *S.-Sauveur*, pièces, no. 48, from the cartulary of the abbey at Saint-Lô, no. 13, where the words 'tam a regis quam a Nigelli iudicibus' are omitted.

[81] Teulet, *Layettes du Trésor des Chartes*, i. 25, no. 22.

[82] *Gallia Christiana*, ix. instr. 127; Appendix F, no. 1. See *supra*, notes 14, 15.

[83] 'In curia mea ante episcopos meos et ante clerum meum': *Livre noir*, no. 38 (1107–1123).

[84] Ordinance of 1135 in *Très Ancien Coutumier*, c. 71; Round, *Calendar*, no. 290; cf. Tardif, *Étude*, p. 48 f.; *infra*, p. 140.

[85] 'Et si aliquis burgensium breve aliquod a prelato pecierit, illud habebit sine precio, preter terram:' *Ordonnances des Rois*, iv. 639, c. 10. The text of these privileges is very corrupt; for *prelato* (cf. DuCange, *s. v.*) we should probably read *pretore* or *preposito*.

king's court administered some form of procedure by sworn inquest; such inquests were certainly held by Henry's command, and within ten years of his death they had developed into regular assizes.[86]

Of the fiscal side of the Norman administration no records have survived anterior to the Exchequer Roll of 1180, but a roll of 1136 is mentioned in the eighteenth century,[87] and a careful study of the later rolls and of the incidental evidence of earlier sources shows that the essential features of the Exchequer of Henry II existed under Henry I and even earlier. As in England, there was no sharp separation between the judicial and the financial duties of the king's officers: in 1123 the *iustitiarii regis* took possession of the county of Évreux and the lands of the rebels and added them to the king's demesne,[88] and after Robert of Bellême had been removed from office in 1112 for failure to render account for the royal revenues in his *vicomtés* of Argentan, Exmes, and Falaise, we find Bishop John of Lisieux in charge of the royal stores at Argentan.[89] The system of collection and account which appears in the later rolls, being based upon the *vicomté* and *prévôté* and not on the newer *bailliage* of the Angevin dukes, plainly goes back to the time when these were the important local areas; and the tithes and specific payments charged against the farms can in many instances be traced back well into the eleventh century.[90] Even the amount of the farm might long remain unchanged, in spite of such a general revision as was made in 1176; the forest of Roumare, for example, was let at the same amount in 1180 as in 1122.[91] An excellent illustration of the continuity of the Exchequer arrangements is furnished by the following extracts from a charter of Henry I for Séez cathedral, in which, as in

[86] See *infra*, Chapter VI.
[87] *M. A. N.*, xvi. p. xxx.
[90] *Supra*, Chapter I.
[88] Ordericus, iv. 453.
[89] *Ibid.*, iv. 303, 305.

[91] ' Et in parco meo Rothomagi totam decimam feni et .c. solidos de foresta mea de Romare, scilicet decimam per annum: ' charter of Henry I in 1122 for Notre-Dame-du-Pré, early copy in Archives of the Seine-Inférieure, *fonds* Bonne-Nouvelle, box D; certified copy in MS. Lat. n. a. 1245, f. 37. In 1180 the tithe is still 100 *solidi* (Stapleton, i. 75). On the revision of 1176 see Powicke, *E. H. R.*, xxii. 23.

a charter for Bocherville,[92] the farm of the *vicomté* is shown to have existed under William the Conqueror:

Ipsis quoque fratribus regularibus damus et confirmamus quindecim libras Rothomagensis monete quas dedi in dedicatione ipsius ecclesie in unoquoque anno habendas, scilicet septem libras et decem solidos in teloneo meo de Falesia et septem libras et decem solidos in teloneo meo de Oximis. . . . Preterea duodecim libras in firma nostra de Argentomo et viginti et unum solidos in teloneo eiusdem ville et sexaginta solidos et decem denarios de teloneo meo de Oximis que dederunt pater meus et mater mea ecclesie Sagiensi ad victum canonicorum duorum, quod antiquitus in elemosina statutum fuerat.[93] . . .

Normandy also offers an interesting parallel to England in the matter of its treasury. Round has shown the significance, for the history of fiscal institutions in England, of Henry I's grants to the French monasteries of Cluny, Tiron, and Fontevrault, especially the grant to Tiron of fifteen marks receivable each year *de thesauro meo in festo Sancti Michaelis Wintonie*, which under Henry II became payable from his treasury at the Exchequer.[94] Now the first of these charters to Fontevrault also contains a charge against the Norman revenues, namely £100 in the rent of the king's mint at Rouen,[95] while a still clearer piece of evidence is found in a charter for the leprosery of Le Grand-Beaulieu at Chartres. Issued originally between 1121 and 1131 and renewed in 1135, this runs as follows: [96]

(17) H. rex Anglorum archiepiscopo Rothomagensi, episcopis, abbatibus, comitibus, iusticiariis Normannie et thesaurariis et omnibus fidelibus suis per

[92] Round, no. 198; Stapleton, i. 68.

[93] See the charter in full in Appendix F, no. 11 (from MS. Alençon 177, f. 98; and MS. Lat. 11058, f. 8). These items are duly charged in the rolls (Stapleton, i. pp. lxxxviii, xcvi, cxxxii, 39, 50, 103), except the payment from the *prepositura* of Falaise, which is 10s. too small in 1180 but appears in full in 1198 (*ibid.*, ii. 414).

[94] *Calendar*, pp. xliii–xlv, nos. 998–1003, 1052, 1053, 1387–1390, 1459, 1460; *Commune of London*, p. 81; Poole, *The Exchequer in the Twelfth Century*, p. 40, note.

[95] Round, nos. 1052, 1459.

[96] *Cartulaire de la léproserie du Grand-Beaulieu*, ed. R. Merlet and M. Jusselin (Chartres, 1909, *Collection de cartulaires chartrains*, ii), no. 1, from a *vidimus* of 1469 in the Archives of the Eure-et-Loir. All the essential phrases are repeated in a charter of Stephen, issued at Évreux in 1136, of which the original is preserved in the same archives (*ibid.*, no. 11; see *infra*, Chapter IV, notes 5, 9, 13). Being witnessed by the earl of Gloucester and Robert 'de sigillo,' Henry's charter cannot be earlier than 1121; in its original form it is anterior to the general confirmation of Innocent II, 13 September 1131 (*Cartulaire*, no. 6).

Normanniam constitutis salutem. Sciatis quia dedi et concessi in perpetuam elemosinam Deo et Sancte Marie Magdalene de Bello Loco et infirmis ibidem Deo servientibus, pro anima patrum et parentum meorum et pro remissione peccatorum meorum et statu et incolumitate regni mei Anglie et ducatus mei Normannie, omni anno X libras Rothomagensium de thesauro meo, et semper eas simul habent ad festum Sancti Michâelis quando firme et pecunia mea colliguntur, et ipsis thesaurariis meis precipio ut eas eis omni anno et termino prenominato sine disturbacione omni et occasione liberent. Hoc itaque donum meum illi ecclesie et fratribus infirmis sine fine mansurum regia auctoritate statuo et adeo michi collata potestate inviolatum permanere confirmo.

Testibus Iohanne episcopo Lexoviorum et Roberto de sigillo et Rogerio de Fiscanno et Roberto comite de Gloecestrie et R[icardo] filio comitis et R[oberto] de Ver et Roberto de Curci, et Gaufrido filio Pagani et Gaufrido de Magnavilla et Roberto de Novo Burgo et Willelmo de Roumaro. Apud Rothomagum. Anno ab incarnatione Domini M°C°XXX° quinto hec carta renovata fuit, quia prior igne combusta erat.

Here we have a Norman treasury as well as Norman treasurers, one of whom can probably be identified in the witness Roger of Fécamp,[97] and we learn that, as in England, Michaelmas was the term when the king's ' farms and money are collected.' No place is mentioned, but the later history of the endowment and the connection of a treasurership with a canonry in Rouen cathedral [98] make it probable that the treasury here mentioned was at Rouen. Stephen repeats all the provisions of his uncle's grant, but Henry II makes it an annual charge, still at Michaelmas, against the *vicomté* of Rouen, where it appears in the Exchequer Rolls.[99] Treasure was stored at other centers also, for at Henry's death we know that the bulk of his treasure was at Falaise,[100] and under Henry II Caen and Argentan were used for the same purpose.[101] The custom of keeping treasure in various royal castles is not, however, inconsistent with a single administration of the treasury of receipt and disbursement.[102]

The English Pipe Roll of 1130 shows the Norman treasury receiving payments on English accounts and certifying credits by

[97] See below, notes 119, 120.
[98] See the following paragraphs.
[99] *Cartulaire du Grand-Beaulieu*, nos. 11, 28, 65; Delisle, *Henri II*, p. 126; Delisle-Berger, no. 434; Stapleton, i. 70.
[100] Ordericus, v. 50; Robert of Torigni, i. 200 f.
[101] Chapter V, note 115.
[102] For England cf. Round, introduction to Pipe Roll 28 Henry II, p. xxiv.

royal writs,[103] the officers who receive the money being Osbert de Pont de l'Arche and Nigel nephew of the bishop of Salisbury. Osbert held a *ministerium camerę curię*.[104] Nigel is styled treasurer in two documents which he witnessed at Rouen,[105] but though he was with the king in Normandy through the early months of 1131, he accompanied him to England in the summer of that year,[106] and it does not appear that his duties or Osbert's were confined to Normandy.[107] Whatever the exact relation of Nigel ' the treasurer ' to the Norman treasury, there was throughout the twelfth century a special treasurer for Normandy. In the Exchequer Rolls of 1180 and later the tithes of the Lieuvin, the *pays d'Auge*, and certain other districts are a fixed charge upon the farms for the benefit of the treasurer of Normandy,[108] a natural extension to one of the royal chaplains of the practice of assigning the tithe of a *vicomté* to a religious house. That this arrangement goes back to the reign of Henry I appears from the following passage in Stephen's confirmation of the possessions of Sainte-Barbe-en-Auge in 1137: [109]

Confirmavi . . . decimam de vicecomitatu de Lesvin et Algia quę sunt de capellaria mea quas Gislebertus de Ebroicis et Robertus filius eius capellani regis Henrici et mei dederunt et concesserunt eidem ęcclesię.

It is not here stated that Gilbert of Évreux and his son were treasurers, but we know from other sources that they were. In the

---

[103] Pp. 7, 13, 37, 39, 54, 63. [104] *Ibid.*, p. 37.

[105] Round, *Calendar*, no. 1388; and the following conclusion of a charter of the chapter of Chartres, issued, as appears from the lists in R. Merlet, *Dignitaires de l'église Notre-Dame de Chartres*, subsequently to 1126: ' Postea vero Mauricius et Petrus, alii fratres, concesserunt hoc ipsum apud Rotomagum et vadimonia sue concessionis transmiserunt per manus domni Henrici prepositi, videntibus et audientibus Andrea de Baldement, Willelmo de Fraxineto, Nigello thesaurario, Heinrico de Richeborc, Radulfo de Mercato, Ansoldo de Bellovidere canonico, Guillelmo de la Ventona, Roberto de la Haie ' (MS. Lat. 5185 I, p. 90, copied from the original).

[106] Round, *Calendar*, nos. 122–124, 287, 373, 1388; *Sarum Documents*, p. 7; Appendix F, no. 10; *Monasticon*, iv. 538, vi. 240, viii. 1271; *E. H. R.*, xxiii. 726.

[107] Cf. the document witnessed by them, *E. H. R.*, xiv. 422, which was probably issued in England. Hubert Hall, *Red Book of the Exchequer*, p. ccc, seeks to identify them with the *milites episcopi* of the *Constitutio domus regis*.

[108] Stapleton, i. pp. xciii, cxxi, 40, 77, 90, 99, 100, 118, 146, 157, 167, 168, 246, ii. 461, 549, 560. Cf. *infra*, Chapter V, note 139.

[109] Original, or pretended original, in the Archives of the Calvados, *fonds* Sainte-Barbe; Round, *Calendar*, no. 570.

history of the foundation of Sainte-Barbe,[110] written at the end of the twelfth century, we read:

Fuit in diebus superioris Henrici regis Anglorum quidam clericus in urbe Rothomagensi nomine Gillebertus, ex clericali et militari prosapia editus. Hic et Rothomagensis ecclesie precentor et prefati regis thesaurarius erat. Cum autem filios quinque haberet iuvenes egregios literis deditos et in curia regis nominatos, primogenitum Willelmum sibi annis iam maturus in thesaurarii officio ex regis beneplacito subrogavit. In quo etiam officio reliqui fratres, quamdiu superstites fuerunt, ac si iure hereditario sibi invicem successerunt. Guillelmus igitur patris potitus officio, cum pro multiplici preclare indolis probitate regis et procerum gratiam et familiaritatem haberet, tandem spreta mundi maleblandientis prosperitate, spreto iuventutis flore, spreto patre dulcique fratrum consorcio, spreto eciam latere regis Anglorum, regi militare disposuit angelorum.

Here we have six successive treasurers. Gilbert [111] must have given up the office some years before 1128, when his son William ' the Treasurer,' having lived as a hermit for a time after his retirement from the court, was made prior of the newly organized community of Sainte-Barbe by its patron Rabel of Tancarville. Gilbert died before 1137,[112] and his fief of Agy, near Bayeux, had been in possession of Sainte-Barbe since 1133 or earlier.[113] William's successor as treasurer was Robert, *secundus natus post*

[110] MS. 1643 of the library of Sainte-Geneviève, f. 57, printed by R. N. Sauvage, *La chronique de Sainte-Barbe-en-Auge* (Caen, 1907), pp. 19-20.

[111] A strict interpretation of Stephen's charter might make Gilbert one of his chaplains, but that is out of the question. ' Gislebertus cantor ' witnesses a charter of Archbishop Geoffrey in 1119 (MS. Lat. 17044, f. 19), but this may have been the Gislebertus cantor who witnesses Archbishop Hugh's charters for Saint-Georges de Bocherville in 1131 (MS. Rouen 1227, ff. 45, 46), for Bec in 1141 (MS. Lat. 13905, f. 90), for Beaubec in 1142 (Archives of the Seine-Inférieure, *fonds* Beaubec), and for Lire in 1145 (Archives of the Eure, H. 438). As Gilbert the treasurer was of clerical descent, he may be that ' Gislebertus filius Rotberti archidiaconi Ebroicensis ' who offered his son Hugh to Jumièges in 1099 (Le Prévost, *Eure*, iii. 46). He can hardly have been the ' Gislebertus filius Bernardi ' who was a canon of Rouen in 1075 (Archives of the Seine-Inférieure, G. 8739).

[112] ' In Baiocassino apud Ageium terram de patrimonio Gisleberti de Ebrois quam filii eius dederunt ęcclesię S. Barbarę pro anima eiusdem Gisleberti qui ibi iacet: ' charter of Hugh, archbishop of Rouen, 1137, confirming the possessions of Sainte-Barbe; original in Archives of the Calvados, *fonds* Sainte-Barbe. The possessions at Agy are described more exactly in original charters of Henry II and Philip, bishop of Bayeux, preserved in the same *fonds;* cf. *Calendar of Charter Rolls*, iii. 308; Sauvage, in *Mémoires de l'Académie de Caen*, 1908, p. 11.

[113] Inquest of military tenants of the bishop of Bayeux in 1133, *H. F.*, xxiii. 701.

Guillelmum, vir in regno nominatissimus,[114] whom we have already
found sitting in the Norman Exchequer.[115] He must have been in
office in 1128 and have continued as late as 1136, since he was a
chaplain of Stephen. Of the other sons we know nothing save
that one was named Richard [116] and that two of the prior's
brothers followed him to Sainte-Barbe. [117] The Master Thomas
of Évreux, who appears as a canon of Rouen in 1165 and subsequently,[118] doubtless belonged to this family. *Rogerus thesaurarius*
witnesses a royal charter at Rouen in 1135,[119] but he is probably
to be identified with Roger, nephew of the abbot of Fécamp, who
was a chaplain of Henry I and Stephen.[120]

The treasurer was not the only chaplain to receive regular
allowances from the Norman revenues, but the sources now available do not permit us to follow the others back or ascertain their
administrative duties. The *dominica capellaria* of Saint-Cande-le-
Vieux at Rouen, for example, tempts our curiosity; its exemption
from the diocese of Rouen requires explanation, and the fact that
the authority of the bishop of Lisieux over it seems to have been
established under John the justiciar suggests some connection
between these chaplains and the royal administration.[121] The
whole subject of the royal chapel is one of great obscurity, for
England as well as for Normandy, and any facts which may be
brought forward concerning it are likely to throw light upon the
history of the administrative system. The scantiness of the Norman material for the early twelfth century likewise leaves us in

[114] Sauvage, *Chronique*, p. 20.   [115] *Supra*, notes 18, 20.
[116] Sauvage, *loc. cit.*, p. 36. He is doubtless the ' Ricardus Ebroicensis canonicus
noster ' who appears, under 15 January, in the obituary of Rouen cathedral: *H. F.*,
xxiii. 359A.
[117] Sauvage, *loc. cit.*, p. 25.
[118] Cartulary of Foucarmont (MS. Rouen 1224), f. 30 (1165); MS. Lat. 17135,
p. 22 (1172); L. de Glanville, *Histoire du prieuré de Saint-Lô*, ii. 326 (1177);
Poupardin, *Chartes de S.-Germain-des-Prés*, no. 156.
[119] Round, *Calendar*, no. 590.
[120] *Ibid.*, nos. 124, 289, 295, 541, 1055; *Ramsey Cartulary*, i. 250; *Monasticon*,
vii. 700.
[121] The whole history of this exemption is obscure. See *Gallia Christiana*, xi. 42,
774; Toussaint Duplessis, *Description de la Haute-Normandie*, ii. 121; H. de
Formeville, *Histoire de l'évêché-comté de Lisieux*, i, pp. xii–xvi; Stapleton, i, pp.
cxxx, cxxxvii.

the dark with respect to other members of that " official class working in the interests of the crown" whose activity at Winchester and elsewhere has been so well illustrated by Round's studies.[122] The following document of 1133–1135 introduces us to two such royal clerks:

(18) H. rex Anglorum archiepiscopo Rothomagensi et iusticiis et baronibus suis de Normannia et vic[ecomiti] et burgensibus et ministris suis de Rothomago salutem. Sciatis quod concedo Oyno episcopo Ebroicensi terram et domum illam de Rothomago que fuit Willelmi Bruni clerici mei quam ipse emit ad opus ecclesie sue de Sancta Maria de Ebroicis de Petro filio ipsius W. Bruni et Rannulfo scriptore meo consensu [123] per .c. sol[idos] Roth[omagensium] quos eis inde dedit. Et ideo volo et precipio quod ipse episcopus et ecclesia sua bene et in pace illam teneant et libere sicut predictus Willelmus unquam melius tenuit et honorabilius. Testibus Adel[ulfo] episcopo Carlol[ensi] et comite Leglrec[estrie] et Rog[ero] de Fisc[anno] et Willelmo de Ely et Radulfo de Hasting[is], apud Rothomagum.[124]

William Brown had been alive in 1130, when he appears as a considerable landholder in Suffolk,[125] and had held lands in Winchester before 1115 in conjunction with William Fitz Odo, probably the constable of that name.[126] Roger Brun occurs in the midst of a group of king's clerks in another document of this period.[127] Apparently we have here another family of royal clerks, and one cannot help surmising some relationship with that Master Thomas Brown, also a landowner in Winchester,[128] who makes his appearance in 1137 at the court of Roger of Sicily, where he rises to high position in the judicial and fiscal administration, and is then recalled by Henry II to a position of ' no mean authority ' in the English Exchequer.[129] It is no part of our present purpose to

---

[122] Compare, besides his article on *Bernard the Scribe*, in *E. H. R.*, xiv. 417–430, the *Victoria History of Hampshire*, i. 430, 536; and R. L. Poole, *The Exchequer in the Twelfth Century*, p. 123 f.

[123] Cartulary G. 6 has ' scriptore concessu meo.'

[124] Évreux cartularies in the Archives of the Eure, G. 122, f. 41v, no. 201; G. 123, no. 193; G. 6, p. 17, no. 11; Round, *Calendar*, no. 289.

[125] Pipe Roll 31 Henry I, p. 99. Ranulf the scribe held lands in Berks: *ibid.*, p. 126.

[126] *Liber Winton.*, ff. 3b, 12b.

[127] *E. H. R.*, xiv. 428; cf. *Ecclesiastical Documents*, ed. Hunter (Camden Society), p. 51.

[128] Pipe Roll 1 Richard I, p. 205.

[129] I have brought together the facts concerning Thomas Brown in an article

enter into the controversy respecting the relation of the Anglo-Norman Exchequer and the Sicilian *diwan* to which these facts in Thomas's biography have given rise. In view of what is now known concerning its Byzantine and Saracen antecedents it can no longer be maintained that the Sicilian fiscal system was imported from England by Thomas Brown; but it is possible that he may have exerted some influence in matters of detail, and it is certainly worth noting that, if we are justified in connecting him with the clerks of the same name under Henry I, he probably had some acquaintance with the workings of Anglo-Norman administration before he entered the service of the Sicilian king.

Precisely to what extent Normandy and England had separately organized governments under Henry I, it is not possible to say without further genealogical study and a more careful examination of the documentary evidence. Wholly distinct the two administrations cannot have been, for so long as kingship was ambulatory and the government centered in the royal household, a considerable number of the king's officers must have been common to the kingdom and the duchy. Thus William of Tancarville, though his castle was in Normandy and though he received a fixed grant from the Norman treasury, is styled ' chamberlain of England and Normandy,' [130] and the seneschalship of Humphrey de Bohun was likewise common to both countries.[131] William Brown we have just seen as a landholder on both sides of the Channel; Simon the dispenser is with the king in Normandy between 1117 and 1120 and in England in 1130.[132] Not only the great body of personal servants, but such departments as the chancery and the chapel, certainly followed the king. Thus in the transfretation of 1120, of which the chroniclers have left some record because of the loss of the White Ship, the king was accompanied by chap-

on *England and Sicily in the Twelfth Century, E. H. R.*, xxvi. 438–443, where (pp. 651–655) the Sicilian fiscal system is also discussed (1911).

[130] Annals of Saint-Wandrille, *Histoire littéraire de la France*, xxxii. 204; cf. Walter Map, *De Nugis*, ed. M. R. James, p. 244. For the grant from the treasury see *Monasticon*, vii. 1066; Stapleton, i. 68, 157.

[131] *Ancient Charters* (Pipe Roll Society), no. 27.

[132] Round, *King's Serjeants*, p. 189; Pipe Roll 31 Henry I, pp. 5, 79.

lains, *dapiferi*, *camerarii*, and *pincerne*.[133] The fiscal administration was naturally more stationary than the household proper, for the collection and disbursement of the revenue had to go on in the king's absence; and, while we know even less of the Norman treasury than of the treasury at Winchester, there was at least a separate treasurer and probably some other permanent officials.[134] Yet in this department too a connection was maintained between the kingdom and the duchy. Treasure was carried back and forth, not only with the king, as on his return from Normandy in 1120,[135] but also at other times, a considerable part of the large sum stored at Falaise at the time of Henry's death having been recently brought from England.[136] Such transshipments must have been accompanied, as under Henry II,[137] by royal officers — indeed the possession of the castle of Porchester by one of the chamberlains of the Exchequer may have been connected with this process of transfer [138] — while some system of balancing accounts between the two treasuries is involved in the practice of receiving payments on one side of the Channel to apply on accounts due on the other. Intercommunication of this sort is, of course, quite compatible with the existence of two separate corps of officials, but the appearance in Normandy of the two chamberlains, Geoffrey de Clinton and Robert Mauduit, as well as such fiscal officers as

[133] *Anglo-Saxon Chronicle;* Henry of Huntingdon, p. 242; William of Malmesbury, *Gesta Regum*, ii. 497. Ordericus (iv. 415-419) mentions by name William, one of the four principal chaplains, William de Pirou dapifer, and Gisulf the scribe. Cf. the transfretation of 1130, John of Worcester (ed. Weaver), p. 33.

[134] There was also a separate Norman mint at Rouen, and pleas concerning the coinage were held *apud arcam monete:* Round, *Calendar*, nos. 1053, 1459; Pipe Roll 31 Henry I, p. 122; *Gallia Christiana*, xi. instr. 157.

[135] Ordericus, iv. 412, 419.

[136] *Ibid.*, v. 50; Robert of Torigni, i. 201.

[137] E. g., Pipe Roll 6 Henry II, p. 47; 13 Henry II, p. 193 f.; 21 Henry II, p. 200.

[138] Round, in *Victoria History of Hampshire*, i. 432; *Ancestor*, v. 207-210. The history of this Mauduit chamberlainship is, in spite of Round's researches, not yet entirely clear. It is not true that, as the editors of the Oxford edition of the *Dialogus* suggest (p. 20), the office of William Mauduit was acquired by William de Pont de l'Arche in 1130, for, apart from the fact that William Mauduit would not be mentioned in the *Constitutio domus regis* if he was no longer in office, we find him receiving money in the *camera curie* in 1130 (Pipe Roll, p. 134) and witnessing as chamberlain in the summer of 1131 (*infra*, Appendix F, no. 11; cf. Round, *Calendar*, no. 107).

Nigel *nepos episcopi* and Osbert de Pont de l'Arche, would seem to indicate that the two administrations were not wholly distinct.[139] In judicial matters the chief link between the kingdom and the duchy was the king, although the officers who came with him from England might also constitute an important element in the meetings of the Norman *curia*. In general, however, the Norman judicial system possessed a considerable measure of distinctness. The cases in which the king sat were more likely to leave a record in the charters, yet we have seen abundant evidence of the activity of the courts in his absence and of the existence, in addition to the local officers, of a body of Norman justices, among whom the justiciar and the two seneschals stand out with such prominence as to suggest that they constituted the nucleus of the Norman central government.

Our conception of Henry's Norman household will depend in large measure upon our interpretation of that curious and unique record, the *Constitutio domus regis*, which contains a detailed list of the officers of the court with their daily stipends and allowances of food, wine, and candles.[140]   Drawn up not long after Henry's death,[141] this is based upon the conditions of his reign and is thus much the earliest of the many household ordinances of European royalty. It is true that in its present form it is not so much an ordinance as an attempt at an up-to-date account of the royal household; but the word *constitutio* points to a formal act, and the consistent use of the future tense shows that in the body of the document we are dealing, not with a mere description, but with the language of one who commands and prescribes. If we call to mind the contemporary mention of Henry's reform in the practices of his courtiers,[142] and particularly the specific statement of

---

[139] Cf. introduction to Oxford edition of *Dialogus*, p. 19, note 3.

[140] *Liber Niger Scaccarii*, ed. Hearne, pp. 341–359 (the best text);   *Red Book of the Exchequer*, ed. Hall, pp. 807–813. For modern discussions, see Hall's introduction, pp. cclxxxvi–ccci; Bateson, *Mediaeval England*, pp. 5–8; Poole, *The Exchequer in the Twelfth Century*, pp. 94–99; Round, *The King's Serjeants and Officers of State*, especially p. 54 ff.

[141] Whether under Stephen, as is generally assumed, or in the early years of Henry II (cf. Liebermann, *Ueber Pseudo-Cnuts Constitutiones de Foresta*, p. 25) does not greatly affect our purpose.

[142] Eadmer, p. 192 f.; William of Malmesbury, *Gesta Regum*, ii. 487.   The re-

Walter Map that he established *scriptas domus et familie sue con-suetudines*, including fixed liveries for the barons of his *curia* and regular allowances for the members of his household,[143] we shall not hesitate to identify this reform with the original nucleus of the *Constitutio*, so far as this can be separated from glosses and later additions. Some elements were doubtless still older, since a charter of the Conqueror[144] in 1070–1071 mentions court liveries, demaine and common bread, candles and candle ends, such as appear in the *Constitutio*, and since many of the serjeanties of the *Constitutio* can be followed back as far as Domesday. As regards place, the *Constitutio* contains no specific reference to either side of the Channel, save for the mention of the *modius Rotomagensis* as a standard of measurement, and this phrase has been used as an argument both for and against the compilation of the document in Normandy.[145] Clearly its scope cannot be restricted to the duchy, for most of the persons therein mentioned are found in possession of lands and offices in England, and the Pipe Roll of 1130 not only shows two of the chief men of the household receiving the *per diem* allowance fixed in the *Constitutio*,[146] but also

form probably antedates 1121, since Robert Peche before becoming bishop ' in cura panum ac potus strenue ministrare solebat ': Florence of Worcester, ii. 75. Another larderer, Roger, had been made bishop in 1101: William of Malmesbury, *Gesta Pontificum*, p. 303.

[143] ' Scriptas habebat domus et familie sue consuetudines quas ipse statuerat: domus, ut semper esset omnibus habunda copiis et certissimas haberet vices a longe provisas et communiter auditas ubicunque manendi vel movendi, et ad eam venientes singuli quos barones vocant terre primates statutas ex liberalitate regis liberationes haberent; familie, ne quis egeret sed perciperet quisquis certa donaria.' *De Nugis Curialium*, ed. James, p. 219 (ed. Wright, p. 210).

[144] Davis, *Regesta*, no. 60.

[145] The Norman view is maintained by Stapleton, *Magni Rotuli*, i, p. xxi; Hall, *Red Book*, p. ccc; id., *Studies in English Official Historical Documents*, p. 163. Poole, p. 95, argues that if the household was settled in Normandy, there would have been no need to call upon the bakers to spend 40*d.* in procuring the measure; but it seems clear that the reference is rather to the purchase of a given quantity of grain. If that is the correct interpretation, we have an illustration of fixed prices for the court's purchases, such as seem to be implied in the passages of Eadmer and William of Malmesbury cited in note 142.

[146] Pipe Roll 31 Henry I, pp. 129, 131, 140, where the liveries of the chancellor and William de Pont de l'Arche the chamberlain are reckoned at 5*s.* a day. When officers served in the *curia*, they were paid from the *camera curie*, so that their wages do not appear in the Pipe Rolls, where they are mentioned for the most

mentions most of its lesser members — ushers, bakers, larderers, cup-bearers, butterymen, naperers, and archers, the velterer and the master of the harriers, *hosarius, scutellarius, bordarius, cortinarius*,[147] the cook who pays half a mark of gold for his father's office,[148] down to the sumpter-man and the serjeants of the chapel and the kitchen.[149] All this, however, does not show that these were members of a purely English household, for the king had spent nearly the whole of this fiscal year in England, and there is no record how many of them accompanied him to Normandy in September.

It is impossible, from the records now extant, to follow out the officers of the *Constitutio* on Norman soil, for we have no Exchequer Rolls for this period and little other material of the sort which has enabled the patient learning and ingenuity of Round to identify so many of the king's serjeants in England. In the absence of any such body of conquered land as in England, it is likely that in Normandy the officers of state were less freely rewarded by land and were dependent in large measure upon the fixed endowments from the ducal revenues of which we find traces here and there. Thus Henry's treasurer, as we have already seen, had the tithes of certain *vicomtés*,[150] and we know that his chamberlain of the family of Tancarville had a fixed grant of £60 from the farm of Lillebonne.[151] Similar charges in the roll of 1180 in favor of the dispenser of Lillebonne [152] and the duke's larderer may also have an early origin.[153] Normandy was familiar with the

part as excused from Danegeld, the amount remitted serving as an accurate measure of the hides which they owned in each county. Cf. Poole, *Exchequer*, p. 125.

[147] Pipe Roll, pp. 1, 4, 15 f., 22 f., 41, 45 f., 51, 56, 59, 61, 72 f., 75 f., 80, 83, 86, 99, 102, 104, 107, 126; and Round, *King's Serjeants*, under these words.

[148] Pipe Roll, p. 84. If the cook Radulphus de Marchia of the *Constitutio* is the Radulfus de Marceio of St. Paul's documents, he was dead before 1127 (9 *Historical MSS. Commission*, p. 65 f.).

[149] Pipe Roll, pp. 102, 107 f., 126; cf. *E. H. R.*, xiv. 423.

[150] *Supra*, note 108; cf. *infra*, Chapter V, note 139.

[151] *Monasticon*, vii. 1066; Stapleton, i. 68.   [152] Stapleton, i. 68.

[153] *Ibid.*, i, pp. lxxxiii, 30, 99, 274, ii. 471, 572, 573. As the alms here charged against the farm of Valognes, like the other fixed charges in the rolls, appear to be arranged in chronological order, the assignment to the larderer is probably earlier than the grant to the chapelry of Valognes, transferred to the abbey De Voto by an early charter of Henry II (Delisle-Berger, no. 135).

system of daily allowances described in the *Constitutio*, for Wace, who would carry this back to the time of Richard the Good and Robert I, speaks of the duke's provision

> De chandeile e de vin e d' altre livreisun,[154]

and tells us that the dignitaries of the household

> Chascun iur orent livreisuns
> E as granz festes dras et duns.[155]

This is confirmed and amplified by a curious charter which bears the royal style of Henry II but on the ground of its witnesses is probably to be assigned to the reign of his grandfather.[156] This document, which gives us the most concrete account of the Norman household, grants to Odoin de Malpalu, the king's serjeant, along with various lands and rights,

'the whole ministry of the king's *panetaria*, with all its appurtenances, with livery in the court every day that the king is at Rouen, namely four pennyworth of bread from the *depensa*, and one sextary of knight's wine from the cellar, and four portions from the kitchen, one of them a large one, two of the size for knights, and one *dispensabile*. And Odoin is to find the king bread in his court, and to reckon by tallies with his dispensers and with all his bakers, and he shall receive the money and give quittances to the bakers. And when the king sends to Rouen for bread, Odoin is to bring it at the king's cost, and every pack horse shall have 12*d.* and every pannier-bearing one 6*d.* and every basket-carrier a pennyworth of bread, and if the bread is brought by water the boatman shall have 6*d.* a journey. When the king makes a journey, Odoin is to have all that is left of the bread of the *panetaria;* and he is to have charge of and jurisdiction over the king's bakers at Rouen and within the *banlieue* of Rouen, and all their forfeitures, and the weighing of bread, and all fines of bread and forfeited bread. Odoin shall also have one free fishery in the Seine, and all his wheat shall be ground in the king's mills of Rouen free of charge, immediately after the wheat which he shall find in the hopper; and he is to be one of the regarders of the king's forests, at the king's cost, and to be quit of pannage in all these forests for all his swine, and every Christmas he is to have twenty shillings or four swine,' etc.[157]

154 *Chronique ascendante*, ed. Andresen (i. 214), line 211.

155 *Roman de Rou*, ed. Andresen, ii, line 799 ff.

156 Delisle, *Cartulaire normand*, no. 14; Delisle-Berger, no. 705; Round, *Calendar*, no. 1280; there is also a copy in MS. Lat. 9067, f. 141v. On the difficult question of the nature and date of this charter, see Delisle, in *B. É. C.*, lxvii. 395–397; Round, in *Archaeological Journal*, lxiv. 73–77; Delisle, *Henri II*, p. 34, note; Round, *Serjeants*, p. 199 f.

157 This is, substantially, Round's analysis.

Here the serjeant remains at Rouen and, apart from his continuing privileges, draws his livery only while the king is there, so that he belongs with the chaplains and porters attached permanently to the royal castles rather than with the officers who follow the king. So in an early charter of Henry II his serjeant Baudri, besides his daily wages as porter and jailer at Rouen and his gifts and liveries as regarder and pannager of the forests, is confirmed as marshal whenever the king sojourns at Rouen, receiving for each of these days six loaves of bread, six portions from the kitchen, and a sextary of wine, besides a shield each year and every Christmas two swine from the larder of Rouen and a beech in one of the forests.[158] Henry II had a way of rewarding his serjeants with town houses, notably in the growing port of Dieppe,[159] and one of his grants of this sort may explain an unexplained officer of the *Constitutio,* namely Ralph le Robeur, or le Bobeur, whom I am inclined to identify with Ralph le Forbeur, who held a house at Bayeux on condition of furbishing the king's hunting arms.[160]

Rouen was doubtless the principal center for these officials of the more local and stationary type,[161] although too much must not be argued from the survival of documents respecting serjeanties which owed their value principally to the later growth of the city. It would still be an anachronism to speak of Rouen as a capital, yet it has special significance in connection with the treasury, and it appears much more frequently than any other Norman place in the king's charters,[162] while his park at Sainte-Vaubourg and his palace at Le Pré were close by.[163] Next to Rouen, Caen holds the

---

[158] Delisle-Berger, no. 212. For another Rouen marshalship see Geoffrey's charter, *infra,* Chapter IV, no. 13; and cf. the services due Henry I from Roland d'Oissel: Delisle, *Cartulaire normand,* no. 2; Round, *Calendar,* no. 1278.

[159] See the *Coutumier* of Dieppe, in Archives of the Seine-Inférieure, G. 851; Delisle-Berger, nos. 115, 329, 398, 479, 709, 713, 719.

[160] 'Servitio furbiandi venabula et alia arma mea': Cartulaire de Normandie (MS. Rouen 1235), f. 24v; Delisle-Berger, no. 723; Valin, p. 151, note 4. Cf. 'Aldwinus forbator' in Pipe Roll 31 Henry I, p. 41.

[161] To the treasurer and serjeants mentioned above should be added ' Robertus capellanus meus de Rotomago': *Monasticon,* vii. 1043, 1099; Round, no. 475.

[162] See Appendix G, supplemented by the great number of charters which cannot be specifically dated.

[163] *B. É. C.,* xi. 438; Stapleton, i, p. cxli; Étienne de Rouen, ed. Omont, bk. iii,

chief place in the description of his enlargement and strengthening of the older Norman castles,[164] and in his itinerary Caen, Falaise, and Argentan appear most frequently after Rouen. The sessions of court and justices at the castle of Caen [165] foreshadow the later meetings of the Exchequer there, while the king's *loricarii* at Argentan are reminders that such strongholds were also needed for sterner work.[166] Henry's sojourns elsewhere are scattered through his itinerary without indicating any such degree of frequency or length of stay; besides the ports of Dieppe and Barfleur and the older towns and fortresses of the interior, they include his newer strongholds on or near the frontier—Verneuil and Vire, Vaudreuil and Lions-la-Forêt, where he died.

Besides the Norman parallels to the serjeants and liveries of the *Constitutio*, there is definite evidence that the officers who accompanied the king to Normandy received the same stipends as in England. In the Pipe Roll of 1130 William de Pont de l'Arche, the chamberlain, has an allowance for the period of sixty-three days intervening between his departure from the king in Normandy and his taking over of the bishopric of Durham,[167] a journey partly in Normandy and partly in England during which he is paid at the uniform rate of 5s. a day fixed in the *Constitutio*. This further shows that the liveries of the *Constitutio* are reckoned in sterling, due allowance being doubtless made for the different standards in Normandy. Moreover, if a difference existed between allowances in England and in Normandy, the *Constitutio* could hardly have avoided mentioning it in tracing the increase in the stipend of the keeper of the seal, Robert, a constant companion of the king in these later years, who was receiving his maximum remuneration in Normandy at the moment of Henry's death. We may conclude that there is no reason for ascribing the

line 55 ff. (Howlett, *Chronicles of Stephen*, ii. 713); Delisle-Berger, no. 523; *Rotuli Chartarum*, p. 3.

[164] On his castles see Robert of Torigni, i. 164, 197; id., in William of Jumièges, ed. Marx, p. 309; Powicke, *Loss of Normandy*, p. 275 f.

[165] *Supra*, no. 5; Deville, *Analyse*, p. 47 f.

[166] Appendix F, no. 21. Note the attestations of the two marshals.

[167] 'In liberatione Willelmi de Pontearcarum de .lxiii. diebus .xv.*l.* et .xv.*s.* ex quo recessit de Rege in Normannia et accepit episcopatum Dunelmensem': p. 129, cf. p. 131.

Constitutio exclusively to either side of the Channel, but, as the compiler speaks particularly of conditions at the time of the king's death, he doubtless had most freshly in mind the household of the last two years of the reign, which were spent in Normandy. Hence the *modius Rotomagensis*, which seems to have been the standard measure of the Norman Exchequer.[168]

This official or semi-official description of the household in Henry's later years may be supplemented by the witnesses to the charters which he issued in Normandy 1133–1135.[169] The most solemn of these, the ordinance respecting the Truce of God which is the only surviving monument of his Norman legislation,[170] was promulgated at Rouen in presence of the archbishop and the bishops of the province, and by the common counsel and consent of the attesting barons who comprised only earls and high officers of the *curia:* Robert, earl of Gloucester, the king's son, his nephew Stephen, the earl of Leicester and Earl Giffard, Brian Fitz Count constable, Robert de Courcy and Hugh Bigod seneschals, William Fitz Odo chamberlain, and William Fitz John, whose office has not been identified. The bishops of Ely and Carlisle and the keeper of the seal are noted as present, but are carefully distinguished from the barons. A charter of the same year issued at Caen [171] adds to Henry's entourage the names of Geoffrey Fitz Payne, Roger the treasurer, and three royal chaplains, Robert archdeacon of Exeter, Richard de Beaufage, and Richard, son of Robert of Gloucester, the last two already designated as bishops respectively of Avranches and Bayeux.[172] Charters of the preceding year [173] add to the names of officers of state who were with

[168] Stapleton, i. 32, 39, where we read of rents and allowances in the Cotentin of ' modii avene ' and ' modii bladii,' 'ad mensuram Rothom[agensem].'

[169] See Appendix G.

[170] *Très Ancien Coutumier*, ed. Tardif, c. 71; Round, *Calendar*, no. 290.

[171] Round, no. 590.

[172] Ordericus, v. 44 f.

[173] Round, nos. 375, 959. See further no. 374; *supra*, no. 18; *E. H. R.*, xxiii. 726, no. iv (*Monasticon*, viii. 1275), which adds William, Earl Warren (*ibid.*, vii. 1113). From the lists of those who were with the king in England just before the transfretation of 1133 (*Monasticon*, vi. 177; Madox, *Baronia Anglica*, p. 158; cf. Round, *Feudal England*, p. 426 f.) it appears that many of these must have crossed with him.

the king at Rouen Robert de la Haie and Humphrey de Bohun seneschals, and Robert de Vere constable. Three other chamberlains, Aubrey de Vere, William of Houghton, and William of Glastonbury, are found at Falaise in a royal charter of the same period,[174] and two marshals appear with the king at Argentan.[175] At Henry's death, 1 December 1135 at Lions, there were present, in addition to his chaplains, the archbishop of Rouen, the bishop of Évreux, the earls of Gloucester, Surrey, and Leicester, and the counts of Meulan and Perche.[176]

In their journeyings to and fro across the Channel the kings of the twelfth century made use of a royal galley (*esnecca*),[177] payments for which are a regular item in the Pipe Rolls of Henry II. In the Conqueror's reign this service seems to have been in charge of Stephen Fitz Airard, who appears in Domesday holding lands in Berkshire, and is probably the ' Stephanus stirman ' who has a house in Warwick and the rent of two houses in Southampton.[178] After Stephen's death the privilege does not seem to have passed to his family, and when his son Thomas claimed the feudal right by placing the White Ship at the disposal of Henry I in 1120, provision had already been made for the king's crossing.[179] Who possessed the *ministerium esnecce* under Henry I and his grandson we learn from a charter issued by Henry II at the beginning of his reign:

Sciatis me reddidisse et concessisse Willelmo et Nicholao, filiis Rogeri generi Alberti, et heredibus Bonefacii et Azonis et Roberti et Radulfi fratrum ipsorum ministerium meum de esnecca mea cum liberatione que pertinet et

---

[174] *Ramsey Chronicle*, p. 284, no. 335; *Ramsey Cartulary*, i. 250.

[175] Appendix F, no. 21.   [176] Ordericus, v. 50 f.

[177] ' Rex Anglie ad suam transfretationem navem propriam solet habere. Cancellarius ei fieri fecit non unam solam sed tres simul naves optimas: ' Fitz Stephen, *Vita S. Thome* (*Materials*, iii. 26). It is not clear whether the *ministerium* of the Hastings *esnecca* which was held under Henry I by the ancestors of Roger of ' Burnes ' (*Abbreviatio Placitorum*, p. 39b) was distinct from the service of the *esnecca* mentioned below. Under Henry II it passed to Hugh de Bec, husband of Roger's sister Illaria, and was claimed under John by Roger's niece Avicia. What may be a Chester *esnecca* appears in 1168 (Pipe Roll, p. 92).

[178] Ordericus, iv. 411; *Domesday Book*, i. 52, 63b, 238. Stephen Fitz Airard also appears in a charter of the early years of Henry I which permits him to grant lands to Ramsey: *Calendar of Charter Rolls*, ii. 102, no. 5 (cf. nos. 7 and 15).

[179] Ordericus, iv. 411.

totam terram Rogeri generi Alberti et feoda omnia que ipse Rogerus tenuit in capite de rege H. avo meo et de quocunque tenuisset die qua fuit vivus et mortuus. [180]

Roger, son-in-law of Albert, is otherwise known. He had held lands in Wallop (Hampshire) before 1130,[181] as well as lands in Southampton which he and his wife gave to the abbey of St. Denis,[182] and he witnessed a royal charter in Normandy which cannot be earlier than 1123.[183] The *ministerium* doubtless came to him from Albert with his wife Avizia, which would carry it well back into Henry's reign. The interesting fact to note is that while none of the names in his family are Anglo-Saxon, and none are necessarily Norman, one at least, Boniface, is evidently Italian,[184] while the names Albert and Azo, as well as the form Avizia, though not necessarily Italian, point toward Italy. The appearance of an Italian shipmaster in charge of the royal galley under Henry I is surely a matter of interest, and suggests that intercourse with the South in this period may well have been more active than is commonly supposed.

[180] British Museum, Campbell Charter, xxix. 9; printed in *Archaeologia*, vi. 116; Delisle-Berger, no. 26. Cf. N. H. Nicolas, *History of the Royal Navy*, i. 433; *Guide to Manuscripts exhibited in the Department of Manuscripts* (1899), p. 41, no. 17.

[181] Pipe Roll 31 Henry I, p. 39.

[182] *Calendar of Charter Rolls*, iii. 337; cf. my paper in *Mélanges Charles Bémont*, p. 78.

[183] Charter for Walter de Beauchamp, given at Vaudreuil: Appendix F, no. 9.

[184] On the rarity of the name Boniface in England in this period see Andrew, in the *Numismatic Chronicle*, fourth series, i. 208.

CHAPTER IV

NORMANDY UNDER STEPHEN OF BLOIS AND GEOFFREY PLANTAGENET[1]

THE conquest of Normandy by Geoffrey of Anjou raises an interesting question for students of Norman history, since by establishing between the two countries a personal union which was to last sixty years it opened the way to Angevin influence in the affairs of the duchy and to the possible modification of Norman institutions in accordance with Angevin practice. The problem of the nature and extent of this influence presents itself in its simplest form during Geoffrey's own reign of six years, not only because the new duke was, unlike his successors, exclusively the product of Angevin training and tradition, but also because under him the Norman and Angevin lands led a life of their own, distinct from that of the larger empire of which they afterward formed a part. Unfortunately the available information is meager, especially with reference to the preliminary elements in the problem, for we know but little of conditions in Normandy under Henry I, and no special study has yet been made of Anjou under Fulk of Jerusalem and his son.[2] In general it appears that the state which Fulk the Red and his descendants hammered out on the borders of the Loire was smaller and more compact than the duchy to the northward, and the government of its rulers was more direct and personal, so that its administrative needs were simpler and seem to have been met without the creation of a fiscal and judicial system like the Norman and without any such fixity of documentary form or rigor of official procedure as are discernible in Normandy by the beginning of the twelfth century.

[1] Revised from *E. H. R.*, xxvii. 417–444 (1912).

[2] For the eleventh century there is an admirable study by L. Halphen, *Le comté d'Anjou au XIe siècle* (Paris, 1906). For the twelfth, a certain amount of useful material is contained in C. J. Beautemps-Beaupré, *Coutumes et institutions de l'Anjou et du Maine*, part ii, i (Paris, 1890); see also F. M. Powicke, *The Angevin Administration of Normandy*, E. H. R., xxi. 625–649, especially 648 f., xxii. 15–42; and his *Loss of Normandy*, ch. ii.

In point of organization there is no ground for considering the Angevin government to have been in advance of the Norman, nor, unless it be in the more immediate control of affairs by the count, is there inherent reason for expecting it to have had the marked effects upon Norman policy which are sometimes ascribed to it. Statements on these matters are, however, premature until more is known of the state of Anjou during this period, but it is possible in the meantime to bring together the Norman evidence for Geoffrey's reign and consider it with reference to the persistence of older institutions as well as to possible innovations. For such a study the death of Henry I forms the natural point of departure.

In Normandy, as in England, the reign of Stephen seems to have had a merely negative importance. After Henry's death the Norman barons invited Theobald of Blois to rule over them, but the news of his brother's accession in England decided them to accept the lord of whom their English fiefs were held. Stephen took the title of duke of the Normans, and had it engraved on his seal, but he used it rarely, even in Norman documents,[3] and never exercised an effective government over the whole of the duchy. The great strongholds of the southern border, Argentan, Exmes, and Domfront, had been promptly handed over to the empress by a loyal *vicomte*, as had also the castles of the count of Ponthieu, notably Séez and Alençon, which were restored to Count William in return for his support of the Angevin party. From this basis, after a short truce, Geoffrey and his followers carried their ravages westward into the vale of Mortain and the Cotentin, and northward as far as Lisieux, while the party of Stephen waited in vain for the arrival of its leader.[4] It was not till March 1137 that the king, accompanied by the queen, the bishops of Winchester, Lincoln, and Carlisle, and his chancellor, Roger,[5] arrived at La Hougue and proceeded by way of Bayeux

---

[3] Delisle, *Henri II*, p. 115 f.

[4] Ordericus, v. 56–78; Robert of Torigni, i. 199 f., 205; John of Marmoutier, in Marchegay, *Chroniques des comtes d'Anjou*, p. 294 (ed. Halphen and Poupardin, p. 225); William of Malmesbury, *Historia Novella*, p. 538; Henry of Huntingdon, p. 260.

[5] See their attestations in Delisle, pp. 117–119, nos. 2–8, 10. For Alexander of Lincoln, see also Henry of Huntingdon, p. 260, and two notifications issued in his favor by Stephen at Rouen and preserved in the Registrum Antiquissimum of

and Évreux to the valley of the Seine. Although he was well received by the Normans, who had been embittered by the excesses of the Angevin soldiery, and was recognized by the French king, Stephen's presence was not sufficient to bring peace to the country. Geoffrey was able to lead an attack on Caen and force money from Norman monasteries as the price of safety for their lands, and after an abortive attempt at an expedition against Argentan, Stephen was, early in July, forced to purchase a truce by the annual payment of two thousand marks. Through this parching summer and until his return to England early in December, Normandy enjoyed whatever of order its duke was able to give it. Certain robber barons were coerced into obedience [6] and the forms of administration were maintained, but Stephen's own partisans were obliged to admit that he was a weak ruler.[7] His strongest support seems to have come from the Norman church: the archbishop of Rouen and four of his suffragans had hastened to his court in England early in 1136; Archdeacon Arnulf of Séez was his chief envoy to Rome in the same year; [8] and most of the

Lincoln Cathedral, nos. 180, 194, a reference which I owe to the kindness of Mr. H. W. C. Davis (cf. *Calendar of Charter Rolls*, iv. 103, no. 29, 140, no. 17). The king was accompanied as far as Portsmouth by Roger of Salisbury and several other members of the *curia* who do not seem to have crossed: *Calendar of Charter Rolls*, iii. 338. On Stephen's sojourn in Normandy see O. Rössler, *Kaiserin Mathilde*, pp. 185–193; Ramsay, *Foundations of England*, ii. 359–364.

His presence at Bayeux is shown by a charter for Montebourg (Delisle, p. 117, no. 1; Robert of Torigni, i. 206), which is dated 1136, and must accordingly have been issued between Stephen's arrival in Normandy, in the third week of March, and Easter (11 April 1137). So a charter for Le Grand-Beaulieu of Chartres (*Cartulaire*, ed. Merlet and Jusselin, no. 11, from the original in the Archives of the Eure-et-Loir) is given at Évreux in 1136 'regni mei vero secundo.' Other points in Stephen's itinerary which appear from the charters but are not mentioned in the chroniclers are Falaise (Round, *Calendar*, no. 611), Lions-la-Forêt (*ibid.*, no. 1404), Rouen (*ibid.*, no. 1055; D. Gurney, *Record of the House of Gournay* (London, 1848–1858), i. 108; *Calendar of Charter Rolls*, iii. 374; *infra*, note 9).

[6] Ordericus, v. 81–91; Robert of Torigni, i. 206 f. On the date of Stephen's return see also Gervase of Canterbury, i. 101; John of Worcester, ed. Weaver, p. 45; Henry of Huntingdon, p. 260.

[7] 'Normannia . . . totam efficaci gubernatore provinciam carere mesta videbat ': Ordericus, v. 91.

[8] Round, *Geoffrey de Mandeville*, pp. 252 f., 260, 262 f. On the attitude of the Norman clergy cf. *Actus Pontificum Cenomannis*, ed. Busson and Ledru (Le Mans, 1901), p. 446.

Norman prelates continued to adhere to him with a loyalty which was to cost them dear at the hands of his successor. It is not surprising that, of the score of Stephen's charters which relate to Normandy,[9] two confirm the bishops in their privileges,[10] and most of the others concern the religious establishments of upper Normandy. Both in form and in substance these documents follow closely the charters of Henry I and assume the maintenance of his administrative system, with its justices, *vicomtes*, and subordinate officers. They also show that the ducal revenues were kept at farm, at least in eastern Normandy [11] — indeed, a fiscal roll of 1136 is said to have once existed [12] — and that the Norman treasurers, among them Robert of Évreux, continued in office.[13] It is, however, noteworthy that only one order to a Norman official has survived, and while it refers to an earlier writ on the same subject, it is perhaps significant that this previous command has not been obeyed: [14]

[9] Delisle, *Henri II*, pp. 117–120, nos. 1–13 (no. 1 is printed without the witnesses in *Gallia Christiana*, xi. instr. 238; nos. 3 and 4 are in Le Prévost, *Eure*, ii. 477, 488; no. 7 is in part in *Neustria Pia*, p. 778, and is indicated, probably erroneously, in the *Inventaire sommaire* as having been in the Archives of the Eure, H. 592); Round, *Calendar*, nos. 9, 239, 291–296, 427, 570, 611, 800, 802, 1055, 1404. Also a charter for Beaubec issued at Rouen (Archives of the Seine-Inférieure, G. 851, f. 57v; Archives Nationales, JJ. 46, f. 37v; printed from a *vidimus* of Charles VI in Gurney, *Record of the House of Gournay*, i. 108); a writ for Bec, printed below, no. 1; a charter for Bec given at Marlborough (MS. Lat. 13905, f. 21v); another addressed to his officers of Wissant and Boulogne and given at Rouen (*ibid.*, f. 86); a charter for the cordwainers of Rouen (La Roque, iii. 149, where it is wrongly attributed to William I); and an agreement in his presence at Rouen in 1137 between the canons of Saint-Évroul and the monks of Notre-Dame de Mortain, notified by Richard, bishop of Avranches (MS. 292, f. 309v, of the Library of Caen, from the original; MS. Lat. 5411, part ii, p. 409; Collection Moreau, lvii. 126; MS. Fr. 4900, f. 70). Of these nos. 11–13 in Delisle and nos. 9, 295, 296, 427, 800, 802 in Round were issued in England, leaving fifteen documents issued in Normandy, if we include the charter for Fontevrault (Delisle, no. 10; Round, no. 1055). To these may be added four others given at Rouen for establishments outside of Normandy, namely one for Boulogne (*Calendar of Charter Rolls*, iii. 374), one for the leprosery of Chartres (*Cartulaire*, ed. Merlet and Jusselin, no. 11) confirming its alms from the Norman treasury, and the two for Lincoln mentioned above, note 5.

[10] Delisle, nos. 5, 11; Round, nos. 9, 291.   [11] Round, nos. 292 f., 570.

[12] It is mentioned in 1790: *M. A. N.*, xvi, p. xxx.

[13] *Supra*, pp. 106–110; charter for Le Grand-Beaulieu of Chartres (*Cartulaire*, no. 11) confirming Henry I's grant of £10 in his Norman treasury.

[14] Fragment of cartulary of Bec in the Archives of the Eure, H. 91, f. 35. Prob-

(1) S. rex Angl[orum] Ing[eranno] de Wasc[olio] salutem. Scias quoniam vehementer miror de hoc quod non fecisti preceptum meum de terra monachorum de Becco de Turfrevilla de elemosina Willelmi Pevrell[i]. Quare tibi precipio quod facias in pace et iuste et quiete terram illam tenere sicut melius tenuerunt die qua rex Henricus fuit vivus et mortuus, ita quod non requiras aliquam novam consuetudinem de hominibus in terra illa residentibus. Teste comite de Mell[ento] apud Pont[em] Ald[omari].

At his departure Stephen left the government of Normandy in the hands of certain justiciars, among whom we have the names of only Roger the *vicomte*, who met his death shortly afterwards in the effort to maintain order in the Cotentin, and William of Roumare,[15] who is mentioned as justiciar in a Rouen document of 18 December 1138.[16] Beyond this point no regular administration of the duchy can be traced, and even in the castles and towns which continued to recognize Stephen his authority must have become merely nominal after the outbreak of the civil war drew the leaders of his party across the sea.[17] William of Ypres and Richard de Luci, who are fighting for him in Normandy in 1138, join him in England at the close of the year; Galeran of Meulan and his brother the earl of Leicester are with him in 1139; and

ably issued in June, when Stephen was at Pontaudemer (Ordericus, v. 85; cf. Delisle, no. 8).

[15] Ordericus, v. 91 f., 105; Delisle, *S.-Sauveur*, p. 28 f.

[16] Printed, *supra*, Chapter III, no. 4; Valin, p. 260; Vernier, no. 61; all from the original in the Archives of the Seine-Inférieure.

[17] The charter of Stephen as count of Mortain, purporting to have been issued at Mortain ' in aula comitis ' in 1139 (*Gallia Christiana*, xi. 478), is false, at least so far as the date is concerned, for Stephen spent that year in England, and the bishop of Avranches was then Richard, not Herbert, whose seal was attached to the accompanying charter (MS. Lat. 5441, ii. 416). Charters of Stephen as count of Mortain are known for Bec (Round, no. 378); for Saint-Étienne (Deville, *Analyse*, p. 18); for the Dames Blanches of Mortain (Stapleton, i, p. lxv); for Savigny (cartulary in Archives of the Manche, no. 211); and for the nuns of Moutons, in the style of the Anglo-Norman writ, as follows: ' St. comes Bolonie et Mortonii Stephano vicecomiti omnibusque suis baronibus atque servientibus salutem. Mando et precipio vobis ut omnes res dominarum Sancte Marie de Mustoñ, scilicet in terra et in vaccis et in aliis bestiis, in pace et quiete dimittatis, easque et quidquid ad eas pertinet honorifice custodiatis et manuteneatis. Tibi autem, Stephane, firmiter precipio ne de aliqua causa implacites eas nisi per me et coram me, quia sunt in mea custodia illisque deffendo ne placitent sine me. Istis testibus: Hamfredo dapifero et Addam de Belnayo et Hamfredo de Camerayo [*or* camerario].' Copies, based on a *vidimus* of 1310, in Archives of the Manche, *fonds* Moutons.

William of Roumare goes over to the empress in 1140.[18] Left to itself, the country quickly fell back into the disorder and bloodshed from which it had never really emerged during Stephen's nine months' sojourn. The descriptions of the Norman anarchy lack something of the realism with which William of Newburgh and the Peterborough chronicler depict conditions on the other side of the Channel, but the account in Ordericus is vivid enough, both in its general summary and its concrete examples, and its venerable author saw no hope of better days when he brought his work to its noble close in 1141.[19]

Yet this same year proved the turning-point in the reëstablishment of ducal authority.[20] Secure in the possession of Argentan

[18] Ordericus, v. 108, 115, 125; Round, *Geoffrey de Mandeville*, pp. 46, 55; Ramsay, *Foundations of England*, ii. 396; *E. H. R.*, xxv. 116.

[19] Ordericus, v. 57–77, 79 f., 89–91, 104–109, 114–117, 130 f., 133. One of the regions which suffered most severely was the Avranchin, where the account of Ordericus (v. 89) and Robert of Torigni (ii. 234) is supplemented by an original notice from the archives of Mont-Saint-Michel (Archives of the Manche, H. 14997; MS. Avranches 210, f. 80v): Certain men of the Mount 'post mortem enim carissimi domini nostri Henrici regis in abbatem dominum suum et contra totius villę salutem nequiter cum pluribus huiusce mali consciis conspirationem fecerunt. Quo comperto a pluribus abbas consilio fidelium suorum eos convenit et super tot et tantos malis conquestus eos alloquitur, quibus negantibus et obtestantibus iterum fidelitatem tam suę salutis quam totius villę iuraverunt. Qui iterum in proditione illa vehementer grassati hominibus alterius regionis ad tantum facinus patrandum adheserunt, iterum allocuti et tercio sacramentis adstricti funditus in malitia sua perseveraverunt. Ad ultimum congregata curia ad dies plurimos constitutos omne iuditium subterfugerunt et sic malitia eorum comperta omnibus patuit. Quo comperto liberales ipsius villę et ipsius provintię proceres super ignominia tanta confusi eos omnino exterminaverunt et sacramento affirmaverunt extunc illos non recepturos nec cum eis deinceps habitaturos. . . . [Rogerius camerarius] post mortem regis Anglie sacramentum irritum fecit, Britanniam cum omni suppellectili petiit, unde multa mala non solum per se verum etiam dux factus inimicorum qui tunc temporis nimia aviditate Normanniam infestabant terre et hominibus ecclesie irrogavit.' It will be noted that in this document there is no trace of ducal authority after Henry's death, and the barons take matters into their own hands.

[20] On Geoffrey's recovery of Normandy see Kate Norgate, *Angevin Kings*, i. 338–342, and the authorities there cited. That, as Miss Norgate says, " the story of this campaign, as told by the historians of the time, is little more than a list of the places taken, put together evidently at random," is true only of William of Malmesbury, who lacked local knowledge. The succession of events in Robert of Torigni and John of Marmoutier is intelligible and consistent, and of the additional places mentioned by William of Malmesbury, Bastebourg and Trevières were apparently the result of special expeditions from Caen and Bayeux, while the others

and the adjoining *vicomtés*, and controlling Caen and Bayeux through his alliance with Robert of Gloucester, Geoffrey of Anjou in 1141 won Lisieux, Falaise, and the country as far as the Seine, and the following year gave him not only the outstanding places in the Bessin, but the county of Mortain, the Avranchin, and the Cotentin.[21] By January 1144 he was able to enforce the submission of the city of Rouen, followed three months later by the surrender of its tower.[22] Although the castle of Arques held out until the summer of the following year, the barons of the duchy had already made their peace with the new duke, who had won over their leader, the count of Meulan, as early as 1141; and even the Norman church, which had received Stephen's nephew as abbot of Fécamp in 1140 and his chancellor as bishop of Bayeux in 1142, was driven to acknowledge the king's defeat. John of Lisieux, the justiciar of Henry I, submitted to Geoffrey just before his death in 1141; the bishop of Avranches led the procession which welcomed the Angevin army to his city in the following year; and even the archbishop of Rouen, *maximus regis propugnator* at the outbreak of the civil war in England, who dated his documents by Stephen's reign as late as 1143, was doubtless present when Geoffrey was received into his cathedral upon the city's surrender, and thenceforth recognized him as ruler of the

— Briquessart, Villers, Plessis, Vire — lay in the direction of Mortain, though not " up the left bank of the Orne."

[21] The chroniclers say nothing of the Channel Islands, although modern writers upon the islands say that Geoffrey sent a certain Raoul de Valmont there to establish the duke's authority and ascertain his rights. It would be interesting to know the origin of this statement. See G. Dupont, *Histoire du Cotentin et de ses Iles* (Caen, 1870), i. 354–357; F. B. Tupper, *History of Guernsey* (Guernsey, 1876), p. 76; E. Pégot-Ogier, *Histoire des Iles de la Manche* (Paris, 1881), p. 133 f. We know very little of the history of these islands in the twelfth century.

[22] As Geoffrey crossed the Seine at Hilarymas and received the submission of Rouen 19 or 20 January, his charter for Château-l'Hermitage, given 28 January 1144 at Mayet (*Archives historiques du Maine*, vi. 45), can hardly belong in this year. On the surrender of Arques in the following year see *Cartulaire de S.-Laud d'Angers*, ed. Planchenault, p. 65. The completion of the conquest as far as the Seine in 1143 is confirmed by a charter of that year given ' Andegavis civitate in anno quo annuente Deo et sancta matre eius partem Normannie que est citra Sequanam adquisivimus ': P. F. Chifflet, *Histoire de l'abbaye de Tournus*, preuves, p. 424 (Juénin, preuves, p. 156).

duchy.[23] Although he had been so styled by his partisans some time before,[24] Geoffrey did not assume the ducal title until the acquisition of Rouen gave him full control of his new dominions and justified his prompt recognition by the king of France.[25]

Geoffrey's reign as duke of Normandy extends from 1144 to early in 1150, when he handed the duchy over to his son Henry, the heir of Matilda and Henry I.[26] This transfer, accomplished

[23] Böhmer, *Kirche und Staat in England und in der Normandie*, p. 313 f. The archbishop still recognizes Stephen in a document of 1143 in *Gallia Christiana*, xi. instr. 23, but acknowledges Geoffrey in charters of 1145 (Pommeraye, *Histoire de S.-Ouen*, p. 425; P. Laffleur de Kermaingant, *Cartulaire de l'abbaye de S.-Michel du Tréport*, p. 31; C. Métais, *Cartulaire de la Trinité de Vendôme*, ii. 331; Collection Moreau, lxi. 188, 206). So Arnulf of Lisieux dates a charter for Fécamp by Stephen's reign in 1142 (Archives of the Seine-Inférieure, *fonds* Fécamp), but attests a charter which recognizes Geoffrey in September 1143 (see the next note), and is soon busy securing the favor of the new prince (*Epistolae*, no. 2). That Geoffrey had been able to put pressure upon the Norman church appears from the instance of the treasurer of Lisieux, who was kept out of his church of Mesnil-Eudes (Calvados) 'propter ducatus divisionem': letters of Bishop John in MS. Lat. 5288, f. 68.

[24] Charter of William, count of Ponthieu, for Vignats, 19 September 1143, witnessed by the bishops of Séez, Lisieux, and Coutances, and three abbots: *Gallia Christiana*, xi. instr. 162. On the other hand Geoffrey is called count in a charter of Reginald of Saint-Valery issued some time before the capture of Dieppe: Round, *Calendar*, no. 1057; Fréville, *Histoire du commerce de Rouen*, ii. 9.

[25] On the assumption of the ducal title, see Delisle, *Henri II*, p. 135 f.; and cf. the date of no. 728 in Round's *Calendar*. According to Robert of Torigni and the annals of Mont-Saint-Michel (ed. Delisle, i. 234, ii. 234), Geoffrey became duke upon the surrender of the tower of Rouen (23 April), but a charter of Ulger, bishop of Angers (Delisle, *Henri II*, p. 135), places 29 June 1145 in the first year of his reign. Lucius II addresses him 16 May 1144 as count of Anjou merely: *Livre noir de Bayeux*, no. 206.

[26] Against the annals of Saint-Aubin (Halphen, *Recueil d'annales angevines*, p. 12), which give 1149, and Miss Norgate's argument for 1148 (*Angevin Kings*, i. 369 f., 377; *Dictionary of National Biography, sub* 'Henry II'), the date of 1150 seems to me clearly established from Robert of Torigni (i. 253), and the annals of Caen (*H. F.*, xii. 780) and Saint-Évroul (Ordericus, v. 162), and especially from the regnal years in certain of Henry's charters. Gervase of Canterbury (i. 142), who is not quite clear as to the year, gives January as the month of Henry's return to Normandy; and two charters for Savigny, given in the eighth year of his reign as duke and issued before the beginning of April 1157, show that he became duke before the end of March (Delisle, pp. 122, 231, 279 f., 515, nos. 30, 30a; Berger, i. 183, confuses the whole matter of these charters by dating Henry's reign from the end of 1150, following an unsupported statement of Delisle, p. 121). A charter of Archbishop Hugh (La Roque, iii. 45) is dated 1150 'principante in Normannia duce Henrico.' On the other hand Geoffrey drops the title of duke in a charter of 28

when the young duke was in his seventeenth year, shows plainly
that the count of Anjou had won and held Normandy for his son
and not for himself, and earlier evidence points to the same conclusion. Besides the few weeks which may have intervened between his return and his assumption of the ducal title in 1150,
Henry was on the Norman side of the Channel from the end of
1146 to the spring of 1149,[27] enjoying the instruction of the most
famous Norman scholar of the time, William of Conches, who
prepared for his use a choice selection of maxims of the Gentile
philosophers;[28] yet even at this tender age his name was used to
give sanction to ducal acts. A charter for Bec[29] and one for Saint-
Wandrille [30] are issued by Geoffrey with the advice and consent
of his son Henry; another confirmation for Bec [31] and one for
Fécamp [32] are issued by the two jointly; while a document of
1147 for Saint-Ouen, attested by Geoffrey's chancellor, Richard

October 1150 (*Liber albus Cenomannensis*, no. 6; cf. Delisle, p. 138) and in a notification at Montreuil, addressed to the archbishop of Rouen, evidently in 1150-
1151 (*infra*, note 90).

[27] On the dates of Henry's crossings see Round, *Geoffrey de Mandeville*, pp. 405-
410.

[28] William's *Dragmaticon* is dedicated to Geoffrey as duke of Normandy and
count of Anjou in an introduction which praises his care for the education of the
young princes (R. L. Poole, *Illustrations of the History of Medieval Thought*, p. 347 f.);
and his treatise on moral philosophy, *De honesto et utili*, is dedicated to Henry before
the assumption of the ducal title. See this work, attributed to Hildebert of Le
Mans, in Migne, clxxi. 1007–1056; and, on its authorship, Hauréau, in *Notices et
extraits des MSS.*, xxxiii, 1, pp. 257–263. Curiously enough, it was used by Giraldus
Cambrensis in writing the *De principis instructione*, where Henry II serves as a
terrible example. Adelard of Bath also appears to have been one of Henry's tutors:
E. H. R., xxviii. 516.

[29] ' Non lateat vos nec quenquam presentium sive futurorum me consilio H. filii
mei et baronum meorum concessisse quod ecclesia Sancte Marie de Becco et monachi
illius ecclesie habeant omnes consuetudines et quietudines et libertates quas habebant
in tempore H. regis. Quapropter ego precipio ut omnes res eiusdem ecclesie sint
quiete et libere in terra et in aqua et in plano et in nemore per totam Normanniam
ab omni consuetudine et vexatione, sicut erant in tempore Henrici regis ' (extract
by Dom Jouvelin-Thibault, in MS. Lat. 13905, f. 85v).

[30] Round, no. 170; Delisle-Berger, no. 9*; Lot, *S.-Wandrille*, no. 78.

[31] " Geofroy duc de Normandie et d'Anjou, Henri 2d son fils, confirment et dé-
clarent que monachi de Becco et omnes res eorum sunt quiete de theloneo et passagio
et pontagio et de omni consuetudine, sicut a retroactis temporibus fuerunt apud
Archas et apud Diepam ": MS. Lat. 13905, f. 85v.

[32] Delisle, p. 508, no. 6*, and facsimile no. 1; Delisle-Berger, no. 8*.

of Bohun, is given by *Henricus ducis Normannorum et comitis Andegavie filius* and addressed to his officers of Normandy.[33] We should also expect to find the empress taking an active part in Norman affairs; but her absence in England from 1139 to 1148 [34] removed her from any share in the events of these critical years on the Continent, nor has any trace been found of her participation in her husband's administration after her return. The lack of documents which can be specifically referred to these two years is, however, probably accidental, for we have a grant of land at Argentan to one of her followers before her departure for England,[35] and several charters, issued in her own name or conjointly with her son, which show her activity in the years immediately following his accession.[36]

The sources of information for the study of Geoffrey's government of Normandy are remarkably scanty and fragmentary. The narrative writers fail us entirely, for Ordericus stops before the conquest is completed, and Robert of Torigni and John of Marmoutier give us nothing beyond an enumeration of campaigns. We are perforce restricted to the charters, among which those of the duke himself, about forty in number, are so fundamental as to call for somewhat special examination. The following list in-

---

[33] *Neustria Pia*, p. 15; La Roque, iv. suppl., p. 10; Delisle, p. 508, no. 3*; Delisle-Berger, no. 5*. Delisle and Berger query the date, but we know that Henry was solemnly received at Bec on Ascension Day, 1147 (Robert of Torigni, i. 243). Henry likewise makes a grant to the nuns of Almenèches as son of Duke Geoffrey: Delisle, *Cartulaire normand*, no. 5; Delisle-Berger, no. 7*.

[34] Delisle, *Henri II*, p. 140, and the older Norman writers give 1147 as the year of her return, which took place 'ante Quadragisimam.' There is some uncertainty because of the confusion of chronology — which is, however, less than has been supposed (see Round, *Geoffrey de Mandeville*, pp. 405–410) — in Gervase of Canterbury, but as he (i. 133) places Matilda's return after the death of Robert of Gloucester (31 October 1147) and just before the council of Rheims (21 March 1148), it would seem to fall in 1148. Rössler, *Kaiserin Mathilde*, pp. 410–412, assumes 1147, but his book has no value for Matilda's later years.

[35] Original in MS. Lat. 10083, f. 3, analyzed in *M. A. N.*, viii. 388; Delisle, p. 141, no. 4; Round, no. 591. As this charter is given at Argentan and witnessed by Matilda's brother Reginald, who attests as earl of Cornwall after 1141 (Round, *Geoffrey de Mandeville*, pp. 68, 271), it must be anterior to her departure in 1139.

[36] Delisle, pp. 126, 141–143, nos. 5–13; Delisle-Berger, nos. 11*, 45*. See also her charters for Silly, Round, *Calendar*, nos. 679 f., 683; and *Sarum Charters*, p. 14 (1148).

cludes such Norman charters of Geoffrey as I have been able to find, arranged, since few of them are dated, in the alphabetical order of the places for whose benefit they were issued:

ALMENÈCHES. Delisle, *Cartulaire normand*, no. 4, and p. 273.

BAYEUX. Probably 1145–1147. Eight charters and writs of Geoffrey: *Livre noir*, nos. 16–19, 24, 25, 39, 100 (1147). Also four reports addressed to him by his justices: nos. 43, 44, 89, 90. These are all, except no. 100, attributed to Henry II in the edition (see, however, the corrections at the end of the second volume), but in the cartulary the initial G appears in every case on the margin. See *A. H. R.*, viii. 618; *infra*, Chapter VI; Delisle, *Henri II*, pp. 137 f., 511, nos. 42*, 43*, where the attribution of the last two to Henry II is corrected by Berger, i. 3. No. 17 is also in the *Livre rouge* (MS. Lat. n. a. 1828, no. 401), of which there is a poor edition by Anquetil (Bayeux, 1909).

BEC. Extracts from two charters, printed above, notes 29, 31.

BEC, priory of Notre-Dame-du-Pré. 27 March 1149, at Bec. Original, printed below, no. 2.

BEC, priory of Saint-Ymer. 1147, at Saumur. MS. Lat. n. a. 2097, p. 9; Collection Lenoir at Semilly, lxxii, 2, p. 169. *Cartulaires de S.-Ymer-en-Auge et de Bricquebec*, ed. C. Bréard (Paris, 1908), p. 7; Round, *Calendar*, no. 360; Delisle, no. 3* A; cf. Delisle-Berger, i. 2.

CLUNY. Before 1147, as it is attested by Hugh, archbishop of Tours. A. Bruel, *Chartes de Cluni*, v. 447; cf. G. F. Duckett, *Charters and Records of Cluni*, ii. 78. In Martène and Durand, *Thesaurus Anecdotorum*, i. 383, it is attributed to a duke R.

COUTANCES. At Saint-Lô. *A. H. R.*, viii. 630; *infra*, Chapter VI, note 95. Cf. Delisle, *Cartulaire normand*, no. 162; *Henri II*, no. 17* A; Delisle-Berger, i. 2. Ascribed to Henry II by Round, no. 960.

ÉVREUX. At Rouen. Printed below, no. 6.

FÉCAMP. (1) At Rouen. Original, misplaced, in Archives of the Seine-Inférieure; modern copies in MS. Lat. n. a. 1245, ff. 122–123; MS. Rouen, 1210, f. 17.[37] (2) With his son Henry; at Rouen. Original, in same archives. Delisle, *Henri II*, no. 6*, with facsimile; Delisle-Berger, no. 8*; Round, no. 126, omitting most of the witnesses.

LESSAY. At Saumur. Original, printed below, no. 3.

LISIEUX, Saint-Désir, and the Knights of the Hospital. 1147, after Easter (?'in Pascha precedenti'), at Mirebeau. Modern copies in Archives of the Calvados. Extract in Grente and Havard, *Villedieu-les-Poëles* (Paris, 1899), p. 6; Round, no. 576, where it is dated at Easter and the wit-

---

[37] ' Gaufredus dux Normannorum et comes Andegavorum omnibus hominibus Fiscanni salutem. Sciatis me vidisse cartam ecclesie Fiscanni que testatur ecclesie Fiscanni portus maris de Stigas usque ad Leregant. Ideo mando vobis et prohibeo quod vos non intromittatis de aliqua re que ad portus istos veniat vel sit, nisi per manum Henrici abbatis vel servientium suorum, quia in ipsis nichil habeo. Teste Raginaldo de Sancto Walerico apud Rothomagum.'

nesses are omitted; *M. A. N.*, xiv. 382, xvii. 325 (translation). Léchaudé, *M. A. N.*, vii. 247, ascribes it to William Rufus!

MARMOUTIER, priory of Héauville. At Argentan. Printed below, no. 7a.

MONTEBOURG. (1) At Argentan. Printed below, no. 4. (2) At Lisieux. Printed below, no. 5.

MORTEMER. 11 October 1147, at Rouen. La Roque, iii. 152, iv. 1396, 1636, suppl., p. 8; *Neustria Pia*, p. 779. Analyzed in *Bulletin des Antiquaires de Normandie*, xiii. 115; Round, no. 1405; cf. *H. F.*, xiv. 511.[38]

PRÉAUX. 1149, at Rouen. Notice of transaction in *curia* sitting at Geoffrey's order. Archives of the Eure, H. 711, no. 453. Printed in Valin, p. 265; cf. Le Prévost, *Eure*, iii. 324.

ROUEN, cathedral. At Rouen. Archives of the Seine-Inférieure, G. 7, p. 793. Printed in Valin, p. 266 (where the undeciphered word is *scilicet*); Delisle-Berger, no. 39*. The initial is left blank in the cartulary, so that the author may be either Geoffrey or Henry II. Delisle, no 37*, ascribes it to Henry, but gives no reason. Geoffrey's authorship seems to me likely from the phrase 'tempore H. regis Anglie,' for in such cases (e. g., *Livre noir de Bayeux*, nos. 27, 28, 32; *Neustria Pia*, p. 15) Henry II adds 'avi mei,' as in the writ for Héauville (Delisle-Berger, no. 29*), which we can compare with an exactly parallel one of his father (no. 7a below).

ROUEN, town. Probably in 1144 and doubtless at Rouen. Incorporated in Henry II's charter: A. Chéruel, *Histoire de Rouen*, i. 241; Round, no. 109; Delisle-Berger, no. 14*.

ROUEN, gild of cordwainers. At Rouen. *Vidimus* of 1267 in MS. Lat. 9067, f. 155v; and MS. Rouen 2192, f. 189. Printed from *vidimus* of 1371 (Archives Nationales, JJ. 102, no. 317) in *Ordonnances des Rois*, v. 416; translated in Chéruel, *Rouen*, i, p. cxiv. Cf. Delisle-Berger, no. 16*.

ROUEN, Henry the Marshal, the duke's serjeant. Probably before 1147, at Rouen. Printed below, no. 13.

ROUEN, leprosery of Mont-aux-Malades. (1) At Rouen. Original writ, printed below, no. 12. (2) Charter notifying the reception of the Palmers of Rouen into confraternity: translation in P. Langlois, *Histoire du prieuré du Mont-aux-Malades-lès-Rouen* (Rouen, 1851), p. 4.

ROUEN, Saint-Amand. At Lisieux. Printed below, no. 7.

ROUEN, Saint-Ouen. 'Gaufredus dux Normannorum et comes Andegavorum confirmat donationem c[omitis] Walterii Giffardi. Testibus Roberto de Novoburgo, Widone de Sabluel.' MS. Lat. 5423, f. 232v.

SAINT-ANDRÉ-EN-GOUFFERN. At Argentan. Printed below, no. 10.

SAINT-ÉVROUL. Probably in 1144. Printed below, no. 8.

SAINT-WANDRILLE. (1) At Rouen. Printed *E. H. R.*, xxvii. 438, note 97; Lot, *S.-Wandrille*, no. 119. (2) At Argentan. *Neustria Pia*, p. 176 (extract); Round, no. 170; in full in Lot, no. 78; Delisle-Berger, no. 9*.

SAVIGNY. (1) At Argentan. Original, Archives Nationales, L. 969; cartulary in Archives of the Manche, no. 408; Round, no. 812. (2) At Ar-

---

[38] The epact in this charter is of 1148, showing that it was calculated from 1 September, as in a charter of Geoffrey in the *Cartulaire de S.-Laud d'Angers*, no. 49.

gentan. *Vidimus*, printed below, no. 11. (3) At Montreuil; 1150–1151. Original, printed below, note 90.

Séez, Saint-Martin. Printed below, no. 9.

For a reign of six years this is a respectable number of documents, if we take into account the relatively small body of Norman charters which has survived from the first half of the twelfth century, and their geographical distribution is significant. Four of the episcopal sees are represented, the archives of the others being an almost total loss, and the monasteries of the list are scattered throughout the duchy, from the ancient establishments in the region of the Seine to Montebourg, Héauville, Lessay, and Savigny on the west. All this bears evidence of an effective rule of the whole land. At the same time it is noteworthy that, if we except the charter for the town of Rouen, which was granted under special circumstances, there are among them all no general enumerations and confirmations of lands and privileges such as are found under Henry I and in still greater number under Henry II.[39] What we have instead is specific grants, letters of protection, declarations of freedom from toll, and orders to the duke's officers to hold inquests, make payments, and maintain rights. The writs bulk large in proportion to the charters. This cannot be mere accident, for the detailed confirmations which are so numerous under Henry II rarely mention his father,[40] but hark back constantly to the conditions of his grandfather's time. We get distinctly the impression of a reign which restores rather than creates, and administers rather than ordains, of a regency rather than a permanent government.

Considered from the diplomatic point of view, Geoffrey's charters show variety, but they also show something of the regularity and definiteness of form which come only from an organized

[39] An apparent exception, the long charter for Bayeux (*Livre noir*, no. 39), is merely a statement of the results of inquests held to determine the ancient rights of the see. The difference from the policy of other dukes may be seen even in the case of Stephen by comparing his detailed confirmation for Montebourg (*Gallia Christiana*, xi, instr. 238) with the charters of Geoffrey for the same abbey printed below, nos. 4, 5.

[40] Later references to Geoffrey's official acts are rare. See *infra*, notes 89, 91, 121; Round, no. 1296; and the grant to Aunay cited in a bull of Eugene III (*Bulletin des Antiquaires de Normandie*, xix. 256).

chancery. That Normandy had the advantage of such a system under Henry I is of course well known, but we cannot speak with equal certainty of conditions in contemporary Anjou. Down to the close of the eleventh century the counts of Anjou, like the kings of France, had not entirely differentiated their chancery from their chapel, the same man appearing at one time as chaplain and at another as chancellor, nor had they developed a regular set of forms for their official acts. Until 1109 at least, the only period which has been carefully studied, almost all of their documents were drawn up by the monasteries in whose favor they were issued,[41] and the evidence of style would indicate that this custom persisted in large measure under Fulk of Jerusalem and even under his son. Geoffrey's Angevin charters have something of the variety, the prolixity, and the narrative form which belong to the monastic notice rather than to the charter proper, and which are in sharp contrast with the brevity and fixity which the Anglo-Norman charter, and especially the writ, has attained before the close of the Conqueror's reign.

Still, mention is found from time to time of the chaplain or notary who composed the document, and especially of Thomas of Loches, the historian of the counts of Anjou, whose attestation appears as early as 1133 and continues as chaplain or chancellor throughout the reign.[42] Thomas also accompanied Geoffrey on his Norman expeditions, for his signature as chancellor appears in documents issued at Argentan, Lisieux, and Rouen, and he witnesses as chaplain a charter given at Bec in 1149.[43] Curiously enough, this last document bears likewise the name of the duke's principal chancellor, Richard of Bohun. Dean of Bayeux since

[41] Halphen, *Le comté d'Anjou*, pp. 192 f., 237. For the confusion of chancellor and chaplain under the Capetians see Prou, *Recueil des actes de Philippe Ier*, pp. liv-lvi.

[42] On Thomas see Mabille's introduction to Marchegay, *Chroniques des comtes d'Anjou*, pp. xiv-xxv; Beautemps-Beaupré, *Coutumes*, part ii, i. 220–222; and now the introduction to Halphen and Poupardin, *Chroniques des comtes d'Anjou*, pp. xxvii-xxxvi.

[43] *Infra*, nos. 2, 4–7a. Thomas is mentioned in a writ of the empress for Cherbourg (Delisle, *Henri II*, no. 84*; Round, no. 938) in a way that suggests (particularly if we conjecture ' tenuerunt ' in the missing portion) that Geoffrey may have given him some part of the considerable possessions of Roger of Salisbury (cf. Round, no. 909) in the Cotentin.

the days of Henry I, Richard bought the chancellorship from Geoffrey by pledging the income of his deanery for an amount which he had much difficulty in paying and which subsequently brought him into trouble with his bishop and with the Pope; and in 1151 he was rewarded with the bishopric of Coutances.[44] Nine of Geoffrey's charters and writs bear his attestation,[45] and as one of these is dated at Saumur,[46] it is plain that he followed the duke beyond the confines of Normandy. No chronological separation between the charters of Richard and Thomas seems possible: the Bayeux writs attested by Richard belong to the early years of the reign; two of the others fall in 1147 [47] and one in 1149; [48] and he appears as chancellor in five documents issued by Henry II.[49] Probably the explanation is that Richard was chancellor in Normandy and Thomas chaplain, as in the charter for Bec, but that in Richard's absence Thomas took the title and perhaps the functions of chancellor, which he had claimed in Anjou as early as 1142.[50]

Richard's work can be tested in two originals, issued at places as far apart as Bec and Saumur, but written by the same scribe [51]

[44] ' Postmodum vero venientis ad nos venerabilis fratris nostri Philippi Baiocensis episcopi suggestione accepimus quod antedictus frater noster pecuniam illam, non pro ecclesie Baiocensis utilitate aut sui honesta necessitate suscepit, sed ut cancellariam sibi nobilis memorie Gaufridi quondam Andegavensis comitis compararet, et cum in capitulo Baiocensi se infra biennium soluturum eandem pecuniam promisisset, licet multum post decanatum habuerit, debitum tamen ipsum, ut promiserat, nequaquam exsolvit ' (Livre noir, no. 185). As Richard continued to hold the deanery, not only for two years but ' multum post,' he evidently became chancellor not long after Geoffrey's conquest of the duchy. He had been dean under Bishop Richard Fitz Samson (ibid., no. 480), who died in 1133, and is mentioned with this title in several Bayeux documents: ibid., nos. 60, 100 (1147), 103 (1146), 106, 207 (1146), 291; cf. Delisle-Berger, no. 20* (1151). On the date of his elevation to the bishopric see Robert of Torigni, i. 257 and note; and cf. Delisle-Berger, nos. 35*, 45*.

[45] Livre noir, nos. 17, 19, 39; Round, nos. 126 (= Delisle, no. 6*, with facsimile; Delisle-Berger, no. 8*), 170, 960, 1405; infra, nos. 2, 3.

[46] Infra, no. 3. [47] Round, no. 1405; Neustria Pia, p. 15. [48] Infra, no. 2.

[49] Delisle-Berger, nos. 5*, 12*, 28*, 40*, 42*. Delisle, p. 88, note, is incorrect.

[50] Cartulaire de l'abbaye du Ronceray, ed. Marchegay, p. 244 (Archives d'Anjou, iii). Halphen and Poupardin, l. c., p. xxix, doubt whether Thomas was really chancellor, the title being at times taken by a mere notary.

[51] That Richard was not himself the scribe is seen from the recurrence of the same hand in the notice printed below (note 90), issued by Geoffrey as count of Anjou at Montreuil-Bellay in 1150–1151, in which Richard is not mentioned.

and showing such resemblances in their formulae that the first, excellently preserved with its seal, may safely be used to supply some of the gaps in the mutilated text of the second. These are:

(2) G. dux Norm[annorum] & com[es] And[egavorum] H. archiep[iscop]o & omnibus ep[iscop]is comitibus baronibus iusticiis Norm[annie] & omnibus suis fidelibus sal[utem]. Notum sit vobis atque omnibus tam presentibus quam futuris quod ego dedi & concessi monachis Sanctę Marie de Becco tres prebendas de Buris, ea conditione quod post quam illę fuerint liberatę a tribus presentibus clericis, scilicet Ivone Hugone atque Alexandro, monachi Sanctę Marię de Prato illas perpetuo libere & quiete possideant. Huius rei sunt testes: Ric[ardus] cancell[arius], Gaufr[edus] Roth[omagensis] decanus, Tomas capellanus, Robertus de Movoburg[o] (*sic*) & alii quam plures. Hoc autem concessum est anno ab incarnatione Domini .M.C.XLIX. in Pascha instanti die dominica de ramis palmarum in Beccensi capitulo.[52]

(3) G. dux Norm[annorum] et comes And[egavorum] H. archiepiscopo & omnibus ep[iscopis comitibus] baronibus iusticiis & omnibus suis servientibus salutem. [Notum sit vobis] atque omnibus hominibus tam presentibus quam futuris quod ego concessi donationem quam Willelmus de Aureavalle fecit ecclesię Sanctę Trinitatis de Exaquio, videlicet de molendino de Sancta Oportuna quod predictę ecclesię dedit cum omnibus consuetudinibus & molta & omnibus rebus que ad illud molendinum pertinebant & de parte illa quam in ecclesia Sanctę Oportunę habebat [ecclesię] Exaquii dedit sicut carta illius testatur. & ut hec dona[tio et concessio] perpetuo fiat sigilli mei testimonio illam confirmari   [T]estes autem inde sunt Ric[ardus] cancellarius, Willelmus de Vernone,   Engelg[erus] de Boh[one], Alex[ander] de Boh[one], Robertus de Montef[orti],   de Sancto Iohanne, Rualocus de Saeio, Iosl[inus] de Tyr[onibus], Pi[ppinus de Tyronibus], Willelmus de [Sai ?], Adam de Sotewast. Apud Salmur[am].[53]

---

[52] Original, sealed *en double queue*, in Archives of the Seine-Inférieure. See the facsimile, Plate 7b. Cf. G. Demay, *Inventaire des sceaux de la Normandie*, no. 20; Porée, *Bec.* i. 397. The phrase 'in Pascha instanti' seems at first sight to indicate that the style of Easter was here used, which would bring the date 9 April 1150. This is, however, inconsistent with the fact that Henry had by this time become duke (*supra*, note 26), and we should need stronger evidence to establish so striking a variation from the practice of beginning the year at Christmas or 1 January, which prevailed in both Normandy and Anjou (Delisle, *Henri II*, p. 230; Halphen, *Le comté d'Anjou*, pp. 237–239). Evidently the phrase has no reference to the beginning of the year, as is likewise true of 'in Pascha precedenti' in the charters of 1147 in *Neustria Pia*, pp. 15, 779, in the latter of which, dated 11 October, the reference to Easter could have no significance under any system of reckoning, a fact overlooked by Berger, *Henri II*, no. 5*. The Bec charter belongs accordingly to 27 March 1149.

[53] Original, with *double queue*, but no trace of seal, in Archives of the Manche, H. 7771. Printed in *Inventaire sommaire*; cf. Delisle, *Henri II*, p. 509, no. 17*B; Berger, i. 2.

No originals have been discovered from the hand of the chancellor Thomas, but we can follow him with some confidence in certain early copies. Let us begin with two charters in the cartulary of Montebourg: [54]

(4) Ego Goffr[edus] dux Norm[annorum] et comes And[egavorum] relatione multorum cognoscens audiendo et audiens cognoscendo quoniam H. rex predecessor meus abbatiam Montisburgi Sancte Marie tanquam propriam capellam nimio dilexit amore diligendo custodivit augmentavit nobilitavit, similiter abbatiam eamdem in mea custodia et in tuitione capio et quicquid ille contulit vel concessit in bosco et in plano et in omnibus consuetudinibus et in omnibus modis unde habent monachi cartas et brevia prefate abbatie diligenter annuo. Insuper illi addo do et concedo in perpetuam elemosinam perpetuo iure habendam pro salute mea et filiorum meorum necnon et predicti regis omniumque predecessorum meorum illam terram que est in suo aisimento inter suam terram et forestam usque ad rivulum sicut oritur et descendit de veteri fonte, et ipsum rivulum cum alveo concedo ita ut rivulus fosseatus sit firma divisa inter eos et forestam, cum constet quia redditus nichil inde foreste minuitur sed melius clauditur munitur atque defenditur.

Testibus Thoma cancell[ario], Alex[andro] de Boh[one], Ric[ardo] de Haia, Ric[ardo] de Wauvilla, W[illelmo] Avenel, Olivier de Albiniaco, Gisleb[erto] archid[iacono], Rob[erto] de Valoniis, Rob[erto] Bordel, Unfr[edo] de Bosevill[a] et aliis multis, apud Argent[omum].

(5) Ego Gaufridus comes Andegavis (*sic*) et dux Normannorum cunctis baronibus meis vicecomitibus ministris et omnibus hominibus meis salutem. Sciatis quod habeo in mea propria custodia abbatiam de Monteburgo omnes monachos et omnes res ad eos pertinentes tanquam meam propriam elemosinam sicut habuit rex Henricus antecessor meus, et concedo abbatie et ipsis monachis quicquid concessit eis predictus rex in omnibus rebus et in omnibus consuetudinibus et unde habent ipsius regis cartas et brevia, et ut habeant omnes consuetudines suas in forestis meis liberas et quietas et focum in Monteburgo, et ut sint quieti a theloneo et consuetudine ubicunque vendant vel emant vel conducant aliquid quod homines eorum possint affidare esse proprium ecclesie et monachorum, et omnes donationes baronum quas dederunt vel dederint ipsi ecclesie. Precipio igitur vobis ut abbatiam et quicquid ad eam pertinet manuteneatis et defendatis et regatis sicut meam propriam elemosinam, ne pro penuria recti inde clamorem audiam.

T[estibus] Will[elmo] de Vernon, Alex[andro] de Bohun, Pag[ano] de Claris Vallibus, Th[oma] cancellario, Rob[erto] de Curc[eio], apud Luxovium. + Preterea concedo eidem abbatie coram supradictis testibus illam terram que est inter suam terram et forestam usque ad rivum et ipsum rivum sicut descendit de veteri fonte et quoddam warlocum quod est in altera parte.

[54] MS. Lat. 10087, nos. 35, 36.

The first of these uses a comparatively untechnical phraseology and has something of the more literary flavor of the Angevin charter. The second, from its substance evidently posterior, is full of the legal terminology of the charters of Henry I on which it is based,[55] and culminates with the characteristically Norman clause, *ne pro penuria recti inde clamorem audiam.*[56] Such repetitions of the language of earlier charters for the same establishment are perfectly natural and are familiar to all students of diplomatics.[57] When, however, we find Thomas adopting the brevity and precision of the Anglo-Norman writ, as well as its typical phrases, we see how thoroughly Norman an institution the chancery of Geoffrey has become. The first of the following relates to the see of Évreux, the second to the nuns of Saint-Amand, the third to Héauville, a priory of Marmoutier:

(6) G. dux Normann[orum] et comes And[egavorum] G[uidoni] de Sablol[io] et Will[elmo] Lovello atque prepositis et ballivis suis de Vernolio et de Nonancort salutem et dilectionem. Mando atque vobis precipio quod episcopo Ebroicensi reddatis omnes decimas suas de Vernol[io] et de Nonancort sicut eas umquam melius habuit in tempore H. regis et sicut carta eius garantizat, ita quod eas habeat prout tempus ierit ad voluntatem suam, et de tempore transacto quicquid ei debetur absque dilatione reddatis. Insuper etiam vobis precipio ne quid inde amittat neque pro refactura molendinorum neque pro augmentatione reddite supradictarum villarum. De pace vero fracta mando vobis quod ei inde quicquid habere debuerit plenarie reddi faciatis, scilicet .ix. libras sicut carta H. regis garantizat. Tibi etiam, Willelme Lovel, precipio quod iusticiam ei facias de Gilleberto nummario (?). Teste Thoma cancellario apud Rothomagum.[58]

(7) G. dux Normann[orum] et comes And[egavorum] R. de Sancto Walerico et ministris suis de Archis salutem. Precipio quod habere faciatis S. Amando decimam suam de forestis de Awi et de Alihermont in denariis

[55] *Supra*, Chapter III, nos. 8–15; Delisle, *Cartulaire normand*, no. 737.

[56] *E. H. R.*, xxvi. 446 f. Can we see Thomas's hand in a writ of Geoffrey in 1146, mentioned in a notice from La Trinité de Vendôme (*Cartulaire*, ii. 343), where we have ' ne amplius super hoc clamorem audiret ' ?

[57] An excellent illustration is furnished by the charter of Geoffrey and Henry for Fécamp (Delisle, *Henri II*, p. 508, no. 6*, with facsimile; Delisle-Berger, no. 8*), which reproduces the language of the early grants of immunity: ' absque ulla inquietatione vel imminutione secularis vel iuditiarie potestatis.' See Appendix B.

[58] Archives of the Eure, G. 122, no. 204, G. 123, no. 196, printed in Le Prévost, *Eure*, ii. 488, who reads ' munario ' before the testing clause where I conjecture ' nummario.' For the charter of Henry I see *Très Ancien Coutumier*, c. 71; Round, *Calendar*, no. 290.

frumento et avena sicut eam melius habuit tempore Henrici regis, quia nolo ut elemosina mea minuatur. Teste Toma cancellario apud Lux[ovium].[59]

(7a) G. dux Norm[annorum] et comes Andeg[avorum] episcopo Constantinensi et iusticiis et vicecomitibus et baronibus Constantini salutem. Precipio et volo quod monachi Sancti Martini Maiorismonasterii de Heavilla teneant omnes terras et ecclesias et decimas et omnes res suas que pertinent ad elemosinam meam de Heavilla ita bene et in pace et honorifice et iuste et quiete sicut melius et quietius tenuerunt tempore regis H. Et nemo eis vel rebus eorum ullam iniuriam vel contumeliam faciat. Teste Thoma cancellario apud Argent[omum].[60]

The triumph of the traditions of the Anglo-Norman chancery can also be seen in documents in which no chancellor is mentioned. The following, which probably belongs to the early part of 1144, is a good example of a brevity which is literary rather than legal in its phraseology: [61]

(8) Notum sit omnibus tam futuris quam presentibus quod ego Gaufridus Andegavorum comes, Fulconis bone memorie Iherusalem regis filius, monachis Sancti Ebrulfi res eorum universas ita habendas et possidendas libere et quiete concedo et affirmo, sicut habebant in tempore regis Hainrici antecessoris mei. Et omnibus communiter ne predictos monachos de rebus suis in causam mittant precipio, insuper illis ne cum aliquo inde placitentur prohibeo, et amicis meis ubicunque fuerint, sicut me diligunt, ut eos manuteneant et ab omnibus defendant cum summa diligentia submoneo et rogo.

The next is similar, though Geoffrey is now duke: [62]

(9) Goffridus dux Normannorum et comes Andegavensium omnibus dapiferis et prepositis villicis et servientibus suis salutem. De his que pertinent ad proprium victum et vestitum monachorum Sancti Martini de Sagio et serviens eorundem monachorum proprium esse eorum affiducare poterit, nullum inde capiatis teloneum aut pedagium aut consuetudinem aliquam minimam vel magnam. Quod si feceritis meum incurretis odium et cum sexaginta solidis reddetis.

[59] Copy by Gaignières in MS. Lat. 17031, p. 137.

[60] *Vidimus* of 1524 after sealed original, " fort consumé en queue simple," in Bibliothèque Nationale, Collection de Touraine, xxxi. 57, no. 8. Cf. *A. H. R.*, xx. 29; Delisle-Berger, no. 29*.

[61] Cartulary of Saint-Évroul, MS. Lat. 11056, no. 681; Round, *Calendar*, no. 637. In the absence of place and witnesses this charter presents some curious features. Geoffrey speaks as successor of Henry I, yet he has not taken the ducal title. The news of Fulk's death, which occurred 10 November 1143 (R. Röhricht, *Geschichte des Königreichs Jerusalem*, p. 229), could hardly have reached his son before the capitulation of Rouen, where Geoffrey remained until his assumption of the ducal title; yet a charter issued at Rouen in such an alien style is rather surprising.

[62] Copy from *Livre rouge* of Séez, in MS. Fr. 18953, pp. 37, 222.

In the following charter the same matter is thrown into the legal language of Henry I's time; indeed, except for the insertion of *sicut mee res proprie*, it reproduces exactly the terms of a writ of Henry for the same monastery: [63]

(10) G. dux Norm[annorum] comes And[egavorum] baronibus et omnibus vic[ecomitibus] et ministris tocius Anglie et Normannie et portuum maris salutem. Precipio quod totum corrodium et omnes res monachorum de abbatia de Vinaz quas servientes eorum affidare poterint pertinere suo dominico victui et vestitui sint in pace et quiete de theloneo et passagio et omnibus consuetudinibus sicut mee res proprie. Et super hoc prohibeo quod nullus eos disturbet iniuste super .x. libras forisfacture. Testibus comite de Pontevio et Alexandro de Bohun et Roberto de Noburg' (*sic*), apud Argentomum.

The following is parallel, but contains a further provision: [64]

(11) G. dux Normannorum et comes Andegav[orum] omnibus baronibus et fidelibus suis et ministris totius Normannie et Cenomannie et portuum maris salutem. Precipio quod totum corredium abbatis de Savign[eio] et monachorum suorum et abbatum qui sunt de obediencia Savign[eii] et omnes res quas ministri sui affidare poterunt esse suas sint quiete de theloneo et passagio et omni consuetudine ubicunque venerint, et prohibeo ne ullus eos super hac re disturbet super decem libras forisfacture. Precipio etiam quod monachi Savigneii totam terram suam et homines et omnes res suas in firma pace teneant et non inde placitent, quia terra et omnes res eorum in mea custodia et defensione sunt et nolo quod aliquis eis inde contumeliam faciat neque de aliqua re eos inquietare presumat.

Teste (*sic*) Guidone de Sabl[olio] et Alexandro de Bohun, apud Argentomagum.

Another writ of a well known type is: [65]

(12) G. dux Norm[annorum] et com[es] And[egavorum] vicec[omitibus] Roth[omagensibus] sal[utem]. Precipio quod tradatis leprosis Roth[omagensibus] xl. sol[idos] Roth[omagensium] singulis mensibus sicut rex .H. eis dedit et carta eius testatur.

T[este] Rob[erto] de Novo burgo, apud Roth[omagu]m.

[63] Cartulary of Saint-André-en-Gouffern, in Archives of the Calvados, f. 22v, no. 90; no. 72 is the writ of Henry I. Note that Geoffrey has even let *Anglie* stand. This type of writ is familiar in England; see, for example, J. Armitage Robinson, *Gilbert Crispin*, p. 150, no. 34. For a quite different Angevin form see *Cartulaire de Tiron*, i. 63.

[64] Copy of 1237 under seal of William, bishop of Avranches, in Archives of the Manche, *fonds* Savigny.

[65] Original, with fragment of *simple queue*, in Archives Nationales, K 23, 15²². See the facsimile, Plate 7a. Printed in Delisle, *Henri II*, p. 136; Langlois, *Histoire*

Further illustration is unnecessary. We recognize not only the sobriety, conciseness, and clearness which Delisle notes as the characteristics of the Anglo-Norman chancery,[66] but also its regular terminology, such as the address, the *nisi feceris* clause,[67] *sicut umquam melius habuit, ne inde amplius clamorem audiam, ita bene,* etc., and the ten pounds' penalty for infringement.[68] In all essential matters Geoffrey's ducal chancery was a Norman institution, and, what is more important, it was an instrument for maintaining the rights which his predecessors had granted and the administration through which they had governed.

Since few of Geoffrey's charters are dated, it is impossible to construct an itinerary or form any estimate of the distribution of his time between Normandy and Anjou. He visited Normandy every year of his reign as duke,[69] but, apart from his sojourns at Rouen and Argentan and an occasional military expedition, the only places at which he can be traced are Bayeux, Bec, Lisieux, and Saint-Lô. By far the greater number of his charters are issued from Rouen, which seems to have acquired new importance as the capital of the duchy. Geoffrey rebuilt the tower and the

---

du prieuré du Mont-aux-Malades-lès-Rouen, p. 397; calendared in Tardif, *Monuments historiques,* no. 516.

[66] *Henri II,* pp. 240–246.

[67] *Livre noir,* no. 24.

[68] A further indication of Norman influence is seen in Geoffrey's second seal, where he takes the title of ' dux Normannorum ' and carries still further the imitation of the Norman type which his father had begun. Only one original of this seal is known to exist (see the facsimile, Plate 7b), attached to a charter for Bec, printed above (no. 2), and described by Demay, *Inventaire des sceaux de la Normandie,* no. 20; but there are also certain drawings (Delisle, *Henri II,* p. 138 f.). On the introduction of the Norman type into Anjou, see G. de Manteyer, *Le sceau-matrice du comte d'Anjou Foulques le Jeune,* in *Mémoires des Antiquaires de France,* lx. 305–338; on the distinction between the ' sigillum ducatus ' and the ' sigillum comitatus,' the *Cartulaire de S.-Laud d'Angers,* no. 83; cf. *Cartulaire de S.-Aubin,* ii. 112.

[69] In 1145 he is at Arques and Rouen (Robert of Torigni, i. 237, 239); in 1146 at Rouen (*ibid.,* i. 242) and Courcy-sur-Dive (charter for Cormery given ' in presentiam meam apud Curciacum super Divam in exercitu meo . . . anno Domini millesimo centesimo quadragesimo sexto regnante Ludovico rege Francorum qui tunc crucem Domini assumpserat ': Bibliothèque Nationale, Collection Housseau, v, no. 1718); in 1147 at Argentan (*Livre noir,* no. 100) and 11 October at Rouen (Round, no. 1405); in 1148 at Fauguernon, near Lisieux (Robert of Torigni, i. 247); 27 March 1149 at Bec (*supra,* no. 2).

bridge over the Seine,[70] and after Rouen became the abode of the empress in 1148[71] a local poet did not hesitate to compare to imperial Rome the ancient and noble city which resembled it so closely in name and claimed Julius Caesar for its founder.[72] To Geoffrey Rouen owed a detailed and comprehensive charter, the earliest of the city's surviving muniments,[73] which restored to the citizens the privileges which they had enjoyed under Henry I, safeguarded particularly their jurisdictional and fiscal immunities, confirmed the gild organization, as represented in the merchant and cordwainers' gilds,[74] and guaranteed the rights of Rouen merchants in England and their monopoly of the commerce of the Seine and the Irish trade of Normandy. Rouen had no rival in political or commercial importance, nor can much trace of municipal life be discovered elsewhere in the duchy during this reign. Verneuil and Nonancourt on the southern border seem to have

[70] Robert of Torigni, i. 239, 242, 368. Cf. A. Deville, *Recherches sur l'ancien pont de Rouen*, in *Précis des travaux de l'Académie de Rouen*, 1831, pp. 171–173.

[71] *Supra*, note 34. Most of Matilda's Norman charters are dated at Rouen or Le Pré: Delisle, *Henri II*, p. 142 f., nos. 6–13; Round, nos. 263, 679 f., 683.

[72]　　　　　' Rothoma nobilis, urbs antiqua, potens, speciosa,
　　　　　Gens Normanna sibi te preposuit dominari;
　　　　　Imperialis honorificentia te super ornat;
　　　　　Tu Rome similis tam nomine quam probitate,
　　　　　Rothoma, si mediam removes, et Roma vocaris.
　　　　　Viribus acta tuis devicta Britannia servit;
　　　　　Et tumor Anglicus et Scotus algidus et Galo sevus
　　　　　Munia protensis manibus tibi debita solvunt.
　　　　　Sub duce Gaufredo cadit hostis et arma quiescunt,
　　　　　Nominis ore sui Gaufredus gaudia fert dux;
　　　　　Rothoma letaris sub tanto principe felix.'

The remaining nine lines are a eulogy of King Roger of Sicily (cf. *E. H. R.*, xxvi. 435): MS. Fr. 2623, f. 114v, printed in C. Richard, *Notice sur l'ancienne Bibliothèque des Échevins de Rouen* (Rouen, 1845), p. 37. ' Imperialis honorificentia ' is, of course, an allusion to the coming of the empress. For the tradition respecting Caesar, see Ordericus, ii. 324, where its size and prosperity are also spoken of.

[73] Chéruel, *Histoire de Rouen*, i. 241; Round, *Calendar*, no. 109; Delisle-Berger, no. 14*. Cf. A. Giry, *Établissements de Rouen*, i. 25–27.

[74] The privileges of the cordwainers are contained in a special charter: *Ordonnances des Rois*, v. 416; *supra*, p. 134. See the similar charters of Henry I, Stephen, and Henry II in La Roque, iii. 149 (cf. Round, no. 107; Delisle-Berger, no. 16*), where the charter of Stephen, found in his name in MS. Lat. 9067, f. 155, is wrongly attributed to William the Conqueror.

continued something of the prosperity which they owed to the fostering care of Henry I,[75] but it is perhaps significant that Geoffrey's charters make no mention of Caen or of its religious establishments, and the fortunes of both Caen and Dieppe waited upon the reëstablishment of close relations with England under his son.[76] Charters and chroniclers are also silent in Geoffrey's reign respecting another phase of local life, namely castle-building, which had been a traditional practice of the Angevin counts at home and played a prominent part in the Norman policy of Henry I and Henry II.[77]

On his visits to Normandy Geoffrey was often accompanied by Angevin barons, such as the seneschal Joslin of Tours and his brother Pippin, Geoffrey de Cleers, and Payne of Clairvaux; but he had also an important Norman following. His most frequent attendants were the seneschal Reginald of Saint-Valery, Robert de Neufbourg, Robert de Courcy, William de Vernon, Guy de Sablé, Alexander and Enjuger de Bohun, Osbert de Cailli, Richard de la Haie, and Enguerran de Vascoeuil. The attestations of the great men of the duchy, such as the counts of Meulan, Roumare, and Ponthieu, appear more rarely, while the subscriptions of the bishops occur only in occasional documents dated at Rouen,[78] where they doubtless attended the more formal meetings of the court, although they played no regular part in the ducal administration. The appearance of Norman barons with Geoffrey in Anjou [79] likewise goes to show that there was no mechanical separation between his two groups of followers; but the regular officers of government were quite distinct in Normandy from

[75] See Henry's charter to Verneuil in *Ordonnances des Rois*, iv. 638; and the documents mentioning these towns in Le Prévost, *Eure*, ii. 476 f., 488, iii. 345, 347; Round, nos. 282 f., 287, 292 f. For Geoffrey's reign see *supra*, no. 6; and Ordericus, v. 132, where the *conventus* of Verneuil in 1141 is estimated at 13,000 men.

[76] For Dieppe under Geoffrey see below, note 97; and Round, nos. 109, 170, 1057 f. The growth of the town under Henry II is seen in the various grants of houses to the king's officers preserved in the *Coutumier de Dieppe* (Archives of the Seine-Inférieure, G. 851): Delisle-Berger, nos. 115, 398, 709, 713, 719.

[77] For the Norman castles of the twelfth century see Powicke, *The Loss of Normandy*, ch. vii.

[78] *Livre noir*, nos. 17, 19; Round, no. 126; Delisle-Berger, no. 8*; *infra*, no. 13.

[79] *Supra*, no. 3; *Cartulaire de S.-Ymer*, p. 7; Round, no. 1058.

those in his other possessions, in which indeed there does not seem to have been entire unity of organization.[80]

It was in this nucleus of administrative officers that the breach of continuity created by time and civil war between the *curia* of Henry I and that of his son-in-law was most serious, yet it is significant that the new recruits came from Normandy and not from Anjou. The change was most marked on the ecclesiastical side, for Henry's justiciar, John of Lisieux, had died in 1141, and Archbishop Hugh and the bishop of Coutances were the only prelates who survived from Henry's time. The bishops had taken Stephen's part; Philip of Bayeux, the most experienced of them in public affairs, had even been his chancellor;[81] and it was not to be expected that Geoffrey would turn to them for confidential advice or place one of them at the head of his administration. Under these circumstances the suppression of the justiciarship was natural, particularly as no such office existed in Anjou. The principal seneschal of Henry I, Robert de la Haie, was also dead,[82] and his son Richard had held Cherbourg for Stephen;[83] so that this dignity fell to a new man, Reginald of Saint-Valery,[84] under whom it seems to have gained something of the relatively greater importance which, in the absence of a justiciar, it had come to possess in Anjou.[85] We hear very little of the other seneschals, although Robert de Courcy, *dapifer* under Henry I, has the same

[80] What has been said above of the chancellors can hardly be considered an exception to the distinctness of Normandy. For Geoffrey's other dominions note the mention of Hugh and Geoffrey de Cleers as seneschals besides Joslin of Tours in Marchegay, *Chroniques des églises d'Anjou*, p. 88 (cf. the documents cited in Delisle, *Henri II*, p. 387 f.); and also the special officers for Maine who appear in a charter given at Le Mans in 1146 (*B. É. C.*, xxxvi. 433).

[81] *Register of St. Osmund*, i. 191 f.; *Calendar of Charter Rolls*, v. 17, no. 8. For Philip's biography see Bourrienne's articles in *Revue catholique de Normandie*, xviii ff.

[82] On his place under Henry I, see *supra*, p. 99. He disappears after Henry's time.

[83] John of Marmoutier, ed. Marchegay, pp. 299–301, ed. Halphen and Poupardin, p. 229 f. If, as John says, Richard was carried off by pirates, he would seem to have returned to Normandy, where he holds an important position under Geoffrey and Henry II. There may, of course, have been two barons of this name; the seneschal, (*infra*, note 88) was a son-in-law of William de Vernon (Stapleton, i, p. cxlv).

[84] On Reginald see Delisle, p. 421.

[85] On the seneschal in Anjou see Beautemps-Beaupré, *Coutumes*, part ii, i, chs. 8, 10; and cf. Powicke, *E. H. R.*, xxi. 649; *Loss of Normandy*, p. 38.

title in one of Geoffrey's charters; [86] and while I have not found the title applied to him before Henry II's reign, I believe that Robert de Neufbourg, whose signature regularly precedes that of Robert de Courcy in the charters,[87] must also have been *dapifer* under Geoffrey before he became chief seneschal under Henry II. The same title may have been restored to Richard de la Haie, who uses it in 1152.[88]

Of actual meetings of the *curia* we have few notices, and these are concerned entirely with its judicial decisions. It was in Geoffrey's court that Philip of Bayeux established his rights over Ducy and Louvières [89] and released to the abbey of Savigny his claim to land in Escures; [90] here also the abbot of Fécamp won

[86] *Livre noir*, no. 19. Robert de Courcy, who was in Normandy in 1138, when he befriended Geoffrey (Ordericus, v. 109), in 1141 (Tardif, *Très Ancien Coutumier*, p. 117; cf. Round, *Calendar*, no. 1198), and in 1145 (*B. É. C.*, xxi. 127, 131), may not be identical with the Robert de Courcy who as *dapifer* attests charters of the empress in 1142 (Round, *Geoffrey de Mandeville*, pp. 170, 183). The Courcy genealogy needs clearing up; see Tardif, *l. c.*; Delisle, p. 440.

[87] *Livre noir*, no. 39; Round, *Calendar*, no. 170; *Neustria Pia*, p. 15; *infra*, Chapter VI, note 95; cf. Delisle-Berger, no. 8*; and the charter for Bec, *supra*, no. 2. Robert de Neufbourg was one of the early partisans of Geoffrey: Ordericus, v. 68. On his position under Henry II see Delisle, pp. 445–447.

[88] See his charters in the Archives of the Manche, H. 4622, 5130; and cf. H. 692. Stapleton, i, p. xxxiv, note, says he was *dapifer* under Geoffrey, but cites no evidence.

[89] ' Quas in curia nobilis memorie Gaufridi quondam Normannie ducis per iudicium obtinuisti ': *Livre noir*, no. 156.

[90] ' H. Dei gratia Rothomagensi archiepiscopo totique capitulo Rothomagensis ecclesię G. Andeg[avorum] comes salutem et dilectionem. Notum sit vobis atque omnibus hominibus tam presentibus quam futuris quod Philipus Baiocensis episcopus in pace dimisit et quietam clamavit terram de Escuris quam ipse adversum monachos Saviniacenses calumpniabatur et quam monachi in tempore regis H. et duorum Baiocensium episcoporum predecessorum eius libere et quiete tenuerant. Illam autem terram dimisit eis quietam et liberam ipse Ph. Baiocensis episcopus in presentia Guillelmi Cenomannensis episcopi et mea aput Cenomannos, presente Raginaldo de Sancto Walerico et Guidone de Sabl[eio] et Gofferio de Brueria atque plurimis aliis. Quare vobis mando ac vos diligenter deprecor ut si Baiocensis episcopus vel aliquis alius super hoc reclamare aut terram calumpniari presumeret, monachi prefati vestram protectionem atque adiutorium inde haberent. Testibus Gaufredo de Claris Vallibus et Guillelmo de Botevilla et magistro Hugone decano Sancti Martini, apud Mosterol[ium].' Original, with *double queue*, in Archives Nationales, L. 969; cartulary of Savigny, in Archives of the Manche, no. 201; Round, no. 809, where the place and witnesses are omitted and Geoffrey's title is arbitrarily altered by the insertion of ' duke of the Normans.' For the date see above, note 26. Another account of the transaction, showing that Hugh de Cleers

control of the port against the townsmen,[91] and the canons of
Rouen established their privileges in the forest of Aliermont.[92] In
these instances the duke appears to have been himself present; [93]
but the *curia* at Rouen, which effected a compromise between the
abbot of Préaux and Enguerran de Vascoeuil, was composed of
iudices, baillivi, and *proceres* under the presidency of Reginald of
Saint-Valery as *dapifer Normannie*,[94] Possibly Angevin precedents may have done something to develop the seneschal's importance on such occasions, but as an itinerant justice he is in no
way distinguished from his associates. As under Henry I,[95] the
judicial authority of the duke seems to have been exercised chiefly
by travelling justices who acted under his writs. Such officers are
constantly found in the inquests held on behalf of the bishop
of Bayeux, specific mention being made of Reginald of Saint-
Valery, Robert de Neufbourg, Robert de Courcy, William de
Vernon, Richard de la Haie, Guy de Sablé, Enjuger de Bohun, and
Galeran, count of Meulan.[96] Certain of these reappear in the same
capacity in other parts of Normandy: Robert de Neufbourg and

was also among those present, is given in the following letter of William, bishop of
Le Mans: ' H. Dei gratia Rotomagensis ecclesie archiepiscopo totique eiusdem
ecclesie capitulo G. eadem gratia humilis Cenomannensis episcopus per bona tem-
poralia immarcescibilis vite coronam feliciter attingere. Discretioni vestre notum
fieri volumus quod Philippus Baiocensis ecclesie episcopus terram de Escuris, quam
abbati et monachis de Savinneio calumpniabatur et quam predictus abbas et monachi solute et quiete in tempore duorum episcoporum predecessorum suorum et
Henrici regis tenuerant, in presentia nostra et domini Gofredi Normannorum
ducis et Andegavorum comitis et Guidonis de Sabloñ et Raginaldi de Sancto
Galerico et Goferii de Brueria et Hugonis de Cleriis et aliorum multorum in pace
dimisit. Hoc ideo vobis scripsimus quod si prefatus episcopus vel aliquis alius
erga ecclesiam Savinneii insurrexerit, prescripte ecclesie, sicut decet sanctos, ius
suum defendatis.' Original in MS. Lat. 9215, Savigny, no. 1; cartulary, no. 202;
omitted by L. Celier, in his *Catalogue des actes des évêques du Mans* (Paris, 1910);
cf. Auvry, *Histoire de la congrégation de Savigny*, iii. 44.

[91] ' Sicut eum disrationavit in curia patris mei et postea in curia mea' : charter
of Henry II, Delisle-Berger, no. 120; Round, no. 132.

[92] Valin, p. 266; Delisle-Berger, no. 39*; cf. *supra*, p. 134.

[93] Pleas ' ante ducem Normannorum ' are mentioned in the charter to Rouen
(Delisle-Berger, no. 14*). In the eulogy of Geoffrey by Étienne de Rouen his justice
is especially praised: *Chroniques des comtes d'Anjou*, ed. Marchegay, p. 313; Howlett, *Chronicles of Stephen*, ii. 772.

[94] Valin, p. 265.   [95] *Supra*, Chapter III.

[96] *Livre noir*, nos. 17, 19, 24, 25, 39, 43, 44, 89, 90.

William de Vernon at Arques and Dieppe; [97] Guy de Sablé, this time with William Lovel, at Verneuil and Nonancourt.[98] In the Cotentin we read of an inquest held at the duke's assize (*in assisia mea*) at Valognes; no justice is mentioned, but four who are otherwise known to have exercised such functions witness the charter of Geoffrey which declares the result.[99] Evidently the system extended throughout the duchy; evidently also the justices were chosen from the principal lay members of the *curia*, without recourse to the clergy.

The problem of chief interest in connection with Geoffrey's justices is their administration of the sworn inquest in the determination of disputes concerning land, a question which need not here be treated at length, as we shall have occasion to discuss it with some fullness later.[100] The evidence comes for the most part from the *Livre noir* of Bayeux and is connected with the active efforts of the bishop, Philip d'Harcourt, for the recovery of his property in the years immediately following the Angevin conquest. For his benefit Geoffrey provided for a general recognition of the demesne, fiefs, and other rights of the see, as well as for the determination by inquest of neighbors of disputes between the bishop and any of his tenants, and he added special writs to individual justices with reference to particular estates and feudal holdings. The facts were determined by the oath of lawful men of the vicinage, and each of the justices in charge made a written return to the duke, four such returns having survived as detailed evidence of the procedure employed. The sworn recognition was also used under Geoffrey to determine the rights of the bishop of Coutances over Tourlaville [101] and those of the chapter of Rouen in the forest of Aliermont; [102] and its diffusion is further shown by

[97] *E. H. R.*, xxvii. 438, note 97; Lot, *S.-Wandrille*, no. 119. Reginald of Saint-Valery was also concerned with Dieppe, where he held the revenues of the port: Round, nos. 1057 f.

[98] *Supra*, no. 6. In the region of Argentan Fulk d'Aunou and Robert de Neuville seem to have been justices: Delisle, *Cartulaire normand*, no. 4, p. 273.

[99] William de Vernon, Enjuger de Bohun, Robert de Neufbourg, and Robert de Courcy: *infra*, Chapter VI, note 95.

[100] *Infra*, Chapter VI.

[101] *Infra*, Chapter VI, note 95.

[102] Delisle-Berger, no. 39*. On the attribution to Geoffrey see above, p. 134.

the practice of submitting the question of a champion's professionalism to the oath of ten citizens of Rouen selected by the
duke's justice,[103] and by a case in the baronial court of the count
of Meulan where the parties put themselves on the verdict of
eight lawful knights.[104] The sworn inquest was nothing new in
Normandy, having been prescribed by Henry I in 1133 to determine the possessions of the bishop of Bayeux,[105] and in employ-
ing it again for the bishop's benefit Geoffrey expressly states that
he is following in Henry's footsteps.[106] It was obviously a Norman, not an Angevin institution. The evidence for its use under
Geoffrey, however, is much more abundant than under the previous Norman dukes, and two writs of his directing his justices to
cause lands of the bishop of Bayeux to be recognized *secundum
assisiam meam* led Brunner to conclude that the duke, whom he
supposed to be Henry II, was here citing a general ordinance
which introduced this procedure as a regular method of trial in
cases concerning land.   No other mention of such an assize has
been found in Geoffrey's reign, and it is possible to interpret the
phrase in other ways; but the reappearance of these words in the
early years of Henry II, along with clear evidence of the use
of the recognition as a remedy regularly open to ordinary litigants, adds weight to Brunner's conclusion.   On the whole, it
seems probable that the regularization and extension of this
form of procedure, which are well attested by 1159, had already
begun under Geoffrey and had perhaps been formulated by him
in some specific document now lost.[107]

Next to the justices, who may be considered as both central and
local officers, came the *vicomtes*, who had since the eleventh century been the principal agents of local administration, charged
with the general oversight of the *vicomté*, and particularly with the

[103] Delisle-Berger, no. 14*.

[104] Valin, pp. 201, 264; Chapter VI, note 128.

[105] *Supra*, Chapter I, p. 15.

[106] ' Vestigiis regis Henrici inherentes qui hoc idem iuramento antiquorum hominum fecerat recognosci. . . . Iuramentum quod rex Henricus fieri fecerat ratum
esse volentes, iuramento eorundem qui tempore regis Henrici iuraverunt et aliorum
recognosci fecimus iura, possessiones, consuetudines, libertates quas ecclesia Baiocensis tempore Odonis episcopi habuerat et habere debebat.' *Livre noir*, no. 39.

[107] See the discussion of this evidence in Chapter VI.

collection of the duke's revenues and the payment of the farm at which their district was let.[108] These fiscal arrangements, which also covered the parallel but inferior jurisdiction of the *prévôts*, show remarkable fixity from the time of William the Conqueror to that of Henry II,[109] and it is not surprising that Geoffrey sought to reëstablish and maintain them, especially since his resources had been diminished by the extensive grants from the ducal demesne which he had been obliged to make as the price of the barons' support.[110] He is careful that the bishop of Évreux shall have his tenths from the farm of Verneuil and Nonancourt,[111] the nuns of Saint-Amand their tithes in the forests of Eaui and Aliermont,[112] the monks of Saint-Wandrille their ancient rights in his rents at Arques and Dieppe, in the proceeds of the fair at Caen, and in the toll of Rouen, Exmes, Falaise, and Argentan.[113] We have the actual writ ordering the *vicomte* of Rouen to pay the lepers of the city the forty shillings monthly which King Henry had given them,[114] and the charter to the citizens of Rouen shows the duke's officers collecting the tolls and customs and wine-dues which are mentioned in the documents of his predecessors.[115] While, however, the *vicomtes* and *prévôts* continued to account to the Exchequer ' for the issues of their more ancient jurisdictions,' the Angevin dukes superimposed upon the local government of Normandy the new area of the *bailliage*.[116] It is not likely that under Geoffrey this new unit acquired any such importance as it possesses in the military returns of 1172; yet the

[108] Stapleton, i, pp. xxxiv–xxxvi, lxi; Delisle, in *B. É. C.*, x. 264 f.; id., *Henri II*, pp. 212–218; *supra*, p. 46 f.

[109] *Supra*, pp. 42–44, 105 f. [111] *Supra*, no. 6.

[110] Robert of Torigni, i. 267. [112] No. 7.

[113] Lot, *S.-Wandrille*, nos. 78, 119. Another example of the continuity of the fiscal system is seen in the empress's grant to Saint-André-en-Gouffern (1151–1154) of 46s. 6d., which had been paid annually to the *vicomte* of Argentan for the *gravaria* of Montgaroult: Round, no. 593; Delisle, p. 142, no. 10.

[114] *Supra*, no. 12. Cf. the charters of the empress and Henry for Le Grand-Beaulieu: Delisle, p. 126; Delisle-Berger, nos. 11*, 45*.

[115] Round, no. 109. On the dues collected at Rouen under the Norman dukes see Charles de Beaurepaire, *La Vicomté de l'Eau de Rouen* (Évreux, 1856), pp. 2, 18–20, 40–52.

[116] Stapleton, i, p. xxxiii f.; *B. É. C.*, x. 259 f.; Powicke, *E. H. R.*, xxii. 22 f.; and, more fully, in his *Loss of Normandy*, pp. 71–73, 103–116.

name *bailia,* probably in the more general sense of an officer's district, occurs first in his reign,[117] and the *baillivi* make their appearance in his charters, where, however, the term, like the more common *ministri,* may have been applied collectively to all below the rank of *vicomte.*[118] We meet also with the duke's constable at Cherbourg,[119] the wardens of his forest of Argentan,[120] his goldsmith at Arques,[121] and his moneyer at Verneuil or Nonancourt,[122] as well as a group of *servientes* — a loose term which in one instance describes those who exercise the duke's authority on the lands of the bishop of Bayeux,[123] and in another denotes the serjeants of Rouen whose offices the charter of the city promises to restore.[124] One hereditary serjeanty of this sort, that of Henry the marshal in Rouen and its *banlieue,* is known in its curious privileges from the document, preserved in a corrupt form, by which Geoffrey conferred it:[125]

(13) G. dux Normenn[orum et] comes Andeg[avorum] . . archiepiscopo Rothomagensi et omnibus episcopis Normennie et comitibus[126] et iusticiis suis salutem.   Noveritis quod ego dedi et concessi Henrico le Mareschal

---

[117] *Livre noir,* no. 24.   Cf. no. 40, issued shortly after Geoffrey's death; and Stapleton, i, p. xxxiv.

[118] *Livre noir,* no. 16; *Neustria Pia,* p. 15; Valin, p. 265; *supra,* nos. 5, 10, 11. Cf. Delisle, pp. 207, 219.

[119] Delisle, pp. 142 f., 409, 513, no. 84*, facsimile, pl. i.   This is a writ of the empress, probably issued between 1151 and 1154, but the constable in question, Osbert de la Heuse, was a companion of Geoffrey (John of Marmoutier, ed. Halphen and Poupardin, p. 174), and had doubtless been placed by him in charge of Cherbourg.

[120] Delisle, *Cartulaire normand,* no. 4.

[121] Charter of Henry II granting 'Waltero cambiatori aurifabro et heredibus suis totam terram Roberti cambiatoris patris sui sitam apud Archas quietam et liberam et totum cambium et totam aurifabricaturam toscius castellarie Archarum et tocius Deppe . . . preterea . . . omnes consuetudines et quittancias et libertates quas pater meus G. comes Andegavorum dedit et concessit Roberto patri suo et carta confirmavit.'   Archives of the Seine-Inférieure, G. 851, f. 55v.; MS. Lat. 9209, Rouen, no. 2; Delisle, *Henri II,* no. 527; Delisle-Berger, no. 719.

[122] *Supra,* no. 6, reading ' Gisleberto nummario.'

[123] *Livre noir,* no. 16.   The general meaning is also found in nos. 3 and 9, *supra.*

[124] Delisle-Berger, no. 14*, where the ' proprium marescallum civitatis ' is also mentioned.

[125] Archives Nationales, JJ. 72, no. 191, based on a *vidimus* of Philip V in 1318. The charter is probably anterior to 1147, as it is witnessed by the count of Meulan. For other serjeanties connected with Rouen under Henry I and Henry II see Chapter III, notes 156–158, and Chapter V, notes 145–147.

[126] MS. *communibus.*

servienti meo sergenteriam de bagnileuca Rothomagensi sicut se proportat de feodo de Pratellis et de feodo de Cailliaco, et dedi eidem Henrico et suis heredibus sergenteriam de Cailliaco sicut se proportat in longum et in latum et sicut extendit de feodo de Cailliaco et de feudo de Pratellis et de feodo de Feritate usque ad partes de Gournayo, et omnia alia ad placitum spate pertinencia, tenenda et habenda dicto Henrico le Mareschal et suis heredibus bene et in pace servientium (*sic*) faciendo. Et volo et concedo quod dictus Henricus le Mareschal et eius heredes habeant omnes robas tallatas omniaque superlectillia et omnia vasa nisi fuerint argentea et aurata, et carnes baconum nisi bacones fuerint integri, et dolium nisi plenum sit vini, videlicet eorum et earum que membra sua forefacient, et de domibus que cremabuntur forefactura que eidem Henricus et eius heredes habeant tantum quantum poterunt sursum percutere de moura [127] spate sue si eques fuerint ignem deffendendo. Volo etiam et concedo quod eidem Henricus et eius heredes habeant suum hardere et suum edificare in foresta mea de Tisone et pasturagia ab omnibus libera et quieta. Et quia volo quod omnia et singula predicta dicto Henrico et eius heredibus rata et stabilia in perpetuum teneantur, hanc presentem cartam munimine sigilli mei confirmavi.

Testibus Hugone Rothomagensi archiepiscopo, Ern[ulfo] Luxoviensi episcopo, Philippo Baiocenso episcopo, Galerano comite Mellendi, Reginaldo de Sancto Walerico, Rogero de Claris vallis (*sic*), Gaufredo de Cleres, apud Rothomagum.

Respecting Geoffrey's policy toward the Norman church, there is little to add to what Böhmer has said on the subject.[128] On three occasions during his reign the effort was made to exercise freedom of election in place of the practice of ducal appointment which had prevailed under Henry I and even under Stephen; but while in each case Geoffrey ended by accepting the candidate so chosen, he asserted his authority with a vigor which left his real control undiminished. He held the property of the see against Arnulf of Lisieux for two years and three months, and restored it then only after the exaction of a heavy payment; Gerard of Séez, elected under questionable circumstances about the beginning of 1144, suffered at the hands of Geoffrey's followers acts of violence which were subsequently compared to the murder of Becket,[129] and was not reconciled to the duke until Easter 1147; the abbot whom monks and pope set over the monastery of Mont-Saint-Michel was compelled to purchase his peace with the duke at a

---

[127] I. e., the blade: Old French *moure, meure* (Godefroy).
[128] *Kirche und Staat in England und in der Normandie*, pp. 310–325.
[129] Giraldus Cambrensis, viii. 301.

price which left his house under a heavy burden of debt.[130] Contests such as these, as well as the long adherence of the prelates to Stephen's cause, make it plain why the bishops play so little part in the secular affairs of the duchy during Geoffrey's reign, the only notable exception being the use of Arnulf of Lisieux as intermediary in the difficulties of 1150 with Louis VII.[131] Apart, however, from the energetic assertion of his claims during vacancies, when he doubtless did much to earn Saint Bernard's characterization of *malleus bonorum, oppressor pacis et libertatis ecclesie*,[132] Geoffrey can hardly be accused of injustice in his dealings with the Norman church. If the case of Bayeux may be taken as an example, we find him placing the full machinery of judicial administration at the bishop's disposal for the recovery of rights and property which had been lost during the anarchy and earlier,[133] and it is significant, in contrast with conditions in Anjou,[134] that no complaints of Geoffrey's exactions in Normandy meet us at the outset of the succeeding reign. It was in accord with the tendencies of the age that the Norman church should in Geoffrey's time be drawn into closer relations with Rome and with the rest of northern France, but it is noteworthy that he did not permit Eugene III or his legates to enter his dominions; [135] and, with due allowance for the inevitable growth of curial influence and of solidarity within the church in this period, it would seem that the ducal prerogative was handed on unimpaired to his successor.

[130] Annals of Mont-Saint-Michel, in Labbe, *Nova Bibliotheca* (1657), i. 352.

[131] *H. F.*, xv. 521; *Oeuvres de Suger*, ed. Lecoy de la Marche, p. 267.

[132] *Epistolae*, no. 348, in Migne, clxxxii. 553. So Peter of Cluny says: ' totius ecclesie Dei que in partibus illis est hostis comes Andegavorum audiatur.' *H. F.*, xv. 637.

[133] *Infra*, pp. 204-212; *Revue catholique de Normandie*, xix. 167-172, 266-272, 295-301. Observe also the enforcement of the fine of £9 for breach of the bishop's peace: *supra*, no. 6.

[134] See the charters of Henry II for Saint-Florent and Fontevrault, in Delisle-Berger, nos. 22*, 27*, 30*.

[135] ' Certus erat se Romanam ecclesiam offendisse, quod nec domnum papam nec aliquem legatum passus erat ingredi terram suam: ' John of Salisbury, *Historia Pontificalis*, in *M. G. H., Scriptores*, xx. 531. Böhmer overlooks this passage. The mission of the legates Alberic and Imarus, upon which he bases his statement that legatine authority was freely exercised in Normandy, belongs to 1144 and hence can hardly be considered typical. *Gallia Christiana*, xi. instr. 80; *Livre noir*, no. 58; *H. F.*, xv. 696 f.

So far as this investigation furnishes an answer to the question with which we started, it is that in his administration of Normandy Geoffrey continued the institutions and the policy of Henry I. The judicial and fiscal system and the organs of local government remain as before, with no trace of Angevin admixture. The personnel of the *curia* undergoes some change, and the seneschal perhaps acquires somewhat greater importance; but if the justiciar disappears, it is only to reëmerge under Henry II, and the department which stands in the most intimate relation to the new ruler, the chancery, is Normanized even to its smallest phrases. Where, as in the case of the sworn inquest, some development appears probable, it roots in the practice of Henry I's reign and follows no discoverable Angevin precedents, nor do we find in Normandy that direct and personal rule which is so characteristic of the government of the counts of Anjou. All the evidence goes to show that Geoffrey observed for himself the policy which at the close of his life he laid down for his son, that of avoiding the transfer of customs or institutions from one part of his dominions to another.[136] How far this advice was followed by Henry II is a problem for the next chapter.

[136] ' Terre vero sue et genti spiritu presago in posterum previdens, Henrico heredi suo interdixit ne Normannie vel Anglie consuetudines in consulatus sui terram, vel e converso, varie vicissitudinis alternatione permutaret: ' John of Marmoutier, ed. Marchegay, p. 292; ed. Halphen and Poupardin, p. 224.

CHAPTER V

THE GOVERNMENT OF NORMANDY UNDER HENRY II[1]

IN the great Plantagenet empire of the twelfth century Normandy held the central place, mediating historically, as well as geographically, between the England which it had conquered a century earlier and the Angevin and Aquitanian lands which shared its Frankish traditions and were beginning to feel with it the nascent centripetal power of the French monarchy. The beginnings of this empire were the result of Norman initiative, and upon Normandy fell the brunt of the attacks under which it collapsed. Yet Normandy, though central, was not dominant. It was bound to its neighbors, not merely by a personal union, but by a common imperial policy, by certain elements of a common administration, and by constant communication and interchange of officials; and it took its place by their side as a member of the strongest and most remarkable state of its time. Be our interest military or economic, ecclesiastical or constitutional, we cannot hope to understand any part of this realm without constant reference to the other parts and to the whole. What is true of the several countries is true of their sovereign. Henry II has too often been viewed merely as an English king, yet he was born and educated on the Continent, began to rule on the Continent, and spent a large part of his later life in his Continental dominions. He was, it is true, not a foreigner, as was William the Conqueror, for England had a share in forming him which it had not in the making of his great-grandfather; yet he is not, even retrospectively, a national figure, either English or French. In a later age he would have been called international, or even cosmopolitan, for he had wide-ranging tastes, and knew the languages of the world from France to Syria.[2]

[1] Revised and expanded from *A. H. R.*, xx. 24–42, 277–291 (1914–1915). A summary was read before the International Congress of Historical Studies at London in April 1913.

[2] 'Linguarum omnium que sunt a mari Gallico usque ad Iordanem habens

It is natural that Henry's reign should have been most thoroughly studied in the land where his descendants still rule, but it is significant of his wider influence that the Continental relations of his legal reforms were first clearly seen by a German jurist, and that the greatest French scholar of our time should have begun his long life of labor with a study of Henry's financial administration and closed it by dedicating to the Continental documents of his reign a masterly volume of the *Chartes et diplômes relatifs à l'histoire de France.* Where Brunner and Delisle are masters, one must perforce follow; yet this period of Norman history is not exhausted, as Powicke has recently shown us, and one may still seek to contribute a bit of new evidence or a new suggestion to the understanding of what will always be a reign of uncommon interest. In presenting the results of any such study much depends on the point of view. When the institutions of Normandy approach those of its Continental neighbors, they will impress the English student more than they impress the French, while other elements which seem familiar and hence commonplace to an English writer become highly significant when seen against a Continental background. The point of view in this chapter is English in the sense that it examines the government of Normandy under Henry II particularly for light which may be thrown upon the government of England in the same period; and, while it is based upon an independent exploration of the available evidence, it will pass lightly over institutions which, like the chancery, are already well understood, or which, like the fiscal system, are interesting chiefly by way of contrast to Continental conditions.[3] The central subject must be the courts of law.

The great obstacle to any careful study of Normandy in this period is the paucity of original information, especially as conscientiam, Latina tantum utens et Gallica,' says Walter Map, *De Nugis Curialium,* ed. M. R. James, p. 237 (ed. T. Wright, p. 227).

[3] For the fiscal system Delisle's study, *Des revenus publics en Normandie au XIIe siècle, B. É. C.,* x, xi, xiii, is still fundamental. For legal matters L. Valin, *Le duc de Normandie et sa cour,* is useful, though inadequate in its use of materials and at times too juristic. F. M. Powicke's *Loss of Normandy,* supplemented at certain points by his articles in *E. H. R.,* xxi. 635–649, xxii. 15–42, gives the best survey of the Angevin period but treats constitutional matters less fully than other aspects of the subject.

trasted with the wealth of record in contemporary England. For Henry's reign the only Norman chronicle is that of Robert of Torigni,[4] pieced out by occasional local annals and by the casual references of English writers to Norman affairs, and there is little to add in the form of letters [5] or other literary remains. Over against the splendid series of the Pipe Rolls, unbroken after 1155, Normandy can show only the Exchequer Roll of 1180 and two fragments of 1184.[6] There is no *Dialogue on the Exchequer* and no Glanvill, and the earliest customal is not earlier than 1199.[7] Henry's charters are fairly numerous, in originals, in cartulary copies, or in the *vidimus* of French kings, and an admirable basis for their study at last exists in Léopold Delisle's *Introduction*,[8] now being followed by the publication of the full texts; yet of those here collected the four hundred or more which relate to Normandy are an insignificant part of the thousands which once existed and from which it would have been possible to reconstruct the whole course of administrative and judicial procedure in the Norman state. The charters of bishops and barons and lesser persons are more numerous and offer much to reward the investigator of local and family history and of legal and economic relations, but they too often tell us what we least want to know, and the result of prolonged explorations is in many respects disappointing.

Equally fatal is the loss of Henry's Norman legislation. At best, as Maitland has reminded us,[9] his law-making was done in

---

[4] Cited from Delisle's edition (Société de l'Histoire de Normandie, Rouen, 1872–1873); Howlett's reprint in the Rolls Series (*Chronicles of Stephen*, iv) is much less useful.

[5] The letters of Arnulf of Lisieux, for example, are disappointing.

[6] Cited from the edition of Thomas Stapleton (London, 1840–1844); the second fragment of 1184 from Delisle's *Henri II*, pp. 334–344. That the Exchequer had other types of rolls appears from the notice of 1186 printed by Delisle, *Mémoires de l'Académie des Inscriptions*, xxiv, part 2, p. 353; and by Valin, p. 278.

[7] E.-J. Tardif, *Le Très Ancien Coutumier*, in his *Coutumiers de Normandie*, i (Rouen, 1881); cf. Viollet, in *Histoire littéraire de la France*, xxxiii. 43–62.

[8] *Recueil des actes de Henri II roi d' Angleterre et duc de Normandie concernant les provinces françaises et les affaires de France*, Introduction, with a fascicle of facsimiles, Paris, 1909; tome i, revised and published by Élie Berger, Paris, 1916; tome ii in press. Cf. my review, *E. H. R.*, October 1917.

[9] *History of English Law*, i. 136. On the legislation of the dukes of Normandy

an informal fashion and has left few monuments, even in England, and for Normandy the only formal ordinances that have been preserved are the levy of the Palestine tax in 1166 and the Continental prototypes of the Assize of Arms and the regulations concerning the Saladin tithe.[10] Here again time has dealt unkindly with records which are known to have existed. The Bec annalist tells of the Christmas court at Falaise in 1159, whose acts he evidently had before him in writing his provokingly meager summary,[11] and three years later we hear of a Lenten assembly at Rouen which seems to have had legislative importance.[12] There were probably, as we shall see, one or more specific assizes establishing the use of the recognition, and tenure by *parage* seems to have been introduced by a definite statute.[13] Now and then, in an age when no line was drawn between legislation and adjudication, there are instances of general enactments in the form of judicial decisions.[14]

Next to the Exchequer Rolls, the fullest information respecting Norman institutions under Henry was contained in the returns from the great general inquests ordered at different occasions in his reign. One of these, the inquest of 1172 concerning military tenures, has long been known and used, but for the others we have little more than a bare mention. In Normandy, as later in England, the new ruler began at once the gradual recovery of the lost portions of his demesne through the machinery of the sworn inquest; and we have record of such inquests held at Caen before 1154 to determine the duke's rights at Bayeux, and, then or shortly afterward, throughout the Bessin,[15] while in 1163 two of

see Tardif, *Étude sur les sources de l'ancien droit normand*, read before the Congrès du Millénaire in 1911, of which the part covering Henry II has not yet appeared. On Henry's early legislation see *infra*, Appendix I.

[10] Gervase of Canterbury, i. 198 (Delisle-Berger, no. 255); Benedict of Peterborough, i. 269, ii. 30. Cf. also the general ordinance concerning the debts of Crusaders issued at Verneuil in 1177, *ibid.*, i. 194; Delisle-Berger, no. 507.

[11] Robert of Torigni, ii. 180; cf. *infra*, Appendix I.

[12] Robert of Torigni, i. 336.   [13] Powicke, *Loss of Normandy*, pp. 69, 101.

[14] See Robert of Torigni, ii. 241; the various reforms attributed to William Fitz Ralph in the *Très Ancien Coutumier*, cc. 60–65; and the unpublished example in Appendix H, no. 9.

[15] *Livre noir*, nos. 13, 35, 138; Delisle-Berger, nos. 68*, 76*, 38. On the procedure see *infra*, Chapter VI.

his justices made inquiry, diocese by diocese, concerning the rents and customs pertaining to the duke and his barons.[16] This was not entirely effectual, and in 1171 the income of the duchy was almost doubled by an inquest held throughout Normandy to ascertain the lands and forest and other portions of the demesne which had been occupied since the death of Henry I.[17] Of this systematic survey we are fortunate in having, besides the references in the Exchequer Rolls [18] and possible indications in cartularies [19] and in the *Coutumier des forêts* of Hector of Chartres,[20] the full returns for the *vicomté* of the Avranchin,[21] which give us an exact picture of the king's rights and his administration in this district. Perhaps we may connect with the same inquest a still more important document of Henry's reign, the so-called *iurea regalis*, preserved in the *Très Ancien Coutumier* [22] and containing a statement of the

[16] Robert of Torigni, i. 344. Roger of Wendover (i. 25) speaks of an 'inquisitio generalis' in England this year, but he plainly has in mind the inquest of knights' fees of 1166. The Inquest of Sheriffs of 1170 is the nearest English analogy to the Norman inquests of 1163 and 1171; see Stubbs-Davis, *Select Charters* (1913), p. 174; and on the returns Round, *The Commune of London*, pp. 125–136.

[17] Robert of Torigni, ii. 28.

[18] Indicated by the phrase 'recuperatus per iuream,' Stapleton, *passim*.

[19] Notably in the cartulary of Fécamp (Valin, p. 269; Delisle-Berger, no. 338), where there is a reference to the rights of the duke as recognized and recorded in his roll; and in the Bayeux cartularies (*Livre noir*, no. 46; *Livre rouge*, no. 46), where the phrase 'recognitum autem fuit' shows that an extract has been made from a more comprehensive document. Being subsequent to the accession of Bishop Henry in 1165, the Bayeux document is not a part of the earlier inquests for this district nor connected with the general inquest of 1163, and the mention of William Fitz John seems to place it before the close of 1172 (see, on the date of his death, Delisle, p. 480, where it should be observed that the entry of 1180 refers to an old account). The portion of the original inquest which concerned the king would naturally be omitted in drawing up a statement for the benefit of the bishop.

[20] Preserved in the Archives of the Seine-Inférieure; see Michel Prévost, *Étude sur la forêt de Roumare* (Rouen, 1904), pp. 354–365. The numerous references to Henry in the *Coutumier*, which appeared to Beaurepaire (*B. É. C.*, lxvii. 508) to point to a general inquest on the forests, seem rather to cite his charters.

[21] Printed by Delisle, pp. 345–347. Cf. Powicke, in *E. H. R.*, xxv. 710 f.; and for the date, Haskins, *ibid.*, xxvi. 326–328; and Appendix K.

[22] Ed. Tardif, pp. 59–65. The *iurea* cannot be later than the death of William Patric in 1174, and it is anterior to 1172 if we accept Sir George Warner's date for the death of William Fitz John (*supra*, note 19); but there is nothing to connect it with any one year, and it may belong with the inquest of 1163 or with the earlier inquiries in the Bessin. In any case, in spite of its general form, it was the result of

duke's reserved jurisdiction and his rights over wardship, *craspice*, wreck, and treasure trove. Ducal example, if not ducal precept, is doubtless responsible for the exact surveys of the possessions of religious houses which were made in this reign and of which the chief Norman instance is the detailed inquest on the manors of La Trinité de Caen.[23] The military inquest of 1172 [24] was a natural consequence of the English inquiry of 1166, itself perhaps suggested by Sicilian precedents,[25] but, save in the case of the bishop of Bayeux [26] and the abbot of Mont-Saint-Michel,[27] we have only the general summary and not, as in the parallel English case, the original returns made by the tenants.

It would be especially interesting to know in some detail the history of Henry's early years as duke, not only because of their importance in forming the youth who was at twenty-one to become ruler of the vast Norman empire, but also because we might then study the institutions of the duchy and the policy of its ruler before the union with England reopened the way to possible modification from without. Unfortunately the thirty ducal charters

a local inquest, for all the jurors are in some way connected with the Bessin and the statement concerning the fishing rights of the bishop of Bayeux and the earl of Chester points to the same region. That William Fitz John was connected with earlier inquests in the Bessin (*infra*, note 74) is pointed out by Tardif (*Étude sur les sources*, i. 12), who, however, knows nothing of the inquest of 1171, in which year William was also justiciar (Round, no. 456; *M. A. N.*, xv. 198). E. Perrot, *Les cas royaux* (Paris, 1910), p. 306 f., assigns the *iurea* to *ca*. 1150.

[23] MS. Lat. 5650, ff. 60v–87, where the mention of William du Hommet (f. 82) shows that the inquests belong to the latter part of this reign and not to the earlier half of the century, as suggested by H. Legras, *Le bourgage de Caen*, p. 37, note. The whole is to be published by R. N. Sauvage in the *Bibliothèque de droit normand*. English examples of monastic inquests in this period are those of the *Ramsey Cartulary*, iii. 224–314; the inquest of 1181 in the *Domesday of St. Paul's;* and the Glastonbury inquisition of 1189. For a writ of Henry II granting the monks of Canterbury permission to hold such inquests on their lands, see Delisle-Berger, no. 425.

[24] *H. F.*, xxiii. 693–699; *Red Book of the Exchequer*, pp. 624–647. On the text see Powicke, in *E. H. R.*, xxvi. 89–93; on the importance of the document for the history of the Norman baronage, see his *Loss of Normandy*, pp. 482–520.

[25] See my discussion in *E. H. R.*, xxvi. 661–664.

[26] *M. A. N.*, viii. 425–431; *H. F.*, xxiii. 699–702. These returns were based on the inquest of 1133 and represent still earlier conditions, *supra*, p. 15.

[27] Robert of Torigni, ii. 296–303; *H. F.*, xxiii. 703–705.

which constitute our sole source for Norman government between 1150 and 1154 give few answers to the many questions we should like to put. So far as they tell us anything, they show the young duke surrounded by his father's advisers and maintaining his father's policy, itself a continuation of the system of Henry I,[28] but we can also discern certain new names which are to rise to importance in the ensuing period. Reginald of Saint-Valery is still seneschal,[29] and so are Robert de Courcy, Robert de Neufbourg,[30] and Richard de la Haie;[31] but Manasses Bisset and Humphrey de Bohun also appear with this title,[32] while William the marshal, Richard du Hommet the constable,[33] and Warin Fitz Gerald the chamberlain [34] are new. Besides Richard de Bohun, who continues to act as chancellor, at least until 1151, we find another chancellor, William,[35] and a chancellor's clerk and keeper of the

[28] *Supra*, Chapter IV. The writ for Héauville in Delisle-Berger, no. 29*, is, save for the witnesses and the insertion of *avi mei*, an exact repetition of the writ of Geoffrey for the same establishment printed above, Chapter IV, no. 7a. The following charter of 1150–1151 for the chapter of Chartres is not in Delisle-Berger: ' H. dux Normannorum G. comiti Mellendi et Willelmo de Hangemara et Roberto de Havilla et omnibus fidelibus suis totius Normannie salutem. Sciatis me resaisisse canonicos Sancte Marie Carnotensis ecclesie de decima et de ecclesia de Havilla, ideoque mando et firmiter precipio quod ecclesiam et decimam teneant in bono et in pace iuste et integre salvis rectis suis omnibus illis hominibus, ubi ea sibi fieri debent, qui in predicta ecclesia aut decima aliquid clamaverint rationabiliter. Testibus Alexandro de Bohun, Willelmo Trosebot, Stephano de Bello Campo, apud Rothomagum ' (MS. Lat. 5185 I, p. 328; not in the printed cartulary). Delisle-Berger also omit a charter of 1152–1154, printed in *Revue catholique de Normandie*, vii. 446.

[29] Delisle-Berger, nos. 8*, 11*, 35*–37*, 44*. See in general the list of witnesses to Henry's early charters in Delisle, p. 133 f., where, however, the official titles are not always given and no distinction is made between Normandy and Anjou.

[30] Robert de Neufbourg is not called seneschal in documents before 1155, but his activity as justice and his precedence in charters make it probable that he held this dignity also under Geoffrey and during the early years of Henry. See Chapter IV, note 87.

[31] Delisle, p. 133 f.; *Livre noir*, no. 7.

[32] Delisle-Berger, nos. 48*–50*, 63*, 65*, 68*, 76*; cf. Vernon Harcourt, *His Grace the Steward*, p. 37.

[33] Delisle-Berger, nos. 50*, 51*, 63*, 65*–68*, 72*, 76*. Humphrey Fitz Odo and William of Roumare also appear as constables (Delisle-Berger, nos. 10*, 42*), and still others appear in no. 55*. For William the marshal see no. 13*.

[34] Delisle-Berger, nos. 48*, 49*, 57*, 76*.

[35] Delisle, p. 88, note; Delisle-Berger, nos. 13*, 15*, 36*, 50*, 52*, 65*. I do not understand why Delisle dismisses the early chancellors with bare mention; certainly Henry's chancery does not begin its history in 1154. See *E. H. R.*, xxxii. 597.

seal, Maurice,[36] who need clearing up. The most notable among these new men is the clever and ambitious Bishop Arnulf of Lisieux, who heads the lists of witnesses to Henry's charters and the list of justices in his *curia*,[37] thus restoring the office of justiciar which his predecessor Bishop John had held under Henry I and which had disappeared under Geoffrey. Of humbler servants we find Odo *hostiarius*, doubtless the usher of this name who appears in the Pipe Rolls and perhaps the Odo of Falaise, *regiorum computator redituum*, who was cured of blindness at the tomb of Becket.[38] The *curia* meets in different parts of Normandy [39] — Rouen, Lisieux, Domfront — and has its share of judicial business: there the abbot of Aunay proves his right to the church of Cenilly, the abbot of Fécamp to his tithes in the neighboring forest, the abbot of Savigny to the land claimed by Robert Fitz Ralph.[40] We get glimpses of a body of justices busy with the holding of sworn inquests and the protection of legal rights;[41] and there are local *vicomtes* and *baillis* and porters, all receiving their orders in the sharp, crisp language of the Anglo-Norman writ.[42]

So far as the sources of information are concerned, the period from 1154 to 1189 is divided into two almost equal parts by the change of the king's style in 1172–1173, which separates his charters into two groups, according as they do or do not contain the words *Dei gratia* in the title.[43] These groups do not differ notably in number, but the materials for the second half of the reign are the fuller, since the charters are there reënforced by the Exchequer Rolls and by a larger number of records of judicial decisions. The earlier period, is, however, the more interesting from a constitutional point of view as being a period of origins, and this

[36] Delisle-Berger, nos. 20*, 37*, 44*.

[37] *Ibid.*, nos. 11*, 34*–37*, 42*, 45*, 68*, 72*, 75*, 76*, 80*. For the disappearance of the justiciarship under Geoffrey, see *supra*, p. 146.

[38] He is the sole witness to Delisle-Berger, no. 38*. For Odo of Falaise see *Materials for the History of Thomas Becket*, ii. 185.

[39] Delisle-Berger, nos. 32*, 67*, 75*; Robert of Torigni, i. 255, 259. Cf. also the large gathering at Bayeux in November 1151: Delisle-Berger, no. 20*.

[40] Delisle-Berger, nos. 32*, 67*, 75*; Appendix H, no. 3.

[41] Delisle-Berger, nos. 28*, 29*, 32*–34*, 41*, 66*, 67*, 80*; *Revue catholique*, vii. 446.

[42] Delisle-Berger, nos. 11*, 14*, 15*, 35*, 36*, 38*, 43*, 66*.

[43] Delisle, pp. 12–38.

is notably true of the years between 1154 and 1164, preliminary to the struggle with the Church and the great legislative measures of the reign in England, but as yet obscure on both sides of the Channel. The possibility of Norman precedents, especially in matters of ecclesiastical jurisdiction and civil procedure, requires a careful sifting of all the information that has reached us from what seems to have been a formative period in Henry's policy.

Let us first consider the administration of justice. Of the judicial business that came before the duke himself in his *curia* we have only the slightest indications,[44] and these tell us next to nothing in the earlier years. Between 1154 and 1164 the king spent half his time in England, while the affairs of his other dominions claimed many of the busy months he passed on the Continent. If Normandy was to have an effective judicial system, it must be organized to work in the king's long absences as well as under his immediate supervision. From his father and grandfather Henry inherited the institution of a regular body of justices, both in the *curia* and in local affairs, which he had only to develop and adapt to the needs of a rapidly expanding ducal jurisdiction. In this process there was doubtless constant experimentation, both with men and with methods, such as we can follow somewhat more closely in England later in the reign; but for the earlier years the Norman evidence happens to be fully as abundant as the English,[45] and shows us some features of the system with reasonable clearness.

First of all there is a distinction between the ordinary justices and the justiciar of Normandy, *iusticia mea Normannie*.[46] Ordinarily, as under Henry I,[47] there would seem to have been two

[44] *M. A. N.*, xv. 198; Delisle, p. 43; *infra*, Appendix H, no. 3. An example from the latter part of the reign is found in an agreement between the abbot of Saint-Pierre-sur-Dive and Gervase de Fresnay, 1 May 1181, ' coram domino rege et iusticia sua ' (original in Archives of the Calvados, *fonds* Saint-Pierre-sur-Dive).

[45] On which see Stubbs, introduction to Benedict of Peterborough, ii, p. lxiv.

[46] Notably in the clause of the king's writs, ' nisi feceris iusticia mea Normannie faciat fieri ': Delisle-Berger, nos. 13, 14, 365, 368, 382; Round, nos. 44, 949; cf. *Livre noir*, no. 37, of Henry I. In other writs we find in the same clause only *iusticia mea:* Delisle-Berger, nos. 38, 91, 99, 155, 206 f., 228 f., 335, 342, 346, 369 f. Sometimes the justice is mentioned by name: *ibid.*, nos. 66* f., 75*, 21, 22.

[47] *Supra*, Chapter III.

justiciars, a bishop and the chief seneschal, who frequently sit together, but at least five persons are known to have acted in this capacity in this period, and the available sources do not enable us to fix their succession and relation to one another with the precision which has sometimes been sought.[48] As under Geoffrey,[49] the courts held by the justiciars are called assizes,[50] often, by way of distinction from the lesser courts, full assizes (*plena assisia*);[51] and if we may judge from a full assize held at Caen in 1157 and attended by the barons from the four great regions of the west,[52] they comprehended several administrative districts. Meetings at Caen and Rouen are frequent, but not sufficiently regular to indicate the existence of a permanent central *curia*, and the justiciars are clearly itinerant. The lack of any rolls prevents our tracing their circuits, but the records of cases are more numerous than those which have been collected for England in the same period.[53] In 1155, before the king had returned from his coronation, Bishop Arnulf of Lisieux and Robert of Neufbourg the chief seneschal, as master justices of all Normandy, hold assizes at Carentan and Domfront.[54] In 1157 they appear in two judgments of the *curia* at Caen,[55] and about the same time in another pro-

[48] Notably by Vernon Harcourt, *His Grace the Steward*, pp. 43–50. His attempt to sustain his theory of the unimportance of the seneschal by explaining away the dapifership of Robert de Neufbourg has been satisfactorily disposed of by Valin, p. 157 f. The charter of Henry II for Savigny (Delisle-Berger, no. 80), in which Harcourt considers Robert's style ʻunofficial embellishment,' is also in the *Cartulaire de Normandie* (MS. Rouen 1235), f. 80v.

[49] ʻIn assisia mea apud Valonias,' *infra*, Chapter VI, note 95.

[50] Robert of Torigni, ii. 241; *M. A. N.*, xv. 197. Note in Henry's writ in *Livre noir*, no. 10, ʻquando fui apud Baiocas ad asisiam meam,' the order to William Patric to be ʻad primam asisam que erit citra Lexovium' (anterior to 1172–1173, Delisle-Berger, no. 335).

[51] ʻIn plena assisia apud Abrincas': Deville, *Analyse*, p. 18; Valin, p. 268; Delisle-Berger, no. 153. ʻIn plena assisia apud Rothomagum': Appendix H, no. 6; cartulary of Saint-Évroul, no. 172. ʻIn plena assisia apud Argentomum': *ibid.*, no. 250 (1190).

[52] ʻIn plenaria curia regis, utpote in assisa ubi erant barones iiii comitatuum': Robert of Torigni, ii. 251.

[53] On records in England, see Pollock and Maitland, i. 156.

[54] Robert of Torigni, ii. 241.

[55] *Ibid.*, ii. 251; *M. A. N.*, xv. 197 (original in Archives of the Orne, H. 3912). Cf. Delisle-Berger, nos. 98, 102.

ceeding, likewise at Caen, in part of which the bishop of Lisieux is in his absence replaced by two barons.[56] Before his death in 1159 we find Robert de Neufbourg in various other cases at Avranches, Bayeux, Caen, and Rouen.[57] In 1157 there appears with him at Rouen Rotrou, bishop of Évreux,[58] who is active in the administration of justice throughout the duchy during the next seven years and is specifically called 'justiciar of Normandy.'[59] At times Rotrou is accompanied by Reginald of Saint-Valery as justiciar,[60] and in 1163 they hold an iter throughout the duchy to ascertain the respective rights of king and barons.[61] Richard du Hommet the constable also appears

[56] Appendix H, nos. 3, 4.

[57] *Livre noir*, nos. 27, 28, 35; Valin, p. 267 f.; *M. A. N.*, xv. 198; Deville, *Analyse*, pp. 18, 42; Delisle-Berger, nos. 21, 22, 38, 121, 153; Round, no. 341; Appendix H, nos. 3-5. He is still ' dapifer et iusticia totius Normannie ' when he retires to Bec in 1159: Robert of Torigni, i. 322, ii. 174. Cf. Delisle, pp. 445-447; Harcourt, p. 46 f.

[58] ' In presencia domini Rotroldi episcopi Ebroicensis et Roberti de Novo Burgo dapiferi et Gualeranni comitis de Mellent et Rogerii abbatis Sancti Wandregisili et Rogerii abbatis Sancti Audoeni Rothomagensis et Hugonis de Gornaio et Godardi de Vallibus et Adam de Wacnevilla et Roberti filii Haimerici, apud Rothomagum. Huius pactionis sunt testes. . . .' Cartulary of Saint-Wandrille, D, ii, 14. The first set of witnesses is different in the other version which follows in the cartulary and is printed by Lot, *S.-Wandrille*, no. 88; Round, no. 172.

The following charter shows Rotrou and Robert de Neufbourg in the court of Galeran, count of Meulan, probably sitting as ducal justices, such as we find under Henry I (Chapter III, no. 16) and later in Henry II's reign (*infra*, note 179): ' Anno etiam ab incarnatione Domini millesimo centesimo quinquagesimo quinto residentibus in curia mea apud Brionnium domino Rotroth venerabili Ebroicensi episcopo et domino Rogerio abbate Becci et honorabili Michaele predicti monasterii patre atque domino Roberto de Novoburgo multisque aliis nobilissimis viris, ego Gualerannus comes de Mellent. . . .' Cartulary of Préaux, no. 68.

[59] Delisle, p. 455 f.; Valin, pp. 268, 270; *infra*, Chapter VI, note 93; Appendix H, nos. 6, 8. A document of Rotrou for Foucarmont (originals in Archives of the Seine-Inférieure; also in MS. Rouen 1224, f. 87) ends: ' Hoc autem totum factum est me presente et audiente et tunc temporis existente iusticia Normannie.' In Henry's great charter for Saint-Étienne, 1156-1161 (Delisle-Berger, no. 154), he attests as ' iustic[ia] Norm[annie].'

[60] Delisle, p. 455; Valin, p. 270; Round, nos. 133, 134, 491; Harcourt, p. 48 f.; Delisle-Berger, nos. 221, 223, 397; and Appendix H, nos. 7, 8. Reginald was absent in the East from 1158 to 1160: Robert of Torigni, i. 316, ii. 166; cf. also Jaffé-Löwenfeld, *Regesta*, no. 10363. Pardons of Danegeld in 1156 (Pipe Roll 2 Henry II, pp. 9 f., 23) indicate that Rotrou and Reginald were already members of the *curia*.

[61] ' Rotrocus episcopus Ebroicensis et Rainaldus de Sancto Walerio fecerunt in

with this title,[62] and Bishop Philip of Bayeux may also have held it.[63]

These courts were doubtless attended by the chief barons and royal officers of the region,[64] some of whom evidently acted as judges, although the title of justice appears rarely in the notices of decisions and our lists of royal officers are so incomplete that in most instances it is impossible to distinguish the officials from the barons. A good example is furnished by an assize held at Bayeux [65] by the bishop of Évreux and Reginald of Saint-Valery between 1161 and 1165, where we find the bishops of Lisieux and Avranches, Richard son of the earl of Gloucester, Godard de Vaux, one of the king's justices, Étard Poulain, one of his *baillis* in the Bessin,[66] Osbert de la Heuse, constable of Cherbourg,[67] Robert Fitz Bernard, *prévôt* of Caen,[68] Graverend d'Évrecy, *vicomte*,[69] Richard de Vaux, *vidame* of the bishop of Bayeux,[70] and Roger d'Arri, canon of Bayeux and later a permanent official of the Exchequer.[71] The *vicomtes* and *baillis* acted as judges in their

Normannia recognoscere iussu regis, per episcopatus, legales redditus et consuetudines ad regem et ad barones pertinentes': Robert of Torigni, i. 344.

[62] A judgment of 1164 is rendered ' apud Cadomum [coram] abbate de Troarno, Ricardo de Humet tunc temporis iustitia regis, Guillelmo filio Iohannis, Renaldo de Gerponvilla, Godardo de Vaux, Guillelmo de Varaville, Iordane Taxone, Ricardo filio comitis, Guillelmo Crasso, Henrico de Agnis, Nicholao de Veies, Graver[endo] de Vrecie, Roberto filio Bernardi, Symone de Scuris, Henrico filio Corbini, Roberto Pigache, Guillelmo Forti, Philippo fratre Vitalis monachi, Guillelmo Gernon, Rogero Darried, Ricardo de Vaux, Iohanne Cumin ': cartulary of S. Wandrille, Q, ii, 36. See also *infra*, Appendix H, no. 6.

[63] He is specially mentioned with Robert de Neufbourg in Delisle-Berger, no. 120, and with Rotrou in Valin, p. 268 (Delisle-Berger, no. 153). Cf. Harcourt, p. 47, note.

[64] 'Interfuerunt huic concordie comes de Mellent, comes Ebroicensis, comes Giffardus, et multi barones et servientes regis de diversis partibus.' Charter of Rotrou: Delisle, p. 455; Le Prévost, *Eure*, i. 551.

[65] *M. A. N.*, xv. 197; Valin, p. 270. Cf. the longer list in the assize at Caen in 1164, *supra*, note 62, in which nearly all these names reappear.

[66] *Infra*, notes 77–79.

[67] Delisle, p. 409.

[68] Delisle-Berger, no. 66*; Robert of Torigni, ii. 251.

[69] *Ibid.*, ii. 248.

[70] *Ibid.*, ii. 258.

[71] See *infra*, note 125, the index to the *Livre noir*, and the list of later assizes in Appendix J.

own districts,[72] where an ordinance of 1159 required them to hold court once a month,[73] and they naturally sat with the justiciars in the larger assizes, where they are sometimes specifically called justices.   Thus William Fitz John and Étard Poulain, the chief royal officers in the Bessin,[74] both with the title of *baillivi regis*,[75] are constantly found in the assizes of Lower Normandy.   William can be traced in the local administration of justice as well as in the assizes, and later in the reign becomes *dapifer*, justice, and *procurator Normannie*.[76]   Étard sits in two cases at Caen in 1157, in one of them apparently with the title of justiciar,[77] is *iusticia regis* at Lisieux in 1161,[78] and appears in the court elsewhere.[79]   He is frequently accompanied by Godard de Vaux, who replaces the bishop of Lisieux at Caen at the beginning of the reign, sits at Caen and Rouen in 1157,[80] and appears at various other sessions at Rouen in this period, often with a certain Adam de Wanneville, who may also have been a justice.[81]   Our information does not permit us to separate the local from the itinerant judges in the records of the assizes, still less to follow the work of the local courts.   Doubtless arrangements varied locally and in the course of the reign, and apparently the confusion of local areas stood in the way of a set of courts as simple and uniform as the English.

[72] Thus at Pontaudemer and in the territory of Brionne, William de Morville is ‘ custos et iusticia iussu regis Henrici ’: cartulary of Pontaudemer (MS. Rouen 1232), ff. 18, 28; Delisle-Berger, no. 368.   At Mortain in 1162–1163 we find the constable, Robert Boquerel (*Analecta Bollandiana*, ii. 527; cf. Delisle-Berger, nos. 79, 364), holding the king's court (Delisle, p. 440; original in MS. Rouen 3122, no. 4); and somewhat later the seneschal of Mortain, Nigel, addressed as one of the king's justices (Stapleton, i, p. lxv; Delisle, pp. 210, 408).   See *infra*, note 170. Cf. ‘ the king's justices of Caux ’ (1154–1165): Sommènil, *Chronicon Valassense* (Rouen, 1868), p. 83.

[73] Robert of Torigni, ii. 180.

[74] Delisle, pp. 366, 479 f.; Tardif, *Très Ancien Coutumier*, p. 110; *Livre noir*, nos. 9, 12; Delisle-Berger, nos. 13, 228.

[75] Delisle, p. 447; *infra*, Appendix H, nos. 3, 4.

[76] *Livre noir*, nos. 27, 28, 35, 36, 46; Robert of Torigni, ii. 31, 251 f.; Delisle-Berger, nos. 66*, 14, 21, 22, 38, 305; *M. A. N.*, xv. 198; *supra*, notes 56, 62.

[77] Robert of Torigni, ii. 252; *M. A. N.*, xv. 197.

[78] *Infra*, note 101.   [79] Appendix H, no. 5.

[80] *Supra*, note 58; *infra*, Appendix H, nos. 3, 4.

[81] *Supra*, notes 58, 59; *infra*, Chapter VI, note 93; Appendix H, nos. 3, 5–8; Delisle, p. 456; Delisle-Berger, no. 366; Round, no. 341; also, perhaps, as justice, in an illegible charter in the Archives of the Manche, H. 212.

The one clear point of special importance is the existence of a well defined system of itinerant justices.

Of even greater interest is the question of procedure, which bears directly upon the development of the jury. This problem will be discussed in detail in the following chapter, so that at this point it is necessary only to indicate its relation to these formative years of Henry's policy. In England, in spite of the occasional employment of the sworn inquest since the Conqueror's time, we have no evidence that it was a normal mode of trial before the appearance of the assize *utrum* in 1164, followed shortly by the other possessory assizes and the grand assize. In Normandy, on the other hand, writs ordering the determination of questions of possession and ownership in accordance with the duke's assize (*secundum assisiam meam*) are found in 1156, as well as in Geoffrey's reign, while we find an ordinary litigant demanding an assize against Saint-Étienne before 1159. In that year a question concerning tithes and presentation is decided by recognition on the duke's court, while at Christmas Henry issued a formal ordinance directing the use of the evidence of neighbors in his local courts. Accordingly it would appear that the recognition had become the normal procedure in certain types of actions concerning land, while the testimony of the vicinage had been prescribed in ecclesiastical courts much as in the Constitutions of Clarendon. That matters had reached this point on the English side of the Channel does not appear from any evidence as yet brought to light, and in the existing state of our knowledge it is highly probable that Henry drew upon the results of his Norman experience in drafting his English assizes. There was, of course, no mechanical transfer, for a restless experimenter like Henry was constantly reshaping his materials, and if we could follow the process in Normandy, we should probably find him modifying in various ways the procedure and the assize which he had inherited from his father. Something, too, must be allowed for the natural development of the institution as it passed into more general use, but the exceptional is not likely to have become normal without some direct action of the sovereign in extending his prerogative procedure to his subjects, and in this respect the evidence available from the years before 1164 places Normandy in advance of England.

There is another field in which the practice of the Norman courts before 1164 has a special interest for England, namely that of ecclesiastical jurisdiction. The struggle between Henry II and Becket, says Maitland,[82] "has a long Frankish prologue"; has it also a Norman prologue ? A short prologue, at least, it must have had, for in February 1162 a great council was held at Rouen, in which Henry " complained of the bishops and their officers and his *vicomtes* and ordered that the provisions of the council of Lille-bonne should be observed." [83] No details are given, but the mention of the local officers and the council of Lillebonne shows plainly that the question was one of encroachments by the Church which his officers failed to prevent. Just which of the canons of this council the king believed to have been violated we can only surmise, but he clearly sought to base his protest, as in England two years later, upon an appeal to ancient and well established practice, as contained in a document which had been drawn up under the Conqueror in 1080 and confirmed by Henry I,[84] and which thus presented a more definite formulation of the "customs, liberties, and dignities of his ancestors " than was at hand in England. From the ecclesiastical point of view, these canons had become somewhat antiquated by 1162, since they referred constantly to local Norman usage rather than to the general principles of canon law which had been more sharply formulated in

[82] Pollock and Maitland, i. 18.

[83] ' Querimoniam faciens de episcopis et eorum ministris et vicecomitibus suis, iussit ut concilium Iulie Bone teneretur: ' Robert of Torigni, i. 336.

[84] The best text of the council of Lillebonne, now preserved in the Archives Nationales, bears the seal of Henry I: Teulet, *Layettes*, i. 25, no. 22; Delisle, *Cartu-laire normand*, no. 1. The canons are also given by Ordericus, ii. 316–323; cf. the analysis given by Tardif, *Étude sur les sources*, pp. 39–43; and *supra*, Chapter I, pp. 30–35. Evidence that they were observed in the twelfth century is found in a charter of Audoin, bishop of Évreux from 1118 to 1139: ' Convocatis ex more ad synodum omnibus presbiteris nostris, circadam quam ab illis exigebam ex concilii Iulibone institutione et ecclesiarum episcopalium Normannie consuetudine, quoniam illa gravari conquerebantur, eorum communi petitione et nostrorum canonicorum intercessione perdonavi ': Archives of the Eure, G. 122, no. 36. The canons of the council were frequently copied in legal collections relating to Normandy.

the interval, and since they recognized the supremacy of the duke and the arbitrament of his *curia* in church matters to an extent which would not have been admitted by the Church in Henry II's time. It is, indeed, highly probable that Henry's complaint was based particularly upon the closing enactment of the assembly of Lillebonne, that the bishops should seize no right of justice or customary dues beyond those there enumerated until they had established their claim in the king's court; but the absence of evidence precludes us from examining the bearing of this canon upon the vexed question of criminous clerks. Some idea of their treatment in Normandy can be gained from a case described by Arnulf of Lisieux, that of a certain Henry, who, apparently before 1166, manufactured false money and put it into circulation at Bayeux. Convicted after confession, it is not stated in what court, he was imprisoned and fettered by the king's officers, but finally much effort of the diocesan secured his release on condition of abjuring the duchy, and he was degraded by the archbishop.[85] An ordinance of 1159 requiring the testimony of neighbors in accusations by rural deans [86] shows that Henry's dissatisfaction with the exercise of jurisdiction by archdeacons and deans had found expression in Normandy as well as in England before the Constitutions of Clarendon, in which it occupies a definite, though subordinate, place.

Still another claim which Henry made in 1164 we are able to test by Norman practice, namely the jurisdiction of the king's court over suits respecting advowson and presentation.[87] In 1159, when the bishop of Coutances had summoned Ralph de la Mouche to show by what right he claimed the presentation of the priest of Mesnil-Drey, a certain Osmund proved his right against Ralph

[85] *Ep.* 123 (Migne, cci. 144). Addressed to N' (this, not Nicolao, is the reading of the MS. used by Giles, St. John's College, Oxford, 126, as Mr. R. L. Poole has kindly ascertained for me), bishop of Meaux, who does not appear to have existed, the text of this letter requires further examination. The priest's brother Amfredus had forfeited his lands and gone into exile fifteen years before, and if Henry's offenses are of the same period, they would fall at least as early as 1166.

[86] Robert of Torigni, ii. 180; cf. Constitutions of Clarendon, c. 6. See *infra*, Chapter VI, note 94; and Appendix I.

[87] Constitutions of Clarendon, c. 1. On the probability of previous English legislation concerning advowsons, see Appendix I.

by sworn recognition in the king's court at Gavray.[88] In another case anterior to 1164 the bishop of Évreux, acting as the duke's justiciar in full assize at Rouen, had adjudged the presentation of Le Sap to the monks of Saint-Évroul against a lay claimant.[89] There are also examples of the bishop's jurisdiction in such cases when one or both of the parties were ecclesiastics,[90] so that there was some foundation for the assertion of Arnulf of Lisieux that such matters had always pertained to the bishop;[91] but the comprehensive inquest of 1205 states specifically that in Henry's reign disputes respecting patronage had to be settled in the duke's court or in the court of the lord of whose fee the church was held,[92] and this is borne out by the documents.[93] Indeed more than a generation before 1164 the monks of Chartres, claiming the church of Chandai in the court of Richer of Laigle, plead in the lay court *iuxta morem Normannie.*[94] In the latter part of Henry II's reign the question whether a holding was lay fee or alms was matter for a recognition in the king's court, as we see from various cases in the cartularies and Exchequer Rolls,[95] as well as from the

[88] Robert of Torigni, ii. 259.

[89] Chapter VI, note 93.

[90] Robert of Torigni, ii. 259; dispute between Archbishop Hugh and the abbot of Préaux, cartulary of Préaux, no. 51; Jordan Taisson *v.* a clerk in the court of Henry, bishop of Bayeux, Archives of the Calvados, H. 5606, 3; cartulary of Saint-Évroul, nos. 231, 233; *infra,* note 125; Appendix H, no. 1.

[91] *Ep.* 116: ' Mota est ei qui presentaverat questio patronatus in iudicio seculari, cum semper ab antiquo cause huiusmodi ad episcopalem audientiam pertinerent.'

[92] Delisle, *Cartulaire normand,* no. 124; Round, no. 1318.

[93] Stapleton, i. 5, 12, 64, 96, 114; cartulary of the chapter of Rouen (MS. Rouen 1193), f. 131; charter of Bishop Lisiard of Séez in cartulary of Saint-Évroul, no. 250 (1190); and the assizes of darrein presentment in Round, no. 438; Delisle, *Jugements de l'Échiquier,* no. 35; the cartulary of Fécamp (MS. Rouen 1207), f. 70v; and Delisle-Berger, no. 651.

[94] *Cartulaire de S.-Père de Chartres,* ii. 607; Round, no. 1257.

[95] Stapleton, i. 55, 64; *B. É. C.,* i. 545; Delisle-Berger, no. 406; charters of Jordan de l'Épesse, in Archives of the Manche, H. 1034, 6452 (printed in *Inventaire sommaire*); charter of John Péril granting ' presentationem ecclesie Sancti Martini de Mairoles (Marolles, canton Lisieux) cum omni iure patronatus eiusdem ecclesie et duas garbas decime eiusdem ville et totius parochie, que recognite fuerunt in assisa apud Monfort tempore domini regis Henrici ad laicum feodum ' (copy of cartulary of leprosery of Lisieux, Archives of the Calvados, H. suppl. 486, f. 9; cf. *infra,* Appendix J, no. 20).

Coutumier and from the inquest of 1205;[96] yet it is not possible
to say how clearly this principle was established in Normandy
before the appearance of the assize *utrum* in the Constitutions
of Clarendon.[97] That this assize had a somewhat independent
history in Normandy may perhaps be argued from the divergence
of the Norman *breve de feodo et elemosina* from the English assize
utrum.[98] While we have clear cases of the decision of questions
of tithes and parish lands in the duke's court before 1164,[99] there
are traces of the bishop's authority here also,[100] and there is some
indication that the two jurisdictions might deal with the same
case, apparently without rivalry.[101] Here, as in all questions concerning the Norman antecedents of the Constitutions of Clarendon, the evidence is interesting but too scanty to be conclusive.
In working back from this document it is always well to remember
Maitland's dictum that " if as regards criminous clerks the Constitutions of Clarendon are the high-water-mark of the claims of

[96] *Très Ancien Coutumier*, c. 18; Delisle, *Cartulaire normand*, no. 124.

[97] The case of the rights of Saint-Évroul over Le Sap cannot be considered an
authentic example of this: *infra*, Chapter VI, note 93.

[98] Brunner, *Schwurgerichte*, pp. 236 f., 324–326; Maitland, *Collected Papers*, ii.
216; Bigelow, *History of Procedure*, p. 4 f.

[99] Robert of Torigni, ii. 259; *infra*, Appendix H, nos. 3, 5, 6. Cf. *Cartulaire de
Notre-Dame de Chartres*, i. 187 (1171); MS. Lat. 5650, f. 80.

[100] E. g., *Neustria Pia*, p. 351 (= Le Prévost, *Eure*, iii. 82); cartulary of Saint-
Évroul, no. 233; Vernier, no. 75; *infra*, Chapter VI, note 109; Appendix H,
no. 9.

[101] Thus (1156–1159) we find the prior of Perrières establishing his right to the
tithe of Épancy (Calvados) in the courts of the bishop of Séez (Collection Moreau,
lxviii. 9), the archbishop of Rouen (*ibid.*, liv. 243; Archives of the Orne, H. 2026),
and the king, the judgment being finally confirmed by Henry: ' teneat bene et in
pace et quiete totam decimam suam de Espanaio sicut eam dirationavit in curia mea
coram iusticiis meis et in curia archiepiscopi Rothomagensis ' (Delisle-Berger, no.
109). We also find the king's justices sitting in the court of Bishop Arnulf of
Lisieux in 1161 in a case between Alice Trubaud and the abbot of Caen against the
abbot of Troarn concerning the advowson of Dives: ' Huius autem actionis sunt
testes et ipsius iudicii cooperatores extiterunt Normannus et Iohannes archidiaconi,
Fulco decanus, Rogerius filius Aini canonicus et alii plures canonici Lexovienses, sed
et barones regis Radulfus de Torneio, Robertus de Montfort, Aicardus Pulcin
iusticia regis ': cartulary of Troarn (MS. Lat. 10086), f. 159; cf. the charters of
Arnulf and Cardinal Henry of Pisa, f. 152v.; and Sauvage, *Troarn*, p. 166, n. 5.
For a case of 1147 ' iustitia archiepiscopi Rothomagensis et comitis de Mellent,'
see Valin, p. 264. See also Round, no. 138; Delisle-Berger, no. 650; Liverani,
Spicilegium Liberianum (Florence, 1864), p. 579.

secular justice, as regards the title to lands they are the low-water-mark." [102]

After 1164 the point of view of our study must be somewhat shifted. Thanks to a series of legislative monuments and treatises which have no Norman analogues, we can trace with some confidence the course of English constitutional development, while our knowledge of Norman affairs is too scanty to permit following the evolution of institutions or policies. The most that we can attempt is to reconstruct the chief elements of judicial and fiscal organization and procedure, in the hope of furnishing an instructive parallel to better known English conditions.

The turning-point in the constitutional history of Normandy during the latter part of Henry's reign is the year 1176, when the death of the seneschal and justiciar, William de Courcy,[103] led the king to appoint in his place as ruler of Normandy Richard of Ilchester, bishop of Winchester, long a trusted officer of the English Exchequer, where he had charge of a special roll and proved himself particularly " alert and businesslike in reckonings and the writing of rolls and writs."[104] Very possibly the constitutional development of Normandy may have lagged behind that of England in the busy years which intervened between the Constitutions of Clarendon and the Assize of Northampton; very likely its administration had fallen into disorder after the rebellion of 1173; certain it is that Richard was excellently qualified by talent and experience to undertake the reorganization of governmental

[102] *Collected Papers*, ii. 216.

[103] On whom see Delisle, *Henri II*, pp. 476–478.

[104] *Dialogus*, bk. i, c. 5 (Oxford ed., p. 77). On Richard see Miss Norgate, in *Dictionary of National Biography*, xlviii. 194; Delisle, pp. 431–434; R. L. Poole, *The Exchequer in the Twelfth Century*, p. 116 ff. It is not quite true, as Miss Norgate says, that we have no trace of his activity during his sojourn in Normandy. He is mentioned in three documents: a charter of Philippa Rosel given at the Exchequer in 1176 (original in British Museum, Add. Ch. 15278; Round, no. 517); an assize which he held at Caen in January, 1177 (*Livre noir*, no. 95; Delisle, p. 347); and an assize held at Montfort ' quo tempore Ricardus Wintoniensis episcopus in Normannia post regem iudex erat et maior iustitia ' (Appendix H, no. 10). A tallage levied by him is still carried on the roll of 1180 (Stapleton, i. 74). Delisle-Berger, no. 569, probably belongs to these years; cf. the witnesses with the justices in Appendix H, no. 10.

business which seems to have been effected during the year and a half which he now spent in Normandy. It is not without significance that the roll of 1176 remained the basis of reckoning for more than twenty years, and that from this year we begin to follow with some clearness and continuity the judicial work of the Norman Exchequer.

It has indeed been maintained that the term exchequer does not previously occur in Normandy, and hence that Richard is the creator of the institution.[105] The author of the *Dialogus*, however, who began his treatise while Richard was in Normandy, refers to the Norman Exchequer as an ancient institution, as old perhaps as the Conqueror,[106] under whom we can trace the regular accounting for the farm of the *vicomtés* which is the essence of such a fiscal system;[107] and the name *scaccarium* occurs in 1171[108] and in a notice of Henry I's reign discovered by Round.[109] At what epoch there was introduced the distinctive method of reckoning which gave the Exchequer its name, is an even darker problem in Normandy than in England. According to an ingenious conjecture of Poole,[110] the employment of the abacus for balancing the royal accounts came to England from the schools of Laon in the reign of Henry I. To me the epoch of its introduction seems probably earlier and connected with the abacists of Lorraine in the

[105] Valin, pp. 116–136. On Valin's own showing we can hardly imagine Richard creating the Exchequer between his arrival toward Michaelmas of 1176 and the regular session of that body, doubtless also at Michaelmas, mentioned in the Rosel charter of that year (see the preceding note).

[106] Bk. i, c. 4 (Oxford ed., p. 66).

[107] *Supra*, pp. 40–44; *E. H. R.*, xxvi. 328 (1911) (a *terra data* under the Conqueror). For accounts which run far back of 1176 see Stapleton, i. 12, 92, 94. On the administrative organization as the essence of the Exchequer cf. Liebermann, *E. H. R.*, xxviii. 153. For the use of tallies under the Conqueror see Stapleton, i, p. xxii.

[108] Delisle, p. 345; cf. *E. H. R.*, xxvi. 326–328 (1911). No reliance can be placed on the early mention of the Exchequer in a highly suspicious charter for Saint-Évroul: Round, nos. 638, 639; Delisle, p. 316; Delisle-Berger, no. 513. There is an important document from the Exchequer, 1178–1180 (Round, no. 1123), which Valin overlooks. His misreading of 'rotulis trium annorum' (p. 135) as a single roll covering three years hardly requires comment.

[109] *E. H. R.*, xiv. 426 (1899); *supra*, Chapter III, note 18.

[110] Poole, *The Exchequer in the Twelfth Century*, pp. 42–59.

preceding century; [111] but in any case the English evidence antedates the Norman, and, although the personnel and the language
of the English Exchequer were Norman, the process may very
well have been, as Poole urges, " from England to Normandy, not
from Normandy to England."

The absence of earlier rolls deprives us of all basis for fixing the
nature of Bishop Richard's reforms, which probably had less to do
with the mechanism of administration than with the reëstablishment of order in the finances through the collection of back
accounts — arrearages of seven, fifteen, even twenty years meet
us in the roll of 1180 [112]—the revision of the farms, and the change
of officials in Normandy and the other continental dominions
which is recorded in 1177. [113] Whatever Richard accomplished, he
did not make the Norman Exchequer a copy of the English, for
in 1178–1179 the author of the *Dialogue*, who had more than
once been in Normandy, tells us that the two bodies differed " in
many points and wellnigh in the most important." [114]

What these great differences were, apart from the absence of
blank farm in Normandy, it is impossible to say, for we have no
Norman *Dialogue*. The terms of the Norman Exchequer are the
same as the English, Easter and Michaelmas; the officers are likewise called barons; the place is fixed at Caen, where the principal
treasury was. [115] One point of divergence which appears from the
rolls is that in Normandy each section begins with a statement of

[111] See my article on *The Abacus and the King's Curia*, E. H. R., xxvii. 101–106
(1912). Norman clerks also were in relations with the schools of Lorraine: Ordericus, iii. 265.

[112] Stapleton, i. 12, 92, 94.

[113] Benedict of Peterborough, i. 198. The words of Ralph de Diceto (i. 424)
' fiscalia diligenter recensens ' need mean no more than is here suggested. On these
points I am glad to find myself in agreement with Powicke (pp. 73–75, 85).

[114] ' In plurimis et pene maioribus dissident:' bk. i, c. 4 (p. 66). Cf. Liebermann,
Einleitung in den Dialogus, p. 111. For Richard Fitz Neal's sojourns in Normandy
see Eyton, *Itinerary*, pp. 112, 190; Delisle-Berger, no. 384.

[115] That the principal treasury was at Caen as early as 1172 is clear from Robert
of Torigni's account (ii. 297) of the deposit there of the barons' returns of that year.
See also Stapleton, i. 56, and another mention on p. 110, where (cf. p. 77; *Rotuli
Normanniae*, p. 50) the treasury at Rouen is likewise important. Treasure was
also kept at Falaise (Stapleton, i. 39), which had been a principal place of
deposit under Henry I (Robert of Torigni, i. 200; Ordericus, v. 50), and at
Argentan (Delisle, p. 334). See Chapter III, p. 107 ff. On the use of castles for

the total amount due, whereas in the Pipe Rolls, until 8 Richard I, this can be discovered only by computation.[116] Variation in nomenclature is seen in the Norman heading *misericordie, promissiones, et fines*, corresponding to the *placita, conventiones*, and *oblata* of the English record. The Norman rolls tell us next to nothing respecting the royal judges and their circuits, while the absence of anything corresponding to Danegeld renders it impossible to trace the members of the *curia* by means of amounts pardoned them. The author of the *Dialogue* was perhaps impressed by the absence from the Norman rolls of the capital headings and other rubrics which he so carefully describes in the English, but so far as we can compare the surviving records the 'great differences' seem to have consisted in externals rather than in essentials. Though the two Exchequers kept their transactions quite distinct,[117] the two sets of rolls rest upon the same fundamental system of accounting,[118] the greater subdivision and local detail of the Norman roll resulting from the existence of a set of governmental areas much more complex and irregular than the English shires. The older *vicomté* and *prévôté* persist in spite of the superposition of the newer *bailliage;*[119] many of the tithes and fixed

the custody of treasure see Round's introduction to the Pipe Roll of 28 Henry II, p. xxiv.

The Pipe Rolls make frequent mention of transshipments of treasure from England to Normandy for the king's use on the Continent, and there is evidence that the various treasuries in the empire were regarded 'as parts of a single system' (Powicke, *Loss of Normandy*, pp. 347–350). For the year 1198 Ramsay (*Angevin Empire*, p. 372) has calculated that the Norman revenue was greater than the English.

[116] Stapleton, i, p. xi; Poole, *The Exchequer in the Twelfth Century*, p. 130.

[117] Thus we rarely find one Exchequer crediting a payment made at the other, as in the case of the relief of Hugh de Gournay: Pipe Roll 32 Henry II, pp. xxviii, 60. For such examples under Henry I, see Chapter III, note 103.

[118] Even to the form of the rolls and the use of tallies: Stapleton, i, pp. ix, xiii, 84; Wace, ed. Andresen, ii, line 2012. Cf. also the parallel treatment of the crown debtors: Stapleton, i, p. xii; Powicke, p. 74. See, however, *infra*, note 215.

[119] In what may be considered our only contemporary description of the Norman Exchequer under Henry II, Wace's account of Richard the Good in his tower, we read (ed. Andresen, ii, lines 2009–2012):

> Venir ad fait de cest pais
> Tuz ses provoz e ses baillis,
> Ses gravereins et ses vescuntes;
> Ses tailles ot e ses acuntes.

On the whole subject of local geography, see Powicke, pp. 61–79, 103–119.

allowances go back to the Conqueror's time or even earlier; [120]
and the farm, less affected by *terre date* than in England, seems to
have undergone little change except in the case of important commercial centers like Rouen, Caen, and Dieppe.[121] The whole sub-
structure of ducal finance was evidently very ancient, and for
that reason in Henry's time quite inadequate, and the rolls show
clearly that, as in England, the chief means for supplementing it
were found in the administration of civil and criminal justice.[122]
However interesting it might be to follow out in detail the points
of agreement and divergence in the methods of the two Exchequers, the fact of primary importance is that, so far as northern
Europe is concerned, England and Normandy stand in a group
by themselves, well in advance of all their neighbors in the
development of a money economy and in the mechanism of fiscal
administration.

As regards its functions as a court, it has recently been argued [123]
that the Exchequer of the Norman dukes was in no sense a judicial
body and was in no wise connected with the later Échiquier de
Normandie. This view is a natural reaction against those writers
who approached the earlier institution with the ideas of an age
when the Exchequer was known only as a court, but it assumes a
breach in that continuity of law and institutions which is in
general so noteworthy in passing from Angevin to Capetian Normandy, and it does not fully realize the fluidity of the Anglo-
Norman *curia*.[124] What we seem rather to find is a *curia* which
sits for fiscal purposes at Caen and for judicial purposes at various
places in the duchy, and which, when Philip Augustus transfers
its fiscal duties to Paris, retains its judicial functions and its
Anglo-Norman name. The chief thing to avoid in tracing its
history is the projection back into the Anglo-Norman period of

---

[120] *Supra*, pp. 42–44.   [121] *Supra*, p. 105; Stapleton, i. 56, 68, 70.

[122] Cf. Delisle, *B. É. C.*, x. 288, xiii. 108 ff.

[123] Valin, pp. 137–139, 249–251; the two passages are not wholly consistent. See,
contra, Powicke, pp. 85, 398.

[124] On the fundamental identity of *curia*, Exchequer, and assizes, see R. de
Fréville, *Étude sur l'organisation judiciaire en Normandie aux XIIe et XIIIe siècles*,
in *Nouvelle revue historique de droit*, 1912, p. 683.

the more fully organized Échiquier which we know from the *Grand Coutumier* and the *arrêts* of the thirteenth century. From the reigns of Henry II and Richard a small but definite body of cases furnishes conclusive evidence of the activity of the Exchequer in judicial matters, and indicates that there was no clear distinction between its competence and that of the *curia regis*.[125] As in England in the same period,[126] it seems probable that the difference was essentially one of place: when the *curia* sat in the Exchequer chamber at Caen, it was said to sit at the Exchequer, when it sat elsewhere it was called simply the *curia*. Certainly the distinction was not, at least among the higher officers, one of personnel, for the same men appear at one time as barons, or justices,[127] of the Exchequer and at another as justices holding assizes in various parts of Normandy.[128]

[125] For cases and transactions before the Exchequer in this period see *M. A. N.*, xv. 198–201; Delisle, p. 349; Valin, pièces, nos. 19, 24, 25, 28; Round, nos. 309, 310, 438, 461, 485 (another version in MS. Lat. 10086, f. 109v), 509 (also in the British Museum, Add. Ch. 15289, no. 2), 517 (original in Add. Ch. 15278; some additional witnesses in the confirmation in Archives of the Calvados, H. 322, no. 3), 560, 606 (where the witnesses are omitted; original in Archives of the Calvados, H. 6607, 301–303), 608, 1123; cartulary of Fécamp, f. 25 (letter of archbishop of Rouen to William Fitz Ralph and the other barons of the Exchequer notifying them of the settlement of a question of presentation in the court of the bishop of Bayeux); *Cartulaire de Normandie*, f. 68v (*infra*, note 127); Archives of the Calvados, H. 5716, 6607 (78–83, 309), 6653 (338–342), 6672 (293–301), 6679 (186–191), 7707; Archives of the Orne, H. 3916 (*infra*, Appendix H, no. 11); and the following passage in Richard's great confirmation of the privileges of Saint-Étienne: 'Recuperavit idem [abbas Willelmus, d. 1179] super Robertum de Veim in curia H. regis patris nostri apud Cadomum hereditagium quod idem Robertus clamabat in tenendo manerio de Veim et de Sancto Leonardo, et super Robertum de Briecuria ecclesiam Sancti Andree de Vilers de qua monachos violenter dissaisierat sed iuditio baronum qui erant ad scacarium apud Cadomum adiudicata est ecclesia predicta Sancto Stephano et restituta ': Archives of the Calvados, H. 1836; cf. Deville, *Analyse*, p. 52. Most of these documents relate to agreements or acknowledgments before the Exchequer, but good examples of judicial proceedings will be found in the last extract; in Valin, nos. 24, 25, 28; in Round, nos. 309, 310, 438 (Delisle-Berger, no. 647); and in the documents given in facsimile in *M. A. N.*, xv.

[126] Poole, *The Exchequer in the Twelfth Century*, pp. 174–182; cf. G. B. Adams, in *A. H. R.*, xviii. 357 (1913).

[127] ' Hoc autem factum fuit apud Cadomum ad scacarium coram iusticiis domini regis tempore Willelmi filii Radulfi senescalli Normannie ': *Cartulaire de Normandie*, f. 68v. So also in Valin, nos. 19, 24; Round, nos. 509, 517. Barons of the Exchequer appear in Valin, no. 25; Round, no. 1123; Delisle-Berger, no. 647.

[128] See the list of assizes, *infra*, Appendix J.

In the sessions of the Exchequer the seneschal naturally presided, accompanied by certain men who bear the title of barons or justices but in the documents are not always distinguishable from the other barons and clerks in attendance. In a charter of 1178–1180,[129] besides William Fitz Ralph the seneschal, we find as barons William du Hommet the constable, Master Walter of Coutances, who had served as clerk of the king's *camera* and keeper of the seal and was perhaps treasurer of Normandy,[130] Osbert de la Heuse, constable of Cherbourg, Ranulf de Grandval, Richard Giffard, and Gilbert Pipart, justiciars of the king, the last two having served as justices in England and as barons of the Norman Exchequer under Richard of Winchester.[131] Later we find most frequently Haimo the butler, the justices William de la Mare and Richard Silvain, Jordan de la Lande, and certain clerks, of whom as many as four appear in one charter of the period.[132] Most of these clerks are only names to us, but we can follow with some clearness two members of the clerical family of Arri, Roger, canon of Bayeux since the early years of Henry's reign and a regular witness in records of the *curia* and Exchequer from 1164 to 1191,[133] and Anquetil, who attests less frequently but receives a livery as clerk of the Exchequer as late as 1198; [134] while another type appears in William Calix, a constant witness from the time of Richard of Ilchester, a responsible disbursing officer in the roll of 1184, and a large money-lender on his own account, forfeiting

[129] *M. A. N.*, xxx. 672 (*cf.* xix. 66); Round, no. 1123.

[130] Delisle, pp. 106–113. The title ' thesaurarius Rothomagensis ' (Delisle, p. 101; Round, no. 34) means treasurer of the cathedral (Delisle-Berger, nos. 510, 567) rather than royal treasurer at Rouen; but Ralph de Wanneville, treasurer of Rouen, was also treasurer of Normandy (Round, no. 21; Stapleton, i. 110), and we know that the office of ducal treasurer had been combined with a canonry in the cathedral from the time of Henry I (*supra*, p. 109 f.). There are relations between the duke and the treasurer of Avranches (Delisle, p. 346) and the treasurer and chaplain of Bayeux (*A. H. R.*, xiv. 471; *Livre noir*, nos. 13, 138, 271, 275) which may have had some significance. For the conversion of the plate of Rouen cathedral to the uses of Henry II, see MS. Rouen 1405, p. 18 (Round, no. 274).

[131] Delisle, pp. 376, 428. [132] Appendix H, no. 11.

[133] *Supra*, note 62; *Livre noir*, nos. 45, 73, 128, 129, 135, 139, 182, 442; Round, nos. 432, 435, 437, 438, 456, 461, 485, 509, 1446, 1447, 1451; Delisle-Berger, no. 689; the Exchequer notices cited in note 125; and the list of assizes in Appendix J.

[134] Stapleton, i. 145, 225, ii. 376, 384; and the lists just cited. Cf. Osmund d'Arri in assizes under Philip Augustus: *Cartulaire de Montmorel*, ed. Dubosc, nos. 34–36.

to the crown at his death a mass of chattels and pledges [135] which suggests on a smaller scale the operations of that arch-usurer William Cade.[136] The rolls show other ecclesiastics active in the business of the Exchequer, notably the king's chancellor, Ralph de Wanneville, later bishop of Lisieux and treasurer of Normandy; [137] but until Henry's faithful clerks are rewarded with the sees of Évreux, Lisieux, and Rouen toward the close of the reign, the higher clergy are less prominent in the administration than they were in his earlier years.[138]

Of those who serve the king in Normandy many have served or will serve him elsewhere; his officers and treasure are passing to and fro across the Channel; his household is ever on the march, and some elements in it are common to the whole Plantagenet empire; yet Normandy has also officers of its own. Some are clerks, such as the treasurer,[139] the subordinates in the Exchequer,[140] and the chaplains of the great castles; [141] some are

[135] Round, no. 517, and index; Stapleton, i, pp. cli, 110, 129, 130, 145, 170, 171, 183, 194–198, 226, 228, 240, ii. 375, 379 (the countess of Richmond as a debtor), 465–469; and the lists cited in note 133.

[136] On whom see *E. H. R.*, xxviii. 209–227, 522–527, 730–732.

[137] Delisle, pp. 99–103.

[138] Yet Froger, bishop of Séez, is said to have been ordered by Alexander III to give up his bishopric or his place in the royal administration (*Mémoires de la Société d'agriculture de Bayeux*, viii. 244); and Nigel Wireker heard in Normandy that the bishops of the English realm attend *curia* and Exchequer so assiduously that they seem ordained ' ad ministerium fisci ' rather than ' ad mysteria ecclesie ' (Wright, *Anglo-Latin Poets*, i. 203).

[139] The relation of the treasurer to the chamberlain on the one hand and to the custody of local treasure on the other is not perfectly clear. In the rolls of 1180 and following the Norman treasurer has an assured income unconnected with service in the king's household and consisting of the tithes of the *vicomtés* of Fécamp, Caux, Auge, Lieuvin, Roumois, and the country between Risle and Seine, and of the great forests of the Seine valley, as well as a special endowment at Vaudreuil (*Rotuli Chartarum*, p. 17; cf. Round, nos. 193, 561). Certain of these can be found in the possession of Henry I's treasurer, and the antiquity and situation of these *vicomtés* may point to an even earlier origin: *supra*, Chapter III, note 108. The duke's chaplain at Bayeux similarly had the tithe of the regards of the forest of Vernai (Stapleton, i. 5). Can this have some connection with a local treasury (*supra*, note 130) ?

[140] *Supra*, notes 132–135; and cf. the clerks who appear in the roll of 1180. Stapleton, i. 37 f., 56–58.

[141] *Ibid.*, i. 5, 90; *Rotuli Normanniae*, pp. 7, 23; *Rotuli Chartarum*, pp. 69, 107, 113.

serjeants, acting as ushers,[142] money-changers,[143] scribes,[144] marshals,[145] pantlers,[146] and larderers;[147] and for local government
there are the keepers of jails, parks and forests,[148] and fairs,[149]
as well as the *vicomtes, prévôts, baillis,* and constables upon whom
the whole system rested — in all a multitude of officials, compared
by Peter of Blois to an army of locusts,[150] with the bureaucratic
element rapidly gaining on the feudal in a way which anticipates
the *gens du roi* of the thirteenth century. Wace, himself a person
of some knowledge of the law,[151] gives us a picture of the growth of
officialism and litigation in his own time in the complaints which
he puts into the mouths of the peasants revolting in 996 against
the *prévôts,* beadles, *baillis* old and new, who leave one not an
hour's peace with their constant summons to pleas of every sort:

> Tant i a plaintes e quereles
> E custummes viez et nuveles,
> Ne poent une hure aveir pais:
> Tute iur sunt sumuns as plaiz:
> Plaiz de forez, plaiz de moneies,
> Plaiz de purprises, plaiz de veies,
> Plaiz de bies faire, plaiz de moutes,
> Plaiz de defautes, plaiz de toutes,
> Plaiz d' aguaiz, plaiz de graveries,
> Plaiz de medlees, plaiz de aies.
> Tant i a prevoz e bedeaus
> E tant bailiz, viels e nuvels,
> Ne poent aveir pais une hure,
> Tantes choses lur mettent sure
> Dunt ne se poent derainier.[152]

[142] Valin, p. 151, note 3; *Rotuli Chartarum,* p. 82; Eyton, *Court, Household, and
Itinerary of Henry II,* p. 9.

[143] Delisle-Berger, nos. 328, 562, 719; Stapleton, i. 77; ' Symon cambitor tunc
prepositus Andeleii ' in cartulary of Mortemer (MS. Lat. 18369), f. 103 (1168).

[144] Hereditary ' scriptor prepositure Cadomi ' in *Olim* (ed. Beugnot), i. 417.

[145] Delisle-Berger, no. 212; *supra,* Chapter IV, no. 13.

[146] Delisle, *Cartulaire normand,* no. 14; *supra,* Chapter III, p. 117.

[147] Stapleton, i. 30, 99, 274, ii. 471, 572 f.; *B. É. C.,* xi. 410, note 14.

[148] Delisle, *Henri II,* p. 209; Delisle-Berger, nos. 171–173, 212. On the Norman
forests at this period see Borrelli de Serres, *Recherches sur divers services publics,
XIIIᵉ siècle,* pp. 406–417.

[149] Delisle, *Henri II,* pp. 210, 271, note, 346.

[150] *Ep.* 95, in Migne, ccvii. 298.   [151] Tardif, *Étude sur les sources,* i. 9, note 4.

[152] Ed. Andresen, ii, lines 841–855. Cf. the extortionate serjeant in *Très Ancien
Coutumier,* c. 64.

Normandy had its full share of the great court days of Henry's reign, when the king kept some great feast amid his barons and officials. Christmas was often spent in this way, at Bayeux, Bur,[153] Domfront, Falaise, twice each at Cherbourg and Argentan, thrice at Caen. The most splendid of these assemblies was the Christmas court of 1182 at Caen. On this occasion Henry's barons were forbidden to hold courts of their own, and they and others flocked to Caen to the number, we are told, of more than a thousand knights. The Young King was there — his last Christmas — and his brothers Richard and Geoffrey, their brother-in-law, Henry the Lion of Saxony, the archbishops of Dublin and Canterbury, with many bishops and abbots.[154] The feudal character of such a *curia* is illustrated by the episode of William of Tancarville, *summus ex feudo regis camerarius*, who pushed his way through the crowd to assert his hereditary right to serve the king and princes and to retain for himself the silver wash-basins, such as his father had thus received and placed in his monasteries of Sainte-Barbe and Saint-Georges de Bocherville; and by the decision of the barons on the following day that the claim had been sustained and the chamberlain vindicated against the accusations of the seneschal and others.[155] A more modern touch is given by the ' full assize ' held shortly afterward by the seneschal, William Fitz Ralph, and attended by barons and others whose names have reached us to the number of nearly eighty.[156]

Throughout the administration of justice the seneschal is the important figure. Something of his enhanced importance was doubtless due to the absences of Henry II and Richard and the decline of the personal justice of the sovereign, but something must also be ascribed to the personality of William Fitz Ralph, who in 1178 came fresh from his experience as itinerant justice in England and held the office until his death in 1200, exerting an

[153] Cf. also the Young King's court at Bur in 1171, attended, among others, by more than 110 knights named William: Robert of Torigni, ii. 31.

[154] Robert of Torigni, ii. 117; Benedict of Peterborough, i. 291.

[155] Walter Map, *De Nugis Curialium*, ed. James, pp. 242–246 (ed. Wright, pp. 232–234); cf. Round, *King's Serjeants*, p. 115 f.; and for the chamberlain's duties, Wace, lines 1873 ff., 2322 ff.

[156] Delisle-Berger, no. 638; Valin, p. 274; Round, no. 432.

influence upon Norman law which may still be traced in the *Très Ancien Coutumier*.[157] As the *alter ego* of the king the seneschal was the head of the whole judicial system, and in his sovereign's absence he alone could preside in the judgment of those who had the privilege of appearing only before the duke or his chief justiciar.[158] We find him holding court, not only at Caen, where the traces of his activity are naturally better preserved, but at Argentan, Bernai, Longueville, Neufchâtel, Saint-Wandrille, and Rouen. With him sit such men as William de la Mare, Richard Giffard, Richard of Argences, and John d'Éraines, archdeacon of Séez, who also in groups of two or three hold assizes in various parts of Normandy.[159] With no help from the Exchequer Rolls and only scattered references in the charters, it is impossible to define the composition of these assizes or determine how often they were held. In the documents the list of justices is often incomplete, and they are frequently indistinguishable from the other witnesses; yet we can identify many of them with the *baillis* and constables who meet us in the rolls, and occasionally an assize is held by a group of constables covering a considerable district. According to the custumal of 1199–1200, a doubtful witness for our period, assizes are held once or twice a year in each *vicomté* and are attended by the ducal officers within the district and by the local lords, who are forbidden to hold their own courts during the session of the assize.[160] Full rolls are kept of the cases considered and the names of the jurors, and the clerks have also

---

[157] Delisle, pp. 219–220, 481–483; Tardif, *Très Ancien Coutumier*, p. 105; Valin, pp. 160–163, where the fines carried in later Pipe Rolls are wrongly taken as evidence that William was justice in England after 1178. The Norman roll of 1180 (pp. 56, 57) shows that he received pay for the full ‚year 1179–1180 and administered justice in a preceding year.

[158] For examples of this privilege see Delisle, pp. 162, 219.

[159] See the list of assizes in Appendix J. Note the assize held by the constables in no. 2.

[160] *Très Ancien Coutumier*, cc. 25–29, 36, 37, 44, 55, 56; Robert of Torigni, ii. 117. R. de Fréville has pointed out (*Nouvelle revue historique de droit*, 1912, pp. 715–724) that the *Très Ancien Coutumier* cannot be taken as an unmixed source for the judicial organization of the Plantagenet period; its statements respecting law and procedure are less likely to have been affected by French influence. The growing importance of the official element in the administration of justice in the twelfth century is well brought out by Fréville (p. 682 ff.), who, however, goes too far in

their little parchments to record the various fines and payments.[161] The theory still survives that all chattels of offenders are forfeited to the duke, for " the function of the sworn affeerers is to declare what goods the offender has ";[162] but there are maximum payments for the various classes of society, and knight and peasant enjoy exemption of their arms and means of livelihood in a way which suggests the well known clause of *Magna Carta*.[163] The justices have a reputation for extortion on technical pretexts,[164] and the Exchequer Rolls show them bent on upholding the dignity and authority of their court by fines for contradiction and foolish speaking, for leaving its session without permission, and for disregarding or transgressing its decrees.[165] There are fines for those who go to the ecclesiastical courts against the justices' orders;[166] and even lords of the rank of Hugh de Longchamp and Hugh de Gournay are heavily mulcted for neglecting the summons to the regard of the forest.[167]

The ordinary local courts of the *vicomte* and *bailli* are not mentioned in the *Très Ancien Coutumier* and have left few traces in the charters. Early in the reign they had been ordered to meet at least once a month;[168] in the Avranchin the *vicomte* held pleas thrice a year in Ardevon and Genest.[169] In Guernsey in 1179, the court of the *vicomte* is still *curia regis*, and he has an official seal.[170]

excluding the non-professional element, and propounds a general theory which inverts the real order of development. His studies of the meaning of the word baron in this period are worth pursuing further.

[161] *Très Ancien Coutumier*, cc. 25, 28, 29, 65.

[162] Pollock and Maitland, ii. 514.

[163] *Très Ancien Coutumier*, cc. 55, 56; *Magna Carta*, c. 20; and on its interpretation, Tait and Pollard, *E. H. R.*, xxvii. 720–728, xxviii. 117.

[164] *Très Ancien Coutumier*, c. 65.

[165] Stapleton, i. 5, 16, 21, 34, 41, 51, 54, 58, 80, 86, 113, 116.

[166] *Ibid.*, i. 21 (' quia ivit in curiam episcopi contra defensum iusticie '), 47, 102.

[167] *Ibid.*, i. 59, 74. On pleas of the forest see the Fécamp cartulary (MS. Rouen 1207), f. 36v.

[168] Robert of Torigni, ii. 180. This is also the period prescribed by Philip Augustus for his *baillis* in 1190: Rigord, ed. Delaborde, p. 100 f.

[169] Delisle, p. 346. Cf. the pleas held by Nigel, seneschal of Mortain: Stapleton, i, pp. lxv, 11; Delisle, p. 408.

[170] ' Actum est hoc in curia domini regis in Guenerreio coram Gisleberto de Hoga tunc vicecomite, et quia sigillum non habebam sigillo Gisleberti de Hoga vicecomitis consideratione et assensu amicorum hanc cartam sigillari constitui ': original, with Gilbert's seal, printed in *Historical MSS. Commission, Various Collections*, iv. 53.

Once the sole agent of the duke in all departments of local administration, the *vicomte* saw his power greatly reduced by the development of the itinerant justices, and we have no means of knowing just what he still retained under the pleas which remained a constituent element of his farm. The newer jurisdictions of the *bailli* and constable have also to be reckoned with, and there were probably differences of local custom as well as changes in the course of the Angevin period. Thus the pleas of the sword regularly stood outside of the local farm [171] and fell naturally to the itinerant justices, yet in the district of Falaise a charter of Henry II specifically reserves them to the *baillis*.[172] The local officers also possessed a minor civil jurisdiction, as we see from a writ in which Henry orders the constable and *baillis* of Cherbourg to do full justice in a certain case unless the land in question be a knight's fee or a burgage of more than a hundred shillings' annual value, in which event the matter doubtless went to the higher court.[173] In general, however, the local writs are administrative

[171] This is specifically stated for the Hiesmois (see the following note), for the Lieuvin (*Rotuli Normanniae*, p. 116), for the castle of Gaillon (Delisle, *Cartulaire normand*, no. 120), and for the *vicomté* of Bonneville and the *prévôtés* of Falaise and Domfront (*ibid.*, no. 111).

[172] *Cartulaire de Fontenay-le-Marmion* (ed. G. Saige), no. 1; Delisle-Berger, no. 701; cf. Valin, p. 227. Later they are held here by the itinerant justices: *Rotuli Normanniae*, p. 20. For the *bailli* of Rouen see Henry's charter in Chéruel, *Histoire de Rouen*, i. 247; Delisle-Berger, no. 526 (on date, see Valin, *Précis* of Rouen Academy, 1911, pp. 9–42).

[173] ' H. Dei gratia rex Angl[orum] et dux Norm[annorum] et Aquit[anorum] et comes And[egavensium] constabulario et baillivis suis de Cesarisburgo salutem. Precipio vobis quod sine dilatione plenum rectum teneatis priori et canonicis Sancte Marie de Voto iuxta Cesarisburgum de terra que fuit Preisie apud Cesarisburgum et de domo quam ipsa eis dedit, quas Willelmus Pichard et uxor Richer' eis diffortiant, nisi sit feodum lorice vel burgagium quod valeat plusquam .c. solidos per annum. Et nisi feceritis iusticia mea Norm[annie] faciat, ne amplius inde clamorem audiam pro defectu recti. T[este] Hug[one] Bardulf dapifero apud Bonam villam.' Original, with fragment of *simple queue*, in Archives of the Manche, H. 1963. Printed from a poor copy by Bigelow, *History of Procedure*, p. 367; Round, no. 949; Delisle-Berger, no. 688. This writ is interesting further as one of the rare Norman examples of a writ of right, approaching more nearly the type addressed in England to the lord (Glanvill, bk. xii, cc. 3, 4) than that addressed to the royal officer (*ibid.*, bk. xii, cc. 11–20). It is indicative of the lesser importance of the local officers in Normandy that the justice appears in the *nisi feceris* clause, as in this writ (cf. those listed in note 46), more commonly than in similar writs in England.

A controversy concerning a mill is settled 30 June 1175, ' in presentia W. de rather than judicial,[174] and throw no light on the work of the local courts, which are plainly less important than in England.

With respect to the criminal jurisdiction of the duke, we have a list of pleas of the sword drawn up before 1174,[175] elaborated at certain points in the earlier part of the *Très Ancien Coutumier*,[176] and confirmed by the fines recorded in the Exchequer Rolls and the cases reserved by Henry in his charters.[177] The enumeration includes murder and slaying, mayhem, robbery, arson, rape, and the plotted assault, offenses against the peace of the house, the plow, the duke's highway and the duke's court, against his army and his coinage. In large measure this list goes back to the Conqueror's time, when many of these pleas had already been granted to the great immunists, lay and ecclesiastical, who still continued to retain them under Henry II.[178] Barons, however, whose courts encroach on the duke's jurisdiction must expect to be fined by his justices,[179] as must those who seek to settle such crimes out of

Huechon conestabularii regis ': *Livre blanc* of Saint-Martin de Séez, f. 13. Cf. the constable of Mortain, *supra*, note 72.

[174] For examples see Round, nos. 25, 26, 131, 205–207, 492 (where the original has ' Beiesino ' in the address), 939, 1282; Delisle, pp. 164 f., 179 f.; *supra*, note 46.

[175] *Très Ancien Coutumier*, c. 70. For the date see *supra*, note 22.

[176] *Très Ancien Coutumier*, cc. 15, 16, 35, 53, 54, 58, 59; cf. Pollock and Maitland, ii. 455.

[177] Round, nos. 375, 382; Delisle, *Cartulaire normand*, no. 16; id., *Henri II*, no. 495. The charter for Cormeilles (Delisle-Berger, no. 707; Round, no. 420) reserves ' incendiariorum iusticia et invasorum euntium et redeuntium ad nostram curiam et retrobanni et auxilio redemptionis nostre et falsariorum monete nostre.'

[178] *Supra*, p. 28 f.; Appendix D. Cf. Powicke, p. 80 ff.; Perrot, *Les cas royaux*, pp. 301–315.

[179] ' Pro placitis ensis iniuste captis ': Stapleton, i. 21. ' Pro duello latrocinii male servato in curia sua . . . pro duello de combustione male servato in curia sua' : *ibid.*, i. 123. On the right of barons to hold pleas of the sword see Chapter I, notes 103, 104; Valin, p. 220 ff.; Powicke, pp. 80–88. That the justices might sit in franchise courts is seen from a charter of John for William of Briouze (*Rotuli Normanniae*, p. 20; see Powicke, *E. H. R.*, xxii. 18) and from the following extract from the cartulary of Savigny (f. 27v): ' Fidelibus universis Guillelmus Avenel salutem. Sciatis quod Robertus pincerna et Guillelmus frater eius in presentia mea in curia comitis in plenaria assissa coram baronibus domini regis concesserunt monachis Savigneii . . . in manu mea qui tunc eram senescallus domini comitis Moretonii.' Cf. the justices in the courts of the bishop of Lisieux and the count of Meulan, *supra*, notes 58, 101. The baron's jealousy of losing his court is illustrated by the following: ' B. de Sancto Walerico maiori et paribus communie Rothomagensis salutem et magnum amorem. Audivi quod vos misistis in placitum Walterum

court.[180] Since the early years of the reign the itinerant justices are proclaiming outlaws in the marketplaces,[181] and men are fleeing the realm for murder, robbery, and similar offenses, which already bear the name of felonies,[182] while their chattels become a large element in the ducal revenues.[183] Nothing is said of their accusation by a jury of presentment, but we have reason for thinking that such juries were in use after 1159,[184] and the chattels of those who fail at the ordeal by water are accounted for in the roll of 1180 as they are in the Pipe Rolls after the Assize of Clarendon.[185] The pleas of the crown are viewed as a source of income analogous to the various portions of the ducal demesne; in the Avranchin, at least, they are in charge of a special officer, or coroner, as early as 1171.[186]

In civil matters the ducal courts had cognizance of disputes concerning church property, so far as these did not come under ecclesiastical jurisdiction,[187] and of such suits concerning land as involved the use of the recognition. From early times the prop-

fratrem meum de masura mea que [est] iuxta atrium Beate Marie de Rothomago. Unde non parum miror, cum non defecerim alicui de recto tenendo. Mando igitur vobis quod dimittatis mihi curiam meam sicut alii barones regis vel etiam minores habent, quia libenter quando requisitus fuero rectum faciam.' Cartulary of the chapter of Rouen (MS. Rouen 1193), f. 112; Delisle, p. 358.

[180] Stapleton, i. 25–27, 32; cf. p. 51; *Très Ancien Coutumier*, c. 36.

[181] Appendix H, no. 4. On the importance of the *fora patrie* in such cases see the *Très Ancien Coutumier*, cc. 36, 37; cf. Wace, ii, line 334; Arnulf of Lisieux, *Ep.* 110.

[182] ' Nisi sint fugitivi de terra mea pro muldro vel furto vel alio scelere ': charter of Henry for Fécamp (1162), in Valin, p. 269; Delisle-Berger, no. 221; Round, no. 133, where a curious misreading of *indictum* makes the document relate to a court instead of a fair. In another charter of 1162 for Fécamp we have (Delisle-Berger, no. 222): ' Habeant meam firmam pacem in eundo morando redeundo, nisi nominati[m] calumpniati fuerint de proditione vel felonia.'

[183] See the *catalla fugitivorum* in Stapleton, i. 4, 7, 10–12, 15, 16, 22, 23, 27, 29, 32–34, 43, 49, 55, 58, 72, 89, 94; Delisle, pp. 335, 339, 340, 343; and cf. *Très Ancien Coutumier*, cc. 36, 37. In the cartulary of La Trinité de Caen, MS. Lat. 5650, f. 84v, we read in an inquest of this reign: ' De feodo Rogeri Terrici fugitivi pro latrocinio inquirendum est ibidem.'

[184] *Infra*, Chapter VI; Appendix I.

[185] Stapleton, i. 62; and for England, Stubbs, *Benedictus*, ii, p. lxii, note.

[186] Delisle, p. 346; *E. H. R.*, xxv. 710 f., xxvi. 326 f. For mention of coroners in England before 1194, see C. Gross, *Coroners' Rolls*, pp. xv–xix.

[187] *Très Ancien Coutumier*, c. 53. Cf. *supra*, p. 172 f. On the prejudice of the author of the *Très Ancien Coutumier* in favor of the Church, see Viollet, in *Histoire littéraire*, xxxiii. 52–55.

erty of churches and monasteries had been assimilated to the
duke's own demesne (*sicut res mea dominica*), and charters repeatedly declare that particular establishments shall be impleaded
only in the king's court, in some cases only before him or his
principal justiciar.[188] The protection of possession by the duke,
praised especially by the author of the first part of the *Très Ancien
Coutumier* as a defense of the poor against the rich and powerful,
is secured, as in England, by recourse to twelve lawful men of the
vicinage. The possessory assizes described in this treatise [189] correspond to the four English assizes, and the Exchequer Rolls
furnish abundant evidence that they were in current use by
1180.[190] On the other hand the principle that no man should
answer for the title of his free tenement without royal writ does
not seem to have been so broadly recognized in Normandy as in
England, nor do we find anything which bears the name of the
grand assize,[191] but its Norman analogues, the *breve de stabilia*
and *breve de superdemanda*, appear in the early Exchequer Rolls,[192]
as does also the writ of right.[193] In the few instances where comparison with Glanvill is possible, the Norman writs seem to have
preserved their individuality of form, while showing general agreement in substance. Even in the duke's court, the law of Normandy has its differences from the law which is being made
beyond the Channel, nor can we see that its development shows
any dependence upon the law of England.[194]

[188] Brunner, *Schwurgerichte*, p. 238 ff.; Delisle, pp. 162, 219.

[189] Cc. 7, 16–19, 21, 23, 57. See Brunner, c. 15, who, however, points out that
the Norman parallel to the assize *utrum*, the *breve de feodo et elemosina*, is a petitory
writ.

[190] E. g., Stapleton, i. 5, 12, 13, 19, 64, 65, 96; cf. 114, 115 (1184). Cf. Brunner,
p. 307.

[191] Brunner, pp. 410–416.

[192] *Ibid.*, pp. 312–317; Stapleton, i. 11, 13, 29; Delisle, p. 339; *Très Ancien
Coutumier*, c. 85, where Tardif (p. lxxv) points out that the appearance of the seneschal's name in the writs carries them back of 1204, when the office was abolished.

[193] *Très Ancien Coutumier*, c. 30; and the numerous payments in the rolls *pro
recto habendo*. For an example see *supra*, note 173.

[194] Cf. the order of Henry III for the maintenance in the Channel Islands of
' assisas illas que ibi temporibus antecessorum nostrorum regum Anglie, videlicet
H. avi nostri, R. regis avunculi nostri, et J. regis patris nostri, observate fuerunt':
Calendar of Patent Rolls, 1216–1225, p. 136.

If we ask what limitations existed upon the ducal authority in Normandy, the answer must be that there were none, beyond the force of feudal custom and the body of law and precedent which the ducal court was creating, and that the only sanction of these was rebellion. Not until 1315, however, did revolt secure a definite formulation of the local rights and liberties of Normandy in the *Charte aux Normands* of Louis X; [195] the scribe who sought to pass off as the work of Henry II a version of *Magna Carta* as reissued in 1225, though he deceived older antiquarians, has long since been discredited.[196] The position of the duke in Normandy required of him none of those chartered promises which are often regarded as the foundations of English liberty. Yet if, with Stubbs,[197] we are to consider the charter of Henry I and its successors as an amplification of the coronation oath, we must not overlook the fact that the coronation oath of the dukes, with its threefold promise of peace, repression of disorder, and justice, is in exact verbal agreement with that of the English king as repeated since Anglo-Saxon times.[198] When, however, we recall that both in England and in Normandy these obligations were explained and accepted with especial care and ceremony at the accession of John,[199] we learn to attach less significance to such promises. And by the time that the Great Charter has declared the king below the law, England and Normandy have started on separate paths of constitutional development.

In the twelfth century, however, the resemblances between Normandy and England stand out the more clearly the further we explore and compare their institutions. There are of course fundamental differences in local government, but the essential central organs of finance and judicature are similarly constituted and fol-

[195] *Ordonnances des Rois*, i. 551, 587. For the revolt see Dufayard in *Revue historique*, liv, lv; Coville, *Les états de Normandie*, pp. 32–40.

[196] Delisle, *Henri II*, pp. 312–316, who by a slip gives 1227 as the date.

[197] *Select Charters*, 9th edition, p. 116. For the opposite view see H. L. Cannon, *A. H. R.*, xv. 37–46.

[198] Compare the two forms in the MS. of Rouen cathedral: *The Benedictional of Archbishop Robert*, ed. H. A. Wilson (Bradshaw Society, xxiv), pp. 140, 158. On the English coronation oath, see Stubbs, *Constitutional History*, i. 163–165; on the Norman ceremony, Valin, pp. 43–45.

[199] Stubbs, i. 553 f.; Roger of Hoveden, iv. 87 f.; *Magna Vita S. Hugonis*, p. 293 f.

low similar methods of work. The matter would be much clearer were it not for the disappearance of many thousands of royal writs which alone could reveal the daily routine of administration on both sides of the Channel; but Henry II had only one chancery, and its methods show remarkable uniformity in all of his various dominions and testify to similar administrative conditions throughout. The chancery was an extraordinarily active and effective mechanism, and we may well join with Delisle in praising its regularity, finish, and irreproachable precision, the terseness and simplicity of its documents, their ' solid and severe elegance.' [200] Its charters and writs, like Glanvill and the *Dialogus*, tell the story of a remarkably orderly and businesslike government, which expected obedience and secured it. A parallel story of order and thrift is told in the records of the Exchequers, in the Norman rolls quite as explicitly as in the English Pipe Rolls. The king's writ is necessary for every new disbursement; his officers must account for every penny of cash and every bushel of grain; the ' seller of justice ' must have his fee or his amercement; the land of the ducal castles is farmed ' up to the very walls.' [201] The thrifty detail of Henry's housekeeping is further illustrated in the inquest concerning his rights in the Avranchin, the only region for which an official statement has been preserved. Besides the ancient farm of the *vicomté*, the king has his monopoly of the fair of Saint Andrew, where even the abbot of the Mount pays his due of wax and pepper; he has his custom of wine in the ' Valley ' and his rights over the ' customary ' houses of the city, including fourpence from each, his meadows, and his chestnut grove; he has recovered by inquest an oven, a bit of land which yields ten quarters of grain, the treasurer's new house, and a room which has encroached on his demesne. The pleas of the crown are also a part of the demesne and have their special custodian, like the fair and the chestnut grove; his men of the neighborhood must bring the chestnuts to the king in Normandy, and he keeps the sacks which they are obliged to furnish for this purpose.[202] The sovereign who

[200] Delisle, *Henri II*, pp. 1 f., 151.
[201] Powicke, *Loss of Normandy*, p. 298.
[202] Inquest of 1171 in Delisle, pp. 345–347; cf. Appendix K.

saves chestnut bags shows equal watchfulness in his own household, wherever it journeys: its written ordinances fix the daily allowances of bread and wine and candle ends, and the master marshal requires tallies of receipt from all its officers.[203] The military bookkeeping is likewise careful: the Norman returns of service in 1172 correspond to the English *cartae* of 1166, and the registers of military obligations extend to minute fractions of a knight's fee. Norman in origin,[204] the military system was by this time as much at home in England as in Normandy, and in both countries it offered convincing evidence of the Norman capacity for methodical and efficient organization.

What more specific elements the Normans contributed to the Anglo-Norman state must remain in large measure a matter of speculation. It would be interesting, were it possible, to ascertain what, in an institutional sense, Normandy had given and received during a century and a quarter of union with England and particularly during more than a generation of membership in the Plantagenet empire. A study of Normandy and England under the Conqueror suggests fields in which Norman influence was exerted, while the reigns of Henry I and Geoffrey show the persistence and further development of the institutions of Normandy; but the process of change under Henry II was too rapid to permit of definite conclusions respecting the influence of one region or set of institutions upon another. Certainly the movement under him was not all in one direction. If the two chief figures in Norman administration in Henry's later years, Richard of Ilchester and William Fitz Ralph, had served an English apprenticeship, there had earlier in the reign been Norman precedents for Henry's English legislation. If the English military inquest of 1166 preceded the Norman returns of 1172, the Assize of Arms and the ordinance for the Saladin tithe were first promulgated for the king's Continental dominions. The order of these measures may have been a matter of chance, for to a man of Henry's temperament it mattered little where an experiment was first tried, but it was impossible to administer a great empire upon his system without using the experience gained in one region

[203] See Chapter III.   [204] See Chapter I.

for the advantage of another. There was wisdom in Geoffrey's parting admonition to his son against the transfer of customs and institutions from one part of his realm to another,[205] but so long as there was a common element in the administration and frequent interchange of officers between different regions, it could not be fully heeded. A certain amount of give and take there must inevitably have been, and now and then it can definitely be traced. On the other hand, it must not be supposed that there was any general assimilation, which would have been a still greater impossibility. Normandy preserved and carried over into the French kingdom its individuality of law and character, and as a model of vigorous and centralized administration it seems to have affected the government of Philip Augustus in ways which are still dark to us.[206] When that chapter of constitutional history comes to be written, if it ever can be written, it will illustrate from still another side the permanent importance of the creative statesmanship of the Norman dukes.

That creative work, so far as we can discern, was completed with the death of Henry II. It is true that no one has yet studied in full detail the law and government of Normandy under Richard and John,[207] and that the materials are in some respects more abundant than under their father. Richard's charters have not been collected,[208] nor does his reign yield any new types of record, but the Exchequer Rolls of 1195 and 1198 are the fullest which have been preserved, and the first Norman customal probably belongs to the year following his death.[209] Under John, as is well

[205] See the quotation from John of Marmoutier at the end of the preceding chapter.

[206] According to Benedict of Peterborough, i. 270, Philip Augustus and the count of Flanders had early imitated the Assize of Arms (cf. Guilhiermoz, *Origine de la noblesse*, p. 227). Ralph of Diceto, ii. 7 f., says Philip followed Henry's administrative policy on the advice of his household. Cf. also *supra*, note 168.

[207] See, however, the discussion of military organization and finance in Powicke, *Loss of Normandy*, chs. vii and viii.

[208] The copies collected by Achille Deville are in MS. Lat. n. a. 1244 and MS. Fr. n. a. 6191. A working list of Richard's charters is given by Cartellieri, *Philipp II. August*, ii. 288–301, iii. 217–233.

[209] Tardif, *Très Ancien Coutumier*, pp. lxv-lxxii; see, however, Viollet, in *Histoire littéraire*, xxxiii. 47–49. No Norman court rolls have been preserved from this period.

known, Normandy has its place in the great series of continuous records which begin with this reign, the charter rolls, patent rolls, and *liberate* rolls, from which material a separate set of Norman rolls was also drawn off.[210] At no period are the workings of administration in the Norman duchy so well known as just before its fall. At no time, one is tempted to add, are they so little worth knowing, save for the illustrations they afford of the government of Henry II. What can be seen only fragmentarily or in outline in his reign is now revealed in explicit detail — the work of the Exchequer and *camera*, the activity of the royal clerks and serjeants, the king's wines and the queen's furs, the royal prisoners and the royal sport, the control over trade and shipping, the strongholds upon which Richard lavished his treasure, the loans and exactions of John. The itinerant justices which had existed since Henry I first meet us by this name under John; [211] the writs presupposed in the earlier Exchequer Rolls can now be read in the *Rotuli de contrabrevibus*.[212] What they offer, however, is new examples, not new principles: there is no evidence of any change in the system of Henry II. The mechanism which in England " was so strong that it would do its work though the king was an absentee,"[213] was in Normandy strong enough to work though the king was present. Even John could not destroy it or seriously weaken it. It would be rash to assert that the fifteen years of Richard and John were not in some degree years of development in Normandy, especially in the field of law, but there is no evidence that they were years of innovation. What was strong and permanent in Norman law and Norman government had been written in before. From an institutional point of view, the interest of these two reigns lies rather in the transition from Angevin to Capetian administration, and it is worthy of note that it is the conditions anterior to 1190, not those of 1204, which the inquests

---

[210] *Rotuli Chartarum,* 1199–1216 (1837); *Rotuli Litterarum Patentium,* 1201–1216 (1835); *Rotuli de Liberate ac de Misis et Praestitis regnante Johanne* (1844); *Rotuli Normanniae in Turri Londinensi asservati* (1835); all edited by Hardy for the Record Commission. The last is reprinted in *M. A. N.,* xv. 89–136.

[211] *Rotuli Chartarum,* p. 59; *Rotuli Normanniae,* pp. 20, 97.

[212] *Rotuli Normanniae,* pp. xv, 22–37, 45–98.

[213] Pollock and Maitland, i. 169.

of Philip Augustus seek to establish.[214] What the new rulers of Normandy preserved and imitated was the work of Henry II and the state-builders who preceded him.[215]

To their Capetian successors the Norman rulers handed over a type of well organized and efficient government such as they had also developed in England. In the fields of finance, judicature, and military organization the modern features of this state, as of its contemporaries in Aragon and Sicily, stood out in sharp relief against the feudal background of the twelfth century. Like theirs, its institutions set strongly in the direction of centralization and royal authority. Unlike them, it had also an element which, while as yet royal, possessed great importance for the future in the development of more popular institutions, the sworn inquest which was to become the jury, the jury of England and of 'kingless commonwealths beyond the seas.' The special interest of the jury in the history of legal procedure and representative government sets it apart for special treatment in the following chapter.

[214] See Delisle, *Cartulaire normand*, nos. 111, 120, 124; *H. F.*, xxiv, preuves, nos. 10, 21, 22, 39, 69.

[215] H. Jenkinson's valuable paper on *The Financial Records of the Reign of King John* (in *Magna Carta Commemoration Essays*, 1917, pp. 244–300) reached me too late for discussion in this chapter. It makes new suggestions concerning the processes of the Norman Exchequer, touching upon the problems of Thomas Brown and Richard of Ilchester, and ascribing noteworthy administrative changes to the reign of John.

CHAPTER VI

THE EARLY NORMAN JURY[1]

THE Continental derivation of the institution of trial by jury is now generally accepted by scholars. First demonstrated in 1872 by Brunner in his masterly treatise on the origin of juries,[2] this view has at length triumphed over the natural disinclination of Englishmen to admit that the palladium of their liberties " is in its origin not English but Frankish, not popular but royal." [3] Whatever one may think of the Scandinavian analogies, there is now no question that the modern jury is an outgrowth of the sworn inquests of neighbors held by command of the Norman and Angevin kings, and that the procedure in these inquests is in all essential respects the same as that employed by the Frankish rulers three centuries before. It is also the accepted opinion that while such inquests appear in England immediately after the Norman Conquest, their employment in lawsuits remains exceptional until the time of Henry II, when they become, in certain cases, a matter of right and a part of the settled law of the land. From this point on, the course of development is reasonably clear; the obscure stage in the growth of the jury lies earlier, between the close of the ninth century, when ' the deep darkness settles down ' over the Frankish empire and its law, and the assizes of Henry II. Information concerning the law and institutions of this intervening period must be sought mainly in the charters of the time, and

---

[1] Revised and expanded from *A. H. R.*, viii. 613–640 (1903).

[2] H. Brunner, *Die Entstehung der Schwurgerichte* (Berlin, 1872). Brunner's results are accepted by Stubbs, *Constitutional History*, i. 652 ff.; Pollock and Maitland, *History of English Law*, i. 138 ff.; J. B. Thayer, *Development of Trial by Jury*, ch. ii; cf. W. S. Holdsworth, *History of English Law*, i. 145 f.; J. Hatschek, *Englische Verfassungsgeschichte* (Munich, 1913), p. 123 f. Valin, *Le duc de Normandie* (1910), pp. 194–220, uses Pollock and Maitland and a few new documents, but makes no use of Brunner or of this chapter as first published in 1903. M. M. Bigelow, *The Old Jury*, in *Proceedings of the Massachusetts Historical Society*, xlix. 310–327 (1916), deals with other questions. Vinogradoff, *English Society in the Eleventh Century*, pp. 6–8, emphasizes the Scandinavian element in the jury of presentment.

[3] Pollock and Maitland, i. 142.

it is upon their evidence that Brunner based his conclusions as to the persistence of the Frankish system of inquest in Normandy. Unfortunately this great historian of law was obliged to confine his investigations to the materials available at Paris, and while further research tends to confirm most of the inferences which his sound historic sense drew from the sources at his disposal, it also shows the need of utilizing more fully the documents preserved in Norman libraries and archives. For the jury, as for other aspects of Norman institutions, these are not abundant, but they enable us to determine some questions which Brunner raised and to illustrate more fully the earlier stages in the development of recognitions. The most important body of evidence, the cartulary of Bayeux cathedral known as the *Livre noir*, is now accessible in print,[4] though unfortunately in an edition marred by many inaccuracies of transcription and defects in dating the documents, so that its evidence can now be subjected to careful analysis and verification.

[4] *Antiquus Cartularius Ecclesiae Baiocensis (Livre noir)*, edited by V. Bourrienne, (Société de l'Histoire de Normandie, Rouen and Paris, 1902–1903). Through the courtesy of the abbé Deslandes I had ample opportunity to examine the MS. at the cathedral in 1902 and again in 1905. A defective analysis of the cartulary was published by Léchaudé d'Anisy, *M. A. N.*, viii. 435–454, and extracts from it are in his papers at the Bibliothèque Nationale (MS. Lat. 10064) and in the transcripts made by him for the English government and preserved at the Public Record Office ('Cartulaire de la Basse Normandie,' i. 46–53). It would be hard to find anything more careless and unintelligent than this portion of Léchaudé's copies, which form the basis of the analyses in Round's *Calendar* (no. 1432 ff.). As a specimen may be cited his account of nos. 34 to 42 of the cartulary: "Suivent neuf autres brefs du même roi Henry II qui n'offrent maintenant pas plus d'intérêt que les vingt-six précédentes." As a matter of fact only three of these documents emanate from Henry II, three being of Henry I, one of Geoffrey, one of Robert, earl of Gloucester, and one of Herbert Poisson; while three of the documents are of decided importance in relation to the Norman jury. Some use was made of the *Livre noir* by Stapleton in his edition of the Exchequer Rolls and by Delisle in his essay on Norman finance in the twelfth century (*B. É. C.*, x–xiii). Brunner used Delisle's copies, from which he published numerous extracts in his *Schwurgerichte*. Sixteen of the documents of most importance for the history of the jury are printed from the London copies by M. M. Bigelow in the appendix to his *History of Procedure* (London, 1880), nos. 40–55, but without any serious effort to determine questions of date and authorship (cf. Brunner in *Zeitschrift der Savigny-Stiftung*, Germ. Abt., ii. 207).

The other Bayeux cartularies preserved at Bayeux (*Livre noir de l'évêché*, MSS. 206–208) and Paris (MSS. Lat. n. a. 1828, 1925, 1926, the last two formerly at Cheltenham) throw no further light on the jury.

One of the most interesting problems in the history of the jury is to determine how and when the procedure by recognition ceased to be an exclusive privilege of the king and became part of the regular system of justice. This extension of the king's prerogative procedure may have been made " bit by bit, now for this class of cases and now for that,"[5] but Brunner believes it can have been accomplished only by a definite royal act or series of acts.[6] The jurists refer to the recognition as a royal favor, an outgrowth of equity, a relief to the poor, while the very name of assize by which the recognition came to be known points to the royal ordinance, or assize, by which it was introduced. The author of this ordinance he considers to have been Henry II. The whole machinery of the various assizes appears in well developed form in the treatise ascribed to Glanvill and written near the close of Henry's reign, whereas none of them has been traced in England back of 1164, when the assize *utrum* makes its appearance in the Constitutions of Clarendon. A charter of King John seems to place the introduction of recognitions in his father's reign, and one of Henry's own writs refers to the grand assize as ' my assize.' The English assizes cannot, then, be older than Henry's accession in 1154; they may be somewhat younger. When we turn to Normandy, we find likewise a full-grown system of recognitions in existence in the later years of the twelfth century, as attested by the earliest Norman customal, the *Très Ancien Coutumier*, and the numerous references to recognitions contained in the Exchequer Rolls of 1180 and the following years.[7] Between these records and Glanvill there is little to choose in point of time, and priority might be claimed for England or for Normandy with equal inconclusiveness.

Brunner, however, discovered in the Bayeux cartulary three documents which not only antedate any mention of assizes so far noted in English sources, but also, he maintained, afford clear proof that the regular establishment of the procedure by recognition was the work of Henry II as duke of Normandy before he

[5] Pollock and Maitland, i. 144.
[6] Ch. xiv, " Die Einführung des ordentlichen Recognitionsprocesses."
[7] *Supra*, Chapter V, note 190.

ascended the English throne. One of these documents, issued in the name of Henry as king and belonging to the year 1156, orders William Fitz John to hold a recognition, by means of the ancient men of Caen, with reference to the rights of the bishop of Bayeux at Caen, and to do the bishop full right according to Henry's assize (*secundum assisam meam*).[8] The other two writs run in the name of a duke of Normandy and count of Anjou whose name is left blank in the cartulary. One of them[9] directs two of the duke's justices to determine by recognition, *secundum asisiam meam*, who was seized of certain fiefs in the time of Henry I; the other commands another justice to hold recognition throughout his district, *secundum assisiam meam*, concerning the fiefs of the bishop of Bayeux, and at the same time threatens one of the bishop's tenants with such a recognition unless he gives up a knight's fee wrongfully withheld from the bishop.[10] While the author of the second and third of these documents (nos. 25 and 24) is not named, the style of duke of Normandy and count of Anjou was used only by Geoffrey Plantagenet and by Henry II between his father's death in 1151 and his coronation as king in 1154.[11] That the duke in question was not Geoffrey, Brunner was led to maintain from the recurrence of the phrase *assisa mea* in the writ of Henry relating to Caen; if ' my assize ' meant Henry's assize in the one case, it must have meant his assize in the other.[12] Inas-

[8] *Livre noir*, no. 27; Bigelow, *History of Procedure*, p. 393, no. 48; La Rue, *Essais historiques sur la ville de Caen*, i. 375; Brunner, p. 302, no. 1; Round, *Calendar*, no. 1443; Delisle Berger, no. 21. Brunner places the document between 1156 and 1159; the king's itinerary fixes it in October 1156. For the text and a fuller discussion of this and the two other documents see below, pp. 209–214.

[9] *Livre noir*, no. 25; Bigelow, p. 393, no. 47; Brunner, p. 302, no. 2; Delisle, *Henri II*, p. 138, no. 6; not in Round.

[10] *Livre noir*, no. 24; Bigelow, p. 392, no. 46; Brunner, p. 302, no. 3; Round, no. 1439; Stapleton, *Magni Rotuli*, i, p. xxxiv; Delisle, p. 137, no. 5.

[11] Henry received the duchy of Normandy from his father in 1150 and became count of Anjou on his father's death, 7 September 1151. His marriage with Eleanor in May 1152 gave him the additional title of duke of Aquitaine, but he did not take this style in his charters until 1153, so that its absence does not prove a document to be anterior to his marriage: see Delisle, pp. 120–133. Nos. 24 and 25, if of Henry, would fall between 1151 and 1153; Brunner places them between 1150 and 1152.

[12] *Schwurgerichte*, p. 303 and note, where the silence of no. 39 in the *Livre noir* is also urged. Brunner's conviction seems to have been fortified by the authority of Delisle (see *Zeitschrift der Savigny-Stiftung*, Germ. Abt., ii. 207), although Delisle

much as the assize referred to is obviously a general ordinance concerning the procedure by recognition, the introduction of this form of procedure is to be ascribed to its author, the young duke Henry II.

Such is the essence of Brunner's argument, which hinges upon two points: the meaning of the phrase *assisa mea*, and the authorship of the two anonymous writs, nos. 24 and 25. In the matter of authorship Brunner, while confident of his interpretation—and his confidence seems to have grown into certitude after the publication of the *Entstehung*[13] — still admitted that a final decision was impossible before the rich treasures of the *Livre noir* should be accessible in print. Now that the published cartulary lies before us, it appears that while the editor follows Brunner in ascribing the critical documents to Henry II, he brings no new evidence to light; the name of the duke does not appear in the printed text. Fortunately, however, a close examination of the manuscript of the cartulary reveals something more. Those familiar with the habits of mediaeval scribes are aware that when, as here, the initial letter was left blank for the rubricator, it was usual to give him some indication of the omitted letter by marking it lightly in the blank space or on the margin.[14] Now an attentive examination of the well thumbed margins of the *Livre noir* shows that the initial was clearly indicated in a contemporary hand, and that not only in nos. 24 and 25 but in ten other documents left anonymous in the edition [15] the initial is G. The author of the writs in ques-

had formerly assigned no. 24 to Geoffrey (*B. É. C.*, x. 260, note 2) and in his last work (*Henri II*, p. 137 f.) comes out decisively for Geoffrey's authorship. Round, who does not calendar no. 25, ascribes no. 24 to Geoffrey (*Calendar*, no. 1439).

[13] In 1896 in a review of Pollock and Maitland he says: " Nach Lage der Urkunden des Liber niger capituli Baiocensis ist es zweifellos, dass die Einführung der Recognitionen in der Normandie 1150–1152 stattfand." *Zeitschrift der Savigny-Stiftung*, Germ. Abt., xvii. 128. Cf. *ibid.*, ii. 207; Holtzendorff, *Encyclopädie der Rechtswissenschaft*, edition of 1890, p. 325; *Political Science Quarterly*, xi. 537; Brunner, *Geschichte der englischen Rechtsquellen* (1909), p. 65.

[14] Where they have often been cut off in binding.

[15] Nos. 16, 17, 18, 19, 39, 43, 44, 89, 90, 100. Throughout the cartulary the initial letter of charters is again and again indicated in this way, only in most of the other cases the rest of the first word was written out in the text, so that the missing letter could readily be supplied without recourse to the margin. The charters of Henry II regularly (no. 436 seems to be the only exception) have something more

tion was accordingly not Henry, but his father Geoffrey. 'My assize' was Geoffrey's assize in the first instance, even if the expression was later adopted by Henry; and if Brunner's contention is sound as to the conclusion to be drawn from the phrase, it was Geoffrey Plantagenet who first established the recognition as a regular form of procedure in Normandy. In continuing the employment of this procedure in Normandy and in extending it to England Henry II was simply carrying out the policy begun by his father. This conclusion necessarily follows if we accept Brunner's premises, but one of them, the phrase *assisa mea*, requires further investigation. Before undertaking, however, to analyze in detail the writs in which this expression is found, it is necessary to place them in their proper setting by tracing the history of the litigation concerning the rights and possessions of the bishop of Bayeux and by examining, as carefully as the material at hand permits, the procedure employed in the bishop's behalf.

The see of Bayeux, which had occupied a position of wealth and importance in the eleventh century, especially in the days of Bishop Odo, the famous half-brother of William the Conqueror, suffered serious losses from the weakness and neglect of Odo's immediate successors, Thorold and Richard Fitz Samson.[16] After Richard's death in Easter week, 1133,[17] "in order that the church

of the duke's name than the initial. In all the charters of Geoffrey, as well as in many others, there is also a marginal 'sic' in what appears to be a somewhat later hand, evidently that of a mediaeval collator. In the *Livre rouge* (MS. Lat. n. a. 1828, f. 154) no. 17 of the *Livre noir* likewise appears with the initial G indicated, this time in the blank space itself.

M. Henri Omont, head of the department of manuscripts of the Bibliothèque Nationale, who happened to visit the chapter library just as I had finished examining the manuscript of the *Livre noir* in August 1902, had the kindness to verify my reading of the marginal initials. So now Delisle, *Henri II*, p. 137, supplemented by Berger, i. 3. In the corrections at the end of the second volume of his edition (1903) Bourrienne ascribes nos. 16–19, 24, 25, 89, and 90 to Geoffrey, but without giving any reason for changing his opinion and without referring to the marginal initials, to which the archivist had called his attention after my visit. The same silence is observed in his articles in the *Revue catholique*, xix (1909), in which considerable use is made of the article in *A. H. R.*, viii. Valin, p. 209 f., overlooks these corrections as well as my readings.

[16] On the history of the possessions of the see cf. Bourrienne's introduction to his edition of the *Livre noir*, p. xxxiii ff.; and his articles on Philip d'Harcourt in the *Revue catholique*, xix ff.　　　　[17] Ordericus Vitalis, v. 31.

of Bayeux might not be utterly ruined," Henry I ordered an inquest to be held, on the oath of ancient men who knew the facts, to ascertain the holdings of the church as they had existed in Odo's time, with respect both to the demesne and to the fiefs of knights, vavassors, and rustics. Accordingly "all these were sworn and recognized and by the king's command restored to the said church," which was confirmed in its possessions by a royal charter.[18] The writ directing this inquest, the record of the returns from the bishop's demesne,[19] and the confirmatory charter are referred to in documents of Geoffrey and Henry II, but they have not come down to us. Fortunately, however, the returns of the inquest relating to military tenures have been preserved and give an idea of the procedure employed. The recognition was held before the king's son, Robert, earl of Gloucester, sent to Bayeux for this purpose immediately after the death of Bishop Richard. Twelve [20] men were chosen, and sworn to tell the truth concerning the fiefs and services; and their returns, besides stating the military obligations of the bishop and the customary reliefs and aids due him, cover in detail the holdings and services of his knights and vavassors, beginning with the principal tenant, Earl Robert himself, whose statement is incorporated verbally into their report.[21]

[18] 'Ne funditus ecclesia predicta destrueretur, provide Henricus rex, avus meus, instituit ut iuramento antiquorum hominum qui rem norant recognoscerentur tenedure iam dicte ecclesie sicut fuerant in tempore predicti Odonis, tam in dominicis quam in feodis militum, vavassorum, et rusticorum. Ipsius equidem tempore hec omnia iurata sunt et recognita et sepe dicte ecclesie precepto eius resignata et munimine carthe sue, quocumque modo a possessione ecclesie alienata essent, reddita sunt et confirmata.' Writ of Henry II, *Livre noir*, no. 14; Brunner, p. 264; Bigelow, p. 389; Delisle-Berger, no. 33*. The inquest of Henry I is also mentioned in a bull of Lucius II (*Livre noir*, no. 206) and in a later writ of Henry II (*ibid.*, no. 32). The date is fixed by a document of Geoffrey (*ibid.*, no. 39): 'post mortem Ricardi episcopi, filii Sansonis.'

[19] ' Recognitum est sicut continebatur in scripto quod factum fuerat secundum iuramentum quod rex Henricus antea fieri preceperat.' *Livre noir*, no. 39; Bigelow, p. 395. That this *scriptum* was not the same as the *carta* seems probable from the different word used and from the preservation of a separate record of the military tenures.

[20] Only eleven are given in the returns, but twelve are named in the *Red Book of the Exchequer*, the name of Helto the constable having been omitted from the Bayeux text.

[21] The document was first published by Léchaudé from a private copy (now MS. Lat. 10064, f. 3) made from a register formerly in the episcopal archives: *M. A. N.*,

How much was accomplished by these proceedings toward the recovery of the bishop's rights, we have no means of knowing. That they were for a time more carefully observed may perhaps be inferred from the fact that the profits of the see would naturally fall to the king during the interval of two years which elapsed before Henry's nominee to the vacant see could be consecrated,[22] and that during this period the king remained in Normandy.[23] However, the new bishop, Richard of Kent, was a son of Robert, earl of Gloucester, and in the stormy times that followed the see seems to have been at the mercy of his father, who soon succeeded in usurping the greater part of its property.[24] The reëstablishment of the bishop's fortunes was the work of Richard's successor, Philip d'Harcourt, bishop from 1142 to 1163, within whose episcopate the evidence of value for the early history of the Norman jury is chiefly found. ' Wise in the wisdom of this world which is foolishness with God,' as the contemporary abbot of Mont-Saint-Michel describes him,[25] Philip seems to have begun his arduous struggle for the recovery of his possessions immediately upon his accession, and to have sought from the beginning the support of the papacy. When his sentences of excommunication proved ineffective in spite of papal sanctions,[26] he made in 1144 the first of a number of journeys to Rome,[27] and 16 May of

viii. 425–431; also in Béziers, *Mémoires pour servir à l'état historique et géographique du diocèse de Bayeux*, i. 142; and in *H. F.*, xxiii. 699–702, which furnishes the best text. These returns are also found in Léchaudé's copies in the Public Record Office (' Cartulaire de la Basse Normandie,' i. 53), but are not mentioned in Round's *Calendar*. Upon them is based the summary of services due from the bishop of Bayeux contained in the *Red Book of the Exchequer* (ed. Hall, pp. 645–647; *H. F.*, xxiii. 699). On the importance of these returns for feudal tenure, see Chapter I, *supra*.

[22] Ordericus, v. 31, 45.　　[23] See Appendix G.　　[24] *Livre noir*, no. 190.

[25] Robert of Torigni, i. 344. Cf. also *H. F.*, xiv. 503; and the *Epistolae* of Arnulf of Lisieux (Migne, cci), no. 6. The various possessions recovered by Philip's efforts are enumerated in a bull of Eugene III of 3 February 1153, *Livre noir*, no. 156.

[26] Bull of Innocent II, 18 June 1143 (probably), *ibid.*, no. 195; bull of Celestine II, 9 January 1144, *ibid.*, no. 179.

[27] He appears in the Pope's presence three times under Eugene III, in 1145 (*ibid.*, no. 173), in 1146 (*ibid.*, no. 207), and in 1153 (*ibid.*, no. 200). His presence at Rome when the bulls were obtained from Lucius II is also attested by a bull of 15 May, in which he appears as a witness: Martène and Durand, *Thesaurus*, iii. 887; Jaffé-Löwenfeld, *Regesta*, no. 8609.

that year obtained from Pope Lucius II three important bulls which mark a turn in the fortunes of the church of Bayeux. One, addressed to Philip himself, enumerated and confirmed the ancient privileges and possessions of the see.[28] The second commanded the clergy and people of the diocese to render due obedience to the bishop, and, after annulling all grants and sales of church property made since the time of Bishop Odo, ordered its restitution to the church of Bayeux on the tenure by which it should be proved, on the oath of lawful witnesses, to have been held in Odo's time.[29] The third bull was addressed to Geoffrey, count of Anjou, who had just succeeded in making himself master of Normandy, and directed him to cause the possessions of the see of Bayeux to be declared by the sworn statement of lawful men of the region, in the same manner as they had been recognized in the time of his father-in-law, Henry I.[30] These bulls were reissued in March 1145[31] by the successor of Lucius, Eugene III, who also rebuked the encroachments of various monasteries and individuals upon the rights of the bishop;[32] but from this point on we need concern ourselves no longer with the acts of the popes, but can turn our attention to the machinery of secular justice which they seem to have set in motion.

For a study of the recognitions held concerning the lands of the bishop of Bayeux under Duke Geoffrey the evidence in the *Livre noir* consists of ten documents emanating from Geoffrey or his justices,[33] and a number of references to these and to others made in documents of Henry II.[34] The inquests to which these writs

[28] *Livre noir*, no. 154.

[29] *Ibid.*, no. 157; Jaffé-Löwenfeld, no. 8612.

[30] *Livre noir*, no. 206.

[31] Only the reissues of the first two have come down to us (*ibid.*, nos. 155, 173), but it is implied in no. 39 that the bull to Geoffrey was likewise repeated.

[32] *Ibid.*, nos. 190, 159 (the Pope's itinerary makes it clear that these are of 1145); 186, 199 (these two may be of either 1145 or 1146); 198 (clearly of 1146); 191 (of 1147 — cf. the Pope's itinerary and no. 41); and 192.

[33] Nos. 16, 17, 19, 24, 25, 39, 43, 44, 89, 90. Bigelow, *History of Procedure*, p. 390 ff., nos. 43–47, 51–55. Cf. Brunner, *Schwurgerichte*, pp. 265 ff., 302. The first letter of each of these is in blank in the cartulary, but in every case G appears on the margin.

[34] Nos. 9, 12, 14, 32, 36; Delisle-Berger, nos. 33*, 13, 14, 72, 228. Of these only nos. 14 and 32 of the *Livre noir* are in Bigelow (nos. 42 and 49).

and charters relate are of course subsequent to the conquest of Normandy by Geoffrey in 1144 and anterior to his relinquishment of the duchy to his son Henry in 1150,[35] and it is altogether likely that they fall after the bulls of Eugene III of March 1145.[36] The documents are issued at various places — Rouen, Le Mans, Bayeux — and witnessed by various of the duke's followers, but none of them are dated, and our knowledge of the itineraries of Geoffrey and his justices is not sufficient to permit of drawing close chronological limits. It is, however, probable that the process of recovering the bishop's possessions began soon after the papal bulls were received, and there is some reason for placing at least two of the documents before the summer of 1147.[37] Clearly the material which has reached us from these inquests is only a portion of what once existed, but it illustrates the different stages in the process of recognition and gives a fair idea of the procedure employed. Apart from the general order to try by sworn inquest all disputes which might arise concerning the bishop's fiefs,[38] a document to which we shall return later, the duke must have provided for a general recognition of the rights and possessions of the see, similar to the one which had been held under Henry I and to that which was afterward ordered by Henry II.[39] This was

[35] For these dates see Chapter IV, *supra*.

[36] 'Predictorum patrum nostrorum Lucii pape et Eugenii litteris commoniti': *Livre noir*, no. 39.

[37] Galeran, count of Meulan, who appears as witness in no. 16 and as the justice who makes the return in no. 89, took the cross at Vézelay in 1146 and followed Louis VII on the second crusade (Robert of Torigni, i. 241; *Chronicon Valassense*, ed. Somménil, Rouen, 1868, pp. 7-9), so that he was away from Normandy from the summer of 1147 until 1149 or thereabouts. The bulls of Eugene III and other documents in the *Livre noir* indicate that the active period in the recovery of the bishop's rights lies between 1145 and 1147. See nos. 159, 189, 190, 199, 186, 207, 198, 191, 192 for the papal bulls, and for the other documents nos. 41, 52, 100-104.

C. Port, in his *Dictionnaire historique de Maine-et-Loire*, ii. 255, says that Geoffrey himself went on the crusade in 1147, but I have found no authority for the statement. Geoffrey issued a charter for Mortemer at Rouen, 11 October 1147, whereas the crusaders started in June: *Bulletin de la Société des Antiquaires de Normandie*, xiii. 115, no. 2; Round, *Calendar*, no. 1405; *supra*, p. 134.

[38] *Livre noir*, no. 16.

[39] The order of Geoffrey for a general recognition has not been preserved, but is clearly presupposed in his charter describing the results of the inquests (no. 39) and in the similar order of Henry II (no. 14).

supplemented, at least in some cases, by special writs issued to individual justices and relating to particular estates.[40] After holding the local inquest each justice made a written return to the duke,[41] and the results were finally embodied in ducal charters.[42]

The course of procedure can be followed most clearly in the various documents relating to the rights of the bishop of Bayeux in the *banlieue* of Cambremer, a privileged portion of an enclave of his diocese lying within the limits of the diocese of Lisieux.[43] The duke issued a writ to Reginald of Saint-Valery, Robert de Neufbourg, and all his justices of Normandy, ordering them to hold a recognition on the oath of good men of the vicinage concerning the limits of the *banlieue*, its customs, forfeitures, and warren, and to put Bishop Philip in such possession of them as his predecessors had enjoyed under William the Conqueror and Henry I.[44] The inquest was held by the duke's justices, Robert de Neufbourg and Robert de Courcy, in the church of Saint-Gervais at Falaise. The jurors were chosen from the old and lawful men residing within the district in question, some of whom had been officers (*servientes*) of the *banlieue* in the time of King Henry, and care was taken to summon a larger number than the justices ordinarily called, eighteen [45] in all, and to see that they represented the lands of different barons. On the basis of what they had heard and seen and knew the recognitors swore to the boundaries of the *banlieue* and to the bishop's tolls, fines, warren, and rights of justice. The justices then drew up returns addressed to the duke, stating the verdict found and the names of the jurors,[46] and on the basis of these the duke issued a charter

[40] Nos. 17, 24, 25. Similar writs are presupposed in nos. 89 and 90 and in no. 36.
[41] Nos. 43, 44, 89, 90.
[42] Nos. 39 (cf. nos. 9, 12, 32), 19 (cf. 18); reference to such a charter in no. 36.
[43] On the *banlieue* (*leugata*) in Normandy see *supra*, p. 49. On the enclave of Cambremer, Béziers, *Mémoires sur le diocèse de Bayeux*, i. 28, iii. 152.
[44] *Livre noir*, no. 17; *Livre rouge*, no. 401.
[45] Eighteen, according to the return of Robert de Neufbourg, but only seventeen names appear in the lists.
[46] Nos. 43, 44 (cf. 32). There are some differences in the two returns: Bourrienne, in *Revue catholique*, xix. 269 f. Each of these returns is in the name of both justices, but in one case the name of Robert de Neufbourg, and in the other that of

embodying the results of the recognition.[47] The inquest concerning the other manors of the bishop was held in the choir of the cathedral at Bayeux by Richard de la Haie, Robert de Neufbourg, Robert de Courcy, and Enjuger de Bohun, specially deputed by the duke for this purpose. The evidence of the recognitors, comprising several ancient and lawful men from each manor, was found to be in entire agreement with the written returns of the inquest held under Henry I, and a statement to this effect was embodied in a charter of the duke, which further specified as belonging to the bishop's demesne the estates of Carcagny and Vouilly, the fosse of Luchon, and " the Marsh and its herbage, including the reeds and rushes."[48] A special charter was also issued for Carcagny and Vouilly.[49] The bishop's forests were likewise the object of an inquest, but the writ and charter issued in this case, though cited by Henry II,[50] have not come down to us.

It will be observed that all the documents so far examined relate to the bishop's demesne, and that, while the preservation of a larger body of material from Geoffrey's time enables us to see more clearly the different stages in the process of recognition, there is no indication that the procedure differs in any way from the practice of Henry I's reign, which it professes to follow. Indeed, so long as the subject-matter of the inquest is the bishop's demesne, it is not likely that there will be much advance in the direction of the trial jury; except that the rights in question are claimed for the bishop instead of for the king or duke, such recognitions as have been described show no significant difference from a fiscal inquest, such, for example, as the Domesday survey. The application of the inquest to the feudal possessions of the bishop,

Robert de Courcy appears first. Brunner (p. 266) suggests the natural explanation that in each case the document was drawn up by the justice whose name appears first. The similar reports of the recognition in regard to Cheffreville (nos. 89, 90) are made by the justices individually.

[47] No. 39, where the facts with regard to Cambremer are set forth at length along with the returns from other domains, the two justices appearing among the witnesses. References to this recognition are also made in nos. 9, 12, 32, and 156.

[48] No. 39, end.

[49] No. 19; Brunner, p. 268. Cf. also the notification in no. 18 of the quitclaim of the fosse of Luchon.

[50] No. 36; Delisle-Berger, no. 14.

on the other hand, brings us a step nearer the later assizes. There
is, it is true, no distinction in principle between recognizing the
bishop's demesne and recognizing his fiefs; but inasmuch as disputes between lord and tenant constitute a large proportion of the
cases arising under the later assizes, the submission of any such
controversy to the sworn verdict of neighbors is a movement
away from the inquest that is primarily fiscal, and toward the
general application of the inquest to suits concerning tenure.
Whether Geoffrey also imitated the example of Henry I in ordering a general inquest with regard to the fiefs of the bishop does not
clearly appear. Henry II indicates that such was the case,[51] and
an extant writ directs one of the duke's justices to have the
bishop's fief in his district recognized,[52] but no set of returns for
the fiefs has been preserved, and the compiler of the list of the
bishop's tenants in the *Red Book of the Exchequer* went back to the
returns of the inquest of Henry I.[53] There is, however, another
writ of Geoffrey relating to the bishop's fiefs which deserves careful attention. It is addressed to all his barons, justices, bailiffs,
and other faithful subjects in Normandy, and provides that " if
a dispute shall arise between the bishop and any of his men concerning any tenement, it shall be recognized by the oath of lawful
men of the vicinage who was seized of the land in Bishop Odo's
time, whether it was the bishop or the other claimant; and the
verdict thus declared shall be firmly observed unless the tenant
can show, in the duke's court or the bishop's, that the tenement
came to him subsequently by inheritance or lawful gift."[54] Here

---

[51] *Livre noir*, no. 14.   [52] *Ibid.*, no. 24.

[53] Pp. 645–647; *H. F.*, xxiii. 699.

[54] ' Volo et precipio quod si de aliqua tenedura orta fuerit contentio inter episcopum et aliquem de suis hominibus, per iuramentum legitimorum hominum vicinie
in qua hoc fuerit sit recognitum quis saisitus inerat tempore Odonis episcopi, vel ipse
episcopus vel ille cum quo erit contentio; et quod inde recognitum fuerit firmiter
teneatur, nisi ille qui tenet poterit ostendere quod tenedura illa in manus suas postea
venerit iure hereditario aut tali donatione que iuste debeat stare, et hoc in curia
episcopi vel in mea.' *Livre noir*, no. 16; Bigelow, p. 390, no. 43; Brunner, p. 265.
It is also provided that no officer shall enter upon the bishop's lands, for judicial or
other purposes, except in accordance with the practice of King Henry's time. The
writ is witnessed at Rouen by the count of Meulan, so that it must be anterior to
the summer of 1147 or, what is much less likely, subsequent to his return from the
East in 1149 or thereabouts.

we have something new, so far as existing sources of information permit us to judge. Instead of a general inquest to be held once for all by the king's officers to ascertain the tenure of the bishop's fiefs, the writ in question confers a continuing privilege — in any controversy that may arise between the bishop and any of his men the procedure by sworn inquest shall be applied. The remedy is designed for the benefit of the bishop, not of his tenants; no attempt is made to deprive the bishop of his court or extend the competence of the court of the duke; but the establishment of the principle that, not merely in this case or in that case, but in any case between the bishop and one of his tenants the oath of lawful neighbors shall decide, is a considerable advance in the extension of the duke's prerogative procedure to his subjects.[55]

It is in the light of this document that we should read the two writs of Geoffrey which make mention of the duke's assize. As they were both witnessed at Le Mans by Payne de Clairvaux[56] and appear together in the cartulary, it is probable that they were issued about the same time. One of them, resembling the later *Praecipe quod reddat*, is directed to Enjuger de Bohun, this time not as one of the king's justices but as in wrongful possession of two fiefs of the bishop of Bayeux at Vierville and Montmartin. He is ordered to relinquish these to the bishop and to refrain from further encroachments; unless the fiefs are given up, Geoffrey's justice Richard de la Haie is directed to determine by recognition, in accordance with the duke's assize, the tenure of the fief in King Henry's time and to secure the bishop in the possession of the rights thus found to belong to him. The writ adds: " I likewise command you, Richard de la Haie, throughout your district [57] to

[55] In such cases, too, the writ could be issued in the duke's name without the necessity of his initiative in every case.

[56] An Angevin knight, who was one of Geoffrey's favorite companions (Halphen and Poupardin, *Chroniques des comtes d'Anjou*, pp. 178, 207) and frequently appears as a witness to his charters, e. g., Round, *Calendar*, no. 1394; MSS. Dom Housseau in the Bibliothèque Nationale, iv, nos. 1505, 1567, 1587, 1614; Delisle, *Henri II*, p. 410.

[57] The proof that Geoffrey is the author of this writ is of importance in connection with this passage because of its bearing upon the date of the institution of *bailliae* in Normandy. For the discussion on this point see Stapleton, i, p. xxxiv; Delisle in *B. É. C.*, x. 260; Brunner, p. 157; *supra*, Chapter IV, note 117.

have the bishop's fief recognized according to my assize and to see that he possesses it in peace as it shall be recognized according to my assize."[58]   The other writ is addressed by Geoffrey to his justices Guy de Sablé and Robert de Courcy, and directs them to ascertain by recognition, according to his assize, who was seized of the fief and service of William Bersic in King Henry's time, and if it is recognized that the bishop of Bayeux was then seized thereof, to secure his peaceful possession.   They are also commanded to determine by recognition, according to the duke's assize, who was seized of the land of Cramesnil and Rocquancourt in Henry's time, and if it be recognized that Vauquelin de Courseulles was then seized of it, to secure him in peaceful possession and prohibit Robert Fitz Erneis and his men from doing him injury, at the same time compelling them to restore anything they may have taken from the estate since the duke issued his precept in relation thereto.[59]

[58] ' G. dux Normannorum et comes Andegavie E[ngengero] de Buhun salutem. Mando tibi et precipio quod dimittas episcopo Baiocensi in pace feudum militis quod Robertus Marinus de ipso tenebat Wirenille et feudum suum quod Willelmus de Moiun de ipso apud Munmartin tenere debet, quod huc usque iniuste occupasti; quod nisi feceris, precipio quod iusticia mea R[icardus] de Haia secundum assisiam meam recognosci faciat predictum feodum episcopi quomodo antecessores sui tenuerunt tempore regis Henrici, et sicut recognitum fuerit ita episcopum in pace tenere faciat.   Et te, Engengere, precor ne de aliquo iniuste fatiges episcopum, quia ego non paterer quod de iure suo aliquid iniuste perderet.   Tibi etiam, Ricarde Lahaia, precipio quod per totam bailiam tuam, secundum assisiam meam, recognosci facias feudum episcopi Baiocensis, et ipsum in pace tenere sicut recognitum fuerit secundum assisiam meam.   Teste Pag[ano] de Clar[is] Vall[ibus], apud Cenomanos.'   *Livre noir*, no. 24; Stapleton, i, p. xxxiv; Brunner, pp. 80, 302; Bigelow, p. 392, no. 46; Round, *Calendar*, no. 1439.

[59] 'G. dux Norm[annorum] et comes Andegavie G[uidoni] de Sableio et R[oberto] de Curc[eio] iusticiis suis salutem.   Mando vobis quod sine mora recognosci faciatis, secundum asisiam meam, de feodo Guillelmi Bersic et de servicio eiusdem quis inde saisitus erat tempore regis Henrici; et si recognitum fuerit quod episcopus Baiocensis inde saisitus esset vivente rege Henrico, ei habere et tenere in pace faciatis.   Preterea vobis mando quod recognosci faciatis, secundum asisiam meam, de terra de Crasmesnil et de Rochencort quis inde saisitus erat tempore regis Henrici; et si recognitum fuerit quod Gauquelinus de Corceliis inde saisitus esset eo tempore, ei in pace tenere faciatis et prohibete Roberto filio Erneis ne aliquid ei forifaciat neque sui homines; et si Robertus filius Erneis sive sui homines aliquid inde ceperint, postquam precepi in Epipphania Domini quod terra esset in pace donec iuraretur cuius deberet esse, reddere faciatis.   Teste P[agano] de Clar[is] Vall[ibus], apud Cenomanos.'   *Livre noir*, no. 25; Brunner, p. 302; Bigelow, p. 393, no. 47; not in Round.

If we compare these writs with the only other special writ of Geoffrey in the *Livre noir*, that directing the recognition concerning the *banlieue* of Cambremer,[60] we find the essential difference to be that whereas in the case of Cambremer it is expressly provided that the facts shall be ascertained by the oath of good men of the vicinage (*faciatis recognosci per sacramentum proborum hominum de vicinio*), in the two other writs no statement is made regarding the procedure except that the facts are to be found according to the duke's assize (*recognosci faciatis secundum asisiam meam*). The same difference appears in the writs of Henry II for Bayeux; indeed, in a single document provision is made for the determination of one question by the verdict of ancient men, and of others in accordance with the assize.[61] The absence from the cartulary of any returns from the justices who were instructed to proceed in accordance with the assize precludes our comparing the procedure; the analogy of the practice in regard to the bishop's demesne and in the matter of his feudal rights at Cheffreville [62] leads us to look for the sworn inquest of neighbors in these cases as well. The word ' assize,' as Littleton long ago pointed out,[63] is an ambiguous term. It seems to have meant originally a judicial or legislative assembly, from which it was extended to the results of the deliberations of such an assembly, whether in the form of statute or of judgment, and was then carried over from the royal or ducal assizes which established the procedure by recognition to that form of procedure itself.[64] In the writs in question ' my assize ' may refer to an ordinance of Geoffrey regulating procedure, it may denote the procedure so

---

[60] No. 17.

[61] No. 27; Delisle-Berger, no. 21.

[62] Nos. 89 and 90 (Bigelow, pp. 398, 399, nos. 54, 55; Brunner, p. 269, ascribing them to Henry II), the returns made by the duke's justices, Galeran of Meulan and Reginald of Saint-Valery, of an inquest held in regard to the respective rights of the bishops of Bayeux and Lisieux at Cheffreville. The bull of Eugene III (no. 156) which enumerates the possessions recovered by Philip d'Harcourt mentions the recovery of fiefs at Ducy and Louvières by judgment of Geoffrey's court, but nothing is said of the procedure and none of the documents are preserved.

[63] *Tenures*, c. 234.

[64] Brunner, p. 299. Cf. Stubbs, *Constitutional History*, i. 614; Murray's *Dictionary, s. v.*

established, or it may conceivably mean only the prerogative procedure of the duke — his not in the sense of origination but of
exclusive possession. Brunner's contention, that the phrase can
refer only to an ordinance by which a particular sovereign introduced the procedure by recognition as a regular remedy throughout Normandy, involves a number of assumptions which need
proof. Even if it be admitted that the assize here mentioned was a
ducal ordinance, the use of the same expression by Geoffrey and
Henry II stands in the way of ascribing the exclusive credit for
the act to either of these rulers, while it is still unnecessary to
assume that the supposed ordinance covered the whole duchy.
There is nothing in either of the writs which goes beyond the
sphere of the bishop's interests,[65] and unless new evidence can be
brought forward for other parts of Normandy, we have no right
to conclude that the supposed ordinance affected any one except
the bishop of Bayeux. Now we have just such a special privilege
for the bishop in the writ providing for the use of the sworn inquest in disputes between the bishop and his men concerning any
tenement.[66] This covers exactly the sort of cases which appear in
the two special writs that mention the duke's assize, and may well
be the assize to which they refer.[67] So far the hypothesis that the
general writ preserved in the cartulary is the much-discussed
assize of Geoffrey seems to meet the conditions of the case, but
it is subject to modification when we examine the documents in
which the word assize appears under Henry II.

[65] It is not specifically stated in no. 25 that Cramesnil and Rocquancourt were
fiefs of the bishop, but we know from other sources that Cramesnil was, and they
were evidently connected. See the inquest of Henry I (*M. A. N.*, viii. 427; *H. F.*,
xxiii. 700; Béziers, *Mémoires*, i. 144); also Béziers, i. 153; and C. Hippeau, *Dictionnaire topographique du Calvados*, p. 90.

[66] No. 16.

[67] There is, it is true, a discrepancy in the periods set as the basis of the recognition; in no. 16 the lands are to be held as in Bishop Odo's time, while in nos. 24 and
25 the tenure of Henry I's time is to be established. The difference is, however, of
no special importance; the documents in the cartulary do not appear to make any
sharp distinction between the two periods, and the writs may well have varied according to circumstances. The returns concerning the feudal rights at Cheffreville
(nos. 89, 90) go back to the tenure of Henry's time, those relating to Cambremer
mention both his and Odo's, while in the latter portion of no. 16 the practice of
Henry's time is to be observed in regard to the immunity of the bishop's lands.

For the reign of Henry II the *Livre noir* yields much less than
for that of Geoffrey, under whom the bishop would seem to have
succeeded in regaining the larger part of his lands and privileges.
The use of the sworn inquest continues — indeed Henry was
compelled to employ it repeatedly for the recovery of his own
ducal rights, which had suffered severely during the anarchy
under Stephen,[68] so that we hear of inquests held in the early
years of his reign to ascertain the duke's demesne and customs at
Bayeux [69] and in the Bessin.[70] On behalf of the bishop of Bayeux
Henry issued not later than 1153 a general precept, which, after
reciting the proceedings under Henry I and Geoffrey, directed the
recognition of the bishop's demesne, fiefs, liberties, and customs by
the oath of ancient and lawful men acquainted with the facts, as
they had been sworn to in the time of his father and grandfather.[71]
In 1156 a similar writ was issued with reference to the bishop's
forests,[72] and while no new recognition seems to have been held
for the *banlieue* of Cambremer, the justices were repeatedly instructed to secure the observance of the bishop's rights there as
defined in Geoffrey's time.[73] The bishop's multure at Bayeux
and his rights in the ducal forests of the Bessin were likewise the
object of a recognition in 1156,[74] and still other inquests related
to his rights at Isigny and Neuilly [75] and his possessions at Caen.
The only matter deserving special remark among these various
inquests is found in the writ of 1156 touching the rights at Caen,
which, like the others, is addressed to the chief local officer,
William Fitz John, and runs as follows: " I command you to
have recognized by ancient men of Caen from how many and
which houses in Caen the bishops of Bayeux were wont to have

[68] Cf. Robert of Torigni, i. 284.

[69] *Livre noir*, nos. 13, 138; Delisle-Berger, nos. 68*, 76*; *M. A. N.*, vii. 179.

[70] *Livre noir*, no. 35; Delisle-Berger, no. 38.

[71] *Livre noir*, no. 14; Bigelow, p. 389, no. 42; Brunner, p. 268; Delisle-Berger,
no. 33*.

[72] *Livre noir*, no. 36; Delisle-Berger, no. 14.

[73] *Livre noir*, nos. 9, 12, 32; Delisle-Berger, nos. 13, 72, 228.

[74] *Livre noir*, nos. 28, 35; Delisle-Berger, nos. 22, 38. Cf. Chapter V, note 19,
supra.

[75] *Livre noir*, no. 46 (also in *Livre rouge*, no. 46), subsequent to the accession
of Bishop Henry in 1165.

rent and profits in the time of King Henry, my grandfather, and what services and customs they had from them. And you shall cause Philip, bishop of Bayeux, to possess the houses fully and justly and in peace according as the recognition shall determine. And you shall do him full right, according to my assize, in respect to the land where the bishop's barns used to stand, and full right in respect to the arable land by the water, according to my assize, and full right in respect to the tithes of woolens at Caen, according to my assize." [76] Here we have again, and three times, the puzzling words *secundum assisam meam*, and Brunner drew from them the conclusion that Henry was the creator of recognitions in Normandy.[77] The phrase is not found in the writ which seems to have been issued at the same time for the recognition of the bishop's multure and his rights in the forests of the Bessin, where, however, there is the difference that the rights in question touched the king's own privileges and were recognized by the jurors specially appointed to swear to Henry's customs and demesne in the Bessin.[78] No other Bayeux document referring to the duke's assize has been found, and there is nothing in this one to show that the assize included anything outside of the bishop's possessions or involved any method of procedure different from " the oath of old and lawful men who know the facts," as prescribed in the general order for the recognition of the bishop's

[76] 'Henricus rex Anglie et dux Normannie et Aquitanie et comes Andegavie Willelmo filio Iohannis salutem. Precipio tibi quod facias recognosci, per antiquos homines Cadomi, quot et quarum domorum in Cadomo episcopi Baiocenses solebant habere censum et redditus tempore Henrici regis avi mei, et que servicia et quales consuetudines inde tunc habebant; et sicut fuerit (MS. fuerat) recognitum, ita in pace et iuste et integre eas facias habere Philippo episcopo Baiocensi. Et plenum rectum ei facias de terra ubi grangee episcopi esse solebant (MS. esse *bis*), secundum assisam meam; et plenum rectum ei facias de terra arabili que est iuxta aquam, secundum assisam meam; et plenum rectum ei facias de decimis   (blank in MS.) et lanifeciorum de Cadomo, secundum assisam meam. Et nisi feceris, Robertus de Novo Burgo faciat.   Teste Toma cancellario apud Lemovicas.' *Livre noir*, no. 27; La Rue, *Essais historiques sur la ville de Caen*, i. 375;   Bigelow, p. 393, no. 48; Brunner, p. 302; Round, no. 1443 (incomplete); Delisle-Berger, no. 21.

[77] *Schwurgerichte*, p. 303.

[78] Writ in *Livre noir*, no. 28; returns, *ibid.*, no. 35: ' per sacramenta iuratorum qui sunt constituti ad iurandas consuetudines meas et dominica mea de Baiocensi.' Delisle-Berger, nos, 22, 38.

rights which was issued by Henry before he became king.[79] This general precept may not be the assize in question, but it certainly covers the ground of the special writ for Caen, and we are not obliged to infer that anything broader was meant by Henry's use of the term assize. Whether he also issued a general writ similar to that of Geoffrey providing for the regular use of the sworn inquest in suits between the bishop and his tenants, it is impossible to say. No such document has been preserved, nor do any of the documents of Henry's time in the *Livre noir* relate to cases where the fiefs of the bishop are concerned.

Taken in themselves and interpreted in their relations to the other Bayeux documents, the three writs which contain the phrase *secundum assisiam meam* do not demonstrate Brunner's thesis that a system of recognitions was created throughout Normandy by a ducal ordinance, whether of Henry II or of his father, for they do not necessarily take us beyond the bishopric of Bayeux and its possessions. On the other hand, there is nothing in the writs inconsistent with such a general ordinance, and any mention of a ducal assize elsewhere in Normandy would point clearly toward some more comprehensive measure establishing procedure by recognition. Such a reference to an assize meets us early in the reign of Henry II in connection with the monastery of Saint-Étienne de Caen. For this favored foundation of the Norman dukes a series of documents, unfortunately less numerous and less detailed than those extant for the see of Bayeux, records various recognitions held in the period between Henry's coronation as king and 1164. In two cases we have the reports of the justices who held the recognition,[80] in others only the royal charter confirming the results.[81] Thus in 1157 an inquest was held at Caen by

[79] *Livre noir*, no. 14; Delisle-Berger, no. 33*.

[80] The charter of Robert de Neufbourg notifying the inquest at Dives (Valin, p. 267; cf. Deville, *Analyse*, p. 42), and the charter of Rotrou of Évreux and Reginald of Saint-Valery relating the recognition at Bayeux (*M. A. N.*, xv. 197; Valin, p. 270). Robert's report on the inquest at Avranches was preserved in the lost cartulary summarized in Deville, *Analyse*, p. 18. On these justiciars see *supra*, Chapter V.

[81] Charter of Henry II issued at Caen between 1156 and 1161: Delisle-Berger, no. 153; extracts in Valin, p. 268. There is also a parallel writ of the king, issued doubtless at the same time, in Delisle-Berger, no. 104; *M. A. N.*, xv, 198. The

the seneschal of Normandy, Robert de Neufbourg, to determine the obligation of the abbey's men, with those of others, to carry in the king's hay at Bretteville and Verson.[82] Before his retirement in 1159 the same seneschal held a detailed recognition at Dives-sur-Mer, on the oath of ten lawful men, respecting the rights of the abbot at Dives and Cabourg;[83] a recognition at Avranches, " by the lawful men of the province," respecting freedom from toll in that city;[84] and a recognition concerning the abbey's rights and possessions at Rouen.[85] Before 1161 the bishops of Évreux and Bayeux and other justices hold an inquest concerning the abbey's rights over houses in its *bourg* at Caen,[86] and between 1161 and 1164 it was determined by recognition before the king's justices, in an assize at Bayeux, that various lands in Cristot and elsewhere were fiefs of Saint-Étienne.[87]

The subjects of these inquiries do not differ from those held for the bishop of Bayeux and others, nor is the procedure in any instance described specifically. One case, however, challenges our special attention. At Rouen " it was recognized that the monks should hold quit their meadows of Bapeaume, with respect to which William, son of Thétion de Fonte, who claimed the right to them (*ius*), failed as regards his claim and the decision of right before Robert and the barons of Normandy in the king's *curia* and as regards the assize which he had demanded with respect thereto." [88] The account is brief, all too brief, for we have only

argument of the editors that this is anterior to the death of Robert de Neufbourg in 1159 applies equally to the longer charter.

[82] Robert of Torigni, ii. 250, no. 34.

[83] Valin, p. 267; Deville, *Analyse*, p. 42.

[84] ' Recognitum etiam fuit in plena assisia apud Abrincas per legales homines provincie ': Delisle-Berger, no. 153; Valin, p. 268; Deville, *Analyse*, p. 18, where it appears that the inquest was held by Robert.

[85] Delisle-Berger, no. 153; Valin, p. 268.

[86] Delisle-Berger, no. 153; Valin, p. 268; Legras, *Le bourgage de Caen*, p. 75, note 1.

[87] *M. A. N.*, xv. 197; Valin, p. 270. The original, with incisions for the seals of the two justiciars, is in the Archives of the Calvados, H. 1883. The date is fixed by the mention of Achard of Avranches (1161–1171) and Rotrou of Évreux, who was translated to Rouen in 1164 or 1165.

[88] ' Et recognitum fuit quod predictis monachis remanserunt sua prata de Abapalmis quieta unde Willelmus filius Thetionis de Fonte, qui in illis clamabat

the summary of the case in a royal charter of confirmation, and language so condensed cannot be rigorously interpreted. We should naturally interpret *ius* in the sense of ultimate right or title (*maius ius*) which it bears in the writs of the period; but it is clearly the claimant, William Fitz Thétion, who demands the assize, and there was no way known to the Anglo-Norman procedure by which the plaintiff could demand an assize on the question of right.[89] If title was the question at issue here, *assisia* might refer to the jury which the claimant might secure after the tenant had put himself upon the assize, the jury then rendering its verdict in spite of the claimant's default. It seems simpler, however, to hold, with Valin, that *ius* is here employed in a general rather than a technical sense, and that the question was one of possession. In any case the essential point is that the party which demanded the assize was the lay claimant, not the monastery, as in the other recognitions for Saint-Étienne. The assize in this instance, therefore, cannot be a special privilege enjoyed by an ecclesiastical establishment, since it is demanded against the monks, nor could such a claimant have put himself upon the assize unless this was a regular method of trial, such as the term comes to denote in England. This assize may, of course, be quite different from the *assisia mea* of the Bayeux documents, for there is nothing to exclude the issuance of more than one ducal ordinance on the subject or, if we take assize merely in its procedural sense, the existence of more than one form of trial established by ducal initiative. Whatever the Bayeux assizes may have been, the assize in the case of Saint-Étienne is more significant, since it is clearly open to the ordinary lay claimant, even against a religious establishment protected by the duke. So far as it goes, it affords conclusive evidence that by 1159 the prerogative procedure has been extended to subjects, at least for one class of cases, much as in the English assize of novel disseisin instituted in 1166.

ius, defecit se de iure et de consideratione recti coram Roberto et coram baronibus Normannie in curia regis et de assisia quam inde requisierat ': Valin, p. 268; Delisle-Berger, no. 153, from *Cartulaire de Normandie*, f. 21v.

[89] Glanvill, bk. ii; *Très Ancien Coutumier*, c. 85; Brunner, *Schwurgerichte*, pp. 312–314; Valin, p. 213 f. Professor G. B. Adams has convinced me that Valin is probably correct in interpreting *ius* in this passage as meaning possession only.

Another instance of what is apparently the ordinary and regular use of the recognition is found, but without any mention of an assize, in 1159, when, in the king's court at Gavray, Osmund, son of Richard Vasce, " on the oath of lawful men, proved his right to the presentation of Mesnil-Drey and two sheaves of its tithe as his ancestors had always had them." Neither Osmund nor his opponent, Ralph de la Mouche, was a privileged person, and this method of trial seems to have been resorted to in the king's court as a matter of course, and hence of right. The probability of some regulation of such suits in Normandy is rendered stronger by the discovery of traces of legislation by Henry in England, between 1154 and 1158, with reference to advowson and presentation.[90] If we could accept the evidence of a charter of Henry for Saint-Évroul, apparently given between 1159 and 1162,[91] the existence of a form of recognition corresponding to the assize *utrum* would be established for Normandy in this period, at least two years before it appears in England. This document, however, which is suspicious in form,[92] does not correspond to the report of the case by the justiciar Rotrou,[93] given between 1164 and 1166,

[90] The notice of the suit is in Robert of Torigni, ii. 259; cf. *supra*, Chapter V, note 88. ' Sacramento legalium hominum ' may conceivably mean party witnesses, but by this time it has become the usual phrase for the sworn inquest. For Ralph de la Mouche cf. a charter of 1158 in Pigeon, *Le diocèse d'Avranches*, ii. 672. On Henry's early English legislation, see Appendix I.

[91] Printed by me, from an incorrect copy from the cartulary of Saint-Évroul, MS. Lat. 11055, no. 24, in *A. H. R.*, viii. 634. Also in the Registres du Trésor des Chartes, JJ. 69, no. 194; Round, no. 641; Delisle-Berger, no. 214, where the date of Abbot Robert's accession, 1159, is overlooked in dating the document.

[92] The charter combines the king's style of the latter half of the reign with a witness who cannot be later than 1162, and contains the suspicious phrase *teste me ipso*, which appears in two other fabrications of this period from Saint-Évroul (Delisle, nos. 347, 362; see pp. 226, 316 f.) and has not yet been found in an original charter of this reign (*ibid.*, p. 226, where too much is made of the occurrence of the phrase in charters for different monasteries, since copyists or forgers might easily carry back a formula common in the succeeding reign). The language of the document is also unusual, quite unlike that of Rotrou's charter, which speaks of but five knights and reports the determination of more limited questions of title. As Henry's charter is also found in a *vidimus* of Matilda, daughter of the monastery's adversary in the suit (cartulary of Saint-Évroul, no. 426; Collection Lenoir, at Semilly, lxxii. 17, lxxiii. 467), its fabrication or modification cannot be placed more than a generation later.

[93] ' Rotrodus Dei gratia Rothomagensis archiepiscopus omnibus ad quos presens

and I believe it to contain a somewhat modernized version of the transaction, prepared in the later years of the twelfth century. Rotrou's charter says nothing of the question of lay fee or alms, but adjudges to the monks, after sworn inquest, full right to the presentation, tithes, and lands belonging to the church in question.

The conclusion that the employment of the recognition was extended and regularized by definite legislative act, rather than by a process of gradual development, is rendered probable, not only by the use of the word assize, but also by evidence of actual legislation in this same period with reference to the sworn inquest in other matters. In 1159 at his Christmas court at Falaise Henry, besides providing that the testimony of the vicinage should be required in support of charges brought by rural deans, commanded his own officers, in the monthly meetings of the local

scriptum pervenerit et precipue ballivis domini regis salutem. Sciatis quod ex precepto domini regis quando per eum per totam Normanniam iusticiam secularem exercebamus, miseratione divina tunc temporis Ebroicensem episcopatum regentes, in plena assisia apud Rothomagum die festo Sancte Cecilie Garinus de Grandivalle et Ricardus Faiel et Rogerus de Moenaio et Rogerus Goulafre et Robertus Chevalier iuraverunt quod ecclesia Sancti Ebrulfi et abbas et monachi eius anno et die quo H. rex filius Willelmi regis fuit vivus et mortuus et postea usque modo presentationem beati Petri de Sap pacifice et quiete habuit in elemosinam cum omnibus decimis et aliis pertinenciis suis et masnagium Willelmi filii Hugonis cum omnibus pertinenciis suis tam in terris quam in aliis rebus possedit. Ipsi vero milites se fecerunt ignorantes utrum cultura que Ardeneta noncupatur ad ius Sancti Ebrulfi vel ad ius domini de Sap verius pertineret, et tamen quandam acram terre in eadem cultura per ecclesiam Sancti Ebrulfi cultam fuisse per sacramentum se vidisse testati sunt. Post obitum vero predicti H. regis residuum predicte culture per abbatem Sancti Ebrulfi cultum fuisse prefati milites necnon et totam illam culturam ad abbatiam Sancti Ebrulfi pocius quam ad dominum de Sappo secundum oppinionem suam pertinere iuraverunt. Nos autem domini regis adimplentes mandatum de consilio baronum ipsius qui presentes erant presentationem predicte ecclesie cum decimis et aliis pertinenciis suis necnon et masnagium iam dictum cum cultura de Ardeneta et aliis omnibus, que sicut dictum est secundum formam regii mandati abbati et monachis eius recognita fuerunt, eisdem de cetero in pace et quiete habenda et possidenda, licet nunquam amisissent, adiudicavimus. Testibus Arnulfo Lexoviensi episcopo, H[enrico] abbati Fiscannensi, Victore abbate Sancti Georgii de Bauchervilla, Galeranno comite Mellenti, comite Patricio, camerario de Tancarvilla, Hugone de Gornaco, Roberto filio Geroii, Nicholao de Stotevilla, Godardo de Vallibus, Roberto filio Hamerici, Roberto de Varvic, Raginaldo de Ierponvilla, Ricardo Beverel, Adam de Walnevilla.' MS. Lat. 11055, no. 172. *A. H. R.*, xx. 38, note 93; now also in Delisle-Berger, i. 353. The discovery of this document led me to modify the view regarding an assize *utrum* which I had expressed in *A. H. R.*, viii. 633 f. (1903).

courts, to " pronounce no judgments without the evidence of neighbors." [94] The exact meaning of this comprehensive language does not appear from the paraphrase in our only source of information, the Bec annalist; it seems, not only to require such use of the accusing jury in ecclesiastical courts as is prescribed in the Constitutions of Clarendon, but also to give it wider scope in the ducal courts, very likely by extending it to criminal accusations before the duke's local judges. Indeed from the language used (*de causis similiter quorumlibet ventilandis*) it is quite possible that the evidence of neighbors was there prescribed in civil cases as well.

That the justices of Geoffrey and Henry II had by this time become familiar with this method of procedure appears from various scattered documents of the period. Thus a charter of Geoffrey in favor of Algar, bishop of Coutances, confirms the verdict of six jurors rendered in accordance with the duke's writ at his assize at Valognes, to the effect that Robert Fitz Neal and his predecessors had held of the bishop and his predecessors whatever rights they had enjoyed in the churches of Cherbourg and Tourlaville and their appurtenances.[95] Another example of a recog-

---

[94] ' De causis similiter quorumlibet ventilandis instituit ut, cum iudices singularum provinciarum singulis mensibus ad minus simul devenirent, sine testimonio vicinorum nichil iudicarent ': Robert of Torigni, ii. 180. Cf. Pollock and Maitland, i. 151. Stubbs says (*Benedict of Peterborough*, ii, p. lix): " This looks very like an instruction to the county court." On the ecclesiastical procedure, see *infra*, p. 226 f., and Appendix I.

[95] ' [G.] dux Normannie et comes Andegavie H. archiepiscopo et omnibus episcopis Normannie, baronibus, iusticiis, et omnibus suis fidelibus, salutem. Notum sit vobis atque omnibus tam presentibus quam futuris quod in tempore meo et Algari Const[anciensis] episcopi fuit iuramento comprobatum per meum preceptum in assisia mea apud Valonias quod Robertus (MS. vob') filius Nigelli et omnes predecessores sui ab Algaro Constanciensi et ab aliis predecessoribus suis Constan[ciensibus] episcopis tenuerant quicquid in ecclesiis de Cesariburgo et de Torlavilla et in omnibus possessionibus ad illas ecclesias pertinentibus habuerant. Hoc vero iuraverunt Ricardus de Wauvilla, Willelmus monachus, Willelmus de Sancto Germano, Willelmus de Bricquevilla, Ricardus de Martinvast, Rob[ertus] de Valonis. Quare ego concedo quod hoc secundum illorum iuramentum ratum sit et perpetuo teneatur. Testes vero huius concessionis sunt: R[icardus] cancellarius, Willelmus de Vernon, Engelg[erus] de Bouhon, Alexander de Bouhon, Jordanus Taysson, Robertus de Novo [Burgo], Robertus de Corceio, Joisfredus de Tur[onibus], G[aufredus] de Cleer, P[ipinus] de Tur[onibus]. Apud Sanctum Laudum.' Cartulary B of the cathedral of Coutances, p. 350, no. 286. Here, as in most of the other documents in this cartulary, the initial is left blank and not indicated, but in this case

nition in the duke's court, probably under Geoffrey and certainly before 1153, is found in a ducal charter for the dean and chapter of Rouen declaring that their rights in the forest of Aliermont, as in the time of Henry I, had been established before the duke by the oath of lawful knights, three of whom are mentioned by name.[96] Between 1151 and 1153 we have a writ of Duke Henry ordering his justiciar, Arnulf of Lisieux, and Robert of Montfort to cause the appurtenances of the church of Saint-Ymer to be recognized by lawful men.[97] Another indication of the prevalence of this method of proof appears, along with clear evidence of the continued use of trial by battle,[98] in the charters of Geoffrey and Henry for the town of Rouen, where, in providing that no citizen shall be held to wage combat against a hired champion, it is prescribed that the fact of the champion's professionalism shall be determined on the oath of ten citizens of Rouen selected by the justice.[99] With regard to the abbey of Savigny,

it is supplied by a *vidimus* of Philip Augustus in the same cartulary (p. 351, no. 288), printed in Delisle, *Cartulaire normand*, no. 162, which refers to this charter as ' autenticum G. ducis Normannie, cuius mandato fuit recognitum in assisia apud Valonias.' This, the only surviving cartulary of Coutances, was still in the episcopal archives when I was permitted to examine it in 1902, but it has since been transferred to the departmental archives at Saint-Lô.

By following Léchaudé and overlooking the *vidimus* Round (*Calendar*, no. 960) was led to ascribe this charter to Henry II; so also Bigelow, *History of Procedure*, p. 367, no. 9. The treatment of this document affords a good illustration of Léchaudé's carelessness. Not only does he omit the last four witnesses, but he quietly inserts Henry's name in his copies — " Henricus &[a] " in the 'Cartulaire de la Basse Normandie,' i. 129; " Henricus R." in MS. Lat. 10068, f. 88, no. 57. Brunner, p. 269, prints the essential portion of the charter and recognizes Geoffrey as its author; so now Delisle, *Henri II*, p. 509, no. 17* A; Delisle-Berger, i. 2. The lost cartulary A, of which a partial analysis is preserved in the archives, contained a copy of the *vidimus* which interpreted G as the initial of a duke William; the text as printed in Dupont, *Histoire du Cotentin*, i. 466, is apparently derived from this source.

[96] Archives of the Seine-Inférieure, G. 7, p. 793; Valin, p. 266, where it is ascribed to Henry II; Delisle-Berger, no. 39*, where the possibility of Geoffrey's authorship is admitted. For the reasons for attributing this charter to Geoffrey, see *supra*, p. 134. For the charter of Henry I, see Appendix F, no. 17.

[97] *Cartulaire de S.-Ymer*, ed. Bréard, no. 6; Delisle-Berger, no. 34*.

[98] Examples of the duel in the duke's court will be found in 1155 in Robert of Torigni, ii. 241; and in 1157 in MS. Rouen 1193, f. 47, where we find among the witnesses ' Mauricio pugile.'

[99] Charter of Geoffrey as confirmed by Henry II soon after he obtained the duchy: Delisle-Berger, no. 14*; *supra*, p. 134.

trial by lawful men of the *villa* is prescribed by a writ of the
Empress Matilda in the case of offenses committed against the
monastery by the foresters or their servants.[100] On behalf of the
duke himself we have no examples of the employment of the inquest under Geoffrey, but numerous instances under Henry II,
early in his reign at Bayeux and in the Bessin, later in the systematic inquiries held by his justices in 1163 and 1171 throughout
the whole of Normandy.[101]

That Geoffrey's reign begins a new stage in the development of
the jury in Normandy may also be argued from such rare instances of the sworn inquest as we find under his predecessors.
The great Bayeux inquest of 1133 is essentially a fiscal inquest,
since the see was then in the duke's hands and its revenues were
accordingly a matter of interest to him.[102] The same holds true
of a writ of William Rufus freeing from *bernagium* a domain of
Bec *donec ego inquiram quomodo fuit tempore patris mei:* [103] if, as
seems probable, the inquiry was to be made by sworn inquest, it
was to determine a fiscal obligation. When we leave these fiscal
inquiries, we no longer find clear examples of inquests of the later
type. The nearest approach is the case of the abbey of Fontenay
under William the Conqueror, who ordered the possessions of the
monastery recorded on oath by the barons of the honor, four of
whom brought testimony of the record to the king's court at

[100] ' M. imperatricis (*sic*) regis H. filia, F. de Tenechebrai salutem. Mando tibi
et precor atque precipio quod permittas senioribus de Savigneio habere et tenere
suam fabricam et alia omnia que ad eos pertinent de elemosina predecessoris mei
regis H. ita libere et quiete sicut ea habuerunt et tenuerunt tempore ipsius regis. Si
autem forestarii vel aliquis alius famulorum eos (MS. eorum) in quoquam forte
molestaverint et inquietaverint, fac inde tractari causam iuste per homines legales
ipsius ville, ita ne amplius inde clamorem audiam pro recti penuria. Si vero alius
aliquis iniuriam eis in aliquo fecerit, manuteneas eos ubique et protegas sicut nostrum dominicum quod habemus protegere ut nostram elemosinam. Teste Roberto
de Curc[eio], apud Falesiam.' Cartulary in the Archives of the Manche, no. 280;
in part in Brunner, p. 241; Delisle, *Henri II*, p. 141, no. 5.

[101] *Livre noir*, nos. 13, 35, 138; Delisle-Berger, nos. 68*, 76*, 38; Robert of
Torigni, i. 344, ii. 28; cf. *supra*, p. 159 f.; *infra*, Appendix K. The inquests for
Fécamp in 1162 (Delisle-Berger, no. 223) and for Mortemer (*H. F.*, xiv. 505) also
touch the rights of the duke.

[102] *Supra*, notes 16–23. Note, however, that Henry's Nostell writ in note 153
was issued in Normandy.

[103] *Supra*, p. 82; Valin, p. 200, note 2.

Caen.[104] In other instances of this period the men who swear are party witnesses, rather than recognitors who render a verdict as representing the knowledge of the community.[105] Even under Henry I the only ducal writ which has reached us (1106–1120) defining the mode of procedure in an inquiry upon oath leaves the monks of Saint-Père de Chartres free to produce their own witnesses or to choose the witnesses for the opposing party:

H. rex Angl[orum] Wigero de Sancta Maria Ecclesia salutem. Precipio ut teneas rectum monachis Sancti Petri Carnotensis de terra eorum ita: siquis eam clamaverit monachi faciant eam probare per suos probos homines, vel illi qui eam clamaverint probare eam faciant per illos quos monachus clegerit. Teste Willelmo de Pirou apud Cadomum.[106]

From the time of Geoffrey no writs have come down prescribing such a procedure.

It would be interesting to know just what Lucius II and Eugene III had in mind when they directed Geoffrey to have the possessions of Bayeux established ' on oath by lawful witnesses,' for the church had its traditions in such matters, as well as the state, and the influence of canonical ideas of proof cannot be wholly ignored as a possibility in tracing the genesis of civil procedure. It is accordingly a matter of some interest to examine the evidence which has reached us respecting the sworn inquest in the ecclesiastical jurisdictions of Normandy in this period.[107] Taking once more the diocese of Bayeux as our point of departure, we find Bishop Philip intervening in a controversy over the limits of certain lands held in alms, in order to secure the consent of the parties to its submission to the verdict of the countryside. " There was a dispute between the canons of Bayeux and Luke, son of Hervé, priest of Douvres, as to what pertained to the alms of the church of Douvres and what to the fief of Luke." After much discussion it was agreed to submit the question to ten men, chosen with the consent of the parties from the assembled parish-

[104] *Gallia Christiana*, xi. instr. 65; cf. Brunner, p. 270; Valin, p. 201.

[105] *M. A. N.*, xv. 196, xxx. 681; cf. Valin, p. 198 f.

[106] Original, formerly sealed *sur simple queue*, MS. Lat. 9221, no. 6. William de Pirou perished on the White Ship in 1120: Ordericus, iv. 418.

[107] Inquests on the manors of monasteries, held probably by royal warrant, fall in a different category: *supra*, Chapter V, note 23.

ioners, " in whose oath the truth of the matter should rest."
Standing before the parish church, this jury declared upon oath
the lands which belonged to the alms of the church; and when
Luke afterward sought to occupy some of the property of the
canons, the jurors were called together at Bayeux and again
recognized the alms of the church, which the bishop enumerates
in his charter.[108] The proceedings in this case, though not held in
accordance with a ducal writ, show all the essential elements of
the recognition—the promissory oath, the free decision, the verdict rendered by chosen men of the vicinage; and if we remember that the jury, in the narrower sense, as distinguished from the
assize, " has its roots in the fertile ground of consent " and " only
comes in after both parties have consented to accept its verdict," [109] the importance of this early example of such a voluntary
agreement is at once evident. In other cases the account of the
procedure is not so specific, but points to the use of the recognition, or something very like it, in connection with the bishop's
jurisdiction. In one of these instances a verdict is mentioned
incidentally in documents of the year 1153 relating to a prebend
created by the bishop out of various elements, among them the
land in Le Val de Port, in the territory of Escures, held by Alexander, son of Téold, which Bishop Philip caused to be recognized
in his presence by the oaths of lawful men of the said Val as
belonging to the demesne of the bishop of Bayeux.[110] Another

[108] ' Erat igitur contentio inter canonicos Baiocenses et Lucam, filium Hervei
sacerdotis de Dovra, quid ad elemosinam ecclesie de Dovra et quid ad feodum
ipsius Luce pertineret. Que controversia, cum diu multumque ventilata agitaretur,
nunc demum in presentia nostra et parrochianorum de Dovra ante ipsius ville
ecclesiam per nos finem sortita est. . . . Vocatis igitur ipsius ville parrochianis
utriusque partis assensu electi sunt decem solum (whose names follow) . . . in
quorum iuramento rei veritas consisteret. Facto igitur prius iuramento has terras
de elemosina ecclesie esse dixerunt . . .' *Livre noir*, no. 63. The charter is not
dated or witnessed, and more definite dates cannot be assigned than the limits of
Philip's episcopate, 1142–1163.

[109] Pollock and Maitland, i. 149. The following is a good example of this principle from the year 1182: ' Coram Radulfo episcopo Lexoviensi composita est
controversia . . . que erat inter monachos Beccenses et Ricardum Cornubiensem
canonicum Lexoviensem arbitris Guillelmo presbytero et duodecim hominibus
iuratis super quasdam decimas apud Falcum et Montemfortem, cuique sua parte
pro iure suo iuxta equitatem attributa ' (MS. Lat. 12884, f. 238).

[110] ' Terra quam tenuit Alexander filius Theoldi in Valle Portus in territorio de

record, from the time of Philip's predecessor, is in the form of a notice witnessed by the bishop and several others, knights as well as clerks, to the effect that four men of Hérils, who are named, have recognized in the presence of the bishop and chapter that the land which Gosselin, succentor of the cathedral, holds at Hérils and the church of the village were given to Gosselin in alms and have always been held by him under such tenure.[111] It might be maintained that these four men of Hérils were party witnesses rather than recognitors, but the language of the document renders it far more likely that they were giving an independent verdict on behalf of the community. It is also possible that in these cases the men were questioned individually, as in the canonical procedure [112] and the later French *enquêtes*, but there is no indication of such an examination, and the use of the words *recognoscere* and *recognitio* points rather to a collective verdict.[113] In a still earlier case, likewise decided before the bishop and chapter, the uncertainty is greater, as nothing is said of the residence of the ancient men who are mentioned or of the capacity in which they appear. Still the matters in controversy, the rights and revenues of the chancellor of the cathedral, are "recognized by the attestation of ancient men" as belonging to the chancellor through the act of Bishop Odo and the continuous possession of former incumbents — just such a question as would naturally be submitted to a

Escures, quam videlicet Philippus, noster episcopus, fecit recognosci esse de dominico Baiocensis episcopi per sacramenta legalium hominum predicte Vallis.' Charter of the chapter of Bayeux, 8 May 1153, *Livre noir*, no. 149; no. 148 is a charter of the bishop to the same effect.

[111] 'Notum sit omnibus tam presentibus quam futuris quod homines de Heriz, et nominatim isti . . . recognoverunt coram Ricardo, Roberti comitis Gloecestrie filio, Baiocensi episcopo, et coram eiusdem ecclesie capitulo terram quam Goscelinus, Baiocensis ecclesie succentor, tenet apud Heriz cum ecclesia eiusdem ville eidem Goscelino in elemosina datam fuisse et eundem sic semper tenuisse. Huius autem recognitionis testes sunt isti: . . .' *Livre noir*, no. 102. Richard was bishop from 1135 to 1142.

[112] For an example of this from the year 1164 see *Livre noir*, no. 49.

[113] Of course *recognoscere* has other meanings, being applied to the certification of a charter, the confession of a criminal, or the admission of another's rights on the part of a claimant, but none of these senses seems to fit the passage in question, where the idea of a formal declaration of fact by a body of men seems clearly implied.

sworn verdict.[114] If such was the procedure employed in this case, it has a special interest as belonging to the pontificate of Richard Fitz Samson and thus falling within the reign of Henry I. How such tribunals came to decide cases of this sort and to employ this form of procedure are questions that cannot be answered until some one has given us a careful study of the Norman ecclesiastical jurisdictions. Indeed, the whole subject of the workings of the ecclesiastical courts in Normandy and elsewhere in the eleventh and twelfth centuries is an important field of investigation and ought to prove fruitful for the history of the transmission of the Frankish *inquisitio* to later times.

In one direction particularly could the history of ecclesiastical procedure in Normandy throw important light upon the origins of the jury, namely with respect to the jury of presentment. It has more than once been remarked that when this makes its first appearance under Henry II, it is as part of the procedure of ecclesiastical courts. At Falaise in 1159 it was ordained that no dean should accuse any one without the testimony of reputable neighbors.[115] At Clarendon in 1164 [116] it is declared that laymen shall be accused only by certain and lawful accusers before the

[114] ' Ceterum, dilecte nobis frater Anulphe, cancellarie ecclesie nostre, cum de hiis que ad ius personatus tui pertinent in capitulo coram Ricardo episcopo et fratribus ageretur, antiquorum virorum et eiusdem episcopi attestatione recognitum est ea que hic subnotata sunt ex institucione Odonis episcopi et tuorum anteces-sorum continua possessione ad ius personatus tui iure perpetuo pertinere. . . . Hec autem omnia in capitulo nostro coram Ricardo episcopo, Sansonis filio, et nobis recognita sunt et postmodum coram successore eius altero Ricardo publica attestatione firmata.' Chevalier, *Ordinaire de l'église cathédrale de Bayeux* (Paris, 1902), p. 419, no. 51. The document is in the shape of a letter from the dean and chapter to the chancellor, and is thus less formal than a charter. The mention of the attestation of the bishop along with that of the ancient men might appear to contradict the view that a sworn inquest was held, but the last sentence makes it plain that the attestation spoken of is that of the subsequent bishop, Richard of Kent, while the facts had been recognized under Richard Fitz Samson.

For similar examples under Hugh, archbishop of Rouen (1130–1164), see the cartulary of Saint-Georges de Bocherville (MS. Rouen 1227), f. 48v; and original charters of Hugh for Fécamp in the Archives of the Seine-Inférieure, *fonds* Fécamp, series Aizier and Étretat. The ' testimonium vicinorum ' appears in the court of the abbot of Préaux 1101–1131: Le Prévost, *Eure*, iii. 301; the recognition by ancient men, in Appendix H, no. 2.

[115] Robert of Torigni, ii. 180. For the immediate antecedents of these measures, see Appendix I.   [116] Constitutions of Clarendon, c. 6.

bishop, and in the absence of such accusers the bishop shall ask the sheriff to have the truth of the matter declared by twelve sworn men of the vicinage. All this calls to mind the synodal witnesses of the bishop's court, as described by Regino of Prüm at the beginning of the tenth century, themselves very likely another offshoot of the Frankish *inquisitio per testes*.[117] What we should like to know is whether the *testes synodales* also survived in the Frankish lands of the west and particularly in Normandy, thus furnishing Henry II with the suggestion which he applied to deans and archdeacons who used more arbitrary methods. Unfortunately no one has sought to answer these questions for France, and the studies of the genesis of the later canonical procedure in Italy take much for granted, after the fashion of too many historians of law.[118] Here, as so often, the Norman evidence is too meager and fragmentary to fill the gap in our knowledge. At one point, however, it offers a suggestion. In the curious arrangement made in 1061 between the bishop of Avranches and the abbot of Mont-Saint-Michel,[119] the men of the Mount had complained that they were subject to constant summons to the bishop's court at Avranches, regardless of war or weather, and were oppressed by the demand for oaths as well as by the fines and forfeitures which they there incurred:

Cogebantur enim venire Abrincas ad respondendum de quacunque accusatione contra christianitatem, nec excusare poterat eos mare insurgens nec Britonum insidie quia preveniri ac provideri poterant, et ita sepe in forifacta et emendationes episcopales incidebant et sepe iuramentis fatiga-

---

[117] See Brunner, *Schwurgerichte*, pp. 458–468; id., *Deutsche Rechtsgeschichte*, ii. 488–494; Hinschius, *Kirchenrecht*, v. 425 ff.; Pollock and Maitland, i. 142, 152.

[118] See particularly Richard Schmidt, *Die Herkunft des Inquisitionsprozesses*, in *Freiburger Festschrift zum 50. Regierungsjubiläum Grh. Friedrichs I* (Leipzig, 1902); id., *Königsrecht, Kirchenrecht, und Stadtrecht beim Aufbau des Inquisitionsprozesses*, in *Festgabe für Rudolph Sohm* (Munich, 1915); Zechbauer, *Das mittelalterliche Strafrecht Siziliens* (Berlin, 1908), pp. 168–247; Max Hoffmann, *Die Stellung des Königs von Sizilien nach den Assisen von Ariano* (Münster, 1915), pp. 84–92. Schmidt, and Niese, *Die Gesetzgebung der normannischen Dynastie im Regnum Siciliae* (Halle, 1910; see my reviews in *E. H. R.*, xxvi. 369–371; *A. H. R.*, xvii. 177), are much too sweeping in their statements as to the Norman origin of Sicilian law, and neither of them has attempted a study of the documentary evidence for the sworn inquest in Sicily.

[119] MS. Lat. 14832, f. 183v; Migne, cxlvii. 265; cf. *supra*, Chapter I, note 137.

bantur. . . . Episcopus vero prefatus, ut erat animo et genere nobilis, petitioni abbatis annuit et archidiaconum suum in Monte eum fecit, ita tamen ut quod bene non faceret vel non posset episcopus corrigeret Abrincis et ecclesiastico iuditio terminaret. De coniugiis autem illicitis, si qui legales testes procederent, apud episcopum audirentur et per sacramentum ipsorum lege dissolveretur quod contra legem presumptum erat. . . .

The jurisdiction here is the ordinary bishop's jurisdiction over laymen (*contra christianitatem*), by the new arrangement handed over to the abbot as archdeacon save in matrimonial cases, where *legales testes* are specially mentioned. What the *iuramenta* were is not specifically stated, but it would seem probable that the oaths required were, at least in part, the presentation of offenders by *fama publica*. If this be the correct interpretation, we have a Norman link midway between Regino and the decrees of Henry II.

Examples of the use of the sworn inquest in baronial courts meet us in other parts of Normandy in the latter part of the twelfth century. Thus the abbot of Saint-Wandrille grants a tenement at La Croisille to be held " as it has been recognized by our lawful and faithful men," [120] and a house at Caudebec with appurtenant rights as these have been recognized by the oath of neighbors.[121] Lawful men are used for the division of land [122] or the assignment of an equivalent holding,[123] and in an

---

[120] ' Sciant omnes presentes et futuri quod ego Walterus abbas S. Wandregisilis concessi Symoni de Cruciola teneuram suam quam in eadem villa de nobis tenet iure hereditario possidendam prout per iuridicos et fideles homines nostros recognita fuerit. . . .' Copy of cartulary in Archives of the Seine-Inférieure, iv. 2084. There are two abbots named Walter in this period, one 1137–1150, the other 1178–1187.

[121] ' Notum sit omnibus tam presentibus quam futuris quod ego Anfredus (1165–1178) abbas S. Wandregisilis et conventus concedimus Willelmo Anglico quietudinem domus sue ab omni consuetudine, salvo tamen censu, et custodiam vivarii nostri de Caldebecco et famulatum eiusdem ville iure hereditario, que ad domum ipsam sicut per iuramentum vicinorum recognitum est pertinent. . . .' Cartulary in Archives of the Seine-Inférieure, G. iii. 24, with list of jurors at end.

[122] ' Terram de Rosello sicut est previsa et ostensa et per legales homines divisa Sancto Martino Sagii ': *Livre blanc* of Saint-Martin de Séez, f. 48v. Cf. the division of land before the duke's justices: Round, *Calendar*, no. 607; MS. Rouen 1227, f. 135v; and an undated piece of the twelfth century in the Archives of the Calvados, *fonds* Saint-Désir de Lisieux: ' De hoc autem requirimus dominum regem et iustitias eius quod nobis haberi faciant intuitum curie.'

[123] ' Tantumdem terre ad valentiam pro ipsa terra arbitrio liberorum virorum ':

agreement for the mortgage of a house at Rouen it is stipulated that the cost of repairs shall be verified by the view of lawful neighbors.[124] Henry, abbot of Fécamp, and Robert, count of Meulan, make an agreement for a general inquest respecting their several rights, six jurors being chosen by each to declare the truth with respect thereto;[125] and a similar inquest by the men of Quillebeuf and Le Marais-Vernier is related by the abbot of Jumièges and Henry de Longchamp.[126] Robert Bertram the younger even admits that he caused his men to render a verdict regarding a presentation ' not of right but by his own might and force.' [127]

Of these baronial cases the most interesting, as regards both date and procedure, is one to which Valin has called attention in the cartulary of Préaux.[128] Two knights of Étréville-en-Roumois, Roger de Lesprevier and Richard, son of Humphrey the priest, claimed in lay fee the dwellings of the parish priests and other appurtenances of the church, whereas the abbot of Préaux claimed them in alms. A term was set before the archbishop and the count of Meulan, the lay lord, at which both parties " placed themselves on the verdict and oath of lawful men, to the number

cartulary of Saint-André-en-Gouffern, in Archives of the Calvados, ff. 61v, 62, nos. 273 f. (1175).

[124] ' Sciant tam presentes quam posteri quod anno incarnationis dominice .M°.C°.LX°.IIII°. Ricardus de Herburvilla invadiavit Simoni Anglico domum suam de atrio Sancti Amandi concessu uxoris sue et heredum suorum pro .lx. et .x. solidis Andegavensium usque ad octo annos tali conditione quod si Simon aliquid de suo in domo reficienda per visum legalium vicinorum suorum expenderit, Simon tailliabit illud in taillia sua et Ricardus ei solvet. . . .' Original in Archives of the Seine-Inférieure, *fonds* Saint-Amand.

[125] Fécamp cartulary (MS. Rouen 1207), f. 36v; extracts in La Roque, iii. 50; Du Cange, under *stalaria*.

[126] Le Prévost, *Eure*, ii. 375; Vernier, no. 194; original in Archives of the Seine-Inférieure, *fonds* Jumièges (1165–1198).

[127] ' Licet in prescriptis ecclesiis instinctu diabolico seu personali odio vel etiam propria malitia ductus diocesiano episcopo personam aliquam aliquando presentaverim et super earundem ecclesiarum presentationibus in curia mea recognitionem iniustam non de iure sed vi et potestate mea per homines meos fieri fecerim, et per recognitionem tunc temporis factam dictarum ecclesiarum quas prior de Sancta Maria de iure et donatione predecessorum meorum antea habuerat michi tam iniuste vendicaverim. . . .' Quasi-original in Archives of the Seine-Inférieure, *fonds* Saint-Ouen.

[128] Valin, p. 264, no. ix; cf. p. 200 f.; and Le Prévost, *Eure*, ii. 63.

of eight, who were sworn " [129] and proceeded to view the holdings in dispute. Their decision in favor of the abbey was opposed by the knights, and a day was fixed in the count's court at Brionne before William Fitz Robert and Robert de Neufbourg as his judges, when the jurors appeared to defend their verdict and Préaux was put in possession of the property as alms. When Richard threatened the abbot, he was locked up in the tower of Beaumont, and only released at another session of the court at Montfort, where he agreed to do homage and service to the abbot for the holding. Now all of this is anterior to the retirement of Robert of Neufbourg in 1159 [130] and quite possibly to the crusade of 1147, so that it falls at the latest in the early years of Henry II and shows, like the contemporary case from Bayeux, that the ' fertile ground of consent ' was already well prepared for his assizes.

Some measure of the progress made in Normandy by the middle of the twelfth century in the development of the recognition, in respect to definiteness of form as well as frequency of employment, may be got by examining the use made of the sworn inquest in the neighboring county of Anjou under Geoffrey Plantagenet and his father Fulk.[131] Although the older methods of trial find

[129] ' In hoc autem stabilito die ecclesia Pratellensis et predicti milites miserunt se in veredicto et iuramento legalium hominum qui octo fuerunt et omnes iuraverunt.'

[130] Robert of Torigni, i. 322, ii. 174. Valin's argument that Richard's journey to Jerusalem mentioned in the document is the Second Crusade, is not decisive; Reginald of Saint-Valery, for example, went to Palestine in 1158 (*ibid.*, i. 316, ii. 166). The other judge, William Fitz Robert, is found with Galeran of Meulan as early as 1143 (Round, no. 380).

For another instance of Robert de Neufbourg in the court of the count of Meulan, see *supra*, Chapter V, note 58, where the presence also of the bishop of Évreux indicates that they were sitting there as ducal justices.

[131] On the courts of Anjou see particularly C. J. Beautemps-Beaupré, *Recherches sur les juridictions de l'Anjou et du Maine pendant la période féodale* (Paris, 1890 ff.), forming the second part of his *Coutumes et institutions de l'Anjou et du Maine*. This elaborate work deals mainly with the later period. The account of Angevin law during the feudal period which the author planned was left unfinished at his death; cf. d'Espinay, *Le droit de l'Anjou avant les coutumes d'après les notes de M. Beautemps-Beaupré* (Angers, 1901). For the judicial institutions of the eleventh century there is a useful study by Halphen in the *Revue historique* (1901), lxxvii. 279-307.

abundant illustration in Angevin charters, one is at once struck with the rare appearance of anything resembling the Norman inquests. The less complete development of the administrative system in Anjou, and the fact that in this period the count generally presided in person in his court, may serve to explain the absence of such writs as are found in Normandy; but any mention of inquests is rare, and in such accounts as we have they are hard to distinguish from other forms of procedure, to which they sometimes seem only accessory. The cases, too, in which anything like the sworn inquest is applied are fiscal, concerning the count's forests, his rights of justice, or his feudal dues. Thus in a controversy between his foresters and the monks of Saint-Aubin Geoffrey calls together his foresters and *segrayers* of the district and adjures "those who had been brought up from infancy in the aforesaid forest and knew the facts well " to declare faithfully and impartially the ancient custom of the forest, neither relinquishing the count's right to the monks nor assigning the monks' right to him.[132] In another case where the matter in dispute concerned the count's right of *fodrium* on a piece of land belonging to the abbey of Saint-Serge, Geoffrey referred the matter to his seneschal, who ordered the local seneschal to take vavassors of the town with him upon the land and render a just judgment; but the question was finally determined by the oath of a witness produced by the monks.[133] Sometimes we find the count selecting men to render a verdict on the matter at issue in a way that suggests a jury of arbitration, as in a case from Fulk's reign touching the count's rights of justice on certain lands. The owner of the land finds seventy-three good men of Angers that know the truth of the

None of these writers discusses the sworn inquest. Cf. the sketch of Angevin institutions in Powicke, *Loss of Normandy*, ch. ii.

[132] 29 May 1129: Bertrand de Broussillon, *Cartulaire de l'abbaye de Saint-Aubin d'Angers*, ii. 408, no. 982; *B. É. C.*, xxxvi. 426, no. 28. Cf. Beautemps-Beaupré, i. 131, note, 143, note. For a similar case at Vendôme see Du Cange, *Glossarium*, under *3. Secretarius* (ed. Favre, vii. 387).

[133] MS. Lat. 5446, f. 295, no. 403 (Gaignières's copies from the cartulary of Saint-Serge). Cf. Beautemps-Beaupré, i. 203, note, where the date is fixed between 31 March 1150 and 7 September 1151. For a somewhat later case of declaration of custom, involving the right to levy *procuratio*, see C. Chevalier, *Cartulaire de l'abbaye de Noyers* (Tours, 1872), p. 651, no. 615.

matter, and gives the count their names; when they have all appeared in court, Fulk selects twelve, who are ordered to swear that they will not conceal the truth for love or hatred.[134] In other cases, however, it does not appear that the arbiters were necessarily neighbors or had any special knowledge of the facts, so that they would seem to have acted as representing the court rather than the countryside.[135] On the whole, while these scanty instances from Anjou show that the verdict of neighbors was occasionally sought in fiscal matters and that a sort of jury of arbitration might sometimes be called by the count, there is nothing to indicate that such modes of procedure were common, clearly defined, or well understood. Compared with such rudimentary institutions as these, it is evident that the Norman recognitions of the same period represent an advanced stage in the evolution of the jury, and that no share can be ascribed to Anjou in its development in Normandy.[136]

The sworn inquest is also found in the Norman kingdom of southern Italy and Sicily, where the judicial organization was in many respects similar to that of Normandy and England,[137] and recent writers are prone to assume that the Sicilian jury was a direct importation from Normandy.[138] While it is true that no examples have been found in the South before the Norman conquest, it is also true that the information for this period is extraordinarily scanty, while we have also to bear in mind the

---

[134] Beautemps-Beaupré, i. 117, note G.

[135] For instances of this sort see Marchegay, *Archives d'Anjou*, i. 409, no. 66; iii. 66, no. 87 (cf. Beautemps-Beaupré, i. 88, 117, 141); Beautemps-Beaupré, i. 116, note B, 136, note B; *Cartulaire de S.-Pierre-de-la-Cour* (*Archives historiques du Maine*, iv), no. 16. On the other hand, in the *Cartulaire d'Azé* (*ibid.*, iii), no. 20, the bishop of Angers puts himself on the verdict of three priests (1130–1135). For fiscal inquests in Maine under Henry II, see Delisle-Berger, nos. 200, 580.

[136] As has been suggested by Powicke, *E. H. R.*, xxii. 15; and Prentout, *La Normandie* (Paris, 1910), p. 57.

[137] See my discussion of the judicial organization in *E.H.R.*, xxvi. 641–651 (1911); and Miss E. Jamison's criticism in her monograph on *The Norman Administration of Apulia and Capua* (*Papers of the British School at Rome*, vi, 1913), which contains a useful list of cases in the royal courts.

[138] E. Mayer, *Italienische Verfassungsgeschichte* (Leipzig, 1909), i. 258; Niese, *Die Gesetzgebung der normannischen Dynastie*, p. 106; and the papers of Schmidt mentioned above, note 118.

possibilities of derivation from the fiscal measures of the later empire as well as from the procedure of the Frankish *missi* in Italy.
In general the legal procedure of the South, under the influence of
Roman law, makes free use of witnesses and written records, so
that it is difficult in many of the documents to distinguish the
individual or party witnesses from the collective jury. The testimony of neighbors, especially aged men, was particularly valued
in determining boundaries, which were regularly fixed by their
evidence, though not always in a way that clearly denotes a real
inquest. Examples of the use of old men of the region in this
indefinite fashion are found at Mileto in 1091,[139] at Squillace in
1098,[140] and in various Sicilian cases of the twelfth century, where
it is regularly stated that Saracens and Christians served together
in this capacity.[141] In the more specific account of a boundary
dispute between Grumo and Bitetto in 1136, the *boni senes
homines* of Bitetto were called *unus ante alium*, although at the
end they took a collective oath as to the term of possession.[142]
In 1158, near Bari, what looks like a collective verdict has to be
confirmed by a party oath of twelve *iuratores*.[143] On the other
hand an unmistakable inquest appears in 1140 at Atina, where
King Roger orders his chamberlain to make diligent inquiry by
suitable men concerning boundaries and royal rights, which were
sworn on the Gospels by twelve of the older men of the city.[144]
Under William I the phrase *isti iurati dixerunt* points to a sworn

[139] Capialbi, *Memorie per servire alla storia della santa chiesa militese* (Naples,
1835), p. 136.

[140] *Regii Napoletani Archivii Monumenta*, v. 245.

[141] Cusa, *I diplomi greci ed arabi di Sicilia*, i. 306, 317, 403; Garufi, *I documenti
inediti dell' epoca normanna in Sicilia* (*Documenti per la storia di Sicilia*, xviii),
nos. 24, 51, 61, 62, 105; id., in *Archivio storico per la Sicilia orientale*, ix. 349 (1912);
Caspar, *Roger II*, Regesten, nos. 9, 81, 145, 232.

[142] Garufi, *I documenti*, no. 13; Caspar, p. 308, note 2; Jamison, no. 5.

[143] Del Giudice, *Codice diplomatico del regno di Carlo I*, i. app. no. 9; Jamison,
no. 47.

[144] 'Precepit statim Ebulo de Mallano regio camerario ut omnia iura regia
necnon et fines tenimentorum civitatis eiusdem diligenter investigaret et per viros
idoneos inquireret solicite. Qui iussis regiis obtemperare paratus, iurare fecit ad
sancta Dei evangelia duodecim homines de antiquioribus civitatis ut ea que idem
dominus rex preceperat fideliter intimarent, quorum nomina hec sunt. . . .' Tauleri,
Memorie istoriche dell' antica città d' Atina (Naples, 1702), p. 92; Caspar, no. 128;
Jamison, no. 9.

inquest in a dispute touching the boundaries of the dioceses of Patti and Cefalù,[145] and a sworn inquest is held by the master chamberlain of Calabria to determine the losses of the church of Carbone.[146] In the same reign we find a clear account of a jury of eight men who are sworn before the king's chamberlain to tell the truth respecting the possessions of San Bartolomeo di Carpineto.[147] In 1183 the justiciars of William II hold a formal inquest to recover lost portions of the king's domain in the vicinity of Gravina.[148] It is particularly under William II that we should expect to find analogies to the Anglo-Norman assizes,[149] but nothing of the kind has been brought to light in the occasional writs that have reached us from this king or his officers,[150] and there is no evidence that the recognition in the Norman kingdom of Sicily was anything more than an occasional expedient for the assistance of the fisc or of some favored church. The inquests in criminal cases under Frederick II raise a different set of problems which lie beyond the limits of the present inquiry.

If now we turn to England, we find an almost complete parallel to the Norman documents. From the time of the Domesday survey examples are extant of fiscal inquests on a large scale, while specific royal writs prescribe the determination of particular cases by sworn inquest.[151] Jurors may be used to render a verdict upon a great variety of questions, even to the marking off of thirty *solidate* of land,[152] and they also appear in baronial jurisdictions,

---

[145] Garufi, *I documenti*, no. 34 (1159).

[146] Minieri Riccio, *Saggio di codice diplomatico di Napoli*, i. 283; Jamison, no. 58 (1163).

[147] Ughelli, *Italia Sacra*, x. app. 369; Jamison, no. 50.

[148] Printed by me, from the original in the Archives of La Cava, in *E. H. R.*, xxvi. 654, note 191. Less definite examples from this reign are in *Studi e documenti di storia e diritto*, xxii. 278 (1178); Tromby, *Storia dell' ordine cartusiano*, iv, p. clxi.

[149] The first mention of an assize seems to be the phrase ' ante assisam domini regis ' in a document of 1155: *Codice diplomatico barese*, v. 191. The so-called Vatican assizes of King Roger do not meet us with this title until later.

[150] See my discussion, *E. H. R.*, xxvi. 444–447 (1911), where certain parallels are pointed out with the Anglo-Norman writs. A *mandatum* of William II, since published (*Quellen und Forschungen des preussischen Instituts*, xvi. 30), should be added to those there cited.

[151] See Sir Francis Palgrave, *Rise of the English Commonwealth*, ii, p. clxxvi ff.; Bigelow, *Placita Anglo-Normannica*; Pollock and Maitland, i. 143.

[152] *Infra*, Appendix F, no. 13.

as when the bishop of Lincoln orders a declaration by the men of Banbury whether a piece of land was once part of his demesne.[153] If we examine more closely the first ten years of Henry II, we find the same practices continuing. The general measures for the recovery of the royal demesne were carried out, it appears, by a sworn inquest throughout the kingdom.[154] The prior and monks of Canterbury are to hold land as they proved their right by the oath of the lawful men of Kent;[155] the nuns of Malling, as it was recognized by the lawful men of the same county.[156] The rights of the church of Ely in the port of Orford are to be sworn by the lawful men of five and one-half hundreds.[157] Twenty-four men have sworn as to the height of the mills of Canterbury in Henry I's time;[158] twenty-four of the older men of Berks are to swear in the county court concerning the market of Abingdon at the same epoch.[159] Before the sheriff and archdeacon twenty-four men swear as to the advowson of Saint Peter's, Derby.[160] In Lancashire land is delimited by the oath of thirty men in accordance with royal writ.[161] The burgesses of Guildford are to have their liberties and customs as these have been recognized before the king and his justices in the county court there held.[162] In a series of records from Rievaulx we have the writ of Henry ordering his sheriff and ministers of Yorkshire to have the waste below Pickering recognized by the lawful men of the wapentake and forest; the report, with the names of the jurors; and the royal confirmation of the land to the abbey as sworn to by the wapentake and recognized before the king's justices in the county court

---

[153] *Eynsham Cartulary*, i. 41, no. 15a (1123–1148). Cf. the writ of Roger of Salisbury published by Massingberd, in Associated Architectural Societies, *Reports and Papers*, xxvii; and one of Henry I for Nostell priory, given by the bishop of Évreux at Évreux, in W. Farrer, *Early Yorkshire Charters*, no. 501.

[154] *Gesta Abbatum S. Albani*, i. 123.

[155] Delisle-Berger, no. 192.

[156] *Calendar of Charter Rolls*, v. 59, no. 19; cf. p. 58, no. 15, which may be somewhat later.

[157] *B. É. C.*, lxix. 550, no. 13.   [158] Delisle-Berger, no. 103.

[159] *Chronicon Monasterii de Abingdon*, ii. 228; Bigelow, *Placita*, p. 200. Cf. *Chronicon*, ii. 221; Bigelow, p. 203.

[160] *E. H. R.*, xxxii. 47.

[161] W. Farrer, *Lancashire Pipe Rolls*, p. 310.

[162] *Register of St. Osmund*, i. 238.

at York.[163] Before 1168 we find the king ordering an inquest in a baronial court in a writ to the earl and countess of Chester commanding them to have recognized by their barons of Lincolnshire whether Arnulf Fitz Peter lost the land of Hunnington by judgment of the court of Henry I.[164]

The fullest set of documents which we have from this period concerns a number of recognitions held to ascertain the rights of the bishop of Lincoln, as regards his justice, warren, burgage, and various local privileges.[165] The king's writs are for the most part addressed to the justices and sheriff of Lincolnshire, although the sheriffs of Nottingham and Derby are also mentioned, and in certain of them the county court is specifically indicated as the place where the recognition is held. Thus in one instance the bishop is to have his right of ferry at Newton on Trent as recognized *in comitatu*,[166] in another the church of Chesterfield is to have its liberties, customs, and tenements " as recognized by the lawful men of the hallmoot of the wapentake."[167] The reeves of Lincoln are directed " without delay to have recognized by the oaths of the more ancient and lawful men of the city, in the presence of the sheriff of Lincolnshire and at his summons, the liberties which the bishops of Lincoln had in their land and burgage at Lincoln in the time of King Henry my grandfather, and what liberties the clerks of the city had at the same time; and as it shall have been recognized, so without delay " they " shall cause Robert, bishop of

---

[163] *Chartulary of Rievaulx* (Surtees Society), nos. 189, 205, 206; W. Farrer, *Early Yorkshire Charters*, nos. 401–403.

[164] ' H. rex Anglorum et dux Normannorum et Aquitanorum et comes Andegavorum Hugoni comiti Cestrie et Matilde comitisse salutem. Precipio vobis quod sine dilatione et iuste faciatis recognosci per barones vestros de Lincolne sira si Arnulfus filius Petri terram de Hunintona in curia H. regis avi mei iudicio amisit et Lucia comitissa et Ran. comes Cestrie illam terram sanctimonialibus de Stikeswalda in elemosinam dederint. Quod si ita recognitum fuerit, faciatis eas bene et in pace et iuste tenere. Et nisi feceritis iusticia mea faciat. Teste M. Bis[set] dapifero meo apud Gloec.' Printed, from the original in the possession of Lady Waterford, in 11 *Historical MSS. Commission's Report*, Appendix vii. 59. The letter of Earl William of Roumare which follows fixes the date as anterior to 1168.

[165] Delisle-Berger, nos. 142, 217–219, 380; *E. H. R.*, xxiv. 308, no. 23; *Calendar of Charter Rolls*, iv. 110, no. 15, 141–145, nos. 21, 23, 37, where various related documents are also given.

[166] *Calendar of Charter Rolls*, iv. 110, no. 15.

[167] *Ibid.*, iv. 141, no. 21.

Lincoln, and his men of Lincoln and the clerks of the city to have all those liberties, without the exaction of any new customs." [168]

Here the parallelism to the Bayeux writs, the chief contemporary group in Normandy, is close and striking, and it should be noted that three of the writs ordering inquests for Lincoln are issued at Rouen and attested by the duke's Norman justiciar, Rotrou of Évreux,[169] so that we should expect close resemblances in procedure. Two notable points of difference, however, stand out. In the first place, the English writs assume as the normal basis for their execution the sheriff and the county court, while in Normandy no such assembly is mentioned. Already the sworn inquest has entered into that intimate relation to the local courts upon which its future history and its future importance in England are to depend. In the second place, the English writs make no mention of a royal assize: *secundum assisiam meam* is found only in Normandy, where the word assize occurs four times before 1159, while in no English document has it been found in this sense before 1164.[170] It is of course possible that instances may come to light in England, it may even be argued that the procedure was already so well established there that reference to the royal assize was no longer necessary; but these remain at present mere possibilities. The evidence for assizes before the Constitutions of Clarendon is Norman, not English; and, for the present at least, Normandy can claim priority, as regards both the term and the procedure which it denotes.

The sworn inquest was introduced into England from Normandy soon after the Conquest. Its history thereafter in the two countries is for some time essentially the same, namely as a prerogative procedure for the sovereign and for those with whom he shares its benefits in particular instances. Then the exceptional becomes general, first for one class of cases and then for another.[171] In England the first clear example of this change is found in the

---

[168] *Calendar of Charter Rolls*, iv. 142, no. 23.

[169] Delisle-Berger, nos. 217–219.

[170] The assizes cited by Bigelow, *History of Procedure*, p. 124, from the early Pipe Rolls denote evidently the *assisa comitatus*. Not until 1166 do these rolls use the word in the sense of royal legislation.

[171] Pollock and Maitland, i. 144.

assize *utrum* of 1164. In Normandy there is evidence earlier, in the assizes of Geoffrey and Henry to which they refer their officers on behalf of the bishop of Bayeux, and in the assize upon which William Fitz Thétion places himself against Saint-Étienne. If we cannot be certain just what these assizes were, we can at least see in them some systematic extension, by ducal act, of the procedure by recognition in cases concerning land. To these we must add the suit brought by Osmund Vasce in 1159, based as it clearly was upon some regular method of procedure open to ordinary litigants, and the ordinance of Falaise in the same year respecting the accusing jury. Thus Normandy is the home of the jury, not only in the sense that it is the source of the sworn inquest so far as England is concerned, but also as the land where we first find it employed as a regular procedure to which suitors can appeal as a matter of right and on which the individual can rely as a protection against arbitrary accusation. Both countries were then to share in its rapid extension to new types of cases by Henry II. England alone was to bring about that combination of the royal inquest with the popular courts which was to give the jury its unique position in the development of individual liberty and representative institutions. Where Normandy sowed, England and all English-speaking lands were to reap.

APPENDICES

APPENDIX A

THE DOCUMENTARY SOURCES OF EARLY
NORMAN HISTORY [1]

THE fundamental difficulty which confronts all students of ducal Normandy is the paucity of documentary evidence. The imposing series of Norman historians — Dudo, William of Jumièges, William of Poitiers, Ordericus Vitalis, Wace, Robert of Torigni — long served to conceal this fact in the pages of the modern writers who, with greater or less skill, paraphrased them into the conventional histories; but the inadequacy of even the best of chroniclers becomes apparent as soon as one attacks any of the fundamental problems of institutions or social conditions. For the tenth century documentary materials never existed,[2] at least in any such abundance as in the neighboring regions of Anjou, Brittany, or Flanders; for the eleventh and twelfth centuries what once existed has in large measure disappeared. It is indeed probable that such sources were always less numerous in Normandy than in England, where the documentary habit had not been broken in the tenth century, and where the Norman Conquest itself produced a monument like the Domesday Survey which was from the nature of the case unique; but we have no reason to suppose that in the twelfth century the records of the central administration were notably different on the two sides of the Channel or that the body of charters and writs showed any such disparity as at present. In the absence of anything

---

[1] See especially Delisle, *Étude sur l'agriculture et la classe agricole en Normandie* (Évreux, 1851), pp. xlv–li; the introduction to his *Cartulaire normand de Philippe-Auguste, Louis VIII, Saint Louis, et Philippe-le-Hardi*, M. A. N., xvi (1852); his *Catalogue des actes de Philippe-Auguste* (Paris, 1856), pp. vi–liii, 525–569; and his *Recueil des actes de Henri II*, introduction, pp. v–xiii. H. Stein, *Bibliographie générale des cartulaires français* (Paris, 1907), lists most of the Norman cartularies, not always accurately (cf. my review, *A. H. R.*, xiii. 322–324). An excellent survey of the materials in the departmental archives is given in the *État général par fonds des archives départementales; ancien régime et période révolutionnaire* (Paris, 1903). Cf. also H. Prentout, *La Normandie* (Paris, 1910), pp. 21–24. A convenient summary by dioceses and religious establishments is given by Dom Besse, in the *Abbayes et prieurés de l'ancienne France*, vii (*Archives de la France monastique*, xvii, 1914).

[2] Cf. *supra*, Chapter I, note 4.

corresponding to Domesday, Glanvill, or the *Dialogue on the Exchequer*, the charters acquire an added importance in Normandy, and it is their loss and destruction which the historian has chiefly to mourn.

The loss of Norman records can be laid to no single period or cataclysm. The Revolution of course did its share in the work of destruction, neglect, or dispersion, as in the case of Bec;[3] but this has often been exaggerated, and the departmental archives and local libraries which were then created seem to have taken over the greater part of what remained in existence. There were losses en route to these establishments, and further losses under the archivists of the Restoration, when numerous pieces disappeared from public repositories only to reappear in certain private collections, but in most instances such material has been recovered or at least placed, so that there is small hope of new discoveries of this sort. The great losses seem to have come before the Revolution, for the scholars of the Old Régime, as their work can be traced in surviving copies, are seen to have had at their disposal relatively few collections which are not still in existence. The Protestants did something in the work of destruction, the Hundred Years' War did more, but much must be ascribed to the frequent fires of the Middle Ages and to the carelessness and neglect of the clergy themselves. As early as the fourteenth century a scribe of Troarn is making extracts from a *Vetus Cartarium* long since disappeared;[4] as late as the Revolution the canons of Coutances are said to have spent days in burning charters which they could no longer read.[5]

Of the nature and extent of the ducal archives themselves it is impossible to speak with much definiteness. An archive of some sort is assumed in the *rotulos et cartas nostras* transferred from Caen to London by order of King John in 1204,[6] but the handful of Exchequer Rolls now preserved in the Public Record Office is but a sorry remnant of what must then have been in the hands of his officers, nor have any rolls of other types survived from earlier reigns.[7] With him begin the

[3] Le Prévost, *Eure*, i. 233 f., 241.

[4] Sauvage, *Troarn*, pp. xxx–xxxiii; cf. *supra*, Chapter III, no. 6; *infra*, Appendix H, no. 1.

[5] Round, *Calendar*, p. xxxi, note.

[6] *Rotuli de Liberate*, p. 102 f. The barons' returns in 1172 were deposited in the royal treasury at Caen (Robert of Torigni, ii. 297), and a summary of them was later copied into the *Red Book* of the Exchequer.

[7] *Supra*, Chapter V, note 6. A brief *extractus memorandi* from John's Exchequer has recently been discovered and published by Legras (*Bulletin des Antiquaires de Normandie*, xxix. 21–31); see further the paper of Jenkinson cited *supra*, p. 195.

short-lived *Rotuli Normanniae* and the Norman entries in the patent and other rolls.[8] After the loss of Normandy the English possessions of Norman religious establishments still furnished an occasion for the enrollment of Norman charters, in the *Cartae Antiquae* and in the numerous *inspeximus* of English sovereigns contained in the charter and patent rolls, and such confirmations were naturally numerous during the occupation of Normandy by Henry V and Henry VI.[9] Certain scattered pieces and a couple of cartularies have in recent years been acquired by the British Museum.[10]

That some public records escaped the process of transfer to England is shown by a fragment of a roll of Stephen cited in 1790 [11] and a fragment of the roll of 1184 discovered by Delisle in the Archives Nationales.[12] Various documents of interest to Norman administration, like the list of knights' fees of 1172, were collected by the officers of Philip Augustus and copied into his registers,[13] yet the only surviving portion of the inquest of 1171 has come to us on the fly-leaf of a copy of Hrabanus Maurus.[14] A semi-official compilation of charters made in the thirteenth century, styled by Delisle the *Cartulaire de Normandie*, should be noted.[15] Formulations of custom, such as the *Consuetudines et iusticie* and the *Iurea regalis*,[16] owe their preservation to private collections of Norman law, and the decisions of Norman courts in the period anterior to the French conquest have reached us only in charters preserved by the interested parties.[17] There are no plea rolls or feet of fines.

Next to the disappearance of the official records of Norman administration, the most serious loss is probably the archives of the bishoprics and cathedrals, of which none has a full series of records for the

[8] *Supra*, Chapter V, note 210.

[9] See the calendars of the Norman rolls of Henry V in appendices to *Reports of the Deputy Keeper*, xli. 671-810, xlii. 313-452; the extracts in *M. A. N.*, xxiii, part 1; and the *Actes de la chancellerie d' Henri VI*, ed. Lecacheux, Rouen, 1907-1908.

[10] Cartulary of the leprosery of Bolleville, Add. MS. 17307; cartulary of the priory of Loders, Add. MS. 15605; and the series of Additional Charters.

[11] *M. A. N.*, xvi, p. xxx f.

[12] *Ibid.*, pp. 109-113; Delisle, *Henri II*, pp. 334-344.

[13] See Delisle's introduction to his *Cartulaire normand* and *Catalogue des actes de Philippe-Auguste*.

[14] Delisle, *Henri II*, pp. 345-347, from MS. Lat. n. a. 1879; *infra*, Appendix K.

[15] Now MS. Rouen 1235. See Delisle, *Cartulaire normand*, p. vii.

[16] Appendix D; Chapter V, note 22.

[17] See Delisle, *Mémoire sur les anciennes collections de jugements de l'Échiquier de Normandie* (Paris, 1864); and cf. *H. F.*, xxiv. 271* ff.

eleventh and twelfth centuries while some have lost practically everything for this epoch. Rouen is the most fortunate, with important cartularies and an extensive *fonds* of pieces in the departmental archives. This *fonds*, however, admirably calendared by Charles de Beaurepaire, contains relatively little anterior to the French conquest, while only two of the cartularies relate to this period,[18] one containing earlier documents having evidently been lost. Évreux is represented by no originals but by a valuable set of cartularies in the Archives of the Eure, extending from the destruction of the cathedral under Henry I. There are no early archives for Séez; a cartulary, the *Livre rouge*, was in the possession of the bishop before the Separation,[19] and copies of the sixteenth century are in the library at Alençon (MS. 177). Lisieux likewise has lost everything for this period, all that remains being a late cartulary of the see in the municipal library and a fragment of the chapter cartulary at Paris.[20] Bayeux has only cartularies, the invaluable *Livre noir* of the chapter and the *Livre noir* of the see still preserved in the cathedral, and the *Livre rouge*.[21] Coutances has much less, only a few documents in the paper cartulary recently transferred from the évêché to the Archives of the Manche.[22] Avranches has left practically nothing save an occasional piece of the twelfth century in its *Livre vert*.[23]

The monastic archives of the duchy have on the whole fared better. The oldest monasteries of importance, Fécamp, Jumièges, Saint-Wandrille, Saint-Ouen, and Mont-Saint-Michel, have transmitted valuable early originals as well as considerable cartularies, while the somewhat later foundations of Caen, Lessay, Saint-Amand, and Troarn are also well represented in the departmental archives. From La Trinité du Mont, Saint-Pierre-de-Préaux, Saint-Évroul, Saint-Taurin, and Saint-Martin de Séez we have only cartularies, in each case of much value for the early period. Important cartularies for the twelfth century are those of Foucarmont, Saint-Georges de Bocherville, the hospital of Pontaudemer, Plessis-Grimould, Saint-André-en-Gouffern, Montebourg, Saint-Sauveur-le-Vicomte, and Savigny. The

[18] The so-called cartulary of Philip d'Alençon, Archives of the Seine-Inférieure, G. 7; and the cartulary of the chapter, MS. Rouen 1193 (copy in MS. Lat. n. a. 1363).

[19] Extracts in MS. Lat. 11058.

[20] MS. Lat. 5288, ff. 68–76.

[21] MS. Lat. n. a. 1828. See *supra*, Chapter VI, notes 4, 15.

[22] *Ibid.*, note 95; cf. *A. H. R.*, viii. 631.

[23] MS. Avranches 206; see Appendix K.

list, however, is long of those houses from which little or nothing has reached us directly for the history of these times: Bec, Bernai, Cerisy, Conches, Cormeilles, Croix-Saint-Leufroy, Grestain, Ivry, Lonlai, Montivilliers, Saint-Désir de Lisieux, Saint-Pierre-sur-Dive, Saint-Sauveur d'Évreux, Saint-Sever, Saint-Victor-en-Caux. In some cases, as Cerisy, Lire, Montivilliers, and Saint-Pierre-sur-Dive, we have *vidimus* of the foundation charters or notices of their beginnings; in others, as Bec, modern copies supply in some measure the loss of the mediaeval pieces.

An important group of ducal charters concerns the Norman possessions of religious houses in other parts of France. Chief among these are Marmoutier, Cluny, Fontevrault, Saint-Julien de Tours, Saint-Florent-lès-Saumur, Saint-Benoît-sur-Loire, La Trinité de Vendôme, Chartres cathedral, Saint-Père de Chartres, Tiron, Saint-Denis de Nogent-le-Rotrou, Le Grand-Beaulieu-lès-Chartres, Saint-Denis and Saint-Martin-des-Champs at Paris, Saint-Martin at Pontoise, Saint-Victor du Mans, Le Mans cathedral, and Saint-Bénigne at Dijon. The most important of these, Marmoutier, had its archives [24] dispersed during the Revolution, but its Norman *chartriers* can in large measure be recovered from pieces preserved in the local priories and especially from the important series of copies in the Bibliothèque Nationale [25] and the library at Tours.[26] In nearly all the other instances mentioned the surviving ducal charters are published in printed cartularies or modern collections of charters.[27]

The principal local repositories of documentary material relating to early Normandy are the departmental archives of the Calvados, Eure, Manche, Orne, and Seine-Inférieure, supplemented by the public libraries of Rouen, Caen, Alençon, and Avranches. Scattered volumes which had remained in the possession of bishops and chapters were claimed by the public archives under the Separation Law, save in the case of the cathedral of Bayeux, which was for the time being constituted a public depository. Only at Rouen do the municipal archives contain material for this period; archives of hospitals are rarely of assistance; there is some scattered matter in the smaller public libraries. The

[24] See P. Colmant, *Les actes de l'abbaye de Marmoutier*, in *Positions des thèses de l'École des Chartes*, 1907.

[25] MSS. Lat. 5441, 12876–12880, MS. Baluze 77.   [26] Particularly MS. 1381.

[27] See, besides the indications in Stein's *Bibliographie des cartulaires*, L.-J. Denis, *Les chartes de S.-Julien de Tours*, in *Archives historiques du Maine*, xii (1912); J. Depoin, *Recueil de chartes de S.-Martin-des-Champs*, in *Archives de la France monastique*, xiii, xvi.

chief collection of originals in private hands is the important body of early Fécamp charters in the Musée de la Distillerie de Bénédictine at Fécamp.[28] The great collection of copies made by Dom Lenoir in the eighteenth century, now the property of the Marquis de Mathan at Saint-Pierre-de-Semilly, is based chiefly upon the registers of the Chambre des Comptes and comprises few early charters.[29] The copies of the abbé de La Rue, concerning especially the history of Caen, are divided among the Collection Mancel at Caen, the libraries of Caen and Cherbourg, and the Bibliothèque Nationale; [30] the *Repertoire des chartes* of de Gerville relating to the Cotentin is now in the Collection Mancel; recently Armand Benet bequeathed to the library of Évreux his copies of ducal and other charters. An older collection of much value for the Cotentin, the copies of Pierre Mangon, is in the library at Grenoble.[31] Of the departmental archives, those of the Eure and Orne have published inventories of the series most important for the early period, G and H; those of the Calvados and the Manche for a portion of H; those of the Seine-Inférieure only for the Rouen portion of G, the rich *fonds* of series H being for the most part still unclassified.[32]

The Archives Nationales are useful, so far as ducal Normandy is concerned, chiefly for the royal *vidimus* contained in the Registres du Trésor des Chartes.[33] There are also scattered pieces in the Layettes du Trésor and in other series, notably S, while there is a fine set of originals for the abbey of Savigny,[34] rescued in 1839 from the garret of the *sous-préfecture* at Mortain.

The Bibliothèque Nationale is exceedingly rich in the manuscript materials for early Norman history.[35] Its resources consist in part of a

[28] *Infra*, Appendix B.

[29] The cartularies used by Dom Lenoir are well known save in the case of a " cartulaire de l'abbaye de Lire trouvé parmi les mss. de la bibliothèque du collège des jésuites de Paris. L'écriture est du 13ᵉ siècle " (xxiii. 453; cf. lxxii, 329 ff.). This seems to be the cartulary used by the editors of the *Monasticon*, vii. 1092–1095.

[30] MSS. Fr. n. a. 20218–20221.

[31] Described by Delisle, in *Annuaire de la Manche*, 1891, pp. 11–42.

[32] For the Seine-Inférieure see P. Chevreux and J. Vernier, *Les archives de Normandie et de la Seine-Inférieure* (Rouen, 1911), which contains a collection of facsimiles.

[33] See in general the introduction to Delisle, *Cartulaire normand*, pp. i–iv, who notes the *vidimus* as far as 1314. I have searched the series of registers to 1380.

[34] L. 966–978, recently renumbered. Other originals are in MS. Rouen 3122. On the history of the archives of Savigny see Delisle's introduction to his edition of the *Rouleau mortuaire du B. Vital* (Paris, 1909).

[35] See in general Delisle, *Le Cabinet des MSS. de la Bibliothèque Nationale* (Paris, 1868–1881), and the lists of acquisitions published biennially by Omont in *B. É. C.*

great number of cartularies and original pieces which have been accumulated since the days of Colbert and which now comprise a very considerable portion of the materials which slipped out of Norman archives and libraries before, during, and after the Revolution; in part, of the copies of modern scholars which preserve matter now lost. The older portion of these copies include the collections of Baluze, Du Cange, Duchesne, Bréquigny, and others; [36] the transcripts accumulated in the eighteenth century for the series of *Chartes et diplômes* and now chronologically arranged in the Collection Moreau; [37] the numerous Norman volumes among the copies of the exact and indefatigable Gaignières; [38] ecclesiastical compilations like the *Monasticon Benedictinum* [39] (MSS. Lat. 12658–12704) and *Miscellanea Monastica* (MSS. Lat. 12777–12780), the *Neustria Christiana* of Du Monstier (MSS. Lat. 10048–10050), the *Hierarchia Normanniae* of Coenalis (MS. Lat. 5201), the materials concerning the diocese of Coutances brought together by Toustain de Billy (MS. Fr. 4900),[40] and the historical collections relating to Bec (MSS. Lat. 12884, 13905), Marmoutier (*supra*, note 25), and Mont-Saint-Michel (MS. Lat. 5430A, MS. Fr. 18947 ff.). To these have been added the papers of most of the principal Norman scholars of the nineteenth century: Achille Deville for Upper Normandy (MSS. Lat. n. a. 1243–1246); Léchaudé d'Anisy for Lower Normandy (MSS. Lat. 10063–10084); Auguste Le Prévost for the department of the Eure (MSS. Lat. n. a. 1837–1838); C. Hippeau for Saint-Étienne de Caen (MSS. Lat. n. a. 1406–1407); and finally the

Certain Norman cartularies are comprised in the considerable group acquired from the library of Sir Thomas Phillipps in 1908 (catalogue by Omont, 1909).

For MSS. of Norman origin in the Bibliothèque Sainte-Geneviève see E. Deville in the *Revue catholique de Normandie*, 1903 ff.

[36] R. Poupardin, *Catalogue des MSS. des collections Duchesne et Bréquigny* (Paris, 1905); *Catalogue de la Collection Baluze* by Auvray and Poupardin (Paris, 1915). Norman cartularies also contributed to the extracts concerning Meulan made by de Blois *ca.* 1650 and now preserved in the Collection du Vexin, iv.

[37] Omont, *Inventaire des MSS. de la Collection Moreau* (Paris, 1891). The Norman copies are chiefly in the hand of Dom Lenoir; volume 341 is devoted to Fécamp.

[38] Chiefly in the volumes classified by monasteries; see also the collections concerning Norman bishops (MSS. Lat. 17022 ff.). The extracts published by Delisle from the collected papers (MSS. Fr. 20899–20917), in *Annuaire de la Manche*, 1893 and 1898, deal with the later period.

[39] Analyzed by Delisle, *Revue des bibliothèques*, vii. 241–267.

[40] Cf. the similar matter in MSS. Fr. 4899–4902, n. a. 154–157. The history of the diocese of Coutances published by the Société de l'histoire de Normandie in 1874 lacks the *preuves*, as do also the histories of Savigny, Jumièges, and Mont-Saint-Michel in the same series.

lifelong accumulations of Léopold Delisle (MSS. Fr. n. a. 21806–21873).[41]

The exploration and publication of these sources have proceeded in an incomplete and unsystematic fashion. In the seventeenth and eighteenth centuries Norman archives were laid under contribution for the *Neustria Pia* of Arthur Du Monstier, the eleventh volume of the *Gallia Christiana*, La Roque's *Histoire de la maison d'Harcourt*, the *Concilia Rotomagensis Provinciae* of Bessin, and the publications of Pommeraye relating to Rouen, as well as for the more general ecclesiastical collections of Mabillon, Martène and Durand, and d'Achery. In the nineteenth century leadership passed to the Société des Antiquaires de Normandie and the Société de l'histoire de Normandie, supplemented by the Norman academies and various local societies and reviews, of which the *Revue catholique de Normandie* in recent years deserves special mention. Among individual scholars Léopold Delisle stands in a place by himself for his thorough acquaintance with Norman history, narrative and literary as well as documentary. De Gerville, who did much to stimulate interest in Norman history at the beginning of the century, was a collector of documents rather than an editor; his younger contemporary Le Prévost, besides his share in the great edition of Ordericus, left behind him a collection of *Mémoires et notes pour servir à l'histoire du département de l'Eure* (Évreux, 1862–1869) which has not always been sufficiently utilized by his successors. Amid the multiplicity of scattered publications relatively few Norman cartularies have been edited, among those of the first importance only the *Cartulaire de la Sainte-Trinité-du-Mont* (ed. A. Deville, 1840) and the *Livre noir* of Bayeux (*Antiquus Cartularius*, ed. V. Bourrienne, 1902–1903).[42] The most extensive publications of this sort (e. g., T. Bonnin, *Cartulaire de Louviers*, Paris, 1870–1883) concern chiefly other periods. Editions by trained scholars are now announced of two important cartularies of the twelfth century, that of La Trinité de Caen by R. N. Sauvage, and that of Mont-Saint-Michel by P. Lecacheux. For the present the most convenient guide to the contents of Norman documents is the *Calendar of Documents Preserved in France* of J. Horace Round (London, 1899). This is unfortunately based upon a set of loose copies in the Public Record Office,[43] and while the editor supplemented these by personal investigation in France and verified a

[41] Also many cartularies copied by him or under his direction.
[42] Cf. *A. H. R.*, viii. 615; *supra*, Chapter VI, note 15.
[43] Cf. *A. H. R.*, viii. 614, note.

certain number from the originals, much material was left untouched and in too many instances the originals were not collated. The analyses of documents and the identification of persons, however, were made with the care and competence which were to be expected from this distinguished master of Anglo-Norman history.

At present the study of the documentary sources needs to be pushed in two directions, the history of monasteries and the ducal charters. In the field of monastic history there is need both of comprehensive studies like the recent monograph of R. N. Sauvage on *L'abbaye de Saint-Martin de Troarn* [44] (Caen, 1911), and of critical editions of early charters, such as Ferdinand Lot has given in his *Études critiques sur l'abbaye de Saint-Wandrille* (Paris, 1913). [45] Such studies furnish the necessary basis for a collection of ducal charters which shall perform for the earlier dukes the labor so admirably done by Delisle and Berger for Henry II. From 1066 on such work must be carried on with the closest attention to the material in England, for which H. W. C. Davis has begun his *Regesta Regum Anglo-Normannorum* (i, Oxford, 1913).

[44] Where, pp. xlv–xlix, other monastic histories are enumerated. One of the best is Porée, *Histoire de l'abbaye du Bec* (Évreux, 1901).

[45] J.-J. Vernier, *Les chartes de l'abbaye de Jumièges* (Société de l'histoire de Normandie, 1916), reached me only after this volume was in type.

APPENDIX B

THE EARLY DUCAL CHARTERS FOR FÉCAMP

THE abbey of Fécamp, " the Saint-Denis of the Norman dukes," [1] was from its foundation in the closest relations with the ducal house, from which it received important grants and privileges; yet its early charters have received singularly little attention from historians. The series in the departmental archives at Rouen, though rich for the later period, contains comparatively few early documents; the earliest originals passed into private hands and were finally acquired by the Musée de la Distillerie de Bénédictine de Fécamp, to the generosity of whose proprietors I am indebted for photographs and opportunities of study on the spot. The cartularies in the Archives of the Seine-Inférieure (no. 16) and in the Public Library at Rouen (MS. 1207) contain little on the early period, but the careful copies of Dom Lenoir at Semilly (volume 76) and in the Collection Moreau at the Bibliothèque Nationale (especially volume 341) are based upon a lost cartulary of the twelfth century as well as upon originals then in possession of the abbey.

An adequate study of this material can be undertaken only as part of a history of the monastery, but the student of Norman institutions cannot avoid an examination of the earliest ducal charters, which offer an exceptionally full series, with several unpublished originals (see the facsimiles in the present volume), and are of much importance for the grants of immunity, the ducal *curia*, and ducal finance. The following list is confined to the charters of Richard I, Richard II, and Robert I, and to certain forgeries based upon them and ascribed to William the Conqueror.[2]

In general the early charters of Fécamp show small trace of the forger's hand, as compared, for example, with the documents of the same period for Saint-Wandrille and Saint-Ouen. At two points, however, Fécamp was tempted to sustain its claims by fabrication, with respect namely to the exemption of Fécamp and certain other parishes from the authority of the archbishop of Rouen, and to the immunity of the monastery from secular jurisdiction. The documentary basis for

---

[1] Prentout, *Étude critique sur Dudon de S.-Quentin*, p. 326.

[2] For three unpublished originals of Robert Curthose, see *infra*, Appendix E, no. 4.

the exemption is not entirely clear,[3] and an interpolation to this effect was attempted in the earliest charter of the monastery, that of Duke Richard I (*infra*, no. 1). No immunity is found in this document, but the first charter of Richard II, issued 30 May 1006 (no. 2), has the following clause:

Tam horum quam eorum quę a patre meo tradita sunt omnis ordinatio exterius et interius in abbatis sibique subiectorum consistat arbitrio, undeque eorum dispositioni resistat persona nulla parva vel magna cuiuscumque officii dignitatisve. Et non solum in rerum ordinatione iustici sed in restituendi abbatis electione . . . a nobis iuste collata utantur libertate.[4]

A specific grant of immunity appears for the first time in no. 5, Richard II's charter *Propitia* of 1025 (1027), in exactly the same terms as in the contemporary charters for Jumièges and Bernai and in the charters of Robert I for Saint-Amand and La Trinité du Mont: [5]

Haec omnia . . . concedo . . . ut habeant, teneant, et possideant absque ulla inquietudine cuiuslibet sęcularis vel iudiciarię potestatis sicuti res ad fiscum dominicum pertinentes.

This is clearly the genuine and standard form of the Fécamp immunity. The general confirmation of Robert I in its expanded text (no. 10B) gives a different statement:

Ista igitur bona et omnia alia quę Fischannensi monasterio olim donata sunt sub solius abbatis potestate et iusticia constituimus ut nullius dignitatis homo aliquando manum intromittere presumat.

The fabrication based upon nos. 5 and 10 and ascribed to William the Conqueror (no. 11) elaborates the exemption with particular reference to Saint-Gervais:

[3] Documents are lacking to confirm the account in the *De revelatione* (*Neustria Pia*, p. 214; Bessin, *Concilia*, ii. 21) according to which the freedom ' ab omni episcoporum iugo et consuetudine ' was granted by Richard II, King Robert, Archbishop Robert, and Benedict VIII; but such an exemption is presupposed in the freedom ' ab omni episcopali consuetudine . . . sicut tenet Fiscannensi ecclesia ' which was granted to Montivilliers in 1035 (*Gallia Christiana*, xi. instr. 326; *infra*, Appendix C, no. 17). For the controversies over exemption at the close of the eleventh century see the *Ordinationes facte in monasterio Fiscanni*, in Mabillon, *Annales*, iv, 668; and the treatises in MS. 415 of Corpus Christi College, Cambridge (Böhmer, *Kirche und Staat*, pp. 180, 183).

[4] King Robert's charter of even date has: ' Sicut nulli ordini, dignitati, potestati, hereditarieque successioni, nostre quinimmo maiestati super idem ius relinquere decrevimus dominationis.' *H. F.*, x. 588.

[5] *Supra*, p. 26. For the later history of the immunity of Fécamp, see Valin, p. 224; Delisle-Berger, no. 57.

Et ab omni servicio archiepiscopali sit libera sicut Fiscanni abbacia, ut nullus meus heres aut archiepiscopus seu alicuius potestatis persona audeat infringere vel violare hanc meam donacionem.

The second of the forgeries attributed to the Conqueror (no. 12), with the related extract concerning Steyning, was prepared primarily for use in England; for the Norman lands it merely repeats the clause of Richard II with the insertion of *vel diminutione*, whereas for the English possessions it repeats the clause in this form and adds

Et quod abbas et monachi ecclesie Fiscannensis vel eorum ministri regiam habeant libertatem et consuetudinem et iusticiam suam de omnibus rebus et negotiis que in terra sua evenient vel poterunt evenire, nec aliquis nisi per eos se inde intromittat, quia hoc totum regale beneficium est et omni servitute quietum.

Such 'royal liberty and justice' was confirmed to the abbey by Henry II.[6]

1

989–990 (?)

Charter of Richard I, with the concurrence of Archbishop Robert and all the bishops of Normandy, granting to Fécamp Mondeville, Argences, (Calvados), Saint-Valery, 'Bretennoles,' and Ingouville (Seine-In-férieure) (together with the exemption of the abbey church and twelve others from all episcopal jurisdiction).

A, original lost; B, copy in lost cartulary of 12th century; C, copy of 12th century in the Public Library of Rouen, MS. 427, f. 151v.

La Roque, *Histoire de la maison d'Harcourt*, iii. 165 (cf. 164), 'extraict des archives de l'abbaye'; *Neustria Pia*, p. 208, from C, omitting several witnesses; Pommeraye, *Sanctae Rotomagensis Ecclesiae Concilia*, p. 60; extract in factum of 1688 (Bibliothèque Nationale, factum 12070, 2), where it is attributed to Richard II. Cf. Mabillon, *Annales*, iv. 57 (62); Bessin, *Concilia*, ii. 21; *Gallia Christiana*, xi. 203, where the text is corrected from B.

The charter is undated but was apparently given at the time of the dedication, the date of which is not given by Dudo, William of Jumièges, or the Fécamp annals (Labbe, *Nova Bibliotheca*, i. 325), but appears as 989 or 990 in the later annalists (Duchesne, *Historiae Normannorum Scriptores*, p. 1017; *H. F.*, x. 317; *Gallia Christiana*, xi. 203). The document cannot in any case be earlier than 989, the year

---

[6] Delisle-Berger, no. 57.

of the accession of Robert to the archbishopric of Rouen (*Annals* of Jumièges, in the Vatican, MS. Regina 553, part 2, f. 6; Ordericus, ii. 365, v. 156; cf. Vacandard in *Revue catholique de Normandie*, xiii. 196); it is fundamental for the dates of the Norman bishops, who are all mentioned by name.

The exemption of the thirteen parishes from the archbishop's jurisdiction, which is found in all the printed texts, is an obvious interpolation, as was pointed out by the editors of the *Gallia*, who note that it does not occur in B. There is no apparent reason for doubting the remainder of the document: a charter of Richard I is specifically cited by Richard II (*infra*, no. 2), and the places here granted are recited in the general confirmation of Richard II (no. 5). The enumeration in this confirmation of other grants of Richard I — Étigues, etc. — may imply other charters of his now lost.

2

30 May 1006, doubtless at Fécamp

Charter of Richard II granting to Fécamp freedom of election according to the custom of Cluny, and adding to the gifts of his father possessions in the following places: Fécamp, ' Giruinivilla' (= Vittefleur ?), Arques, Écretteville, Harfleur, Rouen, Pissy, Barentin (Seine-Inférieure), Aizier (Eure), Hennequeville (Calvados), and five churches in Vaudreuil.

A, original in Musée de la Bénédictine, no. 1; B, copy in Collection Moreau, cccxli. 2, from which the portions in brackets have been restored.

Unpublished; see the facsimile, plate 1. These privileges are confirmed by a charter of King Robert, issued at Fécamp on the same day: collated copies in Musée, nos. 2, 3; printed in *Gallia Christiana*, xi. instr. 8; Mabillon, *Annales*, iv. 170 (185); *H. F.*, x. 587, no. xvi; Pfister, *Robert le Pieux*, catalogue, no. 30.[1]

IN NOMINE SANCTAE ET INDIVIDUAE TRINITATIS DIVINA FAVENTE GRATIA [RICARDUS] COMES ET PATRITIUS.|| Hactenus locum istum vulgaris fama Fiscamnum vocare consuevit, cuius ethimologia perspecta doctores novelli quidam fixum scamnum quidam fixum campum volunt appellari. Rellicto ergo inter contentiosos iudicio huius nominis, causa divini servicii quae ibi

---

[1] The original of Robert's other charter for Fécamp (*H. F.*, x. 587, no. xv; Pfister, no. 33) is in the Musée, no. 1; copy in Collection Moreau, cccxli. 12. For other early grants to Fécamp, see La Roque, iii. 167; Depoin, *Cartulaire de S.-Martin de Pontoise*, p. 342.

agitur quando vel quomodo cepta sit cognoscatur. Sicut in universis terrae partibus sancta mater aecclesia multiplicato gaudet filiorum numero, ita in ipsis exultare cupit operum bonorum incremento. Quorum multis per aliarum exequutiones virtutum occupatis, dum quidam ex transitoriis bonis curas gerunt pauperum, alii sanctorum locis edificandis invigilant, quasi decollatis beneficiis Christo vicissitudinem reddunt, ut cum illo felicius vivant. Quorum exemplo notum sit presentibus et futuris in hoc loco patrem meum comitem Richardum fundamento construxisse aecclesiam in honore sanctae et individuae trinitatis consubstantialis patris et filii et spiritus sancti, eo intentionis voto ut collectus monachorum ordo sub regula Sancti Benedicti viveret et Dei laudibus inserviret. Cuius desiderium ubi mors abstulit imperfectum, ego Richardus comes eius equivocus filius suscepi peragendum, nec multo post divina providentia inventum domnum Wilelmum abbatem et precibus et caput huius crescendę religionis preesse institui. Sub quo iam multiplicatis monachis et multiplicandis temporalibus bonis quae a patre meo huic loco concessa sunt et per cartam firmata, hęc ex hereditario iure concessa super addo: In comitatu scilicet Calciacensi in ipsa villa Fiscamno tertiam partem hospitum quos colonos vocant cum terra arabili quae ad ipsam tertiam partem pertinet, unam partem silvae a publica strata usque ad mare terminatam, et dimidium vectigal; in Giruinivilla cum duobus molendinis quicquid habere visus sum; apud villam Archas tertiam partem piscariae et duas salinas et aliquid terrae arabilis cum prato; aecclesiam Scrotivillae et aliquid terrae arabilis; apud Harofloz .i. mansum cum lx. pensis salis cum .iiii. hacreis prati; in civitate Rotomagensi mansum unum cum ca[p]ella et xxx hacreis terrę arabilis cum vii hacreis prati; et in comitatu eiusdem civitatis ęcclesiam Piscei et aliquid terrae arabilis cum ęcclesia Barentini villae; in vallae Rologiville aecclesiam Sanctae Mariae, aecclesiam Sancti Stephani, ęcclesiam Sanctae Ceciliae, aecclesiam Sancti Saturnini, aecclesiam Sancti Quintini cum capellis subiectis eis et quicquid terrae arabilis et prati ad eas pertinet; super ripam Sequanę Aschei villam et quicquid ibi Trostincus tenuit; Heldechimvillam super mare. Hęc predicto loco perpetualiter habenda concędo, igitur tam [h]orum quam eorum quę a patre meo tradita sunt omnis ordinatio exterius et interius in abbatis sibique subiectorum consistat arbitrio, undeque eorum dispositioni resistat persona nulla parva vel magna cuiuscumque officii dignitatisve. Et non solum in rerum ordinatione iusticia sed in restituendi abbatis electione, ubi morte subtractus fuerit, a nobis iuste collata utantur libertate, ita dumtaxat ut in ipsa electione vel ordinatione abbatis illa per omnia servetur consuetudo quae hactenus in Cluniaco cęnobiorum servata est illu[s]trissimo, unde fons sanctae monasticę religionis per multa iam longe lateque dirivatus loca ad hunc usque Deo profluit propicio. Cuius sanctae religionis observatio ut magis ac magis ad profectum tam meę quam genitoris ac genitricis omniumque fidelium proficiat animarum hoc in Fixiscamnensi monasterio, sicut nulli ordini dignitati potestati heredetarięque successioni relinquere super idem ius decrevimus dominationis, ita si a iam cepta, quod absit, deviaverit rectitudine, nulli illud in pristinum reformanti mercedem denegamus recuperationis, sed et nostrorum super his decretorum invasores violatores sive destructores nisi emendaverint non evadere se sciant maledictionem Dei sed cum diabolo et Iuda proditore pęnas quibunt in inferno sustinere impiorum [ubi v]ermis non morietur et ignis non extinguetur in ęternum. +Ego autem RICHARDUS Norhtmannorum dux, ut hinc mihi merces cumuletur aeterna huiusque cartule testamentum per Widonem notarium meo rogatu conscriptum stipulatione firmetur, subnixa propria signans manu firmavi hisque roborari [rogans t]estibus tradidi. SS Rodulf[i] SS Wilelm[i] SS [EGO WIDO] NOTARIUS IUSSU [DOMNI RICHARDI ILLUSTRISSIMI DUCIS, QUI MISERICORDIAE OPERIBUS VALDE QUIA STUDET] ELEMOSINARIUS VOCATUR, HOC [TESTAMENTUM] SCRIPSI ANNO DOMINICĘ INCARNATIONIS [M̄. VI. INDIC-TIONE IIII. DIE TERTIO ANTE KAL. IUNII V. FERIA DOMINICĘ ASCENSIONIS GAUDIO] CELEBERRIMA, FELICITER.

3

1017–1025 (?)

Charter of Richard II granting for the enrichment of Fécamp lands and churches in Fécamp, Sassetot(?), Limpiville, Trémauville, Ganzeville, Manneville (?), Dun, Barentin, Campeaux, La Carbonière, and Villers-Chambellan [1] *(Seine-Inférieure).*

A, original in Musée de la Bénédictine, no. 2 *bis;* B, copy by Dom Lenoir from A in Collection Moreau, cccxli. 6, from which blurred words in the original have been supplied; C, another copy from A at Semilly, lxxvi. 165; D, copy by A. Deville, MS. Lat. n. a. 1245, f. 110.

Unpublished; see the facsimile, plate 2. Subsequent to 1017, when the predecessor of Maingisus attests as bishop of Avranches; anterior to no. 5. According to Dom Lenoir, " on pense à Fécamp que cette charte est de l' an 1023."

+QUONIAM VERIDICA DIVINARUM SCRIPTURARUM ASSERTIONE|| priscorum-que patrum monimentis expresse edocti id certa ratione comperimus quod quicunque omnipotentis Dei premisso timore speque animatus perhennis vitę aliquod quantulumcumque munusculum sanctę matri aecclesię ex propriis iureque adquisitis rebus contulerit, absque dubio in futuro ei re-compensabitur superni bravii stema; unde ego Richardus huiusce cespitis monarchus, ut credo summi Dei crebrerrimis cordetenus agitatus huiusmodi inspirationis spiculis, quendam locum qui dicitur Fiscamus dicatum in honore summi redemptoris sacris ordinibus monachorum ex more mancipavi quo perpetualiter inibi laudetur nomen Domini. Ut autem devotionis nostrę inconvulsa permaneat ratio, decrevi locum illum ditari et augere. Ad augendam igitur vitam inibi Domino militantium concedo in ipso loco Fiscamo .xii. boñ [2] terrę .xii.que domos; ęcclesiam Beati Stephani cum boñ

---

[1] According to Dom Lenoir the last three are hamlets in the neighborhood of Barentin. Instead of Sassetot one would expect Élétot, as in no. 5.

[2] Delisle, *Étude sur l'agriculture*, p. 537, found no instance of this measure of land, the *bonaria* or *bonata*, in Normandy.

.vi.; ęcclesiam Beati Benedicti cum terra quę est inter duos fluvios et molendino uno; in Saestetoth ecclesiam cum xii. boñ terrę; Leopini villam totam
cum ecclesia et quicquid ad eam pertinet; in Tormodi villa ecclesiam cum
terra unius carrucę; in Gansanvilla ecclesiam cum terra ad eam pertinente; ad
Manonis villam ęcclesiam cum xii. boñ et acri terre; in villa quę dicitur Dunus
.iii. ęcclesias cum .xl.iiii. boñ terrę; ęcclesiam villę que dicitur Barentinus
cum duobus hospitibus et aream molendini unam aquamque villę a gordo de
Pauliaco usque ad fagum comitissę; villam quoque quę dicitur Campelli cum
silva quę est a valle Carbonaria usque ad vallem Villaris. Eo pacto ut hęc
quę prefata sunt inviolabiliter teneant inibi Deo militantes absque ullius
molestia et contradictione sub manu nostrę firmitatis fideliumque nostro-
rumque astipulatione.

+Signum Richardi comitis+Signum Ricardi filii eius+Signum Rotberti
filii eius +Signum Rotberti archiepiscopi +Signum Hugonis Baiocensis
episcopi+Signum Hugonis Ebroicensis episcopi+Signum Mangisi Abrincensis episcopi +Signum Nigelli vicecomitis +Signum Torstingi vicecomitis.

4

15 June 1023, at Rouen

*Grant to Fécamp by Galeran I of Meulan, in the presence of Richard II,
of the toll and péage of Meulan.*

A, quasi-original in Musée de la Bénédictine, no. 28; B, copy therefrom by Dom Lenoir at Semilly, lxxvi. 167.

Unpublished. 'Actum Rothomago (*sic*) .xvii. kal. Iulii indictione
.vi. regnante Rotberto serenissimo rege Francorum ante presentiam
gloriosi Richardi Normannorum ducis et fratris eius Roberti ipsius
urbis archiepiscopi et domini Willelmi iam dicti monasterii abbatis.'
Attestations 'Waleranni, Herberti comitis Cenomannicę civitatis,
Ioffredi comitis Bellimontis castri, Hilduini vicecomitis Mellensis
supradicti castri.'

5

August 1025 (?), at Fécamp

*Great charter of Richard II enumerating and confirming the gifts of his
father, himself, and his followers to Fécamp, including the tithe of his
mint and his camera, to hold on the same conditions as his own demesne.
(Inc. ' Propitia divinę gratiae clementia. . . .')*

A, original in Musée de la Bénédictine, no. 2 *ter;* see the facsimile,
plate 3. There is now no trace of a seal, but according to F (see Delisle,
in MS. Fr. n. a. 21819, ff. 8–12) it still had a great seal in 1503. Dom
Lenoir says: " Il y avoit un sceau appliqué dont la figure étoit ronde.

Il ne subsiste plus, mais on voit encore les incisions faites au bas de la charte pour introduire la cire sur laquelle ce sceau etoit imprimé." B, copy from A by Dom Lenoir, Collection Moreau, cccxli. 8; C, collated copy of 1320 in Musée, no. 4; D, *vidimus* of Philip III formerly in archives of the abbey (cf. Collection Moreau, cccxli. 8); E, copy of D in cartulary, MS. Rouen 1207, f. 1; F, modern copies in Archives of the Seine-Inférieure.

Neustria Pia, p. 215, with innumerable errors; T. Bonnin, *Cartulaire de Louviers*, i. 3, from E; cf. Delisle, *Cartulaire normand*, no. 833.

The date in the original runs as follows, substantially as in *Neustria Pia:* DATA MENSE AUGUSTO CONSIDENTIBUS NOBIS FISCANNI PALATIO ANNO AB INCARNATIONE DOMINI .Î. XXVII. INDICTIONE VIII. REGNANTE ROTBERTO REGE ANNO XXXVI. The same date appears, save for the year of King Robert which is given as the thirty-eighth, in two other charters of Richard II which also show close resemblance in the final clauses: one a *pancarta* for Jumièges preserved in *vidimus* of 1499 and 1533 and in cartulary copies in the Archives of the Seine-Inférieure (Vernier, no. 12, who does not discuss the date); the other the foundation charter of Bernai, preserved only in copies from which it has been edited by Le Prévost, *Eure*, i. 284 (less correctly in *Neustria Pia*, p. 398; extract in La Roque, iii. 165). The impossibility of reconciling the various elements in this date has been evident since the time of Du Monstier and Mabillon (*Annales*, iv. 286), who ascribed the difficulty to an error in copying 1027 instead of 1026 or 1025. We now know that the original has, not only 1027, but a regnal year, the thirty-sixth, which corresponds to no known style of Robert (Pfister, *Études sur Robert le Pieux*, pp. xlii-xliv); yet according to the narrative sources Richard II died 23 August 1026 (*ibid.*, p. 216, note 6; cf. Lot, *S.-Wandrille*, p. 50, note 1). Norman scholars have generally agreed to follow the indiction, which together with the regnal year (38) of the charters for Jumièges and Bernai, gives August 1025 as the date of the three charters and thus brings them into agreement with the chronology of the period so far as it has yet been established. See Le Prévost, *Eure*, i. 283 (cf. however his edition of Ordericus, i. 175, note 2, ii. 10, note 2); Sauvage, *Troarn*, p. 11, note 2.

6

1025–1026

*Grant to Fécamp by Rainald, vicomte of Arques, attested by Richard II,
of all his possessions at Arques and in the county of Arques and at San-
tigny(?), and the churches of Saint-Aubin and Tourville (Seine-Inférieure).*

A, original lost; B, figured copy of *ca.* 1100 in the Archives of the
Seine-Inférieure; C, copy of B by A. Deville, MS. Lat. n. a. 1245,
f. 111.

Published with facsimile by Chevreux and Vernier, *Les archives de
Normandie et de la Seine-Inférieure*, plate 9, from B, which is called an
original of *ca.* 1100, the relation to Richard II being overlooked.

The charter belongs to the very end of Richard II's reign, as its
grants are not included in those confirmed in no. 5, while they are
specifically enumerated by Robert I in no. 10. This charter and its
confirmation by Robert I are cited in a charter of William, count of
Arques, 18 July 1047: original in Musée de la Bénédictine, no. 5 *bis;*
printed in Martène and Durand, *Thesaurus Anecdotorum*, i. 166;
Brussel, *Usage des fiefs* (1750), i. 84.

7

11 April 1028 (or 1034), at Fécamp

*Charter of Robert I authorizing an exchange between Bishop Hugh of
Bayeux and the monks of Fécamp with reference to Argences, and providing that disputes respecting the agreement should be brought before his
court.*

A, original lost; B, copy in lost cartulary of 12th century; C, copy
from B by Dom Lenoir in Collection Moreau, xxi. 9.

Unpublished; cf. *E. H. R.*, xxxi. 264, no. 8; *infra*, Appendix C, p.
272, no. 8.

The omission of any reference to the abbot makes it probable that
this charter belongs to 1028, between the resignation of William of
Dijon and the consecration of John. If the *leuva* of Argences included
in no. 10 had already been granted to the abbey, it would probably be
mentioned specifically in this charter. The prolonged difficulties between the duke and Bishop Hugh are another reason for placing the
charter early in Robert's reign (William of Jumièges, bk. vi, c. 5).

Rotbertus nutu Dei Northmannorum dux omnibus fidelibus nostris
cuiuscumque ordinis, indominicatis scilicet et vavassoribus seu ubicumque

in Christum credentibus, notitiam et commutuationem quam salva fide in memoriam tam presentibus quam futuris litteris tradere disponimus. Notum sit igitur vobis quod Hugo Baiocacensis ҽcclesiҽ episcopus venit ad meam mercedem castro Fiscanni die Cҽnҽ Dominicҽ quҽ habita est eo anno .iii. idus Aprilis, in quo castro in honore summҽ et individuҽ Trinitatis bonҽ memoriҽ avus meus et pater monasterium construxerunt ac villis et ornamentis honorifice decoraverunt et, quod melius est, monachis pro animabus nostris Deo cotidie servientibus deputaverunt. Deprecatus est autem mercedem meam ut apud ipsius monasterii monachos impetrarem ut terram quҽ dicitur Argentias quam prҽnotatus avus meus R. nobilis dux altario eiusdem sanctҽ et individuҽ Trinitatis in dotem tradidit ei commutuarent. Quod post multas eorum excusationes tandem obtinui. Fecerunt itaque per tales tamen convenientias: Episcopus debet dare monachis centum hospites ad presens qui totas diptas reddant et liberos ab omni meo servicio vel costumis per meam auctoritatem et per meum donum in alodum et hereditatem perpetuam, et tres ҽcclesias et xx^{ti} francos homines in locis qui appellantur Boiavilla, Brunvilla, Penloi, Lexartum cum portu piscatorio, cum silvis, pascuis, et omnibus pertinentiis suis, et villam quҽ dicitur Vetus Redum cum molendino et omnibus appendiciis eius; et debet recipere ab ipsis monachis predictam terram, id est Argentias, per tale conventum ut usque dum vixerit teneat et post obitum eius monachi eam statim recipiant, id est ipsam villam Argentias, per meam licentiam sine contradictione alicuius potestatis cuiuslibet ordinis seu magnҽ parvҽque personҽ, sic ex integro cum terris, vineis, molendinis, silvis, pratis, aquis, et mercato forensi seu omnibus appendiciis eius absque ulla calumnia, sicut unquam melius tenuerunt; et ipsos centum hospites quos episcopus donat, sicut prҽdictum est, in prenominatis locis cum omnibus suis appendiciis similiter cum ipsa post obitum episcopi teneant et possideant iure hereditario in alodum ex mea parte concessum sicut predictum est. Notum quoque esse volo quia illa terra quam dat episcopus quorundam hominum calumniis refutata est a monachis postquam has convenientias incҽpimus antequam perficeremus, et postea a me et ab ipso episcopo tali convenientia est data et ab eis recepta ut si per illam calumniam damnum aliquod ipsi monachi habuerint, duas reclamationes in mea corte vel curia faciant, et si tunc ego et episcopus non acquitaverimus eam, monachi per meam licentiam sine contradictione vel malivolentia episcopi vel alicuius hominis reveniant ad villam suam Argentias et recipiant eam et teneant et possideant absque ullo deinceps cambio. Si quis vero contra hanc nostrҽ auctoritatis commutuationem aliquando temerario ausu inferre calumniam presumpserit, primitus ab ipso Deo patre omnipotente et a filio eius unigenito domino nostro et a spiritu sancto sit maledictus et excommunicatus et a beata Dei genitrice Maria et electo archangelo Michaele, Gabriele, Raphaele, et ab omnibus cҽlestium virtutum spiritibus et omnibus patriarchis prophetis apostolis martyribus confessoribus virginibus viduis et omnibus electis Dei, et sit in ҽterna damnatione cum Dathan et Abiron quos vivos terra absorbuit et cum Iuda traditore qui Dominum precio tradidit necnon et cum his qui dixerunt Deo, Recede a nobis, scientiam viarum tuarum nolumus, nisi digna satisfactione emendaverit. Amen.

8

1028–1035

Charter of Robert I restoring to Fécamp Argences and other domains.

A, original lost; B, official copy of 1688 in Archives of the Seine-Inférieure, according to Delisle; these archives and the *fonds* of the barony of Argences in the Archives of the Calvados have been searched without success.

Extracts in Delisle, *S.-Sauveur-le-Vicomte*, pièces, no. 10; cf. *infra*, Appendix C, no. 9.

This charter is evidently posterior to no. 7. Argences is not one of the places claimed by Hugh of Bayeux after Robert's death (*Livre noir*, no. 21.)

9

Ca. 1034–1035

Charter of Robert I granting Saint-Taurin of Évreux in exchange for Montivilliers as a dependency of Fécamp.

A, original lost. Printed in Martene and Durand, *Thesaurus Anecdotorum*, i. 154. Cf. Appendix C, no. 10.

Evidently not long anterior to the foundation of Montivilliers 13 January 1035 (*Gallia Christiana*, xi. instr. 326; *infra*, Appendix C, no. 17).

10

1032–1035

Charter of Robert I enumerating his grants of lands and knights to Fécamp, including the gifts of Rainald of Arques (no. 6).[1]

Supposed originals, unsealed, in Musée de la Bénédictine, with identical witnesses but differences in content: A (no. 3 *bis*), on long, somewhat irregular, unruled piece of parchment, with frequent use of the form *ae* and with crosses in different hands before ten of the witnesses; B (no. 4 *bis*), on broad, ruled parchment, written in a closer hand, with

---

[1] The places mentioned, which lie chiefly in the Pays de Caux, are Petitville, Écretteville, Bernai (Eure ?), Élétot, Arques, Tourville-sur-Fécamp, Argences (Calvados), Ourville, Oissel-sur-Seine, Sorquainville, Bennetot, Biville-la-Martel, Ypreville, Riville, Ermenouville (?), Néville, Anglesqueville, and Caen. Santiniacus villa (cf. no. 6) and Corhulma I have not identified, unless the latter be the 'insula Oscelli que et Turhulmus dicitur' (Ile de Bédanne) of the cartulary of La Trinité-du-Mont, no. 82; cf. Toussaint Duplessis, *Description de la Haute Normandie*, ii. 121, 274.

crosses, apparently in the same hand, before all the witnesses; C, copies by Dom Lenoir in Collection Moreau, cccxli. 12, 15; D, ditto at Semilly, lxx. 525.

Unpublished; see the facsimiles, plates 4 and 5. Extracts in La Roque, iii. 19, iv. 1323; cf. *E. H. R.*, xxxi. 264, nos. 6, 7; *infra*, Appendix C, nos. 6, 7.

Subsequent to the accession of Gradulf as abbot of Saint-Wandrille, whose predecessor died 29 November 1031. Junguené, archbishop of Dol, whose latest attestation in charters is of 1032, seems to have been active in the service of Count Alan III for a year òr two longer; his successor cannot be traced before 1040. See *Gallia Christiana*, xiv. 1045; La Borderie, in *Revue de Bretagne*, 1891, i. 264–267; id., *Histoire de Bretagne*, iii. 10 f.

The signature of Edward the Confessor as king renders it rather likely that neither A nor B is an original, although it is not impossible that he used this title in Canute's lifetime, as in a questionable charter for Mont-Saint-Michel (see Appendix C, p. 273). Further doubt is thrown upon B by the broad grant of authority to the abbot in the last sentence. The contents of A seem to me genuine, and the royal title of Edward would be a natural addition in an early copy.

A and B

In nomine patris et filii et spiritus sancti.[2] Ego Rotbertus filius secundi Richardi nutu Dei Northmannorum ducis et ipse per gratiam Dei princeps et dx (*sic*) Northmannorum notum fieri volo tam presentibus quam futuris ea quae respectu gratiae Dei contuli universorum domino sanctae scilicet et individuę TRINITATI in loco qui dicitur Fiscannus post decessum patris mei pro salute animę meę et predecessorum meorum fratrum quoque et sororum. Quae omnia nominanter subter [3] asscribere volui ne memorię laberentur subsequenti posteritate haec sunt: Pitit villa cum omnibus sibi pertinentiis; quidam [4] homines mei scilicet milites cum omnibus sibi pertinentibus; hii sunt Hundul filius Gosmanni et nepotes eius filii Bloc, Walterius quoque filius Girulfi, filii Gonfredi omnes de Gervinivilla, Torquitil filius Adlec, Iustaldus clericus et Rodulfus laicus fratresque eorum filii Hugonis de Barda villa. Dedi autem terram quae Scrot villa dicitur cum omnibus suis appendiciis. Reddidi etiam totam medietatem Bernai villę cum omnibus que ad ipsam medietatem pertinent ex integro. Dedi etiam villam quae dicitur Eslettot. Reddidi quoque omnem terram quam Rainaldus vicecomes apud Arcas et in Turvilla et Santiniaco villa tenere videbatur cum aeclesiis et molendinis et bosco qui dicitur Appasilva, cum salinis, piscariis, pratis, hospitibus, et omnibus appenditiis suis et omnibus hominibus qui sibi subiecti

---

[2] '+IN NOMINE PATRIS ET FILII ET SPIRITUS SANCT[I A]MEN,' B.

[3] Om. B.   [4] B om. *quidam . . . quae* (before *Scrot villa*).

fuerunt. [Dedi [5] quoque silvam quae Bocolunda [6] dicitur iuxta Fiscannum ex toto. Commutuavi autem eis silvam quam inter duas aquas dicunt ex utraque parte et omnia que ad eam pertinent. Dedi quoque terram quę Hurvilla dicitur quam mea avia pro salute parentum nostrorum et sua Fiscanni loco destinavit, cellarium insuper et vineam. Contuli [7] etiam alios milites, scilicet] Osbertum filium Gosmanni cum suo alodo et Ursonem et Willelmum eius fratrem filios videlicet Anslecci. Donavi apud Argentias leuvam iuxta morem patriae nostrae propter mercatum ipsius villae. Haec omnia pro salute animę meae et parentum meorum soli Deo trino [8] et uno vivo et vero contuli. Siquis autem, quod fieri non credo, contra hanc nostrę preceptionis cartulam contraire aut calumpniam inferre temptaverit, cum Iuda traditore partem habeat si non emendaverit. Ut vero firma et stabilita haec descriptio permaneat, manu propria subter affirmo et fidelibus meis firmare precipio. Reddidi etiam decimam de feriis de Cadumo. Dedi quoque piscariam quod vulgo gordum dicitur apud Oscellum villam. Dedi decimas de pratis in villa que dicitur Corhulma. Donavi nihilominus Ansfredum de Soastichin villa cum omni terra sua ubicunque tenere videbatur.

B

Sed et terram Hugonis de Sortichin villa et de Barda villa ubicunque tenere videbantur de me in Calz et terram Walter filii Girulfi de Hastingivilla et omnem terram filiorum Bloc et terram Hundul filii Gosmanni quam de me tenere videbantur in Calz, id est Bernetot et Buie villam cum aliis sibi pertinentiis et terram Osberti filii Gosmanni omne eius alodum, id est Ypram villam et Rivillam, et terram filiorum Anslec, id est Ermendi villam cum omnibus quę ad ipsam pertinent et omne alodum eorum (?)videbatur in Calz. Dedi quoque Nevillam et omne alodum filiorum Audoeni ubicumque tenere videbantur de me. Dedi terram filiorum Turfredi, id est Angliscavillam et omne alodum eorum in Calz, et terram filiorum Gonberti de Gervini villa et terram Gazel quam de me tenebat in Fischanno, id est campartum de Fischanno et aliquos hospites, et terram Murieldis de Amblida et in Cadomo unum burgarium ad pontum et terram Rotberti de Habvilla. Ista igitur bona et omnia alia quę Fischannensi monasterio olim donata sunt sub solius abbatis potestate et iusticia constituimus ut nullius dignitatis homo aliquando manum intromittere presumat.

A and B

+Signum Rotberti Normannorum ducis. +Signum Willelmi filii eius. +Signum domni Rotberti archiepiscopi. +Signum Rotberti episcopi. Signum Gingoloi archiepiscopi. Signum domni Iohannis abbatis. +Signum Willelmi abbatis. Signum Gradulfi abbatis. Signum Rainerii abbatis. +Signum Durandi abbatis. +Signum Isemberti abbatis. +Signum Edwardi regis. Signum Balduini comitis. Signum Ingelranni comitis.

---

[5] In A the three lines printed in brackets are written more closely over an erasure.
[6] *Buculunda*, B.
[7] B om. *contuli* . . . *Anslecci.*
[8] A. caps.

Signum Gisleberti comitis. Signum Negelli. Signum Osberti senscali(?) +Signum Unfredi vetuli. Signum Richardi vicecomitis. Signum Gozilini vicecomitis. Signum Turstini vicecomitis. Signum Aymonis vicecomitis. Signum Toroldi constabilarii.

11

Forged charter of William the Conqueror confirming Fécamp in possession of Saint-Gervais of Rouen, free from all subjection to the archbishop, as granted by Richard II.

A, pretended original in a late hand, apparently of the fourteenth century, in Musée de la Bénédictine, unnumbered; see the facsimile, plate 6. B, *vidimus* of Pope Benedict XIII, 28 June 1404, copied in Fécamp cartulary (C) and in Archives of the Seine-Inférieure (D).

Delisle, *S.-Sauveur*, pièces, no. 43, from CD; Round, *Calendar*, no. 113, from D. Cf. *A. H. R.*, xiv. 459, note 41.

Delisle declared this charter a forgery because of the combination of William's royal style with witnesses dead long before 1066. Round, p. xxvi, explained the anachronism as an " interpolation by a long subsequent scribe," and assigned the document to " the critical years 1035–1037," with which he found the list of witnesses " wholly consistent "; while F. M. Stenton, *William the Conqueror*, p. 75 f., elaborates from it the entourage of the young duke. The charter is a rank fabrication of a later age. The royal style of 1066 ff. is in the pretended original; the handwriting is painfully imitated; John, who is represented as receiving the original gift from Richard, became abbot under Robert I. The obvious purpose was to strengthen the priory against the archbishop, who is not mentioned in Richard II's original grant (no. 5). The penal clause is copied from Richard's charter. The witnesses are taken bodily from Robert's charter, no. 10; Durand of Cerisy was probably no longer abbot by 1035.

12

Forged charter of William the Conqueror confirming to Fécamp its lands in England with royal liberty and jurisdiction, free from all secular service, and its possessions in Normandy as granted in the charter of his predecessor Count Richard.

A, pretended original in Musée de la Bénédictine, no. 7; B, early copy in Public Record Office, Cartae Antiquae, S. 1; C, cartulary, MS. Rouen 1207, f. 3.

Monasticon, vii. 1082, from B. Cf. *Report of the Deputy Keeper*, xxix. app., p. 42; Davis, *Regesta*, no. 112. The charter in *Neustria Pia*, p. 223, is apparently a truncated copy of this; there is also an extract in La Roque, iv. 2219.

The style of the charter and the extraordinary privileges which it purports to grant are sufficient to condemn it, quite apart from the appearance of the pretended original. A connection with a forged grant concerning the abbot's rights in Steyning, which is abstracted in the charter rolls (*Calendar*, i. 322; Davis, no. 253), has been pointed out by Round, *E. H. R.*, xxix. 348; this may be merely an extract from the fuller charter. As indicated above, the inflation of no. 12 is rather on the English than on the Norman side, where it repeats the language of Richard's charter *Propitia* (no. 5).

APPENDIX C

THE MATERIALS FOR THE REIGN OF ROBERT I[1]

ROBERT I, commonly called Robert the Magnificent or, for no good reason, Robert the Devil, is one of the less known figures in the series of Norman dukes. His reign was brief and left few records, and it was naturally overshadowed by that of his more famous son, yet we shall never understand the Normandy of the Conqueror's time without some acquaintance with the period immediately preceding. The modern sketches are scanty and unsatisfactory, and while the extant evidence does not permit of a full or adequate narrative, they can be replaced only when the available material has been more fully utilized and more carefully sifted. In this direction the publication of a critical edition of William of Jumièges has at last provided the necessary point of departure.[2]

The fundamental account is, of course, the sixth book of the Jumièges chronicler, who expressly declares himself a contemporary of the events therein recounted.[3] For many episodes this is our only contemporary authority, so that it is especially important to fix its value by checking it at the points where we have other evidence, as well as to supplement its meager outline by information found elsewhere. On the narrative side the contemporary material is fragmentary and scattered, consisting of the bare mention of Robert's accession and death in the annals, and of disconnected references in the hagiographical literature. The dates of Robert's accession (6 August 1027) [4] and death (1–3 July

[1] Revised from *E. H. R.*, xxxi. 257–268 (1916). On Robert's reign see, besides the older histories of Normandy, Sir Francis Palgrave, *History of Normandy and England*, iii. 141–190; E. A. Freeman, *Norman Conquest* (1877), ii. 179–191; F. M. Stenton, *William the Conqueror*, pp. 63–72.

[2] Guillaume de Jumièges, *Gesta Normannorum Ducum*, ed. Marx (Rouen, 1914). See my review, *E. H. R.*, xxxi. 150–153.

[3] ' Quorum actus partim intuitu partim veracium relatu comperimus ': bk. vi, c. 1.

[4] C. Pfister (*Études sur la vie et le règne de Robert le Pieux*, p. 216, note), who does not, however, meet all the difficulties of chronology connected with the date of Richard III's death, particularly the irreconcilable elements in the dates of the ducal charters of this period. Cf. Le Prévost, *Eure*, i. 283. Unfortunately the two dated charters of Robert, neither of which is an original, are not decisive as to his accession, that for Cerisy (see list below, no. 3) placing November 1032 in his fifth year,

1035) [5] are fixed by the aid of the local necrologies; the pilgrimage is mentioned by contemporaries like Ralph Glaber [6] and the *Translatio S. Vulganii*.[7] The *Vita Herluini* speaks of his relations with Gilbert of Brionne; [8] the *Translatio Beati Nicasii* places him and his followers at Rouen on 12 December 1032; [9] Hugh of Flavigny [10] describes his reliance upon the counsel of Richard of Saint-Vannes. The most interesting of these writers is the author of the *Miracula S. Wulframni*, a monk of Saint-Wandrille who wrote shortly after 1053 and who characterizes Robert as follows: [11]

Hic autem Rotbertus acer animo et prudens priores suos virtute quidem et potentia exequavit; sed pravorum consultui, utpote in primevo iuventutis flore constitutus, equo amplius attendens regnum quod florens susceperat in multis debilitavit. Verum non multo post, celesti respectus gratia et bona que inerat illi natura et consilii iutus, resipuit et eos quorum pravitate a recto deviaverat a suo consilio atque familiaritate sequestravit sueque iugo potentie versa vice fortiter oppressit ac se in libertatem que se decebat vindicavit atque ita propter preteritorum ignorantiam profectus Hierosolimam profunde penituit. Sed in redeundo malignorum perpessus insidias, qui eius equum (quod iam experti erant) verebantur imperium, veneficio, ut didicimus, apud urbem Niceam occubuit ibique intra sanctam civitatis illius basilicam (quod nulli alii mortalium concessum est) honorifica donari sepultura promeruit. Verum vir tantus non pravorum tantum malignitate quam divino, ut credi fas est, iudicio decessit, qui iam unus eorum effectus erat quibus, ut apostolus conqueritur, dignus non erat mundus.

Here the characterization is fuller than in William of Jumièges,[12] but the fundamental agreement is striking and shows the view of Robert's character which prevailed among ecclesiastical writers. The very phrase 'pravorum consultui' recurs in William [13] and, substan-

and that for Montivilliers (no. 17) placing January 1035 in his eighth. Cf. the question of the date of the charters of Richard II, dated 1027: Appendix B, no. 5.

[5] *H. F.*, xxiii. 420, 487, 579; P. de Farcy, *Abbayes du diocèse de Bayeux*, i. 72. Ordericus, i. 179, gives 1 July.

[6] Ed. Prou, p. 108. Robert is not mentioned in Ralph's life of St. William of Dijon, who died at Fécamp in 1031: Migne, *Patrologia*, cxlii. 720.

[7] *Analecta Bollandiana*, xxiii. 269.

[8] Migne, cl. 697, 699; J. Armitage Robinson, *Gilbert Crispin*, pp. 87, 90. Cf. Robert's relations with Serlo of Hauteville: Geoffrey Malaterra, *Historia Sicula*, bk. i, c. 38 f.

[9] Migne, clxii. 1165 f.

[10] *M. G. H., Scriptores*, viii. 401; cf. *infra*, note 17.

[11] D'Achery, *Spicilegium* (Paris, 1723), ii. 288; Mabillon, *Acta Sanctorum Ordinis S. Benedicti* (Venice, 1734), iii. 353.

[12] Bk. vi, cc. 2, 3, 12.   [13] Bk. vi, c. 3: 'pravorum consultu sponte sibi delegit.'

tially, in a charter of Abbot Gradulf of Saint-Wandrille, shortly after 1035, who saw no occasion for redressing the balance by a glorification at the end:[14]

Quam filius eius et ab illo tercius in regno Robertus, in etate iuvenili perversorum consilio depravatus, supradicto sancto abstulerat confessori. Quo defuncto et a presentibus sublato, filioque illius succedente in regni honore paterno, ego abbas Gradulfus, diu dampnum tam grave perpessus, etc.

Such phrases, taken in conjunction with the troubles with Archbishop Robert and Bishop Hugh of Bayeux described by William of Jumièges,[15] show plainly that there was a strong reaction against the church at the beginning of Robert's reign, a reaction afterwards ascribed to evil counselors and covered up by the all-sufficing merit of the duke's pilgrimage and death.[16] The facts were evidently too flagrant to be ignored by William of Jumièges, favorable as is his narrative to the ducal house; not until the time of Wace could they be entirely passed over. The story that Richard III was poisoned by Robert may be in same way connected with the misdeeds of this period. To these years should probably be referred the troubles between the duke and his barons described by Hugh of Flavigny[17] in his curious account of the diabolical machinations of Ermenaldus the Breton, whom Richard of Saint-Vannes carried off to Verdun after reëstablishing peace in Normandy, but who returned and by means of the wager of battle secured the condemnation of several Norman leaders at the duke's hands.

The next set of authorities consists of the interpolators of William of Jumièges. The first group of interpolations, assigned by Marx to a monk of Saint-Étienne of Caen writing under Robert Curthose, comprises two episodes (c. 8 bis) illustrating Robert's generosity, that of the smith of Beauvais and that of the poor knight, and (c. 11) the story of Robert's magnificence at Constantinople, as exemplified by the mule shod with gold and the fire fed with nuts. No source is cited

[14] Lot, S.-Wandrille, p. 61. Cf. Vernier, no. 13: 'perversorum consiliis illectus.'

[15] Bk. vi, cc. 3, 5. Cf. Fulbert of Chartres, in Migne, cxli. 225; and the losses of Hugh of Bayeux indicated in the Livre noir, no. 21.

[16] On Robert's end cf. Translatio S. Vulganii, in Analecta Bollandiana, xxiii. 269.

[17] M. G. H., Scriptores, viii. 401: ' Inflammatur princeps adversus optimates, fiunt discidia, excitantur iurgia, et uno intestino bello tota debachatur Normannia.' Besides the information accessible to him in the east of France, Hugh had opportunity to become acquainted with Norman traditions during his visit to Normandy in 1096 (ibid., 369, 393 f., 399, 407, 475, 482); his presence in Normandy is proved by an exchange between Saint-Bénigne and Saint-Étienne of Caen which he attests and by a charter of 24 May 1096 which he drafted: supra, p. 75 f.

for the last of these, which was probably, as we shall see, the common property of the period; but the earlier episodes are recounted on the express authority of Isembert, chaplain of the duke and later abbot of Holy Trinity at Rouen,[18] so that they have contemporary value. The additions of Ordericus, made before 1109, are confined to a fuller account of the family of Bellême, for which he could draw on the local traditions of the region.[19] In his *Historia Ecclesiastica* he adds certain further details respecting the reign: the founding of Cerisy (ed. Le Prévost, ii. 11); the reconciliation by the duke of Gilbert of Brionne and the house of Géré (ii. 25); the banishment of Osmund Drengot (ii. 53); the death of Dreux, count of the Vexin, on the pilgrimage (ii. 102, iii. 224 f.); and a fuller account of the relations of the duke to King Henry I, including the grant of the Vexin (iii. 223 f.).

If, as Stubbs thought probable,[20] Orderic's contemporary William of Malmesbury made use of William of Jumièges, he has no confirmatory value where the two accounts agree, as in the mention of the duke's aid to King Henry I or his tears and gifts at the Holy Sepulchre.[21] The Malmesbury chronicler adds the rumor that the pilgrimage was undertaken in atonement for the poisoning of Richard III; the name of the follower guilty of Robert's death, ' Radulfus cognomento Mowinus '; the guardianship by the king of France; and, in very brief form, the story of Arlette so fully developed by Wace, including her dream and the omen attending the Conqueror's birth.[22]

Of subsequent writers much the most important is Wace, who gives a full narrative of the reign which is repeated by Benoît de Sainte-More and the later vernacular chroniclers and has been used without discrimination by modern writers. The question of Wace's sources, first seriously attacked by Gustav Körting in 1867,[23] requires a more thorough treatment upon the basis of the more abundant material and the more critical editions now available. His close dependence on

[18] ' Hoc referre solitus erat de duce Rodberto Isembertus, primum quidem eius capellanus, postmodum vero Sancti Audoeni monachus, et ad extremum abbas Sancte Trinitatis.'

[19] He also gives the name of the commander of the fleet, Rabel, in c. 11. See *infra*, p. 275 and note 41.

[20] *Gesta Regum*, p. xxi, citing the text, p. 161 f. Further investigation is desirable on this point.

[21] *Ibid.*, pp. 211, 227.   [22] *Ibid.*, pp. 211, 285.

[23] *Ueber die Quellen des Roman de Rou* (Leipzig, 1867). It appears from the account of the four sons of William of Bellême (line 2461 ff.) that Wace used the interpolations of Ordericus.

William of Jumièges was clearly demonstrated by Körting, so that he must not be used as an independent authority in the portions on which they agree. At several points, however, in the reign of Robert, Wace offers material not to be found in William, partly by way of amplification, as in the account of the visit of Henry I and the campaigns by land and sea against the Bretons, partly in the form of new episodes. These are:[24] the foundation of Cerisy (ed. Andresen, lines 2305–2312); the poor knight (2313–2338); the clerk who died of joy at the duke's gift (2339–2388); the smith of Beauvais (2389–2430); the stories of Arlette and of the Conqueror's infancy (2833–2930); the investiture of William by the king of France and the guardianship of Alan of Brittany (2979–2994); and the full narrative of the pilgrimage (2995–3252). Something of the substance of the history of the reign, as well as much of its color, depends upon the acceptance or rejection of these elements in Wace's poem.

A professional rhymester writing more than a century and a quarter after Robert's death does not inspire confidence as an historical authority unless the sources of his information can be definitely traced, a task which was long considered unnecessary and unfruitful. " C'est," wrote Édélestand Du Méril in 1862,[25] "une question d'un très-mince intérêt, dont la véritable réponse satisferait bien mal la curiosité: c'était un peu tout le monde." Such vague conclusions are not, however, in accord with the trend of more recent investigation, especially since the publication of Bédier's studies of the mediaeval epic, and the comfortable ' tout le monde ' of earlier belief has in many instances been replaced by particular individuals or monasteries. Can anything of this sort be accomplished in the case of Wace ? The answer is easy if we accept an emendation of Gaston Paris[26] in line 3239, where, speaking of the duke's chamberlain Tosteins who brought back to Cerisy the relics procured at Jerusalem, he says,

De par sa mere fu sis aiues.

This does not make sense, nor does the reading of MS. B, which has ' mis aues.' If, however, we accept B and emend the first pronoun, we have

De par ma mere fu mis aiues,

[24] Cf. Körting's analysis, pp. 51–53.

[25] La vie et les ouvrages de Wace, in Études sur quelques points d'archéologie et d'histoire littéraire (Paris, 1862), p. 269.

[26] Romania, ix. 526 ff. (1880).

which is perfectly intelligible and makes Tosteins the grandfather of Wace. If this be admitted, the whole narrative of the pilgrimage, as well as some of the personal episodes, would come from one of the duke's companions on the journey, not directly, for Wace could not have known a grandfather grown to manhood by 1035, but through the poet's mother.

In some instances the source can be further identified. Thus for the two stories of Robert's generosity we now have the authority of the Abbot Isembert.[27] That of the poor knight Wace reproduces closely, that of the smith of Beauvais he abbreviates; but the inference that he knew them in this form is strengthened by their probable connection with Caen, where he was a *clerc lisant*. On the other hand, the account of Robert's magnificence at the Byzantine court cannot be derived wholly [28] from the interpolation in William of Jumièges, which says nothing of the cloaks used by the Normans as seats and left in the emperor's presence. In this respect the Latin text agrees better with the saga of Sigurd Jerusalem-farer, one of the many forms in which Gaston Paris has traced the story through mediaeval literature.[29] At this point Wace touches the broader stream of popular tradition.

In another portion of his narrative we find a definite and verifiable local source of information.. It is noteworthy that in this part of his work Wace gives prominence to Robert's special foundation, the abbey of Saint-Vigor at Cerisy. Whereas Ordericus and Robert of Torigni barely mention its revival at this time,[30] Wace describes the privileges granted to the establishment by Robert, the sending of the relics thither by the chamberlain Tosteins, and the gifts made early in the Conqueror's reign by Alfred the Giant upon entering the monastery. Here we can test his statements by extant documents.[31] The abbey's jurisdiction is described as follows:

> 2309 E tel franchise lur dunat,
> Cume li ducs en sa terre ad:
> Il unt le murdre e le larun,
> Le rap, le homicide, le arsun.

[27] *Supra*, note 18.   [28] As Marx assumes, *Guillaume de Jumièges*, p. xxii.

[29] *Sur un épisode d'Aimeri de Narbonne*, in *Romania*, ix. 515–546 (1880). Cf. Paul Riant, *Les Scandinaves en Terre Sainte*, p. 196 ff.

[30] Ordericus, ii. 11; Robert of Torigni, ed. Delisle, ii. 195; William of Jumièges, ed. Marx, pp. 252, 255. Cf. Wace, *Chronique ascendante*, line 213.

[31] *Monasticon*, vii. 1073 f.; incomplete in *Neustria Pia*, p. 431; cf. Delisle-Berger, no. 406. For the abbey's possessions, see the *Inventaire sommaire des archives de la Manche*, series H; the index to Longnon, *Pouillés de la province de*

These are not specified in the ducal charter, but there is abundant evidence that such were the crimes regularly included in the grant of ducal *consuetudines* which is there made.[32] Concerning the gifts of Alfred the Giant Wace is more definite:

> 3593 Une vile, Luvres out nun,
> Qui ert de sa garantisun,
> Od tuz les apartenemenz,
> E l'eglise de Saint Lorenz,
> Ovec l'eglise de Taisie
> Fist cunfermer a Ceresie.

Alfred's charter enumerates likewise ' totam terram mcam de Lepori-bus . . . etiam totam terram quam Walterus presbiter de me tenebat in villa que dicitur Taissei '; and we know that these places, the barony of Lièvres and the churches of Tessy-sur-Vire and Saint-Laurent-sur-Mer, were part of the abbey's domain. Specific detail of this sort could be obtained only from the monks of Cerisy, through whom also would come the history of the relics brought by Tosteins, in case we hesitate to identify him as an ancestor of the poet. Wace had of course ample opportunity to converse with monks from Cerisy at Bayeux and at the court of Henry II, from whom they secured charters; but there can be little doubt that he visited the abbey itself, which he locates exactly (lines 3247 f.) between Coutances and Bayeux, three leagues from Saint-Lô, particularly as it was on the natural route between Caen and his native Jersey.[33] As the special foundation of Robert I this monastery would be the natural repository of tradition with respect to him, as Fécamp was for his father and grandfather,[34] and Cerisy may well be the source of other elements in Wace's narra-tive which cannot be distinguished in the absence of any remains of the local historiography.

Our confidence in the general credibility of Wace's account is further strengthened by the confirmation in other chronicles of partic-

Rouen; and Farcy, *Abbayes et prieurés de l'évêché de Bayeux,* Cerisy (Laval, 1887), pp. 78 ff., 259–263.

[32] *Supra,* p. 27; *infra,* Appendix D.

[33] For a later example of the confirmation of Wace by local documentary evi-dence, compare the account of Grimoud du Plessis (lines 4219–4242) with the char-ter in the Bayeux *Livre noir,* no. 3, and the inquest in *H. F.,* xxiii, 699 f.

[34] See J. Bédier, *Richard de Normandie dans les chansons de geste,* in *Romanic Review,* i. 113–124 (1910), and in *Les légendes épiques,* iv. 1–18, 389, 406. For Wace's own sojourn at Fécamp and use of its local traditions, see lines 2246, 2994, 6781–6918, and lines 1356–1359 in Andresen, i. 87; and cf. Gaston Paris, in *Romania,* ix. 597, 610.

ular statements of his which are not found in William of Jumièges. Thus the death of Robert by poison is mentioned by the monk of Saint-Wandrille,[35] as well as by William of Malmesbury,[36] and that of Count Drogo by Ordericus. Ordericus also relates the visit of Henry I at Easter, the grant of the Vexin, and the guardianship of Alan of Brittany.[37]

There remains the question how far the chroniclers are confirmed and supplemented by documentary evidence. Any study of such material must be provisional, until the early Norman charters shall have been collected and critically tested monastery by monastery. Meanwhile a rough list of such charters of Robert I as have come to my notice may serve a useful purpose. In the absence of chronological data the list is arranged by religious establishments; grants of his reign attested or confirmed by Robert are included, but not charters of Richard II in which he appears as a witness.

1. AVRANCHES cathedral. Grants enumerated in notice of Bishop John. E. A. Pigeon, *Le diocèse d'Avranches*, ii. 667, from modern copy.

2. BEC. Consents to grant by Abbot Herluin, 1034–1035. Mabillon, *Annales Ordinis S. Benedicti* (Lucca, 1739), iv. 361; Le Prévost, *Eure*, i. 234.

3. CERISY-LA-FORÊT. Foundation charter of the monastery of Saint-Vigor, 12 November 1032. *Vidimus* of 1269–1313, in Archives Nationales, JJ. 62, no. 96; of 1351, *ibid.*, JJ. 80, f. 340v; *Cartulaire de Normandie* (MS. Rouen, 1235), ff.58v, 84. *Neustria Pia*, p. 431; *Monasticon*, vii. 1073, from Norman rolls of Henry V; Delisle, *Cartulaire normand*, no. 768; Farcy, *Abbayes du diocèse de Bayeux*, i. 78.

4. DIJON, Saint-Étienne. Confirms grants of his predecessors in Normandy. Subsequent to the death of St. William in 1031. Deville, *Analyse*, p. 33; cf. *supra*, Chapter I, note 170; *Analecta Divionensia*, ix. 175.

5. ÉVREUX, Saint-Taurin. Gift mentioned in no. 10.

6. FÉCAMP. Comprehensive enumeration of his gifts to the abbey, 1032–1035. *Supra*, Appendix B, no. 10A.

7. FÉCAMP. Fuller and more suspicious form of no. 6, with identical witnesses. Appendix B, no 10B.

8. FÉCAMP. Charter notifying agreement between the abbey and Hugh, bishop of Bayeux, with reference to Argences. Appendix B, no. 7.

9. FÉCAMP. Charter concerning the restoration of Argences to the abbey. Appendix B, no. 8.

10. FÉCAMP. Charter exchanging Saint-Taurin of Évreux for Montivilliers as a dependency of Fécamp. Appendix B, no. 9.

11. JUMIÈGES. Adds Virville to his father's charter of August 1025 (?). *Vidimus* of 1499 and 1533, and Cartulary 22, in Archives of the Seine-Inférieure, f. 7 ff.; Vernier, no. 12.

---

[35] Mabillon, *Acta*, iii. 353.   [36] *Gesta Regum*, p. 211.

[37] ii. 102; iii. 223–225. Whether Wace and Ordericus are entirely independent is a matter which needs investigation.

12. JUMIÈGES. Subscribes charter of Dreux, count of Amiens, 1031–1035. *Gallia Christiana*, xi. instr. 10; *Neustria Pia*, p. 318; F. Soehnée, *Catalogue des actes de Henri Ier*, no. 37; Vernier, no. 14.

13. JUMIÈGES. Attests charter of Roger of Montgomery. Original in Archives of the Seine-Inférieure; copies, MS. Lat. 5424, f. 184v, MS. Lat. n. a. 1245, f. 175. Vernier, no. 13; J. Loth, *Histoire de l'abbaye de Saint-Pierre de Jumièges*, i. 158.

14. MONT-SAINT-MICHEL. General privilege. Original in Archives of the Manche, H. 14990 (early copy H. 14991). *Mémoires de la Société d' Agriculture de Bayeux*, viii. 252 (1879); Round, *Calendar*, no. 704.

15. MONT-SAINT-MICHEL. Grant of one-half of Guernsey and other specified lands. Original in Archives of the Manche, H. 14992; *vidimus* in Archives Nationales, JJ. 66, no. 1496; cartulary (MS. Avranches, 210), f. 26. *M. A. N.*, xii. 111; Round, no. 705; Delisle, *S.-Sauveur*, pièces, no. 9; G. Dupont, *Le Cotentin* (Caen, 1870), i. 463 f.; V. Hunger, *Histoire de Verson* (Caen, 1908), no. 5 (facsimile).

16. MONT-SAINT-MICHEL. Attests, together with Archbishop Robert († 1037) and others, charter of Edward the Confessor as king granting to the abbey St. Michael's Mount, Cornwall. Cartulary, f. 32v; Delisle, *S.-Sauveur*, pièces, no. 18; Round, *Calendar*, no. 708. Robert's name does not appear in the text printed in the *Monasticon*, vii. 989, ' ex ipso autographo ', and reproduced by Kemble, *Codex Diplomaticus*, iv. 251. Edward's title has generally been considered to render this charter questionable (cf. Freeman, *Norman Conquest*, ii. 527 f.); see, however, Round, no. 706, and *infra*, p. 275.

17. MONTIVILLIERS. Foundation charter of the nunnery, with detailed enumeration of possessions. Given at Fécamp 13 January 1035. Copies in Bibliothèque Nationale, MS. Lat. n. a. 1245, ff. 112, 252; Archives of the Seine-Inférieure, G. 2068. *Gallia Christiana*, xi. instr. 326, from *vidimus*.

18. PRÉAUX. Consents to foundation of abbey. *Gallia Christiana*, xi. instr. 199.

19. PRÉAUX. Attests confused notice of donation by the hermit Peter. Le Prévost, *Eure*, iii. 169, from cartulary in Archives of the Eure (H. 711).

20. PRÉAUX. Notice of his gift of Toutainville to the abbey ' illo anno quo perrexit Robertus comes Ierusalem '. *Gallia Christiana*, xi. instr. 200; *H. F.*, xi. 387; Mabillon, *Annales*, iv. 361 (393); Delisle, *S.-Sauveur*, pièces, no. 12; Le Prévost, *Eure*, iii. 300 (from cartulary).

21. ROUEN cathedral. Charter of restoration issued conjointly with Archbishop Robert. Cartulary (MS. Rouen 1193), f. 32 f.; *vidimus* in Archives of the Seine-Inférieure, G. 2087, 3680. Le Prévost, *Eure*, ii. 520; cf. [Pommeraye] *Histoire de l'église cathédrale de Rouen* (Rouen, 1686), p. 568, where another form of this charter is also mentioned.

22. ROUEN. La Trinité. Confirms the foundation of the abbey and enumerates its possessions, 1030. *Cartulaire de l'abbaye de la Sainte-Trinité*, ed. Deville, no. 1; *Gallia Christiana*, xi. instr. 9; *Neustria Pia*, p. 412; Pommeraye, *Histoire de l'abbaye de Sainte-Catherine*, p. 73.

23–26. ROUEN, La Trinité. Attests four grants to the monastery. *Cartulaire*, nos. 3, 5, 9, 24.

27. ROUEN, Saint-Amand. Confirms foundation. *Vidimus* of Philip the Fair, in 1313, in Archives of the Seine-Inférieure, and in Archives Nationales,

JJ. 49, no. 47; cartulary in Archives of the Seine-Inférieure, f. 5 f. Pommeraye, *Histoire de Saint-Amand*, p. 76; La Roque, iv. 2224 (extract); *Monasticon*, vii. 1100, from Norman rolls of Henry V. The relation of this charter to no. 22, which it closely resembles, and to the confusion respecting the beginnings of Saint-Amand, requires investigation.

28. ROUEN, Saint-Ouen. Adds his confirmation to that of his father in charter of ' Enna Christi famula ': ' Et hoc signum + predictus comes Rotbertus cum suis episcopis atque militibus, scilicet Nigello, Osberno dapifero, atque aliis nobilibus manu sua ' (breaks off). Pretended original, with a duplicate omitting Robert's confirmation, in Archives of the Seine-Inférieure; copy in the Bibliothèque Nationale, MS. Lat. 5423, f. 124v.

28 a. ROUEN. Saint-Ouen. Charter cited by William the Conqueror. MS. Lat. n. a. 1243, no. 19; cf. *Neustria Pia*, p. 23.

29. SAINT-WANDRILLE. Grant of the church of Arques and its dependencies, 1031–1032. Round, *Calendar*, no. 1422; Lot, *S.-Wandrille*, no. 13 (from cartulary in Archives of the Seine-Inférieure).

30. SAINT-WANDRILLE. General confirmation, 1032–1035. Lot, no. 14, where the various copies and editions are given.

31. Sells LE HOMME to his sister Adeliz. Mentioned in charter of Adeliz for La Trinité de Caen. Cartulary in Bibliothèque Nationale (MS. Lat. 5650), f. 17v. Delisle, *S.-Sauveur*, pièces, no. 34; Round, *Calendar*, no. 421.[38]

Not more than three of these documents are originals of charters issued by Robert himself, so that no diplomatic study is possible. It is clear that there was no ducal chancery: not only do we find no signature of chancellor or chaplain, but the varieties of style[39] and substance

[38] The grant of Saint-James to Saint-Benoît-sur-Loire mentioned in the Conqueror's charter of 1067 (Prou and Vidier, *Les chartes de Saint-Benoît*, i. 203), which was ascribed to Duke Robert by Stapleton (i, p. xci), should probably be assigned to his uncle, Archbishop Robert. The charter for Lisieux cited in the *Chronique de S.-Barbe* (ed. Sauvage, p. 26) is probably a charter of Richard II which Robert witnessed: *M. A. N.*, xiii. 9.

[39] Thus the duke calls himself ' Ego Robertus Normannorum comes ' (no. 3); ' ego Robertus gratia Dei dux et princeps Normannorum ' (no. 4); ' ego Rotbertus filius secundi Richardi nutu Dei Northmannorum ducis et ipse per gratiam Dei princeps et dux Northmannorum ' (no. 6); ' Robertus nutu Dei Northmannorum dux ' (no. 8); ' ego Robertus gratia Dei dux Normannorum ' (no. 9); ' ego Robertus comes filius magni Richardi gratia Dei dux et princeps Normannorum ' (no. 15; cf. no. 14); ' Robertus divina auctoritate Normannorum dux et rector ' (no. 17); ' Robertus divina favente clemencia Normanorum dux' (no. 21); ' Robertus divina ordinante providentia Normannorum dux et rector' (nos. 22, 27); ' ego Rodbertus gratia Dei consul et dux Normannorum' (no. 29); ' ego Robertus disposicione divina Normannorum princeps ' (no. 30). In the attestation he appears as 'ego Robertus princeps Norhmannorum gracia Dei dux' (no. 15); 'signum Rotberti marchisi ' (no. 22); ' signum Rotberti Normannorum ducis' (nos. 6, 12); 'signum Roberti comitis et ducis Normannorum ' (no. 30). Cf. *Nouveau traité de diplomatique*, v. 760 f.

point plainly to local authorship. As only the charters for Cerisy and Montivilliers are exactly dated, it is impossible to draw up an itinerary or even to follow in the most general way the duke's progress throughout Normandy. The lists of witnesses, however, are sufficiently full to give us some notion of his entourage, in which four elements can be distinguished. First come the higher clergy, including regularly the duke's uncle, Archbishop Robert, commonly three or four bishops, and less frequently certain abbots; prelates from beyond Normandy appear occasionally, such as the archbishop of Dol (no. 6) and Odilo of Cluny (no. 29). The great lords of Normandy and the adjacent lands come next: Enguerran, count of Ponthieu, Baldwin of Flanders, Gilbert of Brionne, William of Arques, Mauger of Corbeil, Humphrey 'de Vetulis,' Galeran,[40] Rabel, doubtless the commander of the fleet,[41] and on two occasions (nos. 6, 30), in spite of his tender years, the duke's son William. In this group it is possible also to trace the princes who took refuge at the Norman court: King Henry I, 'qui tunc temporibus profugus habebatur in supradicta terra' (no. 29; cf. no. 12); and the ethelings Edward and Alfred, who appear in no. 29 with 'signum Hetuuardi' and 'signum Alureth fratris E.', and in no. 9 with 'signum Hetwardi, signum Helwredi,' while Edward alone is found as king in nos. 6 and 16 — a style which can be explained only by rejecting these charters, at least in their present form, or by admitting that he assumed the royal title during the lifetime of Canute. As compared with their importance in the succeeding reign [42] the group of household officers is small and ill-defined, comprising the seneschal Osbern,[43] who generally appears well up in the list but not always with this title, the constable Turold, who is found at the very end of two apparent originals (nos. 6, 15), and Robert 'pincerna' (no. 15; cf. Round, no. 709); the chamberlains [44] and chaplains [45] mentioned else-

[40] Probably Galeran of Meulan, no. 27. On his difficulties with Robert, see *Neustria Pia*, p. 320; Vernier, no. 16.

[41] Nos. 13, 30. See the interpolation of Ordericus in William of Jumièges, ed. Marx, p. 155. Wace (lines 2795, 2805) calls him Tavel.

[42] *Supra*, p. 50 f.

[43] 'Procurator principalis domus,' he is called by Ordericus: William of Jumièges, ed. Marx, p. 156. Anfredus likewise appears as dapifer in no. 29. 'Gislebertus senescallus' in *Cartulaire de la Trinité*, no. 5, may not be a ducal officer. Cf. L. W. Vernon Harcourt, *His Grace the Steward*, p. 7.

[44] William of Jumièges, p. 107; Wace, line 3237. 'Radulfus camerarius filius Geroldi' is mentioned in no. 20.

[45] Isembert, in William of Jumièges, p. 108; Ernaldus, in Chapter I, note 246 (full text in *Archaeologia*, xxvii. 26).

where do not appear among the witnesses. Probably some of those who sign without title are also members of the household. At the end come the *vicomtes*, ordinarily without designation of districts, and attaining in one case (no. 15) the number of seven. In some instances, as in that of the well known Neal of Saint-Sauveur, *vicomte* of the Cotentin,[46] it is plain that they too may attest without title.

Whether Robert's reign was marked by any acts of legislation, either secular or ecclesiastical, it is impossible to say. The first Norman provincial council of which we have mention is not earlier than 1042,[47] and the earliest formulation of ducal custom comes to us from the sons of the Conqueror.[48] Nevertheless, certain canons of the council of Lillebonne (1080) refer to the practice of Robert's time as the basis of customary right,[49] and respecting cemeteries the reference is so specific as to incline Tardif to the opinion that some actual document of the period is presupposed.[50] In this, as in other matters, it is likely that the conditions of Robert's reign often furnished the norm for that of his son.

[46] On whom see Delisle, *S.-Sauveur*, pp. 2–4, pièces, nos. 1–16.

[47] Bessin, *Concilia Rotomagensis Provinciae*, i. 39. On the date of this council and on all questions concerning early Norman legislation, see E.-J. Tardif, *Étude sur les sources*, i. 29 f.

[48] *Infra*, Appendix D.

[49] Cc. 11, 13, 48, in *Layettes du Trésor des Chartes*, i. 25 ; Ordericus, ii. 316 ff.

[50] *Op. cit.*, i. 40.

APPENDIX D

THE NORMAN *CONSUETUDINES ET IUSTICIE* OF WILLIAM THE CONQUEROR [1]

THE sources for the history of Norman law before the conquest of the duchy by Philip Augustus are, as is well known, exceedingly meager. The earliest law-book, the first part of the *Très Ancien Coutumier*, belongs to the very end of the twelfth century, and the traces of custom and legislation preserved in charters and chronicles are of the most fragmentary and scattered sort.[2] It is, accordingly, all the more imperative, especially in view of the great importance of Norman law in European legal development, to treasure carefully such material as we have; and I venture to think that a text of the year 1091, containing a brief statement of the customs of the duchy under William the Conqueror, has not received sufficient attention from students of Norman, and Anglo-Norman, history and institutions. The text in question was first printed, in an incomplete and sometimes unintelligible form, by Dom Martène[3] under the title ' Normannorum antiquae consuetudines et iustitiae in concilio apud Lillebonnam anno m.lxxx. celebrato confirmatae,' and was reproduced by Mansi as part of the canons of the council.[4] But while in all the manuscripts of the *Consuetudines* they follow immediately the canons of Lillebonne, they do not occur in Ordericus or in the official version of the acts of the council, as sealed by Henry I,[5] and there is nothing in the contents of the two documents which indicates the slightest connection between them. It is plain from the opening sentence that the *Consuetudines* are not an enactment of the Conqueror's reign but the result of an inquest made by

---

[1] Revised from *E. H. R.*, xxiii. 502–508 (1908).

[2] H. Brunner, *Entstehung der Schwurgerichte*, p. 130 ff.; Pollock and Maitland, i. 64 ff.; E.-J. Tardif, *Étude sur les sources de l'ancien droit normand*, i (Rouen, 1911). On the date of the *Très Ancien Coutumier*, see Tardif's edition, pp. lxv–lxxii; Viollet, in *Histoire littéraire*, xxxiii. 47–49.

[3] *Veterum Scriptorum Collectio Nova* (Paris, 1700), i. 226; reprinted in Martène and Durand, *Thesaurus Novus Anecdotorum* (Paris, 1717), iv. 117; from a manuscript of Mont-Saint-Michel, now MS. 149 of the library of Avranches. Reprinted in Migne, *Patrologia*, cxlix. 1329.

[4] *Concilia*, xx. 575.

[5] Ordericus, ii. 316; Teulet, *Layettes du Trésor des Chartes*, i. 25, no. 22.

Robert and William Rufus after his death.[6] As this inquest was held on 18 July at Caen, it must be assigned to 1091 as the only year in the July of which these princes were in Normandy and in friendly relations.[7] The division of territory which they had recently made furnished a natural occasion for ascertaining the ducal rights, or at least for a declaration of such of them (*quia magis necessaria sunt*) as had been most persistently violated during the preceding anarchy.[8]

Over against the adulterine castles of recent origin the inquest declares the law of the Conqueror's time, which not only forbade the building of castles and strongholds, but placed careful restrictions on the making of fosses and palisades (§ 4). With this went the right, so freely used by the Conqueror, of placing garrisons in the castles of his barons and the right of demanding hostages for their loyalty (§ 5). Private war had not been entirely prohibited, but it had been closely limited (§§ 6, 8, 14), just as in 1075 William I had limited the blood-feud without abolishing it.[9]

Ducal and baronial jurisdiction are carefully distinguished, although the line which divides them is not clearly drawn. The list of matters reserved for the duke's jurisdiction is shorter than the enumeration of pleas of the sword which appears a century later in the *Très Ancien Coutumier*,[10] but it must be remembered that the inquest of 1091 expressly disclaims completeness. Assault in the duke's court or on the way to and from it,[11] offenses committed in the host or within a week

---

[6] Cf. Delisle, *B. É. C.*, x. 198; Viollet, in *Histoire littéraire*, xxxiii. 41 f.

[7] For the events of 1091 see Freeman, *William Rufus*, i. 273-293; *supra*, pp. 64 f., 78. H. Böhmer, *Kirche und Staat*, p. 34, note 2, dates the inquest 17 June 1096, mistaking the month and overlooking the fact that in 1096 William Rufus did not cross to Normandy until September (Ordericus, iv. 16). Liebermann, *Gesetze*, i. 597, note, has 1091.

[8] On conditions in Normandy under Robert see *supra*, Chapter II.

[9] 'Instituit legem sanctam, scilicet ne aliquis homo aliquem hominem assalliret pro morte alicuius sui parentis, nisi patrem aut filium interfecisset': Duchesne, *Historiae Normannorum Scriptores*, p. 1018; Ordericus, v. 158; Robert of Torigni, i. 60. The MS. of the Annals of Saint-Étienne in the Vatican (MS. Regina 703A, f. 53v) has, apparently, in place of 'interfecisset,' 'interfectorēf,' while one MS. of Robert of Torigni has 'interfectorem'; the original may have read 'nisi patris aut filii interfector esset.'

On the question of the Conqueror's earlier legislation against disorder see Tardif, *Étude sur les sources*, p. 31 f.; on the interpretation of § 4, C. Enlart, *Manuel d'archéologie française*, ii. 418; Haskins, *The Normans in European History*, p. 152 f.

[10] Ed. Tardif, cc. 15, 16, 35, 53, 59, 67, 69, 70; Pollock and Maitland, ii. 455.

[11] So in the canons of Lillebonne 'assultus in ecclesie itinere' is punished equally with 'violatio ecclesie et atrii.'

of its setting forth or its return, offenses against pilgrims, and violations of the coinage (§§ 1, 2, 12, 13) — these place the offender at the
duke's mercy. Probably the same protection extended over merchants [12] (§ 11) and over the duke's forests [13] (§ 7). All such cases
belong to the duke, but franchise courts may possess jurisdiction over
attacks on houses (*hainfara*), arson, rape, and unwarranted seizure of
sureties (§§ 9, 10) — just as under Edward the Confessor *hainfara* was
one of the pleas which were ordinarily reserved to the crown, but
might be held by a great immunist like the abbot of Westminster or
the bishop of Winchester.[14] Arson, rape, and *hainfara* are mentioned
among the *consuetudines vicecomitatus* [15] in Vascoeuil which the Conqueror granted in the year of his marriage to the abbey of Préaux: [16]

Eodem anno quo in coniugium sortitus est Normannorum marchio Willelmus nomine Balduini comitis filiam dedit Sancto Petro Pratelli consuetudines
quas habebat in quadam terra que Wascolium vulgo vocatur, scilicet hain-
faram, ullac, rat, incendium, bernagium, bellum. Pro quibus abbas eiusdem
loci Ansfridus nomine ei dignam dedit pecuniam, id est .x. libras denariorum,
et orationes loci Pratelli.

Equally interesting is the system of penalties for those *in misericordia ducis*. The authors of the *History of English Law* have made

[12] Merchants had also the protection of the Truce of God in Normandy: *M. G. H.,
Constitutiones et Acta Publica*, ed. Weiland, i. 601, c. 7.

[13] Even priests were comprehended in the forest jurisdiction, as we learn from the
council of Lillebonne.

[14] Pollock and Maitland, ii. 454 f.; Maitland, *Domesday Book and Beyond*,
p. 87 f.; Vinogradoff, *English Society in the Eleventh Century*, pp. 111–114; Steen-
strup, *Normannerne*, iv. 348 ff.; Liebermann, *Gesetze*, ii. 504–506.

[15] So styled in the notice of their regrant by the abbot to Thibaud, son of Norman, shortly afterwards: ' consuetudines vicecomitatus quas a comite ut supra-
scriptum est emerat ' (cartulary of Préaux, no. 439). Compare what Wace (ed.
Andresen, ii, lines 2309–2312) says of Robert I's grant to Cerisy, the text of which
(*Monasticon*, vii. 1073; cf. Appendix C) merely gives freedom from every *consuetudo*:

> ' E tel franchise lur dunat,
> Cume li ducs en sa terre ad:
> Il unt le murdre e le larun,
> Le rap, le homicide, le arsun.'

[16] Cartulary of Préaux, no. 437; now in Valin, pièces, no. 2. In 1106 Robert of
Meulan ' condonavit abbatie sue banleviam et ullac et hainfariam et incendium '
(*ibid.*, no. 347). *Ullac* is a word which I have found only in the Préaux cartulary: in
no. 55 the form is *utlach* and *uthlach;* in Delisle-Berger, no. 675, it is *uthlac*. It
would seem to be connected with the Old Norse *utlagi*, an outlaw, which appears as
ulage or *hulague* in Wace, and it might then mean the harboring of an outlaw

clear how, in the course of the twelfth century, the old system of *bót* and *wite* is replaced by a new criminal law which puts the offender or his property at the king's mercy.[17] As roughly stated by the *Dialogus*,[18] the new system grades offenses into three classes, according as the penalty is forfeiture of movables, of lands and rents, or of life and limb. Now §§ 1–3 and 13 of the *Consuetudines* exhibit precisely the same system, violations of the duke's peace entailing, according to their gravity, the forfeiture of *pecunia*, *terra*, or *corpus*, or of some combination of them; and it is hard to avoid the conclusion that the classification of the *Dialogus* goes back to a Norman original. Against the view of a Norman origin it is not enough to urge the existence of " the preappointed *bót* in Normandy when we can no longer find it in England,"[19] for the principle of amercement may well have existed in Normandy side by side with survivals of the definite penalties which were once found among all Germanic peoples — indeed it is not clear that the provision of the *Consuetudines* in the case of the unforeseen *mêlée* (§ 3), *secundum mensuram forisfacti emendavit*, does not imply the preappointed *bót*.

§ 13 contains the earliest evidence of the ducal monopoly of coinage and the jurisdiction growing out of it.[20] The Bayeux mint is not otherwise known;[21] the Rouen mint is mentioned in a charter of Richard II,[22] and is proved by coins to have existed in the time of William Longsword.[23] The standard of fineness prescribed in § 13 is confirmed by

[17] ii. 458 f. Cf. the discussion of *misericordia* in Liebermann, *Gesetze*, ii. 583 f.

[18] ' Quisquis enim in regiam maiestatem deliquisse deprehenditur, uno trium modorum iuxta qualitatem delicti sui regi condempnatur, aut enim in universo mobili suo reus iudicatur pro minoribus culpis, aut in omnibus immobilibus, fundis scilicet et redditibus, ut eis exheredetur, quod fit pro maioribus culpis, aut pro maximis quibuscunque vel enormibus delictis, in vitam suam vel membra ' (bk. ii, c. 16, ed. Hughes, Crump, and Johnson, p. 149).

[19] Pollock and Maitland, ii. 459.

[20] There are traces of the *iusticia monete* under Henry I. See the charter for Saint-Pierre-sur-Dive, *Gallia Christiana*, xi. instr. 157; Pipe Roll 31 Henry I, p. 122; and cf. *Três Ancien Coutumier*, c. 70.

[21] *B. É. C.*, xiii. 104, note 5; *Bulletin des Antiquaires de Normandie*, xiv. 211, 219.

[22] ' Concedo etiam decimas monete nostrae ex integro.' Charter of 1025 (?) for Fécamp, original in the Musée, no. *2ter*, printed in *Neustria Pia*, p. 217; *supra*, Appendix B, no. 5.

[23] A. Engel and R. Serrure, *Traité de numismatique du moyen-âge*, ii. 380. ' Rannulfus monetarius ' witnesses an early Rouen charter of William the Conqueror (Pommeraye, *S.-Amand*, p. 78); his son Galeran held land in Caen (*Gallia Christiana*, xi. instr. 60). Radulfus appears with this title in a charter of 1061 (Archives of the Manche, H. 14994; Round, no. 711), and this name is found on coins (Engel and

analysis of extant coins of the eleventh century.[24] *Helmarc* is probably to be interpreted as half a mark,[25] which gives a mark of sixteen shillings. This word points to the Scandinavian origin of the mark, which has not been found in France before 1082.[26]

The text of the *Consuetudines* which follows is based upon (A) a manuscript of the twelfth century preserved at the Vatican among the manuscripts of the Queen of Sweden, no. 596, ff. 4–5.[27] The variant readings are taken from (B) the Vatican MS. Ottoboni 2964, ff. 133v–134v;[28] (C) MS. Lat. 1597 B of the Bibliothèque Nationale, ff. 140–141v, a miscellaneous collection of the fifteenth century; and (D) MS. 149, f. 3, of the library of Avranches, which was used by Martène for his edition.[29] The division into paragraphs is that of C, the only manuscript which makes any such division.

Hee [30] *sunt consuetudines et iusticie quas habet dux Normannie in eadem provincia, et Guillelmus rex qui regnum Anglie adquisivit maxime et viriliter eas suo tempore teneri fecit, et sicut hic scripte sunt* [31] *filii eius Robertus et Guillelmus per episcopos et barones suos Cadomi* [32] *recordari fecerunt.*

Hec est [33] iusticia quam rex Guillelmus [34] qui regnum Anglie adquisivit habuit in Normannia, et hic inscripta [35] est sicut Robertus [36] comes Normannie [37] et Guillelmus rex Anglie filii eius et heredes predicti regis fecerunt recordari [38] et [39] scribi [40] per episcopos et barones suos Cadomi [41] xv. kal. Augusti.

1. Et hec est [42] iusticia [43] domini Normannie quod in curia sua vel eundo ad

Serrure, ii. 381). ' Odo monetarius ' appears in a Rouen charter (*Cartulaire de la Trinité*, no. 60).

[24] Sambon finds 44.7 per cent silver in a Rouen denarius of the eleventh century found near Naples (*Gazette numismatique française*, iii. 138, note).

[25] Cf. Du Cange, *s. v.*; *B. É. C.*, x. 198.

[26] Guilhiermoz, *Note sur les poids du moyen âge, ibid.*, lxvii. 210–213. See however *Gallia Christiana*, xi. instr. 74, which may be slightly earlier.

[27] On this manuscript see Pertz's *Archiv*, xii. 296; Auvray in *B. É. C.*, xlix. 637, note 3; Liebermann, *Ueber die Leges Edwardi Confessoris*, p. 59, note 1.

[28] Described by Auvray, *l. c.;* Tardif, *Coutumiers de Normandie*, ii, pp. lii–liv.

[29] This manuscript is of the thirteenth century. Cf. *Catalogue des manuscrits des départements*, x. 68. MS. 551 (A. 373) of the library of Rouen formerly contained ' Consuetudines quas habet dux Normannie in eadem Normannia,' but this portion has been missing since the time of Montfaucon (*ibid.*, i. 130). MS. Rouen 2192, f. 51, contains a modern copy by Le Brasseur, the source of which is not given.

[30] *Hec*, CD; *Hee . . . fecerunt*, om. B. If not official, the title is at least in contemporary language: cf. ' iusticiis et consuetudinibus ' in canon 45 of the council of Lillebonne.

[31] *scripte hic*, C.	[36] *R.*, B.	[40] Om. C.
[32] *eadem*, D.	[37] Om. B.	[41] *eadem*, D.
[33] *cum*, D.	[38] Om. B. *reccedari*, D.	[42] Om. AC.
[34] *Willelmus rex*, B.	[39] Om. BC.	[43] Om. B.
[35] *scripta*, D.		

curiam vel redeundo de curia nullus homo habuit [44] gardam [45] de inimico suo. Et [46] si aliquis inimico suo in via curie vel in curia forisfecit,[47] ita quod ipse sciret [48] quod ille cui malum fecit ad curiam iret vel inde rediret, si probatus inde fuit [49] dominus Normannie habuit [50] pecuniam suam [51] et corpus eius ad suam iusticiam faciendam et terram suam perdidit [52] ita quod nec ipse nec aliquis de parentibus suis eam clamare potuit.[53] Et [54] si defendere potuit quod scienter hoc non fecisset, per pecuniam fuit [55] in misericordia domini Normannie sine perditione terre.

2. Et [56] in via exercitus et in exercitu et in [57] .viii.[58] diebus [59] ante motum determinati exercitus [60] et .viii. diebus post exercitum si aliquis forisfecerit,[61] habuit [62] inde dominus Normannie eandem iusticiam quam de forisfacto sue curie.[63] Nec infra prescriptos terminos exercitus alicui licuit [64] nammum [65] capere, et si fecit [66] per pecuniam emendavit [67] in misericordia domini Normannie.

3. Et si in exercitu vel in curia vel in via curie vel exercitus mislata [68] evenit que pro precedente [69] ira facta non fuerit,[70] et in ea vulneratus vel occisus fuerit [70] aliquis, ille cuius culpa hoc factum est secundum mensuram forisfacti emendavit.[71]

4. Nulli licuit [72] in Normannia fossatum facere in planam terram [73] nisi tale quod de fundo [74] potuisset [75] terram iactare superius sine scabello, et ibi non [76] licuit [77] facere palicium [78] nisi in una regula et illud sine propugnaculis et alatoriis. Et in rupe [79] vel [80] in insula nulli [81] licuit [82] facere fortitudinem, et [83] nulli licuit [84] in Normannia castellum facere,[85] et nulli licuit [84] in Normannia [86] fortitudinem castelli sui vetare domino Normannie [87] si ipse eam [88] in manu sua [89] voluit [90] habere.

5. Et si dominus Normannie filium vel fratrem vel nepotem baronis sui qui non esset miles voluit habere obsidem [91] de portanda fide, nullus sibi contradicere potuit.

[44] Om. C.   [45] *gaurdam*, A; *gardiam*, C; *gardam habebat*, B; *gardam habuit*, D.

[46] *Et . . . suo*, om. B.   [51] *suam pecuniam*, D.   [56] *etiam*, B.

[47] *forisfecerit*, B.   [52] *perdet*, C.   [57] *in .viii. diebus*, om. C; *in*, om. D.

[48] *sciret quod ille*, om. B   [53] *poterit*, C.

[49] *fuerit*, D.   [54] *Et . . . terre*, om. B.   [58] *et octo*, B.

[50] *habebit*, C.   [55] *erit*, C.   [59] *diebus . . . viii.*, om. B.

[60] Here C has *octo diebus et post exercitum octo diebus.*

[61] *-fecit*, C.   [70] *fuit*, B.   [80] *et*, B.

[62] *habebit*, C.   [71] *emendabit*, ACD.   [81] *et nulli*, B.

[63] *curie sue*, BCD.   [72] *liceat*, C.   [82] *liceat*, C.

[64] *licebit*, C.   [73] *plena terra*, B.   [83] *et . . . facere*, om. BD.

[65] *namnum*, C; *nammium*, B.   [74] *profundo*, B.   [84] *liceat*, C.

[75] *popotuisset*, A.   [85] Here D inserts § 6.

[66] *cepit*, BD; *ceperit*, C.   [76] *nulli*, CD; *nullum*, B.   [86] *in Normannia*, om. B.

[67] *emendabit*, BCD.   [77] *licebit*, C.   [87] D inserts *et.*

[68] Om. B; *vis illata*, C.   [78] *palatium*, B.   [88] Om. B.

[69] *precedenti*, BCD.   [79] *ruppe*, B.

[89] *in manu sua*, om. B; *manum suam*, D.

[90] *vellet*, C; *voluit in manu sua*, B.   [91] *ob fidem de portata fide*, B.

6. Nulli [92] licuit [93] in Normannia pro calumnia terre [94] domum vel molendinum ardere vel aliquam vastacionem facere vel predam [95] capere.

7. Nulli licuit [93] in Normannia in forestis ipsius domini hominem assailire [96] vel insidias ponere.

8. Nulli licuit [97] inimicum [98] querendo vel nammum [99] capiendo vexillum [100] vel loricam portare vel cornu sonare neque cembellum mittere post quod insidie remanerent neque de membris suis hominem [101] dampnare sine iudicio, nisi in tali actu vel forisfacto inventus est [102] pro quo membrum perdere debuisset et ibidem perdidisset, et nisi per iudicium curie domini [103] Normannie de hoc quod ad eum pertinet vel iudicio curie baronum de hoc quod ad barones pertinet.

9. Nulli licuit [104] in Normannia hanfare facere [105] vel incendium vel raptum mulieris vel nammum [106] capere quin fieret inde clamor apud eum qui clamorem inde habere debuit.[107]

10. Et si hec facta fuerunt,[108] dominus Normannie [109] habuit [110] inde quod habere debuit [111] in [112] illis locis in quibus habere debuit et barones inde habuerunt [113] quod ad eos pertinuit in illis locis in quibus habere debuerunt.

11.[114] Nulli licuit [115] in Normannia mercatorem disturbare nisi pro suo debito et nisi fideiussor fuisset.

12. Nulli licuit [115] peregrinum [116] disturbare pro aliquo anteriori forisfacto.[117] Et si aliquis [118] fecit,[119] de corpore suo fuit [120] in misericordia domini Normannie.

13. Nulli licuit [121] in Normannia monetam facere extra domos monetarias [122] Rothomagi et Baiocarum et illam mediam argenti et ad iustum pensum, scilicet [123] .viii.[124] solidos in helmarc.[125] Et si aliquis alibi fecit [126] monetam vel ibi fecit [126] monetam falsam, de corpore suo fuit [127] in misericordia domini Normannie. Et si aliquis extra predictas domos [fecit] facere [128] monetam vel in predictis domibus fecit [128] facere [129] falsam,[130] terram suam et pecuniam forisfecit.[131]

[92] *Nulli . . . capere*, inserted in § 4, D.
[93] *liceat*, C.
[94] Om. C.
[95] *predictam*, B.
[96] *assaillire*, C; *assallire*, D; *assallaire*, B.
[97] *liceat*, C; *licuerit*, B.
[98] *in Normannia*, B.
[99] *nammium*, B.
[100] *vexillam*, C.
[101] *hominem de membris suis*, BC; *hominem dampnare de membris suis*, D.
[102] *fuerit*, C; *esset*, B.
[103] *domini . . . curie*, om. B.
[104] *liceat*, C.
[105] Om. B.
[106] *namnum*, C.
[107] *debebit*, C.
[108] *fuerint*, C.
[109] *Normanannie*, A.
[110] *habebit*, C.
[111] *debebit*, C.
[112] *in . . . debuit*, om. BC.
[113] *habuerunt . . . debuerunt*, om. BC; *In illis locis in quibus pertinuit habuerunt quod ad eos habere debuerunt*, B; *Habebunt quod inde habere debebunt in illis locis in quibus debere habebunt et quod ad quemlibet pertinebit*, C.
[114] *Nulli . . . fuisset*, om. D.
[115] *liceat*, C.
[116] *mercatorem*, D.
[117] *facto*, B.
[118] *quis*, C.
[119] *fecerit*, C.
[120] *sit*, C.
[121] *liceat*, C.
[122] *monetarias domos*, CD.
[123] *i*, B.
[124] *octo*, C.
[125] *marca*, B; *helinare*, C.
[126] *fecerit*, C. From this point to the middle of the following paragraph (*iusticiis*) the ends of the lines are wanting in B.
[127] *erit*, C. [128] *fecerit*, C. [129] *fieri*, C. [130] *monetam falsam*, C. [131] *forisfaciet*, C.

Hec autem que superius dicta sunt scripta sunt [132] quia [133] magis necessaria sunt. Remanet autem multum extra hoc scriptum de iusticia monete et reliquis iusticiis Normannie, sed propter hoc quod non scribitur nichil [134] perdunt [135] comes Robertus [136] et rex Guillelmus [137] de iusticia quam pater eorum habuit neque barones de hoc quod habuerunt tempore regis Guillelmi.[138]

14. Nulli licuit [139] pro guerra [140] hominem capere vel redimere nec de bello vel conflictu pecuniam portare vel arma vel equum ducere.[141]

[132] *scripta sunt,* om. C.	[136] Om. B.	[139] *liceat,* C.
[133] *que,* B.	[137] *W,* B.	[140] *uuerra,* B.
[134] *nil,* B.	[138] *Willelmi,* B.	[141] *Et sic finis,* add. C.
[135] *perdent,* C.		

APPENDIX E

UNPUBLISHED CHARTERS OF ROBERT CURTHOSE[1]

1

Shortly after September 1087

Robert confirms to Saint-Étienne of Caen the manor of Vains as granted by his father in his last illness, reserving the toll from those outside the manor.

A, original lost; B, brief cartulary of Vains, MS. Caen 104, f. 150; C, MS. Lat. n. a. 1406, f. 58, from B.

Supra, Chapter II, no. 13. Cf. Deville, *Analyse*, p. 31; and, for the toll, the inquest of 1171 in Delisle, *Henri II*, p. 345.

In nomine sancte et individue trinitatis patris et filii et spiritus sancti. Ego Robertus dux Normannorum et princeps Cenomannorum concedo ecclesie Dei quam W. rex Anglorum pater meus pro salute anime sue et mee, matris mee, fratrum meorum, antecessorum et parentum nostrorum in honore Beati Stephani prothomartyris construxit, donum de manerio de Vain [2] quod idem pater meus in infirmitate qua defunctus est eidem ecclesie fecit, ita integre solide libere et quiete sicut ipse in ea die qua defunctus est idem manerium tenebat. Retineo tamen in manu mea ad censum mei vicecomitatus eiusdem manerii theloneum alivum, hoc est illud theloneum de hominibus qui de foris scilicet venientes in ipso manerio aliquid emunt vel vendunt, theloneum vero residens, hoc est de hominibus in ipso manerio manentibus ceteraque tocius ville de Vaymo, quietum et liberum relinquo et concedo predicte ecclesie.

Ad hanc autem donationem confirmandam consilio meorum fidelium scriptum hoc fieri precipio et manu mea firmavi firmandamque fratri meo Henrico predictisque meis fidelibus tradidi. Huius et[iam] donationis con (*sic*) fieret a patre meo sunt testes Robertus comes Moretonii, Robertus comes de Meullent, Henricus comes frater eius, Yvo Taillebosc, et alii plures.

2

1096

Robert attests an agreement between Gilbert, abbot of Saint-Étienne of Caen, and Gerento, abbot of Saint-Bénigne of Dijon, exchanging Saint-

---

[1] See the full list of Robert's charters, *supra*, pp. 66–70, to which the references by number are made in the text. For convenience the alphabetical order of the beneficiaries has been retained here. Vernier's edition of nos. 6 and 7 arrived after they were in type.

[2] Vains, Manche, canton of Avranches.

285

Hippolyte of 'Curtbertalt' for Saint-Aubert-sur-Orne and Saint-Martin de Longchamps.

A, original, never sealed, in Archives of the Calvados, H. 1847.

Supra, Chapter II, no. 17. Cf. Deville, *Analyse*, pp. 26, 31; Léchaudé, *M. A. N.*, vii. 270, no. 8; Hippeau, *M. A. N.*, xxi. 29, 523; Le Prévost, *Eure*, ii. 323.

The date is fixed by the presence of Abbot Gerento in Normandy in 1096: supra, p. 75. The grant of Longchamps to Saint-Bénigne under Richard II is mentioned in the chronicle of the abbey (*Analecta Divionensia*, ix. 175), which says nothing of this exchange and gives no means of identifying Curtbertalt among the abbey's possessions.

Notum sit omnibus futuris et presentibus quod domnus Gislebertus abbas Cadomensis et domnus Ierento Divionensis fecerunt inter se commutationes quasdam de rebus ad utrasque ęcclesias pertinentibus. Cadomensis enim ęcclesia sita in Normannia habebat in Burgundia ęcclesiam Sancti Ypoliti de Curtbertalt cum appenditiis datis et adquisitis, quam contulit Sancto Stephano Cadomensi Roclenus episcopus Cabilonensis. Similiter Divionensis sita in Burgundia habebat in Normannia ęcclesiam Sancti Alberti cum sibi pertinentibus et ęcclesiam de Longo Campo [1] iuxta silvam quę dicitur Leons cum terris et decimis. Quia ergo res utraque in longinquo posita erat et longinquitas itineris non sinebat tantumdem commodi provenire quantum faceret si esset in vicinio ęcclesię, communi decreverunt consilio ut ęcclesia Cadomensis acciperet ęcclesiam Sancti Alberti cum appenditiis et ęcclesiam de Longo Campo cum terris et decimis, quod erat iuris ęcclesię Divionensis, et ęcclesia Divionensis haberet ęcclesiam Sancti Ypoliti cum omnibus illis quę monachi Sancti Stephani inibi habitantes videbantur possidere. Hęc itaque mutationis conventio facta est communi consilio communi decreto et ut in posterum servaretur stabilitum est cartarum antiquarum commutatione et huius nova conscriptione et abbatum utrorumque et fratrum utriusque ęcclesię subscriptione.

Signum Gisleberti abbatis Cadomensis+ Signum Rodulfi+
Signum Ierentonis abbatis Divionensis+ Signum Humberti monachi+Signum Hugonis capellani+ Signum Roberti monachi+
+Signum Roberti comitis Normannorum filii Willelmi regis Anglorum.

3

1101–1105

Robert grants to Saint-Étienne of Caen a Sunday market and an annual fair at Cheux.

A, original, 42 x 19 centimeters with projecting tag of 14 centimeters, in Archives of the Calvados, H. 1832. Léchaudé, copied by Round,

---

[1] Saint-Aubert-sur-Orne, Orne, canton of Putanges; Saint-Martin de Longchamps, Eure, canton of Étrépagny.

says, "Le sceau de cette charte, scellée en queue, est brisé"; but nothing now remains of it.

Supra, Chapter II, no. 18; Léchaudé, *M. A. N.*, vii. 271, no. 9; Round, no. 451; cf. Deville, *Analyse*, p. 16, where the text gives the names of the bishops of Bayeux and Coutances, Thorold and Ralph; Hippeau, *M. A. N.*, xxi. 495, who says the charter was given at Saint-Pierre-sur-Dive (!).

IN NOMINE sanctę et individuę trinitatis patris et filii et spiritus sancti. Ego Robertus dux Normannorum concedo ęcclesię Dei quam Willelmus rex Anglorum pater meus pro salute animę suę et meę, matris meę, fratrum meorum, antecessorum et parentum nostrorum in honore Beati Stephani Cadomi construxit, habere mercatum ad diem dominicam in manerio de Ceus[1] hereditario et perpetuo iure possidendum et unam feriam in anno ad illum terminum quem abbas et monachi eiusdem ęcclesię elegerint. Quod siquis hanc donationem, scilicet hoc mercatum et hanc feriam quę ego pro salute animę meę et pro salute animę patris mei et matris meę, fratrum meorum, antecessorum et parentum nostrorum ęcclesię Sancti Stephani de Cadomo donavi, eidem ęcclesię auferre aliquo modo temptaverit, concedo ego corde et ore meo et manu mea confirmo ut ex auctoritate Dei patris omni-potentis et filii et spiritus sancti sit excommunicatus et a regno Dei in per-petuum exclusus.

Signum Roberti comitis Normannię+ Signum Eustachii de Bretulio+ Signum Willelmi Rothomagensis archiepiscopi+ Signum Rannulfi episcopi Duhelmensis+ Signum Willelmi camerarii+ Signum episcopi Baiocensis+ Signum Willelmi comitis de Warenna+ Signum Roberti de Monteforti+ Signum Gisleberti de Aquila+ Signum Rainaldi de Aurea valle+ Signum Willelmi de Ferreriis+ Signum Rodulfi Taisson+ Signum episcopi Constantiensis+ Signum Roberti Marmion+ Signum Roberti de Gren-tonis maisnilio+ Signum Roberti Doisnel+

4

1088–1091

(a) *7 July 1088, Robert, when about to cross to England, restores to Fécamp and frees from all secular dues the land of William of Bec, of Hunspath, and of Hunloph, possessions at Ignauville, Bures, and Bouteilles, and land at Fécamp which his father had taken from the abbey.*

(b) *Thereafter Robert grants to the abbey a fair at Fécamp each year as long as the catch of herrings lasts, as well as a meadow for the monks' dairy.*

---

[1] Cheux, Calvados, canton of Tilly-sur-Seulles.

(*c*) *1089–1091, Robert, having defeated Robert of Mortain, son of William of Bec, and given his land to Gohier, again restores it to Fécamp and invests the abbot* per lignum.

A, originals, tied together and retaining portion of attached seal, in Musée de la Bénédictine, no. 6 (fragment of *b* separately preserved as no. 58). As they existed in 1764 they are described by Dom Lenoir as follows: " Cette charte est en quelque façon composée de trois parties. . . . La première et la seconde sont sur une feuille de parchemin de 12 pouces de haut et 13 de large, et la 3ᵉ est sur une autre feuille de parchemin qui a 13 pouces de haut et sept et demi de large, ce qui forme comme deux chartes couchées l'une sur l' autre et jointes ensemble par une lanière d'un cuir blanc fort épais et d'un pouce de large à laquelle est attaché par derrière la grande charte un sceau de deux pouces et demi de diamètre. Ce sceau est d'une espèce de pâte en mastic d'un gris blanc qui s'émie très facilement. Il est si fort endommagé qu'il est impossible d'y rien distinguer." B, copy from A, by Lenoir, Collection Moreau, cccxli, f. 21; C, copies of *a* and *c* in the cartulary, MS. Rouen 1207, f. 14, no. 40, with several of the witnesses omitted; D, copy of C, MS. Lat. n. a. 2412, no. 40.

Supra, Chapter II, nos. 20–22. *a* and *c* are analyzed from C by Round, no. 117, and Davis, no. 297; cf. DuCange, under *gravaria.* Extract from *b* in S. B. de la M. Noel, *Histoire des pêches* (Paris, 1815), p. 379, from *Chronicon Archimonasterii Fiscampnensis,* p. 356.

b and *c* are anterior to the grant of Fécamp to William Rufus in 1091; *c* is posterior to the accession of Abbot Ralph of Séez in 1089.

(*a*) [In nomine sancte et individue trinitatis. Anno ab incarnatione Domini millesimo] LXXXVIII mense Iulio septima die mensis feria vi. [ego Robertus] Dei gratia [dux et princeps Normannorum pro salute] animẹ meẹ et patris mei W. regis Anglorum matrisque meẹ Mathildis reginẹ [et aliorum predecessorum meorum reddo et] concedo ecclesiẹ Sancte Trinitatis Fiscanni et abbati Willelmo Dei providentia [eiusdem ecclesiẹ preordinato pastori terras illas quẹ] antea de casamento prefatẹ ẹcclesiẹ subtractẹ fuerant: scilicet totam terram [Willelmi de Becco quam tenebat de me, simili]ter terram Hunspathi et terram Hunloph de Mamolins et totam terram de Hisnelvilla ¹ [et quicquid ad eam pertinet decimamque molen]dinorum de Buris et duos burgenses cum duabus salinis in villa quẹ dicitur [Butellias terramque burgensium Fiscanni quam] pater meus ira commotus ante obitus sui diem subtraxerat ab eadem ẹcclesia. Has autem [terras reddo et concedo quietas de gravaria] et ab omni laicali consuetudine consilio et nutu Heinrici fratris mei aliorumque [obtimatum meorum quorum subscriptione] presens carta roboratur.

¹ Ignauville, canton of Fécamp; Bures, canton of Londinières; Bouteilles, canton of Offranville, all in Seine-Inférieure.

[Si+gnum Rotberti comitis Signum+ Gisleberti episcopi Ebroicensis]
Si+gnum Henrici comitis +Signum [Willelmi monachi de Archis].

(b) [Ego qui supra Rotbertus Dei gratia dux et princ]eps Normannorum
[concedo] Sanctę Trinitati et ęcclesię Fiscannensi in ipso loco Fiscanni [apud
ęcclesiam Sancti Stephani nundinam unam quę vulgo] feria dicitur omni anno
quandiu captura haringorum duraverit. Et ut [hęc mea concessio firma
maneat signi mei auctorita]te firmavi et fidelium meorum quorum inferius
nomina annotata sunt [attestatione roboravi. Hi sunt] Helias de Sancto
Sydonio, Bernardus de Brus, Willelmus +filius Girardi, et Willelmus Grenet.
Ex parte Sanctę [Trinitatis: Willelmus abbas, Iohannes cellerarius],
Willelmus Malus conductus, et Ingelrannus. Concedo etiam quoddam
pratum quod Grandis campus vocatur ad vacariam unam faciendam ad
opus monachorum.

(c) Post hęc omnia consurrexit adversum me et adversum abbatem
Fiscanni Rotbertus de Moritania filius Willelmi de Becco et in ipsa terra
quam de Sancta Trinitate et Fiscannensi abbate tenebat castrum firmavit et
servitia quę terra debebat contratenuit. At ego Deo auxiliante pariter et fidelibus meis annitentibus non solum eum conquisivi verum et castrum ipsum
destruxi simul et incendi et terram illam Gohero dedi. Quod abbas de cuius
feodo terra erat audiens me inde requisivit, dicens quod terra illa de dominio
sancti antiquitus fuerit et quod ego eam quando in Angliam transire debui
cum aliis terris ecclesię reddiderim. Hoc ego verum esse cognoscens simul
et volens ut suum sancto maneret, Fiscannum veni et terram illam cum aliis
terris ac rebus quę in alia carta annotatę sunt Sanctę Trinitati reddidi et
dedi et inde donationem hoc lignum in manus abbatis misi et utramque
cartam sigillo meo auctorizavi, et hoc ideo feci nequis de cetero existat qui
dicere possit quod terra ista de dominio sancti non fuerit et quod ego eam
ęcclesię non reddiderim et donaverim.

Signum Rotberti+comitis Signum Radulfi+ abbatis Sagii.
Ad hoc barones mei testes fuerunt Goherus, Rotbertus de Donestanvilla,
Radulfus de Grainvilla, Gislebertus filius Raineri, Willelmus filius Girardi,
Willelmus Grenet, Rotbertus filius Turstini, et Gislebertus Belet. Ex parte
Sanctę Trinitatis: Willelmus abbas, Willelmus filius Teoderici, Rogerius de
Scilletot, Ricardus Harela, Iohannis cellerarius, Willelmus Malus conductus,
Hugo de Ichelunt, Ancherus de Nevilla, Ansfredus Bordet, Ingelrannus et
Hugo Gohun.

5

1087–1091

*Robert grants to the abbey of Fécamp the land of Hugh Mursard at
Fécamp.*

A, original lost; B, copy in cartulary, MS. Rouen 1207, no. 35,
omitting the witnesses; C, MS. Lat. n. a. 2412, no. 35, from B.

Supra, Chapter II, no. 23. Probably anterior to the grant of Fécamp
to William Rufus in 1091.

Ego Robertus comes Normannie pro salute anime mee et parentum meorum do atque concedo Sancte Trinitati et domno Willelmo abbati tercio et monachis in Fiscanno Deo servientibus terram Hugonis Mursardi que est in eodem Fiscanno cum domibus et edificiis que in ea sunt, ita liberam et quietam et sine aliqua consuetudine sicut idem Hugo ipsam terram tenuit, ut eam in eternum iure hereditario possideat.

6

30 March 1088

Robert attests a charter of Ralph Fitz Anseré [1] *granting to Jumièges the allod of Beaunay with its appurtenances and the tithe of 'Anslevilla.'*

A, original in Archives of the Seine-Inférieure, *fonds* Jumièges; the entries respecting the execution of the transaction were made in the spaces left vacant by the signatures and list of witnesses. B, copy of the late twelfth century, *ibid.*; C, modern copy by A. Deville, in MS. Lat. n. a. 1243, f. 185, no. 136, where the date is wrongly given as 1087.

Supra, Chapter II, no. 24; Vernier, no. 37; cf. *Histoire de S.-Pierre de Jumièges*, ed. J. Loth, i. 218.

IN NOMINE SANCTĘ ET INDIVIDUĘ TRINITATIS. ANNO IPSO QUO GLORIOSIS-SIMUS ATQUE REVERENTISSIMUS‖ Deoque amabilis Guilelmus rex Anglorum comesque Nortmannię de ista vita nequam assumptus est et ut credimus celestem patriam consecutus est, iii. kal. Aprilis, ego Radulfus filius Anseredi stultum et vanum prospiciens et ad utilitatem meam minus proficiens quod egomet adhuc in ista vita subsistens et potestatem mei habens ut aliis precipiam post mortem meam dare quod vivens melius et utilius pro me pos-sum tribuere, dedimus ego et uxor mea Sanctę Marię et Sancto Petro Gime-giensis monachisque ibi servientibus alodium quod iure hereditario in villa quę vocatur Belnaicus [2] habebam omne sicuti trans ripam citraque ripam fluminis illius villę contra Reinaldum filium Rainerii et Bernardum partior, quod alodium uxori meę in dote dedi eam accipiens. Dedi etiam decimam Anslevillę [3] pro anima mea uxorisque meę et pro animabus domi-norum meorum ad quos hę res pertinebant, concedente et libenti animo donante domino meo Radulfo filio Rogeri Mortemaris ad quem hę res perti-nebant omne quod in his rebus habebat, accipiente ipso die propter istam donationem fraternitatem atque societatem illius loci et quindecim libras Rotomagensium recipiente ab ipsis monachis illius loci; et hoc quod ad istud alodium pertinet quod adiacet in Ulfranvilla [4] et in Bernivoldi villa; [5] et hoc

---

[1] On whom see Lot, *S.-Wandrille*, no. 43 and note.
[2] Beaunay, Seine-Inférieure, canton of Tôtes.
[3] Perhaps Anneville-sur-Seine: Vernier, i, p. cxxxiv.
[4] Offranville, Seine-Inférieure, chef-lieu de canton.
[5] Bernouville, Seine-Inférieure, canton of Offranville.

quod in duobus molendinis illius villę scilicet Belnaici habebam quod ad istud alodium non pertinebat concedimus ut perpetualiter ęcclesia Gemmeticensis possideat, scilicet in terris et in silvis et in aquis etiam et in ęcclesia et in vineis post mortem Radulfi uxorisque eius in dominio; et qui de dominio abstulerit anathema sit.

Signum Radulfi filii + Rogeri Morte maris Signum Mabilię + uxoris eius Signum Radulfi filii Anseredi + Signum uxoris eius + Signum Rogeri Sancti Laurentii militis Radulfi filii Rogeri + Signum Gisleberti Warennę + Signum Ricardi filii Richerii de Aquila + Signum Vuidonis Carcois de Arenis + Signum Vualteri de Wesneval + Signum Hugonis + Signum Bernardi Bellnaci + Willelmi archiepiscopi Rotomagensis +

Signum Rotberti comitis Normannię + Signum Hen +rici comitis fratris eius   Signum Vuillelmi comitis Ebroicensis +

Isti sunt testes ex parte Rodulfi filii Anseredi: Normannus Peignardus, Rotbertus Ivi Maisnerii, Turstenus filius Helewise, Petrus armiger eiusdem Radulfi. Ex parte monachorum: Rotbertus filius Dut, Salomon de Charecclvilla, Radulfus marescallus, Herveus filius Ricardi Oseii, Durandus cellararius, Gislebertus coquulus, Radulfus vastans granum, Herbertus Maloei, Iohannes Grossus, Rotbertus presbiter, et alii multi.

Signum Engelrani filio (*sic*) Hilberti + Vuilelmi cubicularii + Signum Ricardi Bustelli + Signum Engelranni capellani + Signum Iohannis militis + Signum Constantini militis + Benedicti archidiaconi + Fulberti archidiaconi + Ursonis archidiaconi +

Et Guarinus telonarius eiusdem Radulfi recepit easdem quindecim libras Rotomagensium iussu eiusdem Radulfi in villa que dicitur Sancti Victoris[6] et Fulco mercator numeravit. Petrus Bassum villę famulus Radulfi Mortemaris saisivit monachos Gemmeticenses de eodem alodio iussu eiusdem Radulfi videntibus et audientibus hominibus illius villę vidente etiam et audiente Hoello homine eiusdem ęcclesię Sancti Petri Gemmeticensis. Rogerius prior eiusdem loci et Rotbertus filius Dodonis Rodulfusque Montis Durclari cum eo receperunt istam saisitionem et inde habuerunt decem et septem denarios.

7

1091–1095, at Lisieux

Robert confirms a charter of Ralph Fitz Anseré granting to Jumièges half of Étables and the custom of its wood, and invests the monastery therewith.

A, original in Archives of the Seine-Inférieure, the charter proper (*a*) being accompanied by a long and narrow strip of parchment containing (*b*); modern copies in MSS. Lat. 5424, p. 38, and n. a. 1245, f. 189.

[6] Saint-Victor-l'Abbaye, Seine-Inférieure, canton of Tôtes.

Supra, Chapter II, no. 25; Vernier, no. 38. The date is fixed by the accession of Bishop Serlo in 1091 and the death of Abbot Guntard in 1095; Roland of Dol received the pallium in 1093.

(*a*) IN NOMINE SANCTĘ ET INDIVIĘ (*sic*) TRINITATIS PATRIS ET FILII ET SPIRITUS SANCTI.‖ Ego Rodulfus filius Anseredi et uxor mea Girberga medietatem villę de Stablis[1] tam in agris quam in aquis et unum molendinum providentes saluti nostrarum animarum Sanctę MARIAE Gemmetici pari consensu donamus. Denique omnem consuetudinem quam in silva habemus videlicet pasturam nostris animalibus et ligna nobis nostrisque famulis ad calefaciendum necessaria prefatę ęcclesię similiter concedimus. Hanc autem donationem ut inposterum rata foret Rotbertus dux Northmannorum inpresentiarum baronum suorum Luxovii confirmavit. Testes denique huius donationis hi sunt: Signum + Roberti comitis S. Willelmi + archiepiscopi S. Gisleberti + episcopi predictę urbis S. Odonis + episcopi Baioc[ensis] S. Gisleberti + episcopi Ebroic[ensis] S. Serlonis + episcopi Sagii S. Rodulfi Anseredi + S. Girberge uxoris eius S. Roberti comitis Mellent S. Ingelranni + S. Rodulfi Toenei S. Rodulfi Mortui Maris S. Walteri Broc + S. Roberti fili Ansch[etilli] + S. Rol + landi episcopi de Dol Willelmi de Bret[olio] + S. Ricar + di archidiaconi S. Walteri + S. Ful + berti archidiaconi S. Osberni + abbatis[2] + + +

(*b*) DONATIONEM DE STABLIS ROBERTUS DUX Northmannorum PER HOC LIGNUM misit ad Sanctam MARIAM GEMMETICI. Testes autem huius rei sunt: Engelrannus filius Ilberti, Raulfus de Mortuo Mari, Vualterus de Quercu, Robertus filius Anschetilli, Vualterius Broc. Hęc denique facta sunt apud Lexovium per eiusdem loci abbatem Guntardum.

[1] Étables, Seine-Inférieure, canton of Longueville.
[2] Of Bernai.

APPENDIX F

UNPUBLISHED CHARTERS OF HENRY I

WITH two exceptions, the following documents have not been indicated or analyzed by others. It was planned to print a fuller selection from Henry I's unpublished charters, but the difficulties of copying and collation under present conditions have led to the omission of many documents of which published analyses are available. Other charters and writs of Henry are printed above in the text and notes of Chapter III and on p. 223 of Chapter VI.

1

1106–1107, at Rouen

Charter of William, archbishop of Rouen, confirming, with Henry's assent, the church of Notre-Dame at Saint-Sever to Bec as the abbot and monks proved their right before the bishops and barons of Normandy.

A, original, formerly sealed *sur double queue* and now much damaged by gallstones, in Archives of the Seine-Inférieure, *fonds* Bonne-Nouvelle; B, modern copy in MS. Lat. 13905, f. 18v, from which the illegible portions have been supplied; C, modern copy in MS. Lat. 10055, f. 82, ' ex chartulario Beccensi.' Cf. Porée, *Bec*, i. 396, note 2.

The date is fixed by the mention of Thorold, bishop of Bayeux, who is last found attesting in a charter of 7 November 1106 (*Gallia Christiana*, xi. instr. 127), and whose successor came in in 1107. On Thorold's biography see W. Tavernier, in the *Zeitschrift für französische Sprache und Litteratur*, xxxvi ff.

Ego Willelmus Dei gratia Rotomagensis archiepiscopus concedo et confirmo ut ę[cclesia Sanctę Marię Becci iure hereditario] possideat ecclesiam Sanctę Marię de Ermentrudisvilla [1] sicut Willelmus abbas eiusdem loci et monachi deraciocinati sunt eam in capitulo [Sanctę Mar]ię Rotomagensis presente me et episcopis et baronibus Normannie, concedente domino nostro Henrico rege Anglorum et annuentibus supradictis episcopis et baronibus, Turoldo videlicet Baiocensi episcopo et Turgiso Abrincensi et Roberto de Belismo et Roberto comite de Mellent et Eustachio Bononiensi et Henrico comite Augensi et archidiaconis nostris, Fulberto videlicet. Benedicto, [Ricardo, Ursello, et quam plu]ribus aliis clericis [et laicis].

[1] Émendreville, now Saint-Sever, a suburb of Rouen.

2

After 7 October 1118, at Arganchy

Notification by Henry that, with the advice of the archbishops of Canterbury and Rouen and bishops and abbots, he has decided the controversy between Savigny and Saint-Étienne of Caen concerning Mortain.

A, original, with incisions for *double queue*, in the library of Rouen, MS. 3122, no. 2; B, cartulary of Savigny, in Archives of the Manche, f. 6, no. 5. Printed in *Gallia Christiana*, xi. instr. 111, where a line of the text and most of the witnesses are omitted; translated in C. Auvry, *Histoire de la congrégation de Savigny*, i. 290–292. Cf. Deville, *Analyse*, p. 47. The date is fixed by the council of Rouen, 7 October 1118 (Ordericus, iv. 329; cf. Round, *Geoffrey de Mandeville*, p. 423, note).

Ego Henricus Dei gratia rex Anglorum et dux Normannorum, cum archiepiscopis Radulfo Cantuariensi et Gaufrido Rotomagensi et episcopis Ricardo Baiocensi, Turgiso Abrincatensi, Rogerio Constantiensi, Willelmo Exoniensi, Ildeberto Cenomanensi, cum abbatibus etiam et aliis religiosis viris compluribus qui nobiscum huic diffinitioni presentes interfuerunt, consulentes et presentium memorię et futurorum scientię, omnibus catholicę pacis et unitatis cultoribus nostrarum beneficio litterarum manifestare decrevimus qualiter per Dei misericordiam et nostram instantiam inter Eudonem Cadumensium fratrum abbatem et Vitalem Saviniensis monasterii fundatorem super Moritoniensi elemosina quam eidem fratri Vitali ad honorem Sanctę Trinitatis pro amore Dei Willelmus comes contulerat, pacta sit et celebrata concordia . . . [as in *Gallia Christiana*]

Testes enim ex utraque parte subscribi precepimus Stephanum Moritoniensem comitem, Ricardum comitem, Rotbertum filium regis, Hamelinum Meduanensem, Willelmum de Albineio et Nigellum et Hunfridum de Albin[eio], Willelmum camerarium de Tancarvilla, Willelmum Patricium, Thomam de Sancto Iohanne, Willelmum Piperellum de Airam, Gaufridum de Clintona, Rotbertum de Haia Putei, Hugonem de Guilleio, Edwardum Salesberiensem, Rannulfum cancellarium, Iohannem Baiocensis episcopi filium, Rotbertum Peccatum, Gaufridum capellanum, Walterum de Culleio, Rannulfum de Dusseio.

Hec diffinitio fuit diffinita et hec carta sigillata ante me apud Argenteium. Teste (*sic*) episcopo Luxoviensi Iohanne et Eudone Cadumensium monachorum abbate et monachis Wino de Allemania et Nigello et comite de Pertica Rotroco et Rogero Marmione et Ricardo capellano et Symone de Molins et Hamelino de Lesclusa.

3

1119, at Rouen 'in thalamo regis'

Confirmation of charter of Robert, earl of Leicester, on behalf of Bec and Saint-Nicaise of Meulan.

A, original lost; B, modern copy in Bibliothèque Nationale, Collection du Vexin, iii. 171, no. 246.

Anno ab incarnatione millesimo centesimo decimo nono ego Robertus comes Leicestrie do ecclesie Sancte Marie Becci et ecclesie Sancti Nigasii de Mellento decem libras et quinque solidatas terre in manerio de Pinpra in escambium pro terra Radulfi Piquet [1](?) de Blinchefeld que reddebat viii libras et quinque solidos, et pro quadraginta solidos quos debebat pater meus eidem ecclesie Sancti Nigasii in manerio de Hungrefort.[2] Et hoc feci pro deliberatione anime patris mei. Ego Henricus rex Dei gratia rex Anglorum hoc donum concedo et signo et sigillo meo confirmo. Testes Galerannus comes Mellenti, Nigellus de Albegneio, Guillelmus de Tancarvilla, Gaufridus de Magnavilla, Willelmus filius Roberti, Odardus dapifer de Mellento, Ra. Pinter [3](?), Gaufridus de Curvilla, in thalamo regis apud Rothomagum.

4

1117–1119, at Rouen

Writ confirming the nuns of Saint-Amand in their livery at Vaudreuil (Eure).[1]

A, original lost; B, copy in hand of the twelfth century, at the end of quasi-original of foundation charter in Archives of the Seine-Inférieure; C, *vidimus* of Philip IV in 1313, *ibid.*, and Archives Nationales, JJ. 49, f. 26v.

H. rex Anglorum vicecomiti de valle Rodolii salutem. Precipio quod moniales de Sancto Amando ita bene et plenarie habeant liberationem de elemosina mea Rodolii sicut unquam aliquis antecessor illarum eam melius habuit. Et hoc habeant a die illa qua Iohannes Rubi presbiter antecessor earum fuit mortuus in antea. Testibus Radulfo archiepiscopo Cantuariensi et Rannulfo cancellario, apud Rothomagum.

[1] MS. *Piq̄c* followed by a blank.
[2] Pimperne, Blandford (co. Dorset), Hungerford (co. Berks).
[3] MS. *Pit'*.
[1] Cf. Stapleton, i. 111.

5

1106–1120, at Rouen

Order to Hugh de Montfort to restore to the abbot of Bec certain lands of Saint-Philbert-sur-Risle and the church of Saint-Ouen[-de-Flancourt] (Eure).[1]

A, original lost; B, modern copy in MS. Lat. 13905, f. 83, with omissions.

H. rex Anglorum Hugoni de Monteforti salutem. Precipio tibi ut facias resaisiri abbatem de Becco de viginti acris terre que pertinent ecclesie Sancti Philiberti et de ecclesia Sancti Audoeni quas Galefridus dapifer tuus saisivit. Et ecclesiam et decimam fac eum tenere in pace et quiete. . . . Nolo enim ut quis eum placitet de aliqua re unde fuit saisitus die qua dedi tibi honorem de Monfort nisi coram me. Apud Rothomagum.

6

1124, at Évreux

Confirmation to Savigny of the gift of Robert de Tôtes in Escures (Calvados).

A, original sealed *sur simple queue*, in Archives of the Manche, a considerable portion of the seal, in brown wax, still remaining; B, cartulary of Savigny, *ibid.*, f. 51, no. 197, where it is preceded (no. 196) by the charter of Robert, witnessed by Richard, bishop of Bayeux, and dated 1124. Cf. Auvry, *Histoire de la congrégation de Savigny*, i. 404.

H. rex Angl[orum] episcopo Baioc[ensi] et omnibus baronibus et fidelibus suis de Beisin salutem. Sciatis me concessisse ecclesię Sanctę Trinitatis de Savinneio et monachis ibi Deo servientibus donationem terrę quam Rotbertus de Tostis habebat in villa de Scuris et quam Rotbertus Gaufr[ido] abbati et ipsis monachis dedit et concessit in elemosinam concessu Ricardi episcopi Baioc[ensis] de cuius feodo terra ipsa est. Et volo et firmiter precipio ut bene et in pace et honorifice teneant sicut predictus Rotbertus eam eis dedit et concessit in possessionem perpetuam.

T[estibus] Turstino Eboracensi archiepiscopo et fratre eius Oino Ebroicensi episcopo et Iohanne Baioc[ensi], apud Ebroicas.

[1] Saint-Ouen-de-Flancourt, granted to Bec and Saint-Philbert in 1097 (Porée, *Bec*, i. 407), seems more probable than Saint-Ouen-du-Bois-Toustain, which also belonged to Bec (now La Noë-Poulain: Le Prévost, *Eure*, ii. 472).

7

1118–1126, at Rouen

Confirmation to the abbot and monks of Lire of the mills and forge of La Neuve-Lire (Eure).

A, original lost; B, copy in lost cartulary of the thirteenth century formerly " parmi les mss. de la bibliothèque du collège des jésuites de Paris "; C, copy from B by Dom Lenoir at Semilly, xxiii. 453, lxxii. 329; D, extracts from B in Collection Moreau, xlvii. 65.

Robert became earl of Leicester on the death of his father, Robert of Meulan, in 1118; and Ralph of Toeny was dead by 1126 (Ordericus, ii. 404).

Henricus rex Anglie G[aufrido] archiepiscopo Rothomagensi et omnibus episcopis et iusticiariis et abbatibus et baronibus et fidelibus suis totius Normannie salutem. Sciatis me concessisse Deo et ecclesie Sancte Marie de Lyra et abbati et monachis ibi Deo servientibus per petitionem comitis Roberti de Leicestria et Guheri de Morevilla et concessionem eorum molendina de nova Lira et forgiam in eadem villa in elemosinam sicut Radulfus de Witot ea eis reddidit et concessit in elemosinam. Et volo et firmiter precipio ut abbas ea ita bene et in pace et honorifice et quiete in elemosinam ipse et monachi sui teneant sicut ecclesia illa melius et honorificentius tenet aliam elemosinam suam et sicut predictus Radulfus ea eis concessit et reddidit.

Testibus Oino episcopo Ebroicensi et Iohanne episcopo Luxoviensi et Radulfo de Todeneio et Radulfo pincerna et Roberto de Novo Burgo et Ernaldo de Bosco, apud Rothomagum.

8

1127 (?), after 26 August

Confirmation of the gifts of Jordan de Sai and his wife in founding the abbey of Aunay.

A, original lost; B, *vidimus* of Philip VI in 1335, Archives Nationales, JJ. 69, no. 100. Cf. *vidimus* of 1347 in Archives of the Calvados; MS. Lat. n. a. 1245, f. 28.

If the date is correctly given in the *vidimus*, it should replace the date of 1131 usually given for the foundation of Aunay: *Gallia Christiana*, xi. 443; G. Le Hardy, *Étude sur Aunay-sur-Odon*, in *Bulletin des Antiquaires de Normandie*, xix (1897). Otherwise we must emend MCXXXII.

In nomine sancte et individue trinitatis. Ego Henricus Dei gratia rex Anglorum et dux Normannorum anno M°.C°.XXVII°. ab incarnatione Domini, pro salute anime mee ac patris et matris mee uxorumque mearum et prolis mee, donacionem quam fecit Jordains de Saieio et Lucia uxor eius et filii sui, videlicet Engerannus, Gilebertus, Petrus, concessu Stephani comitis Moretoniensis et auctoritate Richardi Baiocensis episcopi, pro animabus suis et antecessorum suorum, ecclesie Sancte Trinitatis de Alneio et domno Viviano abbati et monachis concedo et regali auctoritate confirmo: videlicet ad Alneium partem foreste que est inter inferiorem viam et torrentem, ubi et ecclesiam predictis monachis construxerunt, et ex altera parte eiusdem torrentis de propinquiori terra decem acras et decimam molendinorum suorum et peccorum; et ecclesiam de Herovilla[1]; et in Rinvilla quod habet in ecclesia et in decima; et ecclesias de Cenilleio sicut Gislebertus filius Gunduini possedit, a quo predictus Jordains habuit concessione Richardi Constanciensis episcopi; insuper et terram elemosinariam que pertinet eisdem ecclesiis, et decimam molendinorum de Roumilleio, et ad Haneiras terram duos modios frumenti reddentem, et in Anglia de redditu sexaginta solidos sterlingorum. Hec autem supradicta precipio ut quiete et libere possideant monachi, et hoc propria manu signo sancte crucis corroboro.

9

1123–1129, at Vaudreuil

Notification to the bishop of Worcester and the sheriff and men of Worcestershire that Henry has confirmed to Walter de Beauchamp the land granted him by Adeliza, wife of Urse of Abbetot.

Subsequent to 1123, being witnessed by Geoffrey as chancellor, and anterior to 1130, when Roger 'gener Alberti' was dead (Pipe Roll, p. 39). Eyton (British Museum, Add. MSS. 31941, f. 58, and 31943, f. 79) dates it *ca.* October 1128.

A, original lost; B, copy by Dugdale in his MSS. in the Bodleian Library, L. 18, f. 41, copied for me by the kindness of Professor H. L. Gray.

H. rex Anglorum episcopo Wigornie et vicecomiti et omnibus baronibus et fidelibus suis Francis et Anglis de Wirecestresira salutem. Sciatis me concessisse Waltero de Bellocampo terram que fuit Adeliz uxoris Ursonis de Abbetot, sicut ipsa Adeliz eam ei concessit. Et volo et firmiter precipio ut teneat ita bene et in pace et honorifice et quiete de omnibus consuetudinibus, sicut Urso antecessor suus unquam melius et honorificentius et quietius tenuit in vita sua, cum socha et sacha et tol et theam et infangeneteof et cum omnibus aliis consuetudinibus suis cum quibus Urso unquam melius tenuit, in bosco et plano, in aqua et terra et omnibus aliis locis.

[1] The places mentioned are Hérouville, Ranville, and Asnières in Calvados, and Cenilly and Rémilly in La Manche.

Testibus Gaufrido cancellario et Roberto de sigillo et Willelmo Pevrello Dovre et Willelmo filio Odonis et Willelmo de Pontearcarum et Pevrello de Bellocampo et Pagano de Bellocampo et Roberto filio Willelmi de Stochis et Willelmo Malotraverso et Roberto de Monteviron et Gaufrido de Abbetot et Roberto filio Radulphi de Hastingis et Roberto de Guernai et Roberto filio Fulcheri et Rogero genero Alberti et Iohanne hostiario et Henrico del Broc. Apud Rodolium.

10

February 1131, at Rouen

Grant to Séez cathedral of the fief of William Goth at Laleu (Orne).

A, original lost; B, copy in *Livre rouge* of Séez, f. 77, formerly in possession of the bishop; C, copy from B in MS. Lat. 11058, f. 3.

Henricus Dei gracia rex Anglorum et dux Normannorum archiepiscopo Rothomagensi et episcopis et abbatibus, baronibus et omnibus fidelibus et filiis sancte ecclesie per Normanniam constitutis [1] salutem. Sciatis quod ego Henricus per graciam Dei rex Anglorum et dux Normannorum dedi in elemosinam et concessi pro salute animarum patris et matris mee et parentum meorum et pro remissione peccatorum meorum et pro statu et incolumitate regni nostri et ducatus Normanie Deo et ecclesie sanctorum martirum Gervasii et Prothasii de Sagio in dominium ecclesie et proprium usum episcopi totum feodum Alodii quem tenuit Guillelmus Goth: hoc est quicquid ipse Guillelmus Goth habuit inter Sartam et Tancham tam in terris quam in pratis et aquis et molendinis et silvestribus [2] nemoribus et hominibus et theloneis et consuetudinibus et omnibus omnino rebus, sicut idem Guillelmus quietius et liberius [3] tenuit tempore patris mei. Quem feodum ego emi de mea propria pecunia de Avelina nepte ipsius Guillelmi et Ricardo de Luceio filio ipsius Aveline et iustis heredibus predicti Alodii, quod ipsi, Avelina scilicet et Ricardus et iusti heredes eiusdem feodi, eum in manu Roberti filii comitis Gloescestrie videntibus multis reddiderunt et postea vendicionem istam coram me cognoverunt et confirmaverunt et eam quietam de se et suis heredibus clamaverunt. Et ego predictum feodum Alodii ita liberum et quietum ab eis et omnibus heredibus concedo et confirmo sanctis martiribus Gervasio et Prothasio et episcopo in elemosinam sicut supra dictum est.

Hanc ergo donacionem meam factam anno ab incarnacione Domini millesimo centesimo trigesimo primo laudo et concedo, confirmo et illi [4] ecclesie in perpetuum obtinendam regia potestate et a Deo michi auctoritate collata corroboro. Teste presencia et audiencia Hugonis archiepiscopi Rothomagensis,[5] Iohannis Lexoviensis, Audini [6] Ebroicensis episcopi, Richardi episcopi Baiocensis, Iohannis episcopi tunc Sagiensis, Roberti de sigillo et Nigelli nepotis episcopi de Saresberia, Roberti comitis Gloescestre

---

[1] MS. *constitute.*
[2] MS. *silvestris.*
[3] MS. *quietus et liberus.*
[4] MS. *ille.*
[5] MS. *Hugone archid[iacono] Rothomagensi.*
[6] MS. *Actini.*

filii mei, Guillelmi comitis Warenne et Walerani comitis Mellenti et Roberti comitis Legrecestrie, Roberti de Haia dapiferi et Hugonis Bigot dapiferi et Rabelli cammerarii et Brientii filii comitis conestabularii et Gaufridi de Clintone.[7] Apud Rothomagum mense Februario.

11

Summer 1131, at Dieppe

Confirmation of the establishment of Augustinian canons in Séez cathedral, grant of land at Brighthampton, and confirmation of lands and churches in Normandy and of fixed revenues in the farm of Argentan and the tolls of Exmes and Falaise.

A, original lost; B, collated copy therefrom in 1521 also lost; C, copy from B in *Coppies de tiltres du chartraire* (1633) at Alençon, MS. 177, f. 98; D, copy in *Livre rouge* of Séez, f. 69; E, copy from D in MS. Lat. 11058, f. 8. Extracts in *E. H. R.*, xxiv. 223; Ordericus, iv. 471, note; *supra*, Chapter I, note 174; Chapter III, p. 106. Cf. charter of Bishop John, MS. Lat. 11058, f. 5; incomplete in *Gallia Christiana*, xi. instr. 160.

In nomine sancte et individue trinitatis patris et filii et spiritus sancti amen. Henricus rex Anglorum et dux Normannorum archiepiscopis, episcopis, abbatibus, comitibus, baronibus, et omnibus fidelibus suis tocius Anglie et Normannie salutem. Quoniam regie sublimitatis insignia gerimus et iura Christiane religionis et solicitudinem ecclesiastice defensionis administramus, oportet nos interim omnibus sancte ecclesie filiis benefacere precipueque pauperibus et in Christo religiose viventibus misericorditer subvenire, et quorum preces et vite sinceritas terram elevat celum inclinat unaque iungit superius, eorum quieti atque necessitatibus clementer intendamus ut omnipotentis Dei servicio valeant vacare liberius. Quapropter Sagiensem ecclesiam temporalibus et spiritualibus bonis admodum desolatam ad normam rectioris vite studuimus erigere et ad lucem vere religionis excitare, et quoniam reverende memorie papa Honorius per apostolicas litteras in remissionem peccatorum meorum mihi iniunxerat ut ad regulares canonicos in ecclesia Sagiensi introducendos intenderem et eos de meis facultatibus misericorditer sustentarem; idcirco fratribus regularibus in ipsa Sagiensi ecclesia Dei gratia iam introductis et sub regula Beati Augustini omnipotenti Deo servire studentibus et professis, ipsis inquam eorumque successoribus concedimus atque confirmamus in predicta Sagiensi ecclesia pontificalis sedis potestatem libere et canonice Domino servienti atque ut post decessionem aliorum canonicorum in communes usus regularium statim transeant beneficia prebendarum, ita quod ipsis viventibus constituti redditus eorum nullatenus minuantur.

[7] MS. *Dinī.*

Ipsis etiam fratribus regularibus damus et confirmamus in regno nostro in Anglia decem libratas terre in manerio nostro de Bentona, videlicet Bristelmetonam [1] que est [2] membrum ipsius manerii, et volo et regia auctoritate confirmo ut bene et honorifice et in pace et libere et quiete teneant semper et in perpetuum de hidagiis et geldis et dangeldis et auxiliis et operacionibus, cum socha et sacha et tholl et theam et infangenteof et omnibus consuetudinibus et libertatibus et placitis et querelis et omnibus rebus cum quibus ego tenebam dum esset in meo dominio, et homines eorum placient in hallmoto suo de Bristelmetona in submonicione eorumdem canonicorum vel ministrorum suorum.

Ipsis quoque fratribus regularibus damus et confirmamus quindecim libras Rothomagensis monete quas dedi in dedicacione ipsius ecclesie in unoquoque anno habendas, scilicet septem libras et decem solidos in teloneo meo de Falesia et septem libras et decem solidos in teloneo meo de Oximis. Concedimus etiam atque confirmamus predictis fratribus regularibus donationem eis factam ecclesiarum de Bellimensi pago cum omnibus rebus ad eas pertinentibus, scilicet ecclesiam Sancti Iohannis de Foresta et ecclesiam Sancti Quintini.[3]

Ad dominium autem et proprium usum Sagiensis episcopi damus et confirmamus totum feodum Alodii [4] quem tenuit Guillelmus Ghot, hoc est quicquid ipse habuit inter Sartam et Tancham tam in terris quam in pratis et aquis et molendinis et silvis et hominibus et teloneis et consuetudinibus et omnibus omnino rebus, sicut idem Guillelmus quietius et liberius tenuit tempore patris mei; quem feodum ego emi de nostra propria pecunia de Avelina nepte ipsius Guillelmi et Ricardo de Luccio filio ipsius Aveline et de iustis heredibus predicti Alodii, et ipsi, Avelina scilicet et Ricardus, et iusti heredes eiusdem feodi eum in manu Roberti filii nostri comitis Glocestrie videntibus multis reddiderunt et postea coram me vendicionem istam cognoverunt et confirmaverunt et eam quietam de se et suis heredibus concesserunt. Et ego predictum feodum Alodii ita liberum et quietum ab eis et omnibus heredibus concedo et confirmo sanctis martyribus Gervasio et Protasio in dominium et proprios usus episcopi.

Quecumque etiam preter supradicta ecclesia Sagiensis hodie[2] possidet tam ad proprium usum episcopi quam ad usum canonicorum, hoc est ad usum episcopi dimidietatem burgi Sagii cum terra et pratis que in dominio habet episcopus circa civitatem et dimidietatem telonei ipsius civitatis et villam Floreii [5] cum omnibus suis appenditiis, preterea in Bellimensi pago villam

---

[1] Bampton, Brighthampton (co. Oxford). The land was in the hamlet of Hardwicke, as appears from the heading in the cartularies: ' Charta et confirmatio Henrici regis Anglie de redditibus canonicorum regularium in ecclesia Sagiensi et redditibus eorundem canonicorum in Normannia et in Anglia apud Hardric (E: Hardore) et apud Bristelametone.' Cf. Pipe Roll 31 Henry I, p. 52, from which it would appear that the ten librates were originally in Essex or Herts.

[2] Om. C.

[3] Saint-Jean-de-la-Forêt and Saint-Quentin-le-Petit (Orne).

[4] Laleu (Orne).

[5] Fleuré (Orne).

Sancti Frogentii,[6] que omnia antiquitus tenuit episcopus Sagiensis; ad usum vero canonicorum Bodevillam,[7] [ecclesias de Condeto et de Estretz,][8] et decimam telonei Sagii, scilicet illius partis que est episcopi, et partem mei que dicitur Croleium,[9] et terram que est apud Lurieium,[10] que omnia tempore patris nostri canonici eiusdem ecclesie tenuerunt; preterea duodecim libras in firma nostra de Argentomo et viginti et unum solidos in teloneo eiusdem ville et sexaginta solidos et decem denarios de teloneo meo de Oximis, que dederunt pater meus et mater mea ecclesie Sagiensi ad victum canonicorum duorum, quod antiquitus in elemosinam statutum fuerat.

Hec, inquam, que supradicta sunt et quecumque in futurum nostra vel successorum meorum concessione iuste poterunt adquirere ipsis, scilicet episcopo et canonicis, concedimus et confirmamus. Preterea consuetudines et quietudines quas a tempore patris mei habuerunt tam episcopus quam canonici in terra et in forestis Guillelmi de Belismo ipsis, episcopo scilicet et fratribus regularibus, concedimus atque confirmamus. Quecumque ergo persona contra huius nostre donacionis et constitucionis decretum venire tentaverit, secundo tercioque commonita, nisi digne satisfecerit, regie maiestatis rea nostre vindicte subiacebit.

Et ut hec nostra donatio et constitutio certior habeatur et firmior, propria manu nostra atque sigillo nostro muniri fecimus. Facta est autem atque confirmata hec pagina apud Diepam anno ab incarnatione dominica millesimo centesimo trigesimo primo, me Henrico in Anglia regnante et Normannorum ducatum tenente, Innocentio papa secundo Ausonie cathedre presidente. S. Hugonis archiepiscopi,[11] Audini episcopi Ebroicensis, Ioannis episcopi Lexoviensis, Roberti de Haia dapiferi, Unfredi de Bohun dapiferi, Rabelli camerarii, Guillielmi filii Odonis conestabularii, Guillelmi Maledocti[12] camerarii.

12

After August 1131, at Waltham

Grant to Séez cathedral of ten librates of land, namely Brighthampton, from the king's manor of Bampton.

A, original lost; B, copy therefrom in 1521 also lost; C, copy from B in MS. Alençon 177, f. 103; D, copy in *Livre rouge*, f. 71; E, copy from D in MS. Lat. 11058, f. 11.

---

[6] Saint-Fulgent-des-Ormes (Orne).

[7] This I have not identified.

[8] 'Ecclesias . . . Estretz' is corrected in E in Delisle's hand from 'cum omnibus appendiciis suis,' which is also the reading of C. I do not know the source of Delisle's correction, unless it be a marginal note in D. These churches, Condé-sur-Ifs and Estrées-la-Campagne (Calvados), were both dependencies of Séez cathedral: Longnon, *Pouillés de la province de Rouen*, p. 232.

[9] *Goleium*, E.

[10] Lieurey (Calvados) ?

[11] *Archidiaconi*, CE.

[12] *Maledicti*, C.

Henricus rex Anglie archiepiscopis, episcopis, abbatibus, comitibus, baronibus, vicecomitibus, et omnibus ministris et fidelibus suis Francis et Anglis salutem. Sciatis me dedisse et concessisse ecclesie sanctorum martyrum Gervasii et Protasii de Sagio ad usum canonicorum in dedicatione ipsius ecclesie decem libratas terre de manerio meo de Bentona, videlicet Bristelmetonam que est membrum ipsius manerii, cum omnibus appendiciis suis pro remissione peccatorum meorum et pro animabus patris et matris mee et predecessorum meorum et successorum meorum et pro statu regni nostri. Et volo et firmiter precipio ut bene, honorifice, et in pace et libere et quiete teneant semper et in perpetuum de hidagiis et geldis et danegeldis et auxiliis et operationibus, cum socha et sacha et toll et theam et infangeteof et omnibus consuetudinibus et libertatibus et placitis et querelis et omnibus rebus cum quibus ego tenebam dum esset in meo dominio, in terris et aquis et pratis et pascuis et molendinis et nemoribus et in plano et in omnibus locis, et homines sui placitent in hallimoto suo de Bristelmetona in submonicione canonicorum Sagii vel ministrorum suorum.

Testibus Guilielmo archiepiscopo Cantuariensi et Turstino archiepiscopo Eboracensi et Alexandro episcopo Lincolniensi et Henrico episcopo Wi[n]toniensi et Gilberto episcopo Londiniensi et Rogerio episcopo Salesberiensi et Gaufrido cancellario et Roberto de sigillo et Roberto comite Glocestrie et Waleranno comite de Mellent et Hugone Bigot dapifero et Unfredo de Bouhun dapifero et Milone de Gloecestria et Roberto de Olleio et Pagano filio Ioannis et Eustachio filio Ioannis et Henrico de Ferrariis et Gaufrido filio Pagani et Richardo Basset. Apud Waltham videntibus et audientibus istis confirmata est hec pagina anno ab incarnatione Domini millesimo centesimo trigesimo primo.

13

1107–1133, at Westminster

Order to William of Pont de l'Arche to deliver, on the oath of the men of Bosham, thirty solidates of land in Walton (co. Sussex) in exchange for land which the king has given to Notre-Dame-du-Pré.

A, original lost; B, copy in Public Record Office, Cartae Antiquae, R. 22.

H. rex Anglie Willelmo de Pontearcharum salutem. Libera Willelmo filio Aernulfi .xxx. solidatas terre per sacramentum hominum vicinitatis de Boseham, et hoc de illis .l. solidatas terre quas Robertus tenebat in Waletona, pro escambio terre sue quam ego dedi Sancte Marie de Prato. Et precipio quod ita bene et honorifice et quiete teneat eam sicut melius et honorabilius tenuit terram suam de Normannia. Teste episcopo Saresberie apud Wesmonasterium.

14

1106–1135, or 1154–1173

*Charter of Henry I or Henry II confirming to the monks of Conches
free election and freedom from customs in England and at Dieppe.*

A, original lost; B, incomplete copy in *Coutumier* of Dieppe, Archives of the Seine-Inférieure, G. 851, f. 59.

Henricus rex Anglorum, etc. Sciatis me concessisse et presenti carta mea
confirmasse pro salute anime mee et antecessorum meorum monachis et
ecclesie[1] Sancti Petri de Castellionis domino servientibus liberam et quietam
ellectionem abbatis secundam regulam Sancti Benedicti et quod homines
eorum in Anglia manentes sint liberi et quieti de omnibus consuetudinibus
et querelis ad me pertinentibus. Et in Normannia apud portum qui vocatur
Deppa sint [2] monachi et omnes res eorum et proprii famuli liberi et quieti de
omni passagio et de omni consuetudine in villa, et de omnibus hominibus
eorum ibi manentibus habeant dicti monachi les euces,[3] et si homines eorum
habuerint naves in mari piscantes, quicquid de navibus illis ad me pertinet
amore Dei concedo predictis monachis. *In verbis predictis est tota libertas que
in carta continetur.*

15

1107–1135, at Argentan

*Writ directing that the monks of Troarn shall not be impleaded concern-
ing the castle church at Vire by the monks of La Couture, who defaulted in
their suit before the king at Argentan.*

A, original lost; B, copy therefrom (' sigillata est ') in *Chartrier
rouge*, MS. Lat. 10086, f. 40v.

H. rex Anglorum omnibus baronibus, etc., totius Normannie salutem.
Precipio ne monachi de Truarcio mittantur in placitum aliquando de ecclesia de Vira quam dedi eis in elemosina propter clamorem monachorum de
Cultura, quoniam apud Argent[omum] coram me defecerunt de clamore
quam mihi fecerant, etc. Et ideo per finem iusti iudicii remansit monachis
de Truarcio eadem ecclesia de Vira. Teste H[amone] de Falesia apud
Argent[omum].

16

1107–1135, at Rouen

Writ of protection for Saint-Père of Chartres.

A, original, formerly sealed *sur simple queue*, in MS. Lat. 9221, no. 7.

H. rex Angl[orum] arch[iepiscopo] Roth[omagensi] et ep[iscop]is et omnibus baron[ibus] suis Norm[annie] sal[utem]. Precipio quod abbas S. Petri

---

[1] MS. *ecclesia.*   [2] MS. *sine.*   [3] *ues ?*

Carn[otensis] et monachi teneant ecclesias et terras et elemosinas et omnes decimas et redditus suos de Norm[annia] et omnes quietat[iones] suas ita bene et in pace et honorifice sicut melius tenuerunt tempore patris mei et meo et sicut iuste tenere debuerint. Et prohibeo ne ullus eis super hoc quicquam forifaciat. T[este] ep[iscop]o Lex[oviensi] apud Rothom[agum].[1]

17

1107–1135, at Rouen

Grant to the chapter of Rouen of rights in the forest of Aliermont and the king's share of pleas and forfeitures from the men of Saint-Vaast-d'-Équiqueville and Angreville (Seine-Inférieure).

A, original lost; B, copy in the *Cartulaire de Philippe d'Alençon* in Archives of the Seine-Inférieure, G. 7, p. 792; C, copy in MS. Baluze lxxvii. 123. Round, no. 8.

The name of Robert the *vicomte* places the charter in the earlier part of Henry's reign.

Henricus Dei gratia rex Anglie dux Normannorum archiepiscopo Rothomagensi omnibusque comitibus baronibus et iusticiariis Normannie salutem. Sciatis me dedisse ecclesie Beate Marie Rothomagensi in elemosinam quod decanus eiusdem ecclesie et canonicus qui habet prebendam de Angerville habeant in foresta nostra Dalihermont omnes consuetudines suas liberas et quietas de vivo iacente et mortuo stante et ligna ad herbergagia sibi et hominibus eorum et pasnagium et herbagium et omnes redditus foreste et quicquid ad me pertinet in placitis et catallis forefactis in misericordiis de omnibus de Sancto Vedasto et de Angervilla.

Testibus Iohanne episcopo Lexoviensi, Roberto vicecomite, apud Rothomagum.

18

Ca. 1128–1135

Writ of protection for Saint-Martin of Séez.
A, original lost; B, modern copy in MS. Fr. 18953, p. 45.

Henricus rex Anglorum Odoni vicecomiti de Pembroq salutem. Precipio tibi quod facias abbati et monachos de Sagio tenere omnes res suas in ecclesiis, terris, decimis, elemosinis, et omnibus aliis ita bene et in pace et iuste sicut tenuerunt tempore Arnulphi et Vilfridi episcopi et Walteri Glocesteriensis,[1] ne super hoc eis inde aliqua iniuria fiat et ne super hoc clamorem audiam.

---

[1] Two other originals of Henry I for Saint-Père are in the same MS.: no. 6, printed above, p. 223; and no. 8, printed in the *Cartulaire*, ed. Guérard, p. 640.

[1] Walter's son and successor Miles was in office the year before the Pipe Roll of 1129–1130 (pp. 72, 76, 107).

19

1121–1135, at Rouen

*Confirmation to Bec of a grant of William Peverel in Touffreville
(Eure).*

A, original lost; B, fragment of cartulary of Bec in Archives of the
Eure, H. 91, f. 35.

H. rex Angl[orum] archiepiscopo Rothomagensi et vic[ecomitibus] et
omnibus fidelibus Francis et Anglis de Normannia salutem. Sciatis me concessisse Deo et ecclesie Sancte Marie de Becco et monachis ibidem Deo
servientibus terram et res quas Willelmus Pevr[ellus] eis dedit et concessit in
elemosina de Turfreivilla cum omnibus consuetudinibus et quietacionibus de
pannagio et omnibus rebus que terre simili pertinent et cum quibus Willelmus
liberius tenuit. Quare volo et precipio quod ipsi eam terram et omnia que ad
eam pertinent bene et in pace et libere teneant in perpetua elemosina nunc et
usque in sempiternum sicut Willelmus ea eis dedit et concessit, salva tamen
rectitudine parentum Willelmi si quam in ea habent.

T[estibus] R[oberto] de sigillo et G[aufrido] fil[io] Pag[ani] et A[nselmo]
vic[ecomite], apud Rothom[agum].

20

1124–1135, at Argentan

*Writ of freedom from toll in favor of the monks of Vignats (Saint-
André-en-Gouffern).*

A, original lost; B, copy in cartulary of Saint-André in Archives of
the Calvados, f. 19, no. 72.

H. rex Anglorum baronibus et omnibus vicecomitibus et ministris tocius
Anglie et Normannie et portuum maris salutem. Precipio quod totum corri-
dium et omnes res monachorum de abbatia de Vinaz quas servientes eorum
affidare poterunt pertinere suo dominico victui et vestitui sint in pace et
quiete de theloneo et passagio et omnibus consuetudinibus. Et super hoc prohibeo quod nullus eos disturbet iniuste et super .x. libras forefacture. Testibus episcopo I[ohanne] Sagiensi et comite de Moritonio, apud Argentomum.

21

Ca. 1130–1135, at Argentan

*Grant of a house at Argentan in fief to the king's loricarii Robert and
Hamelin.[1]*

A, original, MS. Lat. 10083, no. 4; B, copy in cartulary of Saint-

[1] Cf. the charter of the Empress Matilda, issued before 1141, when her brother
took the title of earl of Cornwall (Round, *Geoffrey de Mandeville*, pp. 68, 271),

André-en-Gouffern, in Archives of the Calvados, f. 18v, no. 69; C, modern copy in MS. Lat. 10084, no. 37. Cf. *M.A.N.*, viii. 388, no. 136.

H. rex Anglorum iustic[iis] Normannie et vicec[omitibus] et baronibus et fidelibus suis et preposito et omnibus ministris et burgensibus de Argentom[o] salutem. Sciatis me dedisse et concessisse in feodo et hereditate quiete Roberto et Hamelino loricariis meis de Argentom[o] unam mansuram terre in Argentom[o] in fossato inter burgum et calciatam sibi et heredibus suis quietam de omni consuetudine. Quare volo et firmiter precipio quod ipsi eam bene et in pace et quiete et hereditabiliter teneant. T[estibus] R. de Curci et Iohanne mar[escallo] et Wigan[o] mar[escallo] et Rain[aldo] fil[io] com[itis], ap[ud] Argentom[um].

22

1131–1135 (probably after 1133),[1] at Séez

Confirmation to Séez cathedral of a gift by Enguerran Oison of land for the housing of the canons regular.

A, original lost; B, copy therefrom in 1521 also lost; C, copy from B in MS. Alençon 177, f. 104; D, copy in *Livre rouge*, f. 71v; E, copy from D in MS. Lat. 11058, f. 12.

Henricus Dei gratia rex Anglorum et dux Normannorum archiepiscopo Rothomagensi Hugoni, episcopis, abbatibus, comitibus, iusticiariis, baronibus, vicecomitibus, et omnibus fidelibus suis tocius Normannie salutem. Sciatis quoniam Ingelrannus Oison et Guilielmus filius eius coram me et baronibus meis apud Sagium in perpetuam elemosinam concesserunt Deo et ecclesie Sagiensi tres mansuras terre quas idem Ingelrannus de episcopo tenuerat, scilicet mansuram que fuerat Gualteri filii Constantini et aliam que fuit Rogeri Britonis et terciam[2] que fuit Roberti canonici, ad domos regularium et[3] canonicorum eiusdem ecclesie edificandas. Has vero mansuras dedit cum Ingelranno filio suo quem episcopus canonicum regularem fecit ibidem, et pro hac donacione dedit ei episcopus vi. boves et unum palefridum in pretium centum solidorum Cenomannensium. Hanc itaque concessionem[4] in perpetuum valituram eis regia auctoritate confirmavi et sigilli mei impressione munivi.

Testibus Ioanne episcopo Lexoviensi et Galtero filio Pagani et Goscelino de Bailleul et Roberto de sigillo,[5] apud Sagium.

which grants to Robert *loricarius* a house in Caen: original in MS. Lat. 10083, no. 3 (cf. Delisle, *Henri II*, p. 141, no. 4, *M. A. N.*, viii. 388, no. 137).

[1] Subsequent to the general confirmation of 1131 (no. 11), issued apparently on the eve of the king's departure for England, whence he returned in 1133.

[2] *etiam*, C.   [3] So MSS.   [4] *cessionem*, C.   [5] MSS. *Sagio*.

23

1133–1135, at Falaise

Grant of freedom from toll to the nuns of Villers-Canivet.

A, original, torn at the right, formerly sealed *sur simple queue*, in Archives of the Calvados, no. 47–66; B, *vidimus* of G., bishop of Séez, in the same *fonds*, no. 48, from which the gaps have been supplied.

H. rex Angl[orum] iustic[iis] et omnibus vic[ecomitibus] et ministris [tocius Normannie] et portuum maris salutem. Precipio quod totum corredium et [omnes res sanctimon]ialium Sancte Marie de Vilers quas homines earum poterunt [affidare suas] esse dominicas sint quiete de thelon[eo] et passag[io] et omni [alia consuetu]dine. Et nullus eas nec homines earum super hoc iniuste [disturbet super] .x. libras forifacture. Testibus A. episcopo Carlolii et R. comite [Gloecestrie et R. de Ver], apud Falesiam.

APPENDIX G

THE NORMAN ITINERARY OF HENRY I, 1106–1135

OF the twenty-nine years of Henry I's reign as duke more than half were spent in Normandy, so that the history of these Norman sojourns constitutes an essential part of the general history of his rule as well as a not inconsiderable portion of the annals of the duchy. In the absence of any connected narrative of these Norman years, a foundation must be laid by constructing a detailed itinerary, such as Canon Eyton prepared for Henry II, in which the fragmentary statements of the chroniclers shall be supplemented by the evidence of such documents as can be dated and placed with sufficient exactness. Nothing definitive of this sort can be attempted before the completion of this portion of Davis's *Regesta*, but in the meantime the following provisional itinerary may prove of service. A distinction is made between such events and documents as can be assigned to a specific date, and those which can be assigned only to a given year or a particular royal sojourn. No attempt has been made to group the charters which require wider limits: many of Henry's documents can never be dated with any degree of definiteness, while others must await a comprehensive collection and a diplomatic analysis of the more abundant records on the English side of the Channel.[1]

I: 1106–1107

1106 28 September. Battle of TINCHEBRAI. *Supra*, Chapter III, note 6.

FALAISE. Ordericus, iv. 232.

ROUEN. *Ibid.*, iv. 233.

ca. 15 October. LISIEUX. Council. *Ibid.*, iv. 233.

7 November. ROUEN. Court. *Gallia Christiana*, xi. instr. 127.

[1] No special study has been made of Henry's charters. See the notes to Warner and Ellis, *Facsimiles of Royal and Other Charters in the British Museum*, i; many scattered observations of Round; and Birch's paper on his seals in the *Journal of the British Archaeological Association*, xxix. 233–262 (1873). The best study of his itinerary is that of Eyton, British Museum, Add. MS. 31937, f. 122 ff. See also H. F., xii. 934–937; Andrew, in *Numismatic Chronicle* fourth series, i; and Ramsay, *Foundations of England*, ii

1106	30 November.	ROUEN. Chapter III, note 14.
	25 December.	In NORMANDY. *Anglo-Saxon Chronicle.*
1107	January.	FALAISE. Council. Ordericus, iv. 239(?), 269.
	March.	LISIEUX. Council. *Ibid.*, iv. 269.
1106–1107		ROUEN. Charter for Bec: Appendix F, no. 1.

LILLEBONNE. Writs concerning York issued with Queen Matilda (*Historians of York*, iii. 31; *Monasticon*, viii. 1179) belong to this year if this (*Annales Monastici*, Winton, ii. 42) was the Queen's only visit to Normandy.

ROUEN. The same holds true of a charter for Longueville: Round, *Calendar*, no. 219.

1107 Before 14 April. Departure, reaching Windsor before Easter (Eadmer, p. 184; Henry of Huntingdon, p. 236; *A. S. Chronicle*).

II: 1108–1109

1108 July–August, probably *ca.* 1 August. Arrival. Eadmer, p. 197; Robert of Torigni, i. 134; *A. S. Chronicle*.

25 December. In NORMANDY. *A. S. Chronicle.*

1109 March. NEAUFLES. Meeting with Louis VI: Luchaire, *Louis VI*, no. 72.

ROUEN. Letter to Anselm: *Epistolae Anselmi*, bk. iv, no. 93.

25 April. In NORMANDY. *A. S. Chronicle.*

1108–1109 ARGENTAN. Charter for Saint-Pierre-sur-Dive: *Gallia Christiana*, xi. instr. 156; *Neustria Pia*, p. 503; Delisle, *Cartulaire normand*, no. 1219.

CAEN. Vernier, no. 49; Round, no. 156.

ROUEN. Charter for William d'Aubigny: *Calendar of Patent Rolls*, 1327–1330, p. 20.

No place. Letter to Anselm: Eadmer, p. 205.

SAINTE-VAUBOURG. Charter for Ramsey (*Chronicon*, p. 215), attested by Ranulf as chancellor and addressed to Simon I, earl of Northampton, which must be placed in this year if Simon died before 1111 (see Warner and Ellis, *Facsimiles*, i. no. 26).

1109 *ca.* 1 June. Departure.[2] Florence of Worcester, ii. 59; cf. *A. S. Chronicle*.

[2] A grant of 30 June made with Henry's consent to La Trinité de Caen (MS. Fr. n. a. 20221, end), does not require his presence in Normandy at that date.

III: 1111–1113

IIII   August.   Arrival. *A. S. Chronicle; Calendar of Charter Rolls*, iii. 471, no. 4 (charter of 8 August at Waltham ' in transitu ').

1112   2 March.   AVRANCHES. Charter confirming the foundation of Savigny: *Gallia Christiana*, xi. instr. 111; Auvry, *Histoire de la congrégation de Savigny*, i. 157–160 (translation); Round, *Calendar*, no. 792, where the date is incorrectly given as 7 March 1113, a date inconsistent with the chronological elements in the charter, save the regnal years, and with the probabilities of Henry's itinerary.[3] To the long list of witnesses given by Round should be added Nigel d' Aubigny and ' Ricardus sigilli custos.' Cf. the foundation charter of Ralph of Fougères, 25 January 1112, in Martène and Durand, *Thesaurus*, i. 332; and the confirmation of Turgis of Avranches witnessed by Henry in the cartulary of Savigny in Archives of the Manche, f. 170v, no. 657.

    4 November.   BONNEVILLE-SUR-TOUQUES. Condemnation of Robert of Bellême: Ordericus, iv. 305.

               VARREVILLE. Grant of freedom from toll to Savigny: *M. A. N.*, xx. 256.

               No place. Approves grant by Robert of Meulan to Bec of the manor of Chisenbury[4] (co. Wilts): Porée, *Bec*, i. 467.

1113   2–3 February.   SAINT-ÉVROUL. Ordericus, iv. 301 f., v. 196; Round, no. 624.

   [11 February]   BEC. Confirms and seals charter of Hugh of Gournay for Bec: Porée, *Bec*, i. 339. (The year is probably incorrectly given).

   23–28 February.   Near ALENÇON. Meeting with Fulk of Anjou: Ordericus, iv. 306, v. 196.

   Early March.   ROUEN. *Ibid.*, iv. 302, v. 196; Round, no. 624.

   23–30 March.   Near GISORS. Interview with Louis VI: Luchaire, *Louis VI*, no. 158.

   1–3 May.   BELLÊME, siege. Ordericus, iv. 308.

[3] Most of the elements of date can be reconciled by assuming that the style is that of Easter, but the difficulties of the king's itinerary would still stand in the way of 1113.

[4] ' Chilingueburia super Avram ' in MS. Lat. 13905, f. 21v; the correct form Chesingebery in Henry II's confirmation, Delisle-Berger, no. 433.

1113   July.   Departure (Florence, ii. 66), having spent Christ-mas, Easter, and Pentecost in Normandy (*A. S. Chronicle*).

IV: 1114–1115

1114   21 September.   Arrival, via Portsmouth. *A. S. Chronicle;* cf. charter given 13 September at Westbourne (*Calendar of Charter Rolls*, iii. 346, iv. 170; *Monasticon*, ii. 444).

      25 December.   ROUEN. Court at which barons swear allegiance to Prince William. *A. S. Chronicle;* Henry of Huntingdon, p. 239; charter for Tiron in *Cartulaire*, ed. Merlet, i. 27; Round, no. 994.

      (year only)   No place. Charter of confirmation for Saint-Georges de Bocherville: Round, no. 196 (also in *vidimus* in Archives of the Seine-Inférieure and Archives Nationales, JJ. 64, no. 667).

1115   "   No place. Consents to grant of Stephen of Aumale for Aumale: *Monasticon*, vii. 1103 (original in Archives of the Seine-Inférieure).

      Mid-July.   Departure. Florence, ii. 68; *A. S. Chronicle.* (The king was at Westminster 18 September: *Calendar of Patent Rolls*, 1358–1361, p. 7.)

V: 1116–1120

1116 Just after 2 April.   Arrival. *A. S. Chronicle;* Henry of Huntingdon, p. 239; Robert of Torigni, i. 150; cf. Eadmer, p. 237.

1117   No place. Confirms grant to Bec by William Malet of Ménil-Josselin (Eure): MS. Lat. 12884, f. 165; MS. Lat. 13905, f. 21v; Porée, *Bec*, i. 334.

1118   July–August.   SAINT-CLAIR-SUR-EPTE, MALASSIS. Ordericus, ii. 453, iv. 311.

               ALENÇON and vicinity. War with Angevins; cession of territory to Thibaud of Blois. *Ibid.*, iv. 323 f.

  Early September.   Siege of LAIGLE. *Ibid.*, iv. 325–327.

      September.   ROUEN. *Ibid.*, iv. 327; cf. 316.

         "   Campaign against LA FERTÉ-EN-BRAI and NEUF-BOURG. *Ibid.*, iv. 327 f.

    7 October.   Council of ROUEN. *Ibid.*, iv. 329 f.

      October.   ROUEN. Settlement of dispute between Savigny and Saint-Étienne: Appendix F, no. 2.

1118   October.   ARGANCHY. Charter approving this settlement: *ibid.*

"   CAEN. Grant to Saint-Étienne by William d'Aubigny in presence of Henry and his barons at the castle: Deville, *Analyse,* p. 47; 'Emptiones Eudonis,' Chapter III, no. 5.

10–16 November.   Siege of LAIGLE. Ordericus, iv. 331.

December.   Siege of ALENÇON. *Ibid.,* iv. 333; *Chroniques des comtes d'Anjou,* ed. Halphen and Poupardin, pp. 155–161.

1119 16–22 February.   BRETEUIL, FALAISE, CHÂTEAU DE RENOUARD. Ordericus, iv. 337–339.

After 18 May.   LA FERTÉ-FRESNEL. *Ibid.,* iv. 345.

June.   LISIEUX. Court; betrothal of PrinceWilliam. *Ibid.,* iv. 347 f.; cf. *A. S. Chronicle.*

"   ROUEN. Charter for Colchester: *Cartularium S. Iohannis Baptiste de Colecestria,* p. 10.

(probably)   ROUEN. Charter for Colchester: *ibid.,* pp. 4–10; cf. Round, in *E. H. R.,* xvi. 723; *Geoffrey de Mandeville,* pp. 423–427.

Summer.   PONT-SAINT-PIERRE. Ordericus, iv, 348.

"   ÉVREUX, siege and burning. *Ibid.,* iv. 350–352.

20 August.   Battle of BRÉMULE. *Ibid.,* iv. 354–363; Luchaire, *Louis VI,* no. 259.

BRETEUIL. Ordericus, iv. 367 f.

GLOS, LIRE. *Ibid.,* iv. 371.

September.   ROUEN. *Ibid.*

October.   Siege of ÉVREUX. *Ibid.,* iv. 393.

VIEUX-ROUEN. *Ibid.,* iv. 395.

Instructions to bishops going to council of Rheims. *Ibid.,* iv. 373.

Between 22 and 27 November.   GISORS. Interview with Calixtus II. *Historians of York,* ii. 168 ff.; Jaffé-Löwenfeld, nos. 6788–6789; Eadmer, p. 258; Henry of Huntingdon, p. 242.

25 December.   BAYEUX. Charter for Savigny: Round, no. 793.

(year only)   ROUEN. Charter for Bec: Appendix F, no. 3.

1117–1119   ROUEN. Charter for Bec:[5] MS. Lat. 12884, f. 167; *Neustria Pia,* p. 484.

[5] The date of this and the three following documents is fixed by the attestation of Archbishop Ralph of Canterbury, who spent these three years in Normandy, leaving 4 January 1120: Ordericus, iv. 430; Florence of Worcester, ii. 74.

1117–1119	ROUEN. Agreement in his presence between Saint-Wandrille and Cerisy: Lot, *S.-Wandrille*, no. 60.
	ROUEN. Writ for Saint-Amand: Appendix F, no. 4.
1119	ROUEN. Charter for Saint Albans: Matthew Paris, *Chronica Majora*, vi. 39.
1120	No day or place given. Meeting with Louis VI and homage of Prince William. Luchaire, *Louis VI*, no. 298; Lot, *Fidèles ou vassaux?*, p. 202.
Lent.	ARGANCHY. Charter for Colchester: *Cartularium*, i. 42; cf. *E. H. R.*, xvi. 728.
	CAEN. Charters for Colchester, probably about the same time: *Cartularium*, i. 21, 23.
30 May.	VERNON (? ' apud Vercionem '). Interview with the papal legate Conon. *Historians of York*, ii. 186 f.
Before June.	ROUEN. Letter to Archbishop Ralph on behalf of Eadmer: Eadmer, p. 281.
October.	GISORS. Second interview with Conon. *Historians of York*, ii. 189; for the date cf. Mansi, *Concilia*, xxi. 259.
1116–1120	MORTAIN. Charter for Tiron: *Cartulaire*, ed. Merlet, i. 42; Round, no. 995.
	SAINTE-VAUBOURG. Charter for Tiron: *Cartulaire*, i. 41; Round, no. 996.
1116–1120, probably 1120	ROUEN. Charter for Nostell: W. Farrers, *Early Yorkshire Charters*, no. 1433.
1119–1120	BONNEVILLE. Charter for Nostell: *ibid.*, no. 1424.
	ROUEN. Writ for Archbishop Thurstan of York: *ibid.*, no. 1822.
1120 21 November.	BARFLEUR. Charter for Cerisy: *Neustria Pia*, p. 432; *Monasticon*, vii. 1075; Farcy, *Abbayes du diocèse de Bayeux*, pp. 86, 89; Toustain de Billy, *Histoire du diocèse de Coutances*, i. 166; cf. *Revue catholique de Normandie*, x. 441; *M. A. N.*, xxiii, part 1, no. 1474.
25 November.	BARFLEUR. Departure; loss of White Ship. Ordericus, iv. 411–419; *A. S. Chronicle;* Henry of Huntingdon, p. 242; William of Malmesbury, *Gesta Regum*, ii. 496; John of Worcester, ed. Weaver, p. 15.

VI: 1123–1126

1123 11 June.	Arrival, from Portsmouth. Simeon of Durham, ii. 273; *A. S. Chronicle;* Florence, ii. 78; John of Worcester, p. 17; cf. Henry of Huntingdon, p. 245; *Annales Monastici*, i. 11; Round, *Ancient Charters*, no. 10; id., *Geoffrey de Mandeville*, p. 432 f.
June or July.	Confers with archbishops of Canterbury and York on their return from Rome. Florence, ii. 78.
October.	ROUEN. Ordericus, iv. 442.
October, November.	MONTFORT, BRIONNE, PONTAUDEMER, GISORS. Campaign against Hugh de Montfort, Galeran de Meulan, etc. Ordericus, iv. 443–453; Robert of Torigni, i. 163; Simeon of Durham, ii. 274.
1124	Invasion of the VEXIN. Suger, *Louis le Gros*, ed. Molinier, p. 106.
26 March.	CAEN. Robert of Torigni, i. 166.
After 6 April.	ROUEN. Court; condemnation of those taken at battle of Bourgtheroude. Ordericus, iv. 459–463.
16 April.	BEC. *Vita Willelmi tertii abbatis*, Migne, *Patrologia*, cl. 722.
	BRIONNE, SAINTE-VAUBOURG. Porée, *Bec*, i. 287.
18 May–1 June.	ROUEN. *Ibid.*, i. 288.
(year only)	ÉVREUX. Charter for Savigny: Appendix F, no. 6.
1125 " "	ROUEN. Charter for Athelney: *Cartulary* (Somerset Record Society), p. 133.
" "	No place. Charter for Bec: Porée, *Bec*, i. 657.
" "	No place. Charter for Reading, with many witnesses: *Monasticon*, iv. 40; J. B. Hurry, *Reading Abbey*, p. 151.
1126 21 March.	SÉEZ. Dedication of cathedral. Ordericus, iv. 471.
(year only)	SAINTE-VAUBOURG. Decision of controversy between John, bishop of Séez, and Marmoutier: early copy in Archives of the Orne, H. 2159; *M. A. N.*, xv. 197; Round, no. 1191; Barret, *Cartulaire de Marmoutier pour le Perche*, no. 23.
" "	No place. General confirmation for Lessay: original in Archives of the Manche, H. 4607; Round, no. 923. From the names of the witnesses, the confirmation of a charter of Reginald d'Orval for Lessay probably belongs to the same time and place: original in Archives of the Manche, H. 6449; printed in *Inventaire sommaire*; Round, no. 924.

1123–1126(?)　　　No place.　Privilege for Saint-Pierre-sur-Dive: original in Archives of the Calvados; *Gallia Christiana*, xi. instr. 157.

1125–1126 (probably)　ROUEN.　Charter for Hyde Abbey: *Monasticon*, ii. 445 (cf. the witnesses to the charter for Reading, *ibid.*, iv. 41).

1126　11 September.　Departure.　Simeon of Durham, ii. 281 (as of 1127); cf. *A. S. Chronicle;* Henry of Huntingdon, p. 247; William of Malmesbury, *Historia Novella*, p. 528.

VII: 1127–1129

1127　26 August.　Arrival, via Eling.　Simeon of Durham, ii. 282 (as of 1128); cf. Henry of Huntingdon, p. 247; Round, *Feudal England*, p. 268 f.

　　　　(probably)　SAINT-PIERRE-SUR-DIVE.　Charter for Ely: *Monasticon*, ii. 617; cf. Round, *op. cit.*, p. 269.

　　　　(?)　No place.　Charter for Aunay: Appendix F, no. 8.

1128　10 June.　ROUEN.　Knighting of Geoffrey Plantagenet.　On the year see Norgate, *Angevin Kings*, i. 258–260; *Chroniques des comtes d'Anjou*, ed. Halphen and Poupardin, pp. 178–180.

　　17 June.　LE MANS.　Marriage of Geoffrey and Matilda.　See the authors just cited.

Before the end of July.　ÉPERNON.　Invasion of the Mantois.　Henry of Huntingdon, p. 247; Robert of Torigni, i. 175; cf. Luchaire, *Louis VI*, no. 414.

　　October.　ROUEN.　Council.　Ordericus, iv. 495.

　　November.　ROUEN.　Uncertain charter for Saint-Évroul: *Gallia Christiana*, xi. instr. 204; *supra*, Chapter I, pp. 11–14.

　　(year only)　No place.　Charter for Sainte-Barbe: early figured copy in Archives of the Calvados.

　　" "　SÉEZ.　Attests charter of John, bishop of Séez, for Marmoutier.　Barret, *Cartulaire de Marmoutier pour le Perche*, no. 25; Round, no. 1192.

1127–1128　Probably in Normandy.　Confirmation of charter of Count Stephen for Furness Abbey, with inconsistent year, indiction, and epact: *Monasticon*, v. 247.

1129　2 June.　FALAISE.　Whitsuntide court.　*Supra*, Chapter III, no. 3.

1129 (year only)   ROUEN. Charters for Fontevrault: Round, nos. 1052 f., 1459.

1128–1129   ROUEN. Grant to Miles of Gloucester of the lands and constableship of his father: original in British Museum, Cotton Charter xvi. 33. See above, p. 305.

1129 15 July.   Departure. Simeon of Durham, ii. 283; *A. S. Chronicle;* John of Worcester, p. 29. (Henry was in London 1 August: Henry of Huntingdon, p. 250.)

VIII: 1130–1131

1130 *ca.* 1 September.   Arrival, from Portsmouth. Robert of Torigni, i. 182; Pipe Roll 31 Henry I, p. 125; cf. Henry of Huntingdon, p. 252 (Michaelmas); *A. S. Chronicle.*

8 September.   BEC. Robert of Torigni, i. 182.

14 September.   ROUEN. Probably present at consecration of Archbishop Hugh. Robert of Torigni, i. 183.

after 14 September.   ROUEN. Assents to charter of Archbishop Hugh for Aumale: Archives of the Oise, H. 1302; *Gallia Christiana*, xi. instr. 22.

" (?)   ROUEN. Charter for Ramsey:[6] Warner and Ellis, *Facsimiles*, i, no. 11; *Ramsey Cartulary*, i. 242; *Chronicon*, p. 224.

ROUEN. Charter for Notre-Dame-du-Désert: Le Prévost, *Eure*, i. 251; Gurney, *Record of the House oj Gournay*, ii. 739; Round, no. 411.

1131 13 January.   CHARTRES. Meeting with Innocent II. Ordericus, v. 25; Round, no. 1460; cf. Henry of Huntingdon, p. 252; Robert of Torigni, i. 184; William of Malmesbury, *Historia Novella*, p. 534; Jaffé-Löwenfeld, i. 846.

5 February.   ROUEN. *Neustria Pia*, p. 387.

February.   ROUEN. Charter for Séez: Appendix F, no. 10.

[6] The appearance together in this charter of Archbishop Hugh, consecrated 14 September 1130, and William of Tancarville, who died in 1129 (*Histoire littéraire*, xxxii. 204), raises an unsolved problem, unless Hugh was already designated before the king's departure from Normandy in 1129. On the custom of prelates attesting before their consecration see Eyton, Add. MS. 31937, f. 148v; Round, in *Victoria History of Hampshire*, i. 527. A charter of 1133 is dated in the fourth year of Archbishop Hugh: *Cartulaire de Tiron*, i. 205.

1131 9, 10 May. ROUEN. Meeting with Innocent II. Jaffé-Löwenfeld, nos. 7472 f., 7476; William of Malmesbury, *Historia Novella*, p. 534; Robert of Torigni, i. 185; id., in William of Jumièges, ed. Marx, **p. 309; cf.** Round, *Ancient Charters*, p. 30.

    5 or 12 May. ROUEN. Charter for Cluny: Bruel, *Chartes de Cluny*, v, no. 4016; Round, *Calendar*, nos. 1387 f.

    May (1131 ?) VERNON. Meeting with Count Thibaud. Ordericus, iii. 118 f.

    (year only) VAUDREUIL. Charter for Évreux cathedral: Round, no. 287.

    Summer. ARQUES. Charter for Beaumont-le-Roger: *vidimus* in Archives of the Eure, H. 814; copy in cartulary in Bibliothéque Mazarine, MS. 3417; *Cartulaire*, ed. E. Deville, p. 7; Round, no. 373.

    " DIEPPE. Charter for Séez: Appendix F, no. 11; cf. Ordericus, iv. 471, note 4.

1130–1131 ARQUES. Charter for the cordwainers of Rouen: copies in MS. Lat. 9067, f. 154v; MS. Rouen 2192, f. 189; La Roque, iii. 149; Round, no. 107.

    ARQUES. Charter for Saint-Georges de Bocherville: Round, no. 197.

    DIEPPE. Charter for Saint-Wandrille: Lot, *S.-Wandrille*, no. 64; Round, no. 168.

    CAEN. Charter for Saint-Étienne: *Monasticon*, vii. 1071.

    CAEN (?). Charters for Saint-Étienne and confirmation of ' Emptiones Eudonis ': *supra*, Chapter III, no. 5.

    ROUEN. Charters for Fécamp: Round, nos. 122, 123; facsimile of no. 123 in Chevreux and Vernier, *Les archives de Normandie*, no. 33.

1130–1131 (?) ROUEN. Charter for Salisbury cathedral: *Register of St. Osmund*, i. 349.

1131 August Departure, from DIEPPE. *A. S. Chronicle;* Henry of Huntingdon, p. 252; Robert of Torigni, i. 185.

IX: 1133–1135

1133   2 August.   Arrival. *Annals of Rouen*, in Labbe, *Bibliotheca*, i. 368; *Annals of Canterbury*, in Liebermann, *Anglonormannische Geschichtsquellen*, p. 79; Robert of Torigni, i. 192; John of Hexham, ii. 285; John of Worcester, p. 37. William of Malmesbury, p. 535, gives 5 August, but the eclipse was on the 2d.

   (year only)   ROUEN. Charter for Bec: Round, no. 374; Porée, *Bec*, i. 460.

1134   Shortly after 15 April.   MORTEMER. *H. F.*, xiv. 510.

   3 June.   ROUEN. Birth of Henry's grandson Geoffrey, the king being probably at Rouen. Robert of Torigni, i. 192; cf. Porée, *Bec*, i. 293 f., 650.

   (year only)   ROUEN. Charter for Bec: Porée, i. 377–380, 658 f. (two versions); Round, no. 375.

   "   ROUEN. Charter for Coutances cathedral: cartulary now in Archives of the Manche (cf. Chapter VI, note 95), p. 348, no. 284; copy in MS. Fr. 4900, f. 5v; Dupont, *Histoire du Cotentin*, i. 472; Round, no. 959.

1135   Makes three vain attempts to cross to England. Ordericus, v. 45.

   CAEN. Charter for Saint-André-en-Gouffern: Round, no. 590.

   ROUEN. Ordinance concerning the Truce of God: *Très Ancien Coutumier*, ed. Tardif, c. 71; Round, no. 290.

   August–1 November.   SÉEZ, ALENÇON, ARGENTAN, etc. Ordericus, v. 47, 63.

   No place. Confirms grant of William of Warren for Bellencombre: *Monasticon*, vii. 1113.

   No place. Renews charter of 1121–1131 for Le Grand-Beaulieu de Chartres: *Cartulaire*, ed. Merlet and Jusselin, no. 1; *supra*, Chapter III, no. 17.

1133–1135   ARGANCHY. Writ to custodians of the bishopric of Bayeux: *Livre noir*, no. 37. No. 34 is probably of the same period.

   CAEN. Writ for Bayeux cathedral: *ibid.*, no. 8 (probably during the same vacancy).

1133–1135   FALAISE. Charter for Ramsey: *Cartulary*, i. 250; *Chronicon*, p. 284.

        FALAISE. Charter for Villers-Canivet: Appendix F, no. 23.

        ROUEN. Charter for the bishop of Évreux: *supra*, Chapter III, no. 18; Round, no. 289.

        ROUEN. Charter for Lincoln: *E. H. R.*, xxiii. 726, no. 4; *Monasticon*, viii. 1275.

        SÉEZ. Charter for Séez cathedral: Appendix F, no. 22.

1135 25 November. LIONS castle. Ordericus, v. 49.

   1 December. LIONS. Death. *Ibid.*, v. 50.

APPENDIX H

DOCUMENTS CONCERNING NORMAN COURTS, 1139–1191 [1]

1

1139, at Lisieux

Notice of suit before John, bishop of Lisieux, between Richard and Anselm of Dives and the abbey of Troarn concerning the church of Dives (Calvados).

A, original lost; B, copy in lost cartulary of Troarn; C, copy from B ('in veteri cartario folio .xxix. hec repperi') in *Chartrier rouge*, MS. Lat. 10086, f. 159v.

Anno .M°.C.XXXIX. defuncto Herluino presbitero de Diva moverunt Ricardus de Diva et Anselmus frater eius contencionem de ecclesia de Diva contra nos. Dicebant enim quandam partem eiusdem ecclesie esse suam et maxime presentacionem presbiteri. Pro qua causa iussu Iohannis episcopi Lexoviensis perrexerunt in curiam Sancti Petri ante ipsum episcopum, scilicet domnus abbas Andreas et monachi eius cum eo Rannulfus cellararius et Radulfus de Waravilla et Rogerius de Sancto Wandregisilo et Ricardus de Diva et Anselmus frater eius. Et diraciocinati sunt idem abbas et monachi eius quod tota ecclesia Sancte Marie de Diva sua erat et presentacio presbiteri, per testimonium et iudicium predicti episcopi et iudicium qui curiam tenebant et per cartam suam quam inde habebant firmatam manu Willelmi senioris regis et Rogerii de Belmont et Roberti filii eius et manu Hugonis episcopi Lexoviensis et per guarantores suos quos ibi habebant, scilicet Rogerium de Spineto et filios eius et Jordanum de Sulleio; et saisiti redierunt a curia abbas et monachi eius. His interfuerunt Herveus archidiaconus, Normannus archidiaconus, decanus, Rogerius de Monasteriolo, Hugo Teillardus, Willelmus de Capella.[2]

---

[1] For other such documents see *M.A.N.*, xv. 196 ff.; Valin, *pièces justificatives*; and the texts cited *supra*, Chapters V and VI.

[2] Cf. the following letter of Galeran of Meulan: 'I. reverendo Dei gratia Lex-[oviensi] episcopo domino suo et patri G. comes Mellenti salutem. Precor vos quod Dei amore et meo teneatis et custodiatis ecclesiam Sancti Martini de Troarno et monachos et omnes res eorum et nominatim ecclesiam de Diva quam antecessores mei concesserunt et cum Willelmo rege Anglorum a duce Normannorum confirmaverunt predicte ecclesie et monachis, et ut [non] permittatis quod Ricardus de Diva vel Anselmus faciat eis inde aliquam contumeliam vel [blank in MS.]. Teste Roberto de Novoburgo.' *Chartrier rouge*, f. 152; *Chartrier blanc* in Archives of the Calvados, no. 366.

2
20 January 1148, at Lisieux

Notification by Fulk, dean of Lisieux, that in the presence of Rotrou, bishop of Évreux, then administering the see of Lisieux, a piece of land at Mesnil-Mauger (Calvados) has been recognized as alms by the guardian of the honor and the old men of the manor and restored to the priory of Sainte-Barbe.

A, original, with incisions for attachment of seal, in Archives of the Calvados, *fonds* Sainte-Barbe.

Fulco Sancti Petri Lexoviensis ecclesię decanus totusque eiusdem ecclesię conventus dilectis in Christo fratribus Guillelmo priori de Sancta Barba totique ipsius ecclesię conventui salutem et fraternam dilectionem. Quia liberante nos Christo non sumus ancillę filii sed libere, rerum etiam ecclesiasticarum libertati quantum possumus decet nos providere, quatinus eas et ab illicita possessione laicorum liberare studeamus et ab invasione sacrilega premunire. Terram igitur quam Rannulfus et Turulfus filius eius tota vita sua tenuisse dicuntur in elemosina apud Maisnilmalger tempore Rad[ulfi] filii Serlonis et heredum eius Guillelmi et Gauf[redi] et sic, in presentia domini Rotroci Ebroicensis episcopi Lexoviensis episcopatus curam nunc agentis, per Rog[erium] de Hotot qui tunc honorem et heredem de Maisnilmalger habebat in custodia et per antiquos homines eiusdem manerii pro elemosina recognitam, et per manus tam ipsius Rog[erii] quam Gauf[redi] filii Theoderici in manum prefati Rot[roci] episcopi quibusdam ex nobis videntibus et audientibus ut elemosinam redditam, vobis et ecclesię vestrę per manus ipsius episcopi datam in perpetuam elemosinam, assensu et benivolentia predictorum Rog[erii] et Gauf[redi] ceterorumque qui in eorum erant consilio, protestamur. Quandam etiam partem elemosinę de ecclesia Sancti Stephani de Maisnilmalger quam predicti Rannulfus et Turulfus et post eos Guill[elmus] Burgamissam tenuerunt, quam Robertus decanus habebat in custodia, redditam in manu eiusdem episcopi liberam a predictis Rog[erio] et Gauf[redo], vobis nichilominus ab ipso episcopo datam et in perpetuam elemosinam concessam partim vidimus partim audivimus.

Huic actioni presentes affuimus ego Fulco decanus, ex archidiaconis Normannus et Robertus de Altaribus, ex canonicis Rad[ulfus] de Floreio, Rog[erius] filius Amisi, Iohannis archidiaconi vicarius, Guillelmus archidiac[oni] Ricard[i] filius, Gislebertus de Furcis, Turgisus, et alii plures. De exterioribus quoque clericis, Robertus de Hotot decanus qui totius predicti negocii mediator et actor fuit, Rogerius de Dotvilla decanus, Guillelmus de Tebervilla, et Paganus de Grandvilla. Predictam igitur pactionem terrę recognitę et redditę in elemosinam predictus Rog[erius] de Hotot affidavit in manu episcopi Rot[roci] se legitime et fideliter servaturum et contra omnes qui vellent adversari toto posse suo defensurum. Quod totum sicut supra scriptum est testificantes, ex precepto etiam domini Ebroicensis episcopi Rot[roci] conscriptione et sigillo capituli nostri corroboramus, ut Domino

cooperante et sermonem confirmante ratum et indissolubile maneat in perpetuum. Amen. Actum Lexovii in festivitate sanctorum martirum Fabiani
et Sebastiani anno incarnationis dominicę M°.C°.XL°.VIII°.

3

1154–1158, at Caen

*Notification by Robert de Neufbourg, seneschal and justiciar of Nor-
mandy, that Robert,[1] son of Ralph of Thaon, had, in the king's court at
Caen, restored to the abbot and monks of Savigny the tithes and lands at
Thaon (Calvados) to which the abbot had proved his right before the king at
Domfront, and that Robert has given surely for the observance of this.*

A, original lost; B, cartulary of Savigny, in Archives of the Manche,
no. 219.

A. H. R., xx. 32, note 56.

Robertus de Novoburgo sinescallus Normannic archiepiscopo Rothomagensi et episcopis Normannie et consulibus et baronibus et omnibus fidelibus
Henrici regis Anglie salutem. Notum vobis fieri volumus quod Robertus
filius Radulfi de Thaun Cadomo in curia regis coram me qui eram iusticia
Normannie et coram baronibus regis Ricardo abbati et monachis Savigneii
reddidit in pace ac dimisit et in manu abbatis posuit decimas terre eorum de
Thaun et quatuor acras terre, quas ipse Robertus et fratres eius adversus
abbatem et monachos antea calumniabantur et quas ipse abbas et monachi
disrationaverunt in curia regis et coram ipso ad Danfront, et de chatallis
suis misit se in miseratione abbatis et monachorum pro malefactis que ipse et
fratres eius fecerant eis. Et pepigit legitime quod faceret si posset fratres
suos facere et tenere eundem finem cum abbate et monachis quem ipse facie-
bat, et si non posset quod legitime se teneret cum abbate et monachis contra
fratres, et affidavit in manu mea et iuravit super sancta quod ipse hec omnia
que hic diximus legitime teneret et conservaret abbati et monachis. Et hoc
ipsum affidavit Vitalis de Sancto Germano et Ricardus de Babainvilla et alii
amici eius quos abbas voluit. Huius finis et pacis inter Robertum et abbatem
et monachos fuerunt testes Godart de Vaus et Robertus de Sancta Honorina
qui erant in loco episcopi Luxoviarum et Willelmus filius Iohannis et Aitart
Polcin qui erant baillivi regis et Robertus abbas Fontaneti et Ricardus filius
comitis Gloecestrie et Iordanus Taisson et Rualen de Sal et Iohannes de
Guavrei et Willelmus de Vilers et Gaufredus filius Mabile et Robertus filius
Bernardi et Rannulfus Rufellus et Nicholaus de Veieves et Robertus de
Chernellia et multi alii.

---

[1] He also appears in a suit in the king's court under Richard: cartulary of
Savigny, no. 220.

4

1154–1158

Writ of Arnulf of Lisieux and Robert de Neufbourg [the king's principal justices], ordering William Fitz John to cause the friends of Robert of Thaon to give such surety as Robert had given in the preceding document, and directing him further to have Robert's brothers proclaimed in the markets of Caen and Bayeux as under the king's ban.

A, original lost; B, cartulary of Savigny, no. 273.

A. H. R., xx. 33, note 56.

Ernulfus Dei gratia Luxoviensis episcopus et R. de Novoburgo Willelmo filio Iohannis salutem. Mandamus tibi atque precipimus ut facias amicos Roberti de Thaun quos abbas Savigneii tibi nominaverit facere fiduciam eidem abbati et monachis ipsius quam ipse Robertus fecit Cadomi coram nobis, et ut facias fratres Roberti forisbanniri in communi foro Cadomi et Baiocis sicut forisfactos regis.

5

1154–1159

Notification by Robert de Neufbourg, seneschal of Normandy, that Robert Poisson of Foulbec (Eure) has in the king's court and before the king's barons renounced all claim to the church of Épaignes (Eure) in favor of the monastery of Préaux, and has received from the abbot the fief of Ralph the priest subject to the customs which a vavassor owes his lord.

A, original lost; B, cartulary of Préaux in Archives of the Eure, H. 711, no. 78; C, copy from B in MS. Lat. n. a. 1929, no. 75. Cf. Brunner, *Schwurgerichte*, p. 148, note 1; Le Prévost, *Eure*, ii. 125.

Notum sit tam presentibus quam futuris quoniam in curia regis cum ego Robertus de Novoburgo dapifer essem Normannie Robertus Piscis de Fulebecco calumpniam suam de ecclesia de Hispania quietam clamavit ecclesie Sancti Petri Pratellensis tempore Michaelis abbatis. Ipse vero abbas predicto Roberto Pisci feodum quod tenuit Radulfus sacerdos in Hispania reddidit salvis omnibus consuetudinibus quas vavasor compatriota domino facere debet. Et quoniam hec ante meam presentiam in regis curia et ante regis barones factum est, sigilli mei munimento ratum fore in posterum confirmo. Testibus Laurentio archidiacono, Willelmo de Ansgervilla, Godardo [1] de Vallibus, Roberto filio Hemerici, Etardo Pulcin, Roberto de Iuvineio, Gaufredo de Novoburgo, Henrico de Warewic, Gisleberto de Hotot, et aliis.

[1] MS. *Godardus.*

6

1154–1164, at Rouen

Notification that before Rotrou, bishop of Évreux, and Richard du Hommet, constable, as justiciars, the presentation of Brucourt (Calvados) was quitclaimed to Michael, abbot of Préaux, in full assize at Rouen.

A, original lost; B, cartulary of Préaux, in the Archives of the Eure, H. 711, no. 18; C, copy from B in MS. Lat. n. a. 1929, f. 9v.

A. H. R., xx. 33, note 59.

Notum sit tam presentibus quam futuris quoniam cum ego R. episcopus Ebroicensis et Ricardus de Hummeto constabularius regis essemus iusticiarii regis, Galfredus de Bruecourt et Gislebertus de Bruencourt et Robertus filius Matildis in presentia nostra in plena assisia apud Rothomagum clamaverunt quietam imperpetuum presentationem ecclesie de Bruencourt Michaeli abbati et ecclesie Pratellensi, de qua diu controversia inter eos fuerat. Testibus Hugo [*sic*] de Gornaio et Matheo de Gerardivilla et Nicholaus [*sic*] de Stutevilla et G. de Vallibus et Roberto de Pessi et Gisleberto de Vascoil et Roberto de Iuveneio.

7

1154–1175, probably ca. 1160, at Rouen

Grant by the dean, Geoffrey, and the chapter of Rouen of their mill at Maromme (Seine-Inférieure) to the hospital of Saint-Jacques, made in the presence of the king's justices.

A, original, injured, in Archives Nationales, S. 4889, no. 6; B, modern copy, *ibid.*, from which the missing portions of the original have been supplied.

A. H. R., xx. 35, note 79. Frequently cited by Delisle, *Henri II*, who makes the slip of attributing the document to Geoffrey's successor, Robert, and thus placing it after Geoffrey's death in 1175; this error vitiates several of Delisle's biographical notes (pp. 100, 377, 417, 422, 449, 491).

Gaufridus Rothomagensis ęcclesię decanus et tocius eiusdem ecclesię conventus presentibus et futuris salutem. [Not]um esse volumus sancte matris ecclesie filiis quod m[olendinu]m nostrum de Marrona concedimus domui infirmorum de Rothomago [in ec]clesia Sancti Iacobi tenendum in perpetuum sicut tenuerunt iure hereditario Macharius et heredes eius a quibus ipsum emerunt pro .xv. marcis argenti, salvo ibi censu nostro scilicet tribus solidis usualis monete singulis annis in festo Sancti Remigii reddendis. Hec autem em[ptio publice] celebrata est in presentia nostra cui interfuerunt etiam [iustitie regis] Rainaldus de Sancto Walerico, Godardus de Vallibus, [Adam de W]annevilla, Willelmus de Malapalude,[1] Radulfus filius Urselini, Ro[celin filius] Clarembaldi, Rainaldus de Sancto Philiberto.

8

1160–1164, at Rouen

Notification of a decision in the king's court at Rouen, before Rotrou, bishop of Évreux, and Reginald of Saint-Valery as justiciars, adjudging to Gilbert, abbot of Conches, rights in the granary of Varengeville (Seine-Inférieure).

A, original lost; B, cartulary of Conches in the Archives of the Eure, H. 262, f. 101v; C, copy among Delisle's papers from a MS. relating to the family of Chambray, from which the gaps in B have been filled in.

A. H. R., xx. 33, note 59; extract in Delisle, *Henri II*, p. 455.

Rotrodus Dei gratia Ebroisensis episcopus universis sancte matris ecclesie filiis salutem. Notificamus vobis quod Gilbertus Sancti Petri Castellionensis abbas stramen grangie de Warengevilla et palleas cum revaneis iudicio curie domini regis obtinuit contra Mathilde[m] de Monasteris et contra Matheum filium eius disracionavit, quoniam monachos prefate ecclesie inde multum diu placitis et altercationibus indiscussis vexaverant. Hoc autem iudicium factum est apud Rothomagum in monasterio Sancti Gervacii me presente, Reinnoldo de Sancto Walerico iusticia in curia existente plenissima plurimorum virorum qui huius rei testes fuerunt: Arnulphus Luxoviensis episcopus, Frogerius Sagiensis episcopus, Henricus abbas Fiscannensis, Hugo de Gurnaio, Godardus de Vallibus, Robertus de Freschenes, Adam de Martinevilla, Goselinus Rossel, Robertus Harenc de Waldevilla, Rogerius Mahiel, et alii multi.

9

1164–1178

Letter of William de la Seule [1] to Rotrou, archbishop of Rouen, asking him to do justice to the monks of Aunay in their appeal from Richard, bishop of Coutances, with respect to the champart of Saint-Martin-de-Bon-Fossé (Manche), and referring to a recent decision of the king concerning the division of the champart.

[1] William de Malpalu also appears as justice in a document of Richard Talbot for Mont-aux-Malades (Archives of the Seine-Inférieure), where an agreement is sworn to ' coram Willelmo de Mala Palude tunc regis iusticiario.'

[1] On William de la Seule, see Delisle-Berger, i. 278, 301, ii. 365; Deville, *Analyse*, p. 25; *H. F.*, xxiii. 696.

A, original in Archives of the Manche, H. 3.

A. H. R., xx. 27, note 13.

Reverentissimo patri suo et domino carissimo R. Rothomagensi archiepiscopo et omnibus hoc audientibus et recte iudicantibus Willelmus de Sola salutem. Testimonium cuiusdam donationis quam feci monachis de Alneto vobis per litteras meas significare curavi. Habebam quondam in manu mea et adhuc habere poteram si voluissem duas garbas decime in parrochia de Bono Fosseio, ex quibus unam dedi monachis et aliam ecclesię eiusdem ville, persona vero ecclesie suam terciam garbam habuit sibi in pace et habet. Verum tunc temporis talis erat consuetudo circa nos quod tercia tantum garba reddebatur persone, de illis scilicet terris que pro campardo tradebantur, due vero cum eodem campardo tenebantur, que nunc Deo donante et domino rege nostro iudicante ubique in territoriis nostris redduntur, quas monachi et ęcclesia in suam partem volunt habere. Quod quidem rectissimum videtur sed persona contradicit ill[is]. Quam contentionem declarandam domino Ricardo Constantiensi episcopo commiseram et non semel aut secundo me donationem attestante coram ipso iudicium distulit facere. Qua de causa monachi in eius curia aggravati cum Gaufrido milite persona vestram appellaverunt presentiam. Unde obnixe vestram deprecor auctoritatem quatinus vos pro Deo quod unicuique pertinet, et persone et monachis et ecclesie, recta consideratione restituatis. Valete.

10

1176–1178, at Montfort

Notification by William de la Mare of an agreement between Robert Neveu of Trouville and Gilbert of Yainville made before him and the other justices of the king after judgment rendered at an assize at Montfort.[1]

A, original, formerly sealed *sur simple queue,*in Archives of the Seine-Inférieure, *fonds* Jumièges; B, copy thence by Delisle among his papers in MSS. Fr. Printed, with serious errors and omissions, by Valin, p. 271, no. xviii (cf. p. 114); now in Vernier, no. 115.

Ego Willelmus de Mara presentibus omnibus et futuris notam facio concordiam que facta est inter Robertum Nepotem de Turovilla et Gislebertum de Eudonis villa in assisia de Montfort coram iusticiis regis, me scilicet vicecomite Sancte Marię Ecclesię et Willelmo Maleth constabulario de Ponte Abdomari et Hugone de Creissi constabulario Rothomagi et Seherio de Quenci constabulario de Nonantcort et Alvredo de Sancto [Martino] constabulario de Drincort, et quibusdam aliis. Robertus siquidem movebat calumpniam contra Gislebertum de hereditagio suo de Turovilla, scilicet de hospite suo Willelmo Cave et de terra quam habet apud maram de Becco et iuxta domum Morini Planchun. Sed quoniam in eadem assisia coram predic-

---

[1] For the justices mentioned in this document see the biographical notices in Delisle, *Henri II;* and the list of assizes, *infra*, Appendix J.

tis iusticiis recordatum est et recognitum hoc esse rectum hereditagium Gisleberti, pro concordia et pace ab utrisque partibus definitum est ita, Roberto et Gisleberto consencientibus et iusticiis confirmantibus: Gislebertus hominium fecit Roberto et singulis annis ad festum Sancti Michaelis dabit ei duodecim denarios publice monete ut sit inter eos indicium et agmentum firmissime pacis, nichilque amplius faciet ei; et ita hoc modo Gislebertus de ista querela finivit in assisia de Montfort, in curia domini regis coram predictis iusticiis eius. Presentibus his testibus: Rogerio Cellarario, Falcheranno monacho, Roberto Pychart, Radulfo Maisnerio, Rogero Filiolo, Roberto Clarel, Roberto de Leuga, Roberto Belfit, Hermanno Anglico, Matheo Marescal, Hugone de Contevilla, et aliis pluribus. Quo tempore Ricardus Wintoniensis episcopus in Normannia post regem iudex erat et maior iusticia.

11

1189-1191,[1] at Caen

Grant by William de Moult to the nuns of Almenèches of a rent of twenty-five sous Angevin in Moult (Calvados) and all claim to the tithe of Ingouville (Calvados), done at the Exchequer at Caen before William Fitz Ralph, seneschal of Normandy.

A, original, formerly sealed, in Archives of the Orne, H. 3916. Cf. *A. H. R.*, xx. 282, note 28.

Omnibus ad quos presens scriptum pervenerit Willelmus de Mool miles salutem. Noscat universitas vestra quod ego Willelmus intuitu caritatis et antecessorum meorum remedio ecclesie Sancte Marie de Almanesches et monialibus ibidem Deo servientibus dedi et concessi .xxv. solidatas Andegavensium monete in feodo meo laicali apud Mool assignatas, scilicet: in Willelmo filio Leiardi viii. solidos et ii. gallinas, in Gauchero Escorchechine .iii. solidos, in Ricardo Musel .xii. denarios, in Serlone Buffei .ii. sextarios avene ad magnam mensuram de Argentiis et .iii. panes et .iii. gallinas et .xxx. ova, in Hugone filio Willelmi .xii. denarios; prefatis monialibus in puram et perpetuam elemosinam libere et pacifice possidendas. Preterea omni iuri quod Simon filius meus persona ecclesie de Mool super duabus garbis decime de feodo sanctimonialium vendicabat apud Ingulfrevillam penitus renunciavit. Et ut hoc rescriptum perpetue firmitatis robur futuris temporibus optineat nec aliqua possit oblivione deleri, pro me et Simone filio meo sigilli mei munimine roboravi. Actum est hoc apud Cadomum ad scacarium coram Willelmo filio Radulfi tunc Normannie senescallo, testibus his: Anschetillo de Arre, Radulfo de Lexoviis, Daniele, magistro Gaufredo de Cortone, clericis de scacario, R. abbate Sancti Andree de Gofer, Ricardo Haitie, Turofredo de Cyerni, Willelmo filio comitis Iohannis, Henrico de Mool, Radulfo de Rupetra, Ricardo de Argenciis, Radulfo Martel, et aliis pluribus.

[1] Robert became abbot of Saint-André-en-Gouffern *ca.* 1189; William succeeded his father John as count of Ponthieu in 1191.

APPENDIX I

THE EARLY LEGISLATION OF HENRY II

THE record of Henry II's legislation is lamentably incomplete. The chief reason is doubtless that indicated by Maitland, ' the administrative character of his reforms,' embodied usually in instructions to his justices and quickly absorbed ' as part and parcel of the traditional common law ';[1] but the result is none the less fatal for the study of constitutional and legal development. We know nothing, for example, of the establishment of the grand assize, even its date must be recovered by inference;[2] while no formulation of law has reached us anterior to the Constitutions of Clarendon, and no formal ordinance anterior to 1166. The recovery of any texts for these early years is perhaps a vain hope, but it is none the less important to search out all traces of legislative activity on both sides of the Channel, even if its formal expression still escapes us.

The fullest report of any early legislation is given by the Bec annalist in 1159:[3]

Rex Anglorum Henricus ad Natale Domini fuit apud Falesiam, et leges instituit ut nullus decanus aliquam personam accusaret sine testimonio vicinorum circummanentium qui bone vite fama laudabiles haberentur. De causis similiter quorumlibet ventilandis instituit ut, cum iudices singularum provinciarum singulis mensibus ad minus simul devenirent, sine testimonio vicinorum nichil iudicarent, iniuriam nemini facere, preiudicium non irrogare, pacem tenere, latrones convictos statim punire, quemque sua quiete tenere, ecclesias sua iura possidere.

This account reads like a rapid summary, by headings, of the ordinance, and could hardly have been written in this form without some reference to the act itself. Its chief importance, as has already been indicated,[4] consists in its requirement of the accusing jury, which here makes its first appearance under the Anglo-Norman kings. Especially noteworthy is the evident connection between the first provision of this ordinance and § 6 of the Constitutions of Clarendon:

[1] Pollock and Maitland, i. 136.　　　　　[2] See Round, *E. H. R.*, xxxi. 268.
[3] Robert of Torigni, ii. 180.
[4] *Supra*, Chapter VI. Cf. Stubbs, *Constitutional History*, i. 497; Pollock and Maitland, i. 151.

Laici non debent accusari nisi per certos et legales accusatores et testes in presentia episcopi, ita quod archidiaconus non perdat ius suum nec quicquam quod inde habere debeat. Et si tales fuerint qui culpantur, quod non velit vel non audeat aliquis eos accusare, vicecomes requisitus ab episcopo faciet iurare duodecim legales homines de visneto seu de villa, coram episcopo, quod inde veritatem secundum conscientiam suam manifestabunt.[5]

It is true that only the court of the archdeacon is here mentioned, while the ordinance of Falaise speaks only of deans; but the cases which have reached us show both dignitaries associated in the abuses of which the king complains,[6] and in the Inquest of Sheriffs (1170) he groups them together without distinction.[7] The subject was not new in 1164 nor, as we shall see, in 1159.

The exactions of the archdeacon's jurisdiction were one of the serious abuses of the twelfth century. Appointed usually when very young and by family interest, learning their law in the schools of Paris or Bologna, laymen often in all but name, the English archdeacons of the period were notorious for their cupidity and extortion.[8] Men even discussed whether they could be saved — *an possit archidiaconus salvus esse*.[9] Archbishop Theobald, one of their patrons, had twinges of conscience respecting their exactions and seems to have instituted a check upon them in his diocese by the appointment of John of Salisbury as his secretary,[10] in whose correspondence may be found many instances of their misdeeds in the early years of Henry II.[11] It is not surprising that the sixth section of the Constitutions of Clarendon was one of those ' tolerated ' by Alexander III,[12] who was subsequently informed that the archdeacons of the diocese of Coventry, among other things,

[5] Stubbs-Davis, *Select Charters*, p. 165.

[6] See the cases from Scarborough and London mentioned below, and Gilbert Foliot, *Ep.* 24. Cf. also c. 7 of the council of Tours of 1163 (Mansi, xxi. 1178), which shows that the archdeacon's jurisdiction was often sublet to rural deans. For the jurisdiction of a Norman dean in criminal matters see Barret, *Cartulaire de Marmoutier pour le Perche*, no. 18 (1092–1100); for Maine, Celier, *Catalogue des actes des évêques du Mans*, nos. 81, 266, 267.

[7] ' Et similiter inquiratur per omnes episcopatus quid et quantum et qua de causa archidiaconi vel decani iniuste et sine iudicio ceperint, et hoc totum scribatur ': c. 12, Stubbs-Davis, p. 177.

[8] Stubbs, *Seventeen Lectures on the Study of Mediaeval and Modern History* (1900), pp. 152 f., 160, 347–349; id., introduction to Ralph of Diceto, i, p. xxvi f.; L. B. Radford, *Thomas of London* (Cambridge, 1894), p. 163 f.

[9] Cf. John of Salisbury, *Ep.* 166.

[10] Id., *Ep.* 49; Stubbs, *Lectures*, p. 347 f.

[11] John of Salisbury, *Epp.* 27, 34, 69, 80, 89, 93, 107, 118, 166.

[12] *Materials for the History of Thomas Becket*, v. 75; Mansi, xxi. 1194.

were in the habit of extorting 30 $d.$ from every man or woman who went to the ordeal of fire or water.[13]

Just when these abuses first attracted the attention of Henry II is not clear, but it was quite early in his reign. At the outset he was hardly favorably disposed by the fact that he had inherited from Stephen a controversy respecting the punishment of Archdeacon Osbert of York, accused of poisoning his archbishop;[14] and he soon took up the case of a citizen of London despoiled by a dean *et longe aliter iniuriatus quam civem Londoniensem oporteret.*[15] By the beginning of 1158 he had legislated on the subject, as we learn from Fitz Stephen.[16] The narrative tells how a burgess of Scarborough complained to the king at York that the local dean had, without any supporting accuser, accused his wife of adultery and taken twenty-two shillings from him, twenty of which the dean subsequently declared had gone to the archdeacon. Such accusations had already been forbidden by the king, who had the dean brought before him and demanded judgment from his prelates and barons, declaring that the archdeacons and deans of the kingdom got in this way more money in a year than the king himself received:

Quidam decanus abstulerat ei viginti et duos solidos, uxorem ipsius in capitulis plurimis vexans et deferens sine alio accusatore ream adulterii, contra quam consuetudinem rex legem prohibitionis ediderat.

John, treasurer of York, gave it as his opinion that the money should be returned to the burgess and the dean should be at the archbishop's mercy with respect to his office, whereupon Richard de Lucy asked, *Quid ergo domino regi iudicabitis, in cuius iste incidit constitutionem?;* and upon the answer that the king had no claim from a clerk, he left the court. The king appealed to the archbishop but did not follow up the matter, being called over seas in July by the death of his brother Geoffrey.

Here we have two distinct references to previous legislation, the mention of the king's law in the narrative and the reference of Richard de

---

[13] C. 3, X. 5, 37; Jaffé-Löwenfeld, no. 14315 (1174–1181); cf. Maitland, *Domesday Book and Beyond*, p. 282. That some payment was due the archdeacon at such times is assumed by Henry of Huntingdon, himself an archdeacon: *Liber Eliensis*, p. 170. For other forms of archidiaconal exactions see *Cartulary of St. Frideswide's*, i. 33, no. 31; *Ramsey Cartulary*, ii. 152.

[14] John of Salisbury, *Ep.* 122; cf. *Epp.* 108, 110, 111.   [15] Id., *Ep.* 80.

[16] *Materials*, iii, 44 f.; cf. Radford, *Thomas of London*, pp. 193–195. For the presence of the king and Richard de Lucy at York see Farrers, *Early Yorkshire Charters*, no. 419.

Lucy to the *constitutio regis*. The first is specific enough to show that this ordinance dealt with the same problem as that of 1159 and the Constitutions of Clarendon, unsupported accusations against laymen in ecclesiastical courts. That the king intended to pursue the question is further shown by the fact that in all probability he repaid the burgess of Scarborough and thus took over his interest in the case, for in the Pipe Roll of 1158 we find a payment to a merchant of Scarborough *in camera curie* of 22s., the exact amount in question.[17] The problem was postponed by Henry's long absence on the Continent from 1158 to 1163, but it was not forgotten. At Falaise the provision of the earlier *constitutio* is repeated and the requirement of the *testimonium vicinorum* is extended to his own local officers; and soon after his return, he makes the conduct of the archdeacons the first of his grievances against the church at the conference at Westminster.[18]

Another of the ' customs and dignities of the realm ' which Henry asserted in 1164 was the trial of all questions of advowson and presentation in the king's court.[19] Some Norman precedents for this claim have been cited above,[20] but the English evidence still awaits investigation. That Henry II had busied himself with this question in England before 1158 appears from a letter of John of Salisbury[21] to Pope Adrian IV with reference to a dispute concerning the church of Henton between Arnold of Devizes on the one hand and Earl Roger and his clerk Osbert on the other. The archbishop had secured Arnold's restoration to the church, pending a decision of his court:

Cum ergo partibus super hoc dies esset prefixa, ea die iam dictus O. et procuratores comitis adversus prenominatum E. petitorium instituerunt, dicentes ipsum iniuste occupare ecclesiam, quam sine assensu comitis et advocatorum eiusdem ecclesie, quam contra consuetudinem totius ecclesie et regni Anglorum, contra constitutionem regis et antiquam omnium procerum dignitatem ingressus erat manu et violentia predonis, qui prefato comiti totum fundum in quo sepe dicta ecclesia sita est diu abstulerat. Proferebatur insuper mandatum regis quo precipiebamur comiti super advocatione ecclesie sue iustitiam exhibere aut O. pretaxatam ecclesiam restituere, qua post decessum regis contra ipsius edictum fuerat destitutus.

Whereupon Arnold, fearing the influence of his opponents and the king, appealed to the Pope, and Osbert gave up the fight. Evidently the proceedings had begun under Stephen, but the *edictum* was of Henry II

---

[17] Pipe Roll 2–4 Henry II, p. 146.
[18] *Summa cause*, in *Materials*, iv. 201; cf. *Anonymus II, ibid.*, iv. 95.
[19] C. 1. [20] *Supra*, Chapter V, p. 171 f. [21] *Ep.* 6.

and so also, apparently, was the *constitutio*. We cannot press too closely the terms of the writer's classical Latinity, yet while the *edictum* may relate only to the particular case, like the *mandatum*, the *constitutio* is evidently a decree of general scope respecting advowson. If we may turn the classical *iustitiam exhibere* back into the legal *rectum tenere*, the writ to the archbishop (*mandatum*) is also interesting for the early history of the writ of right.

The procedure in such cases in these years is illustrated by the recently published report of an inquest respecting the church of St. Peter, Derby (1156–1159). Twenty-four men, including burgesses, knights, and priests, were summoned by royal writ before the sheriff and the archdeacon; their declaration awarded the advowson to the successors of the lord in whose patrimony the church had been founded.[22]

[22] F. M. Stenton, *An Early Inquest relating to St. Peter's Derby*, in *E. H. R.*, xxxii. 47 f. (1917).

APPENDIX J

NORMAN ASSIZES, 1176–1193 [1]

ASSIZES of the early part of Henry II's reign are noted in Chapter V (*supra*, pp. 165–168). The following list includes such assizes [2] as I have noted in the latter part of this reign and the early years of Richard; when he appears in them William Fitz Ralph regularly has the title of seneschal. The list is based almost entirely upon charters, for the roll of 1180, unlike the contemporary Pipe Rolls, throws no light upon the judges' circuits, save for the mention of William Fitz Ralph on page 57 and of Geoffrey le Moine on page 52 (cf. p. 78 and Round, no. 517); such indications are more abundant in the roll of 1195.

1. 1177, January; CAEN. Richard, bishop of Winchester, Simon de Tornebu, Robert Marmion, William de Glanville as justices. *Livre noir*, no. 95; Delisle, p. 347; Round, no. 1446.

2. 1176–1178; MONTFORT. Justices: William de Mara, *vicomte* of Sainte-Mère-Église, William Malet, Hugh de Cressi, Seher de Quinci, Alvered de Saint-Martin, constables respectively of Pontaudemer, Rouen, Nonancourt, and Neufchâtel (Drincourt). *Supra*, Appendix H, no. 10.

3. No date; MONTFORT. 'Ista autem donatio facta est apud Montemfortem et recitata in plena asisia coram iusticiis domini regis, scilicet Seherio de Quenceio, Alveredo de Sancto Martino, etc.' Fragment of Bec cartulary in Archives of the Eure, H. 91, f. 88v, no. 4.

4. 1178–1179; NEUFCHÂTEL. William Fitz Ralph holds court. Stapleton, i. 57.

5. 1180; ARGENTAN. Agreement 'in plena assissa . . . coram iusticiis domini regis.' Witnessed by William Fitz Ralph, 'qui preerat assisse loco domini regis,' William de Mara, Richard Giffart, John, count [of Ponthieu], Fulk d'Aunou, Ralph Tessun, and others. MS. Lat. 5424, p. 91; Collection Moreau, lxxxiv. 76; Vernier, no. 128.

5a. *Ca.* 1180; CAEN. Fine 'in curia mea coram iusticiis meis.' Round, no. 303; Delisle-Berger, no. 564.

6. Before 1182; ROUEN. Judgment 'in assisa apud Rothomagum in curia mea.' Valin, p. 271; Round, no. 26; Delisle-Berger, no. 586.

7. 1183, January 20; CAEN. 'In curia domini regis . . . in plenaria assissa ' before William Fitz Ralph and many others. Valin, p. 274; Round, no. 432; Delisle-Berger, no. 638.

---

[1] Revised from *A. H. R.*, xx. 289–291 (1915).

[2] General mentions of an assize without indication of date, place, or judges (e. g., Sauvage, *Troarn*, p. 141, note 6) are not included. The list of cases before the Exchequer (Chapter V, note 125) should be compared with this list of assizes.

8. 1183; CAEN (?). William Fitz Ralph and many others, none styled justices, but including William de Mara, Hamo Pincerna, Geoffrey Duredent, Jordan de Landa, Richard Fitz Henry, William de Calux, and Roger d'Arri. Delisle, p. 349; Valin, p. 276; Round, no. 437.

9. 1178–1183; LONGUEVILLE. William Fitz Ralph and many other justices. Valin, p. 273.

10. 1184; SAINT-WANDRILLE. Grant ' in plenaria assisia coram Willelmo filio Radulfi senescallo et iustitia Normannie et multis aliis iusticiis, scilicet Willelmo de Mara, Seherio de Quinceio, Goscelino Rusel.' Collection Moreau, lxxxvii. 157 (cf. f. 159), from lost cartulary of Lire; Le Prévost, *Eure*, ii. 111.

11. 1184; CAEN. ' Hec finalis concordia facta fuit apud Cadomum in assisia coram Willelmo filio Radulfi senescallo Normannie et pluribus aliis qui tunc ibi aderant inter Robertum abbatem Sancte Marie de Monteborc et Henricum de Tilleio de ecclesia Sancte Marie de Tevilla, unde placitum erat inter eos in curia domini regis. . . . Testibus W. de Mara, Hamone Pincerna, W. de Romara, Radulfo de Haia, Rogero de Arreio, magistro Paridi, Radulfo de Wallamint, Iordano de Landa, Roberto de Curle, W. de Sauceio, Iohanne de Caretot, Willelmo Quarrel et pluribus aliis.' Cartulary of Montebourg (MS. Lat. 10087), no. 474.

12. 1185; CAEN. William Fitz Ralph and other justices hold assize; the final decision is given at the Exchequer before an important series of witnesses. Valin, p. 277; Round, no. 438; Delisle-Berger, no. 647.

12a. 1185; LONGUEVILLE. Recognition concerning presentment ' in assisia domini regis.' Delisle-Berger, no. 651.

13. 1186, 30 January; BAYEUX. Henry, bishop of Bayeux, William de Mara, Archdeacon John d'Éraines, and other justices whose names are not given. *Livre noir*, no. 240.

14. 1186; ROUEN. Agreement before William Fitz Ralph and Robert d'Harcourt (without title). Collection Moreau, lix. 106, from the original; cartulary of Fécamp (MS. Rouen 1207), f. 81v; Round, no. 140.

15. 1186; CAEN. Grant in presence of William Fitz Ralph, William de Mara, William Calviz, Richard Fitz Henry, Geoffrey de Rapendun ' tunc baillivus regis,' and others. MS. Lat. n. a. 1428, f. 18, from original at Carleton Castle.

16. 1187; SÉEZ. Grant in assize ' coram iusticiariis domini Henrici regis, scilicet coram Iohanne archidiacono de Arenis et Willelmo de Mara et aliis pluribus.' *Livre blanc* of Saint-Martin of Séez, f. 118v.

16a. 1188–1190; probably at ROUEN. Grant of William, abbot of Mortemer, ' testibus hiis: Iohanne de Constantiis decano Rothomagensi, Willelmo filio Radulphi senescallo Normannie, Roberto de Harecort, Ricardo de Montigneio, Willelmo de Martigneio, Ricardo Ospinel, Willelmo Tolemer, . . . ' Original in Archives of the Seine-Inférieure, *fonds* Saint-Ouen.

17. 1189–1190; BERNAI. *Cartulaire de Notre-Dame de la Trappe* (ed. Charencey), p. 199; cf. Valin, p. 116, note.

18. 1190, August 10; ARGENTAN. Question of presentation ' in curia domini regis. . . . Testibus Iohanne archidiacono Arenensi, Richardo de Argentiis, Willelmo de Obvilla constabulario Falasie, qui prefatam assisiam tenuerant die festi Sancti Laurentii anno primo peregrinationis Philippi regis Francie et Ricardi regis Anglorum.' Cartulary of Saint-Évroul (MS. Lat. 11055), no. 250.

19. 1190, August; SÉEZ. Agreement in assize ' coram iusticiariis domini regis Iohanne Oximensi archidiacono, Ricardo de Hummez comestabulario, W. de Ovilla, Ricardo de Argentiis.' *Livre blanc* of Saint-Martin of Séez, f. 134.

20. 1190; BERNAI. 'Coram Robert de Harecourt et Willelmo de Mara tunc iusticiis, Willelmo Tolomeo clerico, Richardo Sylvano, comite de Alençon, Richard Deri, et pluribus aliis.' An assize at Montfort under Henry II is mentioned. Archives of the Calvados, H. suppl. 486, f. 9; cf. *supra*, Chapter V, note 95.

21. 1190; CAEN. Archives of the Calvados, H. 1872; *M. A. N.*, xv. 199; Round, no. 461.

22. 1191, October; CAEN. William Fitz Ralph, Richard Silvain, Richard d'Argences, Hamo Pincerna, Richard Fitz Henry, Robert, abbot of Fontenay, Roger d'Arri, Eudo de Vaač, Turstin of Ducey, Geoffrey the chamberlain, ' Lucas pincerna, et alii multi ' witness transaction in assize. Archives of the Calvados, H. 1868 (no. 46–18).

23. 1191; ROUEN. Valin, p. 279.

24. 1191; CAEN. Agreement ' in curia domini regis apud Cadomum coram Willelmo filio Radulfi tunc temporis senescallo Normannie et Willelmo de Humetis constabulario domini regis et Roberto Wigorniensi episcopo et Ricardo Selvain et Ricardo de Argentiis, Willelmo Caluz, Ricardo filio Henrici, et pluribus aliis.' Roger d'Arri is among the witnesses. Archives of the Calvados, H. 7077.

25. 1192; ROUEN. Agreement in presence of William Fitz Ralph, William de Martigny, Richard d'Argences, Durand du Pin, and other justices. Chevreux and Vernier, *Les archives de Normandie et de la Seine-Inférieure*, no. 35; Vernier, no. 164.

26. 1187–1193; CAUDEBEC. Agreement ' in plena assisia.' Lot, *Saint-Wandrille*, p. 179, no. 114.

27. Undated; CAEN. Grant of Richard Avenel in *curia* before William Fitz Ralph and the king's justices and barons, witnessed by William du Hommet constable, William de Mara, Hamo Pincerna, Jordan de Landa, Richard Silvain, Richard d'Argences, and others. Archives of the Manche, H. 212.[3]

28. No date; BAYEUX. Grant ' coram iustitiariis scilicet Willelmo Tolemeir et Ricardo de Argentiis dictam assisiam tenentibus.' Archives of the Manche, H. 309.

29. No date; BAYEUX. Grant in assize before William Pesnel, archdeacon of Avranches, William Tolomert, Hamo Pincerna, justices. *Répertoire* of de Gerville (Collection Mancel at Caen, MS. 296), p. 275, no. 21.

---

[3] Cf. Richard d'Argences, Hamo Potelier, and William de Caluz as witnesses in a document of this period: Farcy, *Abbayes de l'évêché de Bayeux*, Fontenay, p. 96.

APPENDIX K

DOCUMENTS FROM THE AVRANCHIN

THE destruction of the records of the bishop and chapter of Avranches, scarcely less complete than the destruction of the cathedral itself, has left us no original documents of the eleventh and twelfth centuries. The only surviving cartulary, the *Livre vert* (MS. Avranches 206), has little that is early; the *Livre blanc* is known only through scattered extracts; the modern copies are few and unsatisfactory.[1] Were it not for the monasteries of Mont-Saint-Michel and Savigny, the whole diocese would have little to tell us of this epoch in its history. Curiously, however, certain documents which have reached us from this region are of unusual significance. The earliest extant notice concerning ecclesiastical jurisdiction is the agreement drawn up between Bishop John and the abbot of Mont-Saint-Michel in 1061.[2] One of the clearest pieces of evidence regarding early knight service is found in a document of the same bishop in 1066.[3] A few years later Mont-Saint-Michel gives us an important convention respecting feudal tenure and jurisdiction,[4] and for the inquest of military tenures in 1172 the only detailed statement is that of its abbot.[5] The only surviving portion of the returns from the great royal inquest of 1171 is that relating to the Avranchin.

[1] See *Archives de la France monastique*, xvii. 91–95; the extracts from documents in E. Le Héricher, *Avranchin monumental et historique* (Avranches, 1845–1865); and the additional pieces in E. A. Pigeon, *Le diocèse d'Avranches* (Coutances, 1888), who has utilized the copies of Guérin in his possession. P. Chesnel, *Le Cotentin et l'Avranchin sous les ducs de Normandie* (Caen, 1912) adds nothing new. A few late copies are in MS. Regina 870 of the Vatican. No ducal charters for Avranches are known save one of Henry II (Pigeon, ii. 661). What once existed may be inferred from later enumerations of the grants of Robert the Magnificent (Pigeon, ii. 667; *supra*, Appendix C, no. 1) and the mention by Lucius III of grants of Henry I: 'Ex dono Henrici primi regis Anglie dimidiam partem nundinarum Sancti Lamberti, decimam nundinarum Sancti Andree, decimam nundinarum de Ponte; in Campo Cervorum duas garbas decime de terra Igerii de Lohf et Ranulfi de Burganoles; decimam molendini de Cantarana; duas . . . (where a gap follows in the MS., *Livre vert*, f. 2v). Cf. Stapleton, ii, p. vi.

[2] Migne, cxlvii. 265; Pigeon, ii. 658; see *supra*, Chapter I, note 137.

[3] Le Prévost, *Eure*, iii. 183; *supra*, Chapter I, note 58.

[4] *Supra*, p. 21.　　　　[5] Robert of Torigni, ii. 296–303.

337

This fragment, copied on the fly-leaf of a text of Hrabanus Maurus from the abbey of La Luzerne, was first published by Delisle in 1909.[6] Headed by a list of twenty-six *milites iuratores* and nine *burgenses iuratores de Abrincis*, it is clearly the return of an inquest. It contains a clear and orderly statement of the royal rights in the *vicomté* of Avranches, including the farm, the proceeds of tolls and the fair of St. Andrew, the parcels of demesne in city and country, and the holdings of the tenants *in capite* in the Avranchin. The pleas of the crown appear as a part of the demesne under a special custodian, who gives us our only glimpse of a Norman coroner.[7] As regards the date of the document, Delisle [8] placed it under Henry II but after the death of Hugh, earl of Chester, in 1181, apparently on the theory, for which the text itself gives no support, that the *vicomté* was in the king's hands at the time of the inquest. Powicke at first [9] assigned it to the reign of Richard because of the phrase *tempore regis H.;* but under Henry II this is constantly used to designate Henry I and can be actually connected with him in the inquest itself, which refers to the grant of the vineyard at Avranches to Savigny by a *rex Henricus* who is in this instance known to have been Henry I.[10] Not only does the inquest belong to the reign of Henry II, but it can be specifically dated therein. It is subsequent to 3 March 1170, for the fief of Gilbert d'Avranches, who was then drowned,[11] has passed to his heir, likewise so returned on the roll of military tenants in 1172; [12] yet this heir, his brother-in-law Fulk Painel, has not yet got possession of the rights over the king's demesne which he enjoys in 1180.[13] Similarly William de Ducey, mentioned in the text as lord of Ducey, died before 1180, when his successor, William de Hueceon, owes a relief for this honor.[14] Certain of

---

[6] *Henri II*, pp. 345–347. The bishop's fiefs are of course not mentioned; they are enumerated when in the king's hands in 1198: Stapleton, ii. 361.

[7] Powicke, *The Pleas of the Crown in the Avranchin, E. H. R.*, xxv. 710 f.

[8] *Henri II*, pp. 333, 387, 420, 423, 448.

[9] *E. H. R.*, xxv. 710. Later he accepted the date here proposed: *ibid.*, xxvi. 326; *Loss of Normandy*, p. 68.

[10] Cartulary of Savigny, in Archives of the Manche, no. 6. Cf. *M. A. N.*, xx. 256; Delisle, *Études sur la classe agricole*, pp. 443, 445; Delisle-Berger, no. 80.

[11] Robert of Torigni, ii. 17; Benedict of Peterborough, i. 4.

[12] *Red Book of the Exchequer*, ii. 640. The abbot's record, however, has been brought up to date: Robert of Torigni, ii. 297.

[13] Stapleton, i, pp. lxviii, 11.

[14] *Ibid.*, i, pp. lxv, 11. Evidence that William de Ducey was dead by 1182, if not by 1179, is also contained in charters of Richard, bishop of Avranches (d. 1182), reciting gifts made in William's last illness to Savigny (cartulary, no. 127; Auvry,

the items recovered by the inquest evidently served as the basis for the corresponding entries in the Exchequer Roll of 1180.[15] There can be no question that the inquiry was held between 1170 and 1180, and these limits can be drawn much closer if we identify the ' Robertus filius Regis ' of the inquest with the Robert Fitz Roy who married Matilda of Avranches and is said by the chronicle of Ford Abbey to have died 31 May 1172.[16] In any case, between 1170 and 1180 there is every reason for ascribing it to 1171, when, according to Robert of Torigni,[17]

Rex Henricus senior fecit investigari per Normanniam terras de quibus rex Henricus avus eius fuerat sasitus die qua obiit. Fecit etiam inquiri quas terras et quas silvas et que alia dominica barones et alii homines occupaverant post mortem regis Henrici avi sui; et hoc modo fere duplicavit redditus ducatus Normannie.

No other records of this investigation are available for comparison, but the Avranchin document is in exact accord with the account of the chronicler, himself writing at Mont-Saint-Michel, and there can be no reasonable doubt that we have here a contemporary, or nearly contemporary, copy of the original returns of the inquest of 1171 in the Avranchin.

The following notice relates to the ecclesiastical rather than to the political institutions of the diocese of Avranches, but it is here printed because it appears to have escaped the attention of local historians. It is found in a manuscript of *ca.* 1200 in the Vatican,[18] MS. Regina 946,

Histoire de la congrégation de Savigny, iii. 188; cf. Delisle-Berger, no. 591, also anterior to 1182) and to Montmorel (*Cartulaire*, ed. Dubosc, no. 113). Both are attested by Ralph, prior of Montmorel, who according to the *Gallia Christiana* (xi. 537) became prior before 1171 and ruled eight years. For other references to William's donations see *Cartulaire de Montmorel*, nos. 8, 10, 12, 109, 110–115, p. 305; Round, no. 721; Pigeon, *Le diocèse d'Avranches*, ii. 671 f.; Le Héricher, *L'Avranchin*, i. 371, 376 f., 387, 423 f., ii. 26, 587.

[15] Stapleton, i. 11; cf. Powicke, *E. H. R.*, xxv. 710.

[16] *Monasticon*, v. 378. Matilda, between 1162 and 1171, grants as ' uxor Roberti filii regis ' to the bishop of Avranches: Pigeon, *Le diocèse d'Avranches*, ii. 339; cf. Delisle-Berger, no. 214. Too much weight must not, however, be attached to the Ford chronicle, which is not earlier than the fourteenth century. The entries which follow in the Avranchin inquest would lead us to expect a possessive in place of the nominative: ' Reinaldus de Cortenai feodum Roberti filii R. in Valle Segie.' This emendation is the more probable since Reginald de Cortenay married the daughter or stepdaughter of Robert (*Monasticon*, v. 378; Stapleton, ii, p. cxlv f.), and Robert may well have died before 1171.

[17] ii. 28.

[18] On the MS. see Pertz's *Archiv*, xii. 311; Liebermann, *Gesetze*, i, p. xlii. This

ff. 72v–74v; certain additions in a different and slightly later hand are printed in italics. The date can be fixed only in general by the age of the codex and by the reference to William de Saint-Jean, who is mentioned in Norman documents from 1133 to 1203.[19] Anterior to the death of William, the text is subsequent to his endowment of La Luzerne in 1162 [20] and to the erection of Montmorel into an abbey not long after 1171.[21] The monasteries mentioned are well known, so that special annotation is unnecessary.

(F. 72v). Prior et conventus monachorum Sancte Mariȩ de Moretonio ab antiquis temporibus, quia in eius iurisdictione sunt, debent episcopo Abrincensi sollennem processionem et annuam procurationem et tam episcopo quam ȩcclesiȩ Abrincensi obedientiam. Similiter sanctimoniales de Moretonio debent sollennem processionem episcopo et tam episcopo quam ȩcclesiȩ Abrincensi obedientiam.

Priorissa autem et conventus sanctimonialium de Moutons subditi sunt episcopo et ȩcclesiȩ Abrincensibus.

Abbatia de Lucerna subdita est episcopo et ȩcclesiȩ Abrincensibus duplici de iure, quia fundata est et sita in episcopatu Abrincensi et quia sita est in feodo Beati Andrȩȩ et episcopi Abrincensis, quem feodum tenet et habet Guillelmus de Sancto Iohanne ab episcopo et inde facit ei ut domino suo hominagium. Abbas vero predicti cenobii debet interesse duabus sinodis et festo hiemali Beati Andrȩȩ, vel si interesse non potest duos mittere de canonicis ecclesie sue. Similiter debet facere et tenetur abbas de Monte Morelli.

Abbatia vero Montis Morelli subdita est episcopo et ȩcclesiȩ Abrincensibus duplici ratione, quia sita est in episcopatu Abrincensi et constituta et fundata in feodo Beati Andrȩȩ et episcopi. Isti duo abbates debent et promittunt obedientiam ecclesie et episcopo Abrincensibus cum ipsi sunt benedicendi.

(f. 73r). Notum sit indubitanter tam presentibus quam futuris quod abbatia Sancti Michaelis de periculo maris tam episcopo quam ecclesie Abrincensi multum est obnoxia, quia de bonis et prediis Beati Andree sibi collatis a Beato Auberto Abrincensi episcopo fundamentum et institutionem accepit et in episcopatu Abrincensi sita est. Unde de antiqua consuetudine ratione obnoxietatis abbas et conventus predicti cenobii singulis annis in hiemali festo Beati Andree debite reddunt ecclesie Abrincensi ut matri ȩcclesiȩ novem pondera cere secundum pondus predicti cenobii, que equivalent et equiponderant quatuor magnis ponderibus communibus et dimidio pon-

is doubtless one of the two MSS. relating to Avranches which are mentioned by Montfaucon, *Bibliotheca Manuscriptorum*, i. 80.

[19] Tardif, *Très Ancien Coutumier*, p. 111 f.; Delisle, *Henri II*, p. 500 f.

[20] *Cartulaire de La Luzerne*, ed. Dubosc, nos. 6, 7; *Neustria Pia*, p. 793 f.; Pigeon, *Le diocèse d'Avranches*, ii. 374–376.

[21] *Gallia Christiana*, xi. 536 f.; cf. *Cartulaire de Montmorel*, ed. Dubosc.

deri. Summa harum librarum est triginta et sex libre cere.[1] Reddunt etiam predictus abbas et monachi debite ecclesie Abrincensi in predicto festo tres libras incensi et episcopo tres libras piperis.[2] Reddit insuper predicta abbatia singulis annis ecclesie Abrincensi in purificatione Beate Marie tres cereos formatos continentes ad minus quatuor libras cere. Reddit preterea decano Abrincensi singulis annis in Pascha Domini .vi. libras Andegavensium monete pro pellitia grisia. Tenetur etiam abbas predicte abbatie interesse hiemali festo Beati Andree nisi legitimam habuerit excusationem, quam si habuerit mittet pro se duos de dignioribus ecclesie sue. Predictus vero abbas quando benedicitur professionem facit et canonicam obedientiam promittit et propria manu firmat et eam obedientiam promittit episcopo et successoribus eius et ecclesie Abrincensi. Monachi autem predicti monasterii singulis annis ecclesiam Abrincensem de antiquo usu, ut matrem ecclesiam cui honorem debent, in die martis post octavas Pentecostes cum sollenni processione tenentur adire et missam in honore Beati Andree sollenniter celebrare. Confirmatio autem electionis abbatis predicti monasterii ad episcopum Abrincensem pertinet. Tenetur etiam predicta abbatia electum Abrincensem in episcopum consecratum cum sollenni processione recipere. Confirmatio vero populi et consecrationes ecclesiarum predicti Montis et ordinationes monachorum et clericorum ad solum episcopum Abrincensem pertinent. Clerici autem predicti Montis bis in anno tenentur interesse sinodo ecclesie Abrincensis. Similiter et abbas Montis Sancti Michaelis eisdem sinodis debet interesse. *Preterea abbas et conventus predicti monasterii debent et tenentur singulis annis reddere episcopo Abrincensi in octavis Penthecostes apud Abrincas per nuncios suos sine requisitione .vii. libras Andegavensium monete.*

(f. 73v). Consuetudo autem est antiqua ut episcopus Abrincensis si voluerit singulis annis ad predictam accedat et veniat abbatiam in ultimo festo Beati Michaelis ad celebrandum ut episcopus ibi divina. In vigilia vero Beati Michaelis habet ex debito antiquo et procurationem et mansionem cum comitatu suo episcopus. In die autem festivitatis post sollennitatem et celebrationem misse habet episcopus cum comitatu suo procurationem et inde post quo voluerit debet recedere. Consuevit preterea episcopus de antiquo usu predictum monasterium adire si voluerit in quarta feria ante Pascha Domini annuatim causa absolvendi monachos et clerum et populum a sarcina peccatorum, et tunc habet ibi episcopus procurationem suam cum suo comitatu. Salva est autem episcopo Abrincensi in predicta abbatia in omnibus canonica iusticia.[3] Prioratus autem predicte abbatie in episcopatu Abrincensi constituti debent de consuetudine episcopo Abrincensi annuam procurationem et priores eorum debent ei obedientiam.

Abbas Sancti Stephani de Cadomo de consuetudine debet interesse hiemali festo Beati Andree in propria persona vel debet mittere unum monachorum suorum cum litteris suis ad probandam rationabilem excusationem sue absentie. Hac vero de causa debet interesse abbas predicto festo ut episcopus

---

[1] Cf. Longnon, *Pouillés de la province de Rouen*, p. 162 (1412).

[2] Cf. the abbot's render to the king: Delisle, *Henri II*, p. 346.

[3] For the bishop's justice over the men of the Mount, see Chapter I, note 137

Abrincensis prioratum suum Sancti Leonardi et priorem et monachos ibi manentes et possessiones eorum manuteneant et contra eis iniuriantes ecclesiastica censura eos defendat et tueatur.

Similiter abbas Sancti Severi debet interesse hiemali festo Beati Andręę de consuetudine vel mittere debet cum litteris suis sufficientem et idoneum excusatorem cum assignatione rationis sue absentię. Hac vero de causa debet interesse abbas Sancti Severi predicto festo quia habet in episcopatu Abrincensi capellam quandam et prioratum cum quibusdam decimis prope Haiam Paganelli, que omnia pertinent ad iurisditionem et defensionem episcopi et ecclesie Abrincensium.[4] *Et in eodem episcopatu habet ecclesiam de Lucerna.*

(f. 74r).[5] Sciant proculdubio omnes tam presentes quam futuri quod inter episcopales ecclesias et sedes provintie Rotomagensis prima et dignior est ecclesia Baiocensis, secunda sedes et dignior post Baiocensem est ecclesia Abrincensis, ut legitur scriptum in quodam libro qui nocte et die est super altare Beate Marie Rotomagensis. Baiocensis vero episcopus est decanus Rotomagensis provintie, subdecanus autem eiusdem provintie est episcopus Abrincensis. Vacante autem sede Baiocensi vel eius episcopo in remotis partibus existente, superstes episcopus Abrincensis sanctum crisma et oleum et sacros ordines et cetera spiritualia ecclesie Baiocensis et eius clericis administrat nec ecclesia Baiocensis aliunde debet ea accipere, et econverso.

In supradicto vero libro qui vocatur Tabule [6] sic scriptum legitur in ecclesia Rothomagensi: Rodomus vel Rothomagus metropolis est. Continet enim sub se sex episcopales civitates, primam scilicet Baiocatarum, secundam scilicet civitatem Abrincatarum, tercia civitatem Evatinorum que dicitur Ebroicas, quartam civitatem Salarium que dicitur Sagium, quintam civitatem Lexoviarum, sextam civitatem Constanciarum.

(f. 74v). Cum omnes ecclesie in quolibet episcopatu constitute in potestate sint diocesanorum episcoporum et subdite sint matri ęcclesię, indubitanter sciatur ab omnibus ecclesiam Sancti Guillelmi Firmati de Moretonio in episcopatu Abrincensi constitutam esse subditam episcopo et ęcclesię Abrincensibus. Debent autem et tenentur canonici predicte ęcclesię episcopum Abrincensem consecratum de antiqua consuetudine cum sollenni processione recipere et ei debent annuam procurationem; cessare vero tenentur a divino servitio et officio ad eius mandatum, quia ei debent obedientiam exhibere ut subditi prelato. Mittunt preterea de inveterata consuetudine duos de canonicis suis ad duas sinodos ęcclesię Abrincensis. Consecratio autem ęcclesię sue et aliarum ecclesiarum suarum et altarium suorum et ordinationes canonicorum et clericorum predicte ęcclesię ad solum episcopum Abrincensem pertinent.

Abbatia Savigneii in episcopatu Abrincensi sita debet episcopo Abrincensi sollennem processionem et annuam procurationem et tam episcopo quam

[4] Cf. Le Héricher, ii. 40.

[5] Evidently this folio or its contents has been reversed, as the two final paragraphs belong here.

[6] Probably the *Liber eburneus*, now MS. Rouen 1405, in which this paragraph is found (p. 26).

ęcclesię Abrincensi canonicam obedientiam, quam abbas cum benedicendus est in ecclesia Abrincensi publice profitetur. Dedicatio autem ecclesie Savigneii et consecratio altarium eius et ordinationes monachorum ad solum episcopum Abrincensem pertinent. Abbas vero Savigneii et abbas Sancti Michaelis de Monte et alii abbates diocesis Abrincensis et omnes principales persone conventualium ecclesiarum episcopatus Abrincensis debent interesse processioni Abrincensis ecclesie ad recipiendum cum honore episcopum Abrincensem redeuntem a sua consecratione, vel debent mittere duos de dignioribus ecclesiarum suarum pro se si non possunt interesse.

INDEX

INDEX

Mediaeval names of persons are arranged alphabetically under the English form of the Christian name. When names of places have been identified, the modern form is given; otherwise the form occurring in the document is used.

Anneville-sur-Seine (Seine-Inf.), 69, 290.
Anquetil d'Arri, 180, 328.
—— de Hotot, 96.
—— priest, 7.
Ansaud de Beauvoir, 108.
Anselm, archbishop of Canterbury, 86, 93, 310.
—— de Dives, 321.
—— *vicomte*, 306.
Ansfred Bordet, 289.
—— abbot of Préaux, 279.
—— abbot of Saint-Wandrille, 228.
—— seneschal, 50, 275.
—— de Sorquainville, 262.
Anslec, sons of, 262.
Anslevilla, 290.
Appasilva, 261.
Aragon, 195.
Archdeacons, hereditary, 7; jurisdiction of, 31, 34, 35, 88, 171, 227, 228, 235, 329–332.
Archives, 221, 241–246; *see* Paris, and the several departments.
Ardeneta, 219.
Ardevon (Manche), 69, 185.
Arganchy (Calvados), 94, 95, 294, 313, 319.
Argences (Calvados), 4, 39, 49, 252, 259–261, 272, 328.
Argentan (Orne), 42, 70, 101, 105–107, 119, 121, 124, 125, 128, 132, 134, 136, 139, 141–143, 151, 152, 165, 176, 183, 184, 300–302, 304, 306, 307, 310, 319, 334, 335.
Arlette, 268, 269.
Arnold of Devizes, 332.
Arnulf, 305.
—— chancellor of Bayeux, 226.
—— of Choques, chaplain of Robert II, 74.
—— bishop of Lisieux, 125, 130, 153, 154, 158, 163, 165–168, 171–173, 188, 203, 219, 221, 324, 326.
—— of Montgomery, 70.
—— fitz Peter, 236.
Arques (Seine-Inf.), 42, 100, 129, 131, 140, 143, 149, 151, 152, 253, 254, 258, 260, 261, 274, 318.

Arras (Pas-de-Calais), abbey of Saint-Vaast, 59.
Arrière-ban, 8, 23, 24, 187.
Ars (Manche), 21.
Asnières (Calvados), 298.
Asselin, chaplain, 91.
Assize, 105, 149, 150, 159, 165–169, 172–174, 179, 180, 184, 187–189, 198–201, 209–219, 234, 238, 325–327, 334–336; of Arms, 23, 159, 192, 193; of Clarendon, 188.
Athelney (co. Somerset), 315.
Atina (province of Caserta), 233.
Atto, 40.
Atzelin, 7.
Auberville (Calvados), 63.
Aubrey de Vere, chamberlain, 121.
Auchy (Seine-Inf.), 67.
Audoin, bishop of Évreux, 111, 170, 296, 297, 299, 302.
Audrieu (Calvados), 70.
Auffai (Seine-Inf.), 49.
Auge, 108, 181.
Aumale (Seine-Inf.), 29, 78, 312, 317. Count: Stephen. Countess: Adeliza.
Aunay-sur-Odon (Calvados), abbey, 135, 163, 297, 316, 326, 327. Abbot: Vivian.
Auvers (Seine-et-Oise), 45.
Auvray, L., 247, 281.
Avelina, niece of William Goth, 299, 301.
Avoué, 36.
Avranches (Manche), 34, 35, 43, 129, 165, 166, 180, 311; archives, 244; bishop of, 8, 18, 19, 34, 35, 37, 76, 87, 167, 227, 228; his rights over monasteries, 340–343; chapter, 43, 180, 272; fair, 191, 337, 338; MSS. at, 33, 41, 59, 69, 128, 142, 244, 245, 273, 277, 281, 337; vineyard, 338. Bishops: Achard, Herbert, John, Maingisus, Michael, Richard.
Avranchin, 8, 9, 128, 129, 160, 185, 188, 191, 337–343.

Bacqueville (Seine-Inf.), 20.
Bailli, bailliage, baillivi, 105, 147, 151, 152, 163, 168, 177, 182–186, 209.

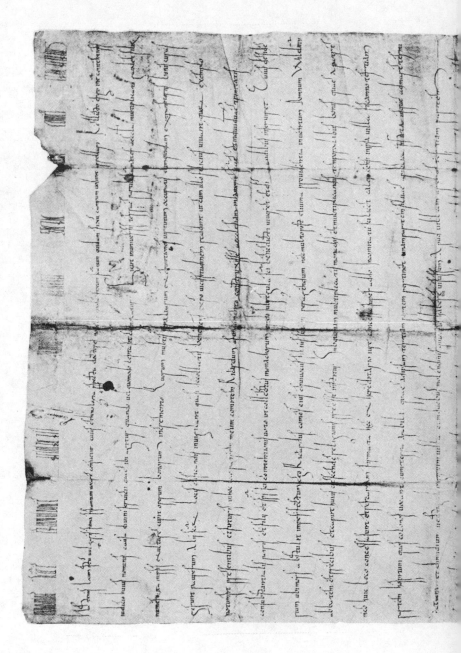

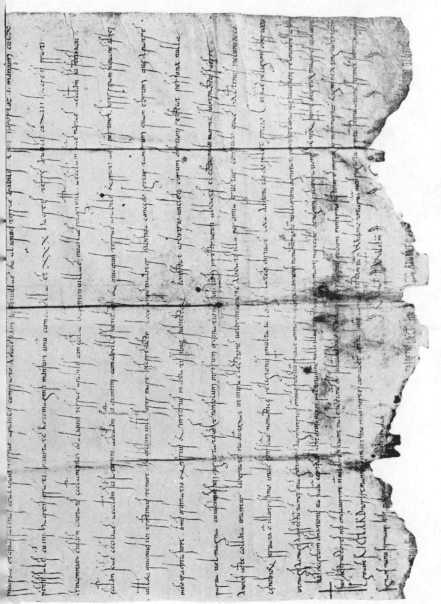

PLATE I. CHARTER *HACTENUS* OF RICHARD II FOR FÉCAMP, 1006 (P. 253, NO. 2).

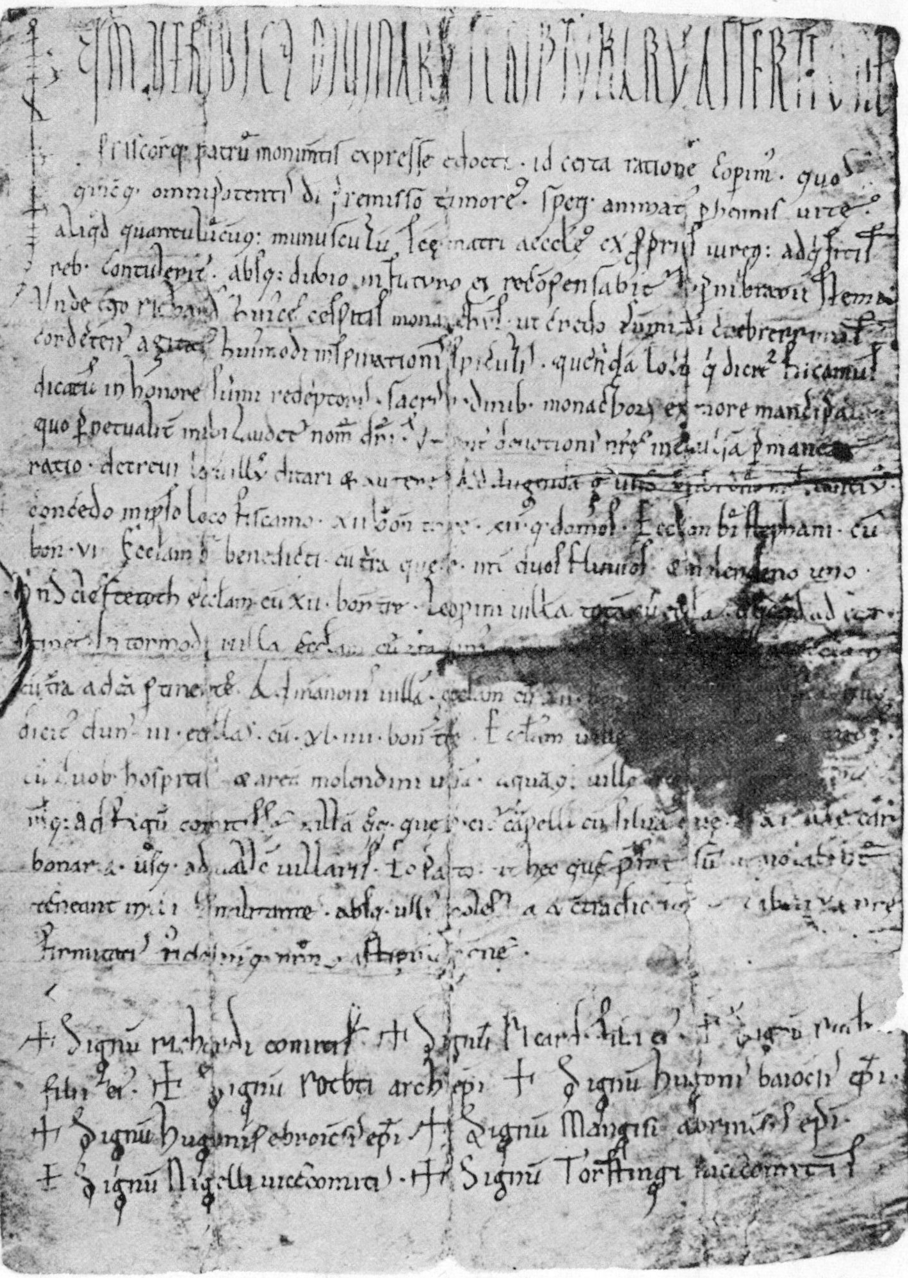

PLATE 2. CHARTER *QUONIAM VERIDICA* OF RICHARD II FOR FÉCAMP (P. 255, NO. 3).

PLATE 3. CHARTER *PROPICIA* OF RICHARD II FOR FÉCAMP, 1027? (P. 256, NO. 5).

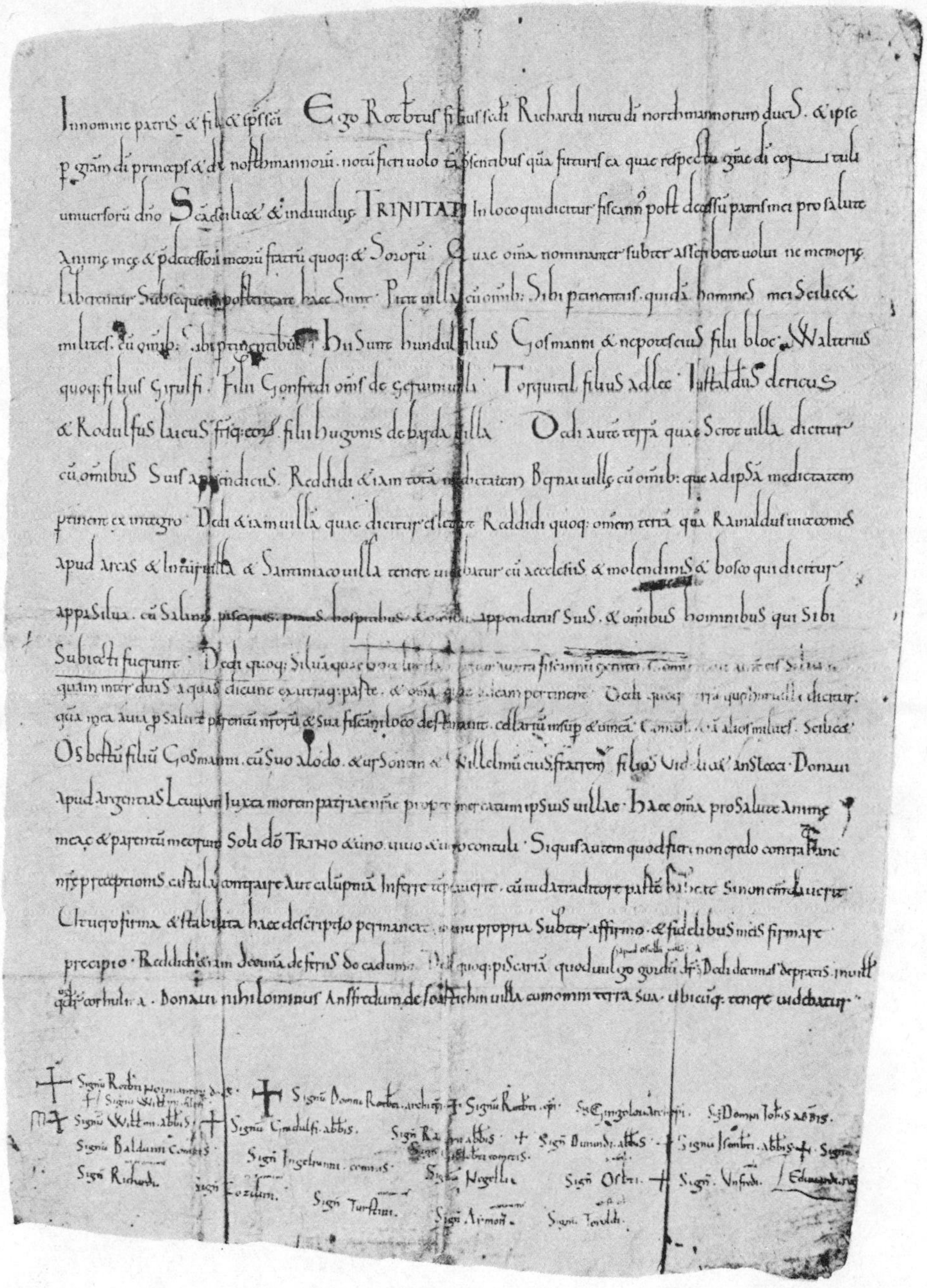

PLATE 4. CHARTER OF ROBERT I FOR FÉCAMP (P. 260, NO. 10A).

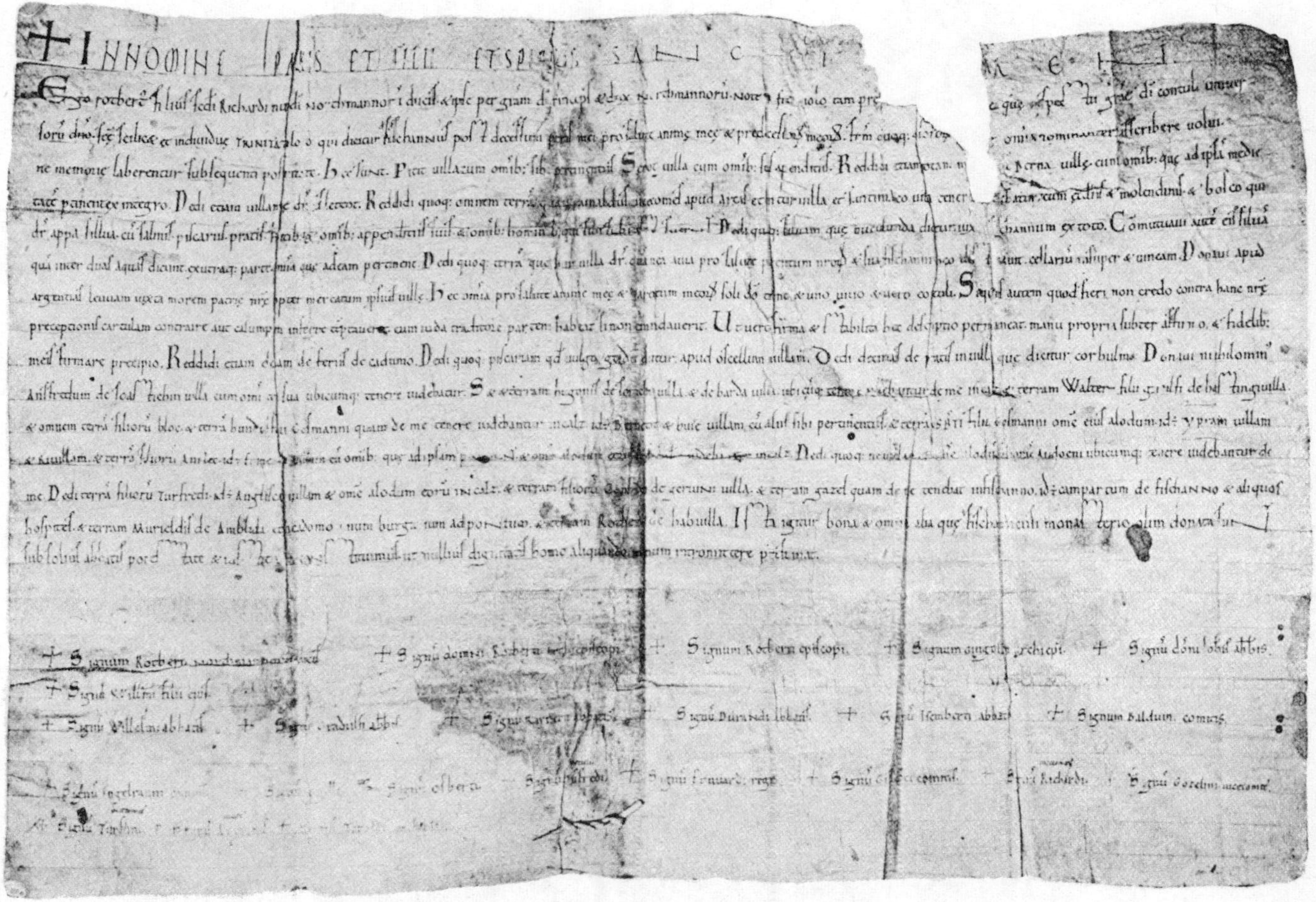

PLATE 5. CHARTER OF ROBERT I FOR FÉCAMP (P. 260, NO. 10B).

PLATE 6. FORGED CHARTER OF WILLIAM THE CONQUEROR FOR FÉCAMP (p. 263, NO. II).

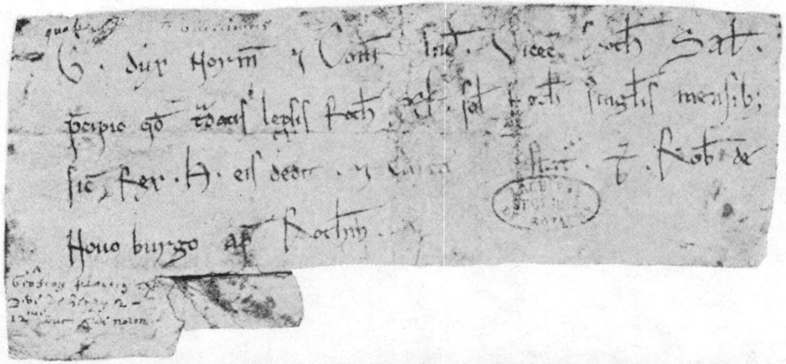

a.

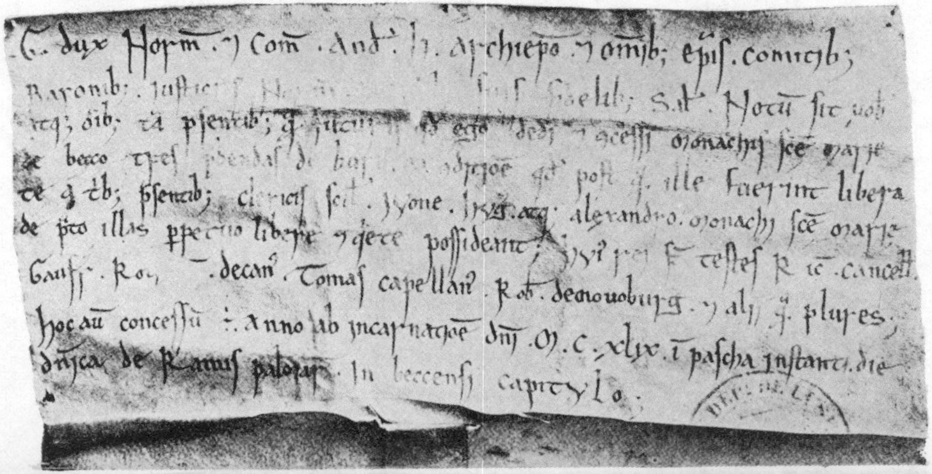

b.

PLATE 7.

a. WRIT OF GEOFFREY PLANTAGENET FOR THE LEPERS OF ROUEN (P. 142, NO. 12).

b. SEALED CHARTER OF GEOFFREY PLANTAGENET FOR BEC, 1149 (P. 138, NO. 2).